POCKET NATURE
WILDLIFE
OF BRITAIN

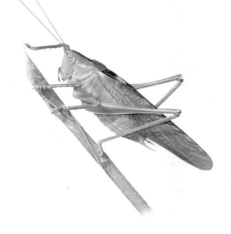

POCKET NATURE

WILDLIFE
OF BRITAIN

DK

DORLING KINDERSLEY

DK

LONDON, NEW YORK, MUNICH,
MELBOURNE, AND DELHI

DK LONDON
Senior Art Editor Ina Stradins
Senior Editor Angeles Gavira Guerrero
Editor Miezan van Zyl
Illustrators Jane Durston, Andy Mackay
Production Editor Tony Phipps
Production Controller Imogen Boase
Senior Managing Art Editor Phil Ormerod
Managing Editor Sarah Larter
Publishing Manager Liz Wheeler
Art Director Bryn Walls
Publisher Jonathan Metcalf

DK DELHI
Designer Neerja Rawat
DTP Coordinator Sunil Sharma
DTP Designer Pushpak Tyagi
Editor Saloni Talwar
Art Director Shefali Upadhyay
Head of Publishing Aparna Sharma

Contributors
Chris Gibson, Jonathan Elphick,
Rob Hume, John Woodward
Kim Dennis-Bryan, Andrew Mackay,
Chris Pellant, Paul Sterry,
George McGavin, Allen Coombes,
Neil Fletcher, David Burnie,
Helen Pellant, Joyce Pitt,
Shelley Evans, Geoffrey Kibby

First published in Great Britain in 2009 by
Dorling Kindersley Limited
80 Strand, London WC2R 0RL

A Penguin Company

Copyright © 2009
Dorling Kindersley Limited

11 12 13 14 15
015-PD124-Apr/2009

A CIP catalogue record for this book
is available from the British Library
ISBN 978 1 4053 2860 9

Reproduced by Colourscan, Singapore
Printed and bound in China by Hung Hing

see our complete catalogue at
www.dk.com

CONTENTS

How this book works

This guide covers more than 900 of some of the most commonly found plant and animal species that inhabit Britain. It opens with a brief introduction, which looks at the landscape and habitats of Britain and includes ten pages that highlight some of the characters to look for when identifying species in the field. The introduction is followed by species catalogues. These catalogues are divided into chapters that focus on key wildlife groups: trees; wild flowers and other plants; fungi and lichens; mammals; birds; reptiles and amphibians; fish; and invertebrates. Each of these chapters contains profiles of the key species that occur in Britain.

Fish

Like reptiles, the number of fish species in Britain has been limited by the effects of the last ice age, though there have been successful introductions of several species from elsewhere. Recent efforts in pollution control have seen fish numbers increase significantly in many rivers, though it takes practice to recognise them when seen from above the water's surface. The species on the following pages are those that are most likely to be encountered when walking by a river, pond, estuary, or the seashore.

△ **CHAPTERS**
Each chapter opens with an introductory page that gives some general information on the group as it relates to Britain.

DISTRIBUTION
Some species profiles include maps that show the European range where the plant or animal occurs.

COMMON NAME

SCIENTIFIC NAME

CLASSIFICATION
The level of classification that best helps to identify and characterize the species is given after the scientific name. Higher Plants: Family; Lower Plants: Phylum; Fungi and Lichens: Kingdom; Algae: Class; Non-arthropod Invertebrates: Phylum; Crustacea: Subphylum; Spiders: Class; Insects: Order; Birds: Family; Fish: Family; Reptiles and Amphibians: Class.

ANNOTATION
Characteristic features of the species are picked out in the annotation.

DETAIL PICTURES
The tinted boxes show variations, including some subspecies, tracks and signs, or simply close-ups of individual parts, such as leaves, flowers, and fruit.

BIRD DISTRIBUTION
Bird profiles include maps that show range and seasonal distribution for each species (see p.16).

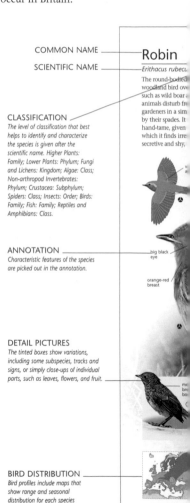

Robin
Erithacus rubecu...

The round-bodied woodland bird ov... such as wild boar a... animals disturb fr... gardeners in a sim... by their spades. It ... hand-tame, given ... which it finds irre... secretive and shy, ...

big black eye

orange-red breast

▽ SPECIES ENTRIES

Each species entry follows the same easy-to-access structure. All consist of a description of the species and a main photograph taken in the species' natural setting in the wild. This is supported by one or more detailed or secondary pictures. Annotations, scale artworks, and a data box add key information and complete the entry.

HABITAT
This describes the natural habitats where the species may be found.

CHAPTER HEADING

BIRDS **353**

...is a shy, skulking ... It is adapted to animals ...all invertebrates that the ...the British Isles, it follows ...orms and grubs turned up ...est of all birds to become ...ealworms or other grubs, ...ss, nesting Robins remain ...ir eggs if disturbed.

LIVES *in open forests and woods, on bushy heaths, and in parks and gardens with hedges and shrubs.*

NOTE
Robins have developed the habit of singing at night under artificial lights, both in suburban areas and alongside car parks and industrial sites.

...pot

bluish grey on sides of neck and chest

...ik, quick tik-ik-ik-ik, high, thin seep; song rich, sweet, ...warble.
...ed nest of leaves and grass in bank or bush; 4–6 eggs; ...-August.
...s spiders, insects, worms, berries, and seeds, ...und.
...ES Dunnock (left), Nightingale (left),
...)

SCALE DRAWINGS
Two small scale drawings are placed next to each other in every entry as a rough indication of species size. The colour illustration or silhouette represents the species featured in the entry.

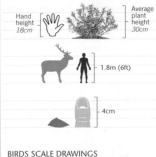

Hand height *18cm*

Average plant height *30cm*

1.8m (6ft)

4cm

BIRDS SCALE DRAWINGS
In the bird scale drawings, the darker drawing represents the bird being described, while the paler drawing is one of four very familiar birds: Mute Swan, Mallard, Pigeon, and House Sparrow. Sizes below are the length from tip of tail to tip of bill.

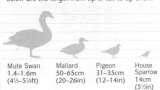

Mute Swan	Mallard	Pigeon	House Sparrow
1.4–1.6m (4½–5¼ft)	50–65cm (20–26in)	31–35cm (12–14in)	14cm (5½in)

SCALE DRAWING
This gives an indication of the size of the species. See panel above.

SYMBOLS
Symbols indicate sex, age, season, view, or in the case of fungi, whether a species is poisonous.

♀ female   ♂ male

● adult   ● immature   ● juvenile

🌱 spring   ☼ summer   🍂 autumn

❄ winter

● upperside view   ● underside view

☠ poisonous   ☠ poisonous but edible after cooking

DATA BOX
Key information relating to the species is encapsulated in a data box. The categories of information are individually tailored for each group of plants or animals, so that the most appropriate details are given for each.

Habitats

Britain contains a wonderful diversity of wildlife habitats within its relatively small area, ranging from lowland marshes to rugged peaks, and from noisy seabird islands to fragrant bluebell woods. Many have been influenced by centuries of human activity, but this in itself has created

unique habitats, like the ancient hedgerows of the southwest and the sheep-cropped turf of chalk downland. And while the wilder fringes offer the most spectacular landscapes, there are pockets of wilderness everywhere, even within the biggest cities.

Coastal

The long coastlines of the British Isles include every type of shore, from sheltered estuaries to wild rocky headlands. They are internationally important breeding and wintering sites for seabirds, which feast on the rich variety of life on the shores and in the shallow seas.

PUFFINS *breed on remote clifftops in the north and west, using their colourful bill to enhance their courtship displays.*

LIMPETS *are superbly equipped for life on exposed rocky shores, with tough conical shells that protect them from wave-tossed stones.*

Freshwater

From tumbling mountain streams to placid lowland rivers and lakes, fresh water provides vital havens for a wide range of life. Many of the most exciting wildlife reserves are centred on wetlands, ranging from reedbeds and fens to acid peat bogs with their fascinating flora.

PALMATE NEWTS *spend much of their time hunting on land, but like all amphibians they spawn in fresh water.*

ROACH *are adaptable fish that live in a wide variety of fresh waters, from small streams to canals and lakes. They often swim in small shoals.*

Mountain and Upland

The rocky mountains and uplands of the north and west provide refuges for many of Britain's most elusive, yet iconic species, such as the Otter, Raven, and Golden Eagle. Heather moorland and peat bog cover vast areas, while ancient woodlands survive in hidden valleys.

PEREGRINES *nest on the highest crags of the uplands, and prey on other birds by using a shattering high-speed dive to kill them on impact.*

RED SQUIRRELS *are common in the pinewoods of northern uplands, which do not suit their rivals, the Grey Squirrels.*

Woodland and Hedgerow

Although most of the woodland that once covered Britain has gone, the landscape is still dotted with small woods that are often linked by a network of hedgerows. In spring the deciduous woodlands are carpeted with flowers, and teeming insect life provides food for breeding songbirds.

BLUEBELLS *create a magical blue haze under leafless trees in early spring – a spectacle virtually unique to Britain.*

SESSILE OAK *is one of just two native oak species, which are both very important micro-habitats for wildlife.*

Grassland and Heath

Created by forest clearance long ago and maintained by centuries of grazing, ancient chalk and limestone grasslands support a rich diversity of flowers and insects. On poor sandy soils the same process created the heaths that are now vital refuges for native reptiles.

MARBLED WHITE *is one of the most typical butterflies of chalk grassland, where the adults fly for just a few weeks in high summer.*

GOLDEN WAXCAP *sprouts from semi-wild mossy grassland in late summer and autumn.*

Identifying Trees

Trees have many characters that can be used to identify them, some obvious, some less so. Note the shape of the tree and where and when it is growing, but also study closely the leaves, flowers, fruit, and bark. Remember that most plants are variable and features such as leaves can differ in size and shape, even on the same tree.

LEAF SHAPE AND COLOUR

Check if the leaf is simple (one individual blade) or compound (divided into leaflets) and how any leaflets are arranged (pinnately or palmately, for example). Some leaves change colour as they mature, or just before they fall in autumn; some leaves are marked with prominent veins or are variegated, consisting of patches of colour. The leaf margin can vary from untoothed to wavy, toothed, spiny, or variously lobed, depending on the species.

prominent veins
toothed margin
leaflet
dark green
glossy

SIMPLE   COMPOUND

FLOWERS AND FRUIT

Note their size, colour, and form, but also consider how and where flowers are borne on the plant. While different types of cone help to distinguish conifers, other trees bear very different forms of fruit, including fleshy, characteristically coloured berries, hard-shelled nuts, and flattened pods.

female opens red
acorn in cup
♀
male opens yellow
♂

SEPARATE MALE AND FEMALE
FLOWERS ON SAME PLANT   FRUIT

BARK

Bark is the distinctive protective outer covering of a tree. As a tree grows, its trunk lays on new layers of wood each season and expands, causing the exterior layers of dead bark to peel or crack. This expansion creates various bark patterns, which are characteristic to each species; it also produces colour and textural differences between young and old specimens.

FLAKING (PLATES)

PATCHY

SMOOTH

RIDGED AND
FISSURED

HABIT

Observing a tree's shape, or habit, can help species identification, but be aware that shape can vary greatly: a tree growing in the open will differ in shape to one of the same species growing in a dense forest. Age is also a factor that can affect the shape of a tree.

SPREADING
Many evergreen trees have open branches, giving them a spreading habit.

COLUMNAR
Some trees are much taller than they are wide.

Identifying Wild Flowers

Occasionally, the flower form or the leaf type alone may be enough to pinpoint a species but, generally, this kind of identification comes with the experience of observing the plant many times in the field. As a beginner, it is important to note all features, including habitat or flowering season, before finally deciding upon a precise identification.

Anatomy

All parts of the flower work together to promote fertilization. The female ovary, found at the base of the style and stigma, is fertilized by the pollen, which is produced by the male anthers. Insects pick up pollen and distribute it to the stigmas of other flowers. The sepals, collectively known as the calyx, and petals surround and protect the reproductive parts. Flowerheads are made up of small flowers called florets. Using the correct terms will add precision to your descriptions and help identification.

petal
stamen (anther and filament)
filament
anther
style
stigma
carpel
FLOWER

Flowers

Flowers are an obvious plant feature, and their colour can assist identification, but be aware of those species that exist in several colour forms. Also note how the individual flowers are clustered together and where, on the plant, they are borne, as well as the number and form of the petals and sepals.

FLOWER ARRANGEMENT

SOLITARY   SPIKE   RACEME   PANICLE

FRUIT

Fruit occur in a huge variety of forms. Closely-related species can often be distinguished by the slight differences in their fruit. It may also be a useful diagnostic feature if the plant is discovered after the flowers have faded or disappeared.

LEAVES

Assess the colour, texture, and shape of the leaves, how they are divided, whether they have toothed margins, and how they are arranged on the stem. Remember that lower leaves may differ from those above.

CAPSULE   BERRIES   MERICAP

LEAF SHAPES

LINEAR   LANCE-SHAPED   ELLIPTICAL

Identifying Fungi

To accurately identify fungi and lichen (a combination of a fungus and an alga), you need to take detailed notes in the field, while the specimens are still fresh and untouched. Take great care when handling, so as not to damage the often delicate surface, or any other diagnostic character. Use a hand lens to study them in detail.

Anatomy

The structure and the anatomical details of all fungi reflect the main function of dispersing their single-celled reproductive spores. The typical fungus has a variably shaped cap lifted up on a central stem. On the underside of the cap are gills, spines, tubes, or fleshy wrinkles where spores are produced and discharged. The cap and stem shape, any surface structures, and the colour are all diagnostic features. Many fungi are covered by a protective tissue (called the universal veil). As the fungus grows, this "veil" ruptures, leaving patches on the cap, stem, or base.

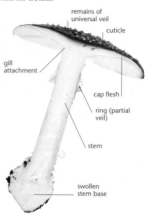

remains of universal veil

cuticle

gill attachment

cap flesh

ring (partial veil)

stem

swollen stem base

Fruitbody shapes

Identifying the shape of the fruitbody is often the first step in identifying the species. The broad classification of fungal groups in this book is based in part on the extraordinary shapes and structures of the fruitbody. Every possible variation may be encountered, many of which are pictured here, from the typical cap, stem, and gills, to fungi with animal-like arms or tentacles.

CAP AND STEM

MULTIPLE BRACKET

EAR-SHAPED

CORAL-LIKE

SKIN-LIKE CRUST

PHALLUS-LIKE

SPONGE-LIKE

TRUMPET-SHAPED

STAR-SHAPED

ANTLER-SHAPED

BALL-SHAPED

BRAIN-LIKE

Texture

Cap textures include many variations, ranging from smooth and sticky to dry, fibrous to scaly. Some species will have an external veil of tissue, which may be thick and skin-like, fine and cobweb-like, or even sticky.

LOOSE SCALES · FIXED SCALES · FIBROUS · SHAGGY-WOOLY · STICKY

Gills

With gilled mushrooms, you should make a note of the gill colour, their general spacing (crowded or widely spaced), and whether they are flexible or brittle. Examine how the gills are attached to the stem; they may be attached narrowly, broadly, or with an indent or notch, or the gills may run down the stem slightly or markedly. Also check whether the gills exude a latex when broken. Gill characteristics are usually constant within a species.

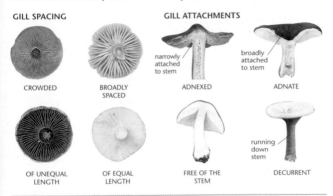

GILL SPACING

CROWDED · BROADLY SPACED

OF UNEQUAL LENGTH · OF EQUAL LENGTH

GILL ATTACHMENTS

narrowly attached to stem — ADNEXED

broadly attached to stem — ADNATE

FREE OF THE STEM

running down stem — DECURRENT

Occurrence

The occurence of a species may distinguish it from similar-looking species. The manner in which it grows – singly, in clusters, in rings etc – can be diagnostic. Also, not all species are common or widespread; some are very rare and exciting to find, and some are also restricted to certain times of the year.

IN CLUSTERS · IN TROOPS · SINGLY · FALSE PARASOLS IN A FAIRY RING

Chicken of the Wood

Oak Polypore

Livid Pinkgill

St. George's Mushroom

COMMON · RARE · LATE SUMMER TO AUTUMN · SPRING TO EARLY SUMMER

Identifying Mammals

Mammals are the only animals that are covered in fur, although only sparsely so in some groups, especially aquatic ones. They are "warm-blooded" (endothermic), and have the ability to maintain a constant internal body temperature, regardless of changing external conditions.

Variations

Not all individuals in a species look the same. There may be differences between the sexes; young mammals may be very different from their parents; the appearance may change with the seasons. Furthermore, there may also be variations between animals from different parts of the geographical range.

Tracks and Signs

Given the often secretive nature, and sometimes nocturnal habits, of many mammals, the best way of recognizing some species is from the signs they leave. These may include droppings, footprints, feeding signs, or distinctive places of shelter, protection, or breeding.

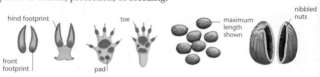

hind footprint

front footprint

toe

pad

maximum length shown

nibbled nuts

Identifying Reptiles

Reptiles were the first group of animals to evolve a wholly terrestrial way of life. Of the 8,000 or so species living today, few are dependent on wet habitats. All reptiles are "cold-blooded" (ectothermic). Unable to generate heat internally, they obtain heat from their environment to function normally. A consequence of cold-bloodedness is a low feeding requirement: many species are able to fast for extended periods of time.

Grass Snake with clutch

REPRODUCTION
Most reptiles produce soft-shelled eggs, which are incubated by warmth from the sun or rotting vegetation. Some, however, retain their eggs internally, producing live young.

SKIN
The texture of the scales that cover the surface of a reptile can impart a characteristic appearance. Detailed examination of the scales, however, is possible only on captive, torpid, or dead specimens.

GRANULAR SMOOTH KEELED

EYES
The colour of the eyes and the shape and orientation (pictured left) of the pupil are important identification features if you can get close enough. Furthermore, the colour of the iris is often highly distinctive.

HORIZONTAL VERTICAL ROUND

Identifying Amphibians

Amphibians were the earliest animal group to exploit terrestrial habitats, but most still lay eggs in water, and the larvae possess external gills for breathing underwater. Being cold-blooded (ectothermic), they often hibernate when it is cold. Conversely, in hot, dry conditions, they may also reduce their activity, a phenomenon called aestivation.

STICKY   WEBBED

FEET
The feet of amphibians show several adaptations to particular lifestyles, sometimes with suction pads for climbing or webbing to aid swimming.

pupil

HORIZONTAL   ROUND   VERTICAL

EYES
The form of the eyes, particularly the shape and orientation of the pupil, is a differentiating feature of many groups.

SMOOTH   WARTY

SKIN
Usually smooth, lacking scales and with a mucus layer, some species may have a characteristic granular covering, which may vary seasonally.

Great Crested Newt

TAIL
Where present, the tail is used for swimming. In males, the tail may bear a distinctive crest in the breeding season.

Identifying Fish

Colour and size are unreliable features to use for indentification purposes because they are highly variable between individual fish. There are, however, other characters which looked at either singly or together make a fish species unique. These features include scales, body shape, fin position, and behaviour.

SCALES
Fish scales vary in size, in shape, and in number. Bony fish have either oval ctenoid scales, which have rough edges, or round cycloid scales, which are smooth. Sometimes the number of scales present on the lateral line are counted and used to identify different fish.

LARGE SCALES   SMALL SCALES   MINUTE SCALES

BODY SHAPE
Fish have evolved into a variety of shapes that reflect their lifestyle. Slim streamlined fish, such as pike, tend to live in turbulent water or may need speed to catch their prey. Deep bodied fish, such as carp, prefer still water, while flat fish, such as the flounders, are often bottom-dwelling, estuarine species.

streamlined shape

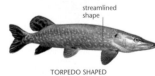

TORPEDO SHAPED

upperside coloured for camouflage

deepest just in front of dorsal fin

DEEP BODIED   FLAT FISH

Identifying Birds

Identifying a bird is usually a process based on a range of information: the place, habitat, time of year, size and shape of the bird, colours, markings, the way it flies and moves, and its general behaviour. While it is not necessary to know the details of anatomy to identify a bird, a little more knowledge adds to the interest and enjoyment. The correct terminology also adds precision to a verbal description.

Anatomy

The coverts on the underside of a bird's wing form a smaller proportion of the wing area than they do on the upperside, but they are arranged in a similar regular pattern of overlapping rows. At the base of the wing, a triangular patch of feathers in the "wingpit" is formed by a group of feathers called the axillaries. The head, belly, breast, and flanks are covered by shorter, less flexible feathers.

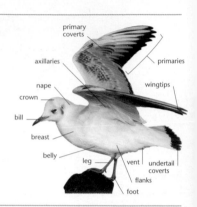

MAPS

Each bird species profile includes a map showing the European range, with different colours reflecting seasonal location.

Summer distribution

Resident all year

Winter distribution

Seen on migration

HEAD MARKINGS

A bird's head markings may include a cap, various different kinds of stripes, such as a superciliary stripe over the eye and an eye-stripe through it, and a bib below the bill.

FEATHER TYPES

Soft down feathers form an insulating underlayer. The head and body are covered with body, or contour, feathers. The wings have small, stiff feathers, wider on one side, called coverts.

DOWN FEATHER **BODY FEATHER** **WING FEATHER**

PLUMAGE

Feathers not only allow flight and keep a bird warm and dry but also add colour, pattern, and shape, which can be useful for display or camouflage.

bold breeding plumage

white for long-distance visual contact

SNOW BUNTING **GANNET**

Location

Similar species often live in different habitats, thus exploiting different feeding or nesting opportunities and avoiding competition with each other. Knowing this is helpful in identifying them. For example, Skylarks occur on open ground, rarely even close to a hedgerow, and may perch on a low fence but not on high wires. Woodlarks, by contrast, live along woodland edges and heaths, often close to bushy cover, and will perch high on a tree or wire.

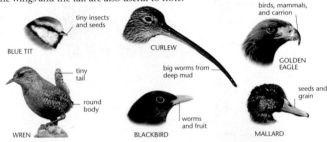

WOODLARK

SKYLARK

Shape and Size

Judging size can be difficult but it is a useful clue to identification. If you see an unfamiliar bird, try to estimate its size against a more familiar one. Also try to judge a bird's a bird's overall shape, including bill and leg lengths. Bill shape is generally related to a bird's diet. The shapes of the wings and the tail are also useful to note.

BLUE TIT — tiny insects and seeds

CURLEW — big worms from deep mud

GOLDEN EAGLE — birds, mammals, and carrion

WREN — tiny tail, round body

BLACKBIRD — worms and fruit

MALLARD — seeds and grain

Flight

Sometimes, the only view you will get of a bird is in flight, when details of plumage and colour are often hard to see. In such cases, the way it flies may be your best clue. Birds have a host of different flight styles: they may fly with long glides on outstretched wings or with constant wing-beats, have shallow or deep beats, flat or arched wings, or hover or dive.

KESTREL HOVERING *Kestrels hunt from the air if there is no perch nearby, hovering as if suspended on a string.*

GOLDFINCH FLOCK
Goldfinches have a particularly light, airy, bouncing flight, with deep, swooping bounds.

Identifying Butterflies and Moths

Some butterfly and moth species are easy to identify, yet within certain groups there are species that are bafflingly similar to one another. By observing physical features, such as colours, markings, and wing shape, along with habitat preferences and geographical range, almost all species can be identified by a persistent beginner.

Anatomy

Butterflies and moths are insects, forming the group – or order – Lepidoptera. Lepidoptera literally means "scale wings" and, indeed, the wings of almost all species in this group are cloaked in scales, which give the wings their colours and patterns. Like other adult insects, the body of a butterfly or moth is divided into three sections: the head, on which are found the eyes, mouthparts, and antennae; the thorax, to which the wings and legs are attached by powerful internal muscles; and the abdomen, which contains many of the vital organs, including the digestive and reproductive systems.

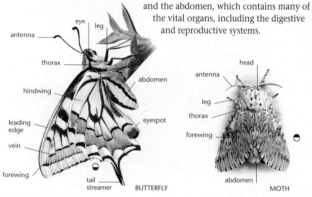

BUTTERFLY

MOTH

Markings and Wing Shape

The wings are generally the most striking part of a butterfly or moth, and their colour and markings offer vital clues to identification. Butterfly and moth wing shape varies remarkably given that their primary role – flight – is purely functional. A peculiar wing shape may also enhance the camouflage.

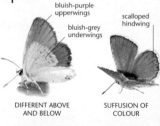

DIFFERENT ABOVE AND BELOW

SUFFUSION OF COLOUR

BAND OF COLOUR

JAGGED MARGIN

EYE SPOTS

FEATHERY PLUMES

Identifying Insects and Spiders

When you find a land-living arthropod, start by deciding which group it belongs to. In general, if it has eight or more pairs of legs and a long body, it is a myriapod; if it has seven pairs of legs, it is a woodlouse. If it has four pairs, it must be an arachnid, and if it has three it is a hexapod.

Anatomy

Insects belong to a large group of animals called arthropods. Other arthropods include arachnids: (spiders and relatives), myriapods (millipedes, centipedes, and relatives), and crustaceans (land-living woodlice and marine species such as shrimps and crabs). Arthropods have a protective outer skeleton, or cuticle, made of a tough material called chitin and pairs of jointed legs. The body segments are arranged to form a number of functioning units. Unlike other arthropods, insects possess only three pairs of legs and they usually have wings. Insect bodies are divided into three separate body sections (head, thorax, and abdomen), whereas arachnids have only two distinct body parts.

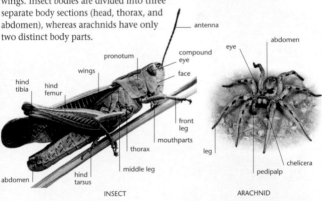

INSECT

ARACHNID

SEX

In many arthropods, the sexes look the same, but in others the male and female differ. Often an appendage is unique to one sex, such as the ovipositor of female horntails.

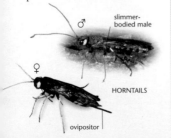

slimmer-bodied male

♂

♀

HORNTAILS

ovipositor

CAMOUFLAGE AND WARNINIG

Many arthropods have dull or mottled coloration as camouflage or are a similar tone to their habitat. Some mimic other, more dangerous, species.

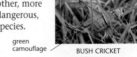

green camouflage

BUSH CRICKET

bee-like appearance

ASSASSIN FLY

Trees

A tree is usually defined as a long-lived woody plant with a distinct main trunk. However, some species have several stems arising from the ground, such as the Hazel and Elder – and although these are technically shrubs, they have been included in this chapter. There are about 60 species of trees that are native to Britain, though there are many others that have been introduced from other parts of the world for their ornamental or commercial value, and are now common and familiar trees, especially in urban areas.

NORWAY
MAPLE

ROWAN

SPANISH
CHESTNUT

YEW

Leyland Cypress

x *Cupressocyparis leylandii* (Cupressaceae)

narrow, columnar habit

A very fast-growing, evergreen tree, the Leyland Cypress has a dense, narrow, columnar habit, tapering towards the top. The tiny, scale-like, dark green leaves have pointed tips. They are borne in small, flattened sprays densely arranged all around the shoots. While male flower clusters are yellow, females are green.

SPHERICAL *green young cones, when produced, ripen to brown the second year after flowering and so appear clustered on the old shoots.*

yellow male flowers

cone 2cm wide

densely arranged leaves

HEIGHT *30m or more.* **SPREAD** *10m.*
BARK *Red-brown and smooth, ridged and flaking with age.*
FLOWERING TIME *Spring.*
OCCURRENCE *Known only in cultivation (several forms are grown, with various foliage colours, especially yellow).*
SIMILAR SPECIES *None.*

Norway Spruce

Picea abies (Pinaceae)

A vigorous evergreen, the Norway Spruce has many cultivars and varieties. Its dark green leaves, with pointed tips, are arranged on orange-brown shoots. Flowers of both sexes bloom separately on the same tree. The reddish male flower clusters become yellow when ripe and releasing pollen; the red female flower clusters develop into brown cones when ripe.

conical tip

CYLINDRICAL, *hanging brown cones have scales that are notched at the tips.*

large, upright tree

female flowers

cone to 15cm long

leaf to 2cm long

male flowers

HEIGHT *50m.* **SPREAD** *15m.*
BARK *Purple, developing scales when mature.*
FLOWERING TIME *Late spring.*
OCCURRENCE *Introduced; widely planted for timber and as an ornamental tree. Native to mainland Europe.*
SIMILAR SPECIES *Sitka Spruce* (P. sitchensis) *has flattened leaves with white lines beneath.*

Scots Pine

Pinus sylvestris (Pinaceae)

YELLOW *male flowers nestle among the rigid and twisted blue-green leaves that are borne in pairs on the shoots; sometimes they have a silvery tinge.*

An evergreen tree, with branches that grow in whorls, the Scots Pine is conical when young, developing a rounded, spreading head on a tall trunk with age. The stout, needle-like leaves are blue-green to blue-grey. Male flower clusters are cylindrical and yellow, and found at the base of young shoots. Female clusters are upright and red, and are scattered in ones or twos at the tips of the young shoots. They mature in the second autumn to egg-shaped, woody green cones that are brown when ripe.

rounded, spreading head

orange to pink bark on upper trunk

NOTE

Many selections, particularly dwarf forms, are cultivated in gardens. Of those that grow into trees, P. sylvestris 'Aurea' has bright yellow leaves in winter, while P. sylvestris 'Fastigiata' is narrowly columnar in habit.

female flower

leaf to 7cm long

male flower

cone to 8cm long

HEIGHT *30m or more.* **SPREAD** *15m.*
BARK *Purple-grey, orange to pink towards top of trunk; deeply cracked, and fissured, flaking into small plates with age.*
FLOWERING TIME *Early summer.*
OCCURRENCE *Scottish highlands; commonly planted and naturalized elsewhere.*
SIMILAR SPECIES *None – its blue-green foliage and coloured upper bark make it easy to recognize.*

Yew

Taxus baccata (Taxaceae)

A broadly conical, evergreen tree, the Yew is often many-trunked. Linear and pointed at the tip, the leaves are dark green above, with two pale bands below, mainly spread in two rows on either side of the shoots. Male flowers grow beneath the shoots, while the tiny green female flowers are borne singly at the ends of the shoots on separate plants. The fruit is a single seed, held in a fleshy, usually red aril. It is open at the top, exposing the green seed, ripening the first autumn. All parts (except the arils) are poisonous. 'Fastigiata', or Irish Yew, is a selection with upright branches and leaves growing all around the shoots.

ROUNDED, *pale yellow male flower clusters, about 3–4mm wide, are found in the leaf axils beneath the shoots.*

conical habit

upright branches

yellow aril

leaf to 3cm long

fleshy red aril with seed

'LUTEA'

NOTE

The Yew is often seen in gardens as hedges or topiary. Many selections have been made, including several with variegated foliage. 'Lutea' is an unusual form with yellow fruit.

HEIGHT *20m.*
SPREAD *10m.*
BARK *Purple-brown, smooth, and flaking.*
FLOWERING TIME *Early spring.*
OCCURRENCE *In woods and thickets, mainly on chalk or limestone; also commonly cultivated.*
SIMILAR SPECIES *None – it is not easily confused with other species, especially when bearing fruit.*

European Larch

Larix decidua (Pinaceae)

This fast-growing species is deciduous. Its slender, soft, bright green leaves, each up to 4cm long, open in early spring, turning yellow in autumn. They are arranged singly on distinctive, long yellow shoots but are borne in dense whorls on short side shoots. Male flower clusters, on the underside of the shoots, are yellow, while the upright female clusters are red or yellow. The egg-shaped cones have upward-pointing scales and ripen in the first autumn after flowering.

OVAL red young cones with upright scales interspersed with needle-like leaves in clusters.

conical habit

thin, drooping branches

female flower cluster

male flower cluster

cone to 4cm long

HEIGHT *30–40m.* **SPREAD** *15m.*
BARK *Grey and smooth; becoming red-brown and cracking into scaly plates with age.*
FLOWERING TIME *Spring.*
OCCURRENCE *Introduced; commonly planted for timber. Native to C. Europe.*
SIMILAR SPECIES *Japanese Larch (L. kaempferi) has cones with out-curving scales.*

Common Juniper

Juniperus communis (Cupressaceae)

This evergreen conifer is of variable habit, from bushy and spreading, to upright. Its sharp-pointed needles are marked with a broad white band on the upper surface, and arranged in whorls of three on the shoots. The flowers are very small; males are yellow and females green, growing in clusters on separate plants. Female plants bear fleshy, blue-black berry-like cones up to 6mm long, covered at first with a white bloom.

PROSTRATE and creeping, or a bushy shrub, or sometimes a tree, this species is of very variable habit.

glossy green needles

leaf to 1.2cm long

cone to 6mm long

bushy, spreading habit

HEIGHT *6m.* **SPREAD** *1–3m.*
BARK *Red-brown with longitudinal ridges; peeling in vertical strips.*
FLOWERING TIME *Spring.*
OCCURRENCE *In scrub on heathland, chalk, and limestone; widely but often locally distributed.*
SIMILAR SPECIES *None.*

Field Maple

Acer campestre (Aceraceae)

Also known as Hedge Maple, this deciduous tree sometimes appears shrubby. The opposite leaves are dark green above, paler and hairy beneath, and turn yellow in autumn. They are heart-shaped at the base and deeply cut into five lobes, which are usually untoothed and pointed. Clusters of green flowers open with the young leaves. When cut, the leaf stalk exudes a milky sap.

round crown

spreading habit

HANGING *in clusters, each fruit has two spreading wings; ripens from green to reddish.*

leaf to 10cm wide

fruit to 2.5cm long, 5cm wide

HEIGHT *15m.* **SPREAD** *10m.*
BARK *Pale brown, with orange fissures, and somewhat corky.*
FLOWERING TIME *Mid- to late spring.*
OCCURRENCE *Woods and hedgerows throughout Britain, particularly on alkaline soils; less common in Scotland.*
SIMILAR SPECIES *None.*

Sycamore

Acer pseudoplatanus (Aceraceae)

The broad crown of this large, deciduous tree spreads with age. Its shoots end in green buds and the opposite leaves are divided into five sharp-toothed lobes. The leaves are dark green above and blue-grey beneath, turning yellow in autumn. Small flowers are borne in dense, drooping panicles, followed by fruit with green or red-flushed wings.

YELLOW-GREEN *flowers hang in pendulous clusters; leaves are palmately lobed.*

broad, columnar head

dense foliage

leaf to 15cm wide

fruit wing to 3cm long

5-lobed leaf

flower cluster to 12cm long

HEIGHT *30m.* **SPREAD** *20m.*
BARK *Pinkish to yellow-grey, flaking in irregular plates when old.*
FLOWERING TIME *Mid-spring.*
OCCURRENCE *Woods, hedgerows, and roadsides throughout Britain and Ireland.*
SIMILAR SPECIES *Norway Maple (p.26) has leaves that are glossy green beneath.*

Norway Maple

Acer platanoides (Aceraceae)

A large, vigorous, deciduous tree with a broadly columnar crown, the Norway Maple has shoots ending in red buds. The large, opposite leaves are divided into five lobes, each with several tapered teeth. Clusters of small, bright yellow flowers open before the young leaves emerge, followed by fruit with large wings.

YELLOW *or red in autumn, the broad, bright green leaves each have five lobes.*

autumn foliage

leaf to 18cm long

fruit to 5cm long

bright yellow flower cluster

HEIGHT *25m.* **SPREAD** *15m.*
BARK *Grey and smooth.*
FLOWERING TIME *Early spring.*
OCCURRENCE *Woods and hedgerows; introduced and naturalized in many areas; commonly planted.*
SIMILAR SPECIES *Sycamore (p.25), which has pendulous flower clusters..*

Common Holly

Ilex aquifolium (Aquifoliaceae)

This evergreen tree is sometimes shrubby, with green or purple shoots. Glossy, dark green, alternate leaves range from oval to oblong. Spiny leaves generally occur on younger trees and lower shoots, while smooth leaves occur on older trees and higher shoots. White or purple-flushed flowers grow in clusters, with males and females on separate trees.

SHINY, *bright red or yellow-orange berries are densely clustered on the branches of female trees.*

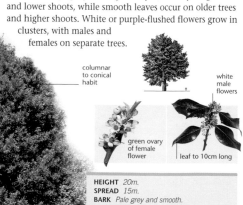

columnar to conical habit

white male flowers

green ovary of female flower

leaf to 10cm long

HEIGHT *20m.*
SPREAD *15m.*
BARK *Pale grey and smooth.*
FLOWERING TIME *Late spring.*
OCCURRENCE *Woods and hedgerows throughout Britain and Ireland.*
SIMILAR SPECIES *None – it is a distinct tree.*

Silver Birch

Betula pendula (Betulaceae)

The young shoots of this deciduous tree are rough to the touch, with numerous small warts. The glossy and dark green leaves are oval to triangular, edged with double teeth, and turn yellow in autumn. Tiny flowers are borne in catkins, the males drooping, and the females upright, and later drooping. The brown fruit clusters break up when ripe. The bark has has deep cracks and knobbly bumps towards the base.

WHITE *bark of mature trees is prominently marked with dark scars and cracks.*

narrow, weeping habit

fruit cluster to 3cm long

leaf to 6cm long

green female

yellow male catkin to 6cm long

HEIGHT *30m.* **SPREAD** *20m.*
BARK *White, often developing black, diamond-shaped, markings at the base of mature trees.*
FLOWERING TIME *Mid-spring.*
OCCURRENCE *Woods, heaths, and mountains, except on chalky soil.*
SIMILAR SPECIES *Downy Birch (B. pubescens), which has hairy leaves.*

Hornbeam

Carpinus betulus (Betulaceae)

Conical when young, the deciduous Hornbeam develops a more rounded outline, the shoots often drooping at the tips. The oval to oblong leaves have prominent veins and are double-toothed at the margins. They are dark green above, paler beneath, and turn yellow in autumn. The tiny flowers are borne in pendulous catkins as the young leaves emerge.

PENDULOUS *fruiting clusters with three-lobed, green bracts are borne in summer.*

broadly spreading habit

leaf to 10cm long

female catkin

fruit cluster

HEIGHT *30m.* **SPREAD** *25m.*
BARK *Pale grey and smooth, fluted on old trees.*
FLOWERING TIME *Early spring.*
OCCURRENCE *Woods and hedgerows mainly in S.E. Britain. It is commonly cultivated.*
SIMILAR SPECIES *None – the fruit is distinct among British trees.*

Alder

Alnus glutinosa (Betulaceae)

SMALL *green unripe fruit are borne in clusters and mature to woody, dark brown cones that remain on the tree during winter.*

The Alder is a deciduous tree of conical habit, whose young green shoots and alternate leaves are slightly sticky to the touch. The dark green, mature leaves, paler beneath, are up to 10cm long; they are widest at the tip, which may be indented, and have a tapering base. The tiny flowers are borne in separate male and female catkins formed during the summer. The males are pendulous and yellow, up to 10cm long; the upright females are red and much smaller, only about 5mm long.

conical habit

green unripe fruit

ripe fruit 2cm long

NOTE

This is the only British native alder. 'Imperialis', a garden selection, is a smaller tree with leaves that are deeply cut into pointed lobes. The Alder is often grown in gardens and parks as an ornamental tree.

HEIGHT *25m.*
SPREAD *12m.*
BARK *Dark grey; cracks into square plates on old trees.*
FLOWERING TIME *Early spring.*
OCCURRENCE *Riverbanks and other wet places throughout Britain and Ireland.*
SIMILAR SPECIES *None – the leaves, broadest at the end with a notched tip, are distinct in shape from other species of Alnus.*

Common Hazel

Corylus avellana (Betulaceae)

Frequently shrubby and forming thickets, this spreading tree has several stems from the base and is often coppiced for its shoots. The alternate, heart-shaped, hairy, dark green leaves turn yellow in autumn. Male flowers appear before the leaves open and female flowers are tiny, with only the red stigmas showing. Partially enclosed in a deeply lobed pale green husk, the edible nuts (cobnuts) are carried in clusters of up to four.

PALE *yellow, pendulous catkins hang from bare shoots, and contain the male flowers.*

multiple stems

leaf to 10cm long

edible nuts

HEIGHT *10m.* **SPREAD** *10m.*
BARK *Grey-brown, glossy, peeling in strips.*
FLOWERING TIME *Late winter to early spring.*
OCCURRENCE *Woods, hedgerows, and thickets throughout Britain.*
SIMILAR SPECIES *This is the only species native to Britain although others are cultivated and sometimes escape from gardens.*

Common Box

Buxus sempervirens (Buxaceae)

This evergreen plant is more often a shrub than a tree. Its opposite, dark green leaves are often blue-green when young. The flowers of both sexes are separate but in the same cluster, the males with conspicuous yellow anthers. The small green fruit are topped with three horns, which are much shorter than the fruit.

OFTEN *a shrub, particularly in exposed positions, but can become a tree in sheltered woodland.*

conical to columnar or spreading habit

leaf to 3cm long

male flowers

fruit to 8mm long

HEIGHT *6m.* **SPREAD** *5m.*
BARK *Grey and smooth, cracking into small squares on older trees.*
FLOWERING TIME *Early spring.*
OCCURRENCE *Beechwoods on alkaline soil. A scarce native of S. Britain; widely planted and naturalized elsewhere.*
SIMILAR SPECIES *None.*

Elder

Sambucus nigra (Caprifoliaceae)

Characterized by a rather twisted growth, and arching branches, the deciduous Elder tree is often shrubby, with several stems sprouting from the base. The leaves, borne in opposite pairs are pinnate, with 5–7 sharply toothed, oval, elliptical, and pointed leaflets. The flowers are followed by glossy black, edible berries, which are green when unripe.

TINY, *creamy white, fragrant flowers are borne in broad, flattened heads up to 25cm wide.*

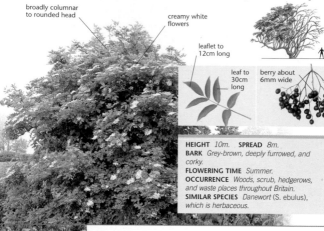

broadly columnar to rounded head

creamy white flowers

leaflet to 12cm long

leaf to 30cm long

berry about 6mm wide

HEIGHT *10m.* **SPREAD** *8m.*
BARK *Grey-brown, deeply furrowed, and corky.*
FLOWERING TIME *Summer.*
OCCURRENCE *Woods, scrub, hedgerows, and waste places throughout Britain.*
SIMILAR SPECIES *Danewort (S. ebulus), which is herbaceous.*

Rhododendron

Rhododendron ponticum (Ericaceae)

The stout shoots of this large, rounded, and evergreen shrub bear alternate, oblong, glossy dark green, untoothed leaves up to 20cm long and 6cm wide. The purple-pink flowers have brownish spots inside. The fruit is a small capsule that splits to release numerous tiny seeds. Rhododendron is an invasive alien, taking over British woodland.

ATTRACTIVE *bell-shaped flowers, to 5cm wide, in rounded clusters at the end of the shoots.*

brownish spots on upper petal

glossy dark green leaf

5-lobed flower

purple-pink flower

prominent stamens

HEIGHT *3m.* **SPREAD** *5m.*
FLOWERING TIME *Late spring to early summer.*
OCCURRENCE *Introduced; native of extreme S.W. and S.E. Europe, and S.W. Asia; hybrids are naturalized in woods throughout most of Britain on sandy or peaty soils.*
SIMILAR SPECIES *Other hybrids in gardens.*

Wayfaring Tree

Viburnum lantana (Caprifoliaceae)

This upright, deciduous shrub has stout, scurfy-hairy shoots. The opposite, oval, dark green leaves are up to 10cm long and 8cm wide, with hair beneath. Small, creamy white flowers are borne in domed heads to 10cm wide. These are followed by flattened, oval berries, each up to 8mm long. Each berry contains a single seed.

SMALL, *white, five-lobed flowers with projecting stamens are borne in dense, domed clusters.*

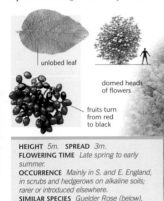

unlobed leaf

domed heads of flowers

fruits turn from red to black

HEIGHT *5m.* **SPREAD** *3m.*
FLOWERING TIME *Late spring to early summer.*
OCCURRENCE *Mainly in S. and E. England, in scrubs and hedgerows on alkaline soils; rarer or introduced elsewhere.*
SIMILAR SPECIES *Guelder Rose (below), which has lobed leaves.*

Guelder Rose

Viburnum opulus (Caprifoliaceae)

A large deciduous shrub, the Guelder Rose is upright when young, and later rounded. The smooth shoots bear opposite leaves with 3–5 toothed lobes that often turn red in autumn. Small white flowers in broad flowerheads up to 10cm wide are surrounded by a ring of sterile flowers.

JUICY *bright red fruits ripen as the leaves start to colour in autumn and are edible if cooked.*

maple-like leaf

smooth shoot

flattened flowerhead

large sterile flowers

HEIGHT *5m.*
SPREAD *5m.*
FLOWERING TIME *Early summer.*
OCCURRENCE *Scrubs, hedgerows, and woods, also commonly planted; widely distributed but less common in the far north.*
SIMILAR SPECIES *Wayfaring Tree (above), which lacks the large, sterile flowers.*

Common Laburnum

Laburnum anagyroides (Leguminosae/Fabaceae)

Also known as the Golden Rain Tree, this deciduous, tree has alternate leaves with three leaflets, each rounded at the tip. They are deep green above, grey-green and whitish beneath, and covered with silky white hair when young. Golden yellow flowers are borne in leafless clusters. The fruit is a slightly rounded, hairy, pale brown pod.

PEA-LIKE, *fragrant, golden yellow flowers are borne in slender, pendulous clusters.*

leaflet to 9cm long

flower to 2.5cm long

broadly spreading habit

HEIGHT 7m. **SPREAD** 3m.
BARK *Smooth and dark grey.*
FLOWERING TIME *Late spring to early summer.*
OCCURRENCE *Introduced and mainly grown in gardens, occasionally naturalized.*
SIMILAR SPECIES *Voss's Laburnum (L. x watereri), which has longer flower clusters.*

Black Locust

Robinia pseudoacacia (Leguminosae/Fabaceae)

Often spreading widely by means of suckers, this is a vigorous, deciduous tree with a broadly columnar head. The alternate, pinnate leaves on red-brown shoots have up to 21 leaflets, usually with a pair of spines at the base. Pea-like, fragrant white flowers hang in clusters to 20cm long, with dark brown pods up to 10cm long.

DARK *blue-green leaves have many elliptical untoothed leaflets that are grey-green beneath.*

leaflet to 5cm long

leaf to 30cm long

flower to 2cm long

columnar habit

HEIGHT 25m. **SPREAD** 15m.
BARK *Grey-brown with deep furrows.*
FLOWERING TIME *Early summer.*
OCCURRENCE *Cultivated, and widely naturalized; native to S.E. USA.*
SIMILAR SPECIES *The cultivated species, Honey Locust (Gleditsia triacanthos) has pink flowers, spiny shoots, and bipinnate leaves.*

Spanish Chestnut

Castanea sativa (Fagaceae)

Also known as the Sweet Chestnut, this deciduous tree was widely introduced outside its native region of southern Europe by the Romans. Its alternate, oblong leaves taper to a point and are edged with numerous teeth. They are glossy, dark green and turn yellow-brown in autumn. The flowers are borne in slender, upright to spreading catkins.

SLENDER, *creamy white flower spikes cover the tree in summer, making for a spectacular sight in parks and gardens.*

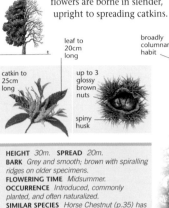

leaf to 20cm long

broadly columnar habit

catkin to 25cm long

up to 3 glossy brown nuts

spiny husk

HEIGHT *30m.* **SPREAD** *20m.*
BARK *Grey and smooth; brown with spiralling ridges on older specimens.*
FLOWERING TIME *Midsummer.*
OCCURRENCE *Introduced, commonly planted, and often naturalized.*
SIMILAR SPECIES *Horse Chestnut (p.35) has larger flower clusters and opposite leaves.*

Common Beech

Fagus sylvatica (Fagaceae)

Zig-zag shoots ending in long, slender-pointed buds characterize this spreading, deciduous tree. It has alternate, dark green, wavy-edged leaves, widest above the middle, with up to ten pairs of veins. Its tiny flowers open with the young leaves, males and females in separate clusters. The more conspicuous males are borne in drooping, rounded, pale yellow heads. The fruit is a woody husk, up to 2.5cm long, and contains one or two edible nuts

SILKY *and hairy when young, the dark green leaves turn bright yellow in autumn.*

spreading habit

yellow autumn foliage

leaf to 10cm long

HEIGHT *30m.*
SPREAD *20m.*
BARK *Pale grey and smooth.*
FLOWERING TIME *Mid-spring.*
OCCURRENCE *Woods in S. England and S. Wales, commonly planted and naturalized further north.*
SIMILAR SPECIES *None.*

English Oak

Quercus robur (Fagaceae)

This oak is a deciduous, spreading tree with smooth shoots. The alternate, widest above the middle, very short-stalked leaves have 5–7 lobes on each side, and are dark green above and blue-green beneath. Flowers are borne in catkins: the males yellow-green and drooping; the females inconspicuous.

LONG-STALKED *acorns are enclosed in a scaly cup, turning brown and developing dark stripes.*

rounded head

spreading habit

rounded head

yellow-green male flowers

leaf to 12cm long

acorn to 4cm long

HEIGHT 35m. **SPREAD** 30m.
BARK Grey with vertical fissures.
FLOWERING TIME Late spring.
OCCURRENCE Woods throughout British Isles.
SIMILAR SPECIES Sessile Oak (below), which has long-stalked leaves and unstalked acorns; Turkey Oak (Q. cerris), which has long scales on the acorn cups and rough leaves.

Sessile Oak

Quercus petraea (Fagaceae)

This is a large, deciduous tree with smooth young shoots. The alternate leaves are borne on stalks up to 1cm or more long and are edged with rounded, untoothed lobes. Dark, slightly glossy green above, they have a thin layer of hair beneath. Male and female flowers are borne separately in catkins: the males yellow-green and drooping; the females inconspicuous.

PROMINENT *and deep vertical ridges develop on the grey bark.*

broadly spreading habit

leaf to 12cm long

acorn to 3cm long

HEIGHT 40m. **SPREAD** 25m.
BARK Grey; vertically ridged in mature trees.
FLOWERING TIME Late spring.
OCCURRENCE Widespread in woods on acidic soil.
SIMILAR SPECIES English Oak (above), which has leaves with very short stalks but long-stalked acorns.

Horse Chestnut

Aesculus hippocastanum (Hippocastanaceae)

The familiar Horse Chestnut is characterized by the large, glossy brown and very sticky buds that appear in winter. Its flowers are white with a yellow blotch that turns red. They are borne in large, upright, conical clusters and are followed by distinctive green fruit that contain up to three glossy brown seeds or conkers. A deciduous tree with a broadly columnar to spreading habit, it has palmate, dark green leaves each with 5–7 large, sharply toothed leaflets with short stalks. The leaves turn orange-red in autumn. 'Baumannii', a selection of this species, has double flowers and no fruit.

LARGE, *creamy white flower clusters – a spectacular sight in spring, in parks, streets, and gardens, where the tree is common.*

columnar to spreading shape

vigorous habit

leaf to 30cm long

flower cluster to 30cm long

HEIGHT *30m.*
SPREAD *20m.*
BARK *Red-brown to grey; flaking in scales on large trees.*
FLOWERING TIME *Late spring.*
OCCURRENCE *Introduced; commonly planted and naturalized. Native to Greece and Albania.*
SIMILAR SPECIES *The commonly planted Red Horse Chestnut (A. x carnea) is a hybrid of this species.*

NOTE

Although commonly planted in parks and large gardens, the origin of this tree was unknown for many years, until it was discovered in the wild in the mountains of N. Greece. The seeds are used in the game of conkers.

Common Ash

Fraxinus excelsior (Oleaceae)

A large, deciduous tree, the Common Ash has stout, smooth shoots and prominent black buds. The opposite, pinnate leaves have up to 13 sharply toothed, dark green leaflets, with a slender, tapered point at the tip. Vigorous shoots from the base may be produced in summer and these often have purple foliage.

TINY *purple flowers in dense clusters have no petals; green fruit are produced in clusters.*

leaf to 30cm long

fruit to 4cm long

broadly columnar habit

HEIGHT *30m or more.* **SPREAD** *20m.*
BARK *Smooth and pale grey when young, developing deep fissures with age.*
FLOWERING TIME *Spring.*
OCCURRENCE *Moist woods and river banks; often on alkaline soils throughout the British Isles.*
SIMILAR SPECIES *None – this is the only ash native to Britain; others are grown in gardens.*

London Plane

Platanus x hispanica (Platanaceae)

This vigorous, large, deciduous tree with a spreading to broadly columnar head has alternate, maple-like leaves with five toothed lobes. Glossy bright green above, the leaves are paler beneath, with brown hair when young. Tiny flowers are borne in pendulous, rounded clusters – male clusters yellow, females red. Dense, rounded fruit clusters persist on the tree over winter, in groups of up to six.

GREY, *brown, and cream, the bark begins to flake conspicuously in large patches with age.*

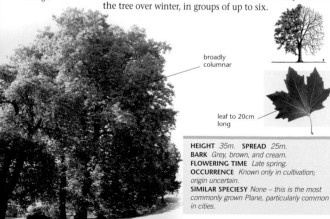

broadly columnar

leaf to 20cm long

HEIGHT *35m.* **SPREAD** *25m.*
BARK *Grey, brown, and cream.*
FLOWERING TIME *Late spring.*
OCCURRENCE *Known only in cultivation; origin uncertain.*
SIMILAR SPECIESY *None – this is the most commonly grown Plane, particularly common in cities.*

Hawthorn

Crataegus monogyna (Rosaceae)

The smooth, thorny shoots of this deciduous species are often somewhat pendulous on old trees. The alternate leaves are oval to diamond-shaped in outline, with a broadly tapered base. They are deeply cut into three or five sharply toothed lobes and are glossy, dark green above and paler beneath. The fragrant white flowers have pink anthers and are borne in dense clusters. These are followed by bright red oval fruit up to 1.2cm wide, each containing a single stone. The Hawthorn is a variable and widely distributed species, often used for hedging.

SHINY, *bright red fruit or hips ripen in attractive clusters at the end of branches from September to October.*

white blossom

broadly spreading habit

flower to 1.5cm wide

leaf to 5cm long

NOTE

The garden selection 'Biflora', known as the Glastonbury Thorn, flowers twice: once in winter or early spring, depending on the weather, and again at the normal time of late spring. It was said to have grown from the staff of Joseph of Arimathea, which he plunged into the ground at Glastonbury when he came to England from the Holy Land.

HEIGHT 10m. **SPREAD** 10m.
BARK Orange-brown; cracked and scaly in old trees.
FLOWERING TIME Late spring.
OCCURRENCE Woods, scrub, and hedgerows; widely distributed throughout the British Isles.
SIMILAR SPECIES Midland Hawthorn (C. laevigata), which has less deeply cut leaves with three to five more or less blunt lobes and fruit containing two stones.

Wild Apple

Malus sylvestris (Rosaceae)

WHITE, *often pink-tinged flowers appear in clusters in April and May.*

This deciduous, spreading tree or shrub sometimes has spiny shoots. The oval to nearly rounded leaves have finely toothed margins and short-pointed tips; they are dark green above, paler below, and smooth or nearly so on both sides when mature. White or pink-tinged flowers, up to 4cm wide, are borne in clusters, followed by small, yellow-green or red-flushed fruit.

spreading habit

leaf to 8cm long

fruit to 4cm wide

HEIGHT *10m.* **SPREAD** *10m.*
BARK *Brown, cracked, and fissured with age.*
FLOWERING TIME *Late spring.*
OCCURRENCE *Woods, thickets, and hedgerows almost throughout the British Isles.*
SIMILAR SPECIES *Other species of Apple are grown in gardens and may be locally naturalized.*

Wild Cherry

Prunus avium (Rosaceae)

FIVE-PETALLED *white flowers, 3cm wide, are borne in clusters just before or as the young leaves emerge.*

A deciduous tree, the Wild Cherry or Gean is conical when young becoming broadly columnar to spreading with age. Elliptic to oblong, the alternate, sharply toothed leaves are up to 15cm long and taper to a short point at the tip. They are bronze when young, maturing to matt dark green, and turn yellow or red in autumn.

spreading habit

profusion of white flowers

fruit to 1cm wide

pink-tinged buds

flower to 3cm wide

HEIGHT *25m.* **SPREAD** *15m.*
BARK *Red-brown, smooth, and glossy at first; peeling horizontally in strips.*
FLOWERING TIME *Spring.*
OCCURRENCE *Woods and hedgerows throughout the British Isles.*
SIMILAR SPECIES *It is distinct among native trees due to its large flowers and large size.*

Blackthorn

Prunus spinosa (Rosaceae)

More a deciduous, thicket-forming shrub than a spreading tree, the Blackthorn has spiny shoots. The small, alternate leaves are broadest at the end, with a toothed margin. They are dark green above; hairy beneath when young. Small white flowers, about 1.5cm wide, are usually borne singly and open on the bare shoots before the leaves emerge.

ROUNDED *blue-black berries are covered with a white bloom; inedible and bitter.*

white flowers clothe shoots in spring

leaf to 4cm long

blue-black fruit

HEIGHT *5m.* **SPREAD** *6m.*
BARK *Dark grey-black.*
FLOWERING TIME *Spring.*
OCCURRENCE *Thickets, wood margins, and hedgerows throughout the British Isles.*
SIMILAR SPECIES *Cherry Plum (P. cerasifera), which flowers earlier, and has edible, plum-like fruit.*

Rowan

Sorbus aucuparia (Rosaceae)

Spreading with age, this deciduous, conical tree has shoots that end in purple buds covered in grey hairs. Alternate, pinnate leaves have up to 15 sharply toothed, taper-pointed, dark green leaflets, which are blue-green beneath. The small white flowers, each with five petals and conspicuous stamens, open in broad heads and develop into berries, which are poisonous when raw.

HEAVY *clusters of rounded orange-red berries, attractive to birds, often weigh down the branches.*

broadly conical habit

flowerhead to 15cm wide

leaf to 20cm long

fruit to 8mm wide

HEIGHT *15m.* **SPREAD** *10m.*
BARK *Glossy grey and smooth, becoming ridged with age.*
FLOWERING TIME *Late spring.*
OCCURRENCE *Widely distributed, except on chalk soils; often planted.*
SIMILAR SPECIES *Service Tree (S. domestica), which has similar leaves but larger fruits.*

Whitebeam

Sorbus aria (Rosaceae)

FIVE-PETALLED *flowers, with numerous white stamens, open in flattened clusters.*

A rounded, deciduous tree, the Whitebeam is conical when young. The shoots are covered with white hairs at first but become smooth with age. Arranged alternately, the oval leaves have sharply pointed teeth; they are white with hairs on both sides when young, becoming smooth and glossy, dark green above.

broadly columnar habit

leaf to 12cm long

fruit to 1.5cm wide

bright red fruit

HEIGHT 20m. **SPREAD** 20m.
BARK Grey and smooth; cracking with age.
FLOWERING TIME Late spring to early summer.
OCCURRENCE In woods, mainly on chalk in southern Britain; widely planted elsewhere.
SIMILAR SPECIES Several other very locally distributed species occur in parts of Britain.

White Poplar

Populus alba (Salicaceae)

DENSE *white hair cover the underside of leaves, they have three to five deep lobes when on vigorous shoots.*

A deciduous tree, the White Poplar is broadly columnar, spreading with age. The alternate leaves have rounded stalks. They have a dense layer of white hair on both surfaces when young, but later become dark green and smooth above. Male and female flowers are borne in drooping catkins on separate plants, the males grey with red anthers, the females green.

spreading habit

leaf to 10cm long

white, hairy young leaves

HEIGHT 30m. **SPREAD** 20m.
BARK Pale grey, dark and fissured at the base of the tree.
FLOWERING TIME Early spring.
OCCURRENCE Introduced and commonly planted; native to mainland Europe.
SIMILAR SPECIES Aspen (right), which has unlobed leaves and flattened leaf stalks.

Aspen

Populus tremula (Salicaceae)

Often found on poor soils, the deciduous Aspen forms large colonies in woods, spreading by means of suckers produced by the roots. Carried on long, flattened stalks, the leaves are edged with rounded teeth. Bronze and hairy when young, the leaves become grey-green above, paler beneath, and turn yellow in autumn. The flowers are borne in drooping catkins, up to 8cm long. The male catkins are grey, the female green, on separate trees.

PENDULOUS *grey male catkins, with red anthers, hang from the bare shoots in early spring.*

leaf to 8cm long

rounded leaf

conical to spreading habit

HEIGHT 20m. **SPREAD** 15m.
BARK Smooth and grey, darker and ridged at the base of old trees.
FLOWERING TIME Early spring.
OCCURRENCE Moist woods throughout Britain, more common in the north.
SIMILAR SPECIES White Poplar (left), which has lobed leaves that are white beneath.

Hybrid Black Poplar

Populus x canadensis (Salicaceae)

Several selections of this very vigorous, deciduous tree with a broadly columnar head, such as 'Robusta', are commonly grown. The broadly oval to nearly triangular, alternate leaves are longer on very vigorous shoots. They are often bronzy red and hairy margined when young, becoming glossy, dark green above. Tiny cottony seeds are released by small green fruit capsules.

DROOPING *catkins of male flowers with red anthers, and green female catkins, are borne on separate trees.*

leaf to 10cm long

pale grey bark

broadly columnar habit

HEIGHT 30m. **SPREAD** 20m.
BARK Pale grey and deeply furrowed.
FLOWERING TIME Early spring.
OCCURRENCE Known only in cultivation; a hybrid between Cottonwood (P. deltoides) and Black Poplar (P. nigra).
SIMILAR SPECIES Black Poplar (P. nigra), which lacks hair on the leaf margins.

Goat Willow

Salix caprea (Salicaceae)

FLOWERS are in catkins; the males are silvery with yellow anthers, the females are green.

This deciduous shrub, sometimes a small tree, is upright when young, later spreading and often branching low down or with several stems, the shoots not ridged beneath the bark. The oval, toothed, alternate leaves are hairy on both sides when young, though the grey-green uppersides becomes smooth in older trees. The flowers are borne in tiny catkins, up to 4cm long, on separate trees. Small green fruit open to release cottony seeds.

multiple stems

leaf to 10cm long

HEIGHT *10m.* **SPREAD** *8m.*
BARK *Grey and smooth; fissured on old trees.*
FLOWERING TIME *Early spring.*
OCCURRENCE *Woods and hedgerows; widely distributed and common.*
SIMILAR SPECIES *None, the size of the broad leaves, hairy beneath, make it distinct.*

Weeping Willow

Salix x sepulcralis 'Chrysocoma' (Salicaceae)

PALE grey-brown, the bark is marked with shallow fissures as the tree ages.

This deciduous, spreading tree has a rounded crown and long, pendulous yellow shoots. The alternate, finely toothed leaves end in tapered points. The flowers are borne in catkins and are mostly male with yellow anthers. The fruit is a small green capsule.

weeping habit

leaf to 12cm long

catkin to 7.5cm long

HEIGHT *20m.*
SPREAD *25m.*
BARK *Pale grey-brown and fissured.*
FLOWERING TIME *Spring.*
OCCURRENCE *Known only in cultivation.*
SIMILAR SPECIES *The species is a hybrid of White Willow (right) and S. babylonica, which was at one time grown in Europe.*

White Willow

Salix alba (Salicaceae)

The common large waterside willow of Europe, White Willow is a vigorous, spreading, deciduous tree, often with drooping shoots. The slender, lance-shaped, finely toothed leaves end in long, tapered points. They are silky and hairy when young, becoming dark green above and blue-green below. The tiny flowers are borne in small catkins as the leaves emerge; the males are yellow, while the females are green and are borne on separate trees.

Small green fruit open to release cottony seeds. The Scarlet Willow (*Salix alba* 'Britzensis') has orange-red winter shoots.

LONG, narrow leaves show their blue-green underside with the slightest breeze blowing along the river bank.

spreading habit

drooping branches

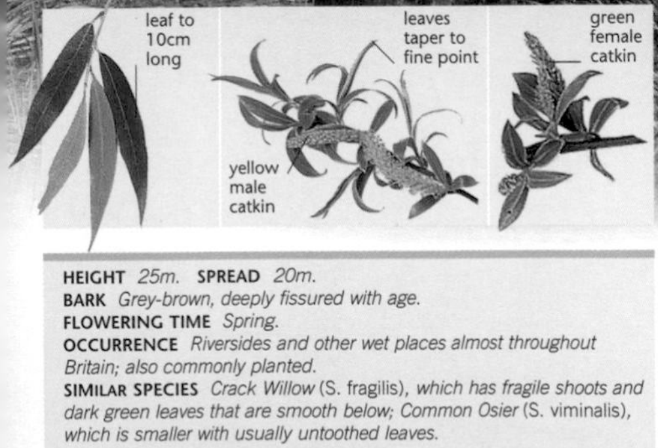

leaf to 10cm long

leaves taper to fine point

yellow male catkin

green female catkin

HEIGHT 25m. **SPREAD** 20m.
BARK Grey-brown, deeply fissured with age.
FLOWERING TIME Spring.
OCCURRENCE Riversides and other wet places almost throughout Britain; also commonly planted.
SIMILAR SPECIES Crack Willow (S. fragilis), which has fragile shoots and dark green leaves that are smooth below; Common Osier (S. viminalis), which is smaller with usually untoothed leaves.

NOTE

The White Willow is pollarded to encourage the growth of young shoots; the wood of Salix alba var. caerulea is highly valued as it is used for making cricket bats.

Common Lime

Tilia x europaea (Tiliaceae)

A hybrid between Small-leaved Lime (*T. cordata*) and Broad-leaved Lime (*T. platyphyllos*), this vigorous and large deciduous tree is broadly columnar in habit, and is often seen with numerous suckers at the base. The rounded to broadly oval, alternate leaves are sharply toothed and end in a short point. They are dark green above, green and smooth beneath except for tufts of hairs in the axils of the veins.

EGG-SHAPED *grey-green fruit are 1.2cm long, and similar to those of the Small-leaved Lime.*

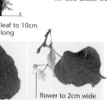

leaf to 10cm long

flower to 2cm wide

broadly columnar habit

HEIGHT *40m.* SPREAD *20m.*
BARK *Grey-brown, shallow fissures with age.*
FLOWERING TIME *Early spring.*
OCCURRENCE *Introduced; widely planted, and sometimes naturalized. Native to Europe.*
SIMILAR SPECIES *Small-leaved Lime, which has blue-green leaf undersides; Broad-leaved Lime, which has hairy leaf undersides.*

Wych Elm

Ulmus glabra (Ulmaceae)

Conical when young, this large, deciduous tree develops a rounded head with age and has rough young shoots. The alternate, oval leaves have unequal halves, with sharp teeth that are larger towards the tip. They are dark green and very rough above, with a short stalk. The flowers are followed by winged green fruit. Dutch Elm (*U. x hollandica*) is a hybrid between Wych Elm and Field Elm (*U. minor*).

SMALL *flowers with red anthers open on the bare shoots in late winter before the leaves emerge.*

rounded head

fruit to 2cm long

leaf to 15cm long

HEIGHT *30m.*
SPREAD *25m.*
BARK *Grey and smooth, becoming ridged in old trees.*
FLOWERING TIME *Late winter.*
OCCURRENCE *Woods and hedgerows, particularly in the north.*
SIMILAR SPECIES *None.*

Wild Flowers and Other Plants

Britain's mild climate and varied geology have led to a vast diversity of plantlife, including not only plants that are easily recognized as wild flowers, but also mosses, ferns, grasses, and seaweeds. Furthermore, its 1,500 native plant species have been augmented over the centuries with at least the same number of introductions from further afield, including some species that were brought by the Romans, some that were accidentally imported in ships' cargoes, and others that simply "escaped" from gardens.

SCARLET
PIMPERNEL

COWSLIP

MAIDENHAIR
SPLEENWORT

TOOTHED
WRACK

Hop

Humulus lupulus (Cannabaceae)

The deeply lobed leaves of the Hop are noticeable round the year as they scramble on twisting stems over bushes and hedges. Male flowers form loose panicles; female flowers, borne on separate plants, form leafy, cone-like catkins that develop into the fruit used to flavour beer.

SCRAMBLES *over or through hedgerows, bushes, and woodland trees, on walls, and up telegraph poles.*

rough, toothed leaf

green male flowers

cone-like fruit

drooping flower panicles

PERENNIAL   twining stems

PLANT HEIGHT *Up to 6m.*
FLOWER SIZE *Male 4–5mm long.*
FLOWERING TIME *July–September.*
LEAVES *Opposite, divided into 3–5 lobes.*
FRUIT *Cone, 2.5–3cm long, with overlapping bracts; pale brown when ripe.*
SIMILAR SPECIES *White Bryony (p.108), which has red berries.*

Common Nettle

Urtica dioica (Urticaceae)

Also known as Stinging Nettle, this plant is well known to all walkers in the countryside, for the leaves and stems are clothed in stiff, needle-like, hollow hairs which break at the slightest touch, releasing an intensely irritating fluid. The tiny flowers are green, sometimes with a reddish tinge, and have yellow stamens.

FORMS *colonies on cultivated and waste ground, roadsides, and scrub; on rich, disturbed soil.*

male flowers in long spikes

coarsely toothed leaves

female flower cluster

stiff, erect stem

PERENNIAL

PLANT HEIGHT *50–150cm.*
FLOWER SIZE *1–2mm wide.*
FLOWERING TIME *May–September.*
LEAVES *Opposite, heart-shaped, toothed, strongly veined, and hairy.*
FRUIT *Small, rounded achene.*
SIMILAR SPECIES *Small Nettle (U. urens), which is an annual and is smaller in size.*

Mistletoe

Viscum album (Loranthaceae)

This evergreen plant, long associated with Christmas, is easily spotted in winter, as its almost spherical form is clearly visible in the bare branches of trees. It is semi-parasitic on its host tree. The small green flowers are less noticeable than the round white berries, whose seeds are distributed by birds.

FORMS *a spherical mass on the branches of deciduous trees, notably poplars, limes, and apples.*

PERENNIAL

forked branches

yellowish green leaves

paired leaves

shiny white berries

PLANT HEIGHT *Up to 2m wide.*	
FLOWER SIZE *Inconspicuous.*	
FLOWERING TIME *February–April.*	
LEAVES *Opposite and paired, resembling rabbits' ears, leathery, with smooth margins.*	
FRUIT *Berries, 6–10mm wide, borne at the fork of stems.*	
SIMILAR SPECIES *None.*	

Japanese Knotweed

Fallopia japonica (Polygonaceae)

Introduced into European gardens in the 19th century, this weed has become widely naturalized and is now a serious pest in some areas. It is easily recognized by its robust and upright habit, broad, triangular leaves on either side of the zig-zag stem, and short spikes of creamy white flowers at the leaf bases.

INVADES *wasteland, roadsides, river banks, and railway embankments.*

pointed tip

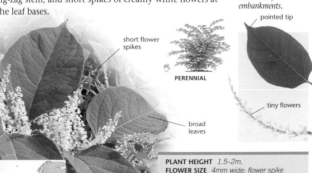

short flower spikes

PERENNIAL

broad leaves

tiny flowers

PLANT HEIGHT *1.5–2m.*	
FLOWER SIZE *4mm wide; flower spike 40–100cm long.*	
FLOWERING TIME *August–October.*	
LEAVES *Alternate, rounded, triangular with a sharp point.*	
FRUIT *Nut with three wings.*	
SIMILAR SPECIES *None.*	

Sheep's Sorrel

Rumex acetosella (Polygonaceae)

The loosely branched flowering spikes of this plant are of varying height and have many whorls of tiny greenish or reddish wind-pollinated flowers. Although male and female flowers are on separate plants, they look identical. Each oblong, stalked leaf has two lobes at the base which point forwards, so the leaf looks like an arrowhead. The leaves have a sharp, acid taste.

GROWS *abundantly in dry meadows, grassy pastures, bare places and heaths, usually on sandy, acid soil.*

arrow-shaped leaf

forward-pointing lobe

reddish flowers

tiny flowers in branched spikes

slender stems

PERENNIAL

PLANT HEIGHT *5–30cm.*
FLOWER SIZE *2mm wide.*
FLOWERING TIME *May–August.*
LEAVES *Basal, alternate, and arrow-shaped.*
FRUIT *Triangular achene, 1.5mm long.*
SIMILAR SPECIES *Common Sorrel (R. acetosa), which is larger with bigger leaves, often turning red in summer.*

Curled Dock

Rumex crispus (Polygonaceae)

This common species may be identified by its leaves. They are long-stalked and rather narrow, with distinctly wavy or crimped edges and strong midribs. The three-parted greenish flowers are arranged in dense whorls along the branched upper stems. The fruit is a rounded achene with three swollen wings or valves, without lobes or teeth.

PROLIFERATES *on cultivated and bare land, fields, rough pastures, and seashores.*

tiny flowers in whorls

branched stems

curled, wavy margin

untoothed fruit valve

narrow leaf base

PERENNIAL

PLANT HEIGHT *30–120cm.*
FLOWER SIZE *2–3mm wide.*
FLOWERING TIME *June–October.*
LEAVES *Basal, alternate, and lance-shaped.*
FRUIT *Achene, 3–5mm long.*
SIMILAR SPECIES *Broad-leaved Dock (R. obtusifolius), which has broad, heart-shaped leaves and toothed fruit valves.*

Bistort

Persicaria bistorta (Polygonaceae)

One of the most attractive members of the dock family, this plant is recognizable by its dense, terminal clusters of pink flowers on long, slender stems, often seen en masse. Each individual flower has five pink petals and eight protruding stamens.

FORMS *colonies or clumps in woodland and in damp, grassy places, such as old meadows and pastures. Often grown in gardens.*

untoothed leaf margin

dense, cylindrical flowerheads

unbranched stems

small pink flowers

PERENNIAL

PLANT HEIGHT *40–100cm.*
FLOWER SIZE *Flowerhead 3–10cm long.*
FLOWERING TIME *June–October.*
LEAVES *Alternate, triangular to arrow-shaped.*
FRUIT *Small, triangular, one-seeded nut.*
SIMILAR SPECIES *Amphibious Bistort (P. amphibium) in terrestrial form has rounded leaves; Redshank (below) has smaller leaves.*

Redshank

Persicaria maculosa (Polygonaceae)

This common weed is most easily recognized by the dark patch in the centre of the leaves, although this is not always present. The leaves are otherwise rather plain, spear-shaped, untoothed, and almost stalkless. The often reddish stems bear numerous small spikes of tiny pink flowers in the leaf axils, each flower seeming to remain tightly closed.

PROLIFERATES *in arable fields, bare wasteland, and damp places such as river banks and floodplains.*

pinkish white flowerhead

branched stems

ANNUAL

dark patch

PLANT HEIGHT *30–80cm.*
FLOWER SIZE *Flowerhead 2–4cm long.*
FLOWERING TIME *June–October.*
LEAVES *Alternate, spear-shaped.*
FRUIT *Shiny black nut, 2–3mm wide.*
SIMILAR SPECIES *Bistort (above); Pale Persicaria (P. lapathifolia), which has unblotched leaves.*

Sea Beet

Beta vulgaris (Chenopodiaceae)

SPRAWLS *over shingle beaches, margins of salt marshes, old sea walls, and grassy embankments. Often close to the tide line.*

There is little in the appearance of this plant to show that it is the forerunner to the modern beetroot, except that the glossy, fleshy leaves and stems are often red-tinged. It has a very prostrate habit, with long, trailing, flowering stems. The tiny greenish flowers are borne in clusters of three on leafy spikes.

slender flower spike

untoothed margin

flowers in small clusters

long leaf stalk

ANNUAL/PERENNIAL

long flower stems

PLANT HEIGHT *20–100cm.*
FLOWER SIZE *2–4mm wide.*
FLOWERING TIME *June–September.*
LEAVES *Alternate, fleshy, untoothed, often red-tinged.*
FRUIT *Corky, swollen segments.*
SIMILAR SPECIES *Fat Hen (below), which has diamond-shaped lower leaves.*

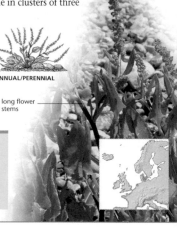

Fat Hen

Chenopodium album (Chenopodiaceae)

FOUND *on rich soil of farmyards, field margins, wasteland, roadsides, and on disturbed soil.*

The lower leaves of this common weed of arable fields are diamond-shaped, lobed, and toothed, while the smaller, lance-shaped upper leaves are usually unlobed and untoothed. The tiny greenish grey flowers are clustered in spikes along the upper branches. Once cultivated as a food source, the plant is now regarded as a pest on farms.

flowers in clusters

grey-green leaves

diamond-shaped lower leaf

lateral flower spike

ANNUAL

toothed margin

PLANT HEIGHT *40–120cm.*
FLOWER SIZE *2–3mm wide.*
FLOWERING TIME *June–October.*
LEAVES *Alternate; lance-shaped upper leaves, diamond-shaped lower leaves.*
FRUIT *Seed enclosed within sepals.*
SIMILAR SPECIES *Spear-leaved Orache (Atriplex prostrata) has arrow-shaped leaves.*

Glasswort

Salicornia europaea (Chenopodiaceae)

This plant is a familiar sight in estuaries, appearing as huge blue-green to red drifts of succulent, upward-pointing fingers protruding from the mud at low tide. The whole plant is edible, although it can be rather woody when mature. The stems are jointed, and the leaves reduced to scales fused to the stem. The flowers are insignificantly tiny, with two barely visible stamens, on fleshy, branched spikes.

PROLIFERATES *in drifts on estuaries, coastal mudflats, and salt marshes.*

ANNUAL

scale-like leaves fused to stem

ascending branches

often red-tinged

PLANT HEIGHT *10–30cm.*
FLOWER SIZE *Spike 1–5cm long.*
FLOWERING TIME *August–September.*
LEAVES *Triangular scales fused to stem.*
FRUIT *Tiny achene.*
SIMILAR SPECIES *Annual Seablite (Suaeda maritima), which has narrow grey-green leaves, and often grows alongside Glasswort.*

Greater Sand-spurrey

Spergularia media (Caryophyllaceae)

Even from a distance, the often extensive mats of this plant brighten salt marshes and coasts with their flowers. The five pink petals are whitish at the base, and interspersed with shorter green sepals. The whorled leaves are linear, fleshy, and flattened on the upper surface; they are rounded below, with a small sheath at the base.

FORMS *small or extensive colonies on drier salt marshes and coastal sands, away from other plants.*

fleshy leaves

papery sheath

PERENNIAL

5-parted flower

petals longer than sepals

starry petals

PLANT HEIGHT *8–20cm.*
FLOWER SIZE *7–12mm wide.*
FLOWERING TIME *May–September.*
LEAVES *Whorled, slightly fleshy.*
FRUIT *Pendent capsule, with three valves.*
SIMILAR SPECIES *Lesser Sand-spurrey (S. marina) and Sand Spurrey (S. rubra), which have petals shorter than the sepals.*

Greater Stitchwort

Stellaria holostea (Caryophyllaceae)

This familiar plant brightens its woodland habitat in spring. Its pure white flowers, in loose clusters, have five deeply notched petals and yellow stamens, with the sepals much shorter than the petals. The rough, oppositely paired leaves persist for many weeks after flowering. The weak stems are often partially supported by other plants.

GROWS *in grassy places, such as woodland, shady field margins, roadsides, and hedgerows.*

PERENNIAL

loosely branched flower stalks

linear leaf

deeply notched petals

large white flowers

yellow centres

NOTE

There are many local names for this plant: "Shirt Buttons", "Milkmaids", "Poor- man's-Buttonhole", and "Poppers", referring to the seed capsules that explode noisily, scattering the seeds some distance away.

PLANT HEIGHT *30–60cm.*
FLOWER SIZE *1.8–3cm wide.*
FLOWERING TIME *April–June.*
LEAVES *Opposite, linear to lance-shaped, untoothed, with long, tapered points, and mostly unstalked.*
FRUIT *Capsule split by six teeth.*
SIMILAR SPECIES *Chickweed (right), which is smaller, with longer sepals; Common Mouse-ear (right), which has hairy leaves.*

Chickweed

Stellaria media (Caryophyllaceae)

This sprawling plant with weak, straggly stems has star-like flowers with five deeply notched white petals, slightly smaller than the green sepals that surround them. The small, oval leaves are hairless, but there is a single line of hairs running along the stem. Chickweed is a ubiquitous weed throughout Britain, with some medicinal properties, and is often fed to poultry as a tonic.

PROLIFERATES *on cultivated land, road verges, and rubbish tips; in pastures and bare places. Tolerates nutrient-rich soils.*

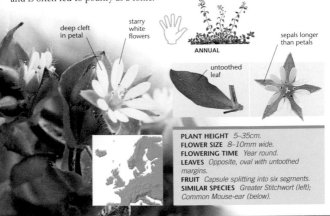

deep cleft in petal

starry white flowers

ANNUAL

untoothed leaf

sepals longer than petals

PLANT HEIGHT *5–35cm.*
FLOWER SIZE *8–10mm wide.*
FLOWERING TIME *Year round.*
LEAVES *Opposite, oval with untoothed margins.*
FRUIT *Capsule splitting into six segments.*
SIMILAR SPECIES *Greater Stitchwort (left); Common Mouse-ear (below).*

Common Mouse-ear

Cerastium fontanum (Caryophyllaceae)

The most distinctive feature of this plant is the covering of fine hairs on the oval leaves, each looking like a mouse's ear. Like Chickweed (above), its flowers each have five deeply notched white petals, but these are the same length as the white-margined green sepals beneath. The fruit capsule is slightly curved and sits within the sepals, looking like a tiny, half-peeled banana.

THRIVES *in moist areas in grassland, sandy places, and shingle banks, usually on neutral or chalky soils.*

sepals as long as petals

PERENNIAL

opposite, unstalked leaves

oval, hairy leaf

curved fruit capsule

PLANT HEIGHT *5–30cm.*
FLOWER SIZE *6–10mm wide.*
FLOWERING TIME *April–October.*
LEAVES *Opposite, oval, and finely hairy.*
FRUIT *Oblong, curved capsule.*
SIMILAR SPECIES *Greater Stitchwort (left) has large flowers with yellow stamens; Chickweed (above), which has sepals longer than petals.*

Bladder Campion

Silene vulgaris (Caryophyllaceae)

INHABITS *rough ground at the edge of fields and roads, and grassy places; often on dry, chalky soil.*

The conspicuous, inflated sepal tubes of Bladder Campion give its flowers the appearance of bladders or old-fashioned bloomers, making it instantly recognizable. The sepal tubes may be greenish, yellowish, or pinkish, with a fine network of veins, and the five deeply notched petals are white. The flowers become fragrant in the evening. The leaves are oval, pointed, and rather wavy-edged.

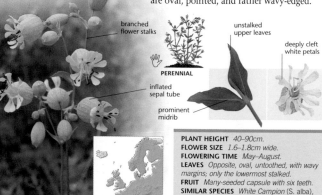

branched flower stalks

unstalked upper leaves

deeply cleft white petals

PERENNIAL

inflated sepal tube

prominent midrib

PLANT HEIGHT 40–90cm.
FLOWER SIZE 1.6–1.8cm wide.
FLOWERING TIME May–August.
LEAVES *Opposite, oval, untoothed, with wavy margins; only the lowermost stalked.*
FRUIT *Many-seeded capsule with six teeth.*
SIMILAR SPECIES *White Campion (S. alba), which does not have an inflated calyx.*

Red Campion

Silene dioica (Caryophyllaceae)

GROWS *in field margins, woodland, and hedgerows; on roadsides and wasteland; in ditches and on rocky slopes.*

In early spring, this plant's tufts of oblong, hairy leaves may be recognizable along woodland paths, but borne later, the profusion of bright, pinkish red flowers on the reddish stems is unmistakable. Male and female flowers are on separate plants; and the fruit capsule enlarges into a flask shape with turned back teeth.

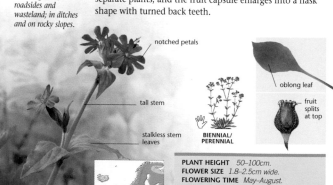

notched petals

oblong leaf

tall stem

fruit splits at top

stalkless stem leaves

BIENNIAL/ PERENNIAL

PLANT HEIGHT 50–100cm.
FLOWER SIZE 1.8–2.5cm wide.
FLOWERING TIME May–August.
LEAVES *Opposite, unstalked, hairy; oval to oblong stem leaves.*
FRUIT *Capsule with ten turned back teeth.*
SIMILAR SPECIES *Corncockle (Agrostemma githago); White Campion (S. alba).*

Ragged Robin

Lychnis flos-cuculi (Caryophyllaceae)

This distinctive marsh-loving plant is easily recognized by the ragged appearance of its bright pink or red flowers. However, each of the five petals is actually rather neatly divided into four finger-like lobes. Below the petals are red-striped sepals that are fused into a tube. The opposite leaves are usually hairy; the basal leaves are almost linear, but the stem leaves are wider or spoon-shaped.

THRIVES in moist grassland, fens, wet woodland, marshes, and streamsides.

loose, spreading petals

slender stems

PERENNIAL

petal cut into 4 narrow lobes

linear leaves

PLANT HEIGHT *30–70cm.*
FLOWER SIZE *3–4cm wide.*
FLOWERING TIME *May–August.*
LEAVES *Opposite, linear or spoon-shaped.*
FRUIT *Capsule, splitting at the tip into five teeth.*
SIMILAR SPECIES *None with such finely divided petals.*

Soapwort

Saponaria officinalis (Caryophyllaceae)

A robust plant found in semi-shaded places, Soapwort has fleshy, veined leaves, which were once gathered and boiled to make a soapy lather for washing. The flowers are in tight clusters, each of the petals broadening towards the tip like an aeroplane propeller, and are notable for their very long, pale green sepal tubes.

FOUND in grassy places, woodland margins, hedgerows, and roadsides; on waste, fallow, and cultivated land.

5 narrow, unnotched petals

pale pink flowers

leafy stem

PERENNIAL

oval to elliptic leaves

long sepal tube

PLANT HEIGHT *60–90cm.*
FLOWER SIZE *2.5–2.8cm wide.*
FLOWERING TIME *June–September.*
LEAVES *Opposite, oval to elliptic, veined.*
FRUIT *Many-seeded capsule with four teeth.*
SIMILAR SPECIES *Hybrids of Red Campion (left) and White Campion (Silene alba) have notched petals and striped calyces.*

White Water-lily

Nymphaea alba (Nymphaeaceae)

This unmistakable aquatic plant has often been hybridized to produce many garden varieties and cultivars. The leaves are rounded and dark green, often with a bronze sheen. They either float on or rise above the water surface. The white flowers, which open only in bright sunshine, are held just at the water surface, each with 20 or more fleshy, oval petals.

COVERS *the surface of still or slow-flowing freshwater in ponds, lakes, and ditches.*

PERENNIAL

numerous stamens and staminodes

large white solitary flower

deep green floating leaf

green-backed outer sepal

PLANT HEIGHT *10cm above water surface.*
FLOWER SIZE *10–20cm wide.*
FLOWERING TIME *June–September.*
LEAVES *Basal, rounded with cleft, split to the stalk, 10–30cm wide.*
FRUIT *Spongy capsule, containing many seeds, that ripens under the water surface.*
SIMILAR SPECIES *Yellow Water-lily (below).*

Yellow Water-lily

Nuphar lutea (Nymphaeaceae)

A robust, aquatic plant, Yellow Water-lily has the largest leaves of any water-lily in the region. The solitary, spherical, deep yellow flowers are small in comparison, and are held on thick stalks. Each flower has five or six large, overlapping, concave sepals and several smaller, narrower yellow petals, which never open fully. They go on to form green fruit.

GROWS *abundantly in freshwater lakes, ponds, dykes, and slow-moving streams and rivers.*

PERENNIAL

stigma rays

flask-shaped green seed capsule

curved stamens

PLANT HEIGHT *Water surface.*
FLOWER SIZE *4–6cm wide.*
FLOWERING TIME *June–August.*
LEAVES *Basal, arising from rhizomes; floating leaves oval, thick and leathery, submerged leaves rounded, thin, and translucent.*
FRUIT *Flask-shaped fruit capsule.*
SIMILAR SPECIES *White Water-lily (above).*

Wood Anemone

Anemone nemorosa (Ranunculaceae)

An early spring flower, Wood Anemone occurs in great sweeps in mature woodland. The white petals, often flushed with pink underneath, open fully only in good light, and follow the direction of the sun. The long-stalked, deeply lobed leaves increase in number after flowering.

FORMS *spectacular drifts in deciduous woodland, coppices, meadows, hedgerows, and mountain ledges.*

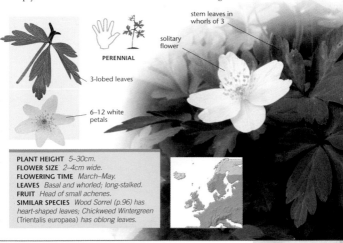

PERENNIAL

stem leaves in whorls of 3

solitary flower

3-lobed leaves

6–12 white petals

PLANT HEIGHT *5–30cm.*
FLOWER SIZE *2–4cm wide.*
FLOWERING TIME *March–May.*
LEAVES *Basal and whorled; long-stalked.*
FRUIT *Head of small achenes.*
SIMILAR SPECIES *Wood Sorrel (p.96) has heart-shaped leaves; Chickweed Wintergreen (Trientalis europaea) has oblong leaves.*

Traveller's Joy

Clematis vitalba (Ranunculaceae)

This scrambling plant produces masses of creamy white flowers in late summer and persistent fruitheads lasting well into winter. These silky, feathery, pompom-like clusters of silvery achenes trail over hedges and trees on long stems that become woody with age, resembling thick rope. The leaves are pinnately divided, with slightly toothed leaflets.

CLAMBERS *over hedgerows and scrub, climbing high up on trees or over old walls; on chalky soil.*

toothed leaflets

numerous stamens

twisting leaf stalks

long stem

PERENNIAL

creamy white flowers

PLANT HEIGHT *4–30m.*
FLOWER SIZE *1.8–2cm wide.*
FLOWERING TIME *July–September.*
LEAVES *Opposite, pinnate, with oval to lance-shaped, toothed leaflets.*
FRUIT *Clusters of feathered achenes; silvery white.*
SIMILAR SPECIES *None.*

Marsh Marigold

Caltha palustris (Ranunculaceae)

The bright golden yellow flowers of this huge buttercup are a striking and unmistakable feature of damp places in early spring. Each flower is composed of five brightly coloured sepals, opening at daybreak to expose up to a hundred stamens. The glossy green leaves are heart-shaped with toothed margins, mostly arising from the base but occasionally rooting at the nodes to form a new clump. The stem leaves are smaller and almost stalkless. In common with many other members of the buttercup family, the whole plant is poisonous.

THRIVES *in damp places in the open or in shade, forming clumps and small colonies in marshes, bogs, stream margins, and wet woodland.*

dark green kidney-shaped leaf

PERENNIAL

large, bright yellow flowers

numerous stamens

long leaf stalk

5 yellow sepals

NOTE

The scientific name – Caltha palustris – of Marsh Marigold comes from the Greek calathos, *which means "cup-shaped", referring to the appearance of the flowers.* Palustris *is from the Latin* palus, *which means "marsh". Double-flowered forms of this plant are often grown in gardens.*

PLANT HEIGHT *30–60cm.*
FLOWER SIZE *2.5–5cm wide.*
FLOWERING TIME *March–June.*
LEAVES *Mostly basal, heart- or kidney-shaped, with finely toothed margins; glossy green; stem leaves almost stalkless.*
FRUIT *Cluster of pod-like follicles, each containing several seeds.*
SIMILAR SPECIES *Globeflower (right), which has spherical flowers and divided leaves. Other buttercups have smaller flowers.*

Globeflower

Trollius europaeus (Ranunculaceae)

A member of the buttercup family, Globeflower owes its distinctive spherical shape to the incurved form of its many lemon-yellow sepals, which enclose the small nectar-secreting petals. This robust plant is hairless, and the flower stems rise above the long-stalked basal leaves. The stem leaves are smaller. The whole plant is poisonous.

FORMS *colonies in damp open grassland, often among rocks or close to streams.*

PERENNIAL

single flower on long stalk

rounded flowers

palmately divided leaves

curved sepals

PLANT HEIGHT *40–70cm.*
FLOWER SIZE *3–5cm wide.*
FLOWERING TIME *May–August.*
LEAVES *Mostly basal, 5–7 palmately lobed, coarsely toothed; smaller stem leaves.*
FRUIT *Many-seeded follicles.*
SIMILAR SPECIES *Marsh Marigold (left) has open flowers and kidney-shaped leaves.*

Creeping Buttercup

Ranunculus repens (Ranunculaceae)

The creeping surface runners of this plant enable it to rapidly colonize entire fields, which may appear entirely yellow in early summer. Each flower has five bright yellow petals. The leaves of Creeping Buttercup are triangular in outline and divided into three coarsely toothed lobes; the middle lobe usually has a short stalk.

THRIVES *in meadows, and other grassy places; on damp soil, forming large colonies.*

triangular leaf

rounded fruit cluster

PERENNIAL

numerous stamens

bright yellow flowers

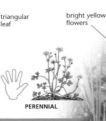

PLANT HEIGHT *10–50cm.*
FLOWER SIZE *1.5–2.5cm wide.*
FLOWERING TIME *May–September.*
LEAVES *Basal, alternate, three toothed lobes.*
FRUIT *Spherical cluster of hooked achenes.*
SIMILAR SPECIES *Lesser Celandine (p.60), Meadow Buttercup (R. acris), and Bulbous Buttercup (R. bulbosus).*

Lesser Spearwort

Ranunculus flammula (Ranunculaceae)

This common buttercup has narrow, spear-shaped leaves in twos or threes. The long-stemmed basal leaves may be broader. Its flowers are in loosely branched clusters, and its stems, which run along the ground and root at intervals, are often reddish.

FORMS *colonies in wet meadows, marshes, or pond margins, often in mountainous areas in the south of its range.*

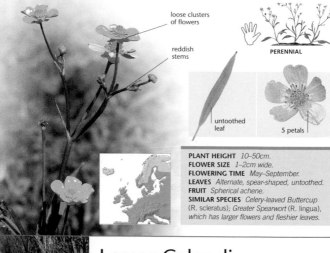

loose clusters of flowers

reddish stems

PERENNIAL

untoothed leaf

5 petals

PLANT HEIGHT	*10–50cm.*
FLOWER SIZE	*1–2cm wide.*
FLOWERING TIME	*May–September.*
LEAVES	*Alternate, spear-shaped, untoothed.*
FRUIT	*Spherical achene.*
SIMILAR SPECIES	*Celery-leaved Buttercup (R. sceleratus); Greater Spearwort (R. lingua), which has larger flowers and fleshier leaves.*

Lesser Celandine

Ranunculus ficaria (Ranunculaceae)

This is the first of the buttercups to appear in spring, and its flowers are easy to recognize with their three green sepals and up to 12 golden yellow petals, which open fully only in bright sunshine. Sometimes, the petals fade to white as they age. The leaves are heart-shaped, deeply cleft, and with blunt tips. Dark glossy green, they are often mottled with purplish or pale markings.

GROWS *in moderately damp, open places, preferring the partial shade of deciduous woodland and hedgerows.*

PERENNIAL

glossy surface

green fruiting head

8–12 narrow petals

blunt leaf tip

PLANT HEIGHT	*7–20cm.*
FLOWER SIZE	*2–3cm wide.*
FLOWERING TIME	*March–May.*
LEAVES	*Mostly basal, heart-shaped.*
FRUIT	*Rounded head of achenes.*
SIMILAR SPECIES	*Creeping Buttercup (p.59) and other members of the buttercup family, which have divided leaves.*

Pond Water-crowfoot

Ranunculus peltatus (Ranunculaceae)

Essentially an aquatic white buttercup, this plant has two kinds of leaves. Those under the water surface are divided into feathery threads, while the leaves that float on the water are rounded, with shallow lobes. The white flowers rise above the water surface on short stems. There are many similar species, but with different leaves.

APPEARS *on the surface of shallow ponds, lakes, ditches, and slow-moving streams, or in mud at the water's edge.*

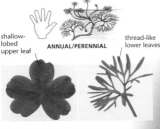

shallow-lobed upper leaf

ANNUAL/PERENNIAL

thread-like lower leaves

5 white petals

numerous yellow anthers

PLANT HEIGHT	Water surface.
FLOWER SIZE	1.5–2cm wide.
FLOWERING TIME	May–August.
LEAVES	Alternate; rounded and lobed upper leaves, thread-like lower leaves.
FRUIT	Collection of achenes.
SIMILAR SPECIES	Frogbit (p.185), which has three-petalled flowers.

Common Meadow-rue

Thalictrum flavum (Ranunculaceae)

The flowers of this plant appear to consist almost entirely of numerous creamy yellow stamens, although there are four tiny sepals. The leaves are divided into distinctive, dark greyish green leaflets, each one usually bearing three points. The leaves are difficult to spot among vegetation but the tall, bright flowerheads are very noticeable.

THRIVES *in damp meadows, fens, and flooded areas, usually among other tall vegetation in lowland.*

fluffy flowerhead

flowers on tall stems

PERENNIAL

3-pointed leaflets

long stamens

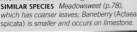

PLANT HEIGHT	0.6–1.5m.
FLOWER SIZE	1–1.5cm wide.
FLOWERING TIME	June–August.
LEAVES	Alternate, pinnately divided.
FRUIT	Achenes twisted together.
SIMILAR SPECIES	Meadowsweet (p.78), which has coarser leaves; Baneberry (Actaea spicata) is smaller and occurs on limestone.

Common Poppy

Papaver rhoeas (Papaveraceae)

Poppies often appear in great profusion in fields or land that has been disturbed after a long period of neglect, as the seeds can lie dormant in the ground for many years, then germinate when brought close to the surface. The deep green leaves are deeply lobed, with toothed margins.

The nodding flower buds are hairy; the flowers have four huge, overlapping scarlet petals, each with a small black blotch at the base. The stamens are also black.

FLOURISHES *in arable fields and field margins, and disturbed and waste ground, on roadsides; often colours whole fields scarlet.*

brilliant red petals

ANNUAL

black centre of flower

pinnately divided leaves

oval fruit capsule

PLANT HEIGHT *30–60cm.*
FLOWER SIZE *7.5–10cm wide.*
FLOWERING TIME *June–September.*
LEAVES *Alternate, pinnately divided, toothed.*
FRUIT *Oval, smooth capsule with holes near the top, filled with numerous tiny black seeds.*
SIMILAR SPECIES *Other poppy species, which have differently shaped or hairy fruit capsules.*

Yellow Horned Poppy

Glaucium flavum (Papaveraceae)

This distinctive and colourful beach flower is easily recognized by its fleshy, grey-green leaves, which are pinnately divided into coarse, toothed segments with an undulating surface. The large, bright yellow flowers have four tissue-like petals and the very unusual fruit is a narrow, elongated capsule.

OCCURS *on shingle or sandy beaches, dunes, sea-cliffs, and very occasionally on waste ground inland.*

grey-green leaves

overlapping petals

large yellow flowers

long, slender capsule

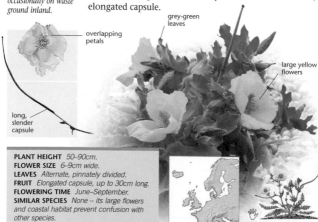

PLANT HEIGHT *50–90cm.*
FLOWER SIZE *6–9cm wide.*
LEAVES *Alternate, pinnately divided.*
FRUIT *Elongated capsule, up to 30cm long.*
FLOWERING TIME *June–September.*
SIMILAR SPECIES *None – its large flowers and coastal habitat prevent confusion with other species.*

BIENNIAL/PERENNIAL

Greater Celandine

Chelidonium majus (Papaveraceae)

An unusual member of the poppy family, this plant has small flowers with four well-separated yellow petals, numerous yellow stamens, and a prominent style in the centre. The same plant may produce flowers for several months and flowering is said to coincide with the presence of swallows (*chelidon* is Greek for swallow). The leaves are pale green, with rounded lobes. Ants are attracted to the oily seeds and often unwittingly carry them off stuck to their bodies.

GROWS *in semi-shaded places such as hedgerows, alongside walls, rocky places, and wasteland, often close to habitation.*

4 separated petals

numerous stamens

pinnate leaves

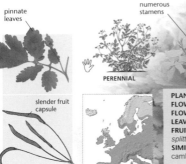

PERENNIAL

slender fruit capsule

PLANT HEIGHT *40–90cm.*
FLOWER SIZE *1.5–2.5cm long.*
FLOWERING TIME *April–October.*
LEAVES *Alternate; pinnate with rounded lobes.*
FRUIT *Linear-oblong, hairless capsule, splitting to release seeds.*
SIMILAR SPECIES *Welsh Poppy (Meconopsis cambrica), which has larger flowers.*

Common Fumitory

Fumaria officinalis (Fumariaceae)

This widespread weed has racemes of upright flowers, each flower with a pouched spur at the back, and two crimson-tipped lips at the front. The weak, straggly stems bear finely divided leaves, each leaflet on its own stalk. The feathery greyish green leaves look almost like smoke, hence the plant's scientific name.

SPRAWLS *over bare ground or grassy places in cultivated fields, wasteland, or pastures, and along roadsides.*

dark-tipped flowers

flowers in racemes

ANNUAL

feathery, divided leaves

thin leaf stalk

pouched spur

PLANT HEIGHT *10–30cm.*
FLOWER SIZE *7–9mm long.*
FLOWERING TIME *May–October.*
LEAVES *Alternate, pinnately divided into lobed, stalked leaflets.*
FRUIT *Single-seeded, round capsule.*
SIMILAR SPECIES *Common Ramping-fumitory (F. muralis) has fewer flowers.*

Garlic Mustard

Alliaria petiolata (Brassicaceae)

The large, triangular leaves of this plant appear in early spring. The four-petalled white flowers are borne at the stem tips, in clusters that seem small for the size of the plant. The flowering stem elongates as the long seed pods develop. When crushed, the leaves have a distinct smell of garlic, which is unusual outside the onion family.

BIENNIAL

FLOURISHES along hedgerows and roads, in woodland margins and among scrub, in the open or semi-shade, on neutral or chalky soils.

small flower clusters

smaller leaves on upper stem

small white flowers

long, thin seed pods

triangular, toothed leaves

PLANT HEIGHT *40–120cm.*
FLOWER SIZE *3–5mm wide.*
FLOWERING TIME *April–June.*
LEAVES *Alternate, triangular to heart-shaped, toothed and stalked.*
FRUIT *Seed pods (siliquas), 2–7cm long, splitting lengthwise when dry.*
SIMILAR SPECIES *Dame's-violet (below).*

Dame's-violet

Hesperis matronalis (Brassicaceae)

The bold clusters of four-petalled white, violet, or pink flowers of this stately plant are easily noticed. The flowers are fragrant only in the evening. The finely toothed, short-stalked leaves are narrow at the base. A native of southern Europe, Dame's-violet is now naturalized in the British Isles.

FOUND in damp, semi-shaded places such as woodland margins, riversides, hedgerows, and road verges; often near settlements.

BIENNIAL/PERENNIAL

4 petals

branched stems

narrow leaf

stalked flowers

PLANT HEIGHT *70–120cm.*
FLOWER SIZE *1.5–2cm wide.*
FLOWERING TIME *May–August.*
LEAVES *Alternate, lance-shaped, toothed.*
FRUIT *Siliquas, 2.5–10cm long, containing many seeds.*
SIMILAR SPECIES *Garlic Mustard (above); Cuckooflower (p.67) has pinnate leaves.*

Wintercress

Barbarea vulgaris (Brassicaceae)

The four-petalled yellow flowers of Wintercress brighten the banks of streams and damp ditches in spring. They are clustered at the top of the stems, which elongate as the long seed pods develop beneath. The lower leaves, which are a rich source of vitamin C, have a large terminal lobe each, while the unlobed upper leaves clasp the stem.

GROWS *close to ditches, ponds, and streams, alongside roads, and in wet places on disturbed soil.*

pinnately lobed lower leaves

branched stems

small yellow flowers

BIENNIAL/PERENNIAL

PLANT HEIGHT *30–90cm.*
FLOWER SIZE *7–9mm wide.*
FLOWERING TIME *May–August.*
LEAVES *Basal leaves, lobed and stalked; alternate stem leaves, unstalked, toothed.*
FRUIT *Narrow siliqua, 1.5–3cm long.*
SIMILAR SPECIES *Hedge Mustard (p.70); Charlock (p.71), which has broader leaves.*

Horse-radish

Armoracia rusticana (Brassicaceae)

This robust and erect plant, whose root is used as a condiment, is mostly without flowers. However, it is easily identified by its stout, shiny leaves, with wavy margins and pale midribs, which have a faint but distinct horse-radish scent. When flowers do occur, they are white with four petals and borne in dense panicles.

FORMS *patches on roadsides, wasteland, and river banks, and along farmland edges.*

oblong, toothed leaves

crinkled leaf surface

panicle of white flowers

PLANT HEIGHT *30–90cm.*
FLOWER SIZE *8–10mm wide.*
FLOWERING TIME *May–July.*
LEAVES *Basal, alternate on flowering stem.*
FRUIT *Silicula, 4–6mm wide, but rare.*
SIMILAR SPECIES *Broad-leaved Dock (Rumex obtusifolius), which has similar leaves and habit before it flowers.*

PERENNIAL

Water-cress

Rorippa nasturtium-aquaticum (Brassicaceae)

SPRAWLS *along ditches, ponds, streams, and wet flushes, sometimes forming colonies.*

The glossy, succulent, edible leaves of Water-cress have a characteristic shape, and grow like a ladder up its fleshy stems. Creeping along freshwater habitats, the plant roots into the mud at intervals or floats on the water surface. It may flower for many weeks, forming rows of long, curved seed pods.

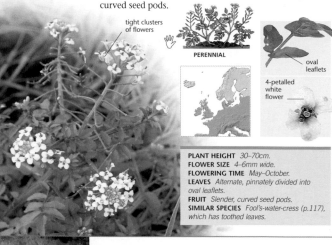

tight clusters of flowers

PERENNIAL

oval leaflets

4-petalled white flower

PLANT HEIGHT *30–70cm.*
FLOWER SIZE *4–6mm wide.*
FLOWERING TIME *May–October.*
LEAVES *Alternate, pinnately divided into oval leaflets.*
FRUIT *Slender, curved seed pods.*
SIMILAR SPECIES *Fool's-water-cress (p.117), which has toothed leaves.*

Hairy Bittercress

Cardamine hirsuta (Brassicaceae)

THRIVES *on wasteland, cultivated and rocky ground, old walls, and in gardens and pavement cracks.*

This common weed of towns and gardens has very small flowers that are easily overlooked. They are in tight clusters at the tips of the gradually lengthening stems, but are usually topped by the long seed pods sprouting from beneath. The narrow, hairy leaves are comprised of well-separated, rounded leaflets in pairs.

ANNUAL/BIENNIAL

large terminal leaflet

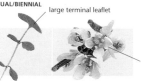

long seed pods

tiny flower clusters

four petals

PLANT HEIGHT *5–30cm.*
FLOWER SIZE *3–4mm wide.*
FLOWERING TIME *February–November.*
LEAVES *Mostly basal, upper alternate, with paired leaflets.*
FRUIT *Siliqua, 2–2.5cm long.*
SIMILAR SPECIES *Cuckooflower (right), which has larger, pinkish flowers.*

Cuckooflower

Cardamine pratensis (Brassicaceae)

Widespread in damp meadows and pastures, this member of the cabbage family is identifiable by its flowers, each with four broad, oval petals ranging from white to lilac or deep pink. The basal leaves have rounded lobes, similar to those of Water-cress (left), and the stem leaves are divided into narrow, well-separated lobes that resemble a ladder.

FAVOURS *damp areas such as verges, river banks, and wet pastures.*

PERENNIAL

clusters of flowers at stem tips

rounded leaflets

yellow anthers

PLANT HEIGHT *Up to 60cm.*
FLOWER SIZE *1.2–1.8cm wide.*
FLOWERING TIME *April–June.*
LEAVES *Loose rosette of pinnately divided leaves; stem leaves with narrower leaflets.*
FRUIT *Slender pod, up to 4cm long.*
SIMILAR SPECIES *Coralroot Bittercress (C. bulbifera) has larger and elliptic leaflets.*

Honesty

Lunaria annua (Brassicaceae)

Introduced from southeast Europe as a garden plant, Honesty is now naturalized in the British countryside. The large purple or white flowers, the heart-shaped leaves, and particularly the fruit, are distinctive. The fruit splits to reveal a persistent silvery membrane, to which the seeds are attached.

OCCURS *on roadsides, banks, wasteland, rubbish tips, and cultivated land.*

BIENNIAL

coarsely toothed leaf

rounded fruit

flowers in clusters

4-petalled flowers

deep green foliage

PLANT HEIGHT *50–100cm.*
FLOWER SIZE *2.5–3cm wide.*
FLOWERING TIME *April–June.*
LEAVES *Alternate, heart-shaped, coarsely toothed.*
FRUIT *Round, flat silicula, 3–5cm wide.*
SIMILAR SPECIES *Dame's Violet (p.64), which is taller with narrower leaves.*

Common Scurvy-grass

Cochlearia offinalis (Brassicaceae)

GROWS *on coastal rocks, salt marshes, sea walls, and motorway verges.*

A variable plant, Common Scurvy-grass has a succulent nature and often prostrate habit, typical of many coastal plants. The long-stalked basal leaves are rounded, while the upper leaves clasp the stem and may be lobed. The four-parted white flowers are in tight clusters above stems that lengthen as the fruit develop.

tight flower clusters

round, fleshy leaves

BIENNIAL/PERENNIAL

heart-shaped base

round seed pod

PLANT HEIGHT *10–40cm.*
FLOWER SIZE *8–10mm wide.*
FLOWERING TIME *April–August.*
LEAVES *Mostly basal, rounded and fleshy.*
FRUIT *Spherical siliculas, with cork-like texture.*
SIMILAR SPECIES *Danish Scurvy-grass (C. danica), which has lilac flowers.*

Shepherd's Purse

Capsella bursa-pastoris (Brassicaceae)

FLOURISHES *even in poor soil, in fields, gardens, cultivated or waste ground, along walls, and in pavement cracks.*

This familiar, ubiquitous plant is variable in size, with tiny, four-petalled white flowers. Below them, rows of heart-shaped seed cases develop along the stem, resembling an old-fashioned leather purse. The leaves are mostly basal in a loose rosette. If Shepherd's Purse is fed to chickens, the egg yolks become darker.

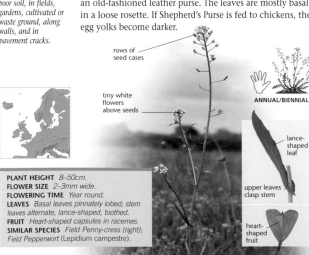

rows of seed cases

tiny white flowers above seeds

ANNUAL/BIENNIAL

lance-shaped leaf

upper leaves clasp stem

heart-shaped fruit

PLANT HEIGHT *8–50cm.*
FLOWER SIZE *2–3mm wide.*
FLOWERING TIME *Year round.*
LEAVES *Basal leaves pinnately lobed; stem leaves alternate, lance-shaped, toothed.*
FRUIT *Heart-shaped capsules in racemes.*
SIMILAR SPECIES *Field Penny-cress (right); Field Pepperwort (Lepidium campestre).*

Field Penny-cress

Thlaspi arvense (Brassicaceae)

The seed pods of this cabbage family member form papery discs with broad, rounded wings that resemble notched coins. When the sun catches the papery discs, they appear to glow yellow. The white flowers are at the top of the branched stems.

FOUND *in disturbed areas such as margins of arable land where the soil is rich, and in wasteland.*

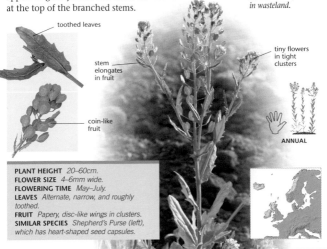

toothed leaves

stem elongates in fruit

coin-like fruit

tiny flowers in tight clusters

ANNUAL

PLANT HEIGHT *20–60cm.*
FLOWER SIZE *4–6mm wide.*
FLOWERING TIME *May–July.*
LEAVES *Alternate, narrow, and roughly toothed.*
FRUIT *Papery, disc-like wings in clusters.*
SIMILAR SPECIES *Shepherd's Purse (left), which has heart-shaped seed capsules.*

Hoary Cress

Cardaria draba (Brassicaceae)

Long associated with coastal areas, often in dry, stony places, this plant is now common along salted roadways. It is easily spotted by the foaming mass of tiny creamy white flowers on its many-branched stems, forming attractive drifts. Each flower has four petals, and develops into a rounded fruit. The toothed, greyish leaves are oblong.

OCCURS *in drifts along roadsides, trackways, and on cultivated and disturbed ground, by the coast.*

unstalked stem leaves

PERENNIAL

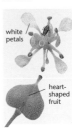

white petals

heart-shaped fruit

PLANT HEIGHT *30–80cm.*
FLOWER SIZE *5–6mm wide.*
FLOWERING TIME *May–June.*
LEAVES *Alternate, oval and coarsely toothed; basal leaves may be untoothed.*
FRUIT *Heart-shaped silicula, 3–4mm long.*
SIMILAR SPECIES *Sea Kale (p.70), which has similar characteristics but is more robust.*

Sea Kale

Crambe maritima (Brassicaceae)

The great clumps of grey-green, waxy leaves of this plant are difficult to miss in the barren expanse of a shingle beach or coastal sands. They are succulent, lobed, and with wavy margins, like those of a cabbage. Large, domed clusters of four-petalled white flowers are produced in profusion.

FORMS *clumps, often close to the shoreline, on shingle beaches and coastal sands, sometimes on cliffs and sea walls.*

dense clusters of white flowers

plant forms large clumps

PERENNIAL

spherical fruit

thick, fleshy leaves

thick, branched stem

PLANT HEIGHT *30–80cm.*
FLOWER SIZE *1–1.5cm wide.*
FLOWERING TIME *June–August.*
LEAVES *Mostly basal, lobed with wavy margins; lower leaves unstalked; grey-green.*
FRUIT *Fleshy siliculas, 8–14mm long.*
SIMILAR SPECIES *Hoary Cress (p.69) is less robust; Wild Cabbage (Brassica oleracea).*

Hedge Mustard

Sisymbrium officinale (Brassicaceae)

A common and coarse-looking weed of wasteland, Hedge Mustard is notable for its clusters of tiny yellow flowers at the end of long, branched stems that elongate further as the fruit develop. The fruit is pressed close to the stem. The lower leaves are divided into jagged lobes, the points of which turn back towards the stem; the upper leaves are narrower.

PROLIFERATES *on bare ground, wasteland, in margins of arable fields, and on roadsides, often with poppies.*

ANNUAL/BIENNIAL

clusters of yellow flowers

jagged leaves

triangular leaf lobe

unnotched petals

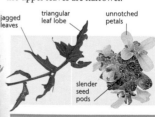

slender seed pods

PLANT HEIGHT *40–90cm.*
FLOWER SIZE *3–4mm wide.*
FLOWERING TIME *May–September.*
LEAVES *Alternate; pinnately divided, stalked lower leaves, narrow, stalkless upper leaves.*
FRUIT *Siliqua, 1–2cm long.*
SIMILAR SPECIES *Wintercress (p.65), which has larger flowers.*

Rape

Brassica napus (Brassicaceae)

Frequently grown as a crop for its oil, this is a tall plant. Its large yellow flowers are usually overtopped slightly by unopened buds, with long seed pods on the elongated stems beneath. The leaves are greyish green with very wavy margins and a pale midrib, the lower ones stalked and lobed, the upper unstalked and clasping the stem.

NATURALIZES *on cultivated land, field margins, roadsides, bare and waste ground, usually close to farmland.*

4-petalled yellow flowers

elongated stems

rounded lobes

slender seed pod

ANNUAL/BIENNIAL

PLANT HEIGHT *50–150cm.*
FLOWER SIZE *1.5–2.5cm wide.*
FLOWERING TIME *May–August.*
LEAVES *Basal leaves stalked and lobed, stem leaves alternate and unstalked.*
FRUIT *Cylindrical siliqua, 5–10cm long.*
SIMILAR SPECIES *Wild Cabbage (Brassica oleracea) has fleshier leaves; Charlock (below).*

Charlock

Sinapis arvensis (Brassicaceae)

One of the commonest yellow crucifers, which used to be a serious arable pest, this plant is rather bristly, with coarsely toothed, lyre-shaped basal leaves that have a wrinkled surface. Its upper leaves are narrower, without lobes, and do not clasp the stem. The flowers have four yellow petals, widely separated to reveal the narrow sepals underneath.

APPEARS *on disturbed ground, roadsides, and rubbish tips, often on chalky soil.*

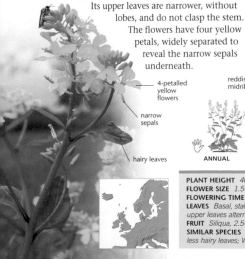

4-petalled yellow flowers

narrow sepals

hairy leaves

reddish midrib

beaked seed pod

ANNUAL

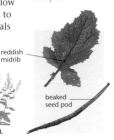

PLANT HEIGHT *40–80cm.*
FLOWER SIZE *1.5–2cm wide.*
FLOWERING TIME *May–October.*
LEAVES *Basal, stalked, coarsely toothed; upper leaves alternate, unstalked, unlobed.*
FRUIT *Siliqua, 2.5–4.5cm long.*
SIMILAR SPECIES *Rape (above), which has less hairy leaves; Wintercress (p.65).*

Sea Rocket

Cakile maritima (Brassicaceae)

In common with many coastal plants living in dry soil, the Sea Rocket has fleshy leaves that retain moisture. They are oblong, bright green, and deeply lobed into rounded "fingers". The pale pink flowers are clustered at the top of the stems, and the fleshy, bullet-shaped fruit has two shoulder-like projections at the base.

FOUND *in open, sandy areas, dunes, and shingle beaches on coastal sites.*

ANNUAL

long, rounded segments

4 petals

pale midrib

clusters of flowers

PLANT HEIGHT *Up to 30cm.*
FLOWER SIZE *6–12mm wide.*
FLOWERING TIME *June–September.*
LEAVES *Alternate, pinnately lobed, fleshy.*
FRUIT *Siliqua, 2cm long, with two segments, the lower one with two projections.*
SIMILAR SPECIES *Cuckooflower (p.67), which has less fleshy leaves.*

Navelwort

Umbilicus rupestris (Crassulaceae)

The coin-shaped leaves of this plant are distinctive, being fleshy and circular, with a dimple in the centre of each leaf (which gives them their name). The flowers have a five-parted tube. This plant can grow in places where there is almost no soil.

RESIDES *on cliffs, rocky outcrops, old walls, and stony banks, from sea-level up to 2,500m.*

bell-like flowers

PERENNIAL

long, tapered spike

dimple in centre

shallowly lobed leaf margin

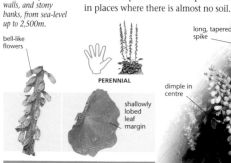

PLANT HEIGHT *15–40cm.*
FLOWER SIZE *8–10mm long.*
FLOWERING TIME *June–August.*
LEAVES *Basal rosettes, circular, fleshy, with the stem attached to the centre.*
FRUIT *Group of follicles with tiny seeds.*
SIMILAR SPECIES *Marsh Pennywort (Hydrocotyle vulgaris) has smaller flowers.*

White Stonecrop

Sedum album (Crassulaceae)

The fleshy, cylindrical leaves of this plant, like little waxy fingers, help it to conserve moisture in the dry conditions in which it lives. The leafy stems are branched at the top, where they bear a mass of starry white flowers. English Stonecrop (*S. anglicum*) is a shorter plant with fewer flowers to each cluster.

APPEARS *on rocks, walls, and dunes, in shingle or on gravel paths, in very dry, exposed places.*

broad, terminal cluster of flowers

5-petalled flowers

succulent leaves

leaves often red-tinged

prominent stamens

PERENNIAL

PLANT HEIGHT *8–20cm.*
FLOWER SIZE *6–9mm wide.*
FLOWERING TIME *June–August.*
LEAVES *Alternate, small, cylindrical, and succulent.*
FRUIT *Cluster of small follicles.*
SIMILAR SPECIES *Biting Stonecrop (below), English Stonecrop (S. anglicum).*

Biting Stonecrop

Sedum acre (Crassulaceae)

The brilliant yellow flowers of this mat-forming, creeping plant, each with five petals and ten stamens, make a bold impact when seen in its dry, bare habitat. The short, blunt leaves, adapted to hold moisture, are succulent and overlap each other close to the tip, often turning partially or wholly red.

FORMS *mats in dry, stony or sandy places such as old walls, embankments, shingle beaches, and rooftops.*

star-shaped flowers

PERENNIAL

flowers in small clusters

red-tinged leaves

PLANT HEIGHT *4–10cm.*
FLOWER SIZE *1–1.2cm wide.*
FLOWERING TIME *May–July.*
LEAVES *Alternate, succulent, 3–6mm.*
FRUIT *Five follicles in star shape, 4mm long.*
SIMILAR SPECIES *White Stonecrop (above), which has similar leaves; Yellow Saxifrage (Saxifraga aizoides), which is bushier.*

Wild Mignonette

Reseda lutea (Resedaceae)

The attractive yellow flowers of this plant have short stalks and deeply notched petals, giving the flowering spike a "fluffy" look, accentuated by its branched, bushy habit. The rough, dark green leaves are pinnately divided into long thin lobes, each with a wavy margin, folding around the midrib. The fruit is an elongated capsule.

OCCURS *on roadsides, embankments, field margins, and dry grassland.*

BIENNIAL/PERENNIAL

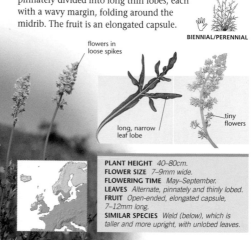

flowers in loose spikes

long, narrow leaf lobe

tiny flowers

PLANT HEIGHT *40–80cm.*
FLOWER SIZE *7–9mm wide.*
FLOWERING TIME *May–September.*
LEAVES *Alternate, pinnately and thinly lobed.*
FRUIT *Open-ended, elongated capsule, 7–12mm long.*
SIMILAR SPECIES *Weld (below), which is taller and more upright, with unlobed leaves.*

Weld

Reseda luteola (Resedaceae)

An easy plant to identify even at a distance, Weld has tall, thin flowering spikes. These are often branched towards the top, and are clothed in hundreds of tiny flowers with deeply cut petals, held very close to the stem. The untoothed leaves, simple but with wavy edges, form a rosette in the first year.

FOUND *on roadsides, field margins, waste or arable land, or grassy places, on chalky soil.*

linear leaf

yellow-green flowers

small fruit capsule

flowers in tall spikes

upright stem

BIENNIAL

PLANT HEIGHT *80–150cm.*
FLOWER SIZE *4–5mm wide.*
FLOWERING TIME *June–September.*
LEAVES *Basal rosette and alternate, lance-shaped, with wavy edges.*
FRUIT *Open-ended capsule, 3–4mm long.*
SIMILAR SPECIES *Wild Mignonette (above) has pinnately divided leaves; Agrimony (p.81).*

Round-leaved Sundew

Drosera rotundifolia (Droseraceae)

The Round-leaved Sundew is usually seen nestling in moss, and its curiously adapted leaves are unmistakable. They are clothed in long, red glandular hairs, each tipped with a drop of sticky liquid. These ensnare an insect hoping to find nectar, whereupon the leaf rolls up and digests the insect inside. The small white flowers of this plant are borne in a loose spike at the top of a leafless stalk, high above the leaves. Each flower has 5–8 sepals and petals.

GROWS *among sphagnum moss and other plants, on bare peat in acid bogs, in moist conditions, and in wet heaths and moors.*

PERENNIAL

rounded leaf blade

white flower

long stalk

leaves with sticky, red hair

NOTE

Sundews live in wet, acidic soils, which are very low in nutrients such as nitrates. Capturing and digesting insects provides the plant with nitrates and phosphates so that it can survive in harsh conditions.

PLANT HEIGHT *5–15cm.*
FLOWER SIZE *5mm wide.*
FLOWERING TIME *June–August.*
LEAVES *Basal, rounded leaf blade, covered with red glandular hairs, and tipped with a drop of sticky liquid.*
FRUIT *Small, many-seeded capsule.*
SIMILAR SPECIES *Great Sundew (D. longifolia), which has narrow, oblong leaves covered in sticky glands.*

Rue-leaved Saxifrage

Saxifraga tridactylites (Saxifragaceae)

This is a diminutive plant but one that is clearly visible in the dry, bare places it inhabits. It is red-tinged, or entirely red in colour, with tiny but characteristic three- or five-lobed leaves, the lower ones often withered. The minute five-petalled white flowers are on long stalks, and each sits in a red calyx, which inflates as the fruit is formed.

INHABITS *dry, rocky, and bare places such as old walls and sandy heaths, on chalky soil.*

ANNUAL

tiny white flowers

reddish stems

flower stalks longer than flowers

lobed lower leaves

PLANT HEIGHT *4–15cm.*
FLOWER SIZE *3–5mm wide.*
FLOWERING TIME *June–September.*
LEAVES *Alternate, fleshy, three- or five-lobed, reddish.*
FRUIT *Two-parted capsule inside the calyx.*
SIMILAR SPECIES *None – this plant is unique with its reddish foliage.*

Meadow Saxifrage

Saxifraga granulata (Saxifragaceae)

The white flowers of this delicate plant stand out among the grasses of old meadows. The flowers are borne in loosely branched clusters of up to 12, on a single, leafless stem arising from a basal rosette of leaves. Bulbils, which are able to form new plants, usually form just below the soil surface, at the base of the lowest leaves.

FOUND *in meadows, pastures, on road verges and rocky places; on chalky soil.*

PERENNIAL

5-petalled flowers

bluntly lobed leaves

rounded petals

PLANT HEIGHT *20–50cm.*
FLOWER SIZE *1.5–3cm wide.*
FLOWERING TIME *April–June.*
LEAVES *Mostly basal rosettes, rounded or kidney-shaped, and bluntly toothed.*
FRUIT *Small, two-parted capsule.*
SIMILAR SPECIES *Grass of Parnassus (right), which has stalked, heart-shaped leaves.*

Opposite-leaved Golden-saxifrage

Chrysosplenium oppositifolium (Saxifragaceae)

Forming golden-green mats in wet woodland, this short plant hugs the ground, spreading by creeping shoots that root at intervals. It has yellow-green leaves and tiny flowers, with bright yellow stamens, in the upper leaf axils.

GROWS *on damp patches or streamsides, in wet woodland and rocks, in shady places.*

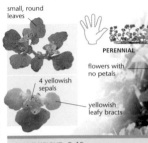

small, round leaves

PERENNIAL

flowers with no petals

4 yellowish sepals

yellowish leafy bracts

PLANT HEIGHT *5–15cm.*
FLOWER SIZE *2–3mm wide.*
FLOWERING TIME *April–July.*
LEAVES *Opposite pairs, bluntly toothed.*
FRUIT *Cup-shaped capsule.*
SIMILAR SPECIES *Alternate-leaved Golden-saxifrage (C. alternifolium), which has alternate leaves that are shinier.*

Grass of Parnassus

Parnassia palustris (Parnassiaceae)

The solitary flowers of this meadow plant have five white petals with greenish veins and a characteristic and unusual arrangement of branched staminodes surrounding the true stamens. Most of the rather waxy leaves are basal and heart-shaped, on long stalks, but there is also a single, centrally placed leaf that clasps the flower stem.

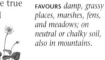

FAVOURS *damp, grassy places, marshes, fens, and meadows; on neutral or chalky soil, also in mountains.*

5-petalled white flower

PERENNIAL

feathery yellow staminodes

heart-shaped leaf

long stalk

PLANT HEIGHT *10–30cm.*
FLOWER SIZE *1.5–3cm wide.*
FLOWERING TIME *June–September.*
LEAVES *Basal, heart-shaped, and long-stalked, having a somewhat waxy appearance, with a single clasping stem leaf.*
FRUIT *Single capsule that splits into four.*
SIMILAR SPECIES *Meadow Saxifrage (left).*

Dropwort

Filipendula vulgaris (Rosaceae)

THRIVES *in meadows and dry grassland, and on roadsides, especially on chalky soil. Prefers open, sunny situations.*

This plant is most easily identified by the small, round, pink-flushed flower buds, which look like beads, borne at the tops of the long, upright stems. The flowers each have six white petals and numerous long stamens; when they open they give the plant a fluffy appearance. The leaves are finely divided into many pairs of leaflets.

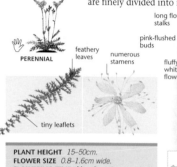

PERENNIAL

feathery leaves

tiny leaflets

numerous stamens

long flower stalks

pink-flushed buds

fluffy white flowers

PLANT HEIGHT *15–50cm.*
FLOWER SIZE *0.8–1.6cm wide.*
FLOWERING TIME *May–August.*
LEAVES *Alternate, most appearing basal, finely divided, and feathery.*
FRUIT *Head of achenes, with 1–2 seeds.*
SIMILAR SPECIES *Meadowsweet (below), which is larger overall, with larger leaflets.*

Meadowsweet

Filipendula ulmaria (Rosaceae)

FLOURISHES *in wet meadows, fens, and tall herb communities, and along river banks, stream margins, and damp road verges.*

This member of the rose family is most attractive when its creamy white flowerheads are seen in great masses along a river bank. The fragrant flowers, each with many stamens, open from the spherical buds at the top of branched stems, which stand tall above other vegetation. The seeds are coiled together like tiny snail shells. The deep green foliage has a rough texture similar to that of elm leaves.

deep green leaves

toothed leaflets

tall, rigid stems

PERENNIAL

spirally twisted seeds

PLANT HEIGHT *60–120cm.*
FLOWER SIZE *4–8mm wide.*
FLOWERING TIME *June–August.*
LEAVES *Alternate, pinnately divided, small leaflets between bigger ones.*
FRUIT *Small collection of achenes, individual fruit tightly coiled.*
SIMILAR SPECIES *Dropwort (above).*

Bramble

Rubus fruticosus (Rosaceae)

The tenacious scrambling stems of the Bramble are covered with vicious thorns and, arching down to the ground, take root to form new plants. Rose-like flowers, present throughout summer, may be any shade from white to deep pink or purple. The edible fruit ripens from green to red to blue-black.

5-petalled flowers

PERENNIAL

OCCURS *in almost any habitat on many types of soil, but favours woodland, hedges, and scrub, where it may form thickets.*

3 leaflets

numerous stamens

cluster of drupelets

PLANT HEIGHT *0.5–2.5m.*
FLOWER SIZE *2–3cm wide.*
FLOWERING TIME *May–September.*
LEAVES *Alternate; divided into three toothed leaflets with prickly surface.*
FRUIT *Cluster of segments or drupelets.*
SIMILAR SPECIES *Field Rose (below) and Dog Rose (p.80), which have larger flowers.*

Field Rose

Rosa arvensis (Rosaceae)

This climbing, straggling rose has white flowers, with the styles forming short columns, protruding about 5mm. Its leaves, borne on sparsely prickled stems, are divided into two or three pairs of small, neat, oval leaflets. The fruit is an oval, bright red hip, emerging from the flower sepals, which fall off when the fruit ripens.

CLAMBERS *over other vegetation in scrub, hedgerows, and woodland margins. May form low bushes.*

styles form column

finely toothed margins

PERENNIAL

white petals

oval, smooth hip

PLANT HEIGHT *Up to 3m if climbing on other shrubs, otherwise 1m.*
FLOWER SIZE *3–5cm wide.*
FLOWERING TIME *June–August.*
LEAVES *Alternate, pinnately divided.*
FRUIT *Smooth, bright red hip, without sepals.*
SIMILAR SPECIES *Bramble (above); Dog Rose (p.80), which has flowers with short styles.*

Dog Rose

Rosa canina (Rosaceae)

Perhaps one of the prettiest wildflowers to grace the countryside in early summer, the Dog Rose has long, arching, thorn-covered stems that clamber over bushes and hedges or occasionally form free-standing bushes. The stems and leaves are free from any hair or glands, and the thorns are hooked at the end like an eagle's beak. The scentless flowers have five white petals that are usually flushed with pale pink, setting off the numerous yellow stamens. The styles form a small dome, rather than a column, in the centre of the flower.

SCRAMBLES *over hedges and bushes, along woodland margins, and in rough, scrubby, grassy places.*

PERENNIAL

pink-flushed petals

numerous yellow stamens

coarsely toothed margins

5–7 leaflets

oval red rosehip

NOTE

The hips have long been used in commercial preparations to ease coughs and sore throats; they may also be fermented to make wine.

PLANT HEIGHT *1–2.5m.*
FLOWER SIZE *4–5cm wide.*
FLOWERING TIME *June–July.*
LEAVES *Alternate, pinnately divided into 5–7 toothed leaflets, with long stipules attached to the leaf stalk.*
FRUIT *Oval to round red hips.*
SIMILAR SPECIES *Bramble (p.79); Field Rose (p.79) has flowers with styles forming a column; other Rosa species with hairy flower stalks.*

Agrimony

Agrimonia eupatoria (Rosaceae)

The long, narrow spires of yellow flowers are highly distinctive in this unusual member of the rose family. The leaves are divided into 3–6 toothed leaflets, with smaller leaflets in between. The hooked spines of the calyx that surrounds the fruit readily attach themselves to animal fur, and to trousers and bootlaces, helping to disperse the seeds to new locations.

FLOURISHES *in tall grassland, meadows, scrub, and woodland margins, and along hedgerows and road verges.*

toothed margins

5 separate petals

up to 20 stamens

PERENNIAL

flowers in long, slender spikes

PLANT HEIGHT *50–100cm.*
FLOWER SIZE *5–8mm wide.*
FLOWERING TIME *June–August.*
LEAVES *Alternate, pinnate, toothed leaflets.*
FRUIT *Cup-shaped and grooved, covered with hooked bristles.*
SIMILAR SPECIES *Weld (p.74). which has smaller, yellowish green flowers.*

Lady's-mantle

Alchemilla vulgaris (Rosaceae)

There are many similar varieties of Lady's-mantle that are difficult to differentiate. *Alchemilla vulgaris* represents an aggregate of several species including *A. xanthochlora* and *A. filicaulis*. They all exhibit the same silky, lobed, grey-green leaves which are covered with downy hairs that repel water. Each tiny flower has four sepals, but no petals.

FOUND *in grassy and rocky places, meadows, woodland margins, and streamsides, at high and low altitudes.*

palmately lobed leaf

tiny green flowers

PERENNIAL

4 stamens

flowers in loose clusters

PLANT HEIGHT *30–60cm.*
FLOWER SIZE *3–4mm wide.*
FLOWERING TIME *May–August.*
LEAVES *Mostly basal with clasping stem leaves; palmately lobed, soft, and hairy.*
FRUIT *Small solitary achene.*
SIMILAR SPECIES *Alpine Lady's-mantle (A. alpina), which is much smaller.*

Salad Burnet

Sanguisorba minor (Rosaceae)

FORMS *large colonies in dry grassland and rocky places, and on roadsides; on slopes and on chalky soil.*

PERENNIAL

The distinctive leaves of this plant are pinnately divided into pairs of tiny, oval leaflets, well separated on the leaf stalk, like a row of little bird's wings. They smell like cucumber when crushed, and may be eaten in salads. The flowerheads open first with the crimson female styles, followed by drooping male stamens with fluffy yellow anthers.

rounded flowerheads

long stem

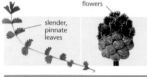

slender, pinnate leaves

crimson female flowers

PLANT HEIGHT *20–50cm.*
FLOWER SIZE *Flowerheads 1–2cm wide.*
FLOWERING TIME *May–July.*
LEAVES *Alternate, pinnately divided with small, toothed leaflets, smelling of cucumber.*
FRUIT *One or two achenes within the calyx.*
SIMILAR SPECIES *Great Burnet (below), which is much larger and has bigger leaves.*

Great Burnet

Sanguisorba officinalis (Rosaceae)

INHABITS *damp meadows and open, grassy places on chalky or rich soil.*

This damp-loving plant is intolerant of grazing or drying out of its habitat. The tall, slender, branched stems bear oval flowerheads with densely packed crimson flowers, often visible above surrounding tall grasses. There are no petals, but deep red sepals and prominent stamens form the flowerheads. The alternate leaves are pinnately divided into about seven pairs of stalked and oval leaflets, dark green above but greyish beneath.

oblong heads of crimson flowers

dark green and greyish leaves

toothed margin

PERENNIAL

PLANT HEIGHT *40–90cm.*
FLOWER SIZE *Flowerheads 1–3cm long.*
FLOWERING TIME *June–September.*
LEAVES *Alternate, with stalked and toothed oval leaflets.*
FRUIT *Tiny achenes.*
SIMILAR SPECIES *Salad Burnet (above), which is smaller and has tiny leaflets.*

Herb Bennet

Geum urbanum (Rosaceae)

Although this leafy member of the rose family has branched
flower stems, there is never a mass of flowers on display at
the same time. Each five-petalled, pale yellow flower is often
partnered by the fruithead, with its characteristic
hooked spines. The toothed leaves are deeply
lobed or divided into leaflets, the stem leaves
with a pair of large leaf-
like stipules at the base.

PROLIFERATES *in
woodland, along
hedgerows, roadsides,
paths, and other
shady places.*

PERENNIAL

hooked styles
of fruithead

rounded
petals

numerous
stamens

coarsely
toothed
leaflets

cluster of
achenes

PLANT HEIGHT *40–70cm.*
FLOWER SIZE *1–1.5cm wide.*
FLOWERING TIME *May–September.*
LEAVES *Basal with pairs of lobed leaflets;
stem leaves with three lobes or leaflets.*
FRUIT *Rounded cluster of hairy achenes.*
SIMILAR SPECIES *Water Avens (below),
which has pendent flowers.*

Water Avens

Geum rivale (Rosaceae)

This graceful plant often hybridizes with the closely related
Herb Bennet (above), resulting in flowers that have features
of both plants. The flowers of Water Avens have pinkish
cream petals and purplish brown sepals that become
upright when the feathery fruit is formed. The leaves are
divided into lobed leaflets; the stem leaves are smaller.

GROWS *in colonies
in marshy grassland,
ditches, meadows, and
wet woodland. Prefers
chalky soil.*

PERENNIAL

pendent
flowers

achenes with
hooked styles

arched flower
stalks

toothed
margin

PLANT HEIGHT *30–50cm.*
FLOWER SIZE *8–15mm wide.*
FLOWERING TIME *April–September.*
LEAVES *Basal pinnate leaves, with 3–6 pairs
of oval to round leaflets; stem leaves trifoliate.*
FRUIT *Collection of achenes.*
SIMILAR SPECIES *Herb Bennet (above);
hybrids, which have pendent yellow flowers.*

Marsh Cinquefoil

Potentilla palustris (Rosaceae)

SEEN *in marshland, fens, bogs, and wet meadows, on acid soil.*

The short-stalked leaves of this plant are pinnately divided into 5–7 serrated leaflets. The distinctive flower has prominent, deep maroon or purplish sepals; the crimson petals are much smaller. The central core of immature achenes is surrounded by dark stamens.

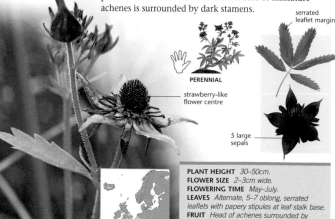

PERENNIAL

strawberry-like flower centre

serrated leaflet margin

5 large sepals

PLANT HEIGHT *30–50cm.*
FLOWER SIZE *2–3cm wide.*
FLOWERING TIME *May–July.*
LEAVES *Alternate, 5–7 oblong, serrated leaflets with papery stipules at leaf stalk base.*
FRUIT *Head of achenes surrounded by persistent calyx.*
SIMILAR SPECIES *None.*

Wild Strawberry

Fragaria vesca (Rosaceae)

CREEPS *along the ground in woods, scrub, rocky places, and hedgerows, and along walls; on chalky soil.*

The fruit of this plant has an excellent flavour, but is much smaller than that of the cultivated variety. The plant creeps by runners, which root to form new plants. Its conspicuous flowers have five rounded white petals, backed with ten green sepals. The leaves have three coarsely toothed leaflets, like a giant clover leaf.

PERENNIAL

veined leaf   green sepals

yellow stamens

fleshy red fruit

PLANT HEIGHT *10–25cm.*
FLOWER SIZE *1.2–1.8cm wide.*
FLOWERING TIME *April–July.*
LEAVES *Mostly basal, with three leaflets.*
FRUIT *Strawberry with seeds on the outside.*
SIMILAR SPECIES *Barren Strawberry (Potentilla sterilis), which has a smaller terminal tooth to each leaflet.*

Silverweed

Potentilla anserina (Rosaceae)

This creeping plant spreads by means of rooting runners. Its leaves are easily recognized by their ladder-like rows of 15–25 serrated leaflets, grey-green above and covered with fine silvery hair below. The solitary flowers, which may not grow in some damp habitats, have rounded yellow petals, with an epicalyx behind each solitary flower.

PROLIFERATES *in open places such as farm tracks, grassy verges, waste, and cultivated ground.*

bright yellow flower

sharply toothed leaflets

PERENNIAL

5–6 large petals

PLANT HEIGHT *5–20cm.*
FLOWER SIZE *1.5–2cm wide.*
FLOWERING TIME *May–August.*
LEAVES *Basal rosettes, pinnate.*
FRUIT *Tight head of achenes.*
SIMILAR SPECIES *Creeping Cinquefoil (P. reptans) has palmately lobed leaves; Tormentil (below) has four-petalled flowers.*

Tormentil

Potentilla erecta (Rosaceae)

A slender, delicate plant that trails through grassland, Tormentil has long, non-rooting flower stems held up by other vegetation. Its bright lemon-yellow flowers have four petals, notched at the tip, in the shape of a cross. The leaves are three-lobed with bluntly toothed, oval segments; there are two smaller stipules at the base.

FORMS *patches in lawns, meadows, heaths, woodland, and on roadsides, preferring acid soil.*

PERENNIAL

solitary lemon-yellow

3-lobed leaf

slender flower stalk

4 petals

PLANT HEIGHT *4–12cm.*
FLOWER SIZE *7–11mm wide.*
FLOWERING TIME *May–September.*
LEAVES *Alternate, three-lobed, toothed.*
FRUIT *Tiny achenes.*
SIMILAR SPECIES *Silverweed (above), which has ladder-like leaves; Creeping Cinquefoil (P. reptans), which has 5 petals.*

Broom

Cytisus scoparius (Fabaceae)

This deciduous shrub has had a long association with people, especially, as its name suggests, in the use of its branches as brooms. The many slender green branches are ridged and angled, producing small oval leaves which may be single or in threes. The strongly scented pealike flowers are borne in leafy spikes.

FORMS *single or clumped bushes in dry, sunny places, woodland edges, heaths, hedgerows, grassland, and coastal cliffs, on sandy soil.*

small stalkless leaflets

slender stems

curled stamens

wide open yellow peaflowers

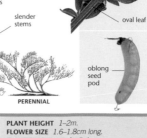

oval leaf

oblong seed pod

PERENNIAL

PLANT HEIGHT *1–2m.*
FLOWER SIZE *1.6–1.8cm long.*
FLOWERING TIME *April–June.*
LEAVES *Alternate, mostly stalkless, very small.*
FRUIT *Hairy, oblong pod, black when ripe.*
SIMILAR SPECIES *Gorse (below), which has spiny stems; Dyer's Greenweed (right), is much smaller overall and has smaller flowers.*

Gorse

Ulex europaeus (Fabaceae)

Although viciously spiked on mature plants, when young, the branches of Gorse are soft and palatable and in rabbit-infested areas, this normally large shrub with ridged stems may grow no more than a few centimetres high. The yellow peaflowers may be seen all through the year, with an arrangement of stamens that shoot out pollen onto visiting bees.

FOUND *in grassy places such as meadows, heaths, woodland margins, or close to the sea. Usually found on light, well-drained soil.*

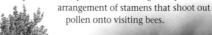

covering of spines

PERENNIAL

hairy sepals

sharp spines

brown pod

PLANT HEIGHT *Up to 2m.*
FLOWER SIZE *1.5–2cm long.*
FLOWERING TIME *January–April.*
LEAVES *Tiny, three-lobed, scale-like when young, soon replaced by branched spines.*
FRUIT *Hairy brown pod, 1.2–2cm long.*
SIMILAR SPECIES *Broom (above) has smaller, oval leaves and no spines on the stems.*

Dyer's Greenweed

Genista tinctoria (Fabaceae)

This subshrub forms small, compact bushes, resembling miniature versions of Broom (left). Its non-spiny branches are sparsely covered with oblong, untoothed leaves, each with a pair of tiny stipules at the base. The yellow peaflowers, borne on the tops of the stems, open out wide so that the two lower wing petals droop downwards.

OCCURS *in meadows, woodland glades, and open scrub, on roadsides and embankments; often on slightly acid soil.*

flowers in stalked spikes

drooping lower petals

narrow seed pod

hairless surface

small, simple leaves

PERENNIAL

PLANT HEIGHT *30–60cm.*
FLOWER SIZE *8–15mm long.*
FLOWERING TIME *May–July.*
LEAVES *Alternate, oblong, and untoothed.*
FRUIT *Pod, hairless, oblong, brown.*
SIMILAR SPECIES *Broom (left), which is larger; Petty Whin (G. anglica), which has small spines on its woody stems.*

Bush Vetch

Vicia sepium (Fabaceae)

This plant uses its long tendrils to scramble over other vegetation. It produces small, tight clusters of peaflowers that vary in colour from a greyish blue to a purplish pink, the standard petal veined with streaks of dark purple. The flowers turn brown once pollinated. The leaves have neat rows of oblong leaflets.

CLAMBERS *over other plants in woodland, scrub, meadows, and hedgerows, avoiding acid soil.*

5–9 pairs of leaflets

PERENNIAL

dark-veined petal

short-stalked flower clusters

PLANT HEIGHT *20–60cm.*
FLOWER SIZE *1.2–1.5cm wide.*
FLOWERING TIME *May–October.*
LEAVES *Alternate, pinnate, toothed stipules.*
FRUIT *Black, hairless pod, 2–3.5cm long.*
SIMILAR SPECIES *Common Vetch (p.88), which has narrower leaflets; Wood Vetch (V. sylvatica), which has larger, paler flowers.*

Common Vetch

Vicia sativa (Fabaceae)

Introduced from southern Europe as a fodder crop for cattle, Common Vetch is now established throughout the British Isles. The ladder-like leaves are pinnately divided, each leaflet with a "needle" at the tip. Each leaf terminates in a long, branched tendril, and at the base are a pair of small, coarsely toothed stipules, each with a black spot. The flowers, usually paired but occasionally solitary, are vivid red to purple, the wing and keel petals usually being a shade darker than the standard petal.

SCRAMBLES *among grasses and other vegetation in cultivated fields, wasteland, roadsides, banks, and scrub.*

narrow, sharply tipped leaflets

ANNUAL

NOTE

The spots on the stipules secrete a sugary substance that attracts ants, which, in turn, help to defend the plant against attack by other insects.

flowers usually in pairs

terminal branched tendril

3–8 pairs of leaflets

red to purple peaflower

slender seed pod

PLANT HEIGHT *50–120cm.*
FLOWER SIZE *1.8–2.5cm long.*
FLOWERING TIME *April–September.*
LEAVES *Alternate, pinnately divided, with 3–8 pairs of oval to lance-shaped leaflets.*
FRUIT *Hairy pod, green, ripening to brown or black, 2.5–7cm long.*
SIMILAR SPECIES *Bush Vetch (p.87), which has broader leaflets; Bitter Vetch (Lathyrus linifolius), which has larger leaves and no tendrils.*

Tufted Vetch

Vicia cracca (Fabaceae)

The deep violet-blue flowers of Tufted Vetch are produced in such profusion that they can be seen from some distance, often alongside roads. Up to 40 bluish violet flowers are clustered into long racemes. The leaves are divided into 6–15 pairs of narrow leaflets. Each leaf terminates in a long, branching tendril, which can support the plant to a considerable height.

twining tendrils

paired leaflets

bluish violet petals

flowers in one-sided racemes

slender stems

PERENNIAL

PROLIFERATES *among tall grasses in meadows, hedgerows, woodland margins, scrub, roadsides, and over coastal rocks and shingle.*

PLANT HEIGHT 0.8–1.8m.
FLOWER SIZE 8–12mm wide.
FLOWERING TIME June–August.
LEAVES Alternate, pinnate, oblong leaflets.
FRUIT Three-lobed capsule, splitting to the base.
SIMILAR SPECIES Lucerne (p.92), which has smaller flower clusters.

Broad-leaved Everlasting Pea

Lathyrus latifolius (Fabaceae)

A vigorous climber, this plant has been introduced throughout Europe where cultivated forms have become naturalized and flower even more freely. The stems and leaf stalks have very broad wings. The leaflets are prominently veined with a pair of stipules at the base.

CLIMBS *over vegetation on rough grassy and bushy sites, roadsides, wasteland, and woodland margins.*

long branching tendril

flower clusters on erect stalks

lance-shaped leaflets

slender fruit pod

PERENNIAL

PLANT HEIGHT 1–3m.
FLOWER SIZE 2–3cm long.
FLOWERING TIME May–July.
LEAVES Broad leaflets with branching tendril.
FRUIT Pod, 5–10cm long, ripening to brown.
SIMILAR SPECIES Narrow-leaved Everlasting Pea (L. sylvestris), which has narrower leaflets and shorter pods.

Meadow Vetchling

Lathyrus pratensis (Fabaceae)

CLAMBERS *and twines through meadow grasses and other vegetation, on roadsides, and in scrub and woodland.*

A member of the pea family, the Meadow Vetchling has thin stems that are slightly winged, and bear a pair of spear-shaped leaflets with a twisting tendril between them. At the base of each leaf-stalk are a pair of large, characteristically arrow-shaped stipules. A tight cluster of bright yellow flowers blooms at the end of a long stem.

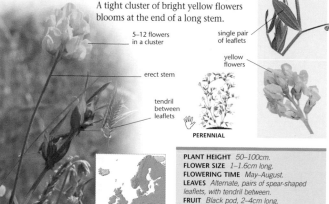

5–12 flowers in a cluster

single pair of leaflets

yellow flowers

erect stem

tendril between leaflets

PERENNIAL

PLANT HEIGHT *50–100cm.*
FLOWER SIZE *1–1.6cm long.*
FLOWERING TIME *May–August.*
LEAVES *Alternate, pairs of spear-shaped leaflets, with tendril between.*
FRUIT *Black pod, 2–4cm long.*
SIMILAR SPECIES *Common Bird's-foot Trefoil (p.95) has flowers clustered in a "crown".*

Common Restharrow

Ononis repens (Fabaceae)

OCCURS *in clumps in meadows, pastures, and grassland, on chalky soil.*

The tough roots and creeping habit of this plant caused problems for farmers before the days of mechanized ploughs. It is a low, bushy plant with woody, hairy stems and rough, trifoliate leaves, each leaflet with oval stipules at the base. The flowers, larger than the leaves, consist of a huge pink standard petal, and white and pink wing and keel petals.

PERENNIAL

flowers in leafy spikes

large standard petal

small trifoliate leaves

oval, toothed leaflet

pink keel petal

white wing petal

PLANT HEIGHT *15–50cm.*
FLOWER SIZE *1.5–2cm long.*
FLOWERING TIME *June–September.*
LEAVES *Alternate, three oval, toothed leaflets.*
FRUIT *Hairy pod, 5–8mm long, containing one or two seeds.*
SIMILAR SPECIES *Spiny Restharrow (O. spinosa), which has stiff spines.*

Ribbed Melilot

Melilotus officinalis (Fabaceae)

As with many other members of the pea family, this plant
has leaves divided into three leaflets. Unlike the rest,
however, the margins of each oval leaflet are gently
toothed as though nibbled away. The tiny peaflowers are
arranged in long, branching spikes,
giving the plant an untidy look;
the seed pods turn
brown when ripe.

GROWS *in clumps
along roadsides and
field edges, on waste or
disturbed ground, and
building sites.*

alternate
leaves

flowers droop
from stems

toothed
margin

slender
flower
spikes

BIENNIAL/
PERENNIAL

PLANT HEIGHT *80–150cm.*
FLOWER SIZE *3–4mm wide.*
FLOWERING TIME *July–September.*
LEAVES *Alternate with three oval leaflets,
sharply toothed.*
FRUIT *Rounded pod with transverse ridges.*
SIMILAR SPECIES *Tall Melilot (M. altissima),
which has hairy black pods.*

Black Medick

Medicago lupulina (Fabaceae)

There are several small, trailing, clover-like species, but Black
Medick may easily be identified by its yellow peaflowers and
clusters of tiny, coiled seed pods, which become jet-black
when ripe. The small yellow flowers are in a crowded,
spherical cluster on a long stalk, while the trifoliate leaves
have a minute terminal tooth on each leaflet.

SPRAWLS *over grassy
places, wasteland, and
recently cultivated or
disturbed land.*

3 oval leaflets

cluster of
10–20 tiny
flowers

ANNUAL

small
teeth

coiled
black
pods

PLANT HEIGHT *10–50cm.*
FLOWER SIZE *Flowerheads 6–10mm wide.*
FLOWERING TIME *May–August.*
LEAVES *Alternate, with three oval leaflets.*
FRUIT *Black pods, 2–3mm long, in clusters.*
SIMILAR SPECIES *Lesser Trefoil (Trifolium
dubium), which has tiny fruit; Spotted Medick
(M. arabica), which has spotted leaves.*

Lucerne

Medicago sativa (Fabaceae)

Also known as Alfalfa, this plant was introduced throughout Europe as a fodder crop for cattle. Its trifoliate leaves are divided into long, slender leaflets, each toothed at the tip. The flowers, in loose clusters, vary in colour from pale pink to deep violet.

FORMS *colonies on cultivated and waste ground, roadsides, and disturbed, rough, grassy areas.*

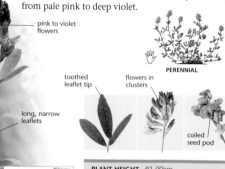

pink to violet flowers

PERENNIAL

toothed leaflet tip

flowers in clusters

long, narrow leaflets

coiled seed pod

PLANT HEIGHT *40–90cm.*
FLOWER SIZE *7–11mm long.*
FLOWERING TIME *June–July.*
LEAVES *Alternate, trifoliate, elliptical leaflets.*
FRUIT *Spiralled pod, 5–6mm wide, with a hole in the centre.*
SIMILAR SPECIES *Tufted Vetch (p.89), which has pinnate leaves and longer flower clusters.*

White Clover

Trifolium repens (Fabaceae)

A familiar grassland plant, White Clover spreads by means of rooting runners. Its three-parted leaves usually have a white band on each leaflet. Rounded heads of white or cream peaflowers may become pinkish brown as they mature, the lower flowers drooping like a wide skirt. The flowers are sweet-scented and a rich source of nectar.

PROLIFERATES *in pastures, commons, lawns, roadsides, heaths, and other grassy places.*

3 oval leaflets

V-shaped, whitish band on leaflet

rounded, cream to white flowerhead

drooping lower flowers

ball-shaped flower cluster

PERENNIAL

PLANT HEIGHT *5–20cm.*
FLOWER SIZE *7–10mm long.*
FLOWERING TIME *June–September.*
LEAVES *Alternate with three oval leaflets.*
FRUIT *Narrow pod with 3–4 seeds.*
SIMILAR SPECIES *Red Clover (right), which has darker red flowers; Strawberry Clover (T. fragiferum) has smaller flowerheads.*

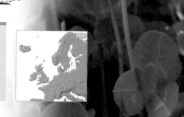

Red Clover

Trifolium pratense (Fabaceae)

Whole fields become crimson with the flowers of this prolific plant, which nourishes the soil with nitrogen, and is excellent fodder for livestock. The round or oblong heads of tightly clustered, pink to red flowers have a leaf directly below them. The leaves are made up of three oval leaflets, often with a V-shaped white mark. The flowers are pollinated by bumblebees. Varieties which have been sown as fodder crops occasionally naturalize and are usually more robust, with paler flowerheads than the truly wild form.

GROWS *in grassy places, old meadows, and wasteland, from lowland up to 3,000m.*

3 oval leaflets

pink petals

PERENNIAL

dense, rounded flowerheads

leaf directly below flowerhead

erect stems

NOTE

Red Clover is an important source of nectar for long-tongued bumble bees, but a decline in old clover meadows has consequently led to a fall in the bumble bee population.

PLANT HEIGHT *20–50cm.*
FLOWER SIZE *Flowerhead 1.5–3cm wide.*
FLOWERING TIME *May–September.*
LEAVES *Alternate, with three oval leaflets.*
FRUIT *Small pod hidden in the calyx.*
SIMILAR SPECIES *White Clover (left); Zigzag Clover (T. medium), has stalked flowerheads, and no leaf directly below; Crimson Clover (T. incarnatum) has longer flowerheads of deep crimson flowers.*

Hop Trefoil

Trifolium campestre (Fabaceae)

A sprawling, clover-like plant, Hop Trefoil has erect stems bearing tight clusters of untidy peaflowers, which ripen from yellow to pale brown, looking like miniature Hop fruit. The single seed of each flower remains hidden within these persistent clusters. The leaves are trifoliate, with oval, minutely toothed leaflets, the central one with a short stalk.

FLOURISHES *in dry, grassy places and on roadsides and wasteland, in well-drained soil.*

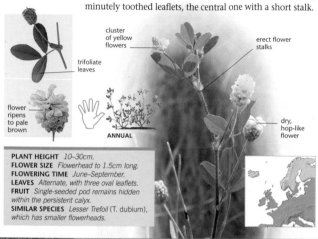

cluster of yellow flowers

erect flower stalks

trifoliate leaves

flower ripens to pale brown

ANNUAL

dry, hop-like flower

PLANT HEIGHT *10–30cm.*
FLOWER SIZE *Flowerhead to 1.5cm long.*
FLOWERING TIME *June–September.*
LEAVES *Alternate, with three oval leaflets.*
FRUIT *Single-seeded pod remains hidden within the persistent calyx.*
SIMILAR SPECIES *Lesser Trefoil* (T. dubium), *which has smaller flowerheads.*

Hare's-foot Clover

Trifolium arvense (Fabaceae)

The dense, fluffy flowerheads are almost like those of grass, but close examination shows that each tiny pink flower is surrounded by a calyx of long, silky hair, which gives the flowerhead the appearance of a hare's foot. The trifoliate leaves are more slender than those of other clovers.

FORMS *mats in dry, grassy areas, scrub, and woodland margins, on sandy soil.*

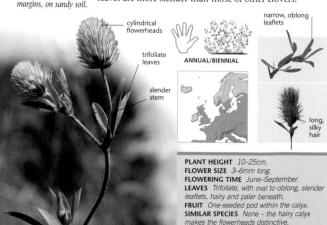

cylindrical flowerheads

narrow, oblong leaflets

trifoliate leaves

ANNUAL/BIENNIAL

slender stem

long, silky hair

PLANT HEIGHT *10–25cm.*
FLOWER SIZE *3–6mm long.*
FLOWERING TIME *June–September.*
LEAVES *Trifoliate, with oval to oblong, slender leaflets, hairy and paler beneath.*
FRUIT *One-seeded pod within the calyx.*
SIMILAR SPECIES *None – the hairy calyx makes the flowerheads distinctive.*

Common Bird's-foot Trefoil

Lotus corniculatus (Fabaceae)

This common member of the pea family produces erect stems topped with fan-shaped clusters of brightly coloured yellow or orange peaflowers with red streaks, which are red-tipped in bud. The fruit cluster is also a fan of long, narrow pods, with a persistent calyx at the base, and resembles a bird's foot.

THRIVES in grassy fields, pastures, scrub, and along roadsides and embankments.

PERENNIAL

cluster of 3–7 flowers

untidy pinnate leaves

red streaks

PLANT HEIGHT 5–30cm.
FLOWER SIZE 1–1.6cm long.
FLOWERING TIME June–September.
LEAVES Alternate, pinnate with oval leaflets, lowest ones at very base of leaf stalk.
FRUIT Brown-black cylindrical pod.
SIMILAR SPECIES Kidney Vetch (below), Greater Bird's-foot Trefoil (L. uliginosus).

Kidney Vetch

Anthyllis vulneraria (Fabaceae)

The colour of the flowers in this unusual member of the pea family varies widely from cream to red, even within the same flowerhead. Each flowerhead is surrounded at the base by thick, downy sepals, which give the plant a woolly and rather robust appearance. The leaves are pinnately divided, like a ladder, each with a large terminal leaflet.

FORMS patches in dry grassland, on cliff-tops, and rocky ledges, often on slopes. Prefers chalky soil, especially near the sea.

PERENNIAL

variable colours for individual flowers

large terminal leaflet

leaf-like bracts below flowerhead

whitish calyx

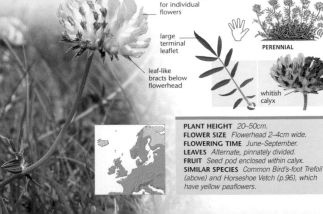

PLANT HEIGHT 20–50cm.
FLOWER SIZE Flowerhead 2–4cm wide.
FLOWERING TIME June–September.
LEAVES Alternate, pinnately divided.
FRUIT Seed pod enclosed within calyx.
SIMILAR SPECIES Common Bird's-foot Trefoil (above) and Horseshoe Vetch (p.96), which have yellow peaflowers.

Horseshoe Vetch

Hippocrepis comosa (Fabaceae)

SEEN *in patches on sunny grassland, often on slopes or cliff-tops, always on chalky*

This plant is an important foodplant for some of the Blue butterfly larvae. The yellow peaflowers with faint reddish veins are arranged like an open fan on a long flower stalk, while the fruithead is an extraordinary collection of twisted pods, each divided into several horseshoe-shaped segments.

fan-shaped flower cluster

PERENNIAL

long flower stalk

neat, pinnate leaves

crimped fruit

PLANT HEIGHT *15–30cm.*
FLOWER SIZE *6–10mm long.*
FLOWERING TIME *May–July.*
LEAVES *Alternate, 4–7 pairs of oval leaflets.*
FRUIT *Pod divided into wavy, horseshoe-shaped segments that separate when ripe.*
SIMILAR SPECIES *Common Bird's-foot Trefoil (p.95), Kidney Vetch (p.95).*

Wood Sorrel

Oxalis acetosella (Oxalidaceae)

FORMS *patches in scrub, woodland, hedgerows, and rocky places, in shade; on humus-rich soils.*

This dainty, creeping plant has bell-like white flowers veined pink or white. Its leaves are distinctive, divided into three drooping, folded, heart-shaped leaflets, which close up in strong sunshine and at night. Bright green above and purplish beneath, they contain a mild acid which gives them a sharp, lemony flavour.

PERENNIAL

leaf folded in centre

solitary flowers

drooping leaflets

5-petalled flower

bell-lke flowers

PLANT HEIGHT *4–10cm.*
FLOWER SIZE *0.8–1.5cm wide.*
FLOWERING TIME *April–June.*
LEAVES *Basal, with three leaflets.*
FRUIT *Capsule 3–4mm long, that explodes, expelling seeds over a distance.*
SIMILAR SPECIES *Wood Anemone (p.57) has six-petalled flowers and divided leaves.*

Wood Crane's-bill

Geranium sylvaticum (Geraniaceae)

The flowers of this species range from pink to violet to purple and are usually arranged in pairs. The petals are paler at the flower centre and do not overlap. The palmate leaves are divided down to the base into broad, coarsely toothed segments, and the entire plant is covered with fine hair. The

PROLIFERATES *along woodland margins, streams, and in mountain pastures.*

beaked fruit, formed from the long styles which remain attached to the seeds, resembles the long bill of a crane or heron.

5–9 lobed leaves

flowers in pairs

unstalked stem leaf

whitish flower centre

PERENNIAL

barely notched petals

PLANT HEIGHT *30–70cm.*	
FLOWER SIZE *2.2–2.6cm wide.*	
FLOWERING TIME *June–July.*	
LEAVES *Mostly basal, palmately lobed leaves.*	
FRUIT *Five mericarps, joined by their styles.*	
SIMILAR SPECIES *Bloody Crane's-bill (below) has more narrowly lobed leaves; Meadow Crane's-bill (p.98), which is a taller plant.*	

Bloody Crane's-bill

Geranium sanguineum (Geraniaceae)

This crane's-bill has flowers with astonishing colours, more akin to a garden cultivar than a wild plant. They are deep purplish pink or cerise and have almost overlapping petals, with a pair of tiny bracts beneath. The distinctive, stalked leaves are almost circular in outline and are deeply divided into finger-like lobes.

PREFERS *shaded places in rocky habitats, open woodland, and glades, on well-drained soil.*

solitary flower on long stem

rounded, slightly notched petals

PERENNIAL

narrow lobes

stalked leaf

PLANT HEIGHT *10–30cm.*	
FLOWER SIZE *2.5–3cm wide.*	
FLOWERING TIME *July–August.*	
LEAVES *Alternate, palmately lobed.*	
FRUIT *Five mericarps, joined by their styles.*	
SIMILAR SPECIES *Wood Crane's-bill (above); French Crane's-bill (G. endressii), which has 5 broad leaf lobes and silky pink flowers.*	

Meadow Crane's-bill

Geranium pratense (Geraniaceae)

GROWS *in meadows, pastures, hedgebanks, and road verges on rich or chalky soil. Garden cultivars of this species sometimes escape into the countryside.*

Distinctive among the geraniums, this plant has violet-blue flowers rather than the more usual pink. The petals are large, and often veined with white or crimson, and make an attractive sight along the verges of country lanes. Also large, the leaves are more or less rounded in outline but very deeply cut, almost to the base, into slender segments, giving them a rather tattered look and differentiating them from many garden cultivars.

toothed leaf segments

hairy stems

PERENNIAL

beaked fruit

petals rounded at tip

lighter veins on petals

NOTE

The beak of geranium fruit is formed from the elongated styles of the flowers. As they dry, they pull on the seeds, which are suddenly released and catapulted away from the plant.

PLANT HEIGHT *60–100cm.*
FLOWER SIZE *2.5–3cm wide.*
FLOWERING TIME *June–September.*
LEAVES *Basal and alternate, palmately lobed into many slender, deeply cut segments.*
FRUIT *Beaked fruit, splitting into five one-seeded portions.*
SIMILAR SPECIES *Wood Crane's-bill (p.97), which has pinker flowers and less deeply cut leaves.*

Hedgerow Crane's-bill

Geranium pyrenaicum (Geraniaceae)

This species has long stems topped with medium-sized flowers – unlike most other pale pink crane's-bills, which have smaller flowers. The pale to mid-pink petals overlap, giving a starry effect. As with other crane's-bills, the fruit is beaked and is usually in pairs.

STRAGGLES *among tall vegetation along hedgerows and woodland margins, and in meadows.*

deeply notched petals

PERENNIAL

blunt-toothed leaf lobes

beaked fruit

flowers in pairs

PLANT HEIGHT *40–60cm.*
FLOWER SIZE *1.4–1.8cm wide.*
FLOWERING TIME *June–August.*
LEAVES *Alternate, palmately lobed.*
FRUIT *Five mericarps with a long beak, hairy, on long, downturned stalk.*
SIMILAR SPECIES Dove's-foot Crane's-bill (G. molle), *which has smaller flowers.*

Herb Robert

Geranium robertianum (Geraniaceae)

The often red-tinged leaves of Herb Robert help it to stand out among other vegetation. The scented leaves are toothed down to the midrib. The small, lobed flowers are bright pink, fading to white at the centre, with two red stripes along their length, and bright orange anthers. The fruit bears a long beak formed by the persistent styles attached to the seeds.

INHABITS *semi-shaded places along old walls, in woodland glades, and banks; also well-drained, rocky or gravelly sites.*

ANNUAL/BIENNIAL

5 rounded petals

flowers in pairs

deeply lobed leaves

thin stalk

long beak on fruit

paired fruit

PLANT HEIGHT *10–50cm.*
FLOWER SIZE *1.4–1.8cm wide.*
FLOWERING TIME *May–September.*
LEAVES *Alternate, stalked, with 3–4 lobes.*
FRUIT *Five mericarps, joined by their persistent styles into a long beak.*
SIMILAR SPECIES Shiny Crane's-bill (G. lucidum) *has smaller flowers and glossy leaves.*

Common Stork's-bill

Erodium cicutarium (Geraniaceae)

FOUND *in dry, sandy places such as heathy grassland, disturbed and bare ground, often near the coast.*

Stork's-bills have even longer beaks on the fruit than the related crane's-bills, and they are often clustered tightly together like a bunch of upright fingers. The feathery leaves are pinnately, rather than palmately, divided. The slightly unequal petals sometimes have a blackish blotch at the base, and begin to fall at midday in sunny weather. The leaves and stems may be eaten raw or cooked in salads, sandwiches, and soups.

ANNUAL/BIENNIAL

petals of unequal length

pink flowers

fine-toothed leaflets

long-beaked fruit

PLANT HEIGHT *10–40cm.*
FLOWER SIZE *0.8–1.8cm wide.*
FLOWERING TIME *June–September.*
LEAVES *Basal and alternate, pinnate.*
FRUIT *Five mericarps joined into a hairy beak, 1–4cm long.*
SIMILAR SPECIES *Musk Stork's-bill (E. moschatum), which has larger flowers.*

Dog's Mercury

Mercurialis perennis (Euphorbiaceae)

COVERS *the floors of woodland, coppices, hedgerows, and shady, rocky places. Male and female colonies may be separate.*

This plant may form extensive carpets of green on woodland floors early in the year, before the trees come into leaf. The green male flowers are on long, erect spikes, while the rather insignificant female flowers are formed on separate plants. Like many members of the spurge family, Dog's Mercury is very poisonous.

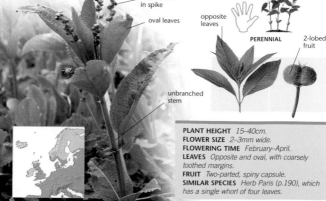

male flowers in spike

oval leaves

opposite leaves

PERENNIAL

2-lobed fruit

unbranched stem

PLANT HEIGHT *15–40cm.*
FLOWER SIZE *2–3mm wide.*
FLOWERING TIME *February–April.*
LEAVES *Opposite and oval, with coarsely toothed margins.*
FRUIT *Two-parted, spiny capsule.*
SIMILAR SPECIES *Herb Paris (p.190), which has a single whorl of four leaves.*

Sun Spurge

Euphorbia helioscopa (Euphorbiaceae)

This spurge produces a clock-like arrangement of yellow-green saucers facing towards the sky, each one made up of whorls of leaf-like bracts that surround the flowers. The flowers themselves are a complex assembly of crescent-shaped glands surrounding the stamens. The smooth, rounded fruit capsule is attached to one side by a small stalk. As with other spurges, the milky juice is very poisonous.

OCCURS on field edges, cultivated or disturbed land, and exposed, dry, or sandy wastelands.

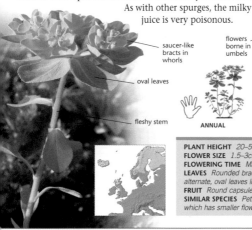

saucer-like bracts in whorls

oval leaves

fleshy stem

ANNUAL

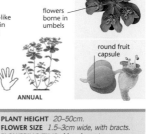

flowers borne in umbels

round fruit capsule

PLANT HEIGHT 20–50cm.
FLOWER SIZE 1.5–3cm wide, with bracts.
FLOWERING TIME May–August.
LEAVES Rounded bracts in whorls at top; alternate, oval leaves lower down.
FRUIT Round capsule on one side of umbel.
SIMILAR SPECIES Petty Spurge (E. peplus), which has smaller flowers.

Wood Spurge

Euphorbia amygdaloides (Euphorbiaceae)

The flowers of Wood Spurge, borne in umbels at the end of an unbranched stem, have no petals. Instead, the ovary is surrounded by curious horned glands and upped by conspicuous yellow-green bracts. The stems may be red-tinged, while the leaves are deep green and untoothed. It exudes a poisonous milky latex that can be irritating to the skin.

FORMS large patches in woodland clearings or coppices, especially among oak or beech.

oblong, untoothed leaf

yellow-green bracts

bracts form a disc

PERENNIAL

PLANT HEIGHT 30–80cm.
FLOWER SIZE 1.5–2.5cm wide, with bracts.
FLOWERING TIME April–June.
LEAVES Alternate, oblong and untoothed, tapered towards the base; deep green.
FRUIT Capsule, 3–4mm wide.
SIMILAR SPECIES Sun Spurge (above), which has whorls of leaves.

Common Milkwort

Polygala vulgaris (Polygalaceae)

The dainty blue flowers of Common Milkwort are the easiest to spot in the grass of its habitat, although it often has magenta or even white flowers. The coloured parts are actually three of the five sepals forming two wings and a hood, while the true petals are tiny, forming a frilly white tuft in the centre.

OCCURS *on short, often grazed grassland, on heaths, commons, and sand dunes.*

fringed white petals

deep green leaves

PERENNIAL

narrow leaf

sepals form hood

wing-like sepals

PLANT HEIGHT *10–30cm.*
FLOWER SIZE *5–8mm long.*
FLOWERING TIME *May–September.*
LEAVES *Alternate, oval-elliptic, untoothed.*
FRUIT *Small, two-lobed capsule.*
SIMILAR SPECIES *Heath Milkwort (P. serpyllifolia), which has opposite lower leaves, and is found on acid soil.*

Himalayan Balsam

Impatiens glandulifera (Balsaminaceae)

Introduced to the British Isles in the 19th century from the Himalayas, this plant has now become an invasive pest in many areas. The succulent, red-tinged stems grow quickly, bearing whorls of pointed leaves with a whitish midrib. Numerous branches produce two-lipped, pendent flowers at the top, each with a pair of almost opalescent sepals that form a sac.

PROLIFERATES *along ditches, river banks, and streamsides, and in damp wasteland and woodland, usually in sheltered situations.*

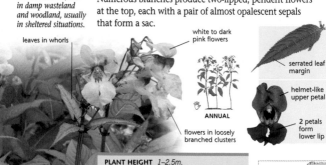

leaves in whorls

white to dark pink flowers

ANNUAL

flowers in loosely branched clusters

serrated leaf margin

helmet-like upper petal

2 petals form lower lip

PLANT HEIGHT *1–2.5m.*
FLOWER SIZE *2.5–4cm long.*
FLOWERING TIME *July–October.*
LEAVES *Opposite or in whorls of 3–5, lance-shaped, finely toothed with pale midrib.*
FRUIT *Spindle-shaped capsule.*
SIMILAR SPECIES *Orange Balsam (I. capensis) is smaller with orange flowers.*

Musk Mallow

Malva moschata (Malvaceae)

The pale powder-pink flowers of this plant are a common sight along roadsides in late summer. They have five distinctly notched petals, with a central column of white to pink stamens, and a sweet, musky scent. The lower leaves are kidney-shaped and toothed, while the upper leaves are deeply divided into narrow segments.

FORMS *clumps along roadsides, hedgerows, and field margins, in meadows and other grassy places.*

PERENNIAL

deeply notched petals

ring of nutlets

lobed lower leaf

segmented upper leaf

PLANT HEIGHT *50–80cm.*
FLOWER SIZE *3–6cm wide.*
FLOWERING TIME *July–August.*
LEAVES *Alternate, palmately lobed, upper leaves more deeply cut into narrow segments.*
FRUIT *Nutlets, surrounded by sepals.*
SIMILAR SPECIES *Common Mallow (below), which has felty, slightly toothed leaves.*

Common Mallow

Malva sylvestris (Malvaceae)

A robust, hairy-stemmed plant frequently found in wasteland, the Common Mallow has flowers with five notched, pink to purple petals, with darker veins along their length, and a long column of pale pink stamens. Behind the petals, the calyx of sepals is backed by three narrow segments – the epicalyx. The felty leaves are rounded, with blunt-toothed margins.

GROWS *in wasteland and along field margins, hedgerows, and road verges.*

thin dark veins on petals

PERENNIAL

shallow toothed lobes

ring of nutlets

PLANT HEIGHT *50–100cm.*
FLOWER SIZE *2–5cm wide.*
FLOWERING TIME *June–September.*
LEAVES *Alternate, shallowly palmately lobed, and toothed, covered in felty hair.*
FRUIT *Ring of nutlets within persistent calyx.*
SIMILAR SPECIES *Musk Mallow (above); Dwarf Mallow (M. neglecta), which is smaller.*

Marsh Mallow

Althaea officinalis (Malvaceae)

The tall Marsh Mallow produces spires of delicately pink-flushed flowers clustered together towards the stem tops, often standing out among reeds or other tall waterside plants. The petals are broader than in other mallows, more deeply coloured towards the middle, and have a column of purplish red anthers in the centre.

FOUND *in salt marshes and damp meadows, by brackish ditches, and on the banks of tidal rivers, usually by the sea.*

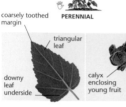

PERENNIAL

coarsely toothed margin

triangular leaf

downy leaf underside

calyx enclosing young fruit

flowers in tight clusters

purplish red anthers

5 broad, slightly notched petals

PLANT HEIGHT *80–150cm.*
FLOWER SIZE *2.5–4cm wide.*
FLOWERING TIME *August–September.*
LEAVES *Alternate, triangular, 3–5 lobes, and long-stalked; softly hairy; greyish.*
FRUIT *Hairy mericarps in a ring, surrounded by the calyx.*
SIMILAR SPECIES *Hollyhock (A. rosea).*

Tree Mallow

Lavatera arborea (Malvaceae)

Impossible to miss in its coastal habitat, this is a robust, tall plant with a woody stem. The large leaves are rounded, with 5–7 lobes that are wrinkled or wavy – an adaptation that helps the plant to conserve moisture in a dry environment. The cup-shaped flowers are a deep magenta-pink, with dark lines radiating out from the centre, and have pale pink anthers.

GROWS *on coasts, on shingle beaches, cliffs, wasteland, rocks, and sand dunes.*

BIENNIAL

dark flower centre

dark-veined petals

wavy lobes

stout stem

PLANT HEIGHT *1–2.5m.*
FLOWER SIZE *3–4cm wide.*
FLOWERING TIME *June–September.*
LEAVES *Alternate, palmate, lobed, downy when young, with pale undersides.*
FRUIT *Cluster of nutlets in a ring.*
SIMILAR SPECIES *Common Mallow (p.103), which has pink-centred flowers.*

Perforate St John's-wort

Hypericum perforatum (Clusiaceae)

There are many similar St John's-worts, but this one may be identified by its round stems, which have two opposite ridges or wings that are more easily felt than seen. The plant has an upright branched habit. Its oval leaves are peppered with tiny, translucent dots, which are visible only when the leaf is held up to the light. They also have a few tiny black glands on the underside, as do the margins of the yellow petals.

OCCURS *singly or in loose clumps in woodland margins, hedgerows, grassy places, on roadsides and banks, in open or semi-shaded places.*

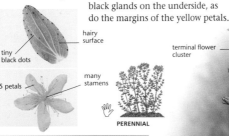

tiny black dots

hairy surface

5 petals

many stamens

terminal flower cluster

PERENNIAL

PLANT HEIGHT *40–80cm.*
FLOWER SIZE *1.8–2.2cm wide.*
FLOWERING TIME *May–September.*
LEAVES *Opposite, oval, and stalkless, with translucent black dots underneath.*
FRUIT *Small, many-seeded capsule.*
SIMILAR SPECIES *Imperforate St John's-wort (H. maculatum), has square stems.*

Field Pansy

Viola arvensis (Violaceae)

This small plant has long and toothed leaves. More obvious are the deeply pinnately divided stipules at the base of the leaf stalks, like little ladders. The flowers of Field Pansy are variable, cream to white with a small or large yellow blotch on the lower petal, and varying degrees of purple streaks. They open fully only in strong sunshine, and are otherwise hidden within the long green sepals.

FOUND *in arable fields, or bare ground, spreading over an entire field; on chalky or neutral soils.*

solitary flower

long green sepals

ANNUAL

5 petals

shallowly toothed margin

pinnately divided stipules

oblong leaf

yellow blotch

PLANT HEIGHT *8–20cm.*
FLOWER SIZE *4–8mm wide.*
FLOWERING TIME *May–October.*
LEAVES *Alternate, oblong, toothed.*
FRUIT *Rounded, green-yellow capsule.*
SIMILAR SPECIES *Eyebright (p.156) has jagged leaves; Wild Pansy (p.107) has larger flowers; other Viola flowers may be white.*

Common Dog-violet

Viola riviniana (Violaceae)

INHABITS *deciduous woodland, grassy heaths, and old pastures, on a variety of soils.*

This is the one of the commonest violets, and may be identified by the distinctly heart-shaped leaves, each ending in a blunt point. The petals are generally spread widely, and there is a stout, gently curved spur at the back, paler in colour than the petals and slightly grooved at the tip. There is a pair of tiny bracts about one third of the way down the flower stem. This is usually the last of the woodland violet species to flower in spring, though also perhaps the most beautiful.

NOTE
The leaves of this and other violets persist for many months after the flowers have faded, and are an important food source for the caterpillars of certain butterflies, especially the Fritillaries.

heart-shaped leaf

PERENNIAL

darker veins in centre of flower

widely spread petals

PLANT HEIGHT *8–20cm.*
FLOWER SIZE *1.4–2.5cm wide.*
FLOWERING TIME *April–June.*
LEAVES *Basal, alternate, and long-stalked.*
FRUIT *Three-parted capsule.*
SIMILAR SPECIES *Sweet Violet (right); Heath Dog-violet (V. canina); Early Dog-violet (V. reichenbachiana), which has narrower petals and a dark purple spur; Heath Violet (V. hirta), which has bracts lower down.*

Wild Pansy

Viola tricolor (Violaceae)

Also known as Heartsease, this plant's flowers are highly variable in colour and form, but always with a few veins pointing to the centre of the flower, and with petals larger than the sepals. This natural ability of the Wild Pansy to hybridize easily with other species has led to the many varieties of garden pansy available.

FOUND *in grassland, neglected and cultivated arable fields, on neutral or acid soils.*

ANNUAL/PERENNIAL

5-petalled flower

narrow, toothed leaf

dark veins on petals

PLANT HEIGHT *10–30cm.*
FLOWER SIZE *1–2.5cm wide.*
FLOWERING TIME *April–October.*
LEAVES *Alternate, oval to elliptical; large, pinnately lobed stipules at the base.*
FRUIT *Three-parted capsule.*
SIMILAR SPECIES *Field Pansy (p.105); Mountain Pansy (V. lutea) has yellow flowers.*

Sweet Violet

Viola odorata (Violaceae)

One of the clues to identifying this tuft-forming species is its early flowering time, when the flowers add a splash of colour to the arrival of spring. They may be deep violet with a spur of the same shade or white with a pink spur, and are sweetly scented. Also characteristic are the two tiny, triangular bracts more than halfway down the stem.

GROWS *in patches in hedgerows, woods, coppices, plantations, and scrub on chalky or neutral soils.*

PERENNIAL

deep violet spur

rounded leaf

solitary flower

kidney-shaped

separate petals

bluntly toothed margin

PLANT HEIGHT *8–15cm.*
FLOWER SIZE *1.3–1.5cm wide.*
FLOWERING TIME *February–May.*
LEAVES *Basal tufts, kidney-shaped.*
FRUIT *Three-valved, hairy capsule.*
SIMILAR SPECIES *Common Dog-violet (left) has more pointed leaves; Marsh Violet (V. palustris), which has darker flowers.*

White Bryony

Bryonia dioica (Cucurbitaceae)

CLIMBS *over hedges and bushes in scrub, and at woodland margins, on lime-rich soil at low altitudes.*

Unrelated to Black Bryony (p.192), this plant climbs by means of tendrils borne near the base of the fig-like leaves. Male and female flowers, both greenish white, are borne on separate plants, the male in longer-stalked clusters than the female, which have the developing berries beneath them. The poisonous berries are bright red when ripe.

PERENNIAL

5-lobed leaves

5-petalled flowers

coiled tendrils

small red berries

PLANT HEIGHT 2–3m.
FLOWER SIZE 1–1.8cm wide.
FLOWERING TIME May–September.
LEAVES Alternate; divided into five deep lobes.
FRUIT Poisonous, bright red berries.
SIMILAR SPECIES Hop (p.46), which has three-lobed leaves and pale brown fruit.

Common Rock Rose

Helianthemum nummularium (Cistaceae)

INHABITS *dry areas, with short turf and thin soil over chalky rock, up to 2,500m.*

Thin, crumpled yellow petals like tissue paper distinguish this plant of grassy, rocky places. The five petals are backed by three large, striped sepals and two tiny ones. Drooping buds and developing fruit also display these characteristic stripes. The small, oblong, and rather stiff leaves are in opposite pairs, and the stems are woody.

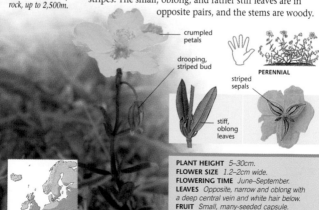

crumpled petals

drooping, striped bud

PERENNIAL

striped sepals

stiff, oblong leaves

PLANT HEIGHT 5–30cm.
FLOWER SIZE 1.2–2cm wide.
FLOWERING TIME June–September.
LEAVES Opposite, narrow and oblong with a deep central vein and white hair below.
FRUIT Small, many-seeded capsule.
SIMILAR SPECIES White Rock Rose (H. appeninum), which has white flowers.

Purple Loosestrife

Lythrum salicaria (Lythraceae)

Purple spires of this plant can be seen towering over other vegetation in damp areas. The erect, square, ridged stems bear stalkless leaves in whorls of three below but in opposite pairs above. They branch towards the top, bearing tiered ranks of flowers in tight whorls, each flower with five purple petals that are wrinkled and tissue-like. It often grows with the unrelated Yellow Loosestrife (p.126).

FORMS *clumps in damp sites such as marshes and wet meadows, alongside rivers, ponds, and ditches; also at the edges of reedbeds.*

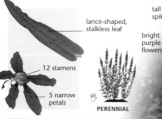

lance-shaped, stalkless leaf

tall flower spikes

bright purple flowers

12 stamens

5 narrow petals

PERENNIAL

PLANT HEIGHT *70–150cm.*
FLOWER SIZE *1–1.5cm wide.*
FLOWERING TIME *June–August.*
LEAVES *Whorled below, opposite above, lance-shaped, untoothed, and stalkless.*
FRUIT *Capsule containing many seeds.*
SIMILAR SPECIES *Rosebay Willowherb (p.110) has alternate leaves and larger flowers.*

Enchanter's-nightshade

Circaea lutetiana (Onagraceae)

The tiny white flowers of this plant are easily spotted in the gloom of its preferred habitat. The petals are deeply notched; the sepals and anthers are rosy-pink. Several flowers are arranged loosely along the leafless, upright stems, often above rows of drooping club-shaped, bristly fruits that attach themselves to clothing. The leaves are elliptical, with a barely toothed margin, and are noticeably veined.

OCCUPIES *dark and shaded corners of woodland, gardens, and pathways, under hedges or bushes.*

rosy-pink anthers

pink sepals

white flowers

leafless stem

elliptical leaf

PERENNIAL

PLANT HEIGHT *20–60cm.*
FLOWER SIZE *4–7mm wide.*
FLOWERING TIME *June–August.*
LEAVES *Opposite, elliptical.*
FRUIT *Semi-pendent achene with bristles.*
SIMILAR SPECIES *Upland Enchanter's Nightshade (C. x intermedia), which is almost identical but rarely sets fruit.*

Large-flowered Evening-primrose

OCCURS *on waste and disturbed ground, embankments, roadsides, rubbish tips, and sand dunes, on well-drained soil.*

Oenothera erythrosepala (Onagraceae)

As the name indicates, the flowers of the Evening-primrose open just before sunset. It takes just a few minutes for the sepals to curl back and the four pale primrose-yellow petals to unfurl, but by noon the next day, this begins to wilt. The plant produces flowers every day for several weeks.

lance-shaped leaf

sepals covered with red hair

crinkled leaf margin

very large yellow flowers

BIENNIAL

PLANT HEIGHT *80–150cm.*
FLOWER SIZE *5–8cm wide.*
FLOWERING TIME *June–September.*
LEAVES *Alternate, lance-shaped, with crinkled margins and a pale midrib.*
FRUIT *Four-valved capsule.*
SIMILAR SPECIES *Common Evening-primrose (O. biennis) has no red hair on sepals or stems.*

Rosebay Willowherb

Chamerion angustifolium (Onagraceae)

Spreading by means of underground rhizomes, this plant can form an extensive patch or colony, which may really be a single plant. Flowers are borne on tall, pyramidal spikes; each has four, rounded rose-pink petals and eight drooping stamens. The flowers at the tip may still be in tight bud when the lower ones have formed fruit. The narow, pointed leaves have finely toothed, often rather wrinkled margins.

THRIVES *in disturbed sites such as woodland clearings, river banks, and roadsides; also where the ground has been burned.*

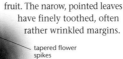

tapered flower spikes

rose-pink flowers

wavy leaf margin

pale midrib

8 stamens

rounded petals

PERENNIAL

PLANT HEIGHT *80–150cm.*
FLOWER SIZE *2–3cm wide.*
FLOWERING TIME *June–September.*
LEAVES *Alternate, lance-shaped.*
FRUIT *Slender, four-valved capsule, containing numerous fluffy seeds.*
SIMILAR SPECIES *Purple Loosestrife (p.109); Great Willowherb (right).*

Great Willowherb

Epilobium hirsutum (Onagraceae)

This tall, hairy plant forms large patches at the edges of wet areas. Born in racemes, the saucer-shaped flowers are deep pink with four-lobed creamy white stigmas. They give rise to long, downy fruit capsules that peel back to reveal many light, hairy seeds. The narrow leaves are stalkless or clasp the stem.

PROLIFERATES *in damp, open sites, such as river banks, reedbeds, lake margins, and marshes.*

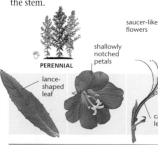

saucer-like flowers

shallowly notched petals

PERENNIAL

lance-shaped leaf

capsules split lengthwise

PLANT HEIGHT *1–1.8m.*
FLOWER SIZE *1.5–2.5cm wide.*
FLOWERING TIME *June–September.*
LEAVES *Mostly opposite, occasionally whorled, lance-shaped, coarsely toothed.*
FRUIT *Capsule with four segments.*
SIMILAR SPECIES *Rosebay Willowherb (left), which has flowers in distinct spikes.*

Broad-leaved Willowherb

Epilobium montanum (Onagraceae)

A slender plant of semi-shaded places, this willowherb usually just has a few pale pink flowers with four deeply notched petals arranged in a cross. Despite the plant's name, the oval leaves are not particularly wide, but are broader than those of similar species. The rounded, slender stems are reddish.

INHABITS *sheltered spots on woodland margins, along ditches, hedgerows, and old walls; also in gardens.*

oval leaves

few flowers in loose clusters

strongly veined leaf

toothed margin

4-lobed stigma

notched petals

PERENNIAL

PLANT HEIGHT *30–75cm.*
FLOWER SIZE *6–12mm wide.*
FLOWERING TIME *May–August.*
LEAVES *Opposite, oval, toothed, and veined.*
FRUIT *Long, slender capsule, with purplish tinge, producing fluffy seeds.*
SIMILAR SPECIES *American Willowherb (E. ciliatum), which has narrower leaves.*

Dogwood

Cornus sanguinea (Cornaceae)

OCCURS *in woodland margins, hedgerows, and scrub on limestone soil.*

Dogwood is easily recognized at any time of year, for the bare red shoots are very conspicuous, even in winter. The leaves have a distinctive wavy margin and deep-set veins. They turn a deep crimson in early autumn, before the leaves of other trees have begun to turn colour. The 4-petalled flowers are produced in an umbel-like, cream or greenish white cluster.

PERENNIAL

wavy edge to leaf

crimson leaf

black berries

rounded clusters of flowers

prominent leaf veins

PLANT HEIGHT *1–4m.*
FLOWER SIZE *8–10mm wide.*
FLOWERING TIME *June–July.*
LEAVES *Opposite, elliptical, green becoming gold then crimson, wavy edged, deep-veined.*
FRUIT *Rounded black berry, 5–8mm wide.*
SIMILAR SPECIES *C. sericea, which has brighter red twigs and white berries.*

Ivy

Hedera helix (Araliaceae)

CLIMBS *deciduous and coniferous trees, even in dense shade. Trails over walls, buildings, rocks, and hedgerows.*

An evergreen, woody climber, Ivy is a familiar sight in woodland. The leaves are a shiny deep green but it is only the young leaves that have the classic three- or five-lobed triangular shape. The mature leaves on the flowering stems are quite different, being oval, without lobes. The flowers, in yellow-green clusters, are some of the latest to bloom in the year, providing valuable nectar for bees.

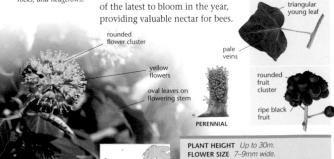

triangular young leaf

rounded flower cluster

pale veins

yellow flowers

oval leaves on flowering stem

rounded fruit cluster

ripe black fruit

PERENNIAL

PLANT HEIGHT *Up to 30m.*
FLOWER SIZE *7–9mm wide.*
FLOWERING TIME *September–November.*
LEAVES *Alternate; untoothed leaves.*
FRUIT *Green berries that turn brown, then black when ripe.*
SIMILAR SPECIES *Black Bryony (p.192) has longer twining stems and smaller flowers.*

Cow Parsley

Anthriscus sylvestris (Apiaceae)

One of the first members of the carrot family to bloom in spring, Cow Parsley is also one of the most familiar, often forming crowds of frothy white flowerheads along roadsides. The deeply divided leaves may appear during winter. They are slightly hairy, and each has a small sheath at the base of the leaf stalk. The ridged and hollow stems are unspotted.

GROWS *in masses along roadsides, woodland margins, and hedgerows, and in meadows and pastures. Prefers moist soil.*

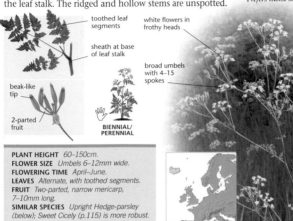

toothed leaf segments

sheath at base of leaf stalk

white flowers in frothy heads

broad umbels with 4–15 spokes

beak-like tip

2-parted fruit

BIENNIAL/PERENNIAL

PLANT HEIGHT *60–150cm.*
FLOWER SIZE *Umbels 6–12mm wide.*
FLOWERING TIME *April–June.*
LEAVES *Alternate, with toothed segments.*
FRUIT *Two-parted, narrow mericarp, 7–10mm long.*
SIMILAR SPECIES *Upright Hedge-parsley (below); Sweet Cicely (p.115) is more robust.*

Upright Hedge-parsley

Torilis japonica (Apiaceae)

This plant resembles a smaller version of Cow Parsley (above), but appears much later in the year. The umbels of tiny white, pink, or pale purplish flowers are relatively small and spaced out on widely branching slender stems, showing up clearly against the dark background of hedges. The leaves are like small, neat fern fronds.

FOUND *on the edges of hedgerows and grassy woodland, and on roadsides.*

small, neat umbels

fern-like leaves

slender, branched stems

coarsely toothed leaflets

flowers may be pink in bud

tiny flowers

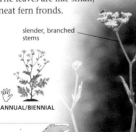

ANNUAL/BIENNIAL

PLANT HEIGHT *50–120cm.*
FLOWER SIZE *Umbels 3–4cm wide.*
FLOWERING TIME *July–September.*
LEAVES *Alternate and pinnately divided.*
FRUIT *Egg-shaped mericarp, 3–4mm long, and covered in tiny spines.*
SIMILAR SPECIES *Cow Parsley (above), Sweet Cicely (p.115).*

Fool's Parsley

Aethusa cynapium (Apiaceae)

The most distinguishing feature of this delicate plant is the long bracteoles that hang beneath the flowers; these form smaller umbels than in the similar Wild Carrot (below). The stems are ridged and leaves are finely divided. Fool's Parsley is poisonous so care should be taken if found growing near salad vegetables.

INHABITS *cultivated land at edges of crops, wasteland, gardens, and roadsides.*

ANNUAL

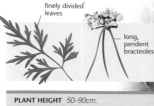

finely divided leaves

long, pendent bracteoles

flowers in umbels

PLANT HEIGHT *50–90cm.*
FLOWER SIZE *3–6cm wide.*
FLOWERING TIME *June–October.*
LEAVES *Alternate, finely divided.*
FRUIT *Egg-shaped, ridged mericarp, 3–4mm long, divided into two parts.*
SIMILAR SPECIES *Cow Parsley (p.113); Wild Carrot (below); Sweet Cicely (right).*

Wild Carrot

Daucus carota (Apiaceae)

This is one of the easiest members of the carrot family to identify. The umbels of flowers are domed and often pink at first and then flatten out, turning white. Very close examination often reveals a purple flower in the centre of the umbel. There is a spreading ruff of bracts beneath the umbel, which turns brown and contracts as the fruit develops.

PREFERS *grassy and waste places, roadsides, dry cliffs, and field margins. Prefers dry, open situations.*

BIENNIAL

outer florets larger than inner ones

long flower stems

finely divided leaves

dense fruit clusters

PLANT HEIGHT *30–100cm.*
FLOWER SIZE *Umbels 5–10cm wide.*
FLOWERING TIME *June–August.*
LEAVES *Alternate, finely divided.*
FRUIT *Two-parted mericarp, 2–4mm long, in a cluster that looks like a bird's nest.*
SIMILAR SPECIES *Fool's Parsley (above), which has smaller umbels and long bracteoles.*

Sweet Cicely

Myrrhis odorata (Apiaceae)

A member of the carrot family, Sweet Cicely is highly aromatic and has often been used for flavouring food. The hollow stems smell strongly of aniseed when crushed. The plant often grows tall and bushy, and has large, fern-like leaves and white flowers. The plant's most distinctive feature is its narrow, two-parted fruit.

GROWS *in semi-shade in damp meadows, woodland margins, pastures, and streamsides, and on roadsides, mainly in mountains.*

finely divided leaves

densely packed flower umbels

PERENNIAL

long, narrow fruit

ridged surface

PLANT HEIGHT *0.8–1.8m.*
FLOWER SIZE *Umbels 5cm wide.*
FLOWERING TIME *May–July.*
LEAVES *Alternate, finely pinnate and fern-like; pale green, occasionally with white spots.*
FRUIT *Elliptical mericarp, beaked at the tip.*
SIMILAR SPECIES *Cow Parsley (p.113), which is less robust and has small fruit.*

Pignut

Conopodium majus (Apiaceae)

A small, delicate plant of grassland and woods, Pignut has feathery leaves, the upper ones almost hair-like, the lowest leaves having withered by flowering time. It bears white flowers in loose umbels, each with spokes that have tiny bracts beneath. The plant has small, edible brown tubers with a pleasant nutty taste, which used to be gathered in quantity by children.

INHABITS *meadows, woodland edges and clearings, road verges, and hedgerows.*

white flowers in loose umbels

PERENNIAL

slender, erect stems

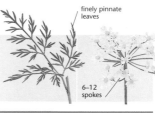

finely pinnate leaves

6–12 spokes

PLANT HEIGHT *20–50cm.*
FLOWER SIZE *Umbels 3–7cm wide.*
FLOWERING TIME *May–July.*
LEAVES *Alternate, finely divided and feathery; hair-like upper leaves.*
FRUIT *Ridged mericarp, 3–4mm long.*
SIMILAR SPECIES *Burnet-saxifrage (Pimpinella saxifraga), Sanicle (Sanicula europaea).*

Ground-elder

Aegopodium podagraria (Apiaceae)

FORMS *colonies on shaded wasteland and roadsides, in open woodland, and close to human habitation.*

An invasive plant that creeps to cover large areas by means of its underground stolons, Ground-elder may be a persistent weed in gardens. The soft leaves resemble those of the Elder tree (p.30). Introduced to Britain by the Romans, the leaves were cooked and eaten as spinach. The delicate white flowerheads show up well in shade.

small, delicate flowers

branched umbels

PERENNIAL

broad, toothed leaflets

flowers in umbels

PLANT HEIGHT *30–80cm.*
FLOWER SIZE *Flowerhead 4–7cm wide.*
FLOWERING TIME *May–July.*
LEAVES *Basal and alternate, divided into three broad, toothed leaflets.*
FRUIT *Mericarp, oval and finely ridged.*
SIMILAR SPECIES *Cow Parsley (p.113), which has more finely divided leaves.*

Hemlock Water-dropwort

Oenanthe crocata (Apiaceae)

FLOURISHES *in damp sites by fresh water, in ditches, and along rivers and streams.*

This robust member of the carrot family is one of the most poisonous plants in Europe, responsible for the deaths of many cattle. It has large white flowerheads and triangular leaves divided into leaflets of the same shape. Its damp habitat is a key to identification.

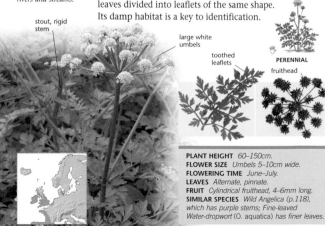

stout, rigid stem

large white umbels

toothed leaflets

PERENNIAL

fruithead

PLANT HEIGHT *60–150cm.*
FLOWER SIZE *Umbels 5–10cm wide.*
FLOWERING TIME *June–July.*
LEAVES *Alternate, pinnate.*
FRUIT *Cylindrical fruithead, 4–6mm long.*
SIMILAR SPECIES *Wild Angelica (p.118), which has purple stems; Fine-leaved Water-dropwort (O. aquatica) has finer leaves.*

Fool's-water-cress

Apium nodiflorum (Apiaceae)

This water-loving member of the carrot family is unusual in that its flowers arise midway along the stems, opposite leaf junctions, rather than at the end. There are 3–12 widely separated spokes to each umbel, the tiny flowers in small clusters. The leaves are divided into oval leaflets in a ladder-like fashion.

SPRAWLS *along ditches, slow streams, marshes, and lake and river margins. May clamber on long stems among other vegetation.*

alternate leaves

off-white flowers in rounded clusters

PERENNIAL

toothed leaflets

small umbels

PLANT HEIGHT *30–90cm.*
FLOWER SIZE *Umbels 3–6cm wide.*
FLOWERING TIME *June–August.*
LEAVES *Alternate, pinnately divided.*
FRUIT *Two-parted mericarp, 1–2mm long.*
SIMILAR SPECIES *Water-cress (p.66), which has different flowers; Lesser Water-parsnip (Berula erecta), which has terminal umbels.*

Hemlock

Conium maculatum (Apiaceae)

All parts of the Hemlock plant are poisonous, but the seeds contain the greatest amount of coniine, which is fatal. Hemlock is extremely tall and robust and one of the easiest of the carrot family to identify. The ridged, hollow stems are clearly blotched with purple. The lower leaves are large and triangular, while the upper ones are smaller.

FOUND *at the margins of damp places such as ditches, rivers, and streams; also grows on wasteland and roadsides.*

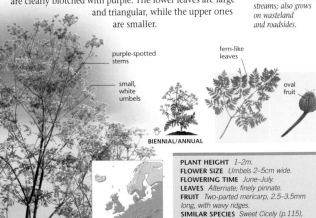

purple-spotted stems

small, white umbels

fern-like leaves

oval fruit

BIENNIAL/ANNUAL

PLANT HEIGHT *1–2m.*
FLOWER SIZE *Umbels 2–5cm wide.*
FLOWERING TIME *June–July.*
LEAVES *Alternate; finely pinnate.*
FRUIT *Two-parted mericarp, 2.5–3.5mm long, with wavy ridges.*
SIMILAR SPECIES *Sweet Cicely (p.115), which does not have red-spotted stems.*

Wild Angelica

Angelica sylvestris (Apiaceae)

The stout purplish stems and round, pink- to brown-tinged flowerheads make this tall member of the carrot family easy to identify. The neatly divided leaves are quite different from those of Hogweed (below) with which it may grow. Wild Angelica is often seen towering above other vegetation.

GROWS *among tall herb communities, in damp meadows and wet woodland; also along river banks.*

large, rounded flowerheads

purple stems

inflated sheath base of upper leaves

PERENNIAL

neat leaf segments

PLANT HEIGHT *1–2m.*
FLOWER SIZE *Umbels 8–20cm wide.*
FLOWERING TIME *July–September.*
LEAVES *Alternate, pinnately divided into neat, oval segments.*
FRUIT *Two-parted mericarp, 4–5mm long.*
SIMILAR SPECIES *Hogweed (below), Giant Hogweed (Heracleum mantegazzianum).*

Hogweed

Heracleum sphondylium (Apiaceae)

This familiar, coarse weed lacks the grace of its relatives in the carrot family. The unpleasant-smelling flowerheads are dirty white, broad, and flat-topped, the outer petals of each umbel having clearly larger petals. Each leaf has an inflated sheath where it joins the stem.

DOMINATES *rough areas such as hedgerows, roadsides, woodland margins, and embankments.*

grey-white flowers

large, flat umbels

coarsely divided leaves

BIENNIAL

flattened fruit

PLANT HEIGHT *0.6–2m.*
FLOWER SIZE *Umbels 10–20cm wide.*
FLOWERING TIME *June–September.*
LEAVES *Alternate, pinnately divided into big, toothed lobes with rough surface; dark green.*
FRUIT *Two-parted mericarp, 7–10mm long.*
SIMILAR SPECIES *Wild Angelica (above) has more finely divided leaves; Hemlock (p.117).*

Wild Parsnip

Pastinaca sativa (Apiaceae)

A member of the carrot family, Wild Parsnip is the parent of cultivated parsnip, but the sap from the leaves and stems can cause intense skin irritation, especially in sunlight. Its leaves

OCCURS *in grassland on roadsides, on scrub, wasteland, and embankments, on dry, chalky soil.*

flat leaflets

are divided into large leaflets, the lower ones long-stalked, the upper ones much smaller and almost stalkless. The yellow-ochre flowers are borne in flat-topped umbels.

coarsely toothed

yellow-ochre flowers

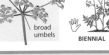
broad umbels

BIENNIAL

ridged stems

PLANT HEIGHT *60–100cm.*
FLOWER SIZE *Umbels 4–10cm wide.*
FLOWERING TIME *July–August.*
LEAVES *Alternate, pinnately divided.*
FRUIT *Two-parted mericarp, 6mm long, elliptical with ringed ridges.*
SIMILAR SPECIES *Alexanders (below); Fennel (Foeniculum vulgare) has hair-like leaves.*

Alexanders

Smyrnium olusatrum (Apiaceae)

One of the earliest members of the carrot family to flower, this is a robust, clump-forming, very leafy plant. The leaves are divided into three groups of three flat leaflets, the upper ones arranged oppositely on the stem and often yellowish in colour. The five-petalled yellow or greenish yellow flowers are borne in tight, domed umbels without bracts.

FORMS *clumps or patches by the sea, and along salted roads inland.*

rounded flower umbels

broad, flat leaflets

long leaf stalk

yellow flowers

BIENNIAL

PLANT HEIGHT *80–150cm.*
FLOWER SIZE *Umbels 4–8cm wide.*
FLOWERING TIME *April–June.*
LEAVES *Alternate at base, opposite at top, divided into three groups of three leaflets.*
FRUIT *Oval mericarp, black when ripe.*
SIMILAR SPECIES *Wild Parsnip (above), which is less leafy, with flat umbels.*

Sea Holly

Eryngium maritimum (Apiaceae)

GROWS *in small patches or extensive colonies along the coast, chiefly on sand dunes and sometimes on shingle.*

This member of the carrot family is unmistakable for many reasons. Most distinctive are its bluish or greenish grey leaves. They are stiff and waxy, undulating like dried leather, and are coarsely toothed, with each tooth ending in a sharp spine. The upper leaves are unstalked while the lower leaves are long-stalked. A tight ruff of bracts below blue-violet tint, reflecting the colour of the blue flowers. The final clue to identity is the habitat, for the plant is restricted to sandy coasts.

PERENNIAL

waxy, grey-green leaves

tiny blue flowers

spiny bracts below flowerhead

whitish leaf veins

rounded flowerhead

NOTE

The root of this plant was popular in the 17th century as a candied sweetmeat; the candied root was also used as an expectorant.

PLANT HEIGHT *30–60cm.*
FLOWER SIZE *Flowerhead 1.5–3cm wide.*
FLOWERING TIME *June–September.*
LEAVES *Basal and alternate, roughly rounded, lobed and toothed into spines; bluish or greenish grey.*
FRUIT *Mericarp with overlapping scales.*
SIMILAR SPECIES *Milk Thistle (Silybum marianum), which has green rosette leaves with white veins, but pink flowers.*

Common Wintergreen

Pyrola minor (Pyrolaceae)

The tiny flowers of this plant resemble those of Lily-of-the-Valley (p.189) but are arranged on all sides of the straight, upright stem. They have five, bell-like petals that are white or tinged with pink, and an enclosed, straight style which does not protrude. The leaves, from which wintergreen oil is extracted, are oval, rather leathery and mostly arranged in loose rosettes.

FOUND *in damp places, woodland, moors, marshes, and mountains.*

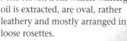

bell-like flowers

PERENNIAL

oval leaves

finely toothed margin

PLANT HEIGHT *10–25cm.*
FLOWER SIZE *6mm wide.*
FLOWERING TIME *June–August.*
LEAVES *Mostly basal in loose rosette.*
FRUIT *Round capsule, splitting into five segments.*
SIMILAR SPECIES *Lily-of-the-Valley (p.189), which has flowers only on one side.*

Cowberry

Vaccinium vitis-idaea (Ericaceae)

This small, neat shrubby plant is a member of the heather family. The five-petalled, bell-shaped flowers are in tight clusters. They are white with a pinkish tinge and the pointed tip of each petal is turned slightly outwards. The leathery leaves have downturned margins. The berries have a bitter taste.

GROWS *in coniferous woodland, moors, mountains, and heaths, on acid soil; forms colonies.*

oblong leaves

notched leaf tip

PERENNIAL

upturned petal tip

round red berries

PLANT HEIGHT *30–70cm.*
FLOWER SIZE *5–8mm wide.*
FLOWERING TIME *May–August.*
LEAVES *Alternate, oblong.*
FRUIT *Rounded red berry, 5–10mm wide.*
SIMILAR SPECIES *Bilberry (p.122), which has black berries; Bearberry (Arctostaphylos uva-ursi), which has darker pink flowers.*

Bilberry

Vaccinium myrtillus (Ericaceae)

This compact, deciduous shrub appears in clumps. The ridged, angled stems bear soft, oval leaves with short stalks. Tiny flowers, green or flushed with red, hang in loose clusters, going on to form small black berries covered in a whitish bloom. The berries are edible, but being sparsely distributed on the plant, take time to gather.

OCCURS on moors and heaths, in deciduous or coniferous woodland, on dry, acid soil.

PERENNIAL

pale green leaves

bell-shaped flowers

bluish black berry

PLANT HEIGHT 20–50cm.	
FLOWER SIZE 4–6mm wide.	
FLOWERING TIME April–June.	
LEAVES Alternate, oval, toothed.	
FRUIT Fleshy black berry, 5–8mm wide.	
SIMILAR SPECIES Cowberry (p.121), which has red berries; Bog Bilberry (V. uliginosum), which has blue-green leaves.	

Cranberry

Vaccinium oxycoccus (Ericaceae)

A straggling plant that can be easily missed, Cranberry has slender, creeping stems and small, oval leaves with whitish undersides. The curious shape of the pink flowers, with their recurved petals and columns of purple and yellow anthers, recall that of the unrelated Bittersweet (p.149). The large berries are orange-red with brown speckles.

CREEPS over sphagnum and other mosses in bogs, moors, heaths, and damp woodland.

wiry reddish stems

recurved petal

PERENNIAL

long-stalked, pink flowers

anthers in spike

orange-red berries

tiny leaves

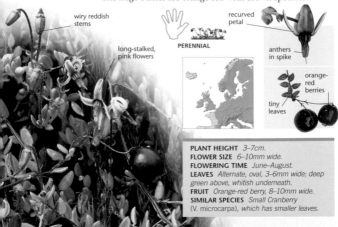

PLANT HEIGHT 3–7cm.	
FLOWER SIZE 6–10mm wide.	
FLOWERING TIME June–August.	
LEAVES Alternate, oval, 3–6mm wide; deep green above, whitish underneath.	
FRUIT Orange-red berry, 8–10mm wide.	
SIMILAR SPECIES Small Cranberry (V. microcarpa), which has smaller leaves.	

Heather

Calluna vulgaris (Ericaceae)

With its woody stems and scale-like leaves, Heather is well adapted to habitats with low-nutrient soil; it may grow slowly, but it lives for a long time. The tiny leaves, in pairs on small branches, overlap each other almost like the shoots on moss. They are somewhat leathery, becoming rough to the touch as they mature, but are surprisingly soft when young and provide an important food source for caterpillars and gamebirds such as grouse. For this reason, the plant is cut or burnt on grouse moors to stimulate further young growth. Each flower has prominent sepals and a protruding style, with eight hidden anthers.

FORMS *carpets on heaths, moors, bogs, acid soil, and dry, sandy banks, and in pine or birch woods.*

PERENNIAL

numerous flowers

very dense flowerheads

NOTE

Heather was an invaluable resource for peasant communities; the stiff, woody branches were used for thatching roofs, strengthening wattle-and-daub clay walls, and in household articles.

pale pink to purple flowers

leaves crowded on stem

PLANT HEIGHT *20–80cm.*
FLOWER SIZE *3–4mm long.*
FLOWERING TIME *July–September.*
LEAVES *Opposite, closely pressed on short branches, tiny and scale-like.*
FRUIT *Small, many-seeded capsule.*
SIMILAR SPECIES *Bell Heather (p.124), which has larger, darker flowers, and linear leaves in whorls.*

Bell Heather

Erica cinerea (Ericaceae)

This evergreen shrub often grows scattered among other plants in the same family, such as Heather (p.123), but also forms large expanses on its own. The flowers are slightly flared at the mouth and are borne in whorls or clusters on short stems. The tiny, leathery leaves are in whorls of three on very short stems, so they appear bunched together.

GROWS in small or extensive colonies on the dry, acid, sandy soil of heaths and moors, or in clearings in open pine woodland.

magenta-purple flowers

PERENNIAL

tiny, linear leaves

bell-shaped flowers

short leaf stems

woody stems

PLANT HEIGHT 20–60cm.
FLOWER SIZE 5–7mm long.
FLOWERING TIME July–September.
LEAVES Whorled, tough, needle-like, and hairless, on very short stems; green to bronze.
FRUIT Small, dry, hairless capsule.
SIMILAR SPECIES Heather (p.123), which has paler flowers and overlapping leaves on stems.

Scarlet Pimpernel

Anagallis arvensis (Primulaceae)

The brilliant red petals of this diminutive plant are easily spotted when the flowers open in bright sunshine. Occasionally, blue-flowered forms occur. The oval, shiny leaves have tiny black dots underneath, while the fruit is a tiny, rounded capsule that splits around the middle.

GROWS on wasteland, in fields and field margins, and coastland; on dry, well-drained soil.

yellow anthers

opposite, oval leaves

shiny leaves

ANNUAL

5-petalled flowers

toothed margin

PLANT HEIGHT 5–15cm.
FLOWER SIZE 4–7mm wide.
FLOWERING TIME May–September.
LEAVES Opposite, oval, and unstalked.
FRUIT Small, rounded capsule.
SIMILAR SPECIES Sea Milkwort (Glaux maritima) has short-stalked flowers; Pheasant's Eye (Adonis annua) has feathery leaves.

Cowslip

Primula veris (Primulaceae)

Entire meadows are often coloured in spring by the abundant yellow flowers of Cowslip. Borne in tight clusters on each stem, or scape, they are fragrant, with a long, yellow-green calyx and five petals that form a tube, opening slightly to reveal an orange mark on each petal. The leaves form a rosette close to the ground and in long grass or semi-shade, they may grow longer.

GROWS *in meadows and dry, grassy places; also on embankments, usually on chalky soil; prefers open situations.*

PERENNIAL

nodding flowers

oblong leaf

pale midrib

flower tube

neatly toothed edge

5 notched petals

PLANT HEIGHT *10–25cm.*
FLOWER SIZE *7–14mm wide.*
FLOWERING TIME *April–May.*
LEAVES *Basal rosette, oblong; with wrinkled surface; dark green.*
FRUIT *Many-seeded capsule.*
SIMILAR SPECIES *False Oxlip (P. veris x vulgaris), which has fewer one-sided umbels.*

Primrose

Primula vulgaris (Primulaceae)

The pale yellow flowers of Primrose signal the arrival of spring. Each flower is on a solitary stalk and has a long, tubular calyx and broad yellow petals, often with orange markings in the centre (although other colours occur in garden cultivars). As distinctive as the flowers, the oblong, toothed leaves are in basal rosettes.

PROLIFERATES *in deciduous woodland, along embankments, in meadows, and on grassy roadside verges.*

pale midrib

pale yellow flowers

bright green leaves

PERENNIAL

5 notched petals

PLANT HEIGHT *10–15cm.*
FLOWER SIZE *2–4cm wide.*
FLOWERING TIME *February–May, or earlier.*
LEAVES *Basal, oblong, with wrinkled surface and margin, pale midrib.*
FRUIT *Many-seeded capsule.*
SIMILAR SPECIES *Oxlip (P. elatior), which has one-sided clusters of flowers.*

Creeping-Jenny

Lysimachia nummularia (Primulaceae)

This creeping plant can be easily missed among taller vegetation. Once discovered, however, there is no mistaking its cup-shaped yellow flowers nestling along the twining stem. The leaves, arranged in opposite pairs like a ladder, are rounded to oval, decreasing in size along the stem. When produced, the fruit capsule is on a long stalk.

CREEPS *along in damp habitats, in woodland, pond and stream margins, and ditches.*

PERENNIAL

smaller leaves at top of stem

cup-shaped flowers

oval leaves

broad sepals

PLANT HEIGHT *3–6cm.*
FLOWER SIZE *1.2–1.8cm wide.*
FLOWERING TIME *May–July.*
LEAVES *Opposite, rounded to oval.*
FRUIT *Five-parted capsule, rarely produced.*
SIMILAR SPECIES *Yellow Pimpernel*
(L. nemorum), *which has less ladder-like leaves and narrow sepals.*

Yellow Loosestrife

Lysimachia vulgaris (Primulaceae)

This tall plant punctuates the landscape of marshes and fens with its golden yellow flowers and orange centres. The flowers are grouped in panicles produced from the upper leaf axils. The leaves are sometimes dotted with black or orange glands and have bluish green undersides. The fruit capsule often occurs in the same cluster as the buds or open flowers.

INHABITS *tall vegetation in moist habitats such as streamsides, fens, and wet meadows, on neutral or chalky soil.*

oval leaf

spherical fruit capsule

PERENNIAL

tightly clustered yellow flowers

5-petalled flower

whorl of 3–4 lower leaves

PLANT HEIGHT *60–150cm.*
FLOWER SIZE *1.5–2cm wide.*
FLOWERING TIME *July–August.*
LEAVES *Opposite on upper stem, whorls of 3–4 below, oval to lance-shaped.*
FRUIT *Spherical, five-parted capsule.*
SIMILAR SPECIES *Dotted Loosestrife (L. punctata), which has flowers in narrow spikes.*

Thrift

Armeria maritima (Plumbaginaceae)

This plant forms cushions of narrow grey-green leaves that persist throughout the year. In summer, it produces long-stalked, bright pink flowerheads, each with papery scales surrounding the base, transforming the coastal scenery with extensive patches of colour. The plant is variable in height, with taller forms on inland sites.

FORMS *mats on cliffs, coastal rocks, and salt marshes, and inland on sandy grassland.*

grass-like leaves

spherical flowerheads

sheath below flowerhead

pink flowers

PERENNIAL

PLANT HEIGHT *5–30cm.*
FLOWER SIZE *Flowerhead 1.5–3cm wide.*
FLOWERING TIME *April–August.*
LEAVES *Basal, linear.*
FRUIT *Small, one-seeded capsule, with a papery wall.*
SIMILAR SPECIES *Common Sea-lavender (below), which has oblong to elliptical leaves.*

Common Sea-lavender

Limonium vulgare (Plumbaginaceae)

The wiry stems of this plant branch at the top and bear tight heads of pink to lilac flowers, each flower surrounded by papery bracts. The cut flowers retain their colour well and are commonly used in dried flower arrangements. The narrow, basal leaves, each with a single prominent vein, taper to a stalk about half the length of the leaf blade.

FOUND *in extensive carpets on the mud of salt marshes, colouring large areas with its flowers.*

single-veined leaf

long leaf stalk

tight clusters of flowers

tough, leafless stems

5-petalled flowers

PERENNIAL

PLANT HEIGHT *20–40cm.*
FLOWER SIZE *6–8mm long.*
FLOWERING TIME *July–September.*
LEAVES *Basal, oblong to elliptical.*
FRUIT *Small capsule, surrounded by a persistent papery calyx.*
SIMILAR SPECIES *Thrift (above), which has unbranched stems.*

Yellow-wort

Blackstonia perfoliata (Gentianaceae)

This plant has a distinctive arrangement of leaves in that each pair is fused together around the stem – the upper pairs occurring where the stems branch. Unusually for a member of the gentian family, the flowers have up to eight starry petals, which open almost flat.

GROWS *on grassland and other rocky, open places on well-drained, dry chalky soil.*

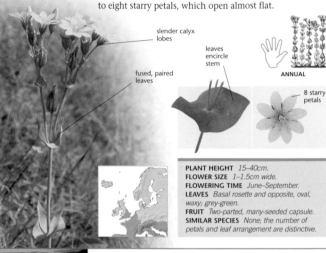

slender calyx lobes

fused, paired leaves

leaves encircle stem

ANNUAL

8 starry petals

PLANT HEIGHT *15–40cm.*
FLOWER SIZE *1–1.5cm wide.*
FLOWERING TIME *June–September.*
LEAVES *Basal rosette and opposite, oval, waxy; grey-green.*
FRUIT *Two-parted, many-seeded capsule.*
SIMILAR SPECIES *None; the number of petals and leaf arrangement are distinctive.*

Common Centaury

Centaurium erythraea (Gentianaceae)

The pink flowers of Common Centaury stand out among the grasses of the plant's natural habitat. They each have five elliptical petals, which are fused below into a tube about twice as long as the narrow sepals, and are borne in flat-topped clusters. The waxy, pale green leaves are arranged in a basal rosette, and in opposite pairs on the branching stems.

FLOURISHES *in grassy habitats on chalky or sandy soil, such as pastures, heaths, and among scrub.*

untoothed leaf margin

yellow-orange anthers

petals fused into long tube

BIENNIAL

flowers in clusters

PLANT HEIGHT *10–40cm.*
FLOWER SIZE *1–1.5cm wide.*
FLOWERING TIME *June–September.*
LEAVES *Basal rosette and opposite, elliptical, three-veined stem leaves.*
FRUIT *Two-parted capsule, with waxy seeds.*
SIMILAR SPECIES *Lesser Centaury (C. pulchellum), which has no basal rosette.*

Autumn Gentian

Gentianella amarella (Gentianaceae)

Flowers of this small gentian usually have five short petal lobes which form a long tube at the base, but occasionally there are only four. Usually bluish violet, they may also be dull purple or magenta. The calyx also has four or five lobes of equal width.

GROWS *in short turf in pastures and other dry, grassy areas, and on dunes; on chalky soil and slopes.*

clustered flowers

BIENNIAL

clearly veined leaves

5 petal lobes

PLANT HEIGHT *10–30cm.*
FLOWER SIZE *1.4–2cm long.*
FLOWERING TIME *June–October.*
LEAVES *Basal rosette and opposite, lance-shaped; deep grey-green.*
FRUIT *Capsule, splitting into two parts.*
SIMILAR SPECIES *Field Gentian (G. campestris), which has bluish lilac flowers.*

Privet

Ligustrum vulgare (Oleaceae)

Privet is a looser, more open-growing shrub than the familiar Garden Privet (*L. ovalifolium*). It is nevertheless densely branched, with smooth greyish bark, and freely forms small panicles of white flowers when growing in a sunny position, followed by small, mildly poisonous black berries. The leaves are usually evergreen, being dark, glossy, and clearly veined.

OCCURS *in woodland margins, hedgerows, and embankments.*

panicles of small white flowers

PERENNIAL

4-petalled flower

glossy leaves

shiny black berries

PLANT HEIGHT *1–3m.*
FLOWER SIZE *4–6mm wide.*
FLOWERING TIME *May–June.*
LEAVES *Evergreen, opposite, lance-shaped, with glossy surface.*
FRUIT *Shiny black berry, 6-8mm wide.*
SIMILAR SPECIES *Garden Privet (L. ovalifolium), which has broader leaves.*

Bogbean

Menyanthes trifoliata (Menyanthaceae)

RISES *up out of pools of water in bogs, fens, mountains, and lake margins; often forming large colonies.*

This plant is unmistakable when seen en masse, with its white blossoms dotted over the surface of acid bog pools. The flowers appear in a loose cluster on a single stem. Rosy-pink in bud, the fully open flowers are white, each petal with an extraordinary fringe of long white hair that give the flower a fluffy appearance. The rather fleshy, trifoliate leaves rise up out of the water.

pink buds

flowers in loose clusters

fleshy, elliptical leaflets

PERENNIAL

petals fringed

trifoliate leaves

PLANT HEIGHT *10–35cm.*
FLOWER SIZE *1.4–1.6cm wide.*
FLOWERING TIME *April–June.*
LEAVES *Basal, fleshy, and bean-like leaflets.*
FRUIT *Egg-shaped capsule that splits into two halves when ripe.*
SIMILAR SPECIES *Water Violet (Hottonia palustris), which has no aerial leaves.*

Fringed Water-lily

Nymphoides peltata (Menyanthaceae)

FORMS *large patches on the surface of slow-moving rivers and streams, ponds, lakes, and in ditches.*

Like its close relative, the Bogbean (above), this aquatic plant has petals with a delicately fringed margin of tiny hairs; they may also appear creased or slightly folded. The long-stemmed, bright yellow flowers are held just above the water surface. Rounded, dark green leaves, sometimes purple blotched, have a slit to the centre where the stalk joins the leaf. They are much smaller than those of other water-lilies.

PERENNIAL

bright yellow flower

long stem

creased petals

deep leaf cleft

5 petals

PLANT HEIGHT *Up to 10cm above water surface.*
FLOWER SIZE *3–4cm wide.*
FLOWERING TIME *June–September.*
LEAVES *Whorled, on long stems, rounded.*
FRUIT *Egg-shaped capsule.*
SIMILAR SPECIES *Yellow Water-lily (p.56), which has spherical flowers.*

Lesser Periwinkle

Vinca minor (Apocynaceae)

The shiny, deep green leaves and trailing stems of this plant may carpet large areas of woodland in spring – only a few flowers may occur in such shaded places. The flowers are violet-purple, occasionally white, with each petal twisted and blunt-ended, resembling a ship's propeller. The calyx at the base of the long petal tube has tiny, triangular teeth.

FORMS *extensive mats in woodland, coppices, hedgerows, banks, and rocky ground, often in deep shade.*

glossy, deep green leaves

violet-purple flower

PERENNIAL

blunt-edged petals

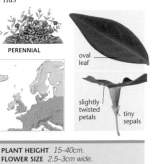

oval leaf

slightly twisted petals

tiny sepals

PLANT HEIGHT *15–40cm.*
FLOWER SIZE *2.5–3cm wide.*
FLOWERING TIME *March–May.*
LEAVES *Opposite, oval to elliptic, short-stalked.*
FRUIT *Forked capsule, 2.5cm wide, but rare.*
SIMILAR SPECIES *Greater Periwinkle (V. major) has larger flowers with long sepals.*

Squinancywort

Asperula cynanchica (Rubiaceae)

This small, ground-hugging plant forms masses of pink blooms. The tiny flowers, at the ends of slender, many-branched stems, are white or pink, with four petals fused at the base to form a tube. Like other members of the bedstraw family, the leaves are in whorls, but they are very small and narrow.

SEEN *as cushions of flowers on short, dry chalk grassland or sand dunes.*

pink or white flowers

branched flower stems

small linear leaves

four petals

PERENNIAL

PLANT HEIGHT *5–30cm.*
FLOWER SIZE *3mm wide.*
FLOWERING TIME *June–September.*
LEAVES *Whorled, linear or lance-shaped.*
FRUIT *Tiny, two-parted mericarp, finely warty.*
SIMILAR SPECIES *Field Madder (p.134) and other bedstraws, which generally have broader leaves.*

Sweet Woodruff

Galium odoratum (Rubiaceae)

This neat, attractive plant has whorls of 6–9 elliptical leaves up the stem, each with tiny prickles along the margin. The white flowers form small, branched clusters, set off by the leaf whorl beneath them. The leaves contain an aromatic substance called coumarin, which is used to flavour liqueurs.

GROWS *in the shade of deciduous woodland and hedgerows, sometimes forming extensive patches, usually on chalky soil.*

PERENNIAL

4-petalled flowers

6–9 elliptical leaves

small flower clusters

PLANT HEIGHT *10–30cm.*
FLOWER SIZE *4–7mm wide.*
FLOWERING TIME *May–June.*
LEAVES *Whorls, elliptical.*
FRUIT *Nutlet, 2–3mm wide, with bristles.*
SIMILAR SPECIES *Cleavers (below), which is a scrambling plant; Hedge Bedstraw (right) which has smaller leaves.*

Cleavers

Galium aparine (Rubiaceae)

A common hedgerow plant, Cleavers is especially well known to walkers and dog-owners because the entire plant is covered in hooked hair that help it to clamber wover other vegetation, but it may also stick (cleave) to clothing or fur. The paired, rounded fruit are also studded with hooked spines to facilitate their distribution. The tiny white flowers are borne in sparse clusters at the leaf-bases.

SCRAMBLES *over and through vegetation in scrub or on hedgerows, wasteland, and also cultivated sites.*

flowers in small clusters

hooked hair

4 petals

bristly, paired fruit

ANNUAL

whorls of narrow leaves

sharp-pointed leaves

PLANT HEIGHT *30–150cm.*
FLOWER SIZE *2mm wide.*
FLOWERING TIME *May–August.*
LEAVES *Whorls of 4–6, narrow and elliptical.*
FRUIT *Mericarps with hooked bristles.*
SIMILAR SPECIES *Hedge Bedstraw (right) and Sweet Woodruff (above); Heath Bedstraw (G. saxatile) and Marsh Bedstraw (G. palustre).*

Hedge Bedstraw

Galium mollugo (Rubiaceae)

Masses of creamy white flowers are produced by this scrambling plant along hedgerows and roadsides. Each tiny flower has four petals in the form of a cross, and is borne in loose, many-branched clusters. The leaves are small with rough prickly margins, and the stem is smooth and square. Hedge Bedstraw does not grow on acid soil, unlike the similar Heath Bedstraw.

CLAMBERS *over hedgerows, scrub, dry grassland, meadows, and along roadsides.*

many-branched flower clusters

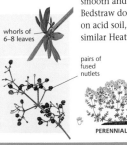

whorls of 6–8 leaves

pairs of fused nutlets

creamy white flowers

PERENNIAL

PLANT HEIGHT *40–150cm.*
FLOWER SIZE *2–3mm wide.*
FLOWERING TIME *June–September.*
LEAVES *Whorls, oblong.*
FRUIT *Fused nutlets, black when ripe.*
SIMILAR SPECIES *Sweet Woodruff (left); Lady's Bedstraw (below) has yellow flowers; Heath Bedstraw (G. saxatile) is shorter.*

Lady's Bedstraw

Galium verum (Rubiaceae)

The tiny flowers of Lady's Bedstraw seem, at a distance, like candyfloss. Each flower has four well-separated petals and is grouped into a branched, greenish yellow panicle, which is highly fragrant. The leaves are borne in whorls of 8–12 tiny, shiny dark green leaflets arranged around the thin, wiry stems. The tiny fruits turn black when ripe.

INHABITS *dry, open grassy places, banks, and roadsides; also sand dunes and other places near the sea.*

PERENNIAL

greenish yellow flowers

whorl of tiny leaves

dense, branched panicles of flowers

PLANT HEIGHT *20–80cm.*
FLOWER SIZE *2–3mm wide.*
FLOWERING TIME *June–September.*
LEAVES *Whorls of 8–12 small, linear leaves; dark green.*
FRUIT *Fused black nutlets.*
SIMILAR SPECIES *Hedge Bedstraw (above), which has creamy white flowers.*

Crosswort

Cruciata laevipes (Rubiaceae)

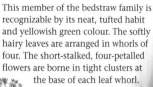

tiny, pale yellow flowers

This member of the bedstraw family is recognizable by its neat, tufted habit and yellowish green colour. The softly hairy leaves are arranged in whorls of four. The short-stalked, four-petalled flowers are borne in tight clusters at the base of each leaf whorl.

INHABITS *road verges, meadows, pastures, hedgerows, and scrub, often close to taller, sheltering vegetation.*

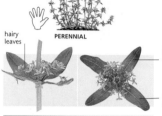

PERENNIAL

hairy leaves

flowers in clusters

3 main leaf whorls

erect stems

neat whorls of 4 leaves

PLANT HEIGHT 20–50cm.
FLOWER SIZE 2–3mm wide.
FLOWERING TIME April–June.
LEAVES Whorls of four, elliptical.
FRUIT Rounded, smooth nutlets, black when ripe.
SIMILAR SPECIES None; the whorls of four leaves are distinctive.

Field Madder

Sherardia arvensis (Rubiaceae)

This low, bristly plant often goes unnoticed among taller vegetation. The pointed, oval leaves have prickly margins, and, as in other bedstraws, are borne in distinct whorls around square stems. The stems have downward-pointing bristles, and the pink flowers are borne in small clusters at the tip, with a ruff of green bracts below each cluster.

SPRAWLS *close to the ground in grassy places and on bare ground, preferring chalky soil.*

whorl of 4–6 leaves

tiny, 4-petalled flowers

leaf-like bracts

ANNUAL

PLANT HEIGHT 5–30cm.
FLOWER SIZE 3mm wide.
FLOWERING TIME May–September.
LEAVES Whorled, oval to elliptical, with prickly margins.
FRUIT Bristly nutlets, in pairs.
SIMILAR SPECIES Squinancywort (p.131), which has narrow leaves.

Hedge Bindweed

Calystegia sepium (Convolvulaceae)

This familiar weed may completely cover hedges and fences with its white flowers in late summer, often becoming a serious garden pest. The tough, sinuous stems twist and wind themselves around other plant stems or any other object in their path, and produce heart-shaped leaves at intervals. The

CLIMBS *over hedges, other tall plants, scrub, woodland margins, fences, and poles. Prefers damp soil.*

bold white flower unfurls like an umbrella, and has two green sepals at the base.

heart-shaped leaf

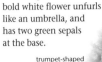
trumpet-shaped white flowers

bracts do not overlap

PERENNIAL

PLANT HEIGHT *1–3m.*
FLOWER SIZE *3–3.5cm wide.*
FLOWERING TIME *July–September.*
LEAVES *Alternate, arrow- or heart-shaped.*
FRUIT *Rounded green capsule.*
SIMILAR SPECIES *Black Bryony (p.192), which has smaller flowers; Field Bindweed (below), which usually has pink flowers.*

Field Bindweed

Convolvulus arvensis (Convolvulaceae)

A fast-growing plant, this bindweed twines itself around other plants in an anti-clockwise direction, or sprawls along the ground. The leaves are either arrow-shaped with sharp, backward-pointing lobes at the base, or oblong. The trumpet-shaped flowers are usually pink with white stripes, but may be pure white or dark pink.

TWINES *around stems of other plants, fences, and other objects, and along hedgerows; on waste or arable land.*

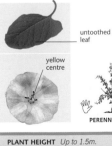
untoothed leaf
yellow centre

striped petals

rounded or arrow-shaped leaves

PERENNIAL

PLANT HEIGHT *Up to 1.5m.*
FLOWER SIZE *2–2.5cm wide.*
FLOWERING TIME *June–September.*
LEAVES *Alternate; arrow-shaped or oblong.*
FRUIT *Rounded, many-seeded capsule.*
SIMILAR SPECIES *Hedge Bindweed (above); Sea Bindweed (Calystegia soldanella), which has fleshy leaves.*

Common Comfrey

Symphytum officinale (Boraginaceae)

This robust and bushy, damp-loving plant has bristly, spear-shaped leaves. The leaf base continues down the stem to the next leaf joint, forming a pair of wings. The tubular flowers appear in a coiled spray like a scorpion's tail, opening in sequence, and are creamy white, pink, or violet. Common Comfrey was once grown in cottage gardens for its efficacy in healing wounds and mending broken bones.

FLOURISHES *in damp places such as river and stream margins, marshes, fens, wet woodland, and damp meadows.*

stalkless leaf

bell-shaped flowers

PERENNIAL

bushy habit

tubular flowers

spear-shaped leaves

PLANT HEIGHT *80–150cm.*
FLOWER SIZE *1.2–1.8cm long.*
FLOWERING TIME *May–July.*
LEAVES *Alternate and basal; stalkless, untoothed, and coarsely hairy.*
FRUIT *Four shiny nutlets.*
SIMILAR SPECIES *Russian Comfrey (S. x uplandicum), which has blue flowers.*

Viper's-bugloss

Echium vulgare (Boraginaceae)

The long, bristly stems of this plant arise from a rosette of leaves formed in the first year, and are clothed in masses of five-petalled, deep purple flowers. Each cluster or cyme of flowers unfurls along the stem like a scorpion's tail, the buds gradually changing from pink to violet as they mature. The leaves and bracts are rough and hairy.

FLOURISHES *in dry, open places, road verges, cliffs, shingle, sand dunes, heaths, and grassy banks, often on disturbed soil.*

coiled flower buds

scarlet protruding stamens

narrow, stalkless leaves

funnel-shaped flowers

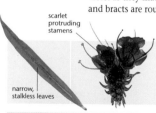

BIENNIAL

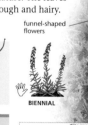

PLANT HEIGHT *50–100cm.*
FLOWER SIZE *1.5–2cm wide.*
FLOWERING TIME *June–September.*
LEAVES *Basal rosette and alternate, narrow-elliptical to lance-shaped, unstalked; bristly stem leaves.*
FRUIT *Four nutlets at base of persistent calyx.*
SIMILAR SPECIES *None.*

Bugloss

Anchusa arvensis (Boraginaceae)

This erect, extremely bristly plant has rough, alternate
leaves with undulating and slightly toothed margins. The
lower leaves are stalked, but the smaller upper leaves are
unstalked and clasp the stem with heart-shaped bases.
The tiny, five-petalled blue flowers are borne in clusters,
each with a white centre and a curved
tube at the base. A common plant in
farmland, it may grow hidden
among rows of cereal crops.

GROWS *on arable
fields, field margins,
waste and bare land,
and sandy heaths,
especially near the sea.*

fine bristles

5-petalled
blue flower

unstalked
upper leaf

white centre

ANNUAL

PLANT HEIGHT *15–60cm.*
FLOWER SIZE *4–6mm wide.*
FLOWERING TIME *May–September.*
LEAVES *Alternate, rough and bristly.*
FRUIT *Four nutlets at the base of the calyx.*
SIMILAR SPECIES *Green Alkanet (below),
which has larger flowers; Forget-me-nots
(p.138), which have untoothed leaves.*

Green Alkanet

Pentaglottis sempervirens (Boraginaceae)

The large, slightly bristly, basal leaves of Green Alkanet are
formed early in the year. Covered with fine hair, they are
somewhat wrinkled, and paler beneath. The flowering
shoots are distinctive, bearing coiled clusters of blue
flowers, darker than those of the
related forget-me-nots (p.138), each
with a pure white throat and
spreading, rounded petals.

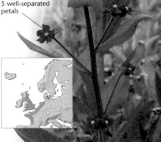

PROLIFERATES *in damp,
semi-shaded sites
along woodland
margins, hedgebanks,
and roadsides, often
close to habitation.*

oval
basal
leaf

long stalk of
basal leaf

untoothed
leaves

flowers
in small
clusters

white
centre

5 well-separated
petals

PERENNIAL

PLANT HEIGHT *40–80cm.*
FLOWER SIZE *8–10mm wide.*
FLOWERING TIME *April–July.*
LEAVES *Basal leaves, oval, long-stalked and
hairy; alternate stem leaves, unstalked.*
FRUIT *Four nutlets, rough, netted on surface.*
SIMILAR SPECIES *Bugloss (above), Borage
(Borago officinalis), which has black stamens.*

Wood Forget-me-not

Myosotis sylvatica (Boraginaceae)

GROWS *in semi-shaded situations in woodland rides and clearings, road verges, and damp meadows.*

There are several species of forget-me-nots in Europe, all of which have the same basic flower structure of sky-blue petals with a yellow centre, as well as hairy leaves (the name Myosotis means "mouse's ear"). The chief differences between them are the size of the flowers and the preferred habitat. The Wood Forget-me-not has the largest flowers and is found in woodland.

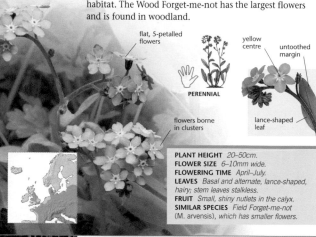

flat, 5-petalled flowers

yellow centre

untoothed margin

PERENNIAL

flowers borne in clusters

lance-shaped leaf

PLANT HEIGHT *20–50cm.*
FLOWER SIZE *6–10mm wide.*
FLOWERING TIME *April–July.*
LEAVES *Basal and alternate, lance-shaped, hairy; stem leaves stalkless.*
FRUIT *Small, shiny nutlets in the calyx.*
SIMILAR SPECIES *Field Forget-me-not (M. arvensis), which has smaller flowers.*

Water Forget-me-not

Myosotis scorpioides (Boraginaceae)

FORMS *colonies in wet places along rivers and streams, in marshes, ditches, and meadows, on neutral soil.*

This species appears less hairy than most forget-me-nots, as the hairs lie very flat on the stems and leaves. The stems look fleshy, befitting its moist habitat. The flower cluster, a cyme, is coiled in bud and resembles a scorpion's tail when it uncoils. Pink in bud, the flowers open sky-blue.

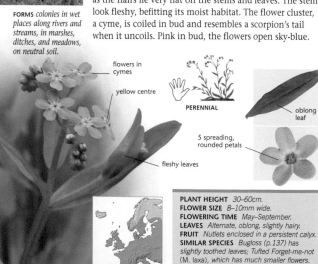

flowers in cymes

yellow centre

PERENNIAL

oblong leaf

5 spreading, rounded petals

fleshy leaves

PLANT HEIGHT *30–60cm.*
FLOWER SIZE *8–10mm wide.*
FLOWERING TIME *May–September.*
LEAVES *Alternate, oblong, slightly hairy.*
FRUIT *Nutlets enclosed in a persistent calyx.*
SIMILAR SPECIES *Bugloss (p.137) has slightly toothed leaves; Tufted Forget-me-not (M. laxa), which has much smaller flowers.*

Hound's-tongue

Cynoglossum officinale (Boraginaceae)

This is a roughly hairy plant, with soft, hairy, greyish green leaves with a coarse texture. It forms a distinct tuft, sending up long branching cymes that uncoil to reveal a row of five-petalled, very dark crimson or dull purplish flowers, which have a characteristic smell of mice. Four large, bristly nutlets are squeezed tightly into the outspread calyx.

OCCURS *among scrub, in rough grassland, or alongside hedgerows, on chalky soil.*

funnel-shaped flowers

BIENNIAL

untoothed leaves

4 nutlets | hooked bristles | 5 petals | dark centre

PLANT HEIGHT *40–70cm.*
FLOWER SIZE *6–10mm wide.*
FLOWERING TIME *May–August.*
LEAVES *Alternate, lance-shaped.*
FRUIT *Four nutlets, with hooked bristles.*
SIMILAR SPECIES *Green Hound's-tongue (C. germanicum), which has hair only on the undersides of its leaves.*

Vervain

Verbena officinalis (Verbenaceae)

A wiry, hairy, and rather rough plant, Vervain has long, square, branching stems bearing tall spikes of surprisingly small flowers. These are pink with white centres, and each have five asymmetric lobes, appearing almost two-lipped. The opposite leaves are strongly pinnately lobed, and coarsely toothed. Vervain, once used as a charm against snake bites, has a long history of medicinal and sacred uses.

GROWS *in bare, rocky places, on wasteland and roadsides, avoiding acid soil.*

deeply lobed leaf

narrow flower spikes

pink flowers

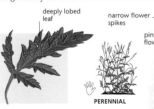

PERENNIAL

tough, wiry stems

PLANT HEIGHT *50–75cm*
FLOWER SIZE *4–5mm wide.*
FLOWERING TIME *June–September.*
LEAVES *Opposite; pinnately lobed and coarsely toothed, the lower leaves more strongly lobed than the upper.*
FRUIT *Four ribbed nutlets.*
SIMILAR SPECIES *None.*

Bugle

Ajuga reptans (Lamiaceae)

FOUND *in mats in damp areas of woodland rides and shady grassland, or along hedgerows.*

oval leaf

prominent flower lobes

Bugle only produces fertile seed in small quantities, and spreads chiefly by long runners, which form roots and new shoots at intervals. These runners die off in winter, but the following spring, the dormant, newly-rooted plants produce densely-flowered spikes. The blue flowers each have a reduced upper lip. The stems are hairy on two opposite sides only, with a dark purple line on the corners.

PERENNIAL

violet-flushed leaves

flowers in whorls

square stem

PLANT HEIGHT *10–25cm.*
FLOWER SIZE *1.4–1.7cm long.*
FLOWERING TIME *April–June.*
LEAVES *Opposite, oval.*
FRUIT *Four small nutlets.*
SIMILAR SPECIES *Self-heal (p.145) has tightly clustered 2-lipped flowers; Ground Ivy (p.145) has toothed leaves and 2-lipped flowers.*

Wood Sage

Teucrium scorodonia (Lamiaceae)

FORMS *tufts in dry and often sandy, open woods, grassland and hedgerows, and on heaths and dunes.*

One-sided spikes of yellow-green flowers and wrinkled leaves, similar in appearance to the leaves of the culinary sage, make this plant distinctive. Close examination of the flowers shows that they have only one lip, which is slightly lobed, so that the brown stamens are exposed. The leaves are in opposite pairs and the stems are square, as in other members of the mint family.

flowers in leafless spikes

square stems

PERENNIAL

wrinkled, toothed leaf

maroon anthers

one-lipped flower

PLANT HEIGHT *30–50cm.*
FLOWER SIZE *8–9mm long.*
FLOWERING TIME *July–September.*
LEAVES *Opposite pairs, oval, toothed, with heart-shaped bases.*
FRUIT *Four nutlets within the calyx.*
SIMILAR SPECIES *None; the leafless flower spikes are distinctive within the mint family.*

Skullcap

Scutellaria galericulata (Lamiaceae)

Not easy to spot among the taller vegetation of its marshland habitat, this member of the mint family produces just a few flowers, always in pairs, often quite low down on the square stem, at the base of the leaves. The bright violet-blue flowers have a distinctive shape, especially in bud, when they look like a pair of tiny, downy boxing gloves. The bluntly toothed leaves are oval to lance-shaped.

OCCURS *in damp places, wet meadows, marshes, margins of rivers, streams, and ditches, often among taller vegetation.*

violet-blue flowers

leafy stems

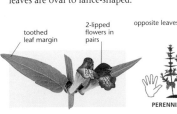

toothed leaf margin

2-lipped flowers in pairs

opposite leaves

PERENNIAL

PLANT HEIGHT *30–50cm.*	
FLOWER SIZE *1–1.8cm long.*	
FLOWERING TIME *June–September.*	
LEAVES *Opposite, oval to lance-shaped, with blunt teeth.*	
FRUIT *Four nutlets at base of calyx.*	
SIMILAR SPECIES *Lesser Skullcap (S. minor), which has smaller, pink flowers.*	

Red Dead-nettle

Lamium purpureum (Lamiaceae)

One of the earliest plants to flower in the year, this plant is a member of the mint family. It does not sting as it is not related to common nettles. The smaller, upper leaves, bunched together at the top of the plant, are flushed with purple, while the two-lipped flowers are pink to red.

INVADES *cultivated, disturbed, and waste ground, roadsides, and gardens; also alongside walls.*

coarsely toothed leaves

ANNUAL

upper lip

straight tube

purple-flushed upper leaves

flowers in whorls

PLANT HEIGHT *8–25cm.*	
FLOWER SIZE *1–1.8cm long.*	
FLOWERING TIME *March–December.*	
LEAVES *Opposite, oval, and toothed.*	
FRUIT *Four tiny nutlets at the base of calyx.*	
SIMILAR SPECIES *Black Horehound (p.143); Wild Basil (p.146); Hedge Woundwort (p.144), which has heart-shaped leaves.*	

White Dead-nettle

Lamium album (Lamiaceae)

The leaves of this plant resemble those of common nettles, but do not have stinging hairs. Like other members of the mint family, this plant has a square stem and leaves on opposite sides. Two-lipped white flowers emerge in tight whorls, and bloom for many months.

INHABITS *grassy roadsides, wasteland, and hedgerows; on rich soil, particularly where disturbed.*

coarsely toothed leaf margin

large, pure white flowers

hairy upper lip

black anthers

alternate leaves

PERENNIAL

PLANT HEIGHT *20–50cm.*
FLOWER SIZE *1.8–2.5cm long.*
FLOWERING TIME *April–November.*
LEAVES *Opposite; oval to heart-shaped, stalked, with toothed margins.*
FRUIT *Four small nutlets.*
SIMILAR SPECIES *None with such large white flowers.*

Yellow Archangel

Lamiastrum galeobdolon (Lamiaceae)

A plant that brightens the landscape with its striking colour in spring, Yellow Archangel has unusually large flowers for a member of the mint family. Each two-lipped flower is bright butter-yellow, with red markings on the lower lip. The paired leaves are almost triangular in outline, with coarse teeth.

GROWS *in shady woodland, hedgerows, and coppices, on heavy clay or chalky soil.*

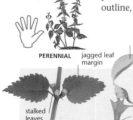

PERENNIAL

jagged leaf margin

2-lipped flower

flowers in tight whorls

large, pointed leaves

red streaks on lower lip

stalked leaves

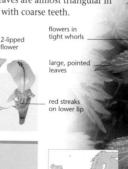

PLANT HEIGHT *20–50cm.*
FLOWER SIZE *1.7–2.1cm wide.*
FLOWERING TIME *April–June.*
LEAVES *Opposite, almost triangular.*
FRUIT *Four nutlets at base of calyx.*
SIMILAR SPECIES *Yellow Rattle (p.157); Large-flowered Hemp-nettle (Galeopsis speciosa) has flowers with a violet blotch.*

Black Horehound

Ballota nigra (Lamiaceae)

This hairy, scruffy-looking plant has an unpleasant smell when the leaves are crushed. It has two-lipped, reddish mauve flowers, in compact whorls along the upper stem, with distinctive, sharply pointed calyces; these turn brown or black, giving the plant a dirty appearance.

FOUND *in hedgerows and woodland edges; on rich, neutral or chalky soil.*

toothed leaves

whorls of flowers

erect stems

PERENNIAL

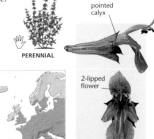

pointed calyx

2-lipped flower

PLANT HEIGHT *50–100cm.*
FLOWER SIZE *1.2–1.5cm long.*
FLOWERING TIME *June–September.*
LEAVES *Opposite, narrow and toothed.*
FRUIT *Four nutlets at the base of the calyx.*
SIMILAR SPECIES *Red Dead-nettle (p.141); Hedge Woundwort (p.144); Common Hemp-nettle (Galeopsis tetrahit).*

Betony

Stachys officinalis (Lamiaceae)

The bright magenta flowerheads of Betony, with leaf-like bracts drooping below them, are hard to miss among the grasses with which it grows. The plant has a neater appearance than many of its relatives in the mint family, with square stems bearing 2–4 pairs of narrowly oval, deep green leaves, with rounded teeth. Betony was used medicinally for centuries and as a protective charm by the Anglo-Saxons.

GROWS *in dry, grassy places, in heaths, woodland, and hedgerows.*

rounded teeth

2-lipped flower

tapered flower spike

whorls of magenta flowers

PERENNIAL

PLANT HEIGHT *20–75cm.*
FLOWER SIZE *1.2–1.8cm long.*
FLOWERING TIME *June–October.*
LEAVES *Opposite, narrowly oval, toothed.*
FRUIT *Four small nutlets within the calyx.*
SIMILAR SPECIES *Wild Basil (p.146); Hedge Woundwort (p.144); Common Hemp-nettle (Galeopsis tetrahit).*

Hedge Woundwort

Stachys sylvatica (Lamiaceae)

The dark claret or dull purple flowers of Hedge Woundwort do not seem bright enough to attract insects in their shady woodland habitat, but they do have some white markings that guide bees and flies to the throat of the flower to help pollination. The leaves give off a strong, foetid smell that may also entice insects. They are distinctly heart-shaped, with a wrinkled surface and toothed margin. The square stems have crimson ridges on the corners and are clothed in glandular hair.

FOUND *in woodland margins, cultivated or wasteland, and along hedgerows and footpaths, in semi-shaded situations.*

NOTE

The Hedge Woundwort and other Stachys species have a long medicinal history. They have been used since the time of the ancient Greeks in poultices for wounds and to help staunch bleeding.

flowers in whorled spike

dull purple petals

calyx with equal teeth

square stems

PERENNIAL

toothed margin

heart-shaped base

pale markings on lower lip

2-lipped flower

PLANT HEIGHT *60–100cm.*
FLOWER SIZE *1.3–1.8cm long.*
FLOWERING TIME *June–September.*
LEAVES *Opposite, heart-shaped, with toothed margins; short-stalked upper leaves, long-stalked lower leaves.*
FRUIT *Four nutlets at the base of the calyx.*
SIMILAR SPECIES *Black Horehound (p.143); Betony (p.143); Marsh Woundwort (S. palustris), which has pink flowers and grows in marshes.*

Ground Ivy

Glechoma hederacea (Lamiaceae)

Although this plant may flower throughout summer, it is in early spring that extensive mats bloom with bluish mauve, sometimes pink, two-lipped flowers that have pink spots on the lower lip. In summer, Ground Ivy spreads by sending long, leafy runners over the ground, much like Ivy (p.112).

GROWS *in mats on bare ground, field margins, woodland rides and clearings, and along hedgerows; prefers damp places.*

PERENNIAL

red-tinged upper leaves

long leaf stalk

large, blunt teeth

flowers in whorls

2-lipped flower

PLANT HEIGHT *10–25cm.*
FLOWER SIZE *1.5–2.2cm long.*
FLOWERING TIME *March–September.*
LEAVES *Opposite, kidney-shaped or rounded, long-stalked, coarsely toothed.*
FRUIT *Four nutlets in persistent calyx.*
SIMILAR SPECIES *Bugle (p.140), which has untoothed leaves and one-lipped flowers.*

Self-heal

Prunella vulgaris (Lamiaceae)

This plant forms distinctive oblong flowerheads, tightly packed with often purplish calyces. A pair of sharp bracts and rounded, dark-margined leaves below each flower, make the whole flowerhead look like a fir-cone. The flowers, each with a long, hooded upper lip, are usually deep blue, but colonies of pure pink flowers are often seen.

FORMS *patches in grassy places, lawns wasteland, and woodland clearings, or among scrub.*

finely pointed teeth on calyx

PERENNIAL

dark bracts below each flower

dark lines on square stems

oval leaf

hooded upper lip

PLANT HEIGHT *15–30cm.*
FLOWER SIZE *1.3–1.5cm long.*
FLOWERING TIME *June–November.*
LEAVES *Opposite, oval to lance-shaped, very slightly toothed.*
FRUIT *Four nutlets at base of calyx.*
SIMILAR SPECIES *Bugle (p.140), which has one-lipped flowers in leafy spikes.*

Wild Basil

Clinopodium vulgare (Lamiaceae)

GROWS *in dry, grassy places along woodland margins, hedgerows, and on embankments; prefers chalky soil.*

Although Wild Basil is not the culinary herb, it is faintly aromatic, with a scent similar to thyme. A rather weak and straggly plant, it has dense whorls of deep pink flowers clustered around the upper leaf bases. The lower sepals of the calyx are slightly longer and more slender than the upper ones. The hairy leaves are oval and gently toothed.

flowers in dense whorls

oval leaves

bluntly toothed margin

2-lipped flower

PERENNIAL

spiky calyx

PLANT HEIGHT *40–75cm.*
FLOWER SIZE *1.2–2cm long.*
FLOWERING TIME *July–September.*
LEAVES *Opposite, toothed, and hairy.*
FRUIT *Four nutlets at the base of calyx.*
SIMILAR SPECIES *Red Dead-nettle (p.141), which has purple-flushed leaves; Betony (p.143) has darker leaves with larger teeth.*

Gipsywort

Lycopus europaeus (Lamiaceae)

THRIVES *in wet areas such as pond margins, boggy woodland, and edges of reedbeds, often growing among taller vegetation.*

Instantly recognizable in its habitat, this plant has very distinctive leaves. They are oval to elliptical, with large, jagged, forward-pointing teeth, and are arranged in opposite pairs at well-spaced intervals along the stem. The whorls of tiny white flowers, patterned with minute purple dots, are clustered very tightly on the stem, and each has a rather spiny calyx of sepals.

evenly spaced leaves

jagged teeth

tiny dots on petals

tight whorl of flowers

PERENNIAL

spiny calyx

PLANT HEIGHT *30–80cm.*
FLOWER SIZE *3–4mm long.*
FLOWERING TIME *July–September.*
LEAVES *Opposite, oval to elliptical.*
FRUIT *Four nutlets.*
SIMILAR SPECIES *Corn Mint (Mentha arvensis), which has pinker flowers, more rounded leaves, and a sickly smell.*

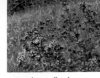

Wild Marjoram

Origanum vulgare (Lamiaceae)

Commonly cultivated as the herb oregano, this bushy plant often grows in large colonies, filling the air with its strong scent. The oval leaves are short-stalked, and are covered with tiny glands. Flowers, with protruding stamens, are borne in dense clusters on the much-branched stems. The two-lipped, pink petals are surrounded by prominent crimson sepals and bracts.

FOUND *in woodland, rough grassland, and scrub; along roadsides and hedgerows; prefers chalky soil.*

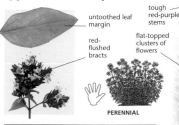

untoothed leaf margin

tough red-purple stems

red-flushed bracts

flat-topped clusters of flowers

PERENNIAL

PLANT HEIGHT	*30–50cm.*
FLOWER SIZE	*4–7mm long.*
FLOWERING TIME	*July–September.*
LEAVES	*Opposite, untoothed, strongly aromatic; bright green.*
FRUIT	*Four nutlets within the calyx.*
SIMILAR SPECIES	*Wild Thyme (below) is smaller and has a distinctly different scent.*

Wild Thyme

Thymus polytrichus (Lamiaceae)

The scent of thyme is released when the leaves of this plant are crushed, although it is not the species grown for culinary use. The slender, hairy, square stems bear tiny leaves, and dense clusters of pink flowers with red sepals at their tips. In the Brecklands of Norfolk, this species is replaced by *T. serpyllum*, which is almost identical but with rounded stems.

FORMS *creeping mats, often in the short, grazed turf of chalk grassland; also heaths, banks, and dunes.*

pink flowers in dense heads

PERENNIAL

oval leaf

2-lipped flower

red sepals

PLANT HEIGHT	*4–10cm.*
FLOWER SIZE	*5–6mm long.*
FLOWERING TIME	*May–September.*
LEAVES	*Opposite, oval, up to 8mm long.*
FRUIT	*Four nutlets in the persistent calyx.*
SIMILAR SPECIES	*Wild Marjoram (above); Large Thyme (T. pulegioides), which has hairs only on the angles of the square stems.*

Water Mint

Mentha aquatica (Lamiaceae)

FLOURISHES *at the edges of ponds and lakes, often in water, or in the damp parts of freshwater marshes.*

The strong, sickly sweet scent of this plant is noticeable even without bruising the leaves. Its large flowerheads are bunched on top of one another, the flowers having two-lipped lilac-pink petals and crimson sepals, the prominent, protruding stamens giving them a fluffy appearance. The leaves are oval and toothed, the lower ones short-stalked, and often tinged with red.

fluffy flowerhead

red-tinged leaf

toothed leaf margin

long stamens

2-lipped flower

PERENNIAL

PLANT HEIGHT 4–8m.
FLOWER SIZE 4–6mm long.
FLOWERING TIME July–September.
LEAVES Opposite, oval, coarsely toothed.
FRUIT Four nutlets at the base of the calyx.
SIMILAR SPECIES Corn Mint (M. arvensis), which has stems ending in leaves, not flowers; hybrids also occur frequently.

Deadly Nightshade

Atropa belladonna (Solanaceae)

INHABITS *semi-shaded places in old quarries, ruins, and woodland, usually among scrubby vegetation.*

A medium-sized, shrub-like plant, Deadly Nightshade looks innocuous, but is highly poisonous. Shiny black and slightly flattened, the berries are said to taste sweet, but are fatally poisonous. They can be identified by the persistent, five-sepalled calyx at the base of the fruit. The leaves are oval and pointed. Each flower is solitary in the upper leaf base.

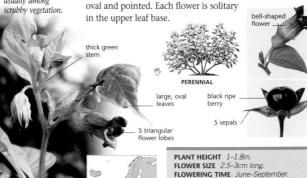

thick green stem

bell-shaped flower

large, oval leaves

black ripe berry

5 sepals

PERENNIAL

5 triangular flower lobes

PLANT HEIGHT 1–1.8m.
FLOWER SIZE 2.5–3cm long.
FLOWERING TIME June–September.
LEAVES Alternate, oval, pointed and untoothed, on short stalks.
FRUIT Black berry, 1.5–2cm wide, with persistent five-sepalled calyx, highly poisonous.
SIMILAR SPECIES None.

Black Nightshade

Solanum nigrum (Solanaceae)

This common bushy weed has flowers similar to those of the potato plant, with which it often grows. Each consists of a yellow cone of anthers surrounded by five white petals. These later form clusters of poisonous, round berries, which ripen from green to black. The stems are blackish, and the variable leaves are slightly toothed or lobed.

pointed, oval leaves

PREFERS *wasteland, bare soil, and rich cultivated ground, often with crops.*

starry, white and yellow flowers

reflexed petals

shiny fruit

short anthers

ANNUAL

PLANT HEIGHT *10–50cm.*
FLOWER SIZE *1–1.4cm wide.*
FLOWERING TIME *July–October.*
LEAVES *Alternate, oval to broadly triangular.*
FRUIT *Clusters of round berries, ripening from green to black.*
SIMILAR SPECIES *Bittersweet (below); Green Nightshade (S. physalifolium) has green stems.*

Bittersweet

Solanum dulcamara (Solanaceae)

The flowers of this poisonous woody climber are instantly recognizable as they are similar to those of the related tomato and potato. The five slender petals surround cone-shaped bright yellow anthers. These form clusters of green fruit that later ripen to orange and finally to red, persisting long after the leaves have withered. The leaves have deeply cut lobes.

CLAMBERS *over hedges and other vegetation in scrub, marsh, and fens; also sprawls over shingle beaches.*

cone of yellow stamens

large terminal lobe

PERENNIAL

swept-back purple petals

egg-shaped berries

PLANT HEIGHT *1–2.5m (20cm on shingle).*
FLOWER SIZE *1–1.5cm wide.*
FLOWERING TIME *May–September.*
LEAVES *Alternate, arrow-shaped, untoothed, 3–5 lobes, short stalks.*
FRUIT *Red, egg-shaped berry.*
SIMILAR SPECIES *Potato (S. tuberosum), which grows as a short bushy plant.*

Great Mullein

Verbascum thapsus (Scrophulariaceae)

Usually much taller than Dark Mullein (right), this plant has characteristic dense spires of bright yellow flowers. The first flowers to open are at the base of the spike, but as this elongates and branches, flowers open at intervals along it. Each flower has five spreading, rounded lobes, and stamens that have white filaments. The leaves of this plant are soft, thick, and felty. Grey-green in colour, they are covered with fine, branched hairs, and are easily identifiable in the plant's first year, when this biennial does not flower.

FOUND on wasteland and banks, rough, dry grassland, along roadsides, and in stony places; often on disturbed soil.

tall spires of yellow flowers

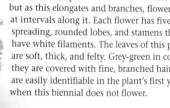

NOTE

The tiny hairs, which give the leaves of this plant a velvety look, ignite easily and were once used to make lamp wicks.

BIENNIAL

grey-green leaf

untoothed margin

rounded flower lobes

PLANT HEIGHT 0.5–2m.
FLOWER SIZE 1.2–3.5cm wide.
FLOWERING TIME June–August.
LEAVES Alternate, densely packed together, oblong to elliptical, thick and velvety.
FRUIT Small, many-seeded capsule.
SIMILAR SPECIES Dark Mullein (right); White Mullein (V. lychnitis) has white flowers; Hoary Mullein (V. pulverulentum) has very woolly leaves.

Dark Mullein

Verbascum nigrum (Scrophulariaceae)

The upright yellow flower spikes of this robust plant make it easy to spot. Each flower has prominent purple hairs on the stamens, which contrast with the five yellow petals. Unlike Great Mullein (left), which has soft, velvety leaves, it has glossy, dark green leaves that are paler beneath, with gently toothed margins. The basal leaves are in tufts.

OCCURS *on roadsides, embankments, dry grassland, and along hedgerows, often in semi-shade.*

tall, narrow flower spike

oval petals

purple stamens

PERENNIAL

oblong leaf

PLANT HEIGHT *50–100cm.*
FLOWER SIZE *1.8–2.5cm wide.*
FLOWERING TIME *June–September.*
LEAVES *Alternate, oblong, long-stalked.*
FRUIT *Small, many-seeded capsule.*
SIMILAR SPECIES *Agrimony (p.81), which has lobed leaves; Great Mullein (left), which is larger, with velvety leaves and white stamens.*

Common Toadflax

Linaria vulgaris (Scrophulariaceae)

The tufted spikes of Common Toadflax flower late into the autumn. Each lemon-yellow flower is composed of two closed lips, the lower with two orange bosses (palette), and a slender, tapering spur which hangs downward. Only large bees are able to push the lips apart to reach the nectar. The narrow leaves grow spirally up the stem.

GROWS *in clumps on roadsides, meadows, embankments, field margins, and other open, grassy places.*

2-lipped flower

orange boss

PERENNIAL

alternate leaves

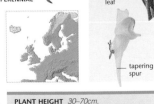

linear leaf

tapering spur

PLANT HEIGHT *30–70cm.*
FLOWER SIZE *2–3.5cm long.*
FLOWERING TIME *July–October.*
LEAVES *Alternate, linear, untoothed.*
FRUIT *Large, oval capsule, split near apex.*
SIMILAR SPECIES *Garden snapdragons (Antirrhinums), which sometimes become naturalized, and occur in a range of colours.*

Purple Toadflax

Linaria purpurea (Scrophulariaceae)

A robust plant originating from southern Italy, Purple Toadflax is becoming increasingly naturalized in wasteland close to human habitation. The long, slender, almost wiry spikes are composed of whorls of two-lipped, purple flowers, each with a slender spur at the back, reminiscent of a snapdragon. The grey-green leaves are linear, whorled at the bottom, but alternate at the top.

SEEN *on cultivated and waste ground, on or along old walls and pavements, close to human habitation.*

slender flower spikes

PERENNIAL

deep purple flowers

dark-veined flower

linear leaf

slender spur

PLANT HEIGHT *60–100cm.*
FLOWER SIZE *0.9–1.5cm long.*
FLOWERING TIME *June–August.*
LEAVES *Whorls at bottom, alternate higher up, linear.*
FRUIT *Small, rounded capsule.*
SIMILAR SPECIES *Pale Toadflax (L. repens), which has pale lilac flowers with darker veins.*

Ivy-leaved Toadflax

Cymbalaria muralis (Scrophulariaceae)

Originally from southern Europe, this plant is now found further afield. The long, trailing stems are reddish, with fleshy, lobed leaves similar in shape to those of Ivy (p.112). The long-stemmed flowers have two lilac or violet lips, with two central yellow patches and a short spur.

LIVES *in nooks and crannies, old walls, pavements, and rocky places, in shaded areas.*

5–9 broad lobes

PERENNIAL

slender reddish stems

yellow patch

lilac or violet petals

short spur

PLANT HEIGHT *10–25cm.*
FLOWER SIZE *9–15mm long.*
FLOWERING TIME *May–September.*
LEAVES *Alternate, palmately lobed, fleshy.*
FRUIT *Small capsule, opens by irregular slits.*
SIMILAR SPECIES *Ivy (p.112), which has similar leaves; Round-leaved Fluellen (Kickxia spuria), which has oval leaves.*

Ground Ivy

Glechoma hederacea (Lamiaceae)

Although this plant may flower throughout summer, it is in early spring that extensive mats bloom with bluish mauve, sometimes pink, two-lipped flowers that have pink spots on the lower lip. In summer, Ground Ivy spreads by sending long, leafy runners over the ground, much like Ivy (p.112).

GROWS *in mats on bare ground, field margins, woodland rides and clearings, and along hedgerows; prefers damp places.*

long leaf stalk

large, blunt teeth

PERENNIAL

flowers in whorls

red-tinged upper leaves

2-lipped flower

PLANT HEIGHT *10–25cm.*
FLOWER SIZE *1.5–2.2cm long.*
FLOWERING TIME *March–September.*
LEAVES *Opposite, kidney-shaped or rounded, long-stalked, coarsely toothed.*
FRUIT *Four nutlets in persistent calyx.*
SIMILAR SPECIES *Bugle (p.140), which has untoothed leaves and one-lipped flowers.*

Self-heal

Prunella vulgaris (Lamiaceae)

This plant forms distinctive oblong flowerheads, tightly packed with often purplish calyces. A pair of sharp bracts and rounded, dark-margined leaves below each flower, make the whole flowerhead look like a fir-cone. The flowers, each with a long, hooded upper lip, are usually deep blue, but colonies of pure pink flowers are often seen.

FORMS *patches in grassy places, lawns wasteland, and woodland clearings, or among scrub.*

finely pointed teeth on calyx

PERENNIAL

dark bracts below each flower

dark lines on square stems

oval leaf

hooded upper lip

PLANT HEIGHT *15–30cm.*
FLOWER SIZE *1.3–1.5cm long.*
FLOWERING TIME *June–November.*
LEAVES *Opposite, oval to lance-shaped, very slightly toothed.*
FRUIT *Four nutlets at base of calyx.*
SIMILAR SPECIES *Bugle (p.140), which has one-lipped flowers in leafy spikes.*

Wild Basil

Clinopodium vulgare (Lamiaceae)

GROWS *in dry, grassy places along woodland margins, hedgerows, and on embankments; prefers chalky soil.*

Although Wild Basil is not the culinary herb, it is faintly aromatic, with a scent similar to thyme. A rather weak and straggly plant, it has dense whorls of deep pink flowers clustered around the upper leaf bases. The lower sepals of the calyx are slightly longer and more slender than the upper ones. The hairy leaves are oval and gently toothed.

flowers in dense whorls

oval leaves

bluntly toothed margin

2-lipped flower

PERENNIAL

spiky calyx

PLANT HEIGHT *40–75cm.*
FLOWER SIZE *1.2–2cm long.*
FLOWERING TIME *July–September.*
LEAVES *Opposite, toothed, and hairy.*
FRUIT *Four nutlets at the base of calyx.*
SIMILAR SPECIES *Red Dead-nettle (p.141), which has purple-flushed leaves; Betony (p.143) has darker leaves with larger teeth.*

Gipsywort

Lycopus europaeus (Lamiaceae)

THRIVES *in wet areas such as pond margins, boggy woodland, and edges of reedbeds, often growing among taller vegetation.*

Instantly recognizable in its habitat, this plant has very distinctive leaves. They are oval to elliptical, with large, jagged, forward-pointing teeth, and are arranged in opposite pairs at well-spaced intervals along the stem. The whorls of tiny white flowers, patterned with minute purple dots, are clustered very tightly on the stem, and each has a rather spiny calyx of sepals.

evenly spaced leaves

jagged teeth

tiny dots on petals

tight whorl of flowers

PERENNIAL

spiny calyx

PLANT HEIGHT *30–80cm.*
FLOWER SIZE *3–4mm long.*
FLOWERING TIME *July–September.*
LEAVES *Opposite, oval to elliptical.*
FRUIT *Four nutlets.*
SIMILAR SPECIES *Corn Mint (Mentha arvensis), which has pinker flowers, more rounded leaves, and a sickly smell.*

Wild Marjoram

Origanum vulgare (Lamiaceae)

Commonly cultivated as the herb oregano, this bushy plant often grows in large colonies, filling the air with its strong scent. The oval leaves are short-stalked, and are covered with tiny glands. Flowers, with protruding stamens, are borne in dense clusters on the much-branched stems. The two-lipped, pink petals are surrounded by prominent crimson sepals and bracts.

FOUND *in woodland, rough grassland, and scrub; along roadsides and hedgerows; prefers chalky soil.*

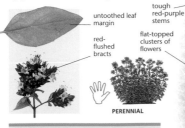

untoothed leaf margin

tough red-purple stems

red-flushed bracts

flat-topped clusters of flowers

PERENNIAL

PLANT HEIGHT *30–50cm.*
FLOWER SIZE *4–7mm long.*
FLOWERING TIME *July–September.*
LEAVES *Opposite, untoothed, strongly aromatic; bright green.*
FRUIT *Four nutlets within the calyx.*
SIMILAR SPECIES *Wild Thyme (below) is smaller and has a distinctly different scent.*

Wild Thyme

Thymus polytrichus (Lamiaceae)

The scent of thyme is released when the leaves of this plant are crushed, although it is not the species grown for culinary use. The slender, hairy, square stems bear tiny leaves, and dense clusters of pink flowers with red sepals at their tips. In the Brecklands of Norfolk, this species is replaced by *T. serpyllum*, which is almost identical but with rounded stems.

FORMS *creeping mats, often in the short, grazed turf of chalk grassland; also heaths, banks, and dunes.*

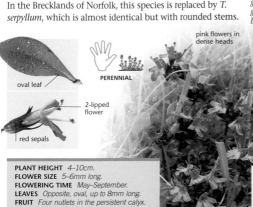

pink flowers in dense heads

oval leaf

PERENNIAL

2-lipped flower

red sepals

PLANT HEIGHT *4–10cm.*
FLOWER SIZE *5–6mm long.*
FLOWERING TIME *May–September.*
LEAVES *Opposite, oval, up to 8mm long.*
FRUIT *Four nutlets in the persistent calyx.*
SIMILAR SPECIES *Wild Marjoram (above); Large Thyme (T. pulegioides), which has hairs only on the angles of the square stems.*

Water Mint

Mentha aquatica (Lamiaceae)

The strong, sickly sweet scent of this plant is noticeable even without bruising the leaves. Its large flowerheads are bunched on top of one another, the flowers having two-lipped lilac-pink petals and crimson sepals, the prominent, protruding stamens giving them a fluffy appearance. The leaves are oval and toothed, the lower ones short-stalked, and often tinged with red.

FLOURISHES *at the edges of ponds and lakes, often in water, or in the damp parts of freshwater marshes.*

fluffy flowerhead

red-tinged leaf

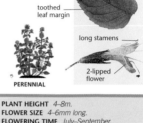

toothed leaf margin

long stamens

2-lipped flower

PERENNIAL

PLANT HEIGHT *4–8m.*
FLOWER SIZE *4–6mm long.*
FLOWERING TIME *July–September.*
LEAVES *Opposite, oval, coarsely toothed.*
FRUIT *Four nutlets at the base of the calyx.*
SIMILAR SPECIES *Corn Mint* (M. arvensis), *which has stems ending in leaves, not flowers; hybrids also occur frequently.*

Deadly Nightshade

Atropa belladonna (Solanaceae)

A medium-sized, shrub-like plant, Deadly Nightshade looks innocuous, but is highly poisonous. Shiny black and slightly flattened, the berries are said to taste sweet, but are fatally poisonous. They can be identified by the persistent, five-sepalled calyx at the base of the fruit. The leaves are oval and pointed. Each flower is solitary in the upper leaf base.

INHABITS *semi-shaded places in old quarries, ruins, and woodland, usually among scrubby vegetation.*

thick green stem

large, oval leaves

5 triangular flower lobes

PERENNIAL

bell-shaped flower

black ripe berry

5 sepals

PLANT HEIGHT *1–1.8m.*
FLOWER SIZE *2.5–3cm long.*
FLOWERING TIME *June–September.*
LEAVES *Alternate, oval, pointed and untoothed, on short stalks.*
FRUIT *Black berry, 1.5–2cm wide, with persistent five-sepalled calyx, highly poisonous.*
SIMILAR SPECIES *None.*

Black Nightshade

Solanum nigrum (Solanaceae)

This common bushy weed has flowers similar to those of the potato plant, with which it often grows. Each consists of a yellow cone of anthers surrounded by five white petals. These later form clusters of poisonous, round berries, which ripen from green to black. The stems are blackish, and the variable leaves are slightly toothed or lobed.

pointed, oval leaves

PREFERS *wasteland, bare soil, and rich cultivated ground, often with crops.*

starry, white and yellow flowers

reflexed petals

shiny fruit

short anthers

ANNUAL

PLANT HEIGHT *10–50cm.*
FLOWER SIZE *1–1.4cm wide.*
FLOWERING TIME *July–October.*
LEAVES *Alternate, oval to broadly triangular.*
FRUIT *Clusters of round berries, ripening from green to black.*
SIMILAR SPECIES *Bittersweet (below); Green Nightshade (S. physalifolium) has green stems.*

Bittersweet

Solanum dulcamara (Solanaceae)

The flowers of this poisonous woody climber are instantly recognizable as they are similar to those of the related tomato and potato. The five slender petals surround cone-shaped bright yellow anthers. These form clusters of green fruit that later ripen to orange and finally to red, persisting long after the leaves have withered. The leaves have deeply cut lobes.

CLAMBERS *over hedges and other vegetation in scrub, marsh, and fens; also sprawls over shingle beaches.*

cone of yellow stamens

large terminal lobe

PERENNIAL

egg-shaped berries

swept-back purple petals

PLANT HEIGHT *1–2.5m (20cm on shingle).*
FLOWER SIZE *1–1.5cm wide.*
FLOWERING TIME *May–September.*
LEAVES *Alternate, arrow-shaped, untoothed, 3–5 lobes, short stalks.*
FRUIT *Red, egg-shaped berry.*
SIMILAR SPECIES *Potato (S. tuberosum), which grows as a short bushy plant.*

Great Mullein

Verbascum thapsus (Scrophulariaceae)

FOUND *on wasteland and banks, rough, dry grassland, along roadsides, and in stony places; often on disturbed soil.*

Usually much taller than Dark Mullein (right), this plant has characteristic dense spires of bright yellow flowers. The first flowers to open are at the base of the spike, but as this elongates and branches, flowers open at intervals along it. Each flower has five spreading, rounded lobes, and stamens that have white filaments. The leaves of this plant are soft, thick, and felty. Grey-green in colour, they are covered with fine, branched hairs, and are easily identifiable in the plant's first year, when this biennial does not flower.

tall spires of yellow flowers

NOTE

The tiny hairs, which give the leaves of this plant a velvety look, ignite easily and were once used to make lamp wicks.

BIENNIAL

grey-green leaf

untoothed margin

rounded flower lobes

PLANT HEIGHT *0.5–2m.*
FLOWER SIZE *1.2–3.5cm wide.*
FLOWERING TIME *June–August.*
LEAVES *Alternate, densely packed together, oblong to elliptical, thick and velvety.*
FRUIT *Small, many-seeded capsule.*
SIMILAR SPECIES *Dark Mullein (right); White Mullein (V. lychnitis) has white flowers; Hoary Mullein (V. pulverulentum) has very woolly leaves.*

Dark Mullein

Verbascum nigrum (Scrophulariaceae)

The upright yellow flower spikes of this robust plant make it easy to spot. Each flower has prominent purple hairs on the stamens, which contrast with the five yellow petals. Unlike Great Mullein (left), which has soft, velvety leaves, it has glossy, dark green leaves that are paler beneath, with gently toothed margins. The basal leaves are in tufts.

OCCURS *on roadsides, embankments, dry grassland, and along hedgerows, often in semi-shade.*

tall, narrow flower spike

PERENNIAL

oblong leaf

oval petals

purple stamens

PLANT HEIGHT *50–100cm.*
FLOWER SIZE *1.8–2.5cm wide.*
FLOWERING TIME *June–September.*
LEAVES *Alternate, oblong, long-stalked.*
FRUIT *Small, many-seeded capsule.*
SIMILAR SPECIES *Agrimony (p.81), which has lobed leaves; Great Mullein (left), which is larger, with velvety leaves and white stamens.*

Common Toadflax

Linaria vulgaris (Scrophulariaceae)

The tufted spikes of Common Toadflax flower late into the autumn. Each lemon-yellow flower is composed of two closed lips, the lower with two orange bosses (palette), and a slender, tapering spur which hangs downward. Only large bees are able to push the lips apart to reach the nectar. The narrow leaves grow spirally up the stem.

GROWS *in clumps on roadsides, meadows, embankments, field margins, and other open, grassy places.*

2-lipped flower

orange boss

PERENNIAL

linear leaf

alternate leaves

tapering spur

PLANT HEIGHT *30–70cm.*
FLOWER SIZE *2–3.5cm long.*
FLOWERING TIME *July–October.*
LEAVES *Alternate, linear, untoothed.*
FRUIT *Large, oval capsule, split near apex.*
SIMILAR SPECIES *Garden snapdragons (Antirrhinums), which sometimes become naturalized, and occur in a range of colours.*

Purple Toadflax

Linaria purpurea (Scrophulariaceae)

A robust plant originating from southern Italy, Purple Toadflax is becoming increasingly naturalized in wasteland close to human habitation. The long, slender, almost wiry spikes are composed of whorls of two-lipped, purple flowers, each with a slender spur at the back, reminiscent of a snapdragon. The grey-green leaves are linear, whorled at the bottom, but alternate at the top.

SEEN *on cultivated and waste ground, on or along old walls and pavements, close to human habitation.*

slender flower spikes

PERENNIAL

deep purple flowers

dark-veined flower

linear leaf

slender spur

PLANT HEIGHT 60–100cm.	
FLOWER SIZE 0.9–1.5cm long.	
FLOWERING TIME June–August.	
LEAVES Whorls at bottom, alternate higher up, linear.	
FRUIT Small, rounded capsule.	
SIMILAR SPECIES Pale Toadflax (L. repens), which has pale lilac flowers with darker veins.	

Ivy-leaved Toadflax

Cymbalaria muralis (Scrophulariaceae)

Originally from southern Europe, this plant is now found further afield. The long, trailing stems are reddish, with fleshy, lobed leaves similar in shape to those of Ivy (p.112). The long-stemmed flowers have two lilac or violet lips, with two central yellow patches and a short spur.

LIVES *in nooks and crannies, old walls, pavements, and rocky places, in shaded areas.*

5–9 broad lobes

PERENNIAL

slender reddish stems

yellow patch

lilac or violet petals

short spur

PLANT HEIGHT 10–25cm.	
FLOWER SIZE 9–15mm long.	
FLOWERING TIME May–September.	
LEAVES Alternate, palmately lobed, fleshy.	
FRUIT Small capsule, opens by irregular slits.	
SIMILAR SPECIES Ivy (p.112), which has similar leaves; Round-leaved Fluellen (Kickxia spuria), which has oval leaves.	

Common Figwort

Scrophularia nodosa (Scrophulariaceae)

A tall, robust plant, Common Figwort has surprisingly small flowers, which in bud look like beads on stalks. They are borne on square stems, usually opening one at a time within a cluster. Each flower has a notched, purplish brown upper lip, which forms a little hood over the pouched lower lip, with two of the four stamens protruding.

GROWS *in damp places, along stream and river banks, in meadows and open woodland.*

oval leaf

PERENNIAL

bead-like flower buds

yellow stamens

hooded upper lip

branching stems

PLANT HEIGHT *60–100cm.*
FLOWER SIZE *7–9mm long.*
FLOWERING TIME *June–September.*
LEAVES *Opposite, oval, with finely toothed margins and wrinkled surface.*
FRUIT *Two-parted, rounded capsule.*
SIMILAR SPECIES *Water Figwort (S. auriculata), which has winged stems.*

Brooklime

Veronica beccabunga (Scrophulariaceae)

Brooklime is a distinctive plant, with its fat, succulent stems flushed red around the leaf-joints. The flowers form loose clusters on long stalks that arise from the leaf bases. Each flower is a rich blue, with a small white "eye" ringed with scarlet. The hairless leaves are also a little succulent and have a wavy margin.

wavy-edged leaf

PERENNIAL

INHABITS *margins of ponds, ditches, rivers, and permanently damp parts of marshes and wet meadows.*

deep blue flowers

red ring around white centre

red-tinged succulent stems

PLANT HEIGHT *20–60cm.*
FLOWER SIZE *5–8mm wide.*
FLOWERING TIME *May–September.*
LEAVES *Opposite, oval to elliptical, slightly fleshy, toothed; deep green.*
FRUIT *Small, round capsule.*
SIMILAR SPECIES *Blue Water-speedwell (V. anagallis-aquatica) has longer leaves.*

Germander Speedwell

Veronica chamaedrys (Scrophulariaceae)

The flowers of this plant are an exceptionally deep and vivid blue, with a contrasting white "eye" in the centre and two divergent protruding stamens. The flower stalks are produced from the base of hairy, stalkless leaves. Close examination of the hairy stems reveals that the hairs are in two neat, opposite rows.

PROLIFERATES *in shady grassy areas, alongside woodland, hedgerows, among scrub, and on embankments.*

4 petals of unequal size

PERENNIAL

white centre

coarsely toothed leaves

PLANT HEIGHT *20–40cm.*
FLOWER SIZE *9–12mm wide.*
FLOWERING TIME *March–July.*
LEAVES *Opposite, oval, coarsely toothed, and unstalked.*
FRUIT *Small heart-shaped capsules.*
SIMILAR SPECIES *Common Field Speedwell (below), which has flowers with a white petal.*

Common Field Speedwell

Veronica persica (Scrophulariaceae)

Introduced into Europe in the early 19th century, this species has become a common sight on farmland in many places. The lowest of the four petals is smaller than the others and is usually white, the others being violet with dark radiating veins. The oval, hairy leaves are very short-stalked, with just a few coarse teeth.

FLOURISHES *on disturbed soil such as wasteland, and among farmland crops.*

ANNUAL

dark-veined flower

lower petal usually white

oval leaf

coarsely toothed leaves

PLANT HEIGHT *5–20cm.*
FLOWER SIZE *8–12mm wide.*
FLOWERING TIME *Year round.*
LEAVES *Mostly alternate, lower ones opposite.*
FRUIT *Heart-shaped capsule.*
SIMILAR SPECIES *Germander Speedwell (above); Green Field Speedwell (V. agrestis) has white flowers with a blue upper petal.*

Foxglove

Digitalis purpurea (Scrophulariaceae)

Recognizable even in its first year, by the rosettes of large, wrinkled, hairy leaves, Foxglove is unmistakable in the following year when the tall flower stems are formed. As many as 60 or more pink to purple flowers droop in one-sided spikes. The whole plant is poisonous.

PROLIFERATES *on heaths, in woodland clearings and margins, and along road verges, hedgerows, and banks; mostly on acid soil.*

tapered flower spikes

tubular flowers

BIENNIAL/ PERENNIAL

wrinkled leaf surface

blunt, hairy leaf

many-seeded fruit capsule

PLANT HEIGHT *1–2m.*
FLOWER SIZE *4–5.5cm long.*
FLOWERING TIME *June–September.*
LEAVES *Basal rosette at first, followed by alternate stem leaves; oval, densely hairy.*
FRUIT *Capsule expelling numerous seeds through three slits at the tip.*
SIMILAR SPECIES *Great Mullein (p.150).*

Common Cow-wheat

Melampyrum pratense (Scrophulariaceae)

The yellow flowers of this plant brighten shaded woodland in late summer. The two-lipped flowers are arranged in neat pairs, each one often tipped red or becoming wholly red with age. The leaves and flower bracts are in pairs and swept back away from the flowers so that they look like ranks of wings along the slender stems.

FOUND *in shady corners and along paths in deciduous and coniferous woodland; prefers acid soil.*

long, narrow leaf

ANNUAL

tubular flower

toothed bracts

leaves swept back at angles

paired flowers

PLANT HEIGHT *15–30cm.*
FLOWER SIZE *1–1.8cm long.*
FLOWERING TIME *June–August.*
LEAVES *Opposite, narrowly lance-shaped, bracts with long teeth at base.*
FRUIT *Small capsule splitting along one side.*
SIMILAR SPECIES *Yellow Rattle (p.157), which has inflated sepals and toothed leaves.*

Red Bartsia

Odontites verna (Scrophulariaceae)

This wiry, hairy plant with arching stems, is often flushed red. Each one-sided flower spike has a three-lobed lower lip and a hooded upper lip from which the stamens protrude. Long, leaf-like bracts spread below each flower. The paired leaves have long veins.

THRIVES *in fields, meadows, pastures, wasteland, and trampled ground; also along footpaths.*

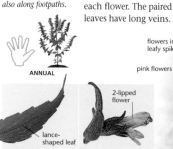

ANNUAL

flowers in leafy spikes

pink flowers

lance-shaped leaf

2-lipped flower

PLANT HEIGHT *15–40cm.*
FLOWER SIZE *8–10mm long.*
FLOWERING TIME *June–September.*
LEAVES *Opposite, spear-shaped, few teeth.*
FRUIT *Hairy capsule, with ridged, oval seeds.*
SIMILAR SPECIES *Common Lousewort (right) has pinnate leaves; Subsp. serotina of S. Britain has shorter bracts.*

Eyebright

Euphrasia species (Scrophulariaceae)

There are about 20 *Euphrasia* species in Britain, but they are extremely difficult to tell apart. All have the same basic structure of small, two-lipped flowers, the lower lip being three-lobed. The flowers are usually white or lilac with a yellow blotch and purple streaks. The leaves, sometimes purple-flushed, are small and stalkless, with jagged teeth. The plant is semi-parasitic on the grasses with which it grows.

INHABITS *grassy sites, heaths, sand dunes, and on woodland edges, usually in small patches.*

flowers in short spikes

ANNUAL

2-lipped white flowers

branched stem

toothed leaf margin

3-lobed lower lip

purple veins

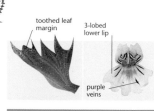

PLANT HEIGHT *5–25cm.*
FLOWER SIZE *5–7mm long.*
FLOWERING TIME *June–September.*
LEAVES *Opposite, with jagged toothed margins, stalkless.*
FRUIT *Capsule, splitting lengthwise.*
SIMILAR SPECIES *Field Pansy (p.105), which has oblong, shallowly toothed leaves.*

Common Lousewort

Pedicularis sylvatica (Scrophulariaceae)

This tufted, compact plant has densely crowded leaves and flowers. The flowers are pale pink, each with a three-lobed lower lip and a hooded upper lip, emerging from a papery calyx that expands in fruit. The leaves are divided into small, "frilly" leaflets with crisped edges.

GROWS *in clumps in damp areas of heaths, bogs, moors, grassy places, and woodland.*

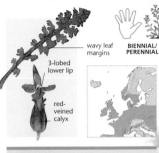

elongated upper lip

wavy leaf margins

BIENNIAL/ PERENNIAL

3-lobed lower lip

red-veined calyx

PLANT HEIGHT *10–25cm.*
FLOWER SIZE *2–2.5cm long.*
FLOWERING TIME *April–July.*
LEAVES *Alternate, pinnately lobed, fern-like.*
FRUIT *Capsule in the inflated, hairless calyx.*
SIMILAR SPECIES *Red Bartsia (left) has opposite, spear-shaped leaves; Marsh Lousewort (P. palustris) has longer leaves.*

Yellow Rattle

Rhinanthus minor (Scrophulariaceae)

This partially parasitic plant derives water and minerals from the adjoining root systems of grasses. The small, rather squat, yellow flowers have two lips, with tiny violet teeth on the upper lip. The calyx is extremely inflated and, when ripe and dry, the enclosed capsule and its seeds rattle when moved by the wind. The narrow leaves are dark green.

GROWS *in open, grassy places on roadsides, banks, and pastures; prefers chalky soil.*

leaves clasp stem

toothed upper lip

inflated, dry calyx

serrated leaf margins

ANNUAL

PLANT HEIGHT *20–40cm.*
FLOWER SIZE *1.3–1.5cm long.*
FLOWERING TIME *May–August.*
LEAVES *Opposite, lance-shaped, unstalked.*
FRUIT *Round capsule, with a short beak, enclosing winged seeds.*
SIMILAR SPECIES *Yellow Archangel (p.142); Common Cow-wheat (p.155).*

Common Butterwort

Pinguicula vulgaris (Lentibulariaceae)

The pale yellow-green leaves of Common Butterwort have a very sticky surface that attracts small insects. These become trapped when they alight and are digested by the plant, as the leaf margins roll in slightly. The solitary purple flowers have a whitish centre and a spur at the back.

FORMS *small colonies in wet, acid locations such as bogs, moors, heaths, and damp rocks, often along streams.*

flower spur

leafless stem

PERENNIAL

rounded petals

pale yellow-green leaf

PLANT HEIGHT *8–18cm.*
FLOWER SIZE *1.5–2cm wide.*
FLOWERING TIME *May–July.*
LEAVES *Basal rosette, elliptical with in-rolled margin, fleshy and sticky; yellow-green.*
FRUIT *Small, erect, many-seeded capsule.*
SIMILAR SPECIES *Pale Butterwort (P. lusitanica), which has pale lilac flowers.*

Honeysuckle

Lonicera periclymenum (Caprifoliaceae)

The delightful fragrance of Honeysuckle flowers, most noticeable on warm summer evenings, is designed to attract pollinating moths. The plant trails over the ground or climbs high into trees, bearing oblong leaves. In clusters of up to 12, the two-lipped flowers may be white or cream to dark peach, darkening as they mature, followed by a cluster of berries.

CLIMBS *over hedges, fences, or high up a tree to form a "bush" midway; trails on ground in woodland.*

long flower tube

bright red berries

protruding stamens

whorl of flowers

PERENNIAL

PLANT HEIGHT *1–6m*
FLOWER SIZE *3.5–5cm long.*
FLOWERING TIME *June–October.*
LEAVES *Opposite, oblong to elliptical, untoothed.*
FRUIT *Red berries.*
SIMILAR SPECIES *Fly Honeysuckle (L. xylosteum), which has flowers in pairs.*

Greater Plantain

Plantago major (Plantaginaceae)

This common weed of wasteland has distinctive thick, dark green leaves that form a flat rosette close to the ground. The plant becomes even more conspicuous when the long, upright flower spikes develop. Varying in length, these bear many tiny green flowers, which for a short while produce purple to yellowish or brown anthers.

FOUND *in bare areas in wasteland, on field margins, and on paths. Also in lawns.*

large, rounded leaf

spikes of tiny green flowers

PERENNIAL

basal leaf rosettes

long stalk

PLANT HEIGHT *10–45cm.*
FLOWER SIZE *1–2mm wide.*
FLOWERING TIME *June–October.*
LEAVES *Basal rosette, rounded, thick with long stalks, and veined; dark green.*
FRUIT *Small capsule enclosing several tiny seeds.*
SIMILAR SPECIES *None.*

Ribwort Plantain

Plantago lanceolata (Plantaginaceae)

This common grassland weed can be easily overlooked until its most noticeable feature – the anthers – are mature. These are large and white, forming a conspicuous ring around the flowerhead, whose tiny brown sepals give it a rusty look. The leaves, clustered in a tuft at the base, have raised veins on their undersides. The tough and fibrous flower stems are also furrowed.

FORMS *extensive patches in meadows, roadsides, pastures, and untended lawns; on neutral soils with little shade.*

parallel veins on leaf

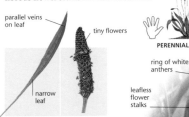

tiny flowers

PERENNIAL

tapering, rusty flowerheads

ring of white anthers

leafless flower stalks

narrow leaf

PLANT HEIGHT *20–50cm.*
FLOWER SIZE *4mm wide.*
FLOWERING TIME *April–October.*
LEAVES *Basal, linear to almost elliptical, with toothed or entire margins.*
FRUIT *Capsule containing boat-shaped seeds.*
SIMILAR SPECIES *Spiked Rampion (Phyteuma spicatum), which has oval leaves.*

Common Valerian

Valeriana officinalis (Valerianaceae)

This plant of damp places has white flowerheads that may be flushed with pink. Each flower is five-lobed, narrowing to a tube with a pouched base. The leaves comprise long, narrow leaflets giving a ladder-like appearance, although the upper leaves are much smaller.

OCCURS *along river and stream margins, in wet meadows, ditches, pastures, and damp woodland.*

slender leaflets

ladder-like leaves

5-lobed flower

dense, branched flowerheads

pinkish white flowers

PERENNIAL

PLANT HEIGHT *1–1.8m.*
FLOWER SIZE *3–5mm long.*
FLOWERING TIME *June–August.*
LEAVES *Opposite, pinnately divided into lance-shaped, toothed leaflets.*
FRUIT *Achene with a pappus of hairs.*
SIMILAR SPECIES *Dwarf Elder (Sambucus ebulus), which has larger leaves.*

Red Valerian

Centranthus ruber (Valerianaceae)

A distinctive plant when in full flower through the summer months, this native of the Mediterranean is now a popular garden plant and naturalized throughout Britain. The waxy leaves, in opposite pairs, clasp thick, erect stems. Flowers are usually deep red, but pink and white forms are also common.

CLINGS *to coastal rocks and cliff faces, old walls and monuments, usually near the sea, on shingle beaches and sandy places.*

oval, grey-green leaf

long, slender flower tube

spur at flower base

lobed, unequal petals

broad clusters of flowers

thick, erect stems

PERENNIAL

PLANT HEIGHT *50–80cm.*
FLOWER SIZE *8–12mm long.*
FLOWERING TIME *July–September.*
LEAVES *Opposite, oval, fleshy, and usually untoothed, clasping the stem; grey-green.*
FRUIT *One-seeded nut with a feathery pappus.*
SIMILAR SPECIES *Common Valerian (above).*

Common Figwort

Scrophularia nodosa (Scrophulariaceae)

A tall, robust plant, Common Figwort has surprisingly small flowers, which in bud look like beads on stalks. They are borne on square stems, usually opening one at a time within a cluster. Each flower has a notched, purplish brown upper lip, which forms a little hood over the pouched lower lip, with two of the four stamens protruding.

GROWS *in damp places, along stream and river banks, in meadows and open woodland.*

oval leaf   PERENNIAL

yellow stamens

bead-like flower buds

hooded upper lip

branching stems

PLANT HEIGHT *60–100cm.*
FLOWER SIZE *7–9mm long.*
FLOWERING TIME *June–September.*
LEAVES *Opposite, oval, with finely toothed margins and wrinkled surface.*
FRUIT *Two-parted, rounded capsule.*
SIMILAR SPECIES *Water Figwort (S. auriculata), which has winged stems.*

Brooklime

Veronica beccabunga (Scrophulariaceae)

Brooklime is a distinctive plant, with its fat, succulent stems flushed red around the leaf-joints. The flowers form loose clusters on long stalks that arise from the leaf bases. Each flower is a rich blue, with a small white "eye" ringed with scarlet. The hairless leaves are also a little succulent and have a wavy margin.

INHABITS *margins of ponds, ditches, rivers, and permanently damp parts of marshes and wet meadows.*

wavy-edged leaf

PERENNIAL

deep blue flowers

red ring around white centre

red-tinged succulent stems

PLANT HEIGHT *20–60cm.*
FLOWER SIZE *5–8mm wide.*
FLOWERING TIME *May–September.*
LEAVES *Opposite, oval to elliptical, slightly fleshy, toothed; deep green.*
FRUIT *Small, round capsule.*
SIMILAR SPECIES *Blue Water-speedwell (V. anagallis-aquatica) has longer leaves.*

Germander Speedwell

Veronica chamaedrys (Scrophulariaceae)

The flowers of this plant are an exceptionally deep and vivid blue, with a contrasting white "eye" in the centre and two divergent protruding stamens. The flower stalks are produced from the base of hairy, stalkless leaves. Close examination of the hairy stems reveals that the hairs are in two neat, opposite rows.

PROLIFERATES *in shady grassy areas, alongside woodland, hedgerows, among scrub, and on embankments.*

4 petals of unequal size

white centre

PERENNIAL

coarsely toothed leaves

PLANT HEIGHT *20–40cm.*
FLOWER SIZE *9–12mm wide.*
FLOWERING TIME *March–July.*
LEAVES *Opposite, oval, coarsely toothed, and unstalked.*
FRUIT *Small heart-shaped capsules.*
SIMILAR SPECIES *Germander Speedwell (below), which has flowers with a white petal.*

Common Field Speedwell

Veronica persica (Scrophulariaceae)

Introduced into Europe in the early 19th century, this species has become a common sight on farmland in many places. The lowest of the four petals is smaller than the others and is usually white, the others being violet with dark radiating veins. The oval, hairy leaves are very short-stalked, with just a few coarse teeth.

FLOURISHES *on disturbed soil such as wasteland, and among farmland crops.*

ANNUAL

lower petal usually white

oval leaf

dark-veined flower

PLANT HEIGHT *5–20cm.*
FLOWER SIZE *8–12mm wide.*
FLOWERING TIME *Year round.*
LEAVES *Mostly alternate, lower ones opposite.*
FRUIT *Heart-shaped capsule.*
SIMILAR SPECIES *Germander Speedwell (above); Green Field Speedwell (V. agrestis) has white flowers with a blue upper petal.*

coarsely toothed leaves

Foxglove

Digitalis purpurea (Scrophulariaceae)

Recognizable even in its first year, by the rosettes of large, wrinkled, hairy leaves, Foxglove is unmistakable in the following year when the tall flower stems are formed. As many as 60 or more pink to purple flowers droop in one-sided spikes. The whole plant is poisonous.

PROLIFERATES *on heaths, in woodland clearings and margins, and along road verges, hedgerows, and banks; mostly on acid soil.*

tapered flower spikes

tubular flowers

BIENNIAL/ PERENNIAL

many-seeded fruit capsule

wrinkled leaf surface

blunt, hairy leaf

PLANT HEIGHT *1–2m.*
FLOWER SIZE *4–5.5cm long.*
FLOWERING TIME *June–September.*
LEAVES *Basal rosette at first, followed by alternate stem leaves; oval, densely hairy.*
FRUIT *Capsule expelling numerous seeds through three slits at the tip.*
SIMILAR SPECIES *Great Mullein (p.150).*

Common Cow-wheat

Melampyrum pratense (Scrophulariaceae)

The yellow flowers of this plant brighten shaded woodland in late summer. The two-lipped flowers are arranged in neat pairs, each one often tipped red or becoming wholly red with age. The leaves and flower bracts are in pairs and swept back away from the flowers so that they look like ranks of wings along the slender stems.

FOUND *in shady corners and along paths in deciduous and coniferous woodland; prefers acid soil.*

toothed bracts

long, narrow leaf

ANNUAL

leaves swept back at angles

tubular flower

paired flowers

PLANT HEIGHT *15–30cm.*
FLOWER SIZE *1–1.8cm long.*
FLOWERING TIME *June–August.*
LEAVES *Opposite, narrowly lance-shaped, bracts with long teeth at base.*
FRUIT *Small capsule splitting along one side.*
SIMILAR SPECIES *Yellow Rattle (p.157), which has inflated sepals and toothed leaves.*

Red Bartsia

Odontites verna (Scrophulariaceae)

This wiry, hairy plant with arching stems, is often flushed red. Each one-sided flower spike has a three-lobed lower lip and a hooded upper lip from which the stamens protrude. Long, leaf-like bracts spread below each flower. The paired leaves have long veins.

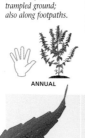

THRIVES *in fields, meadows, pastures, wasteland, and trampled ground; also along footpaths.*

ANNUAL

lance-shaped leaf

2-lipped flower

flowers in leafy spikes

pink flowers

PLANT HEIGHT *15–40cm.*
FLOWER SIZE *8–10mm long.*
FLOWERING TIME *June–September.*
LEAVES *Opposite, spear-shaped, few teeth.*
FRUIT *Hairy capsule, with ridged, oval seeds.*
SIMILAR SPECIES *Common Lousewort (right) has pinnate leaves; Subsp. serotina of S. Britain has shorter bracts.*

Eyebright

Euphrasia species (Scrophulariaceae)

There are about 20 *Euphrasia* species in Britain, but they are extremely difficult to tell apart. All have the same basic structure of small, two-lipped flowers, the lower lip being three-lobed. The flowers are usually white or lilac with a yellow blotch and purple streaks. The leaves, sometimes purple-flushed, are small and stalkless, with jagged teeth. The plant is semi-parasitic on the grasses with which it grows.

INHABITS *grassy sites, heaths, sand dunes, and on woodland edges, usually in small patches.*

flowers in short spikes

ANNUAL

2-lipped white flowers

branched stem

toothed leaf margin

3-lobed lower lip

purple veins

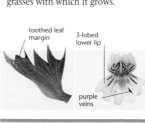

PLANT HEIGHT *5–25cm.*
FLOWER SIZE *5–7mm long.*
FLOWERING TIME *June–September.*
LEAVES *Opposite, with jagged toothed margins, stalkless.*
FRUIT *Capsule, splitting lengthwise.*
SIMILAR SPECIES *Field Pansy (p.105), which has oblong, shallowly toothed leaves.*

Common Lousewort

Pedicularis sylvatica (Scrophulariaceae)

This tufted, compact plant has densely crowded leaves and flowers. The flowers are pale pink, each with a three-lobed lower lip and a hooded upper lip, emerging from a papery calyx that expands in fruit. The leaves are divided into small, "frilly" leaflets with crisped edges.

GROWS *in clumps in damp areas of heaths, bogs, moors, grassy places, and woodland.*

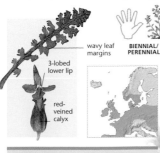

elongated upper lip

wavy leaf margins

BIENNIAL/ PERENNIAL

3-lobed lower lip

red-veined calyx

PLANT HEIGHT *10–25cm.*
FLOWER SIZE *2–2.5cm long.*
FLOWERING TIME *April–July.*
LEAVES *Alternate, pinnately lobed, fern-like.*
FRUIT *Capsule in the inflated, hairless calyx.*
SIMILAR SPECIES *Red Bartsia (left) has opposite, spear-shaped leaves; Marsh Lousewort (P. palustris) has longer leaves.*

Yellow Rattle

Rhinanthus minor (Scrophulariaceae)

This partially parasitic plant derives water and minerals from the adjoining root systems of grasses. The small, rather squat, yellow flowers have two lips, with tiny violet teeth on the upper lip. The calyx is extremely inflated and, when ripe and dry, the enclosed capsule and its seeds rattle when moved by the wind. The narrow leaves are dark green.

GROWS *in open, grassy places on roadsides, banks, and pastures; prefers chalky soil.*

leaves clasp stem

toothed upper lip

inflated, dry calyx

serrated leaf margins

ANNUAL

PLANT HEIGHT *20–40cm.*
FLOWER SIZE *1.3–1.5cm long.*
FLOWERING TIME *May–August.*
LEAVES *Opposite, lance-shaped, unstalked.*
FRUIT *Round capsule, with a short beak, enclosing winged seeds.*
SIMILAR SPECIES *Yellow Archangel (p.142); Common Cow-wheat (p.155).*

Common Butterwort

Pinguicula vulgaris (Lentibulariaceae)

The pale yellow-green leaves of Common Butterwort have a very sticky surface that attracts small insects. These become trapped when they alight and are digested by the plant, as the leaf margins roll in slightly. The solitary purple flowers have a whitish centre and a spur at the back.

FORMS *small colonies in wet, acid locations such as bogs, moors, heaths, and damp rocks, often along streams.*

flower spur

leafless stem

PERENNIAL

rounded petals

pale yellow-green leaf

PLANT HEIGHT *8–18cm.*
FLOWER SIZE *1.5–2cm wide.*
FLOWERING TIME *May–July.*
LEAVES *Basal rosette, elliptical with in-rolled margin, fleshy and sticky; yellow-green.*
FRUIT *Small, erect, many-seeded capsule.*
SIMILAR SPECIES *Pale Butterwort* (P. lusitanica), *which has pale lilac flowers.*

Honeysuckle

Lonicera periclymenum (Caprifoliaceae)

The delightful fragrance of Honeysuckle flowers, most noticeable on warm summer evenings, is designed to attract pollinating moths. The plant trails over the ground or climbs high into trees, bearing oblong leaves. In clusters of up to 12, the two-lipped flowers may be white or cream to dark peach, darkening as they mature, followed by a cluster of berries.

CLIMBS *over hedges, fences, or high up a tree to form a "bush" midway; trails on ground in woodland.*

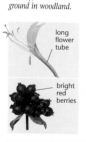

long flower tube

bright red berries

whorl of flowers

protruding stamens

PERENNIAL

PLANT HEIGHT *1–6m.*
FLOWER SIZE *3.5–5cm long.*
FLOWERING TIME *June–October.*
LEAVES *Opposite, oblong to elliptical, untoothed.*
FRUIT *Red berries.*
SIMILAR SPECIES *Fly Honeysuckle* (L. xylosteum), *which has flowers in pairs.*

Greater Plantain

Plantago major (Plantaginaceae)

This common weed of wasteland has distinctive thick, dark green leaves that form a flat rosette close to the ground. The plant becomes even more conspicuous when the long, upright flower spikes develop. Varying in length, these bear many tiny green flowers, which for a short while produce purple to yellowish or brown anthers.

FOUND *in bare areas in wasteland, on field margins, and on paths. Also in lawns.*

large, rounded leaf

long stalk

spikes of tiny green flowers

basal leaf rosettes

PERENNIAL

PLANT HEIGHT *10–45cm.*
FLOWER SIZE *1–2mm wide.*
FLOWERING TIME *June–October.*
LEAVES *Basal rosette, rounded, thick with long stalks, and veined; dark green.*
FRUIT *Small capsule enclosing several tiny seeds.*
SIMILAR SPECIES *None.*

Ribwort Plantain

Plantago lanceolata (Plantaginaceae)

This common grassland weed can be easily overlooked until its most noticeable feature – the anthers – are mature. These are large and white, forming a conspicuous ring around the flowerhead, whose tiny brown sepals give it a rusty look. The leaves, clustered in a tuft at the base, have raised veins on their undersides. The tough and fibrous flower stems are also furrowed.

FORMS *extensive patches in meadows, roadsides, pastures, and untended lawns; on neutral soils with little shade.*

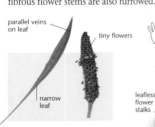

parallel veins on leaf

tiny flowers

narrow leaf

PERENNIAL

tapering, rusty flowerheads

ring of white anthers

leafless flower stalks

PLANT HEIGHT *20–50cm.*
FLOWER SIZE *4mm wide.*
FLOWERING TIME *April–October.*
LEAVES *Basal, linear to almost elliptical, with toothed or entire margins.*
FRUIT *Capsule containing boat-shaped seeds.*
SIMILAR SPECIES *Spiked Rampion (Phyteuma spicatum), which has oval leaves.*

Common Valerian

Valeriana officinalis (Valerianaceae)

OCCURS *along river and stream margins, in wet meadows, ditches, pastures, and damp woodland.*

This plant of damp places has white flowerheads that may be flushed with pink. Each flower is five-lobed, narrowing to a tube with a pouched base. The leaves comprise long, narrow leaflets giving a ladder-like appearance, although the upper leaves are much smaller.

slender leaflets

ladder-like leaves

5-lobed flower

dense, branched flowerheads

pinkish white flowers

PERENNIAL

PLANT HEIGHT *1–1.8m.*
FLOWER SIZE *3–5mm long.*
FLOWERING TIME *June–August.*
LEAVES *Opposite, pinnately divided into lance-shaped, toothed leaflets.*
FRUIT *Achene with a pappus of hairs.*
SIMILAR SPECIES *Dwarf Elder (Sambucus ebulus), which has larger leaves.*

Red Valerian

Centranthus ruber (Valerianaceae)

CLINGS *to coastal rocks and cliff faces, old walls and monuments, usually near the sea, on shingle beaches and sandy places.*

A distinctive plant when in full flower through the summer months, this native of the Mediterranean is now a popular garden plant and naturalized throughout Britain. The waxy leaves, in opposite pairs, clasp thick, erect stems. Flowers are usually deep red, but pink and white forms are also common.

broad clusters of flowers

thick, erect stems

oval, grey-green leaf

long, slender flower tube

spur at flower base

lobed, unequal petals

PERENNIAL

PLANT HEIGHT *50–80cm.*
FLOWER SIZE *8–12mm long.*
FLOWERING TIME *July–September.*
LEAVES *Opposite, oval, fleshy, and usually untoothed, clasping the stem; grey-green.*
FRUIT *One-seeded nut with a feathery pappus.*
SIMILAR SPECIES *Common Valerian (above).*

Teasel

Dipsacus fullonum (Dipsacaceae)

Shaped like the blade of a spear, the leaves of Teasel are unmistakable, with a bold white midrib armed with long prickles underneath, and many lateral veins creating a rather wavy margin. The opposite leaves are joined together around the stem, and may collect pools of rainwater in wet weather. The flowerhead is a dense collection of stiff, straight spines, between which the lilac-blue flowers emerge. They open in a concentric ring about one third of the way up the head, and then spread upwards and downwards simultaneously.

FLOURISHES *in rough, grassy places and along embankments, roadsides, river and stream banks, hedgerows, and woodland margins.*

stiff spines

NOTE

Fuller's Teasel (D. sativus) is a variety cultivated (mostly in Somerset) for its flowerheads, which have flexible hooked spines used for "fleecing" or raising the knap of woollen cloth.

whorl of long bracts below flowerhead

BIENNIAL

white midrib

florets open in concentric rings

dried, bristly fruithead

PLANT HEIGHT *1–2m.*
FLOWER SIZE *Flowerhead 4–8cm long.*
FLOWERING TIME *July–October.*
LEAVES *Basal rosette in first year; opposite stem leaves, lance-shaped with spines on lower midrib, fused around stem.*
FRUIT *Small achene.*
SIMILAR SPECIES *Small Teasel (D. pilosus), which has white flowerheads; Fuller's Teasel (D. sativus), which has recurved spines in the flowerhead.*

Devil's-bit Scabious

Succisa pratensis (Dipsacaceae)

FLOURISHES in meadows and heaths, in dry or moist conditions, in the open or in light shade of scrub, on chalky to slightly acid soils.

Entire meadows may be coloured purple by swathes of this plant in late summer. The flowers are generally darker than other scabious species, and form a rounded rather than flat-topped head. Each tubular floret is the same in shape and size, without larger petals on the outside. When in bud, the flowerhead is like a collection of green or purple beads but later, when the flowers open and the stamens protrude, it comes to resemble a pincushion.

prominent pale midrib

protruding stamens

PERENNIAL

florets of equal size

small linear bracts below flowers

rounded flowerhead in bud

PLANT HEIGHT *50–100cm.*
FLOWER SIZE *Flowerhead 1.5–2cm wide.*
FLOWERING TIME *July–October.*
LEAVES *Basal leaves, lance-shaped with a white midrib; stem leaves opposite and toothed.*
FRUIT *One-seeded achene.*
SIMILAR SPECIES *Sheep's-bit (Jasione montana) does not have protruding stamens.*

Field Scabious

Knautia arvensis (Dipsacaceae)

GROWS in meadows, pastures, open woodland, hedgerows, and roadside verges; generally on chalky soil.

This is the largest and most robust of the scabious family flowers and may be recognized by its large leaves dissected into narrow, pointed lobes, though the basal ones are usually undivided. The flowerhead is a collection of pinkish lilac, tubular florets. The narrow bracts below the flowerhead are about the same length as the florets.

long, slender flower stem

tubular florets

ruff of bracts below flowerhead

PERENNIAL

pinnately lobed leaf

enlarged outer petals

PLANT HEIGHT *50–100cm.*
FLOWER SIZE *Flowerhead 2–4cm wide.*
FLOWERING TIME *July–September.*
LEAVES *Basal rosettes; upper leaves opposite and pinnately lobed.*
FRUIT *Achene with a feathery calyx attached.*
SIMILAR SPECIES *Devil's-bit Scabious (above) has simpler leaves and is darker in colour.*

Harebell

Campanula rotundifolia (Campanulaceae)

The scientific name *rotundifolia* refers to the round basal leaves, which have almost always withered away by flowering time. By contrast, the stem leaves are linear, the lowest ones lance-shaped. It is the dainty nodding bells, however, that are the noticeable feature of the plant: a rich sky-blue with five pointed lobes, usually in a very loose cluster.

SEEN *in dry, grassy places, such as commons, heaths, banks and hills; on rocky ground and sand dunes.*

PERENNIAL

5-lobed corolla

tiny calyx

nodding bells

linear stem leaf

PLANT HEIGHT *20–50cm.*
FLOWER SIZE *1.2–2cm long.*
FLOWERING TIME *July–September.*
LEAVES *Basal leaves rounded, usually withered by flowering time; stem leaves alternate, narrow, and untoothed.*
FRUIT *Pendent capsule.*
SIMILAR SPECIES *None.*

Clustered Bellflower

Campanula glomerata (Campanulaceae)

This plant is easily identified by the close grouping of the flowers at the top of the stems, giving it a rather top-heavy look. Each upright flower is deep blue-violet in colour, the five petals fused into a long bell shape but with pointed lobes at the mouth and a fold along the length of each. The slightly toothed stems and leaves are roughly hairy.

INHABITS *dry, rough grassland, and meadows; also along roadsides and among scrub, on chalky soil.*

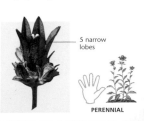

5 narrow lobes

flowers clustered at top of stem

bell-shaped flowers

PERENNIAL

PLANT HEIGHT *15–30cm.*
FLOWER SIZE *1.5–2cm long.*
FLOWERING TIME *July–September.*
LEAVES *Basal leaves oval to lance-shaped, stem leaves narrower and clasping the stem.*
FRUIT *Capsule containing many seeds.*
SIMILAR SPECIES *Nettle-leaved Bellflower (C. trachelium) has loose racemes of flowers.*

Hemp Agrimony

Eupatorium cannabinum (Asteraceae)

Tall and robust, Hemp Agrimony has characteristic lobed leaves and red stems, which begin growing long before the flowerheads open. The flower heads are composed of tubular pink florets with long, protruding stamens. Each group of five to six florets is enclosed by crimson-tipped bracts.

FORMS clumps on road verges, in spaces left by tree clearance, and in damp areas such as margins of rivers, streams, and ditches.

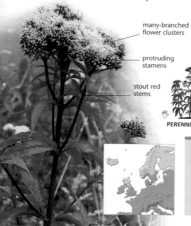

many-branched flower clusters

protruding stamens

stout red stems

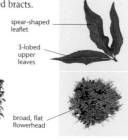

spear-shaped leaflet

3-lobed upper leaves

broad, flat flowerhead

PERENNIAL

PLANT HEIGHT *90–150cm.*
FLOWER SIZE *2–5mm wide.*
FLOWERING TIME *July–September.*
LEAVES *Opposite, palmately lobed, toothed leaflets – lower leaves with five lobes and upper leaves with three lobes or undivided.*
FRUIT *Achene with a hairy pappus.*
SIMILAR SPECIES *None.*

Daisy

Bellis perennis (Asteraceae)

A familiar plant, Daisy is easily recognized. The small, central yellow disc of the solitary flower is surrounded by numerous white rays which are tinged pink on the undersides, visible when the flower closes in the evening or when in bud. The hairy leaves are often bluntly toothed, and crowded into a tight rosette. The leaves and flowers of this plant may be added to salads, though the leaves have a mildly sour flavour.

ASSOCIATED with old grassland, this plant is now ubiquitous on railway embankments, lawns, roadsides, and short turf by the sea.

solitary flower

central yellow disc florets

PERENNIAL

spoon-shaped leaf

white rays tinged pink below

PLANT HEIGHT *5–10cm.*
FLOWER SIZE *Flowerhead 1.5–2.5cm wide.*
FLOWERING TIME *Year round.*
LEAVES *Basal, spoon-shaped with short stalk.*
FRUIT *Simple achene, with no feathery attachment.*
SIMILAR SPECIES *Oxeye Daisy (p.169), which has larger flowers, but can be very short.*

Goldenrod

Solidago virgaurea (Asteraceae)

The stiff, erect stems of Goldenrod may produce a single spike of yellow flowers or many branches bearing golden bunches of flowers. Each flower is actually a mass of tiny florets, the outer ones with a single petal or ray. The leaves are narrow and slightly toothed, the lower leaves are long-stalked and broader.

INHABITS *dry, grassy places, open woods, heaths, meadows, and rocky sites.*

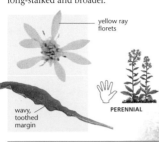

yellow ray florets

branched flower spikes

wavy, toothed margin

PERENNIAL

PLANT HEIGHT *10–60cm.*
FLOWER SIZE *Flowerhead 1.5–1.8cm wide.*
FLOWERING TIME *July–September.*
LEAVES *Alternate, variable but narrow.*
FRUIT *Achene with a brown pappus, forming a clock.*
SIMILAR SPECIES *Common Ragwort (p.173), which is more bushy and has divided leaves.*

Canadian Goldenrod

Solidago canadensis (Asteraceae)

Having escaped from gardens, this robust plant now forms patches or small colonies in the wild. The golden yellow flowerheads are arranged on many horizontal branches, both flowerheads and branches decreasing in size up the stem. The whole spike tends to lean over in one direction, giving the inflorescence a one-sided look.

GROWS *in patches on roadsides, railway embankments, bare ground, wasteland, and field margins.*

tall flower spike

lance-shaped leaves

numerous tiny flowerheads

toothed leaf margin

leafy stem

PERENNIAL

PLANT HEIGHT *1–2m.*
FLOWER SIZE *Flowerhead 5–6mm wide.*
FLOWERING TIME *August–October.*
LEAVES *Alternate, lance-shaped, with toothed margins.*
FRUIT *Achene with a short pappus.*
SIMILAR SPECIES *None, the tall, pyramidal one-sided spikes are characteristic.*

Sea Aster

Aster tripolium (Asteraceae)

Most easily observed at low tide, this plant may be almost engulfed by the incoming sea over salt marshes. The daisy-like flowers have narrow, rather untidy, pale lilac or purple ray florets, though sometimes these are missing altogether, leaving only the bright yellow disc florets on the short column of bracts. The leaves are fleshy and rounded in cross-section.

FORMS *large colonies in salt marshes and estuaries, often inundated by high tide.*

yellow disc florets

linear stem leaf

BIENNIAL

fleshy stems

pale lilac ray florets

PLANT HEIGHT *30–70cm.*
FLOWER SIZE *1–2cm wide.*
FLOWERING TIME *July–October.*
LEAVES *Alternate, linear to lance-shaped, succulent.*
FRUIT *Achene with a hairy pappus.*
SIMILAR SPECIES *Michaelmas-daisy (below), which grows inland.*

Michaelmas-daisy

Aster novi-belgii (Asteraceae)

This garden plant was introduced into Britain from North America along with several other *Aster* species which have since hybridized, making identification difficult. However, they are all robust plants with white to blue or purple ray florets and yellow centres, and small leaves that clasp the wiry stems.

PROLIFERATES *on fens, wasteland, commons, roadsides, and river or stream banks.*

branched clusters of flowers

ray florets around yellow centre

red-tinged stems

unstalked stem leaf

PERENNIAL

PLANT HEIGHT *80–150cm.*
FLOWER SIZE *2.5–4cm wide.*
FLOWERING TIME *September–October.*
LEAVES *Alternate, oval to lance-shaped, hairy.*
FRUIT *Achene with a hairy pappus.*
SIMILAR SPECIES *Sea Aster (above) grows near the sea; there are several hybrids of Michaelmas-daisy which are common.*

Fleabane

Pulicaria dysenterica (Asteraceae)

This member of the daisy family may be differentiated from its relatives by the flat-topped disc in the centre of its flower, and numerous very narrow or linear rays, which are often somewhat ragged. The stems are grey with woolly hairs, and the leaves, which clasp the stem, have a finely wrinkled surface, wavy edges, and are greyish beneath.

PERENNIAL

OCCURS *in extensive colonies in damp grassland, meadows, and marshes, and by ditches and canals.*

daisy-like flowerhead

flat disc

many narrow rays

leaf clasps stem

clock of achenes

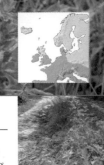

PLANT HEIGHT *40–60cm.*
FLOWER SIZE *1.5–3cm wide.*
FLOWERING TIME *July–September.*
LEAVES *Alternate, arrow-shaped, wrinkled surface with wavy edges, clasping the stem.*
FRUIT *Clock of hairy, brown achenes.*
SIMILAR SPECIES *Common Ragwort (p.173), which is more bushy and has divided leaves.*

Pineappleweed

Matricaria discoidea (Asteraceae)

This delicate plant has daisy-like green flowers, with only the central disc and no ray florets. Not only do the flowers look similar to a pineapple but the plant smells like one too. Although well established in Britain, this is probably a 19th-century introduction from northeast Asia.

PROLIFERATES *on bare paths, in wasteland, and cultivated fields; withstands trampling.*

domed, bud-like flowerhead

thread-like foliage

finely divided leaves

central disc

ANNUAL

PLANT HEIGHT *10–30cm.*
FLOWER SIZE *5–9mm wide.*
FLOWERING TIME *May–November.*
LEAVES *Alternate, pinnately divided into narrow segments.*
FRUIT *Achenes with a pappus of hair.*
SIMILAR SPECIES *Scentless Mayweed (p.169), when not in flower.*

Yarrow

Achillea millefolium (Asteraceae)

This plant may form large drifts of white flowers among the dry grasses of late summer. The erect stems are very tough and hairy. Numerous small flowers are borne in clusters, and are usually white but may be tinged with pink. The yellow anthers soon turn brown, making the flowers look rather dirty. The dark green leaves have a strong, pungent aroma.

FORMS *patches in dry grassland, meadows, and on embankments and roadsides.*

PERENNIAL

stiff, green leaves

fine leaf segments

flowers may be tinged pink

flat-topped flowerheads

hairy, erect stems

PLANT HEIGHT *40–80cm.*
FLOWER SIZE *4–6mm wide.*
FLOWERING TIME *July–October.*
LEAVES *Alternate, feathery, divided into many fine segments; aromatic when crushed.*
FRUIT *Achenes with no pappus.*
SIMILAR SPECIES *Sneezewort (below) has narrow, toothed leaves; Wild Carrot (p.114).*

Sneezewort

Achillea ptarmica (Asteraceae)

Closely related to Yarrow (above), Sneezwort inhabits damp sites and often grows among taller vegetation. It has daisy-like flowerheads, each with a distinct, pale greenish white disc surrounded by white rays, and borne in loose clusters. The scentless leaves are small, narrow, and undivided, but finely toothed.

FOUND *in damp, grassy places, marshes, and meadows, on heavy, acid soil.*

linear, deep green leaves

PERENNIAL

disc of tubular florets

white flowerheads

PLANT HEIGHT *20–50cm.*
FLOWER SIZE *Flowerhead 1.2–1.8cm wide.*
FLOWERING TIME *July–September.*
LEAVES *Alternate, lance-shaped to linear.*
FRUIT *Achene, no pappus, 1.2–1.8cm wide.*
SIMILAR SPECIES *Yarrow (above), which has smaller flowerheads and feathery leaves with a pungent aroma.*

Scentless Mayweed

Tripleurospermum inodorum (Asteraceae)

This attractive plant forms bushy masses, and bears larger flowers than other mayweeds, each with a solid, dome-shaped, central yellow disc. The leaves are fleshy, very finely divided and feathery, and have no scent. In Scented Mayweed, the disc is hollow and the plant has a looser habit and a chamomile scent.

FLOURISHES *on disturbed soil of arable fields, and on wasteland, roadsides, and bare ground.*

large, daisy-like white flowerheads

thread-like leaves

domed centre

PERENNIAL/BIENNIAL

robust, bushy habit

PLANT HEIGHT *20–60cm.*
FLOWER SIZE *2–4cm wide.*
FLOWERING TIME *June–October.*
LEAVES *Alternate, finely divided, and fleshy.*
FRUIT *Simple achene without hair.*
SIMILAR SPECIES *Scented Mayweed (Chamomilla recutita); Sea Mayweed (Matricaria maritime), which is coastal.*

Oxeye Daisy

Leucanthemum vulgare (Asteraceae)

Although very variable in height, there is no mistaking the Oxeye Daisy for the common Daisy (p.164), as its flowerheads are much larger. These comprise a bright yellow disc surrounded by a ring of white ray florets that are borne singly on stems. The leaves are bright green, becoming small and clasping the stem towards the top of the plant.

GROWS *profusely in grassy meadows and on wasteland; also along embankments and road verges.*

small leaves on upper stem

PERENNIAL

broad, spreading ray florets

prominent yellow central disc

coarsely toothed margin

spoon-shaped leaf

large flowerhead

PLANT HEIGHT *20–70cm.*
FLOWER SIZE *Flowerhead 2.5–5cm wide.*
FLOWERING TIME *May–September.*
LEAVES *Alternate and basal; spoon-shaped.*
FRUIT *Small single-seeded achenes.*
SIMILAR SPECIES *Daisy (p.164), which has smaller flowers; Scentless Mayweed (above), which has finer leaves; Corn Marigold (p.170).*

Tansy

Tanacetum vulgare (Asteraceae)

FORMS *small patches in waste or cultivated land, on roadsides, and riverbeds, on a variety of soils.*

This tall, aromatic plant is recognizable by its tight clusters of rayless flowerheads. These are often flat-topped on much-branched stems, and look like a collection of yellow buttons. The deeply divided leaves, with many tiny, regular teeth, are distinctive too. The whole plant is robust yet graceful, forming small patches where it grows.

tight clusters of flowerheads

fern-like leaves

PERENNIAL

button-like yellow flowerheads

PLANT HEIGHT *80–120cm.*
FLOWER SIZE *8–12mm wide.*
FLOWERING TIME *July–September.*
LEAVES *Alternate, pinnately divided, small toothed, fern-like.*
FRUIT *Simple achene with no pappus.*
SIMILAR SPECIES *None; the fern-like leaves and button-like flowers make it distinctive.*

Corn Marigold

Chrysanthemum segetum (Asteraceae)

APPEARS *among cereal crops and in fields where herbicides are not used; escapes into the wider countryside.*

Although this medium to tall plant appears quite robust, it soon flops over if not supported by neighbouring vegetation in its favoured cornfield habitat. The fleshy leaves are deeply lobed and toothed; the upper leaves clasp the stem at their base. The golden yellow flowerheads, however, are the most striking feature of this plant. They have broad, overlapping rays that are slightly toothed at the ends.

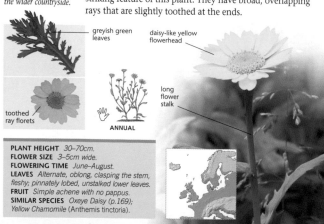

greyish green leaves

daisy-like yellow flowerhead

toothed ray florets

ANNUAL

long flower stalk

PLANT HEIGHT *30–70cm.*
FLOWER SIZE *3–5cm wide.*
FLOWERING TIME *June–August.*
LEAVES *Alternate, oblong, clasping the stem, fleshy; pinnately lobed, unstalked lower leaves.*
FRUIT *Simple achene with no pappus.*
SIMILAR SPECIES *Oxeye Daisy (p.169); Yellow Chamomile (Anthemis tinctoria).*

Mugwort

Artemisia vulgaris (Asteraceae)

A common wasteland plant with insignificant flowers, Mugwort can be distinguished from similar plants by its lower leaves. They are delicate and finely lobed, very dark green above, but bright silvery below, with distinct veins. The margins remain green, giving the leaf an "outlined" look. The flowerheads, with pale grey bracts, open golden yellow but quickly turn reddish brown.

FLOURISHES *on wasteland, disturbed ground, and rubbish tips, and in farmyards, in bare, rich soil.*

numerous tiny flowerheads in clusters

erect stems

finger-like leaf lobes

reddish brown florets

PERENNIAL

PLANT HEIGHT *80–150cm.*
FLOWER SIZE *Flowerhead 3–4mm wide.*
FLOWERING TIME *June–September.*
LEAVES *Alternate, oval in outline, lobed.*
FRUIT *Tiny, hairless achene.*
SIMILAR SPECIES *Wormwood (A. absinthium), which has yellower flowers, and more rounded leaf lobes.*

Coltsfoot

Tussilago farfara (Asteraceae)

This plant flowers early and is one of the first of the daisy family to dot the February landscape with its flowerheads. Each is a small disc encircled by narrow rays, on a stem with overlapping scales like an asparagus tip. The leaves, with tiny, black-tipped teeth, grow large in summer.

FOUND *in damp places, cultivated land, roadsides, spoil-heaps, embankments, and woodland edges.*

leafless stems

hair-like yellow rays

PERENNIAL

PLANT HEIGHT *10–25cm.*
FLOWER SIZE *1.5–2.5cm wide.*
FLOWERING TIME *February–April.*
LEAVES *Basal, horse hoof-shaped, downy, white and hairy beneath; appear after flowers.*
FRUIT *Clock of feathered achenes.*
SIMILAR SPECIES *Winter Heliotrope (p.172), which has vanilla-scented flowers.*

angled leaf

cluster of achenes

long stalk

Butterbur

Petasites hybridus (Asteraceae)

The leaves of this plant, although small at flowering time, grow up to a metre wide, and were once used for wrapping butter. The white or pink flowerheads are borne in dense, cone-like spikes, female and male flowers on separate plants; male flowers have short stalks.

OCCURS *in colonies alongside streams, rivers, ditches, and in damp woodland and meadows.*

conical spike of flowers

kidney-shaped leaf

irregular toothed margin

tight flowerheads

PERENNIAL

PLANT HEIGHT *70–150cm.*
FLOWER SIZE *Female flowerhead 3–6mm wide; male flowerhead 7–12mm wide.*
FLOWERING TIME *March–May.*
LEAVES *Basal, kidney-shaped, felty beneath.*
FRUIT *Clock of achenes with a hairy pappus.*
SIMILAR SPECIES *White Butterbur (P. albus), which has white flowers and smaller leaves.*

Winter Heliotrope

Petasites fragrans (Asteraceae)

This winter-flowering plant produces small clusters of pinkish white flowers that smell pleasantly of vanilla. Small, rounded leaves appear at the base on short stalks, which grow throughout the following summer, long after the flowers have faded. Lance-shaped bracts grow along the flowering stem.

SPREADS *by means of underground runners, to form large clumps on footpaths, stream margins, and disturbed ground; in damp sites.*

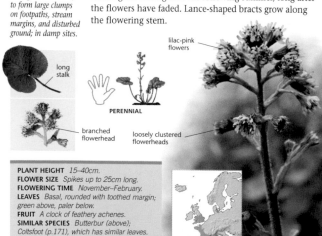

lilac-pink flowers

long stalk

PERENNIAL

branched flowerhead

loosely clustered flowerheads

PLANT HEIGHT *15–40cm.*
FLOWER SIZE *Spikes up to 25cm long.*
FLOWERING TIME *November–February.*
LEAVES *Basal, rounded with toothed margin; green above, paler below.*
FRUIT *A clock of feathery achenes.*
SIMILAR SPECIES *Butterbur (above); Coltsfoot (p.171), which has similar leaves.*

Groundsel

Senecio vulgaris (Asteraceae)

A common, ubiquitous weed, Groundsel is found in flower at almost any time of year. It has many-branched stems topped with small yellow flowerheads, which soon become tufts of white pappus hairs, although occasionally there is a form with a few short, yellow rays. The leaves are pinnately and untidily lobed.

FLOURISHES *in gardens, wasteland, cultivated land, road verges, and open habitats.*

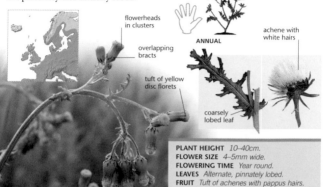

flowerheads in clusters

overlapping bracts

ANNUAL

achene with white hairs

tuft of yellow disc florets

coarsely lobed leaf

PLANT HEIGHT *10–40cm.*
FLOWER SIZE *4–5mm wide.*
FLOWERING TIME *Year round.*
LEAVES *Alternate, pinnately lobed.*
FRUIT *Tuft of achenes with pappus hairs.*
SIMILAR SPECIES *Canadian Fleabane (Conyza canadensis), which has similar tiny flowers, but is taller, with linear leaves.*

Common Ragwort

Senecio jacobaea (Asteraceae)

A widespread weed of cultivation, Common Ragwort forms extensive colonies. It proliferates in pastures for horses, but is poisonous to livestock, especially when dried and palatable. It produces loose clusters of bright yellow daisy-like flowerheads, each with 12–20 spreading rays above linear, black-tipped bracts. The stems are ridged and the leaves are pinnately divided.

THRIVES *in disturbed soil of pastures, wasteland, rubbish tips, and roadsides.*

deeply lobed leaves

black-tipped bracts

BIENNIAL/ PERENNIAL

long, spreading rays

branched stems

PLANT HEIGHT *80–150cm.*
FLOWER SIZE *Flowerhead 1.5–2.5cm wide.*
FLOWERING TIME *June–October.*
LEAVES *Alternate, curling up at edges.*
FRUIT *Achene with pappus of long hairs.*
SIMILAR SPECIES *Goldenrod (p.165), which has narrow leaves; Fleabane (p.167), which has arrow-shaped leaves*

Carline Thistle

Carlina vulgaris (Asteraceae)

This plant appears in its first year as an easily overlooked basal rosette of leaves. However, if touched or sat upon, its spiky, needle-like spines soon make their presence felt. The flowerheads are composed of tubular, yellow-brown disc florets, surrounded by stiff, curved, straw-coloured bracts. The fruiting head persists for many months.

GROWS *in meadows and dry grassland, usually among short turf on chalky soil.*

ray-like bracts

densely leafy stems

fruiting head

BIENNIAL

feathered seeds

wavy, spiny leaf

PLANT HEIGHT	15–50cm.
FLOWER SIZE	2–4cm wide.
FLOWERING TIME	July–September.
LEAVES	Basal rosette at first, alternate, narrow, stiff, spiny, cottony on underside.
FRUIT	Achene with pappus of yellow hairs.
SIMILAR SPECIES	Dwarf Thistle (p.176), which has pink flowers without spiny bracts.

Greater Burdock

Arctium lappa (Asteraceae)

This robust plant, with thick, branched stems, has large, rough leaves that appear longer than the flowers. Resembling those of thistles, the flowers themselves are reddish purple or pink and are surrounded by numerous hooked green spines or bracts, which form a much larger, spiny ball. These readily attach themselves to fur or clothing thereby helping to distribute the seed.

FORMS *large clumps in woodland clearings and wasteland, and alongside roads and hedgerows; dislikes deep shade.*

slightly toothed margin

BIENNIAL

hooked bracts surround flowerhead

large, stalked leaves

spiny bracts

PLANT HEIGHT	80–160cm.
FLOWER SIZE	Flowerhead 2–2.5cm wide.
FLOWERING TIME	July–September.
LEAVES	Basal and alternate, oval to heart-shaped, with a rough surface.
FRUIT	Achene with a pappus of hairs.
SIMILAR SPECIES	Spear Thistle (right), which has bristly leaves; Lesser Burdock (A. minor).

Marsh Thistle

Cirsium palustre (Asteraceae)

Easily identified even at a distance by its very tall, slender stature, this thistle has spiny wings along the length of its stems. The narrow leaves are pinnately lobed and, as well as being spiny, are covered in dark purplish hairs, especially when young. The small and pinkish red flowers are crowded in clusters at the top of the stems.

INHABITS *damp areas in pastures, meadows, marshy ground, and wet woods, in less disturbed places than many other thistles.*

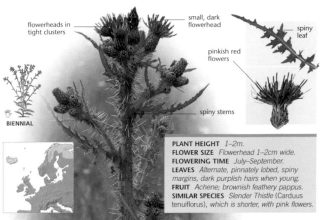

flowerheads in tight clusters

small, dark flowerhead

spiny leaf

pinkish red flowers

spiny stems

BIENNIAL

PLANT HEIGHT *1–2m.*
FLOWER SIZE *Flowerhead 1–2cm wide.*
FLOWERING TIME *July–September.*
LEAVES *Alternate, pinnately lobed, spiny margins, dark purplish hairs when young.*
FRUIT *Achene; brownish feathery pappus.*
SIMILAR SPECIES *Slender Thistle (Carduus tenuiflorus), which is shorter, with pink flowers.*

Spear Thistle

Cirsium vulgare (Asteraceae)

One of the most imposing and prickly of thistles, Spear Thistle has deep green leaves. They are shaped rather like a spearhead, with long, pinnate lobes, each ending in a spine. The stems are also covered in little irregular, triangular wings that are armed with spines. Part of the flowerhead is enclosed by green bracts, each tapering to a sharp point. The flowers themselves are reddish purple and fan out from the top.

PROLIFERATES *on wasteland, dry, grassy sites, embankments, scrub, and roadsides, on chalky soil.*

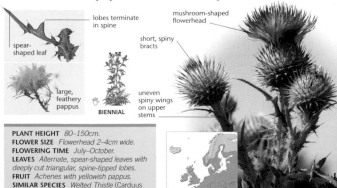

lobes terminate in spine

mushroom-shaped flowerhead

spear-shaped leaf

short, spiny bracts

large, feathery pappus

BIENNIAL

uneven spiny wings on upper stems

PLANT HEIGHT *80–150cm.*
FLOWER SIZE *Flowerhead 2–4cm wide.*
FLOWERING TIME *July–October.*
LEAVES *Alternate, spear-shaped leaves with deeply cut triangular, spine-tipped lobes.*
FRUIT *Achenes with yellowish pappus.*
SIMILAR SPECIES *Welted Thistle (Carduus crispus), which has smaller flowerheads.*

Creeping Thistle

Cirsium arvense (Asteraceae)

ABOUNDS *in pastures, wasteland, and farmland; may form large colonies.*

PERENNIAL

The stems of this spreading, persistent plant are hairy but, unlike many other thistles, have no spines or wings. Its narrow, toothed leaves, although spiny, are slightly softer too. The flowers are pale red to pink, or sometimes lilac. They are borne above narrow bracts, which are softly spiny. This untidy plant produces prodigious quantities of feathery yellow-brown seeds.

small pinkish flowerheads

spineless, hairy stems

narrow, wavy leaf

feathery pappus

PLANT HEIGHT 60–100cm.
FLOWER SIZE Flowerhead 1.5–2.5cm wide.
FLOWERING TIME June–September.
LEAVES Alternate, thin-spined, hairy beneath.
FRUIT Achene, brownish feathery pappus.
SIMILAR SPECIES Saw-wort (Serratula tinctoria), which has spineless, pinnate leaves with finely toothed margins.

Dwarf Thistle

Cirsium acaule (Asteraceae)

GROWS *in the short turf of chalk grassland, in pastures, and rabbit-infested areas.*

This plant is stemless, making it the easiest of the thistles to identify, and the very large flowerhead is stalkless, or on a very short stalk. The leaves are in a tight rosette held flat to the ground. They have sharp spines on the margins and hairs on the surface, as a defence against being grazed.

leaf rosette

single purple flowerhead

overlapping spineless bracts

spiny leaf margin

PERENNIAL

narrow leaf

linear florets

PLANT HEIGHT 5–12cm.
FLOWER SIZE Flowerhead 2.5–4cm wide.
FLOWERING TIME June–September.
LEAVES Basal rosette, pinnately lobed.
FRUIT Achene with a white feathery pappus.
SIMILAR SPECIES Carline Thistle (p.174), which may be short-stemmed, and has similar leaves but yellowish flowers.

Greater Knapweed

Centaurea scabiosa (Asteraceae)

More imposing than Common Knapweed (p.178), this
bristly plant has stiff, slender stems. The large flowerhead
has branched outer florets, which spread out in a ring.
They are sterile and serve to attract bees to the flower.
The bracts at the base of the flowerhead are also
distinctive: green with a horseshoe-shaped fringe of black
or brown hairs, and neatly overlapping like tiles on a roof.
The soft, delicate, grey-green leaves are pinnately lobed,
the upper leaves much smaller and unlobed. When the
fruit has been dispersed, the bracts open out to form a
shiny, pale brown saucer.

FOUND *in rough
grassland and
meadows, on road
verges, among scrub,
on embankments
and cliff tops.*

PERENNIAL

large, solitary
flowerhead

overlapping
bracts

NOTE

*The roots and seeds
of this plant are
known for their
diuretic properties.
Combined with
pepper, they were
once used as a
remedy for loss
of appetite. Do
not attempt.*

lobed lower
leaves

spreading
outer
florets

inner
florets

PLANT HEIGHT *80–120cm.*
FLOWER SIZE *Flowerhead 3.5–5cm wide.*
FLOWERING TIME *July–October.*
LEAVES *Alternate, pinnately divided into narrow lobes – somewhat
ladder-like.*
FRUIT *Achene topped with bristly hair.*
SIMILAR SPECIES *Cornflower (C. cyanus); Perennial Cornflower
(C. montana), which has blue florets and oblong, unlobed leaves.*

Common Knapweed

Centaurea nigra (Asteraceae)

THRIVES *in meadows, among scrub, and on road verges and embankments; absent from grazed areas.*

The stems of this common, colourful plant have many branches, each topped with a tight, neat head of reddish purple florets, all of equal length. Below this are overlapping dark or black bracts, each with a fringe of untidy hairs. The narrow leaves are pointed, sometimes with a few large teeth lower down.

PERENNIAL

prominent midrib

overlapping bracts

tubular florets

PLANT HEIGHT *50–100cm.*
FLOWER SIZE *Flowerhead 2–3cm wide.*
FLOWERING TIME *June–September.*
LEAVES *Alternate, narrow, usually untoothed.*
FRUIT *Achene with short bristly hairs, enclosed by bracts.*
SIMILAR SPECIES *Saw-wort (Serratula tinctoria); Greater Knapweed (p.177).*

Cat's-ear

Hypochaeris radicata (Asteraceae)

OCCURS *in meadows, lawns, on roadsides, and other grassy places; prefers slightly acid or sandy soils.*

This plant can be difficult to distinguish from other dandelion-like plants. Its hairy leaves have very broad teeth and are in a loose, untidy rosette. The leafless flower stems are sometimes branched and have tiny, scale-like, dark-tipped bracts resembling miniature cats' ears. The outer ray florets of the yellow flowerheads are tinged green beneath.

PERENNIAL

yellow ray florets

yellow flowerhead

leafless stem

broadly toothed margin

oblong leaf

greenish tinge on underside

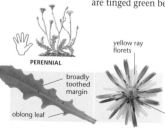

PLANT HEIGHT *20–60cm.*
FLOWER SIZE *Flowerhead 2–3cm wide.*
FLOWERING TIME *June–September.*
LEAVES *Basal rosette, oblong, lobed, hairy.*
FRUIT *Cluster of hairy achenes.*
SIMILAR SPECIES *Hawkweed (p.183), which has unlobed leaves; Autumn Hawkbit (right), which has deeper lobed leaves.*

Chicory

Cichorium intybus (Asteraceae)

The tall, flowering spikes of Chicory are an unmistakable sight among the grass on road verges and wasteland. Each flower is made up of broad, strap-like ray florets that are sky-blue, an unusual colour for the daisy family. It is cultivated as a salad vegetable; the roots and young shoots are also roasted, ground, and then blended with coffee.

FOUND *in grassy places and fields, and on road verges, wasteland, and embankments, on chalky soil.*

flowers in tall spikes

green flower bracts

lobed lower leaf

spreading ray florets

PERENNIAL

stiff, upright stem

PLANT HEIGHT 60–100cm.	
FLOWER SIZE 2.5–4cm wide.	
FLOWERING TIME July–October.	
LEAVES Alternate; upper leaves spear-shaped and toothed, lower leaves pinnately lobed.	
FRUIT Achene without a pappus.	
SIMILAR SPECIES None.	

Autumn Hawkbit

Leontodon autumnalis (Asteraceae)

This small, neat plant comes into its own in late summer, when many similar-looking species have had their main flowering period. The stems are slightly branched, with a few tiny bracts, and are topped by yellow-rayed flowerheads. The leaves are in a basal rosette and are very narrow, with long lobes that are thinner than those of Dandelion (p.181).

INHABITS *grassy places, roadsides, short-turf pasture, and rocky habitats, preferring chalky soil.*

PERENNIAL

yellow rays

tiny bracts

long, thin leaf

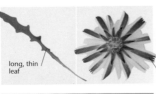

red stripes underneath rays

PLANT HEIGHT 5–40cm.	
FLOWER SIZE Flowerhead 2–3cm wide.	
FLOWERING TIME June–October.	
LEAVES Basal rosette, hairless, lobed.	
FRUIT Achene with pappus of white hairs.	
SIMILAR SPECIES Cat's-ear (left), which has hairy leaves; Mouse-ear Hawkweed (p.183), which has unlobed leaves.	

Bristly Oxtongue

Picris echioides (Asteraceae)

GROWS *in rough grassy places, abandoned fields, roadsides, and wasteland.*

Easily recognized by the white pimples on the leaves, each one with a hooked bristle in the centre, this rough plant is covered with bristly hair. The upper leaves clasp the stem and the lower ones are stalked. The flowerheads are made up of pale yellow rays, with curved bracts curling up at the base.

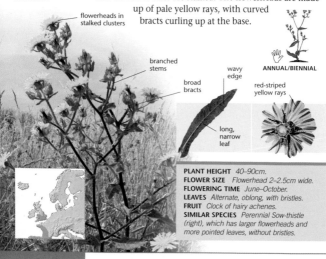

flowerheads in stalked clusters

branched stems

broad bracts

wavy edge

ANNUAL/BIENNIAL

long, narrow leaf

red-striped yellow rays

PLANT HEIGHT *40–90cm.*
FLOWER SIZE *Flowerhead 2–2.5cm wide.*
FLOWERING TIME *June–October.*
LEAVES *Alternate, oblong, with bristles.*
FRUIT *Clock of hairy achenes.*
SIMILAR SPECIES *Perennial Sow-thistle (right), which has larger flowerheads and more pointed leaves, without bristles.*

Goat's-beard

Tragopogon pratensis (Asteraceae)

OCCURS *among tall grasses in meadows, on road verges and embankments, and alongside paths.*

This stately member of the daisy family stands robust and erect. It has few branches, its stems are ridged, and the leaves are tapered to fine tips. In Britain and western France, there is a form whose flowerheads have very short ray florets, inside a ring of lance-like bracts. The continental form has long ray florets, but both forms are folded tightly shut by midday.

tapered leaf

spreading ray florets

CONTINENTAL FORM

clock-like fruithead

single row of bracts

stem swells slightly below flowerhead

thick stem

solitary flowerhead

ANNUAL/ BIENNIAL/ PERENNIAL

PLANT HEIGHT *40–75cm.*
FLOWER SIZE *Flowerhead 1.8–4cm wide, depending on length of rays.*
FLOWERING TIME *June–July.*
LEAVES *Alternate, linear to lance-shaped.*
FRUIT *"Clock" of white feathery achenes forming a whitish ball, up to 12cm wide.*
SIMILAR SPECIES *None.*

Perennial Sow-thistle

Sonchus arvensis (Asteraceae)

Although superficially similar to other sow-thistles and dandelion-like plants, this bristly plant is distinctive. Its very large flowerheads, commonly seen in late summer and early autumn, sit on a base of sticky, hairy bracts. The whole plant is tall and stiff with greyish leaves, and produces milky latex when cut.

GROWS *on disturbed and cultivated ground, wasteland, abandoned fields, and along streams and rivers.*

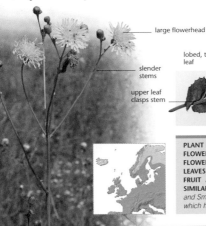

large flowerhead

slender stems

upper leaf clasps stem

lobed, toothed leaf

PERENNIAL

yellow ray florets

PLANT HEIGHT *80–150cm.*
FLOWER SIZE *4–5cm wide.*
FLOWERING TIME *July–October.*
LEAVES *Alternate, lobed, and toothed.*
FRUIT *Achene with white pappus.*
SIMILAR SPECIES *Bristly Oxtongue (left) and Smooth Sow-thistle (S. oleraceus), which have smaller flowerheads.*

Dandelion

Taraxacum officinale (Asteraceae)

Dandelions create a swathe of yellow during spring. Their flowerheads are made up of about 200 ray florets and have a ruff formed by the lower bracts. They are borne on unbranched, hollow, shiny, reddish flower stems, which exude milky-white juice if broken. The leaves have backward-pointing terminal lobes and are on winged stalks.

PROLIFERATES *in bare and grassy places, lawns, pastures, road verges, open woodland, and alongside paths.*

arrow-shaped leaf lobe

solitary flowerhead

clock of white hairs

PLANT HEIGHT *5–30cm.*
FLOWER SIZE *Flowerhead 2.5–4.5cm wide.*
FLOWERING TIME *March–October.*
LEAVES *Basal rosette, deeply lobed and toothed, pale midrib.*
FRUIT *Clock of achenes with a hairy pappus.*
SIMILAR SPECIES *Many similar Taraxacum species, all with solitary, shiny, hollow stems.*

PERENNIAL

Nipplewort

Lapsana communis (Asteraceae)

This common plant is easily recognized by its branched, slender stems bearing slim, neat buds and many small dandelion-like flowerheads. The leaves are broad, dark-tipped, slightly toothed, and are unlobed, except for the basal leaves, which are stalked and have two or more lobes.

INHABITS *semi-shaded sites alongside paths, open woodland, waste and disturbed land, old walls, and gardens.*

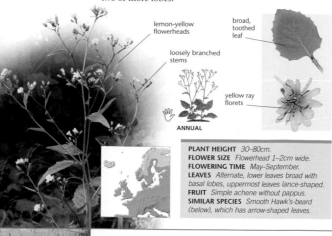

lemon-yellow flowerheads

loosely branched stems

broad, toothed leaf

yellow ray florets

ANNUAL

PLANT HEIGHT *30–80cm.*
FLOWER SIZE *Flowerhead 1–2cm wide.*
FLOWERING TIME *May–September.*
LEAVES *Alternate, lower leaves broad with basal lobes, uppermost leaves lance-shaped.*
FRUIT *Simple achene without pappus.*
SIMILAR SPECIES *Smooth Hawk's-beard (below), which has arrow-shaped leaves.*

Smooth Hawk's-beard

Crepis capillaris (Asteraceae)

A dandelion-like plant with many branched flowering stems, Smooth Hawk's-beard has small flowerheads, with the outer ray florets tinged red underneath. Below the rays are two sets of green bracts, one long, and the other shorter at the base. The upper leaves clasp the stem; the lower leaves are lobed.

FORMS *small colonies in grassy places, such as pastures, wasteland, and cultivated land.*

tapered point

clasping base of upper leaf

yellow ray florets

flowerheads in clusters

green bracts

ANNUAL/BIENNIAL

PLANT HEIGHT *30–80cm.*
FLOWER SIZE *Flowerhead 1–1.5cm wide.*
FLOWERING TIME *June–September.*
LEAVES *Alternate, narrow upper leaves; basal rosette of lobed, toothed lower leaves.*
FRUIT *Small achene with white hairs.*
SIMILAR SPECIES *Cat's-ear (p.178), which has larger flowers and hairy leaves.*

Mouse-ear Hawkweed

Pilosella officinarum (Asteraceae)

This plant spreads by overground runners or stolons that occasionally take root. The leaves, in basal rosettes, are densely white-felted beneath, with a few long, bristly white hairs on the surface. The lemon-yellow flowerheads are on leafless stalks, the rays striped red beneath.

FOUND *in dry grassy sites such as pastures, roadsides, and lawns, on acid or chalky soils.*

solitary flowerhead

PERENNIAL

oblong leaf

red-striped rays

slender runners

> **PLANT HEIGHT** *5–20cm.*
> **FLOWER SIZE** *Flowerhead 1.8–2.5cm wide.*
> **FLOWERING TIME** *June–September.*
> **LEAVES** *Basal rosette, oblong, untoothed with long hairs above, white-felted below.*
> **FRUIT** *Small achene with brownish pappus.*
> **SIMILAR SPECIES** *Autumn Hawkbit (p.179), which has lobed leaves and no runners.*

Common Hawkweed

Hieracium vulgatum (Asteraceae)

The hawkweeds are a complex group of species, divided further to include hundreds of "microspecies", which are difficult to differentiate. Common Hawkweed represents a group of these, recognizable by the loose rosette of mostly basal leaves that are oval to lance-shaped. They are toothed, but never lobed, and are crowded towards the base. The slender stems are branched at the top and the yellow ray florets have hairy bracts beneath them.

OCCURS *in rocky and grassy habitats, open woodland, heaths, cliff-tops, and other dry places.*

toothed margin

bright yellow flowerhead

leafless stem

ray florets

PERENNIAL

> **PLANT HEIGHT** *30–80cm.*
> **FLOWER SIZE** *2–3cm wide.*
> **FLOWERING TIME** *June–September.*
> **LEAVES** *Mostly basal, oval to lance-shaped with short stalk.*
> **FRUIT** *Achene with brittle brown pappus.*
> **SIMILAR SPECIES** *Cat's-ear (p.178), which has lobed leaves and a white pappus.*

Arrowhead

Sagittaria sagittifolia (Alismataceae)

A semi-aquatic plant, Arrowhead has large, arrow-shaped leaves that rise up on long stalks out of the water. It also has smaller, elliptical leaves that float on the surface, and these are the first to appear in spring. The three-petalled flowers, in whorls of three, are white with dark purple centres; male flowers sit above the females.

INHABITS *margins of shallow, freshwater lakes, slow-moving rivers and streams, and ditches.*

PERENNIAL

long-lobed leaf

white flowers with purple anthers

unbranched stem

3 petals

PLANT HEIGHT *60–100cm.*
FLOWER SIZE *2–2.5cm wide.*
FLOWERING TIME *July–August.*
LEAVES *Basal, arrow-shaped; smaller, elliptical leaves on water surface.*
FRUIT *Round, knobbly, bur-like achene.*
SIMILAR SPECIES *Water-plantain (below), which has smaller flowers.*

Water-plantain

Alisma plantago-aquatica (Alismataceae)

This plant forms a large tuft of spear-shaped leaves at the edges of standing water, and these are often more obvious than the small flowers borne on the tall, widely branching stems. Each flower has three white petals, which may have a pinkish tinge, and numerous yellow anthers. Each flower lasts for a day and only opens in the afternoon.

FOUND *in ponds, streams, lakes, marshes, and rivers, in the water or in mud at the water's edge.*

PERENNIAL

long-stalked flowers

flowers in whorls

untoothed margin

white or pinkish petals

PLANT HEIGHT *30–100cm.*
FLOWER SIZE *6–10mm wide.*
FLOWERING TIME *June–August.*
LEAVES *Basal and elliptical to oval, long-stalked, with a pointed tip.*
FRUIT *Tight cluster of in-curved achenes.*
SIMILAR SPECIES *Arrowhead (above); Flowering Rush (right).*

Flowering Rush

Butomus umbellatus (Butomaceae)

Although the narrow leaves of this aquatic plant look similar to those of a rush or sedge, the Flowering Rush is unrelated and, unlike them, it produces elegant umbels of reddish flower stalks. The flowers have three petals, red-striped beneath, with three smaller sepals in between, and several dark-tipped stamens. In cross-section, the leaves are triangular at the bottom, thinning out to a flat blade at the top.

GROWS *in shallow water at the edges of rivers, streams, ditches, and ponds; prefers recently cleared areas.*

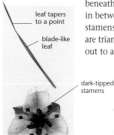

leaf tapers to a point

blade-like leaf

dark-tipped stamens

PERENNIAL

crimson flower bud

cup-shaped flower

umbrella-like flowerhead

PLANT HEIGHT *80–150cm.*
FLOWER SIZE *1.6–2.6cm wide.*
FLOWERING TIME *July–August.*
LEAVES *Basal, linear, tapering, with a broad sheath at the base.*
FRUIT *Six follicles, fused together, red–purple.*
SIMILAR SPECIES *Water-plantain (left), which has smaller flowers and broad leaves.*

Frogbit

Hydrocharis morsus-ranae (Hydrocharitaceae)

Floating on the water surface, this pretty plant looks like a miniature water-lily (p.56). Each leaf is rounded, with a heart-shaped base, often with a bronze tinge. The flowers have three white petals and a yellow centre and the male and female flowers are borne on separate plants. Frogbit spreads by means of long runners under the water, rooting at intervals.

OCCURS *in unpolluted, slow-moving water of ditches, ponds, lakes, and canals.*

PERENNIAL

rounded leaves

curved veins on leaf

wrinkled petals

white flowers with yellow centres

PLANT HEIGHT *Water surface.*
FLOWER SIZE *1.8–2cm wide.*
FLOWERING TIME *June–August.*
LEAVES *In whorls from runners, rounded with heart-shaped base; often tinged bronze.*
FRUIT *Small capsule.*
SIMILAR SPECIES *Marsh Pennywort (Hydrocotyle vulgaris), which is not aquatic.*

Broad-leaved Pondweed

Potamogeton natans (Potamogetonaceae)

The broad leaves of this aquatic plant appear to be hinged at the base, enabling them to float flat on the water surface, while longer, narrower leaves are submerged. The tiny green flowers, which have no petals, are borne in short spikes held above the water. Unusually for a water plant, they are wind-pollinated – contact with water sterilizes the pollen.

COVERS *the surface of nutrient-rich, freshwater ponds, ditches, and slow rivers. May colonize cleaned-out ponds.*

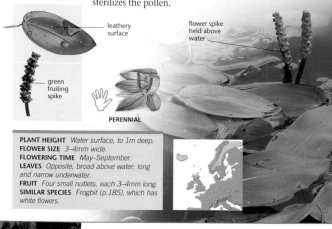

leathery surface

green fruiting spike

flower spike held above water

PERENNIAL

PLANT HEIGHT *Water surface, to 1m deep.*
FLOWER SIZE *3–4mm wide.*
FLOWERING TIME *May–September.*
LEAVES *Opposite, broad above water; long and narrow underwater.*
FRUIT *Four small nutlets, each 3–4mm long.*
SIMILAR SPECIES *Frogbit (p.185), which has white flowers.*

Bog Asphodel

Narthecium ossifragum (Liliaceae)

This colourful plant forms large colonies within its very specific habitat. Greenish to orange stems rise from a clump of strap-shaped leaves, and buds in a neat spike open from the base upwards to produce yellow flowers, each with six furry stamens. As the fruit develops, the stems and dry sepals become fiery orange.

FOUND *only in acid bogs, moors, and heaths in damp areas, particularly on hills and mountains.*

yellow-green flower buds

orange-red fruit capsules

starry, bright yellow flower

6 petals

PERENNIAL

PLANT HEIGHT *15–40cm.*
FLOWER SIZE *1–1.6cm wide.*
FLOWERING TIME *July–September.*
LEAVES *Basal, strap-shaped, short, often orange-flushed; small, bract-like stem leaves.*
FRUIT *Narrow, oblong, three-parted capsule, orange-red.*
SIMILAR SPECIES *None.*

Bluebell

Scilla non-scripta (Liliaceae)

An easily recognizable plant, the Bluebell forms dense carpets of blue over the woodland floor, where it blooms just as the trees are coming into leaf. The fragrant, nodding, violet-blue (rarely white or pink) flowers have creamy white anthers. They are clustered on one side in groups of five to fifteen, each flower ending with two blue membranous bracts on its base. The narrow, dark green leaves, which rise from the base may persist for some weeks after flowering.

FORMS *carpets in woodland and scrub; found on hedgebanks and sea-cliffs in the far west of its range.*

PERENNIAL

NOTE

The "bluebell woods" of Britain and Ireland, often written about over the centuries, are considered to be some of the most spectacular floral displays in Europe.

fleshy, leafless flower stalks

blue bracts

strap-shaped, dark green leaf

bell-shaped flowers

6-parted flower forms a tube

PLANT HEIGHT *25–50cm.*
FLOWER SIZE *1.5–2cm long.*
FLOWERING TIME *April–June.*
LEAVES *Basal, linear to lance-shaped.*
FRUIT *Small, three-parted capsule.*
SIMILAR SPECIES *Spanish Bluebell (S. hispanica), which is a more robust plant with broader bells and blue anthers; frequently escapes gardens.*

Ramsons

Allium ursinum (Liliaceae)

Woodland floors can be carpeted with this vigorous plant in spring, and the scent of garlic may be overpowering when a colony of Ramsons is in full bloom. There are two or three bright green leaves, each rising directly from the bulb below the ground. Each cluster of up to 25 star-shaped flowers is enclosed within two papery spathes before it opens out.

GROWS *in extensive colonies in deciduous woodland, scrub, banks, and hedgerows.*

PERENNIAL

umbels of 6-petalled white flowers

pointed tip

bright green leaf

2 spathes enclose buds

PLANT HEIGHT *30–45cm.*
FLOWER SIZE *1.2–2cm wide.*
FLOWERING TIME *April–June.*
LEAVES *Basal, growing directly from the underground bulb; broadly elliptical.*
FRUIT *Small, three-parted capsule.*
SIMILAR SPECIES *Lily-of-the-Valley (right) has diminutive flowers borne in racemes.*

Three-cornered Leek

Allium triquetrum (Liliaceae)

One of the most distinctive of the *Allium* species, this plant is easily recognized by its nodding head of bell-like flowers all facing in one direction. The petals of each flower overlap for much of their length, never opening out fully, and each has a narrow green stripe, visible on both the inside and the outside of the flower. The stems are markedly triangular in cross-section, with sharp edges. The leaves have a prominent keel so they too are somewhat triangular in cross-section.

SEEN *in damp, semi-shaded spots such as woodland clearings, grassy places, and road verges; often cultivated.*

spathe encloses young flowers

drooping head of flowers

PERENNIAL

narrow green stripe

strongly angled stem

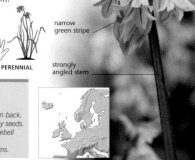

PLANT HEIGHT *20–45cm.*
FLOWER SIZE *1.8cm long.*
FLOWERING TIME *March–May.*
LEAVES *Narrow, tapering, with keel on back.*
FRUIT *Three-parted capsule with many seeds.*
SIMILAR SPECIES *White forms of Bluebell (p.187); Drooping Star-of-Bethlehem (Ornithogalum nutans) has round stems.*

Lily-of-the-Valley

Convallaria majalis (Liliaceae)

Although the leaves of this plant are simple in shape, they are distinctive when seen in pairs along the woodland floor. The small, fragrant white flowers are like little bells, borne in a loose raceme on one side of the stalk, and develop into poisonous red berries. The plant spreads by means of underground runners.

FORMS *patches in dry woodland, mountain meadows, and on limestone pavements. Grown in gardens and escapes from cultivation.*

PERENNIAL

bell-shaped flowers

leaves in pairs

elliptical leaves

deep green leaves

pendent red berries

one-sided raceme of flowers

PLANT HEIGHT *15–25cm.*
FLOWER SIZE *5–8mm long.*
FLOWERING TIME *May–June.*
LEAVES *Basal in pairs, elliptical and untoothed.*
FRUIT *Pendent, poisonous red berries.*
SIMILAR SPECIES *Ramsons (left) has similar leaves; Common Wintergreen (p.121).*

Butcher's Broom

Ruscus aculeatus (Liliaceae)

The leaf-like structures of this spiky, evergreen plant are in fact flattened extensions of the stems called cladodes. The stems themselves are upright, and branched on the upper part of the plant. The small green flowers appear directly on the surface of the cladodes and each has three petals and three sepals, the male flowers with purple anthers.

OCCURS *in ancient woodland, scrub, and hedgerows, even in deep shade. Also in rocky places by the sea. Prefers dry conditions.*

bright red berry

tough, spine-tipped cladodes

dark green leaves

flowers with 3 petals and 3 sepals

PERENNIAL

finely grooved stem

PLANT HEIGHT *25–80cm.*
FLOWER SIZE *3–5mm wide.*
FLOWERING TIME *January–April.*
LEAVES *Alternate, leaf-like structures (cladodes), rigid, elliptical with pointed tips.*
FRUIT *Red berry, 1–1.5cm wide, borne singly.*
SIMILAR SPECIES *None, but may be mistaken for a small Holly (p.26) bush.*

Herb Paris

Paris quadrifolia (Liliaceae)

This unusual member of the lily family bears a whorl of just four leaves halfway up the stem. Above these it produces a single flower, which has four very slender green petals and sepals, and eight yellowish stamens. The most notable feature is the large blackish fruit capsule in the centre, which splits to reveal red seeds. A low-growing plant, it may also spread by means of underground rhizomes.

FOUND in patches in ancient woodland and other shady habitats on chalky soil.

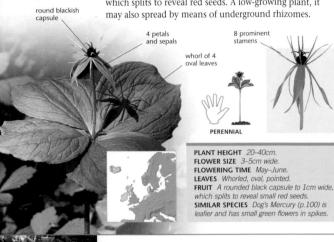

round blackish capsule

4 petals and sepals

whorl of 4 oval leaves

8 prominent stamens

PERENNIAL

PLANT HEIGHT *20–40cm.*
FLOWER SIZE *3–5cm wide.*
FLOWERING TIME *May–June.*
LEAVES *Whorled, oval, pointed.*
FRUIT *A rounded black capsule to 1cm wide, which splits to reveal small red seeds.*
SIMILAR SPECIES *Dog's Mercury (p.100) is leafier and has small green flowers in spikes.*

Solomon's-seal

Polygonatum multiflorum (Liliaceae)

This plant has leaves arranged alternately, in two rows on either side of the long, arvching, round stems. Each leaf is oval and pointed, with distinct parallel veins, and the margin is untoothed. Hanging in small clusters of 1–6 from the leaf axils, the nodding, unscented, green-tipped white flowers are like elongated bells. The fruit persists on the plant into autumn.

GROWS in shady places in ancient woodland and along hedgerows, on chalky soil.

PERENNIAL

alternate leaves in two rows

narrow, bell-shaped flowers

long stem

round black berries

PLANT HEIGHT *40–70cm.*
FLOWER SIZE *1–2cm long.*
FLOWERING TIME *May–June.*
LEAVES *Alternate, oval, pointed.*
FRUIT *Black berry with bluish bloom, 1cm wide.*
SIMILAR SPECIES *Angular Solomon's-seal (P. odoratum) has larger, scented flowers.*

Summer Snowflake

Leucojum aestivum (Amaryllidaceae)

The daffodil-like leaves of Summer Snowflake are tall, strap-shaped, and dark green. The flower stalk (scape) unfurls to reveal 3–6 bell-shaped flowers, each having six white petals with a green spot at the tip. Spring Snowflake is similar but has solitary or paired flowers that open in early spring.

INHABITS *moist places close to rivers and streams, marshes, wet meadows, and damp woodland. Grown in gardens and frequently naturalized.*

tall, tapered leaves

PERENNIAL

6 petals

ovary below petals

green spot at tip of each petal

leaf-like spathe

nodding flowers

PLANT HEIGHT *30–50cm.*
FLOWER SIZE *1.5–2.2cm long.*
FLOWERING TIME *April–June.*
LEAVES *Basal, strap-shaped.*
FRUIT *Small, three-parted capsule.*
SIMILAR SPECIES *Snowdrop (below), which is smaller, with three sepals; Spring Snowflake (L. vernum), which is smaller.*

Snowdrop

Galanthus nivalis (Amaryllidaceae)

Among the earliest of plants to flower, the Snowdrop first pushes its two slender grey-green leaves up through the bare earth, and these are followed by the flower stalks. Each bears a solitary white flower with three sepals, and three shorter notched petals streaked green on the inside. The fruit is rarely formed as the plant most often spreads by division of the bulbs.

FORMS *patches in scrub, woodland, and shady meadows, and on banks. Cultivated and naturalized.*

PERENNIAL

3 white sepals

3 shorter petals

double flower

green streaks

nodding flower

clump-forming habit

PLANT HEIGHT *10–20cm.*
FLOWER SIZE *1.5–2cm long.*
FLOWERING TIME *January–March.*
LEAVES *Basal, strap-shaped.*
FRUIT *Small, three-parted capsule.*
SIMILAR SPECIES *Summer Snowflake (above); Spring Snowflake (Leucojum vernum), which has six green-tipped petals.*

Wild Daffodil

Narcissus pseudonarcissus (Amaryllidaceae)

This tuft-forming plant has leafless stems (scapes). The solitary flowers are made up of six outer, pale primrose yellow tepals (petal-like sepals and petals), and a central trumpet (corona), which is a darker, more opaque yellow. Each flower has a green or brown papery spathe at the base. The grey-green basal leaves are flat and fleshy. The fruit capsule contains many seeds, helping extensive colonies to develop.

FORMS *colonies in ancient deciduous woodland and meadows, on river banks, and along hedgerows.*

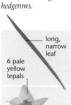

long, narrow leaf

6 pale yellow tepals

yellow stamens

triangular, slightly twisted tepals

papery spathe

trumpet-shaped, deep yellow corona

PERENNIAL

PLANT HEIGHT *30–50cm.*
FLOWER SIZE *2.5–4cm long.*
FLOWERING TIME *March–May.*
LEAVES *Basal, linear, 6–12mm wide, 2–5 in number, fleshy; grey-green.*
FRUIT *Three-parted capsule, with many seeds.*
SIMILAR SPECIES *Cultivated varieties, which have flowers ranging in shape and colour.*

Black Bryony

Tamus communis (Dioscoreaceae)

The glossy, heart-shaped leaves of this climbing plant are unmistakable. The greenish yellow flowers are borne on long, trailing stems; the male flowers in slender spikes and the female flowers in shorter clusters on separate plants. The shiny red berries are long-lasting but poisonous; although the plant is related to yams, its black tuber is poisonous too.

CLAMBERS *over hedges, woodland trees, and scrub; also twines over wire fences; usually at low altitudes.*

PERENNIAL

6-lobed flowers

twining stems

male flowers in drooping spikes

cluster of red berries

PLANT HEIGHT *Up to 4m.*
FLOWER SIZE *3–6mm wide.*
FLOWERING TIME *May–July.*
LEAVES *Alternate, heart-shaped; dark green.*
FRUIT *Red, fleshy berries.*
SIMILAR SPECIES *Ivy (p.112), which has flowers in umbels; Hedge Bindweed (p.135), which has trumpet-shaped white flowers.*

Yellow Flag

Iris pseudacorus (Iridaceae)

This marsh-loving iris may be identified by its base, where the flat leaves grow one inside another, layered to form a chevron pattern. The leaves are bright grey-green, each with a slightly raised midrib. There is no mistaking the brilliant yellow iris flowers. Each has three fall petals with faint brown markings, supported by a green leaf-like spathe, and three erect standard petals that are smaller and unmarked.

THRIVES in marshes and other wet places such as pond and river banks, margins of reedbeds, and ditches.

pointed leaf tip

flattened, sword-like leaf

orange-brown seeds

brown fruit capsule

brilliant yellow flowers

PERENNIAL

> **PLANT HEIGHT** 1–1.5m.
> **FLOWER SIZE** 7–10cm wide.
> **FLOWERING TIME** June–August.
> **LEAVES** Basal, flat; bright grey-green.
> **FRUIT** Three-parted capsule that splits to reveal hard, irregular orange-brown seeds.
> **SIMILAR SPECIES** Sweet Flag (p.194) has tiny flowers; yellow form of Stinking Iris (below).

Stinking Iris

Iris foetidissima (Iridaceae)

The tufts of strap-like leaves of the Stinking Iris are evergreen, and most easily seen in winter. They give off a strong smell like that of roast meat and a more offensive odour if crushed. Yellow and purple petals of the flowers sometimes occur as dull violet-brown. The inner petals are actually modified styles. Berries remain until early winter.

GROWS in shady corners of woodland, alongside hedgerows and embankments, in dampish areas.

purple outer petals

PERENNIAL

dark-veined purple petals

notched, yellowish inner "petals"

numerous bright red berries

3-parted fruit capsule

> **PLANT HEIGHT** 40–70cm.
> **FLOWER SIZE** 5.5–8cm wide.
> **FLOWERING TIME** May–July.
> **LEAVES** Basal and alternate, sword-shaped, up to 2.5cm wide, strong-smelling.
> **FRUIT** Three-parted capsule, with red berries.
> **SIMILAR SPECIES** A form with yellow flowers, (var. citrina) is a frequent garden escape.

Sweet Flag

Acorus calamus (Araceae)

The leaves strongly resemble those of other waterside plants, but are wrinkled on one side and smell of tangerines when crushed. The rarely produced flower spike is borne halfway up the plant. It is cylindrical, appearing at an angle to the flattened stems, and consists of a tightly packed cone of very tiny yellow flowers, each with six stamens.

INHABITS *the muddy margins of reedbeds, ponds, and slow-flowing streams, often among other similar-looking plants.*

section of narrow, stiff leaf

wrinkled on one side

PERENNIAL

tapered point

yellow flower spike

PLANT HEIGHT *80–120cm.*
FLOWER SIZE *Flower spike up to 9cm long.*
FLOWERING TIME *June–July.*
LEAVES *Basal, sword-shaped, with distinct midrib and wrinkled surface on one side.*
FRUIT *Berry, but does not ripen in Britain.*
SIMILAR SPECIES *Branched Bur-reed (right), Yellow Flag (p.193), and Reed Mace (right).*

Lords and Ladies

Arum maculatum (Araceae)

The arrow-shaped leaves of this plant are a deep green colour. They are often spotted with dark blotches, and have a wrinkled surface. A large yellow-green bract (spathe) pushes up from the base of the plant and unfurls to reveal the brown flower spike (spadix). This is warm and scented to attract flies down to the true flowers, which are hidden in the bulge below.

FOUND *in shade in woodland or scrub, alongside hedgerows, particularly close to paths, or on dry banks.*

PERENNIAL

large yellow-green spathe

club-shaped brown spadix

wrinkled, arrow-shaped leaves

deep green leaf

occasional black blotches

green to orange-red fruit

berries borne on short stalk

PLANT HEIGHT *15–35cm.*
FLOWER SIZE *Spathe 10–20cm long.*
FLOWERING TIME *April–May.*
LEAVES *Basal, arrow-shaped and wrinkled; dark green, often with dark blotches.*
FRUIT *Red berries.*
SIMILAR SPECIES *Large Cuckoo Pint (A. italicum), which has white-veined leaves.*

Branched Bur-reed

Sparganium erectum (Sparganiceae)

The leaves of this plant are similar to those of iris and bulrush. The flowers, however, are distinctive. The branched flowering stem has a number of female flowerheads ranged along it, with the male flowerheads at the top. As the fruit is formed, the female flowerheads swell to become a spiky ball or bur. The plant spreads with the aid of rhizomes.

FOUND *on the edges of freshwater ponds, ditches, lakes, slow-moving rivers, and streams; may grow among other plants with similar leaves.*

male flowerheads in spikes

round female flowerheads in clusters

strap-shaped leaf

white anthers

PERENNIAL

PLANT HEIGHT *80–150cm.*
FLOWER SIZE *1–2cm wide.*
FLOWERING TIME *June–August.*
LEAVES *Basal, strap-shaped, stiff, and erect.*
FRUIT *Single-seeded drupe, borne on the female bur.*
SIMILAR SPECIES *Unbranched Bur-reed (S. emersum), is smaller with floating leaves.*

Reed Mace

Typha latifolia (Typhaceae)

This robust, often invasive plant is also known as Bulrush. It has stout stems and grows from rhizomes in shallow water or mud. The leaves are erect and flat. The flowers are distinctive, borne in two dense spikes, one above the other. The dark brown, felty "cigar" is actually a collection of female flowers. The yellow male flowers appear in a narrower spike immediately above this.

PROLIFERATES *in wetland habitats such as pond and river margins, marshes, and ditches, always with its base in water.*

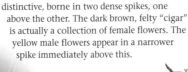

dense, cylindrical spikes of flowers

tall, sword-like leaves

yellow male flowering spike

fruiting spike

cigar-like female spike

PERENNIAL

PLANT HEIGHT *1.5–2.8m.*
FLOWER SIZE *Female spike up to 15cm long.*
FLOWERING TIME *July–August.*
LEAVES *Mostly basal; flat, sword-like, and erect; up to 2cm wide; greyish green.*
FRUIT *Capsule containing light, fluffy seeds.*
SIMILAR SPECIES *Branched Bur-reed (above), which has yellow-green flowerheads.*

Broad-leaved Helleborine

OCCURS in shady areas of deciduous woodland, scrub, roadsides, and banks, preferring chalky soil.

narrow bract under flower

Epipactis helleborine (Orchidaceae)

This *Epipactis* species is unusual in that it grows and flowers at the darkest, shadiest time of year, when most other woodland plants are dormant. These orchids are able to do this with the help of a fungus around their roots that provides them with extra nourishment. Up to 50 flowers are borne in long spikes, each a complex shape of greenish sepals and petals, with a large pink, crimson, or white lower lip, recurved at the tip.

greenish sepals

winged side petals

recurved lower lip

broad, veined leaf

smooth fruit capsule

PERENNIAL

PLANT HEIGHT *50–80cm.*
FLOWER SIZE *Lower lip 1cm long.*
FLOWERING TIME *July–August.*
LEAVES *Spirally arranged, oval to elliptical, strongly veined.*
FRUIT *Pendent, many-seeded capsule.*
SIMILAR SPECIES *Marsh Helleborine (E. palustris), which has narrower leaves.*

Bird's-nest Orchid

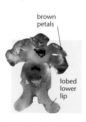

FOUND in shady areas of deciduous woodland, particularly beech but also hazel. Blends into leaf-litter so is difficult to spot.

Neottia nidus-avis (Orchidaceae)

Lacking chlorophyll, this orchid instead derives its nutrients from a fungus within its root system that breaks down dead organic material. The whole plant is yellowish brown. There are numerous flowers, each with brown petals, a long lower lip, and small, papery bracts at the base. The leaves are reduced to papery, overlapping scales on the stem and the mass of tangled roots resembles a bird's nest.

brown petals

lobed lower lip

PERENNIAL

many-flowered spike

yellowish brown stem

PLANT HEIGHT *20–40cm.*
FLOWER SIZE *Lower lip 8–12mm long.*
FLOWERING TIME *May–July.*
LEAVES *Alternate, papery scales.*
FRUIT *Capsule, containing many seeds.*
SIMILAR SPECIES *Common Broomrape (Orobanche minor); other broomrapes, which have tubular, two-lipped flowers.*

Common Twayblade

Listera ovata (Orchidaceae)

This common and widespread orchid bears only two prominently veined, broad, oval leaves near the base of the plant and produces a single flowering stem, at the top of which is a spike of numerous yellow-green flowers. Each flower has a long, grooved, and deeply forked lower lip. The leaves are more noticeable than the flower stem, but may quickly be devoured by insects.

OCCURS in semi-shaded woods, scrub, meadows, marshy ground, and dunes, on a variety of soils.

numerous flowers on upper stem

unbranched veins

tall, erect stem

forked lower lip of flower

PERENNIAL

PLANT HEIGHT 20–60cm.
FLOWER SIZE Lip 7–15mm long.
FLOWERING TIME May–July.
LEAVES Basal, simple, two broad, oval leaves on each plant.
FRUIT Capsule, containing many tiny seeds.
SIMILAR SPECIES Man Orchid (Aceras anthropophorum) has long, narrow leaves.

Autumn Lady's-tresses

Spiranthes spiralis (Orchidaceae)

This small orchid is difficult to spot even in short grassland, but once seen is easily recognized. Numerous tiny flowers, each with a frilly-margined lower lip, are borne in a spiral up the spike. The greyish green leaves, in a basal rosette, wither by flowering time, but the following year's rosette is often present next to the flowering spike.

THRIVES in some years, absent in others, on dry grassland, lawns, and dunes, preferring chalky soil.

white flowers

flower spike

oval, fleshy leaf

yellowish lower lip

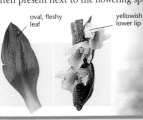

PERENNIAL

PLANT HEIGHT 8–15cm.
FLOWER SIZE 4–6mm long.
FLOWERING TIME August–September.
LEAVES Basal rosette, scale leaves on stem.
FRUIT Capsule containing many tiny seeds.
SIMILAR SPECIES Creeping Lady's-tresses (Goodyera repens), of N. Scotland, which has fewer flowers in a less obvious spiral.

Lesser Butterfly Orchid

Platanthera bifolia (Orchidaceae)

GROWS in various habitats such as bogs, heaths, pastures, and woodland margins; on a variety of soils.

This attractive orchid has just two oblong, shiny leaves arising from the base. It produces a stout spike, with a few scale-like leaves, bearing vanilla-scented, creamy or greenish white flowers. The outer sepals are thinly triangular, but most noticeable is the very long, thin, unlobed lower lip, increasingly green towards the tip, with a long spur behind. The two small yellow anthers are parallel to each other.

butterfly-like flower

slender, unlobed lip

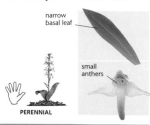

narrow basal leaf

small anthers

PERENNIAL

PLANT HEIGHT *30–45cm.*
FLOWER SIZE *Lower lip 6–12mm long; spur 2.5–3cm.*
FLOWERING TIME *May–July.*
LEAVES *Basal, oblong.*
FRUIT *Capsule containing many tiny seeds.*
SIMILAR SPECIES *Greater Butterfly Orchid (P. chlorantha), which is larger in all parts.*

Fragrant Orchid

Gymnadenia conopsea (Orchidaceae)

SEEN singly or in large, loose colonies on dry grassland and scrub, preferring slopes on chalky soil; also in undisturbed fens.

This orchid's densely packed flowering spikes vary in size, but always have a delicate vanilla scent. Each pink, sometimes lilac, flower has a lower lip with three small, round lobes, wing-like sepals at either side, and a long, slender curving spur drooping down behind. The leaves are bright green, without any spots or markings, and are grooved along the middle.

PERENNIAL

erect stem

small flowers in dense spikes

long, narrow leaf

3-lobed lower lip

long spur

PLANT HEIGHT *20–40cm*
FLOWER SIZE *Lower lip 4–6mm long.*
FLOWERING TIME *June–July.*
LEAVES *Alternate, simple, and linear.*
FRUIT *Capsule containing many tiny seeds*
SIMILAR SPECIES *Pyramidal Orchid (right), which has shorter, more conical flower spikes of a darker colour.*

Common Spotted Orchid

Dactylorhiza fuchsii (Orchidaceae)

Even before the flowering spike has developed, this orchid is identifiable by the dark blotches on its shiny, deep green leaves. Borne in spikes, the flowers have wing-like sepals set high up, and a lower lip deeply lobed into three and patterned with looping lines and dots. The colour of the petals ranges from white and pink to reddish purple, but always with the dots on the lower lip.

OCCURS *in colonies in open woods, meadows, fens, and marshes, on road verges and among scrub, on chalky soil.*

narrow leaf

rounded blotches

pattern on lip

flowers in dense spikes

solitary stem

PERENNIAL

PLANT HEIGHT *20–45cm.*
FLOWER SIZE *Lower lip 1–1.2cm long.*
FLOWERING TIME *June–July.*
LEAVES *Basal rosette at first, then alternate.*
FRUIT *Capsule containing many tiny seeds.*
SIMILAR SPECIES *Heath Spotted Orchid (D. maculata), which has circular, brown leaf spots and a shallow-lobed lip.*

Pyramidal Orchid

Anacamptis pyramidalis (Orchidaceae)

The triangular shape of the newly formed flower spike gives this plant its name. The small, neat flowers are pale pink or, more often, deep pink, or cerise. They have no veins or spots but each has a long, slender spur at the back, from which butterflies and moths sip nectar.

PROLIFERATES *in open, grassy places, lightly grazed pastures, dunes, downland, scrub, and on roadsides. Prefers well-drained, chalky soil.*

dense, conical flowerhead

tapered point

unspotted leaf

deep pink flower

3-lobed lip

PERENNIAL

sheath-like upper leaf

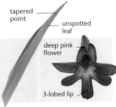

PLANT HEIGHT *20–40cm.*
FLOWER SIZE *Lip 6–8mm long.*
FLOWERING TIME *June–August.*
LEAVES *Alternate, lance-shaped, pale green.*
FRUIT *Capsule containing many tiny seeds.*
SIMILAR SPECIES *Fragrant Orchid (left), which has longer, cylindrical flower spikes that are lighter in colour.*

Early Purple Orchid

Orchis mascula (Orchidaceae)

GROWS *singly or in loose colonies in semi-shady, grassy places such as woodland, scrub, and road verges, and sometimes out in open grassland.*

Often the first orchid to appear in spring, this plant may also be identified by the long, dark purple blotches on the dark green leaves. The lower lip of the flower appears narrow, as it is folded back, and it has a pale patch towards the base, with a variable amount of darker spots. The sepals, with a long spur behind them, are swept upwards like wings. Their fragrance is pleasant at first but soon degenerates to an animal-like odour. They often grow among Bluebells (p.187), flowering at the same time, but may also be seen in more open situations.

PERENNIAL

long, narrow spike of flowers

erect stem

long dark blotches

dark green leaf

upward-pointing spur

paler patch on lip

NOTE

The round tubers of the Early Purple Orchid contain a great deal of starch; traditionally, this was ground and mixed with milk, honey, and spices to make a nutritious drink called "salep".

PLANT HEIGHT *20–50cm.*
FLOWER SIZE *Lower lip 7–9mm long.*
FLOWERING TIME *April–May.*
LEAVES *Basal, lance-shaped.*
FRUIT *Capsule containing many tiny seeds.*
SIMILAR SPECIES *Green-winged Orchid (O. morio), which has green-tinged sepals with purple veins; Common Spotted (left), Broad-leaved (left), and Lapland Marsh (D. lapponica) Orchids all have spotted leaves.*

Fly Orchid

Ophrys insectifera (Orchidaceae)

Often hidden in shady undergrowth, this slender orchid can be difficult to spot. It has narrow, pale green leaves and a single long flower stalk bearing a loose spire of 2–12 narrow flowers that look like flies. They have green sepals and a long, three-lobed chocolate-brown lip with a violet patch (speculum).

FOUND *in semi-shaded grasses in woodland, coppices, road verges, and scrub; on chalky soil.*

PERENNIAL

widely spaced flowers

green sepals

violet patch

lobed lip resembles a fly

slender flower stalk

PLANT HEIGHT *30–60cm.*
FLOWER SIZE *Lip 9–13mm long.*
FLOWERING TIME *May–June.*
LEAVES *Alternate, simple, thin and narrow.*
FRUIT *Capsule containing many tiny seeds.*
SIMILAR SPECIES *Bee Orchid (below); Early Spider Orchid (O. sphegodes), which has a much larger lower lip.*

Bee Orchid

Ophrys apifera (Orchidaceae)

The *Ophrys* species of orchids have an unusual flower shape, which mimics the form of a bee or wasp. In most species, the flower is pollinated by male insects, but in the Bee Orchid – unusually – the flowers are almost always self-pollinated. Each flower has three pink sepals, a narrow green hood, and a large, bulbous, dark chocolate brown lip.

INHABITS *woodland margins, meadows, embankments, and road verges; prefers chalky soil.*

leaf edges turned inwards

flowers in loose spikes

green hood

shiny, pale green leaf

furry, dark brown lip

3 prominent pink sepals

yellow markings on lip

PERENNIAL

PLANT HEIGHT *25–45cm.*
FLOWER SIZE *Lower lip 1–1.3cm long.*
FLOWERING TIME *May–June.*
LEAVES *Mostly basal, forming loose rosettes, oval to lance-shaped; pale green.*
FRUIT *Capsule containing many tiny seeds.*
SIMILAR SPECIES *Late Spider Orchid (O. fuciflora) has a broader lip with a central tooth.*

Toothed Wrack

Fucus serratus (Phaeophyceae)

This seaweed is distinctive, flattened, and olive-green. The reproducing male plants, however, assume a golden colour from the swollen reproductive frond tips. After reproduction the fertile fronds are shed, and this, along with damage from storms, leads to a lower dominance of this species. The fronds are often covered by the white spiral tubes of the worm *Spirorbis spirorbis*.

INHABITS *sheltered rocky shores; dominant below the Bladder Wrack zone.*

frond split into two

serrated frond edge

SIZE *Length to 70cm, or up to 2m in very sheltered conditions; frond about 2cm wide.*
REPRODUCTION *May–October, peaking in late summer.*
DISTRIBUTION *All British and Irish coasts.*
SIMILAR SPECIES *None – the serrated frond margins distinguish it from the bladderless Horned Wrack (F. ceranoides), and Spiral Wrack (F. spiralis).*

Bladder Wrack

Fucus vesiculosus (Phaeophyceae)

A common mid-shore seaweed, the Bladder Wrack has distinctive pairs of gas-filled bladders on its fronds, on either side of the midrib. The bladders help the frond to reach sunlight at high tide, when light penetration is limited by sediment stirred up by waves. In season, the tips of the fronds develop swollen, warty, forked reproductive bodies.

OCCURS *in the middle intertidal zone of rocky shores; also in estuaries and brackish water.*

almost spherical, paired gas bladders

dark olive-brown fronds

prominent midrib on frond

SIZE *Length to 1.5m; shorter with increased exposure.*
REPRODUCTION *Mid-winter to late summer.*
DISTRIBUTION *All British and Irish coasts.*
SIMILAR SPECIES *On exposed shores, a short, bladderless form occurs, which is similar to Horned Wrack (F. ceranoides), but the latter is found only in sheltered, low-salinity water.*

Oarweed

Laminaria digitata (Laminariaceae)

Also known as Tangle or Sea Girdle, this familiar kelp attaches to rocks by means of a domed, claw-like holdfast, often home to colonies of barnacles and algae. The smooth, flexible stalk, or stipe, is oval in cross-section and gives rise to broad, glossy dark brown fronds that are divided into finger-like segments and lack a midrib.

ATTACHES to rocks on the lower shore down to a depth of 20m in clear waters.

glossy brown fronds

frond variably divided

frond battered by wave action

SIZE Length to 2m.
REPRODUCTION By spores, year round.
DISTRIBUTION Common on all coasts of Britain and Ireland except Yorkshire to Kent.
SIMILAR SPECIES Young L. hyperborea, which has a brittle stipe that is circular in cross-section and lighter brown fronds; L. saccharina, which has unlobed fronds with ruffled edges.

Knotted Wrack

Ascophyllum nodosum (Phaeophyceae)

Sometimes known as Egg Wrack, the single, egg-shaped, gas-filled flotation bladders of the Knotted Wrack are found at intervals along the strap-like frond. It is often found on the mid-shore, brown seaweed zone, especially where it is sheltered. In exposed conditions, it still survives, but is reduced to a tattered tuft of stem bases.

OCCURS on rocky shores, sometimes extending into estuaries.

raisin-like reproductive bodies

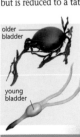

older bladder

young bladder

branched frond

SIZE To 2m long, although can be longer in favoured areas.
REPRODUCTION April–June.
DISTRIBUTION All British and Irish coasts.
SIMILAR SPECIES None, although small, battered examples could be mistaken for Channelled Wrack (Pelvetia canaliculata), but the stalked reproductive bodies of Knotted Wrack are distinctive.

Carragheen

Chondrus crispus (Rhodophyceae)

With flat fronds, dividing into two up to five times, Carragheen, or Irish Moss, is fan-shaped. However, its shape, size, and colour vary according to habitat conditions: smaller plants with narrower lobes are found in more exposed conditions. It turns green in strong sunlight. Underwater, the tips of the fronds are often iridescent.

OCCURS *on rocky shores, at lower intertidal levels, in rock pools, and estuaries.*

PERENNIAL

divided fronds

fronds usually purplish red

flat fronds

runded frond tips

narrow stalk

SIZE *Length to 20cm.*
REPRODUCTION *Autumn–Spring; reproductive bodies are small swellings on one side of the frond tips.*
DISTRIBUTION *All British and Irish coasts.*
SIMILAR SPECIES *False Irish Moss (Mastocarpus stellatus), which has curved branch margins and obvious reproductive outgrowths at the frond tips.*

Gut Weed

Enteromorphia intestinalis (Ulvophyceae)

Previously and perhaps more commonly known as *Enteromorpha intestinalis*, Gut Weed forms an inflated frond, resembling an intestine. Its holdfast is small and disc-like, and may become detached from the rock allowing this seaweed to rise to the water surface, where it continues to grow in floating masses. It requires high nutrient levels, and so is very well developed near sewage outfalls.

ATTACHES *to rocks and stones on sandy or muddy shores; abundant in low-salinity areas.*

ANNUAL

pale to bright green fronds

tube-like fronds

irregular constrictions

SIZE *Length to 80cm.*
REPRODUCTION *All year round, but concentrated in the summer in the north; coordinated with the phases of the moon.*
DISTRIBUTION *All British and Irish coasts.*
SIMILAR SPECIES *Other members of the genus* Enteromorpha *can be very similar and difficult to tell apart. E. linza and E. compressa are similar but have flattened fronds.*

Sea-lettuce

Ulva lactuca (Ulvophyceae)

A widespread green seaweed, tolerant of most conditions except extreme exposure, Sea-lettuce is found throughout the intertidal zone. It thrives in brackish water, but is also found in shallow inshore waters. Its flat frond is often split or divided, and has a wavy edge. Fertile plants can be recognized by changes to the marginal colour of the frond, becoming yellowish green in male plants and dark green in the female.

INHABITS *brackish water; found in estuaries and on rocky shores; also free-floating.*

PERENNIAL

translucent green frond

wavy edge

dark green female plant

SIZE *Length to 40cm.*
REPRODUCTION *Vegetative and sexual; all year round.*
DISTRIBUTION *Ubiquitous on all British and Irish coasts.*
SIMILAR SPECIES *Monostroma grevillei, which is smaller, funnel-shaped; Udotea petiolata, which has long-stalked fronds.*

Bog Moss

Sphagnum palustre (Sphagnaceae)

One of the commonest mosses, occurring throughout the British Isles, Bog Moss, one of several closely related sphagnum mosses, can tolerate a wide range of dampness. The unique character of these mosses is that the individual stems continue growing upwards while the lowest parts die back to form peat. They can hold up to 20 times their own weight in water – each tiny leaf contains some empty cells and acts like a sponge. Bog Moss has robust, branched stems, crowded with concave leaves.

OCCURS *in wet places such as bogs, fens, damp hollows, and flushes in woods on wet heaths.*

whitish green leaves

SIZE *Stems to 25cm high.*
REPRODUCTION *Small black spore-producing capsules in summer.*
DISTRIBUTION *Throughout the British Isles; internationally important populations found in Britain and Ireland.*
SIMILAR SPECIES *Distinguishing Sphagnum species often needs microscopic examination.*

Common Hair Cap

Polytrichum commune (Polytrichaceae)

Easily recognized, no other moss forms such tall tussocks as the Common Hair Cap. It has strong, erect stems and toothed leaves, each with a transparent sheathing base. The fruiting capsules, with their golden pointed caps, are a common sight in summer, young capsules being particularly conspicuous as they are covered by a golden-haired cover or calyptra.

FORMS *tussocks in bogs, damp heath, moorland, and in damp acid flushes in woodland.*

PERENNIAL

narrow leaves

box-shaped capsule

stalk up to 12cm

SIZE *Erect stems to 50cm high.*
REPRODUCTION *Spores in beaked, box-shaped, long-stalked fruiting capsules.*
DISTRIBUTION *Throughout the British Isles.*
SIMILAR SPECIES Polytrichum formosum, *which is similar in appearance when it is in luxuriant growth, but has shorter stems and capsule stalks.*

Large White-moss

Leucobryum glaucum (Leucobryaceae)

The Large White-moss can be easily recognized, even from a distance. The individual stems support lance-shaped leaves that taper from a broad base to a pointed tip. The tightly packed, greyish green cushions, which form patches, are only very loosely attached to the soil and occasionally become detached. They can continue to survive and if the cushions overturn, they can form "moss balls".

INHABITS *woodland floors, under beech, oak, and conifers, and bare peaty slopes and bogs in moorland.*

PERENNIAL

moss ball

dense cushion

SIZE *Patches varying from a few centimetres to 1m wide.*
REPRODUCTION *Fruiting capsules are rarely produced, in autumn.*
DISTRIBUTION *Throughout the British Isles, especially associated with beech woods.*
SIMILAR SPECIES *None.*

Mnium hornum

Mnium hornum (Mniaceae)

This very common woodland moss can be seen in most woods in the British Isles. In spring, the pale green young leaves contrast strongly with the rather dull, darker older leaves. Individual plants are either male or female, the females, producing spore-bearing cylindrical capsules borne on reddish stalks.

FOUND *on soil, rocks, and tree bases, in all types of woodland with acidic conditions.*

PERENNIAL

pendulous capsule

leaves taper at tip

toothed leaves

SIZE *Individual stems to 4cm high, leaves 4–5mm long.*
REPRODUCTION *Cylindrical fruiting capsules borne on 2–6-cm long reddish stalks.*
DISTRIBUTION *Throughout the British Isles.*
SIMILAR SPECIES *Catherine's Moss (Atrichum undulatum), which has narrow, wavy-edged leaves and curved capsules.*

Cord Moss

Funaria hygrometrica (Funariaceae)

A common, tufted species, Cord Moss has sharp-tipped leaves, the upper ones being larger. Its favoured habitat is bonfire sites, where it forms pale green carpets with a profusion of pear-shaped capsules on yellow stalks. The capsules are green at first, changing to yellow-brown, and becoming strongly furrowed and brown when fully mature.

COLONIZES *bare soil in woods, moorland, heaths, greenhouses, and gardens; cracks on roadsides, and bonfire sites.*

immature green capsule

mature brown capsules

yellow stalk

PERENNIAL

SIZE *Tufts 2–15mm high.*
REPRODUCTION *Spores produced in pear-shaped capsules on long stalk or seta to 3–5cm tall.*
DISTRIBUTION *Throughout the British Isles.*
SIMILAR SPECIES *Leptobryum pyriforme, which is less common and has extremely narrow leaves and glossy red-brown capsules.*

Common Tamasisk Moss

Thuidium tamariscinum (Thuidiaceae)

GROWS *in shady places on the ground in woodland, particularly on heavy clay soil.*

The stems of this species are regularly branched into three divisions, giving it a very fern-like appearance. The bright green or golden "fronds" are roughly triangular in outline. The main stems are dark green or almost black, with broadly triangular or heart-shaped leaves; the leaves on the branches are narrower, tapering to a long point. All the leaves are toothed towards the tip.

fern-like appearance

SIZE *To 2–3cm high, branches to 20cm long.*
REPRODUCTION *Fruit capsules are extremely rare.*
DISTRIBUTION *Throughout the British Isles.*
SIMILAR SPECIES Hylocomnium splendens, *which has distinctive red stems and is particularly common in upland woods in the north and west of the British Isles.*

Marchantia polymorpha

Marchantia polymorpha (Marchantiaceae)

This shiny green, ribbon-like plant is one of Britain's commonest liverworts. Its stems repeatedly divide in two as they grow. Throughout the year, the plant reproduces asexually by forming gemmae, which look like tiny green eggs. However, in spring and summer, it sprouts male and female reproductive structures with stalks.

FOUND *in marshy ground and wet streamsides, on soil in flowerpots, outside or under glass.*

female reproductive structure with spreading rays

spores released from underside

female structure

cup containing gemmae

SIZE *Width of stem (thallus) 1–3cm.*
STEM *Glossy dark to light green, with a central midrib. Surface has a hexagonal pattern, created by internal air chambers.*
REPRODUCTIVE STRUCTURES *3–4cm high.*
DISTRIBUTION *Throughout the British Isles.*
SIMILAR SPECIES *Crescent-cup Liverwort (right), which has narrower ribbons.*

Crescent-cup Liverwort

Lunularia cruciata (Lunulariaceae)

A familiar sight in greenhouses and damp corners in gardens, this bright green liverwort is thought to have arrived in Britain in Roman times. It gets its name from its crescent-shaped gemmae cups – reproductive structures that look like minute fingernails. Like other ribbon-shaped liverworts, it grows by repeatedly dividing in two, but it rarely forms spores.

GROWS *along shady stream-banks, but is more often found in flowerpots and under glass.*

densely-branched stems often overlap

gemmae produced in cups

SIZE *Width of stem (thallus) 0.5–1cm; spread 5–15cm.*
STEM *Bright green, except when dry, without a pronounced midrib.*
REPRODUCTIVE STRUCTURES *Crescent-shaped gemma cups.*
DISTRIBUTION *Throughout the British Isles.*
SIMILAR SPECIES *None.*

Pellia epiphylla

Pellia epiphylla (Pelliaceae)

In early spring, this shade-loving liverwort is often covered with black spore capsules, which grow on translucent hair-like stalks. The plant itself is a deep glossy green. Given enough space, its stems lie flat, but when crowded the plant often becomes cushion-like, as the stems arch upwards to catch the light. The capsules split open when the spores are ripe, revealing a tuft of brownish hairs.

FREQUENTLY *seen on damp, acidic ground close to streams, and in waterlogged soil in upland areas. Absent from limestone regions.*

lobes often overlap

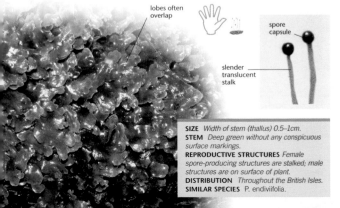

spore capsule

slender translucent stalk

SIZE *Width of stem (thallus) 0.5–1cm.*
STEM *Deep green without any conspicuous surface markings.*
REPRODUCTIVE STRUCTURES *Female spore-producing structures are stalked; male structures are on surface of plant.*
DISTRIBUTION *Throughout the British Isles.*
SIMILAR SPECIES *P. endiviifolia.*

Bracken

Pteridium aquilinum (Dennstaedtiaceae)

GROWS *abundantly on open hillsides, moors, and heaths, and in open woods.*

Often covering entire hillsides, Bracken is difficult to eradicate and is regarded as a pest. It grows from branching rhizomes, which produce tall fronds. The young, pale green, tri-pinnate fronds first appear as "shepherds' crooks", unfurling as they grow. The undersides of the blades are hairy; the upper sides darker and hairless. Pinnule margins are untoothed and inrolled.

sori covered by inrolled edge

autumn colour

unfurling pinnae

sturdy frond

PLANT HEIGHT *Up to 4m.*
FROND DIVISION *Tripinnate.*
SORI *Continuous around, and covered by inrolled pinnule margins.*
SPORES RIPE *August–October.*
DISTRIBUTION *Throughout the British Isles. It can tolerate a wide range of climates.*
SIMILAR SPECIES *None.*

Male Fern

Dryopteris filix-mas (Dryopteridaceae)

FLOURISHES *in woods, hedgebanks, and screes, and among rocks.*

One of Britain's commonest ferns, the Male Fern has a tuft of fronds, shaped like a large shuttlecock, arising from its rootstock. Pointed, pale brown scales grow on the stalks. The bi-pinnate frond blade tapers at both ends and is mid-green in colour. Individual pinnules have broad bases, blunt tips, and toothed margins.

fronds arranged like a shuttlecock

large sori close to midrib

unfurled young frond

PLANT HEIGHT *Up to 1.2m.*
FROND DIVISION *Bipinnate.*
SORI *On veins on the underside of pinnule, covered by a kidney-shaped indusium.*
SPORES RIPE *August–November.*
DISTRIBUTION *Throughout the British Isles.*
SIMILAR SPECIES *Several Dryopteris species, especially Golden-scaled Male Fern (D. affinis).*

Soft Shield-fern

Polystichum setiferum (Dryopteridaceae)

The fronds of Soft Shield-fern grow in a drooping circle around the top of the rootstock. Large, pale brown, sharply pointed scales clothe the stalk. The bi-pinnate frond blade is soft, coloured mid-green above and paler beneath, especially when fresh. The pinnules have short stalks and a blunt angle at the base, with a much enlarged lobe on one side. The pinnule teeth end in fine hair-like points.

PREFERS *wetter areas, growing in woods, hedge banks, and rocky places.*

pinnule teeth with hair-like points

dopping frond tip

PLANT HEIGHT *Up to 1.5m.*
FROND DIVISION *Bipinnate.*
SORI *On either side of pinnule midrib; covered by a round indusium.*
SPORES RIPE *July–September.*
DISTRIBUTION *England, Wales, southern Scotland and Ireland.*
SIMILAR SPECIES *P. aculeatum.*

Hard Fern

Blechnum spicant (Blechnaceae)

Hard Fern is a distinctive, tufted species with two types of frond. Bright green, shiny, sterile fronds spread out over the ground, forming rosettes, and surround erect, narrow, fertile fronds. Both types of blade are pinnate and hairless, the fertile fronds bearing linear sori, extending from the pinna base to its tip and covered by linear indusia. The sterile fronds are vergreen, while the fertile ones die in autumn.

FAVOURS *acid soils, on heaths and moors and in woods, especially in upland areas.*

tufted growth

SIZE *Sterile fronds to 15cm, fertile fronds to 75cm.*
FROND DIVISION *Pinnate.*
SORI *Linear, extending the length of the pinna, with a linear indusium.*
SPORES RIPE *August–November.*
DISTRIBUTION *Throughout the British Isles.*
SIMILAR SPECIES *None.*

Common Polypody

Polypodium vulgare (Polypodiaceae)

PREFERS *acid soils, and is found growing on tree trunks, walls, rocks, and banks.*

Common Polypody is seen in small groups of evergreen fronds. The pinnae are straight-sided, shallowly toothed and almost joined at the base, often with blunt tips. Most of the pinnae are of equal length, tapering gradually along the final quarter or so of the blade to the tip. Round sori are borne on either side of the midrib, with no indusia.

pinnae almost joined at base

round sori

SIZE *Frond length to 25cm.*
FROND DIVISION *Pinnate.*
SORI *Round, on either side of the midrib, without an indusium.*
SPORES RIPE *July–September.*
DISTRIBUTION *Throughout the British Isles.*
SIMILAR SPECIES: *Western (P. interjectum) and Southern Polypody (P. cambricum).*

Hart's-tongue

Phyllitis scolopendrium (Aspleniaceae)

GROWS *in woods, hedgebanks, rocky places, and on damp walls.*

Even in the depths of winter, the glossy, bright green fronds of Hart's-tongue brighten up dark corners in woods and rocky places, growing in dense tufts. The stalk is clothed with sharply pointed brown scales, and both stalk and midrib are dark purple-brown, becoming green towards the tip. The blade is strap-shaped and undivided, usually with wavy margins.

wavy margin on blade

sporangia in parallel rows

SIZE *Frond length to 50cm.*
FROND DIVISION *Undivided, strap-shaped.*
SORI *Linear, in pairs along the underside of veins, each covered by a linear indusium.*
SPORES RIPE *July–November.*
DISTRIBUTION *Throughout; absent from most of northern Scotland.*
SIMILAR SPECIES *None.*

Wall-rue

Asplenium ruta-muraria (Aspleniaceae)

The dark-based stalks of Wall-rue are often longer than the leaves. Persisting through the winter, the fronds grow in dense tufts and are dark green and tough. The leaflets are fan-shaped, their pinnules varying in shape, with wedge-shaped bases and rounded teeth on the edges. Linear sori are situated on the veins on the lower surface of the pinnules.

LIVES *in calcareous areas, on walls, rocks, and limestone pavements; on cracks in walls in acid soil.*

sori on veins of pinnules

dark green fronds

fan-shaped pinna

SIZE *Frond height to 15cm, usually less than 10cm.*
FROND DIVISION *Usually bipinnate.*
SORI *On veins on lower surface of pinnules.*
SPORES RIPE *June–October.*
DISTRIBUTION *Throughout; absent from much of Scotland.*
SIMILAR SPECIES *None.*

Maidenhair Spleenwort

Asplenium trichomanes (Aspleniaceae)

This attractive, evergreen fern bears tufts of pinnate fronds. The stalk is purplish black or brownish, hairless, and shiny, and the midrib has the same characteristics. Small, slightly toothed pinnae grow from each side of the midrib, giving the frond a long, linear outline. Sori lie between the midrib and the pinna margin, each covered by a linear indusium.

GROWS *in walls, on ledges, or in crevices between rocks or stones.*

rounded pinnae

linear sori

dark stalk

SIZE *Frond length to 20cm.*
FROND DIVISION *Pinnate.*
SORI *Linear, between midrib and pinna edge.*
SPORES RIPE *August–November.*
DISTRIBUTION *Throughout the British Isles.*
SIMILAR SPECIES *Green Spleenwort (A. viride), which has a green midrib and stalk.*

Common Horsetail

Equisetum arvense (Equisetaceae)

FLOURISHES *in damp, grassy and waste places and cultivated ground.*

In spring, the pale, pinkish brown, fertile stems of Common Horsetail, also called Field Horsetail, appear above ground. As they wither, the plant produces green, sterile stems. The fertile stems are unbranched and fleshy, with toothed sheaths covering the stem joints. Each fertile stem has at its tip a long, blunt-ended reproductive cone that bears the sporangia.

branched
sterile
stem

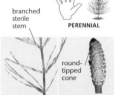

PERENNIAL

fleshy
fertile
stem

round-
tipped
cone

SIZE *Fertile stems to 25cm, sterile to 80cm.*
BRANCHES *Simple, rigid.*
CONES *On fertile stems, which appear before the sterile stems.*
SPORES RIPE *April–May.*
DISTRIBUTION *Throughout the British Isles.*
SIMILAR SPECIES *Other horsetails, especially Great Horsetail (below).*

Great Horsetail

Equisetum telmateia (Equisetaceae)

THRIVES *in damp areas with soft soil, such as clay.*

A robust, patch-forming perennial of damp places, the Great Horsetail is the largest British species of this prehistoric group of plants, which once dominated the Earth. It has distinctive fertile and sterile shoots. The unbranched, white fertile shoots, topped with a spore cone, usually emerge in spring before the more persistent, "bottlebrush-like" sterile summer shoots.

slender cone at top
of fertile stem

tall sterile stem

green branches in
dense whorls

stout
whitish
stem

PERENNIAL

SIZE *Sterile stems to 1.5m, occasionally more; fertile stems to 50cm tall.*
BRANCHES *In whorls at each stem joint.*
CONES *Narrowly conical, to 8cm long.*
SPORES RIPE *March–April.*
DISTRIBUTION *Throughout, except for most of Scotland.*
SIMILAR SPECIES *Common Horsetail (above).*

Common Couch

Elytrigia repens (Poaceae)

Also known as Twitch, Common Couch is a pernicious weed, which spreads by rhizomes, or underground stems. The fertile stems are erect and the unbranched inflorescence consists of unstalked spikelets alternately arranged on opposite sides of the axis. The flowers are usually unawned.

FLOURISHES *on cultivated and waste ground, rough grassland, roadsides, and field margins.*

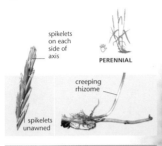

spikelets on each side of axis

PERENNIAL

creeping rhizome

spikelets unawned

spike-like inflorescence

SIZE *Up to 1.2m high.*
LEAVES *Dull green, flat, usually hairless.*
INFLORESCENCE *Spike-like; spikelets unstalked, consisting of several flowers, and alternately arranged on opposite sides of the axis; June–August.*
DISTRIBUTION *Throughout the British Isles.*
SIMILAR SPECIES *Perennial Rye-grass (below).*

Perennial Rye-grass

Lolium perenne (Poaceae)

Tolerating trampling, and re-growing strongly after cutting, Perennial Rye-grass has been widely cultivated in Britain for over 300 years. Several flowering stems grow together, giving it a tufted appearance. The inflorescence is long, narrow, and flattened, with green or purplish, flat spikelets. They are unstalked, and the flowers lack awns.

FLOURISHES *in pastures, sports grounds, and lawns, where it is often sown, and on roadsides and waste ground.*

greenish, sometimes purple, flat spikelet

PERENNIAL

narrow edge of spikelet pressed against axis

blunt ligule

SIZE *Up to 60cm or more.*
LEAVES *Hairless, flat (folded when young), with narrow projections at the base.*
INFLORESCENCE *Long, narrow, flattened; spikelets flattened, alternate. May–August.*
DISTRIBUTION *Throughout the British Isles.*
SIMILAR SPECIES *Italian Rye-grass (L. multiflorum).*

Wall Barley

Hordeum murinum (Poaceae)

The smooth stems of Wall Barley may be tufted or solitary, erect or spreading. The dense, spike-like inflorescence is composed of many groups of three spikelets, each spikelet consisting of a single long-awned flower. The middle spikelet of each group is unstalked, with both male and female reproductive organs, while the other two are male or barren. There are no sterile shoots.

GROWS *on waste ground and roadsides, particularly at the foot of walls.*

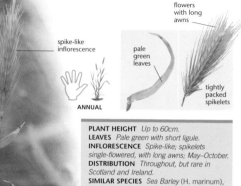

flowers with long awns

spike-like inflorescence

pale green leaves

tightly packed spikelets

ANNUAL

PLANT HEIGHT *Up to 60cm.*
LEAVES *Pale green with short ligule.*
INFLORESCENCE *Spike-like; spikelets single-flowered, with long awns; May–October.*
DISTRIBUTION *Throughout, but rare in Scotland and Ireland.*
SIMILAR SPECIES *Sea Barley (H. marinum), which has blue-green leaves.*

False Brome

Brachypodium sylvaticum (Poaceae)

The leaves of False Brome are a distinctive bright yellowish green, often hairy, and have blunt ligules. Its growth is tufted, with sterile and fertile stems. The inflorescence is a nodding spike, with stalked spikelets arranged alternately on opposite sides of the axis. Each spikelet is made up of several green, awned flowers. Although it is a plant of shady places, it often persists in the open when trees and bushes are removed.

INHABITS *woods and hedgerows, persists on roadsides and grassland after the clearing of trees and bushes.*

nodding flowerheads

yellow-green leaves

spikelet of awned flowers

PERENNIAL

PLANT HEIGHT *Up to 1m.*
LEAVES *Often hairy, with blunt ligules.*
INFLORESCENCE *Spike-like; spikelets stalked, composed of several awned flowers; flowers July–August.*
DISTRIBUTION *Throughout the British Isles.*
SIMILAR SPECIES: *Tor-grass (B. pinnatum), which has erect inflorescences.*

Timothy

Phleum pratense (Poaceae)

The tall flowering stems of this grass are smooth and usually swollen at the base. The leaves are flat with pointed tips and blunt ligules. At the top of each flowering stem is a dense flower spike, made up of many green or purple-tinged, one-flowered spikelets, each flower with two short awns. Non-flowering shoots are also produced.

GROWS *on grassland, roadsides, and waste ground, often cultivated for hay and grazing.*

cylindrical spike

tufted growth

flat, hairless leaves

spike of short-talked spikelets

PERENNIAL

PLANT HEIGHT *Up to 1.5m.*
LEAVES *Hairless, flat, with blunt ligules.*
INFLORESCENCE *Cylindrical to 20cm long; spikelets numerous, with awned flowers; flowers June–August.*
DISTRIBUTION *Throughout the British Isles.*
SIMILAR SPECIES *Smaller Cat's-tail (P. bertolonii) has pointed ligules and is smaller.*

Meadow Foxtail

Alopecurus pratensis (Poaceae)

One of the earliest flowering grasses, coming into flower in April, Meadow Foxtail is an attractive, tufted species with smooth flowering and non-flowering stems. The leaves are flat and hairless, with blunt ligules. Numerous spikelets, each containing a single flower, form a dense, soft, narrowly cylindrical inflorescence with a blunt top. The flowers are awned and softly hairy, with purple or yellow anthers.

FLOURISHES *in grassy places, especially on rich, damp soil.*

purple anthers

softly hairy inflorescence

tufted growth

PERENNIAL

PLANT HEIGHT *Up to 1.2m.*
LEAVES *Flat, hairless, with blunt ligules.*
INFLORESCENCE *Narrow, cylindrical, dense and soft; spikelets with a single awned flower produced April–June.*
DISTRIBUTION *Throughout the British Isles.*
SIMILAR SPECIES *Marsh Foxtail (A. geniculatus) has stems bent near the base.*

Sweet Vernal Grass

Anthoxanthum odoratum (Poaceae)

OCCURS in meadows, pastures, moors, and heaths, flourishing in a wide range of soils and situations.

Flowering as early as April, Sweet Vernal Grass is a variable, tufted species, producing both flowering and non-flowering shoots, the former erect, unbranched, and smooth. The narrow, yellow-green flower spikes are composed of many short-stalked, three-flowered spikelets.

flowers have 2 anthers

narrow flower spike

PERENNIAL

finely pointed leaves

spikelet with awned flowers

PLANT HEIGHT *Up to 50cm.*
LEAVES *Variable, fringed with hairs at the base, with a blunt, toothed ligule.*
INFLORESCENCE *Spike; spikelets short-stalked, three-flowered; flowers with one bent and one straight awn; April–July.*
DISTRIBUTION *Throughout the British Isles.*
SIMILAR SPECIES *None.*

Crested Dog's-tail

Cynosurus cristatus (Poaceae)

GROWS abundantly in meadows and pastures and on roadsides, on a wide range of soils.

Crested Dog's-tail is a tufted grass with erect, smooth stems and usually hairless leaves, which are rough towards the pointed tip. The ligules are short and blunt. All the spikelets grow on one side of the axis, forming a dense, stiff, spike-like inflorescence. The spikelets are of two kinds – fertile ones, consisting of several awned flowers and flattened sterile ones.

flattened spikelets

stiff, one-sided inflorescence

leaf rough towards tip

awned flowers

PERENNIAL

PLANT HEIGHT *Up to 75cm.*
LEAVES *Usually hairless, rough towards the tip, with short, blunt ligule.*
INFLORESCENCE *Spike-like, dense; sterile spikelets flattened, fertile spikelets with several awned flowers; June–August.*
DISTRIBUTION *Throughout the British Isles.*
SIMILAR SPECIES *None.*

Common Bent

Agrostis capillaris (Poaceae)

A tufted grass with a creeping rootstock, Common Bent produces erect flowering and non-flowering stems. The flowering stems are slender with an open, branching inflorescence; the hair-like branches grow in whorls, each dividing again and bearing spikelets at the tips. Awns are usually absent but the flower sometimes has a short one.

FLOURISHES *on heaths, moors, and pastures, especially on poor, acid soil.*

slender stems

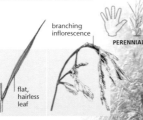

branching inflorescence

PERENNIAL

flat, hairless leaf

PLANT HEIGHT *Up to 70cm high.*
LEAVES *Smooth, with short, blunt ligules.*
INFLORESCENCE *Open, branched, and spreading; flowers usually without awns; June–August.*
DISTRIBUTION *Throughout the British Isles.*
SIMILAR SPECIES *Creeping Bent (A. stolonifera), which has long, pointed ligules.*

Marram

Ammophila arenaria (Poaceae)

Spreading widely from extensive, branching rhizomes, Marram grows in large tufts, its tough rhizomes binding the loose sand of coastal dunes. The rigid, greyish green leaves are sharply pointed and inrolled, ribbed on the upper surface and smooth beneath, with long ligules. The spike-like, cylindrical inflorescence is made up of many overlapping, one-flowered spikelets. There are no awns on the flowers.

BINDS *the loose sand of dunes with its tough, spreading rhizomes; often planted to control erosion.*

overlapping spikelets

tapering spike

sharply pointed leaf

PERENNIAL

straw-coloured spikelets

greyish green leaves

PLANT HEIGHT *Up to 1.2m.*
LEAVES *Greyish green, with sharp points, inrolled margins, and long ligules.*
INFLORESCENCE *Spike-like, straw coloured, tapering towards the tip; spikelets containing a single awnless flower; June–August.*
DISTRIBUTION *Throughout, on coasts.*
SIMILAR SPECIES *None.*

Common Reed
Phragmites australis (Poaceae)

Extensively creeping rhizomes mean that Common Reed often forms dense reedbeds, an important habitat for a wide range of other plants and animals. The nodding, purplish flowers contain silky hairs, which are especially obvious when fruiting: caught by low autumn sunlight, they create a beautiful golden glow over vast areas of wetland.

THRIVES *in fresh to brackish water, to one-third the salinity of sea water, in upper salt marshes, lagoons, and marsh ditches, often in large stands.*

silky-hairy inflorescence

dark purple inflorescence

greyish green leaf

PERENNIAL

PLANT HEIGHT Up to 3m or more.
LEAVES Greyish green, blades flat, spreading, with a fringe of short hairs as the ligule.
INFLORESCENCE Long, soft, purple, branched; spikelets with long silky hairs and unawned flowers; August–October.
DISTRIBUTION Throughout the British Isles.
SIMILAR SPECIES None.

Tufted Hair-grass
Deschampsia caespitosa (Poaceae)

As its name suggests Tufted Hair-grass is a tufted species that forms large tussocks. The leaves are ribbed on their upper surface and smooth beneath. Smooth, erect flowering stems carry a delicate inflorescence. The spikelets are two-flowered and silvery, green, or purple in colour. Each flower has a straight awn.

FLOURISHES *in damp, rough grassland, wet woods, ditches, and marshes.*

much-branched inflorescence

rough-edged leaves

PERENNIAL

hair-like branches

PLANT HEIGHT Up to 2m.
LEAVES Hairless, ribbed above, with rough ribs and margins and long, pointed ligules.
INFLORESCENCE Branched; spikelets with two awned flowers; June–August.
DISTRIBUTION Throughout the British Isles.
SIMILAR SPECIES: Wavy Hair-grass (D. flexuosa), has short, blunt ligules.

Yorkshire Fog

Holcus lanatus (Poaceae)

Softly downy all over and velvety to the touch, Yorkshire Fog is a very common grass of pastures and meadows. The erect flowering and non-flowering stems are bent at the base and grow in tufts. The leaves have a fairly short ligule. The inflorescence can be spreading or fairly compact, erect or nodding, and is branched, with short-stalked spikelets which may be pale green or whitish, but are often pinkish or purple.

GROWS *in pastures, meadows, and open woods, tolerating a wide range of soils, wet or dry.*

softly downy leaf

pinkish spikelets

stalked spikelets

erect, or drooping, inflorescence

softly downy stem

PERENNIAL

> **PLANT HEIGHT** *Up to 1m.*
> **LEAVES** *Softly downy, with a fairly short ligule.*
> **INFLORESCENCE** *Spreading or compact, branched; flowers with inconspicuous hooked awns; May–August.*
> **DISTRIBUTION** *Throughout the British Isles.*
> **SIMILAR SPECIES** *Creeping Soft-grass (H. mollis), which has densely hairy joints.*

Cock's-foot

Dactylis glomerata (Poaceae)

A very common grassland plant, Cock's-foot has compressed non-flowering shoots and sturdy flowering stems. The greyish green leaves are folded at first and later open out flat. They are rough, with pointed tips and long ligules. The one-sided inflorescence consists of stalked, oval clusters of densely grouped spikelets, the clusters growing on rough, spreading branches.

FLOURISHES *in meadows and pastures and on roadsides.*

pointed leaf tip

lowest inflorescence branch spreading

densely clustered spikelets

greyish green leaf

short awns

PERENNIAL

> **PLANT HEIGHT** *Up to 1.4m.*
> **LEAVES** *Folded at first, later flat, greyish green, rough, with long ligules.*
> **INFLORESCENCE** *One-sided, consisting of dense clusters of spikelets; spikelets with several shortly awned flowers; May–November.*
> **DISTRIBUTION** *Throughout the British Isles.*
> **SIMILAR SPECIES** *None.*

Annual Meadow-grass

Poa annua (Poaceae)

Flowering throughout the year, Annual Meadow-grass is one of Britain's commonest grasses. Its name is not always accurate, as it is sometimes a short-lived perennial. The tufted stems are usually spreading, quite often horizontal at the base and rooting at the lowest joints. Inflorescence branches are borne singly or in pairs.

GROWS on cultivated and waste ground, paths and roadsides; on a wide range of soils.

spikelet of unawned flowers

protruding anthers

hairless leaf

triangular inflorescence

ANNUAL/PERENNIAL

PLANT HEIGHT *Up to 25cm.*
LEAVES *Hairless, fresh pale green, often crinkled when young; ligule pointed.*
INFLORESCENCE *Branched; spikelets with several unawned flowers; January–December.*
DISTRIBUTION *Throughout the British Isles.*
SIMILAR SPECIES *Rough Meadow-grass (P. trivialis), which is usually much taller.*

Red Fescue

Festuca rubra (Poaceae)

Because it is so variable, Red Fescue is often divided into several subspecies. Its growth can be tufted or creeping. The leaves are extremely narrow and may be flat or folded, green, greyish green, or bluish green, their sheaths completely enfolding the stem. The ligules are very short. Small green, bluish, or purple spikelets are borne on the inflorescence branches and the flowers usually have short awns. Non-flowering shoots are also produced.

GROWS in grassy places, on sand dunes and salt marshes.

branched inflorescence

purplish spikelets

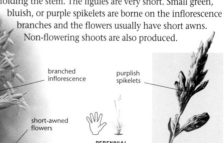

short-awned flowers

PERENNIAL

PLANT HEIGHT *Up to 75cm.*
LEAVES *Very narrow, flat or folded; sheaths tightly closed; ligules very short.*
INFLORESCENCE *Spikelets green, bluish green, or purple; May–July.*
DISTRIBUTION *Throughout the British Isles.*
SIMILAR SPECIES *Sheep's Fescue (F. ovina), another very variable species.*

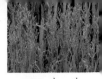

Soft Brome

Bromus hordeaceus (Poaceae)

Notable for its variability, Soft Brome is a common species, divided into several subspecies. This plant is clothed with soft hairs. Its stems are erect or spreading, slender or sturdy. The inflorescence is usually branched and bears plump spikelets with awned flowers, but may be unbranched, with a single spikelet.

INHABITS *meadow and other grassy places, roadsides, waste ground, dunes, and sea cliffs.*

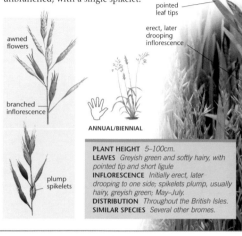

awned flowers

branched inflorescence

plump spikelets

pointed leaf tips

erect, later drooping inflorescence

ANNUAL/BIENNIAL

PLANT HEIGHT *5–100cm.*
LEAVES *Greyish green and softly hairy, with pointed tip and short ligule*
INFLORESCENCE *Initially erect, later drooping to one side; spikelets plump, usually hairy, greyish green; May–July.*
DISTRIBUTION *Throughout the British Isles.*
SIMILAR SPECIES *Several other bromes.*

False Oat-grass

Arrhenatherum elatius (Poaceae)

Also known as Tall Oat-grass, False Oat-grass is a commonly found loosely tufted perennial. It has erect, shiny flowering stems. The flat leaves have pointed tips and short ligules, and are usually hairless. Whorls of branches form a long, somewhat spreading inflorescence. Each of the shiny spikelets comprise two flowers with long, straight awns.

FLOURISHES *in grassland and on roadsides, hedgebanks, and waste ground, on most types of soil.*

inflorescence with whorls of branches

long, straight awn

two-flowered spikelets

PERENNIAL

PLANT HEIGHT *Up to 1.8m.*
LEAVES *Flat, usually hairless, with pointed tips and short, blunt ligules.*
INFLORESCENCE *Somewhat spreading; spikelets shiny; May–September.*
DISTRIBUTION *Throughout the British Isles.*
SIMILAR SPECIES *Downy Oat-grass (Helictotrichon pubescens) has pointed ligules.*

Common Club-rush

Schoenoplectus lacustris (Cyperaceae)

GROWS *in still water, in lakes, ponds, canals, and ditches, and also in slow-moving rivers.*

Also known as Bulrush, a name which was wrongly given, but is now accepted, for Reedmace (*Typha latifolia*), Common Club-rush has tall, rounded stems. The strap-like leaves grow from below the water-line. The inflorescence is branched and made up of stalked clusters of unstalked spikelets with smooth, reddish brown glumes. Each egg-shaped spikelet contains several bisexual flowers, each with three stigmas.

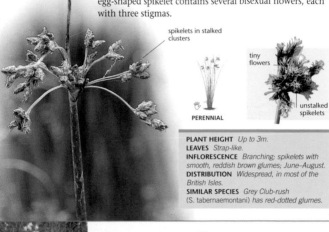

spikelets in stalked clusters

tiny flowers

unstalked spikelets

PERENNIAL

PLANT HEIGHT *Up to 3m.*
LEAVES *Strap-like.*
INFLORESCENCE *Branching; spikelets with smooth, reddish brown glumes; June–August.*
DISTRIBUTION *Widespread, in most of the British Isles.*
SIMILAR SPECIES *Grey Club-rush (S. tabernaemontani) has red-dotted glumes.*

Common Cottongrass

Eriophorum angustifolium (Cyperaceae)

FLOURISHES *in bogs and wet places on acid soil.*

Also known as Bog Cotton, Common Cottongrass is more conspicuous in fruit than in flower. Long, creeping rhizomes produce scattered, erect stems which are three-sided at the top. The leaves are dark green in summer, turning deep red in autumn. Several spikelets with smooth stalks grow together in drooping clusters. The brown fruit have long, white, unbranched hairs, brightening wet ground with their snowy tassels.

cottony white hairs on fruit

drooping clusters of fruiting spikelets

three-sided stem

PERENNIAL

PLANT HEIGHT *Up to 70cm.*
LEAVES *Three-sided at tip; short ligule.*
INFLORESCENCE *Drooping clusters; spikelets smooth stalked; flowers with yellow anthers; flowers April–May; fruits May–July.*
DISTRIBUTION *Mainly in west and north.*
SIMILAR SPECIES *Hare's-tail Cottongrass (E. vaginatum) has a single, erect spikelet.*

False Fox-sedge

Carex otrubae (Cyperaceae)

With densely tufted growth, False Fox-sedge has
three-sided stems that are smooth towards the base but
rough above. The erect, bright green leaves are keeled,
with a pointed tip, rough margins, basal projections, and
a pointed ligule. The inflorescence consists of numerous
overlapping flower spikes growing all around the
axis. Each flower has a pale orange-brown
glume with a green
midrib. The fruit is
smooth and glossy.

GROWS *in damp
grassland, marshes
and ditches;
prefers clay soil.*

fruiting
spikes
look
prickly

overlapping
flower
spikes

dense
inflorescence

PERENNIAL

PLANT HEIGHT *Up to 1m.*
LEAVES *Bright green, with rough margins.*
INFLORESCENCE *Composed of numerous
flower spikes; fruits July–September.*
DISTRIBUTION *Mainly southern and eastern
Britain and in Ireland.*
SIMILAR SPECIES *True Fox-sedge
(C. vulpina) has wings on the stem angles.*

Common Sedge

Carex nigra (Cyperaceae)

The stems of Common Sedge may be solitary or tufted. The
leaves are greyish green on both sides, with rounded ligules.
There are one or two male flower spikes at the top of the
stem, with one to four female spikes below. The female
spikes are usually overlapping, the upper ones erect,
with a few male flowers at the top, the lower
nodding, all having purple-black glumes with a
broad, pale midrib. The female flowers have
two stigmas, and the fruit has a tiny beak.

FLOURISHES *in bogs
and dune slacks and
wet, grassy places, on
acid, neutral, or
calcareous soil.*

male flower
spike

female
flower
spike

PERENNIAL

PLANT HEIGHT *Up to 70cm.*
LEAVES *Greyish green, with a rounded ligule.*
INFLORESCENCE *1–2 male flower spikes
above 1–4 female; fruits June–August.*
DISTRIBUTION *Throughout the British Isles.*
SIMILAR SPECIES *Glaucous Sedge (C. flacca)
has leaves that are green on their upper
surface, and the flowers have three stigmas.*

Remote Sedge

Carex remota (Cyperaceae)

Stems of Remote Sedge form dense tufts with drooping leaves.
Flower spikes at the top of the inflorescence are closely
grouped, lower down they are widely spaced.
Upper flower spikes are male at the top and
female below; the lower ones are entirely
female. The glumes are pale brown
with a green midrib. The leaf-like
bract below the lowest spike is
longer than the inflorescence.

INHABITS *woods,
hedgerows, shady
banks, sides of ditches,
and other damp places.*

pale brown glumes

upper
spikes

female
flower
spike

PERENNIAL

PLANT HEIGHT *Up to 75cm.*
LEAVES *Narrow and drooping, with a
rounded or blunt ligule.*
INFLORESCENCE *Long; upper flower spikes
closely grouped; glumes pale brown with a
green midrib; fruits July–August.*
DISTRIBUTION *Throughout the British Isles.*
SIMILAR SPECIES *None.*

Pendulous Sedge

Carex pendula (Cyperaceae)

The stems of this distinctive sedge are smooth and bluntly
three-sided and bear one or two male spikes above four
or five elegantly drooping, long female spikes. The male
glumes are brownish, narrow and pointed, the shorter
female glumes red-brown, with a pale midrib. There
three-sided fruit is short-beaked. The
leaves are long and strap-shaped.

FLOURISHES *in
damp woods and on
streamsides, especially
on clay soils.*

male
spike

browinsh
male
glumes

female
spike

PERENNIAL

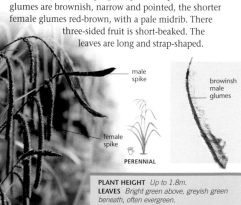

PLANT HEIGHT *Up to 1.8m.*
LEAVES *Bright green above, greyish green
beneath, often evergreen.*
INFLORESCENCE *1–2 male spikes above
4 or 5 drooping females; fruits June–July.*
DISTRIBUTION *Mostly S. and E. England.*
SIMILAR SPECIES *Wood Sedge (C. sylvatica),
which is a much smaller plant.*

Greater Pond Sedge

Carex riparia (Cyperaceae)

Growing in tufts, the stems of Greater Pond Sedge are sharply three-sided and rough. There are three to six overlapping male flower spikes, their sharply pointed glumes dark brown with a paler midrib and margins.

FORMS *large patches on riversides and pond margins, also in marshes and ditches.*

Below them are one to five overlapping female spikes; the upper stalkless, the lower stalked. The female glumes are sharply pointed and purplish brown, with a paler or green midrib.

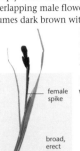

female spike

broad, erect leaves

PERENNIAL

dark brown glumes

yellow stamens

overlapping male spikes

PLANT HEIGHT *Up to 1.3m.*
LEAVES *Broad, erect, greyish green, with a blunt or rounded ligule.*
INFLORESCENCE *3–6 male spikes above 1–5 females; fruits June–September.*
DISTRIBUTION *Mainly south-east England.*
SIMILAR SPECIES *Lesser Pond Sedge (C. acutiformis) has blunt-pointed male glumes.*

Soft Rush

Juncus effusus (Juncaceae)

Widespread and common in a variety of damp habitats, Soft Rush often forms extensive patches, becoming a pest in pastures. It is a deceptive plant, for what look like leaves are, in fact, barren stems, and although the flower clusters seem to emerge part-way up the fertile stems, they are actually on the end, the green part above the cluster being a bract, not a continuation of the stem. The brown, egg-shaped fruit is normally shorter than the flowers.

GROWS *in damp, often grassy places, in overgrazed, poorly drained fields; also in ditches and bogs.*

loosely clustered flowers

smooth bright green stems

PERENNIAL

PLANT HEIGHT *Up to 1.2m, usually less.*
LEAVES *None; stems glossy bright green.*
INFLORESCENCE *Loose flower clusters; June–July.*
DISTRIBUTION *Throughout the British Isles.*
SIMILAR SPECIES *Compact Rush (J. conglomeratus) has stems which are dull and distinctly ridged, and compact flower clusters.*

Hard Rush

Juncus inflexus (Juncaceae)

FAVOURS *neutral or calcareous soil, inhabiting damp grassland, marshes, ditches, and other wet habitats.*

Tufts of hard, bluish green, strongly ridged stems are characteristic of Hard Rush. The flower clusters arise at the base of a long bract, which looks like a continuation of the slender stem. They are rather loose, with brown flowers borne on more or less erect stalks of unequal length. The brown fruit are egg-shaped, with a tiny point at the top.

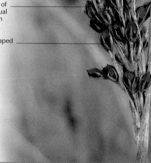

stalks of unequal length

egg-shaped fruit

brown flowers

PERENNIAL

PLANT HEIGHT *Up to 1.2m.*
LEAVES *None.*
INFLORESCENCE *Loose cluster of more or less erect stalks, with brown flowers; May–July.*
DISTRIBUTION *Throughout, except for most of Scotland.*
SIMILAR SPECIES *Compact Rush (J. conglomeratus) has compact flower clusters.*

Jointed Rush

Juncus articulatus (Juncaceae)

FLOURISHES *in damp grassland, marshes, on wet moorland, pond edges, and riversides.*

A very common and widely distributed species, Jointed Rush grows from a creeping rootstock. The leaves have internal cross-partitions, hence the name "Jointed". At the top of the stem is a branching inflorescence comprising small clusters of dark brown flowers with pointed segments. The brown, egg-shaped fruit is abruptly narrowed to end in a small point.

clusters of flowers

branching inflorescence

PERENNIAL

pointed flower segments

PLANT HEIGHT *Up to 60cm.*
LEAVES *Curved and flattened, with internal cross-partitions.*
INFLORESCENCE *Branched, with small clusters of dark brown flowers; July–August.*
DISTRIBUTION *Throughout the British Isles.*
SIMILAR SPECIES *Sharp-flowered Rush (J. acutiflorus) has rounded, unflattened leaves.*

Toad Rush

Juncus bufonius (Juncaceae)

Toad Rush has erect, spreading or trailing stems. Narrow leaves are produced at the base and on the stems. The inflorescence is made up of spreading branches bearing clusters of greenish white flowers with pointed segments. The brown, egg-shaped fruit is usually pointed and is the same length as, or shorter than, the inner flower segments.

GROWS *in bare damp places, widely distributed, and common.*

branched inflorescence

pointed flower segments

clusters of greenish white flowers

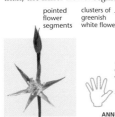

ANNUAL

PLANT HEIGHT *Up to 50cm, usually less.*
LEAVES *Narrow, at base and on stems.*
INFLORESCENCE *Branching, with clusters of greenish white flowers; June–September.*
DISTRIBUTION *Throughout the British Isles.*
SIMILAR SPECIES *Leafy Rush (J. foliosus) has erect stems, broader leaves, and dark lines on the flower segments.*

Field Wood-rush

Luzula campestris (Juncaceae)

Producing short runners, Field Wood-rush forms extensive colonies. The leaves are narrow and grass-like, tapering to a fine point, and fringed with long white hairs. The chestnut brown flowers have very conspicuous yellow anthers. The globular brown fruit is shorter than the flower segments.

FLOURISHES *in short grassland, preferring calcareous or neutral soil.*

pointed flower segments

one flower cluster unstalked

chestnut brown flowers

PERENNIAL

PLANT HEIGHT *to 25cm, but usually less.*
LEAVES *Grass-like with hairy margins.*
INFLORESCENCE *Several flower clusters, one unstalked, the others stalked; April–May.*
DISTRIBUTION *Throughout the British Isles.*
SIMILAR SPECIES *Heath Wood-rush (L. multiflora) favours acid soil, lacks runners, and flowers May–June.*

Fungi and Lichen

This group includes many more organisms than those that could simply be called mushrooms or toadstools. A vast range of forms exist, including brackets, puffballs, clubs, bird's-nests, and lichens, which are living partnerships of a fungus and an alga. There are over 4,000 species of larger fungi recorded in Britain. The object that we usually refer to as the fungus, most often seen during the autumn, is actually only the fruiting body of an organism (called the mycelium) that is largely microscopic and underground.

ORANGE PEEL FUNGUS

BUTTER CAP

FALSE MOREL

MAP LICHEN

Fly Agaric

Amanita muscaria (Amanitaceae)

The striking red cap with white spots makes this species the classic "toadstool" of children's storybooks. Depending on age and weathering, the colour of the fungus varies, tending to wash out with rain. The cap – domed when young, flattened later – can vary in colour from vivid red to orange or even a very pale orange-yellow. Its margin is grooved and the surface covered in wart-like white veil scales which wash off in the rain. The gills, stem, and drooping stem ring are all white; the stem has a scaly surface and a volval swelling at the base. Extremely toxic, the Fly Agaric can cause severe symptoms if eaten.

FOUND in troops and rings on the ground in woods, growing with birch and spruce, more rarely with beech.

red to orange-red cap

cap to 15cm wide

wart-like cap scales

scaly stem base

crowded gills

white gills free from stem

volval swelling at stem base

SECTION

NOTE

Collect the fungus carefully so that the volval swelling on the stem base is visible. Without it, rain-washed specimens, which do not have any white spots or ring, could be mistaken for red species of Russula.

SPORES *Off-white.*
FRUITING *Summer to late autumn.*
OCCURENCE *Common throughout.*
EDIBILITY *Highly poisonous.*
SIMILAR SPECIES *Orange Grisette (A. crocea), which is more golden orange and without a ring; red species of Russula, which have no ring or volva.*

Panthercap

Amanita pantherina (Amanitaceae)

This extremely poisonous species has high concentrations of muscarin and other toxins. Its smooth, rounded cap flattens out with age and varies from light to dark brown. The stem has a bulbous base that has a gutter-like margin and a series of narrow girdles on the upper edge. There is a pendent ring about half way up the stem, and the upper surface is smooth and ungrooved.

FRUITS *in leaf litter in woodland, both broadleaf and coniferous, usually on alkaline soil.*

cap 5–12cm wide

white veil scales on cap

stem 5–10cm high

light to deep brown cap

flattened mature cap

radial grooves along cap margin

ring half way up stem

young cap rounded

bulbous stem base with gutter

SPORES *White.*
FRUITING *Summer to autumn.*
OCCURENCE *Rare to locally frequent.*
EDIBILITY *Highly poisonous.*
SIMILAR SPECIES *Grey Spotted Amanita (A. spissa), which has a grey-brown cap with greyish veil scales, no margin or girdles on the stem bulb, and a ring that is high on the stem.*

The Blusher

Amanita rubescens (Amanitaceae)

The pinkish brown cap of The Blusher can be mottled with lighter, pale pink areas with age, after heavy rain, or even if the weather has been particularly hot. The grey to pink cap scales can be dense and warty or more fleecy and sparse, making it difficult to identify at first. White to pinkish grey, the stem is often stout with a swollen base that has remains of volval bands.

GROWS *singly and in groups, in woodland – both broadleaf (such as birch, beech, and oak) and conifer (such as pine and spruce).*

crowded off-white gills

swollen stem base

scaly, pinkish brown cap

cap 6–18 cm wide

white to pinkish grey stem

SECTION

large floppy, furrowed ring on stem

SPORES *White.*
FRUITING *Early summer to late autumn.*
OCCURENCE *Common and widespread.*
EDIBILITY *Poisonous when raw, edible on being cooked.*
SIMILAR SPECIES *Panthercap (above), which is poisonous, has a grooved cap margin, white veil scales, and a distinctly rimmed bulb.*

Death Cap

Amanita phalloides (Amanitaceae)

Variability in colour makes this poisonous fungus tricky to identify. The cap can vary from yellowish green to bronze, greyish, and even, though rarely, white. It is always radially streaked with a smooth cap margin. The gills and stem are white, though the stem is sometimes flushed with the cap colour and banded with faint zig-zag marks. The stem has a white, drooping, slightly grooved ring, which may fall off.

GROWS *in woodland of all types, including grassy fringes or parks; associated with broadleaf trees, such as beech, oak, and hazel, on rich soils.*

immature, green-capped fruitbody

streaky cap surface

white gills

banded stem

large, baggy white volva

SPORES *White.*
FRUITING *Summer to autumn.*
OCCURENCE *Widespread with host trees.*
EDIBILITY *Highly poisonous.*
SIMILAR SPECIES *False Deathcap (below) smells of raw potato; Tricholoma sejunctum lacks the ring and volva; Agaricus species have no volva and brown gills.*

False Deathcap

Amanita citrina (Amanitaceae)

The smooth-edged cap of this fungus can either be lemon-yellow or pure white, and when young is covered in a map-like mosaic of detachable white or beige scales. The crowded gills are whitish yellow. There is a drooping ring at the top of the stem and a rounded bulb with a distinct rim at the base. The flesh smells strongly of raw potatoes, especially when rubbed.

FOUND *singly or in troops in woodland, on acidic soil; grows with conifers or broadleaf trees (beech, oak, and birch).*

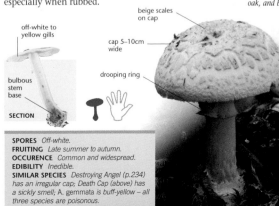

off-white to yellow gills

beige scales on cap

cap 5–10cm wide

drooping ring

bulbous stem base

SECTION

SPORES *Off-white.*
FRUITING *Late summer to autumn.*
OCCURENCE *Common and widespread.*
EDIBILITY *Inedible.*
SIMILAR SPECIES *Destroying Angel (p.234) has an irregular cap; Death Cap (above) has a sickly smell; A. gemmata is buff-yellow – all three species are poisonous.*

Destroying Angel ☠

Amanita virosa (Amanitaceae)

Fatally poisonous, as the common name suggests, this species is pure white all over. The often sticky cap is pointed and egg-shaped when immature and later flattens out. The slender, shaggy stem has a floppy ring at the top, which is often torn, and an egg-like volva enclosing the base. This fungus develops a sickly sweet odour with age.

FOUND *in damp woodland on acidic soils, especially with birch or conifers.*

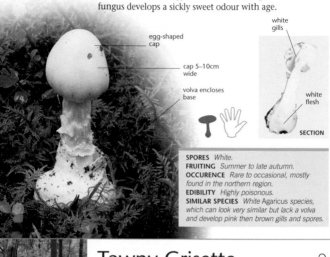

egg-shaped cap

cap 5–10cm wide

volva encloses base

white gills

white flesh

SECTION

SPORES *White.*
FRUITING *Summer to late autumn.*
OCCURENCE *Rare to occasional, mostly found in the northern region.*
EDIBILITY *Highly poisonous.*
SIMILAR SPECIES *White Agaricus species, which can look very similar but lack a volva and develop pink then brown gills and spores.*

Tawny Grisette ☠

Amanita fulva (Amanitaceae)

This species has a conical to umbonate, smooth, dull tawny-brown cap with few, if any, scaly patches and a grooved margin. Its smooth, pale to light brown stem is ringless and at its base, which is often buried in soil, has a thick persistent off-white and tan-brown volva. The Tawny Grisette has white to cream gills, which are crowded and free from the stem.

GROWS *singly or in small troops, in broadleaf woods but occasionally with conifers.*

cap up to 8cm wide

crowded free gills

white to cream gills

hollow stem

pale to light brown stem

dull tawny-brown cap

off-white and brown volva

SECTION

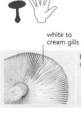 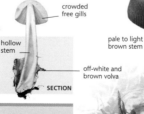

SPORES *White.*
FRUITING *Summer to autumn.*
OCCURENCE *Common and widespread throughout.*
EDIBILITY *Edible only when cooked.*
SIMILAR SPECIES *Orange Grisette (A. crocea), which is bright orange; A. vaginata, which is pale grey.*

Deer Shield

Pluteus cervinus (Pluteaceae)

The pale fawn to buff or dark brown cap of the Deer Shield is variable in size as well as colour. It has a felty centre and becomes greasy when wet. The gills are cream, later deep pinkish brown. The club-shaped stem is white with blackish brown fibres. The flesh is white and thick, with a musty, radish-like smell.

FOUND *on dead stumps, logs, branches, and fallen timber, also on sawdust; in woods, parks, and gardens.*

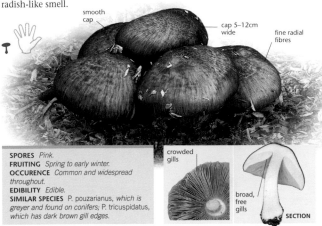

smooth cap

cap 5–12cm wide

fine radial fibres

SPORES *Pink.*
FRUITING *Spring to early winter.*
OCCURENCE *Common and widespread throughout.*
EDIBILITY *Edible.*
SIMILAR SPECIES *P. pouzarianus, which is greyer and found on conifers; P. tricuspidatus, which has dark brown gill edges.*

crowded gills

broad, free gills

SECTION

Stinking Dapperling ☠

Lepiota cristata (Agaricaceae)

The small, domed cap of the Stinking Dapperling is white with red-brown scales concentrated at the centre, growing paler as they spread out. The free gills are white to pale cream and crowded. The white stem becomes dull brown lower down and has a silky surface. At the top of the stem is a thin, easily detached white ring. The gills and white flesh strongly smell of fresh rubber or chemicals.

SEEN *in small groups, usually in grass along woodland paths, field edges, and on lawns; prefers rich soil.*

free cream gills

dark spot at centre of cap

scales radiate outwards from centre

cap 2–4cm wide

tough, thin stem

SPORES *White.*
FRUITING *Summer to late autumn.*
OCCURENCE *Common and widespread.*
EDIBILITY *Poisonous.*
SIMILAR SPECIES *Other species of Lepiota, which differ in colour of scales; several are fatally poisonous, including Star Dapperling (L. josserandii), which has pinkish brown scales.*

Parasol

Macrolepiota procera (Agaricaceae)

This is a well-known, edible species that often grows very large. The egg-shaped young cap soon expands and flattens with a large central umbo. It has a pale buff-brown surface with dark, flattened scales radiating out from the centre. The free gills are broad and pale cream, while the tall, club-shaped stem is firm and pale buff with numerous bands of dark brown scales. There is a large, double ring on the stem which can be moved up and down when it gets old. The flesh is whitish in colour and bruises to dull yellowish red.

FOUND *in small troops in meadows, fields, and woodland clearings, as well as in dune grassland and on roadsides.*

dark scales radiate out from centre

cap 10–30cm wide

large stem ring

dark scales on tall stem

white to cream gills

dark umbo

bulbous stem base

SPORES *White.*
FRUITING *Summer to late autumn.*
OCCURENCE *Common and widespread throughout the region.*
EDIBILITY *Edible and tasty.*
SIMILAR SPECIES *M. fuliginosa, which has a grey-brown cap with dark brown scales; M. permixta, which often has pinkish gills and its flesh stains a deeper red-brown; The Blusher (p.232).*

NOTE

The Parasol can be easily distinguished by its banded stem. The toxic Blusher (p.232), with which it may be confused, has detachable cap scales.

Horse Mushroom

Agaricus arvensis (Agaricaceae)

This is a well-known edible species formerly cultivated in rural districts. Often quite large, the fungus has a mainly smooth, rounded white cap, becoming dull bronze-yellow with age. The cap may crack into fibres when exposed to hot sun. Its similarly coloured stem is smooth below a large, soft, floppy ring that hangs down from the top.

OCCURS *in grass meadows, parks, or near broadleaf woods. Also in gardens on manured soil.*

gills age from pale pink to brown

soft, floppy ring

SECTION

cap 6–10cm wide

cylindrical to club-shaped stem

white cap ageing to dull yellow

flattened, thimble-shaped young caps

SPORES *Dark brown.*
FRUITING *Summer to late autumn.*
OCCURENCE *Occasional to frequent everywhere.*
EDIBILITY *Edible and tasty.*
SIMILAR SPECIES *A. macrocarpus is more robust and prefers woodlands; A. osecanus is whiter and prefers chalky soil.*

Field Mushroom

Agaricus campestris (Agaricaceae)

The edible Field Mushroom has a flattened white cap with bright pink gills when young. Later the cap may turn pinkish grey, while the gills become chocolate brown. It has a short, tapering or cylindrical stem with a very fragile ring that is often visible as just a faint zone at the top of the stem.

FOUND *often in large numbers, forming fairy rings in grassy meadows and field and grass verges.*

cap 4–10cm wide

finely scaled white cap

small, fragile ring

white flesh

SPORES *Dark brown.*
FRUITING *Summer to late autumn.*
OCCURENCE *Common and widespread.*
EDIBILITY *Edible.*
SIMILAR SPECIES *Agaricus lutosus, which is smaller with purplish scales in the cap centre, and stains dull yellow.*

young pink gills

short, stout stem

SECTION

Yellow Stainer

☠

Agaricus xanthodermus (Agaricaceae)

A toxic species easily confused with other field mushrooms, the Yellow Stainer is bright white throughout when young, becoming a dirty orange-brown in patches when older. When young, the whole mushroom very easily bruises a bright chrome-yellow, especially in the stem base; this is less obvious when it is older. The gills change from grey to pink to brown as it ages, and the fungus has a strong, unpleasant, chemical smell, like that of ink.

SEEN *in grassland or woodland edges, in bare soil, grass, or bark mulch, especially in man-made habitats like parks and cemeteries.*

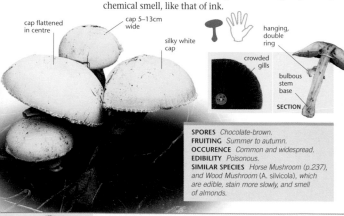

cap flattened in centre

cap 5–13cm wide

silky white cap

crowded gills

hanging, double ring

bulbous stem base

SECTION

SPORES *Chocolate-brown.*
FRUITING *Summer to autumn.*
OCCURENCE *Common and widespread.*
EDIBILITY *Poisonous.*
SIMILAR SPECIES *Horse Mushroom (p.237), and Wood Mushroom (A. silvicola), which are edible, stain more slowly, and smell of almonds.*

Shaggy Inkcap

Coprinus comatus (Coprinaceae)

Also known as the Lawyer's Wig, this fungus has an egg-shaped or elongated cap covered in shaggy scales when young – hence the common name. A narrow ring around the middle of the stem elongates as the fungus matures, lifting the cap upwards. The cap and white gills gradually blacken to release the spores – until the cap dissolves entirely and only the stem remains.

GROWS *in small troops in grassy areas, and on roadsides, often where soil has been disturbed.*

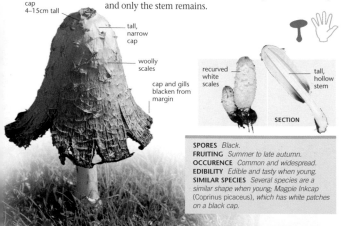

cap 4–15cm tall

tall, narrow cap

woolly scales

cap and gills blacken from margin

recurved white scales

tall, hollow stem

SECTION

SPORES *Black.*
FRUITING *Summer to late autumn.*
OCCURENCE *Common and widespread.*
EDIBILITY *Edible and tasty when young.*
SIMILAR SPECIES *Several species are a similar shape when young; Magpie Inkcap (Coprinus picaceus), which has white patches on a black cap.*

Common Inkcap ☠

Coprinus atramentarius (Coprinaceae)

This species is edible except when mixed with alcohol in any form. It causes palpitations and sickness even when alcohol is consumed days after the fungus is eaten. The egg-shaped cap has a red-brown centre and a smooth surface that is ridged. The cap expands slightly and gradually becomes inky black, liquifying from the margin, which can be lobed. Its stem has a ring-zone.

grey to grey-brown cap

SEEN *in clusters in humus-rich places, often on buried wood of broadleaf trees, in woods and gardens.*

cap to 7cm wide

reddish brown fibres

free gills

hollow white stem

SECTION

SPORES *Black.*
FRUITING *Spring to autumn.*
OCCURENCE *Common and widespread.*
EDIBILITY *Potentially poisonous; edible with extreme caution.*
SIMILAR SPECIES *C. acuminatus has a pointed umbo on the cap; C. romagnesianus has cap with reddish orange flattened scales.*

Glistening Inkcap

Coprinus micaceus (Coprinaceae)

An egg-shaped, bright tan to brown, clustering, inedible fungus, the Glistening Inkcap is often found in large groups. The caps appear pleated, and are darker in the centre with a pale cream line at the edge. They are covered in fine, powdery granules which make the cap surface glisten, though these can rub off with age. The brittle stems are pale by contrast, and the gills turn inky black with age.

OCCURS *often in dense clusters on and around the base of rotting trees and fallen broadleaf wood of all kinds.*

cap to 4cm wide

brown gills edged white

silvery stem

SECTION

"pleated" egg-shaped caps

SPORES *Black.*
FRUITING *Late spring to early winter.*
OCCURENCE *Common and widespread.*
EDIBILITY *Inedible.*
SIMILAR SPECIES *C. domesticus, which has a yellow mat around the base; Psathyrella clusters, which have no granules or pleats on the cap.*

Ringed-blue Roundhead

GROWS *singly or in small groups on debris in broadleaf and coniferous woods, or among moss in pasture or on roadsides.*

Stropharia aeruginosa (Strophariaceae)

The distinctive blue-green domed cap of this species has fleecy white scales at the margin when young, which fade to ochre-yellow. The gills are brownish violet with a frosted white edge. There is a prominent though fragile ring on the stem, which is whitish above the ring and pale blue-green below, with fleecy scales.

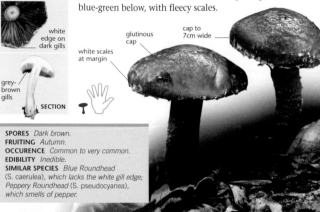

white edge on dark gills

grey-brown gills

SECTION

glutinous cap

white scales at margin

cap to 7cm wide

SPORES *Dark brown.*
FRUITING *Autumn.*
OCCURENCE *Common to very common.*
EDIBILITY *Inedible.*
SIMILAR SPECIES *Blue Roundhead (S. caerulea), which lacks the white gill edge; Peppery Roundhead (S. pseudocyanea), which smells of pepper.*

Deadly Fibrecap ☠

Inocybe erubescens (Cortinariaceae)

Dangerously poisonous due to high levels of the toxin muscarine, this species is entirely ivory-white with a rounded to strongly umbonate cap, splitting into radial fibres. Its gills, grey-buff then deep brown, are almost free from the stem. The solid, cylindrical stem is fibrous. All parts of the fungus stain deep pinkish red when scratched. This early fruiting species has a pleasant odour and can be easily mistaken for some edible fungi.

GROWS *with broadleaf trees, particularly beech, on warm calcareous soil, especially southern slopes.*

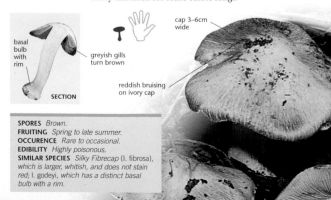

basal bulb with rim

greyish gills turn brown

SECTION

cap 3–6cm wide

reddish bruising on ivory cap

SPORES *Brown.*
FRUITING *Spring to late summer.*
OCCURENCE *Rare to occasional.*
EDIBILITY *Highly poisonous.*
SIMILAR SPECIES *Silky Fibrecap (I. fibrosa), which is larger, whitish, and does not stain red; I. godeyi, which has a distinct basal bulb with a rim.*

Sulphur Tuft

Hypholoma fasciculare (Strophariaceae)

Domed when young, the yellow-edged caps are more orange
at the centre, becoming funnel-shaped and undulating when
older. The stem is yellow and fibrous, its ring-zone becoming
brownish purple with fallen spores. The gills are a garish
yellow-green when young, darkening to a purplish black
with age. The flesh of the Sulphur Tuft is very
bitter and can cause severe stomach upsets.

SEEN *in tufts, often in
large numbers, growing
on the rotting wood
of both conifers and
broadleaf trees.*

sulphur-yellow cap

darker centre on caps

cap to
7cm wide

green and purplish
black gills

stem
yellow
at top

darker
stem base

SPORES *Purple-brown.*
FRUITING *Summer to autumn.*
OCCURENCE *Common and widespread.*
EDIBILITY *Poisonous.*
SIMILAR SPECIES *Brick Tuft (H. lateritium)
and Snakeskin Brownie (H. marginatum),
which have whitish gills and a silky white
stem layer when young.*

Shaggy Scalycap

Pholiota squarrosa (Strophariaceae)

An easily recognizable species, the Shaggy Scalycap has
dense, dark brown scales on its light yellow cap and stem.
The upturned, pointed scales cover both the rounded cap
and the lower part of the tough stem below the ring-
zone. Its crowded gills are straw-yellow when young,
later becoming brown, and the pale yellow flesh
smells of radishes.

FOUND *clustered at the
base of broadleaf
trees, especially beech
and ash.*

rounded,
scaly cap

yellow gills
turn brown

scaly
stem

cap to
15cm wide

upturned
brown
scales

SPORES *Brown.*
FRUITING *Late summer to early winter.*
OCCURENCE *Common and widespread.*
EDIBILITY *Inedible.*
SIMILAR SPECIES *Golden Scalycap
(P. aurivella), which is golden-yellow with
flat scales; Spectacular Rustgill (Gymnopilus
junonius), which lacks cap scales.*

Funeral Bell ☠

Galerina marginata (Strophariaceae)

This is a seriously poisonous fungus and its characteristics should be carefully noted to avoid confusion with similar edible fungi. Its cap is initially convex and then flattened. Rather thin-fleshed, it is reddish brown to honey-coloured when dry. The stem has lengthwise fibres and a ring at the top, which frequently tears and may not be complete.

FOUND *in small to large clumps on rotten logs and stumps of conifers and broadleaf trees; common on bark mulch in gardens.*

smooth cap surface

cap 2–5cm wide

margin lined when moist

pale yellow-ochre gills

stem paler on top

SPORES *Brown.*
FRUITING *Spring to early winter.*
OCCURENCE *Occasional to frequent and widespread.*
EDIBILITY *Highly poisonous.*
SIMILAR SPECIES *Sheathed Woodtuft (below), which has scales below the ring; Honey Fungus (p.250), which has white spores.*

Sheathed Woodtuft

Kuehneromyces mutabilis (Strophariaceae)

The convex, leathery, date-brown to yellow cap of this popular, edible species soon expands to become umbonate and is fairly thick-fleshed and aromatic. When wet, the surface is smooth or even sticky. The most distinctive characteristic is that the cap becomes much paler ochre from the centre outwards as it dries. The gills are ochre-brown, joined to the stem with a slight tooth, and run a little way down the stem.

OCCURS *in small or large clumps on dead or rotten logs and stumps of broadleaf trees, rarely on conifers.*

centre turns pale on drying

smooth, 2-tone cap

dark, scaly stem

cap 2–6cm wide

broad gills

pale brown flesh

SECTION

small ring

SPORES *Brown.*
FRUITING *Spring to early winter.*
OCCURENCE *Occasional to frequent, and widespread.*
EDIBILITY *Edible.*
SIMILAR SPECIES *Funeral Bell (above) is poisonous, has fibres and no scales below the ring; Honey Fungus (p.250) has white spores.*

The Miller

Clitopilus prunulus (Entolomataceae)

Very variable in shape, the white to greyish cap of The Miller can be domed to quite flat, or even funnel-shaped. The gills are crowded and run down the stem, white at first, but turning pink when mature. Similarly coloured, the stem may be shorter than the cap diameter. This fungus has a floury smell and tastes of fresh meal.

FOUND *along woodland paths, in gardens, and parks; in groups in broadleaf and coniferous woods.*

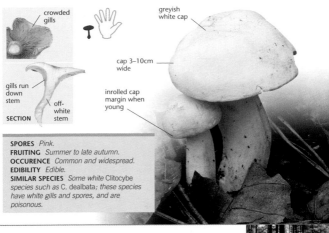

crowded gills

greyish white cap

cap 3–10cm wide

gills run down stem

off-white stem

SECTION

inrolled cap margin when young

SPORES *Pink.*
FRUITING *Summer to late autumn.*
OCCURENCE *Common and widespread.*
EDIBILITY *Edible.*
SIMILAR SPECIES *Some white Clitocybe species such as C. dealbata; these species have white gills and spores, and are poisonous.*

Yellow Knight

Tricholoma equestre (Tricholomataceae)

The cap of this species is bronze- to orange-yellow, sometimes with scales, especially at the centre. It has bright yellow gills, even when young. The stem, which is also yellow, has a slightly fibrous texture and the whitish yellow flesh has a mealy smell. The Yellow Knight varies considerably in stature from slender to robust.

OCCURS *singly or in troops on the ground with conifers, especially pine; also broadleafs such as beech.*

scales on cap

yellow-brown cap

SPORES *White.*
FRUITING *Autumn to early winter.*
OCCURENCE *Rare to occasional.*
EDIBILITY *Edible and tasty.*
SIMILAR SPECIES *Plums and Custard (Tricholomopsis rutilans); Soapy Knight (T. saponaceum) has a soapy smell; T. bufonium has a gassy smell.*

cap to 14cm wide

Wood Blewit

Lepista nuda (Tricholomataceae)

Wood Blewit's cap is violet- to grey-brown or pinkish lavender. Smooth and rounded, it soon expands, and has a slightly inrolled margin. The gills are pale bluish lilac when young, becoming pinker with age. The stout, fleshy stem becomes browner when old, and has a white, scurfy appearance towards the top. Pleasantly scented, the flesh is marbled with buff-ochre.

FOUND *often in large groups or in circles in broadleaf woods, gardens, roadsides, or rich composted areas.*

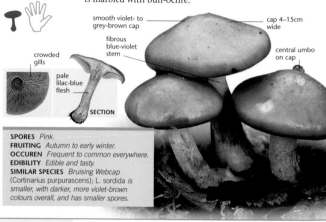

smooth violet- to grey-brown cap

cap 4–15cm wide

fibrous blue-violet stem

central umbo on cap

crowded gills

pale lilac-blue flesh

SECTION

SPORES *Pink.*
FRUITING *Autumn to early winter.*
OCCUREN *Frequent to common everywhere.*
EDIBILITY *Edible and tasty.*
SIMILAR SPECIES *Bruising Webcap (Cortinarius purpurascens); L. sordida is smaller, with darker, more violet-brown colours overall, and has smaller spores.*

Ivory Funnel 💀

Clitocybe dealbata (Tricholomataceae)

This small to medium fungus is extremely poisonous. The cap is funnel-shaped or flat, and cream to pinkish beige with a white bloom that makes it look frosted. It can be zoned or blotched and sometimes cracks when old. White to greyish cream gills run slightly down the creamy beige stem. Ivory Funnel can smell mealy when young and can easily be mistaken for several edible species.

GROWS *in grassy places including lawns, parks, gardens, cemeteries, fields, meadows, wood edges, and coastal dunes.*

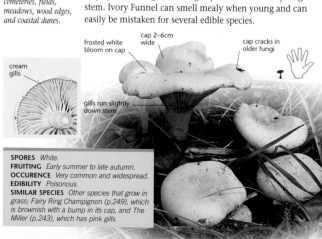

frosted white bloom on cap

cap 2–6cm wide

cap cracks in older fungi

cream gills

gills run slightly down stem

SPORES *White.*
FRUITING *Early summer to late autumn.*
OCCURENCE *Very common and widespread.*
EDIBILITY *Poisonous.*
SIMILAR SPECIES *Other species that grow in grass; Fairy Ring Champignon (p.249), which is brownish with a bump in its cap, and The Miller (p.243), which has pink gills.*

Common Funnel

Clitocybe gibba (Tricholomataceae)

The funnel-shaped cap and stem of this delicate, edible species are pale buff-brown to pinkish beige. The cap often has a small umbo at the centre and its surface is dry and felty. The thin, crowded gills run down the stem, which is slender and fibrous. Faintly smelling of bitter almonds, the flesh has a mild taste.

APPEARS *in small groups, usually in leaf or needle litter in mixed woods, often along paths.*

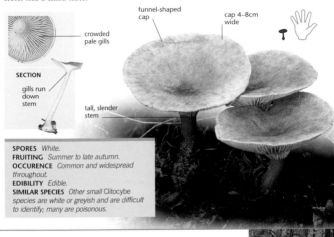

crowded pale gills

funnel-shaped cap

cap 4–8cm wide

SECTION

gills run down stem

tall, slender stem

SPORES *White.*
FRUITING *Summer to late autumn.*
OCCURENCE *Common and widespread throughout.*
EDIBILITY *Edible.*
SIMILAR SPECIES *Other small Clitocybe species are white or greyish and are difficult to identify; many are poisonous.*

Clouded Funnel

Clitocybe nebularis (Tricholomataceae)

A rather variable, mid-grey species, the Clouded Funnel has a felty grey cap, domed when young, later becoming largely flattened to deeply funnel-shaped, with a wavy margin. The margin is often paler and inrolled, and the entire cap surface becomes increasingly dusted with a white bloom. The club-shaped stem has a strong, distinctive, and slightly unpleasant smell.

APPEARS *in troops and rings – often in large numbers late in the year – or occasionally singly, in leaf litter in woods.*

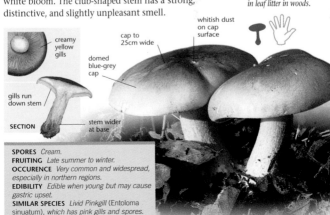

creamy yellow gills

cap to 25cm wide

whitish dust on cap surface

domed blue-grey cap

gills run down stem

SECTION

stem wider at base

SPORES *Cream.*
FRUITING *Late summer to winter.*
OCCURENCE *Very common and widespread, especially in northern regions.*
EDIBILITY *Edible when young but may cause gastric upset.*
SIMILAR SPECIES *Livid Pinkgill (Entoloma sinuatum), which has pink gills and spores.*

Aniseed Funnel

Clitocybe odora (Tricholomataceae)

APPEARS *singly but often in troops or rings, sometimes in large numbers in leaf litter.*

Not many fungi are blue-green and this unusual colour, along with a strong smell of aniseed, distinguishes this edible fungus. The rounded cap is often inrolled at the margin and becomes flat to slightly depressed with age. It also fades to grey-green and rarely, white. The creamy yellow gills run slightly down the stem.

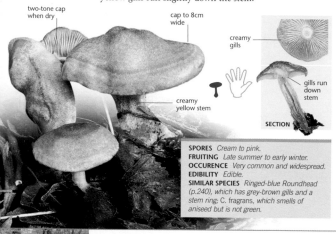

two-tone cap when dry

cap to 8cm wide

creamy gills

gills run down stem

creamy yellow stem

SECTION

> **SPORES** *Cream to pink.*
> **FRUITING** *Late summer to early winter.*
> **OCCURENCE** *Very common and widespread.*
> **EDIBILITY** *Edible.*
> **SIMILAR SPECIES** *Ringed-blue Roundhead (p.240), which has grey-brown gills and a stem ring; C. fragrans, which smells of aniseed but is not green.*

Deceiver

Laccaria laccata (Tricholomataceae)

FOUND *in mixed woods and heaths, as well as in sphagnum bogs; common everywhere.*

The small, rounded cap of the Deceiver soon flattens, varying from pale pinkish brown to orange-ochre, with a smooth to slightly scurfy surface. The gills are thick, widely spaced, and pale pink, and are often dusted with white, powdery spores. Its stem is slender, pinkish brown, and fibrous. This species lacks a distinctive smell or taste.

cap 2–4 cm wide

thick gills

scurfy scale at cap centre

> **SPORES** *White.*
> **FRUITING** *Almost throughout the year.*
> **OCCURENCE** *Very common throughout.*
> **EDIBILITY** *Edible.*
> **SIMILAR SPECIES** *Scurfy Deceiver (L. proxima), which is larger (5–7 cm wide) and taller, with a very scurfy cap and fibrous stem; it smells like a radish.*

Amethyst Deceiver

Laccaria amethystina (Hydnangiaceae)

When fresh and moist, the Amethyst Deceiver's cap, stem, and gills are an intense, almost luminous, a violet-amethyst, making it one of the most attractive woodland fungi. The cap is dry to felty, with a central navel, and paler marginal stripes. As the fungus dries, it turns a drab greyish violet and is difficult to recognize. The gills are thick and widely spaced, while the stem is slender, tough, and very fibrous. The stem usually has a white, cottony-felty base. This edible species does not have a distinctive taste or smell.

OCCURS *usually in small troops in both broadleaf and coniferous woods, especially in wet areas.*

cap 2–5cm wide

violet-amethyst in all parts

thick, widely spaced gills

hollow stem centre

SECTION

slender, fibrous stem

SPORES *White.*
FRUITING *Summer to late autumn.*
OCCURENCE *Common to very common throughout.*
EDIBILITY *Edible.*
SIMILAR SPECIES *Bicoloured Deceiver (L. bicolor), which has a brownish cap with lavender-blue gills and a brownish stem with a violet base.*

NOTE

At first sight, you might think this species has violet spores, but as the gills mature they are clearly dusted with white spores.

Clustered Toughshank

Collybia confluens (Tricholomataceae)

OCCURS *in dense clusters both in broadleaf and coniferous woods, also in thick leaf litter or needles.*

The dense clumps of fruitbodies and an aromatic smell help to identify this inedible species. The cap is pale tan to greyish buff, thin, tough, and domed to flattened. Narrow and crowded, the gills are white to cream. The buff to deep brown stem is hollow, tough, and hairy with a dry surface. Several stems are fused together at the base.

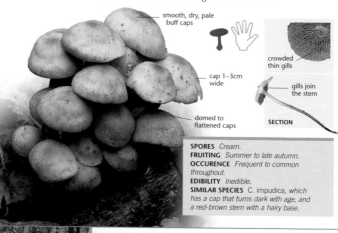

smooth, dry, pale buff caps

crowded thin gills

cap 1–3cm wide

gills join the stem

domed to flattened caps

SECTION

SPORES *Cream.*
FRUITING *Summer to late autumn.*
OCCURENCE *Frequent to common throughout.*
EDIBILITY *Inedible.*
SIMILAR SPECIES *C. impudica, which has a cap that turns dark with age, and a red-brown stem with a hairy base.*

Butter Cap

Collybia butyracea (Tricholomataceae)

SEEN *in both broadleaf and pine woods in leaf litter, often in large numbers or fairy rings.*

This is a common species, producing an umbonate, red-brown to grey-brown cap, with a much darker area at the centre. The greasy feel to the cap is a key feature. The gills are white to pale cream and appear almost free. Slender at the top and swelling to a broad club at the bottom, the stem is dry, fibrous, and darker at the base.

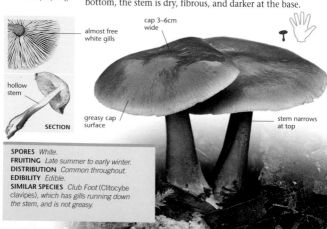

almost free white gills

cap 3–6cm wide

hollow stem

greasy cap surface

stem narrows at top

SECTION

SPORES *White.*
FRUITING *Late summer to early winter.*
DISTRIBUTION *Common throughout.*
EDIBILITY *Edible.*
SIMILAR SPECIES *Club Foot (Clitocybe clavipes), which has gills running down the stem, and is not greasy.*

Fairy Ring Champignon

Marasmius oreades (Tricholomataceae)

A popular edible species, the Fairy Ring Champignon has very tough, fleshy fruitbodies. The entire fungus is pale buff-tan, darker when wet, much paler when dry and sun-baked. The rounded or domed cap soon expands, becoming flatter with a broad umbo with age, and is smooth. The broad gills are almost free of the stem, and are pale cream to buff. The tough stem is dry, slightly powdery to touch, and off-white to pale buff.

FORMS *circles or arcs in short turf in meadows, parks, gardens, and near roadsides.*

broad, widely spaced gills

rounded or smooth domed cap

pale buff cap

cap 2–5cm wide

gills free of stem

white to buff flesh

SECTION

tough, dry stem

SPORES *White.*
FRUITING *Spring to late autumn.*
OCCURENCE *Common throughout.*
EDIBILITY *Edible and tasty.*
SIMILAR SPECIES *Ivory Funnel (p.244), which is highly poisonous – it has a white, frosted-looking cap, and gills that run very slightly down a stem that is not as tough.*

Velvet Shank

Flammulina velutipes (Tricholomataceae)

This widely eaten species grows clustered on wood. It has a smooth, sticky, orange-brown cap, which is domed and inrolled at the margin. Very rarely, a white form of this species also occurs. The gills are yellowish and moderately spaced, producing white spores. Tapering to the base, the stem is smooth and yellow at the top and distinctly velvety and black towards the base.

FOUND *clustered in tufts on a variety of broadleaf trees. Prefers decaying wood or old, standing trees.*

cap to 6cm wide

orange-brown cap

smooth yellowish stem

yellow gills

SPORES *White.*
FRUITING *Late autumn to early spring.*
OCCURENCE *Occasional to widespread.*
EDIBILITY *Edible.*
SIMILAR SPECIES *Sulphur Tuft (p.241) has purplish green gills and purple spores, and is poisonous; Common Rustgill (Gymnopilus penetrans) has spotted orange-brown gills.*

Honey Fungus

Armillaria mellea (Tricholomataceae)

FORMS *large, dense clusters in woods, parks, and gardens. Parasitic mainly on broadleaf trees, especially beech and oak. Also known to attack garden shrubs.*

This common, edible fungus is one of the most confusing for the beginner to identify as it has such a variable appearance. It is now reclassified as a group of closely related separate species. Growing in clusters, the fruitbodies are firmly joined together at the base. The cap can be domed, flattened, or funnel-shaped and wavy, and varies in colour from honey-brown, to yellowish or olive, with a darker brown centre covered in sparse brownish scales. The gills are white, becoming spotted brown. Often tapering, the brownish stem is darker towards the base, sometimes with lighter fibres. It has a thick, woolly, cream or yellow-tinged ring. The young, fresh caps should be cooked well.

well-spaced gills

darker stem base

cap 3–15cm wide

tapering stems

SPORES *White.*
FRUITING *Autumn.*
OCCURENCE *Very common and widespread.*
EDIBILITY *Edible but can cause gastric upset.*
SIMILAR SPECIES *A. ostoyae, which has more scales, a brown-tinged ring, and is most likely to cause stomach upsets; A. cepistipes, which has darker greyish scales with a more fragile ring; A. gallica, which is less clustered with a bulbous stem base.*

Common Bonnet

Mycena galericulata (Tricholomataceae)

This common but inedible fungus differs from other species of *Mycena* in its tough stem and gills that turn pinkish with age. The bell-shaped cap is grey-brown; the pale grey gills are broad, medium-spaced, and have connecting veins. The smooth, shiny stems are tough, and often have a long rooting base.

APPEARS *in tufts or dense clumps, on or around the stumps of broadleaf trees.*

bell-shaped to convex cap

cap 1–6cm wide

grey-brown cap

pale to pinkish grey gills

smooth, tough stem

SECTION

SPORES *White.*
FRUITING *Summer to early winter.*
OCCURENCE *Common and widespread throughout.*
EDIBILITY *Inedible.*
SIMILAR SPECIES *Clustered Bonnet (below), which has a rancid smell, and a stem that is deep reddish brown lower down.*

Clustered Bonnet

Mycena inclinata (Tricholomataceae)

Growing in dense clumps, the smooth, bell-shaped caps of this pretty species are whitish grey, becoming browner with age, and often have a toothed margin. The white to cream gills are narrow, joined to the stem, and smell of soap or candles. Smooth and shiny, the stems are cream above and deep reddish brown below, often woolly-white at the base.

FOUND *in clumps on dead stumps and logs of broadleaf trees, occasionally on standing trees.*

toothed margin

older fungi turn brown

cap 2–4cm wide

SECTION

red-brown below

gills join stem

stem bases fuse together

SPORES *White.*
FRUITING *Summer to late autumn.*
OCCURENCE *Frequent to common throughout.*
EDIBILITY *Inedible.*
SIMILAR SPECIES *M. maculata, which has a smooth cap margin, purplish brown stem, and red-brown spots on the cap and gills.*

Oyster Mushroom

Pleurotus ostreatus (Polyporaceae)

INHABITS *dead or dying hardwood trees, rarely on conifers, often found on the side of standing trees at a great height.*

The rounded, oyster-shaped caps of this species grow in large clumps, often with several fruitbodies overlapping each other. The caps vary from pale brown to deep blue-grey, and may often have a whitish woolly coating at the centre in wet and cold weather. Crowded white gills run down the very short, or almost absent stem, and are often home to small insects. The white flesh of this edible fungus has a pleasant smell and taste, and a firm, meaty texture. This species is very easy to cultivate and is a popular food item.

many overlapping fruitbodies

smooth cap surface

very crowded gills

SPORES *Pale lavender.*
FRUITING *Autumn to early winter.*
OCCURENCE *Common and widespread.*
EDIBILITY *Edible.*
SIMILAR SPECIES *Branching Oyster (P. cornucopiae), which forms dense trumpet-shaped clusters with distinct stems; P. pulmonarius, which is paler.*

Porcelain Fungus

Oudemansiella mucida (Tricholomataceae)

OCCURS *in large numbers on fallen dead wood or on the trunks of standing beech trees, deeply rooted into the wood.*

The Porcelain Fungus has a slimy, pure white to pale grey cap that resembles glistening porcelain, and is difficult to grip. The stem has a narrow ring that is white above and grey on the underside. The base of the stem is often dark brown and the broad, widely spaced gills are white and attached to the stem.

wrinkled at centre

cap 3–10cm wide

gills attached to stem

widely spaced gills

thin ring at top of stem

bulbous stem base

ring grey below, white above

tough, thin stem

SECTION

SPORES *White.*
FRUITING *Late autumn to early winter.*
OCCURENCE *Common and widespread throughout.*
EDIBILITY *Edible.*
SIMILAR SPECIES *White or grey species of Mycena, which also grow on wood but are not slimy and do not have a ring on the stem.*

Scarlet Waxcap

Hygrocybe coccinea (Hygrophoraceae)

The greasy scarlet cap, stem, and gills of this species make it one of the most brightly coloured grassland fungi. It is distinguished from other red waxcaps by the minute lumps on its umbonate cap. The red gills have a yellowish edge, but may sometimes be entirely yellow. Occasionally paler, the stem is smooth, dry, and compressed with a groove along its length.

FOUND *singly but often in scattered groups in grassland not treated chemically, including pastures, lawns, and churchyards.*

cap up to 6cm wide

central umbo

greasy cap

reddish gills

paler stem flesh

SECTION

SPORES *White.*
FRUITING *Late summer to early winter.*
DISTRIBUTION *Common and widespread.*
EDIBILITY *Edible.*
SIMILAR SPECIES *Crimson Waxcap (H. punicea) is larger with a streaky stem; Splendid Waxcap (H. splendidissima) has a rippled stem; H. marchii is more orange.*

Blackening Waxcap ☠

Hygrocybe conica (Hygrophoraceae)

One of the most common waxcaps, this species occurs in a variable range of colours, combining yellow, orange, tomato-red, and even olive-green tones with grey and black. The one constant feature that enables easy recognition of this poisonous species is the slow blackening of the entire fruitbody with age and after collection.

GROWS *singly and in small groups in grassland, including lawns and parks, and occasionally in woods.*

cap colour variable

conical cap

fruitbody turns black

cap to 5cm wide

sticky, fibrous cap

gills narrowly attached to stem

yellow gills

finely fibrous stem

SECTION

SPORES *White.*
FRUITING *Late summer to early winter.*
OCCURENCE *Occasional to very common, widespread.*
EDIBILITY *Poisonous.*
SIMILAR SPECIES *Dune Waxcap (H. conicoides); Persistent Waxcap (H. persistens), which is also yellow but does not blacken.*

Golden Waxcap

Hygrocybe chlorophana (Hygrophoraceae)

This small yellow waxcap has pale whitish to lemon-coloured gills. It is waxy to the touch and so slimy on the cap that when wet, it is often difficult to hold. The compressed yellow stem may have a groove along its length. The stem base is whitish while the upper portion, near the gills, is often finely powdery.

FOUND *singly or often in some numbers, in grassland, especially short mossy patches free from chemical fertilizers.*

flattened, lemon-yellow cap

cap to 7cm wide

whitish yellow gills

flattened, yellow stem

yellow flesh

SECTION

SPORES *White.*
FRUITING *Late summer to early winter.*
OCCURENCE *Occasional to common, widespread.*
EDIBILITY *Edible.*
SIMILAR SPECIES *H. ceracea has a dry stem and gills; H. glutinipes has a sticky cap and stem; H. persistens has a dry cap.*

Parrot Waxcap

Hygrocybe psittacina (Hygrophoraceae)

A small, bell-shaped, brightly coloured waxcap with a very slimy cap, this species has a vivid mixture of colours. It is predominantly green, yellow, and orange but sometimes also blue, lilac, and pink. Coloured like the cap, the gills often have a paler edge. The stem is also slimy with a rippled surface and nearly always has a hint of green at the top.

APPEARS *singly or in troops in grassland or, less often, in woods with moss.*

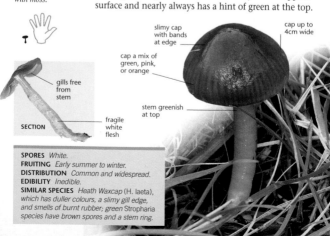

slimy cap with bands at edge

cap up to 4cm wide

cap a mix of green, pink, or orange

gills free from stem

stem greenish at top

fragile white flesh

SECTION

SPORES *White.*
FRUITING *Early summer to winter.*
DISTRIBUTION *Common and widespread.*
EDIBILITY *Inedible.*
SIMILAR SPECIES *Heath Waxcap (H. laeta), which has duller colours, a slimy gill edge, and smells of burnt rubber; green Stropharia species have brown spores and a stem ring.*

False Saffron Milkcap

Lactarius deterrimus (Russulaceae)

One of the most brightly coloured milkcap species, the cap, gills, and stem of this fungus are all a rich salmon-orange, becoming mottled green with age, frost, or bruising. Its gills exude orange milk which may slowly darken. Sticky when moist, the cap may be funnel-shaped with faint, darker concentric zones. The smooth stem easily bruises green.

GROWS *usually in rings or troops; associated solely with spruce in all types of locations, including parks and roadsides.*

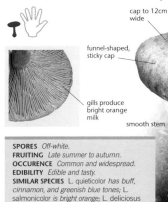

cap to 12cm wide

fruitbody bruises green

funnel-shaped, sticky cap

gills produce bright orange milk

smooth stem

SPORES Off-white.
FRUITING Late summer to autumn.
OCCURENCE Common and widespread.
EDIBILITY Edible and tasty.
SIMILAR SPECIES *L. quieticolor* has buff, cinnamon, and greenish blue tones; *L. salmonicolor* is bright orange; *L. deliciosus* has a stem covered with small pock marks.

Oakbug Milkcap

Lactarius quietus (Russulaceae)

The smell of engine or bed bugs is the clue to identifying the Oakbug Milkcap. Rounded to slightly depressed, the cap is a reddish- to grey-brown with faint but distinct darker zones. The gills are pale brown while the smooth stem is usually darker than the cap and club-shaped. When scratched, the fungus bleeds an unchanging white milk.

ASSOCIATED *with oaks, often in partial fairy-rings around a tree, in leaf litter and grass.*

depressed cap

darker spots

cap 3–8cm wide

pale brown flesh

crowded gills

SECTION

SPORES Cream.
FRUITING Late summer to early autumn.
OCCURENCE Common to very common throughout.
EDIBILITY Inedible.
SIMILAR SPECIES Yellowdrop Milkcap (*L. chrysorrheus*), which is paler, yellower, and bleeds abundant milk that turns yellow.

Charcoal Burner

Russula cyanoxantha (Russulaceae)

The cap of this very variable species is usually shades of purple, lavender, or violet; however, it may also be partly or entirely green. The gills are very flexible and feel greasy or oily when touched, unlike the brittle and dry gills of most *Russula* species. The sturdy stem is white to dull cream in colour. Quite tough, it turns brittle when old.

OCCURS singly, or in small groups, in broadleaf woods, especially beech but also under conifers, on acid soil.

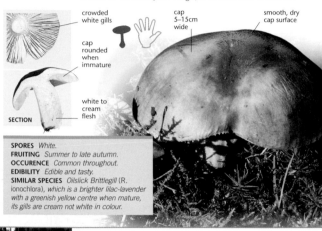

crowded white gills

cap rounded when immature

cap 5–15cm wide

smooth, dry cap surface

white to cream flesh

SECTION

SPORES *White.*
FRUITING *Summer to late autumn.*
OCCURENCE *Common throughout.*
EDIBILITY *Edible and tasty.*
SIMILAR SPECIES *Oilslick Brittlegill (R. ionochlora), which is a brighter lilac-lavender with a greenish yellow centre when mature, its gills are cream not white in colour.*

The Sickener ☠

Russula emetica (Russulaceae)

This striking and common species has a bright scarlet-red cap contrasting with pure white stem and pale gills. The stem is often tall and cylindrical while the cap is smooth, domed to flattened, and depressed when old. The skin of the cap peels off almost completely. White to pale cream in colour, the gills are medium-spaced. The mildly poisonous, crumbly white flesh has no particular smell.

APPEARS usually in wet, mossy, or even boggy areas in conifer woods, singly but often in small troops.

medium-spaced gills

cap to 10cm wide

smooth, glossy surface

domed to flattened cap

club-shaped stem, often hollow

scarlet-red cap

SPORES *White.*
FRUITING *Summer to late autumn.*
OCCURENCE *Common and widespread.*
EDIBILITY *Poisonous.*
SIMILAR SPECIES *R. silvestris, which is more pinkish red, and grows with oaks or pines on dry sandy soils; R. mairei, which looks and tastes very similar but grows with beech.*

Ochre Brittlegill

Russula ochroleuca (Russulaceae)

The cap of this very common species is a dull ochre yellow to slightly greenish yellow, rather dry and matt, and slightly grooved at the margin. The gills are pale cream and brittle while the whitish stem may be slightly encrusted with dull yellow at the base and turns greyish with age or when very wet. The soft, brittle flesh is odourless.

ASSOCIATED *with a wide variety of both broadleaf and coniferous trees, usually on acid soils.*

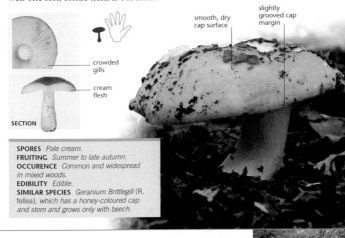

smooth, dry cap surface

slightly grooved cap margin

crowded gills

cream flesh

SECTION

SPORES *Pale cream.*
FRUITING *Summer to late autumn.*
OCCURENCE *Common and widespread in mixed woods.*
EDIBILITY *Edible.*
SIMILAR SPECIES *Geranium Brittlegill (R. fellea), which has a honey-coloured cap and stem and grows only with beech.*

Bay Bolete

Boletus badius (Boletaceae)

A popular edible species, this bolete has a rounded cap that soon expands and flattens. It is deep bay brown to reddish brown, or even pale orange-brown in colour in some forms. When dry, the cap is finely felty or velvety to smooth, but when wet it may be quite sticky. The tubes and pores start pale cream and age to greenish yellow. The whitish flesh, and the tubes and pores bruise blue when cut.

SEEN *in small groups in needle or leaf litter in both broadleaf and coniferous woods, on acid soils.*

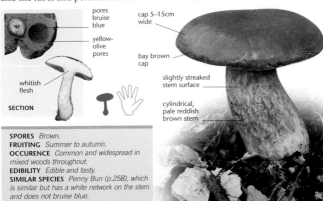

pores bruise blue

yellow-olive pores

whitish flesh

SECTION

cap 5–15cm wide

bay brown cap

slightly streaked stem surface

cylindrical, pale reddish brown stem

SPORES *Brown.*
FRUITING *Summer to autumn.*
OCCURENCE *Common and widespread in mixed woods throughout.*
EDIBILITY *Edible and tasty.*
SIMILAR SPECIES *Penny Bun (p.258), which is similar but has a white network on the stem and does not bruise blue.*

Penny Bun

Boletus edulis (Boletaceae)

Among the most famous edible fungi, the Penny Bun, also known as Cep Steinpilz and Porcini, grows in both deciduous and coniferous woodland. It can be a very large, robust fungus and has a yellow-brown to dark brown cap that appears toasted on the outer surface. The usually swollen, pale brown stem has a fine network of white veins over the upper half, while the pores are white turning yellowish to olive when old. Widely sought-after for its white flesh that does not stain on being cut, the Penny Bun has a pleasant smell and mild taste.

FOUND *in leaf litter or moss of deciduous and coniferous woods, associated with a large variety of different trees.*

bun-shaped brown cap

cap to 25cm wide

network of veins

pores start white then turn yellowish olive

white flesh

SECTION

swollen, pale brown stem

NOTE

Before cooking, check the flesh for maggot holes, and for yellowish stains, which may be caused by parasites. These affected portions can be cut out, but if badly damaged, discard the entire fruitbody.

SPORES *Olive-brown.*
FRUITING *Summer to late autumn.*
OCCURENCE *Common to very common, and widespread.*
EDIBILITY *Edible and tasty.*
SIMILAR SPECIES *B. aereus, which has a darker, black-brown cap and a dark brown network on the stem; B. aestivalis, which has a pale biscuit-brown cap and stem, and a dry, roughened cap surface. Both are edible.*

Red Cracking Bolete

Boletus chrysenteron (Boletaceae)

Fine cracks appear on the older, olive-brown caps, revealing the dull reddish flesh beneath, which give this species its name. The angular pores are yellow to dull olive and the flesh is white to pale yellow. Yellowish and streaked red below, the slender stem has fine red dots and fibrous lines. The stem, pores, and flesh stain slightly blue.

OCCURS *in woodland, on a wide range of soil types, although prefers acid soils.*

olive-brown cap

cap 3–10cm wide

yellow to olive pores

slightly notched tubes

red flesh in cracks

SECTION

SPORES *Brown.*
FRUITING *Summer to autumn.*
OCCURENCE *Occasional to common and widespread in the British Isles.*
EDIBILITY *Edible.*
SIMILAR SPECIES *Sepia Bolete (B. porosporus), which has a dull sepia brown cap without red in the cracks.*

Suede Bolete

Boletus subtomentosus (Boletaceae)

As its common name suggests, the cap of this species is velvety and suede-like in texture, and varies in colour from yellow or yellow-brown to olive or reddish brown. Its tubes and pores are bright yellow. The usually slender stem is yellowish, often with brown dots or ridges at the top. The flesh is pale whitish yellow and does not stain when cut or bruised. Although it is edible, it tastes quite bland.

OCCURS *in woodland, on a wide range of soil types, although prefers acid soils.*

yellow pores

pores bruise blue

felty cap surface

cap 3–6 cm wide

whitish yellow flesh

SECTION

yellow tubes

SPORES *Brown.*
FRUITING *Summer to autumn.*
OCCURENCE *Common and widespread throughout.*
EDIBILITY *Edible.*
SIMILAR SPECIES *B. ferrugineus, which has a brighter rust-brown cap, white flesh, and a raised net on the stem.*

Brown Birch Bolete

Leccinum scabrum (Boletaceae)

Reaching large sizes, this common species has a dark to medium- or buff-brown cap, which is smooth and sticky when wet. The off-white tubes and pores turn pale brown with age. Often tall, the cylindrical or club-shaped stem is cream with tiny blackish brown scales. The cream flesh hardly changes colour when cut or bruised.

ASSOCIATED with birch, singly or in small clumps, often in damper areas.

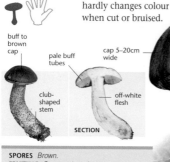

buff to brown cap

pale buff tubes

cap 5–20cm wide

club-shaped stem

off-white flesh

SECTION

smooth surface

blackish scales on stem

SPORES *Brown.*
FRUITING *Summer to autumn.*
OCCURENCE *Common and widespread throughout.*
EDIBILITY *Edible.*
SIMILAR SPECIES *Mottled Bolete (L. variicolor), which has a mottled grey-brown cap.*

Slippery Jack

Suillus luteus (Gomphidiaceae)

Like all *Suillus* species, Slippery Jack is associated with conifers, in this case pines. It has a slimy, convex, cap whose skin is easily peeled. The stout off-white stem has a large, floppy ring at the top, which covers the pores when young; it has dark dots above the ring, while the stem below and the underside of the ring are purple.

FOUND in large groups, in coniferous forests, only under two-needled pine trees.

cap 5–10cm wide

pale yellow pores

pale yellowish-white flesh

SECTION

slimy purple-brown cap

large, floppy ring

SPORES *Brown.*
FRUITING *Summer to autumn.*
OCCURENCE *Common and widespread throughout.*
EDIBILITY *Edible with caution – it is essential to remove the cap skin which may be toxic.*
SIMILAR SPECIES *Suillus collinitus, which is ochre-brown and lacks a ring.*

Brown Rollrim ☠

Paxillus involutus (Paxillaceae)

Although widely eaten in some areas, this controversial species has a variable or cumulative toxin, so it should definitely not be eaten. The yellow-brown cap has a strongly inrolled, woolly margin. Yellowish gills run down the short brown stem and bruise deep brown on handling; they are soft, thick, and easily separated from the flesh.

GROWS *in small troops, associated with a number of trees; often in wet, boggy places.*

soft, thick gills

broad, depressed cap

inrolled margin

pale yellow-brown flesh

cap 5–15cm wide

thick stem

deep brown bruising

SECTION

SPORES *Brown.*
FRUITING *Spring to late autumn.*
OCCURENCE *Common throughout.*
EDIBILITY *Poisonous.*
SIMILAR SPECIES *Alder Rollrim (P. rubicundulus), which grows only under alders, is usually smaller with a few, flattened, reddish brown scales on the cap.*

Wood Hedgehog

Hydnum repandum (Hydnaceae)

This common, highly prized edible species has soft but brittle ochre spines below the cap, which are easily rubbed off. The cap has a depressed centre and is irregularly shaped. It is dry to felty in texture, and pale cream to pinkish ochre in colour. The stem is fairly smooth. It has very solid whitish flesh that usually discolours pinkish.

GROWS *in rings, troops, or clusters in conifer as well as broadleaf woodland, especially with spruce, pine, oak, and birch.*

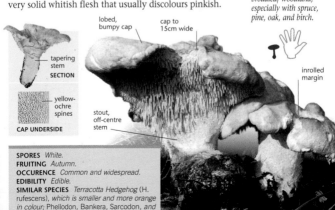

lobed, bumpy cap

cap to 15cm wide

tapering stem

SECTION

yellow-ochre spines

CAP UNDERSIDE

stout, off-centre stem

inrolled margin

SPORES *White.*
FRUITING *Autumn.*
OCCURENCE *Common and widespread.*
EDIBILITY *Edible.*
SIMILAR SPECIES *Terracotta Hedgehog (H. rufescens), which is smaller and more orange in colour; Phellodon, Bankera, Sarcodon, and Hydnellum species, which have tough flesh.*

Chanterelle

Cantharellus cibarius (Cantharellaceae)

FOUND *often in moss, it is associated with pines and spruce but also with oak, beech, and birch.*

The smooth golden cap of this edible species forms a broad, flattened trumpet, often slightly depressed in the middle, with a wavy margin. The pale apricot-yellow underside is wrinkled, with gill-like veins running down the short stem. The flesh is thick, with a pleasant apricot scent, and bruises orange to red. The true Chanterelle produces a pinkish yellow spore deposit unlike the deadly *Cortinarius* species.

gill-like blunt veins

SECTION

depressed cap centre

cap 2–12cm wide

wavy, cap margin

short, solid stem

SPORES *Ochre-yellow.*
FRUITING *Summer to late autumn.*
OCCURENCE *Occasional to common; widespread but becoming rarer.*
EDIBILITY *Edible and tasty.*
SIMILAR SPECIES *Deadly Webcap (Cortinarius rubellus) and Fool's Webcap (Cortinarius orellanus) are both orange with brown spores.*

Horn of Plenty

Craterellus cornucopioides (Cantharellaceae)

FOUND, *often in large troops, in leaf litter of broadleaf woods, on rich, alkaline soil. Frequently on slopes in deep leaf litter.*

The distinctive Horn of Plenty is difficult to mistake for any other species. The pale whitish grey outer surface is finely wrinkled and has a frosty white bloom. The flesh has a peppery, spicy flavour and a sweet aromatic odour. The fungus can be difficult to spot amongst leaf litter but when it is found, it will usually be in large numbers. It dries well and can be ground to use as a spice or flavouring.

SECTION

thin, fibrous flesh

grey-brown to black inner surface

hollow trumpet-shaped fruitbody

fruitbody 3–10cm tall

whitish bloom on outer surface

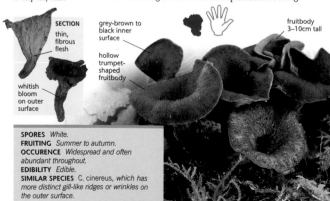

SPORES *White.*
FRUITING *Summer to autumn.*
OCCURENCE *Widespread and often abundant throughout.*
EDIBILITY *Edible.*
SIMILAR SPECIES *C. cinereus, which has more distinct gill-like ridges or wrinkles on the outer surface.*

Candlesnuff Fungus

Xylaria hypoxylon (Xylariaceae)

This species has two distinct states in its lifecycle. At first, it resembles a snuffed out candle-wick with a slender black base and pointed, powdery, white tips (from asexual spores) that are branched like antlers. When older, it is like a pointed club with a rough, pimply surface in which mature spores are formed.

FOUND *in large numbers on dead wood of logs, stumps, and branches in broadleaf woods.*

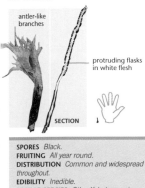

antler-like branches

white tips

protruding flasks in white flesh

fruitbody 1–6cm tall

SECTION

SPORES *Black.*
FRUITING *All year round.*
DISTRIBUTION *Common and widespread throughout.*
EDIBILITY *Inedible.*
SIMILAR SPECIES *Other Xylaria species are larger and more club-like. Coral fungi are usually found on the ground and are brittle.*

Southern Bracket

Ganoderma australe (Ganodermataceae)

At times a massive bracket, this perennial species forms broad, semi-circular shelves, building up a new layer of tubes each year; the flesh is very thick where it joins the tree. Its rich reddish brown upper surface lacks granules but is irregular and lumpy. The tubes and pores are pale cream and bruise reddish brown, while the tough flesh is a dark red-brown.

GROWS *on old stumps and standing broadleaf trees, such as beech, oak, and lime, rarely on conifers.*

fibrous, dark brown flesh

SECTION

powdery layer of spores

fruitbody 10–60cm wide

SPORES *Brown.*
FRUITING *All year round.*
OCCURENCE *Common throughout.*
EDIBILITY *Inedible.*
SIMILAR SPECIES *Artist's Bracket (G. applanatum), which is thinner, with paler flesh, often with pockets of whitish tissue.*

Birch Polypore

Piptoporus betulinus (Fomitopsidaceae)

The Birch Polypore is the cause of death of a great many trees. The fungus starts as a round, brownish ball emerging from the trunk, and later expands to form a kidney-shaped bracket. The leathery upper surface is pale brown, while the blunt margin is white. The white flesh is corky and fragrant. Despite its pleasant smell, it tastes bitter and is inedible. One of the few bracket fungi that is host specific, it is hardly ever absent in any birch woodland.

ASSOCIATED *only with birch, on living and dead standing trees; also on fallen logs.*

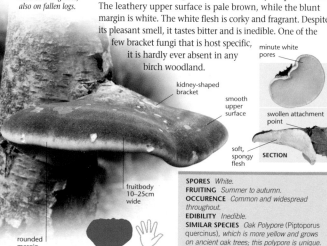

kidney-shaped bracket

smooth upper surface

minute white pores

swollen attachment point

soft, spongy flesh

SECTION

fruitbody 10–25cm wide

rounded margin

SPORES *White.*
FRUITING *Summer to autumn.*
OCCURENCE *Common and widespread throughout.*
EDIBILITY *Inedible.*
SIMILAR SPECIES *Oak Polypore (Piptoporus quercinus), which is more yellow and grows on ancient oak trees; this polypore is unique.*

Dryad's Saddle

Polyporus squamosus (Polyporaceae)

The change from young to old in the Dryad's Saddle is quite dramatic. When immature, it appears as a rounded brown lump with a flattened top. This gradually expands to form a wide, round or kidney-shaped shelf or bracket with a stout stem at the inner edge, making the species appear somewhere between a cap and stem and bracket fungus. The white flesh smells strongly of flour when young.

FOUND *usually low down on standing broadleaf trees in woods, parks, and gardens; sometimes on fallen logs.*

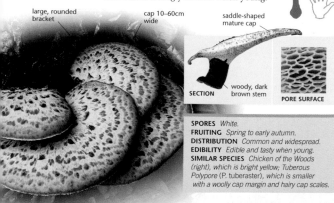

large, rounded bracket

cap 10–60cm wide

saddle-shaped mature cap

SECTION

woody, dark brown stem

PORE SURFACE

SPORES *White.*
FRUITING *Spring to early autumn.*
DISTRIBUTION *Common and widespread.*
EDIBILITY *Edible and tasty when young.*
SIMILAR SPECIES *Chicken of the Woods (right), which is bright yellow; Tuberous Polypore (P. tuberaster), which is smaller with a woolly cap margin and hairy cap scales.*

Chicken of the Woods

Laetiporus sulphureus (Polyporaceae)

Bright yellow when fresh and forming large, tiered clusters of fan-shaped fruitbodies, Chicken of the Woods is one of the most spectacular bracket fungi. When very young, the fruitbodies are almost orange with a meat-like texture. However, they decay quite rapidly – the colour fades to pale buff and the flesh becomes cheesy and crumbles easily.

SEEN *on living trees, rarely on dead trunks. Commonest on broadleaf trees such as oak; also on yew.*

fan-shaped fruitbody

bright yellow bracket

SECTION

bracket 10–50cm wide

soft flesh

fruitbody in tiered clusters

SPORES *White.*
FRUITING *Late spring to early autumn.*
OCCURENCE *Very common and widespread.*
EDIBILITY *Edible when young, but can cause stomach upsets.*
SIMILAR SPECIES *Giant Polypore (below) is never bright yellow; Oak Polypore (Piptoporus quercinus) is yellowish brown with white pores.*

Giant Polypore

Meripilus giganteus (Bjerkanderaceae)

The Giant Polypore lives up to its name and typically produces massive tiers or rosettes of soft, fleshy, fan-like brackets arising from a common basal stem. The brackets are ochre-brown, the pores whitish, and all parts of the fungus bruise grey to blackish. It always grows on or close to the ground, at the base of trees, around stumps, or on buried roots.

GROWS *at the base of trees and around stumps, with oak and beech, but also with a variety of other species.*

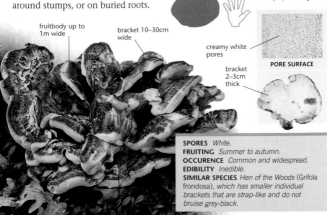

fruitbody up to 1m wide

bracket 10–30cm wide

creamy white pores

PORE SURFACE

bracket 2–3cm thick

SPORES *White.*
FRUITING *Summer to autumn.*
OCCURENCE *Common and widespread.*
EDIBILITY *Inedible.*
SIMILAR SPECIES *Hen of the Woods (Grifola frondosa), which has smaller individual brackets that are strap-like and do not bruise grey-black.*

Beefsteak Fungus

Fistulina hepatica (Fistulinaceae)

This edible, soft-fleshed bracket looks like a bright red clown's nose when it first emerges from its host tree. It rapidly expands to a tongue shape, becoming a darker blood-red. On the underside, the pale yellow pores become reddish with age and bruising, and are easily separated. Acid- to sour-tasting when old, the Beefsteak Fungus is best consumed when young and fresh.

FOUND *singly or scattered on host trees, especially oak. Often found on living trees but also occurs on dead, fallen, or cut wood.*

kidney-shaped, blood-red bracket

sticky upper surface

marbled flesh

flesh oozes red droplets

bracket to 25cm wide

SPORES *White.*
FRUITING *Summer to autumn.*
OCCURENCE *Occasional to common, especially in the south.*
EDIBILITY *Edible.*
SIMILAR SPECIES *Resin Bracket (Ganoderma resinaceum) and Cinnamon Bracket (Hapalopilus nidulans) both have hard flesh.*

Stinkhorn

Phallus impudicus (Phallaceae)

The best-known member of the *Phallaceae* family, the Stinkhorn is also one of the smelliest, often smelt before it is seen. The smell, when very diluted, is reminiscent of hyacinths but is more unpleasant as one nears the fungus. Hatching from a large egg, lined by a gelatinous substance, the stout white stem is spongy and hollow. It is topped by a thimble-shaped, honeycomb-like cap, covered with the greenish spore mass.

SEEN *usually close to old stumps and dead wood, in both broadleaf and conifer woods, also in sand dunes.*

fruitbody 15–20cm tall

cylindrical stem

large white egg

papery skin

stem inside egg

SECTION

SPORES *Olive-brown.*
FRUITING *Summer to autumn.*
OCCURENCE *Very common throughout.*
EDIBILITY *Edible in egg stage.*
SIMILAR SPECIES *Sand Stinkhorn (P. hadriani), which is usually found on sand dunes, has a pinkish lilac egg and its cap is larger in proportion to the stem.*

Giant Puffball

Calvatia gigantea (Lycoperdaceae)

This impressive fungus is easily recognized by its sheer size, ranging from that of a small football to the size of a sheep – for which it has reportedly been mistaken. It is generally round but with irregular lobes and occasional fissures. When immature and edible, it is creamy white, with firm white flesh throughout and a thick leathery skin that can be easily peeled away. On maturing, the Giant Puffball becomes dark olive-brown, drying out to become polystyrene-like.

PREFERS *nutrient-rich sites in fields and hedgerows, and often near manure heaps and nutrient-loving plants.*

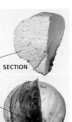

fruitbody to 50cm wide

creamy white when immature

thickened base

SECTION

flesh turns yellow-brown with age

SPORES *Olive-brown.*
FRUITING *Summer to autumn.*
OCCURENCE *Occasional and widespread throughout.*
EDIBILITY *Edible only when young.*
SIMILAR SPECIES *Mosaic Puffball* (Handkea utriformis), *which is smaller, pear-shaped, with a granular to scurfy appearance.*

Stump Puffball

Lycoperdon pyriforme (Lycoperdaceae)

The very young fruitbodies of the Stump Puffball are covered in granular spines, but these are quickly shed to leave a soft, smooth surface. At the base of each fruitbody is a white, root-like strand. Unlike other puffballs, this species always grows on rotten wood, usually in very large clusters.

GROWS *in large, dense clusters on rotten wood such as stumps, buried wood, or fallen trunks.*

cream to buff when young

opening for spore-release

fruitbody 2–3cm wide

smooth surface

root-like strand

SECTION

SPORES *Brown.*
FRUITING *Summer to winter.*
OCCURENCE *Very common throughout.*
EDIBILITY *Edible when young and white.*
SIMILAR SPECIES *None – although other Puffballs may grow on rotten wood, none has the distinct, root-like strand at the stem base.*

Common Puffball

Lycoperdon perlatum (Lycoperdaceae)

ABUNDANT *in small clusters or scattered troops on the ground, occasionally on rotten wood, in broadleaf and conifer woods.*

Like all Lycoperdon species, the Common Puffball produces its spores inside the upper part of the fruitbody and, when mature, releases them through an opening which develops at the top. To do this, the fungus relies on rain drops. When a drop falls on the upper part of the fruitbody, spores puff out of the opening, rather like working a miniature bellows.

brown spore mass

fruitbody browns with age

tiny, conical spines

firm flesh

SECTION

SPORES *Brown.*
FRUITING *Summer to late autumn.*
DISTRIBUTION *Common and widespread.*
EDIBILITY *Edible when young and white throughout.*
SIMILAR SPECIES *Other puffball species lack the Common Puffball's distinctive conical spines.*

Common Earthball ☠

Scleroderma citrinum (Sclerodermataceae)

GROWS *singly or in small groups with broadleaf trees on pathsides and banks, in acid woodland and heaths.*

At first glance this might be confused with a large puffball, but the scaly yellow surface is distinctive. The fruitbody is much heavier and, if cut in two, reveals a thick, fleshy layer containing a dense black mass of spores, which are released when the fruitbody falls apart. It also has a characteristic smell of old rubber.

scaly, yellowish surface

fruitbody 5–15cm wide

dense black spore mass

SECTION

SPORES *Dark brown.*
FRUITING *Summer to late autumn.*
OCCURENCE *Very common and widespread throughout.*
EDIBILITY *Poisonous.*
SIMILAR SPECIES *Potato Earthball (S. bovista) prefers less acid ground and has a smoother, greyer surface with a thin skin.*

Collared Earthstar

Geastrum triplex (Geastraceae)

This is one of the largest and most common earthstars. Young fruitbodies are onion-shaped with a distinct point on top. When mature, the woody outer surface splits and opens out into a star, revealing the puffball-like inner ball which contains the spores. It has a distinctive thick, raised collar around the ball, hence the common name.

FOUND *in small troops in broadleaved woods, along roadside hedgerows, in scrub, and on sand dunes.*

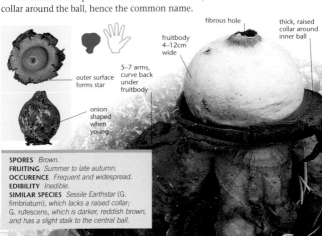

outer surface forms star

onion shaped when young

5–7 arms, curve back under fruitbody

fruitbody 4–12cm wide

fibrous hole

thick, raised collar around inner ball

SPORES *Brown.*
FRUITING *Summer to late autumn.*
OCCURENCE *Frequent and widespread.*
EDIBILITY *Inedible.*
SIMILAR SPECIES *Sessile Earthstar (G. fimbriatum), which lacks a raised collar; G. rufescens, which is darker, reddish brown, and has a slight stalk to the central ball.*

Yellow Brain

Tremella mesenterica (Tremellaceae)

Like a soft, gelatinous flower, this edible species forms irregular, wrinkled, and folded flabby fruitbodies. The colour varies from almost white or translucent to bright golden-yellow. When dry, it shrivels to become hard, tough, and dark orange, but revives with rain to continue spore production. Spores are produced all over the outer surface.

FOUND *usually on fallen wood of broadleaf trees and piles of brushwood; parasitic on crust fungi species.*

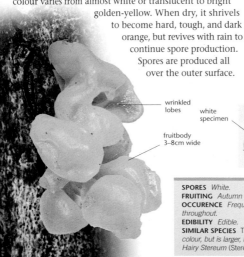

wrinkled lobes

fruitbody 3–8cm wide

white specimen

SPORES *White.*
FRUITING *Autumn to winter.*
OCCURENCE *Frequent and widespread throughout.*
EDIBILITY *Edible.*
SIMILAR SPECIES *T. aurantia is a similar colour, but is larger, more leafy, and parasitizes Hairy Stereum (Stereum hirsutum).*

Jelly Rot

Phlebia tremellosa (Meruliaceae)

INHABITS *the rotten wood of fallen trees, both broadleaf and conifers, creeping over the surface.*

When growing on the underside of logs, this species is often flattened and crust-like against the surface, but it can form narrow shelves or irregular caps several centimetres across on the sides or top of a log. These are soft and rubbery to the touch, whitish and hairy on the upper side, and yellow-orange and minutely wrinkled on the underside. When dry, they can become very tough and leathery. The margin of the caps is usually white and irregular in shape.

shelf to 15cm wide

top turned green by algae

SPORES *White.*
FRUITING *Autumn to early winter.*
OCCURENCE *Uncommon but widespread throughout.*
EDIBILITY *Inedible.*
SIMILAR SPECIES *Other crust fungi lack the dense, tiny wrinkles on the underside and are not as rubbery in consistency.*

White Saddle

Helvella crispa (Helvellaceae)

GROWS *singly or in troops among leaf litter in broadleaf woods, often on disturbed ground along roadsides or tracks.*

White Saddle is probably the commonest and most conspicuous of the saddle fungi. The stem is white with deep, irregular ridges and furrows, while its spore-bearing cap is cream to pale buff, with irregular lobes. White Saddle is a relative of the morels but, unlike them, it is an autumn-fruiting fungus. Though it is said to be eaten after drying or repeated boiling, it is actually poisonous and best avoided.

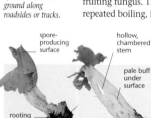

spore-producing surface

hollow, chambered stem

fruitbody 2–6cm wide

pale buff under surface

rooting base

SECTION

deeply ridged stem

SPORES *White.*
FRUITING *Late summer to autumn.*
OCCURENCE *Common and widespread.*
EDIBILITY *Poisonous.*
SIMILAR SPECIES *Elfin Saddle (H. lacunosa), which has a grey-black cap; Pouched False Morel (Gyromitra infula), which has a smoother stalk and brown cap.*

Morel

Morchella esculenta (Morchellaceae)

One of the most well-known edible species, the Morel is collected in large numbers in Europe, Asia, and America. The large, sponge-like cap is a bright ochre-yellow to reddish brown, very crisp, and brittle. The cap is fused at the base to the club-shaped, white or pale brown stem. When young, the cap is darker brown with white wrinkles and takes two weeks or more to mature.

FOUND *among herbaceous plants in open woods, especially near dying elms, ash, and old apple trees.*

honeycomb-like cap

cap 5–12cm wide

paler margins

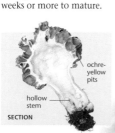

ochre-yellow pits

hollow stem

SECTION

SPORES *Ochre.*
FRUITING *Early summer to late autumn.*
OCCURENCE *Common and widespread.*
EDIBILITY *Edible and tasty when cooked.*
SIMILAR SPECIES *M. elata has grey black conical caps with more vertical ridges. Most Morel species seem to be forms of this very variable species.*

False Morel

Gyromitra esculenta (Helvellaceae)

Although widely eaten, False Morel can be dangerously poisonous, even deadly. It has a distinctive wrinkled red-brown cap folded back over a short, strongly furrowed whitish stem. The chambers of the hollow stem can be seen in cross-section. The very thin cap is fused to the stem at irregular intervals. False Morel is known to contain a poison destroyed by cooking.

SEEN *in conifer woods in sandy soils or in wood chippings.*

wrinkled, brain-like cap

cap 5–15cm wide

hollow stem

SECTION

SPORES *White*
FRUITING *Spring to early summer.*
OCCURENCE *Locally common.*
EDIBILITY *Poisonous, although edible if expertly cooked – best avoided.*
SIMILAR SPECIES *G. infula, which has a simpler, saddle-shaped cap, slender whitish lavender stem, and grows in autumn.*

furrowed, white stem

Orange Peel Fungus

Aleuria aurantia (Otideaceae)

Resembling a piece of orange peel, the underside of the bright orange fungus cup is covered in short, downy white hairs. The margin is inrolled, becoming more flattened and wavy with lobes at the edge with age. The vivid colour may fade in older specimens with thin, brittle, and pale flesh. A short base, which may be off-centre, attaches the cup to the ground.

GROWS *in groups, often in large numbers, on bare ground or grass; favours disturbed man-made sites such as dirt or gravel tracks.*

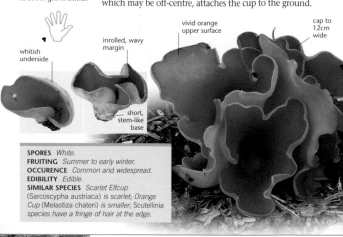

whitish underside

inrolled, wavy margin

short, stem-like base

vivid orange upper surface

cap to 12cm wide

SPORES *White.*
FRUITING *Summer to early winter.*
OCCURENCE *Common and widespread.*
EDIBILITY *Edible.*
SIMILAR SPECIES *Scarlet Elfcup (Sarcoscypha austriaca) is scarlet; Orange Cup (Melastiza chateri) is smaller; Scutellinia species have a fringe of hair at the edge.*

Dog Lichen

Peltigera canina (Peltigeraceae)

Consisting of large leafy structures that are attached lightly to the substrate by small roots called rhizines, members of the genus *Peltigera* are easily recognized. It is, however, often difficult to identify the exact species. Texture of the upper surface and colours are variable. *Peltigera canina* has a grey brown upper surface while the lower surface is fleecy. Its spore-producing capsules consist of reddish brown discs located on the wavy edges of the leafy lobes.

FOUND *on dry calcerous and sandy soil; occurs on damp rocks and trees, and on healthy acidic soil.*

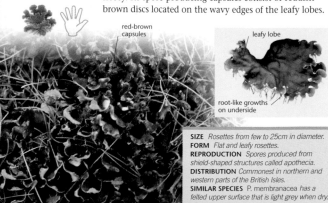

red-brown capsules

leafy lobe

root-like growths on underside

SIZE *Rosettes from few to 25cm in diameter.*
FORM *Flat and leafy rosettes.*
REPRODUCTION *Spores produced from shield-shaped structures called apothecia.*
DISTRIBUTION *Commonest in northern and western parts of the British Isles.*
SIMILAR SPECIES *P. membranacea has a felted upper surface that is light grey when dry.*

Oak Moss

Evernia prunastri (Parmeliaceae)

Lichens that are attached only at the base are called fruticose and *E. prunastri* is the commonest in this group. It has no official English name but is known as *Mousse de Chene* (oak moss) in France. It has a strap-shaped body, with fork-like branches hanging down from the basal attachment. The upper surface of the branches is grey-green but the undersides are white. This distinguishes members of the genus *Evernia* from *Ramalina* species, which are grey-green on both surfaces. Oak Moss had many uses in the past. It was once ground up with rose petals to make a hair powder to whiten wigs and kill off head lice.

FOUND *on trees, shrubs, soil, and fences; early colonizer of twigs and shrubs in towns; sometimes occurs on rocks.*

flat, irregular branches

grey-green above

white below

SIZE *Branches 1–2cm long, to as much as 6cm in very clean air.*
FORM *Shrubby.*
REPRODUCTION *Brown or pinkish, spore-producing discs, but these are very rarely produced.*
DISTRIBUTION *Throughout the British Isles.*
SIMILAR SPECIES *Ramalina farinacea, which is grey-green on both upper and lower surfaces and rarely grows on rock.*

NOTE

Oak Moss is commercially harvested in south-central Europe and exported to France for use in the perfume industry. It adds to the scent and also acts as a fixative, making the perfume last.

Sunburst Lichen

Xanthoria parietina (Teloschistaceae)

GROWS *on rocks and trees along coasts and inland, including walls, roofs, and tombstones.*

The most common yellow-orange lichen, the Sunburst Lichen is characteristically, though not exclusively, maritime. It is tolerant of both salt spray and nitrogen enrichment, and so is often best developed around favoured perching sites for seabirds. It also contributes to the characteristic lichen colour zones of yellow and grey lichens at the high water mark upwards on rocky cliffs.

bright orange-yellow thallus in the open

orange fruiting disc with pale, raised margin

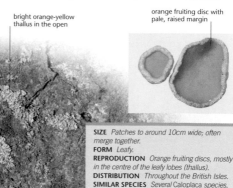

SIZE *Patches to around 10cm wide; often merge together.*
FORM *Leafy.*
REPRODUCTION *Orange fruiting discs, mostly in the centre of the leafy lobes (thallus).*
DISTRIBUTION *Throughout the British Isles.*
SIMILAR SPECIES *Several Caloplaca species, which lack the raised leafy lobes.*

Map Lichen

Rhizocarpon geographicum (Rhizocarpaceae)

FORMS *mosaics across the surface of hard acid rock, especially in upland areas; rare in the lowlands.*

Map Lichen consists of a very distinctive glossy yellow-green crust sitting on a black plate of tissue containing the reproductive structures. The crust is made up of individual parts called areoles. Angular in shape, each areole is outlined by a black margin so that the crust with its black network resembles crazy paving. Small, black spore-bearing structures are usually very abundant within the network.

cracked, yellow-green mosaic

irregular green patches

CLOSE-UP

SIZE *Individual crusts 2–3cm in diameter.*
FORM *Flat crust.*
REPRODUCTION *Small, slightly concave black spore-bearing structures about 1–2mm in diameter.*
DISTRIBUTION *Throughout the British Isles.*
SIMILAR SPECIES *Rhizocarpon lecanorinum, which is matt rather than glossy on the crust.*

Mammals

In many ways mammals represent our most-loved wildlife, but the majority of them are rarely seen, as they lead secretive and often nocturnal lives. Most baby mammals are nourished by milk from their mothers and many are cared for long after they have finished suckling. Some mammals live alone and only come together to mate and raise their young. Other species are social – living in groups that range from small family units to large herds. The Rabbit and the Grey Squirrel, which are actually introduced species, are perhaps the most familiar of mammals to many of us.

WOOD MOUSE

RABBIT

RED FOX

GREY SEAL

Western Hedgehog

Erinaceus europaeus (Insectivora)

Hedgehogs, characterized by their covering of protective spines up to 3cm long and short dark legs are familiar animals in parks and gardens. There are three European species, with the Western Hedgehog being the only one in the British Isles. A noisy forager and largely nocturnal, this hedgehog hibernates in nests of dry grass and leaves.

FOUND *in lowland grassland and open woods; very frequently in gardens.*

ROLLED DEFENSIVE POSTURE

face and limbs hidden

creamy brown spines, often dark-tipped

covered in spines above

hind to 3cm long

droppings to 4cm long

front to 2.5 cm long

SIZE *Body 20–30cm; tail 1–4cm.*
YOUNG *One or two litters of up to six; June–September.*
DIET *Earthworms and other invertebrates; birds' eggs and nestlings; some plant material.*
STATUS *Common.*
SIMILAR SPECIES *None.*

Common Mole

Talpa europaea (Insectivora)

Common Moles are rarely seen above ground, but their presence is easily noted from the spoil heaps (molehills) resulting from their burrowing activity, which continues day and night throughout the year. They are least visible in the heat of summer when their invertebrate prey is forced down to deeper, more moist soil levels. The dispersal of young animals is largely above ground.

FAVOURS *grassland, cultivated areas, and deciduous woodland; avoids places that are prone to flooding.*

dark velvety fur

front to 4mm long, formed by claws only

hind to 2cm

small, but open, eyes

large front feet

spoil heap from tunnelling

MOLEHILL

large front feet

SIZE *Body 11–16cm; tail 2–4cm.*
YOUNG *Usually a single litter of 3–4; May–June.*
DIET *Insect larvae and subterranean invertebrates. Rarely forage on surface.*
STATUS *Common.*
SIMILAR SPECIES *None.*

Common Shrew

Sorex araneus (Insectivora)

Like all shrews, the Common Shrew is a small, active but secretive animal, its elongated snout bearing long sensory bristles. Adults are distinctly three-coloured, with a brown back, creamy underside, and chestnut flanks. In contrast, juveniles have a paler overall appearance, and a thicker tail, which bears tufts of bristly hair. Common Shrews are active by day and night, throughout the year.

FREQUENTS *all habitats with significant ground cover, particularly rough grassland.*

front to 8mm

hind to 1.2cm

droppings 2–4mm long

reddish flanks

dark brown back

small, inconspicuous eyes and ears

slender, pointed muzzle

pale underparts

SIZE *Body 5.5–9cm; tail 3–6cm.*
YOUNG *Up to four litters of 6–7; April–August.*
DIET *Worms, woodlice, spiders, beetles, and other ground-dwelling invertebrates; seeds.*
STATUS *Common.*
SIMILAR SPECIES *Pygmy Shrew (below).*

Pygmy Shrew

Sorex minutus (Insectivora)

The Pygmy Shrew is distinctly smaller than most other widespread shrews in Britain and Europe. Its upper fur is a relatively pale, medium brown colour, which merges into the whitish underside. The tail is relatively long and broad, covered by a dense clothing of hairs. It is active by both day and night, with alternating periods of foraging and rest.

FOUND *in a very wide range of lowland and upland grassy heath and scrub habitats.*

droppings to 4mm long

slender, pointed muzzle

small eyes

hind print to 1.2cm long

front print to 8mm long

very small ears, hidden in fur

no distinct flank colour

more whitish underside

SIZE *Body 4–6cm; tail 3–4.6cm.*
YOUNG *Two litters of 4–7; April–August.*
DIET *Ground-dwelling invertebrates, especially beetles, spiders, and woodlice.*
STATUS *Common, usually less abundant than Common Shrews in the same habitats.*
SIMILAR SPECIES *Common Shrew (above).*

Water Shrew

Neomys fodiens (Insectivora)

A large species, the Water Shrew is usually found in damp areas, as its name would suggest. It is a good swimmer, aided by fringes of hair on the feet and a keel of silvery hairs on the tail. Water Shrews are largely nocturnal foragers, leaving piles of food remains around their feeding sites. They build tunnels near water and live in nests made of dry grass and leaves.

LIVES *in a variety of aquatic habitats, from seaweed-covered boulders to mountain streams at high levels.*

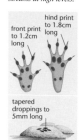

front print to 1.2cm long

hind print to 1.8cm long

tapered droppings to 5mm long

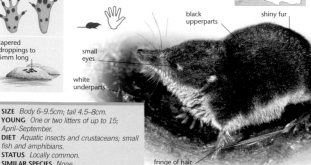

black upperparts

shiny fur

small eyes

white underparts

fringe of hair on feet

SIZE *Body 6–9.5cm; tail 4.5–8cm.*
YOUNG *One or two litters of up to 15; April–September.*
DIET *Aquatic insects and crustaceans; small fish and amphibians.*
STATUS *Locally common.*
SIMILAR SPECIES *None.*

Lesser Horseshoe-bat

Rhinolophus hipposideros (Chiroptera)

Often forming large communal roosts, the Lesser Horseshoe-bat is the smallest species of its group in Europe. Winter roosts, in which it hibernates between November and March, are largely underground, in caves, tunnels, and cellars, but breeding colonies are mostly to be found in buildings.

FOUND *in well-wooded areas, usually associated with limestone geology; hunts close to the ground, usually below 5m.*

greyish ears without a tragus

tapering sella

pale grey below

pale brown membrane

droppings to 8mm long

wings enfold the body completely at rest

wingspan 19–25 cm

SIZE *Body 3.5–4.5cm; tail 2.5–3.3cm.*
YOUNG *Single young; June–August.*
DIET *Small insects and spiders.*
ECHOLOCATION *110kHz.*
STATUS *Vulnerable; scarce and declining.*
SIMILAR SPECIES *Greater Horseshoe-bat (R. ferrumequinum), which is much larger.*

Brown Long-eared Bat

Plecotus auritus (Chiroptera)

Very long ears, up to 4cm long, serve to distinguish the
long-eared bats from all other species. At rest, the ears are
folded back over the body, although the long, narrowly
triangular tragus remains erect. Its thumb is more than
6mm long. The ears and face of the Brown Long-eared Bat
are pinkish brown, while the fur on its upperparts is pale
brown, fading to whitish below. Its flight is graceful and
swooping, often with well-controlled hovering as it
gleans insects off the foliage of trees.

PREFERS *well-wooded,
open areas, such as
parks and gardens;
roosts in buildings and
trees throughout the
year, and occasionally
underground in winter.*

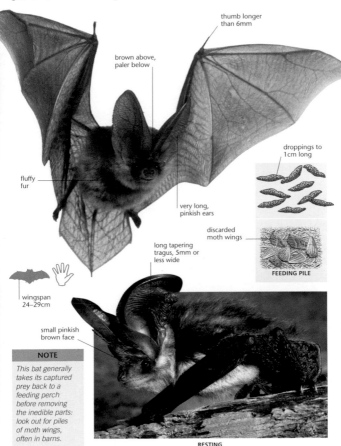

thumb longer
than 6mm

brown above,
paler below

fluffy
fur

very long,
pinkish ears

droppings to
1cm long

discarded
moth wings

FEEDING PILE

long tapering
tragus, 5mm or
less wide

wingspan
24–29cm

small pinkish
brown face

RESTING

NOTE

*This bat generally
takes its captured
prey back to a
feeding perch
before removing
the inedible parts:
look out for piles
of moth wings,
often in barns.*

SIZE *Body 3.5–5.3cm; tail 3.5–5.5cm.*
YOUNG *Single young (occasionally two); June–July.*
DIET *Flying insects, especially moths; spiders and other invertebrates.*
ECHOLOCATION *50kHz, though only very quietly.*
STATUS *Common.*
SIMILAR SPECIES *Grey Long-eared Bat (P. austriacus), a southern
species with darker skin and underfur.*

Common Pipistrelle

Pipistrellus pipistrellus (Chiroptera)

OCCURS *in lowland habitats, including woodland and urban areas, especially around water; roosts in buildings and trees.*

The commonest bat over most of Britain and Europe, Common Pipistrelle is also the smallest. As with other pipistrelles, the wing membrane extends outside the calcar, but the thumb is relatively short. It is a strongly colonial bat and it is quite common to find maternity roosts of more than a thousand females. Its hunting flight is rather jerky, usually below 10m in height. Activity continues later into the autumn than most other bats.

uniformly brown fur

long, blunt tragus

short thumb

droppings to 0.8cm long

wingspan 18–24cm

SIZE *Body 3.3–5.2cm; tail 2.5–3.6cm.*
YOUNG *Single litter of 1–2; May–August; mostly breed every other year.*
DIET *Small flying insects.*
STATUS *Common, though declining.*
ECHOLOCATION *45kHz.*
SIMILAR SPECIES *Other pipistrelles.*

Daubenton's Bat

Myotis daubentonii (Chiroptera)

INHABITS *open wooded areas; summer roosts in cracks in trees and buildings, and under bridges.*

Small to medium-sized, Daubenton's Bat often feeds low over still or slow-moving water. It swims well and is capable of taking flight off the surface of water. In winter, it roosts in underground sites with high humidity, where torpid specimens often covered in dew are found. It occupies rock crevices and may also be found among screes on cave floors.

droppings to 9mm long

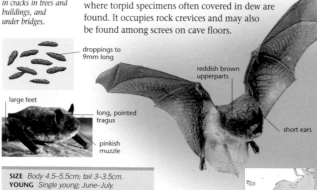

reddish brown upperparts

short ears

large feet

long, pointed tragus

pinkish muzzle

SIZE *Body 4.5–5.5cm; tail 3–3.5cm.*
YOUNG *Single young; June–July.*
DIET *Flying insects, such as caddisflies.*
ECHOLOCATION *45kHz.*
STATUS *Common.*
SIMILAR SPECIES *Natterer's Bat (M. nattereri); Common Pipistrelle (above).*

wingspan 23–27cm

Noctule

Nyctalus noctula (Chiroptera)

The largest widespread British bat, Noctules are relatively visible as a result of their early emergence from roosts, up to an hour before dark. Typically, they fly high (at 50m or more), but it is not difficult to find them even in the dark because the echolocation calls can be picked up on a bat detector at a range of 200m. Noctules also produce an audible (to most people) loud metallic chirp in flight.

FEEDS *over open woodland, summer roosts in tree holes, winter roosts in rock crevices as well.*

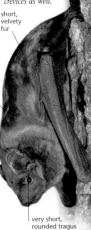

short, velvety fur

pale brown below

rich redbrown fur

droppings to 1.4cm long

wingspan 32–45cm

short, rounded ears

very short, rounded tragus

SIZE *Body 6–8cm; tail 4–6cm.*
YOUNG *Single litter of 1–3; June–July.*
DIET *Large flying insects.*
ECHOLOCATION *25kHz.*
STATUS *Common.*
SIMILAR SPECIES *Serotine (below); Leisler's Bat (N. leisleri), which is smaller and darker.*

Serotine

Eptesicus serotinus (Chiroptera)

The Serotine is often seen feeding at dusk with Swifts (p.348), though at a somewhat lower level than Noctules (above). In reasonable light, the dark upperparts can be seen to

FAVOURS *open and lightly wooded habitats in lowlands; roosts in buildings, occasionally tree holes, and in winter may be found underground.*

dark wing membranes

contrast with the more yellowish underparts. At rest, the dark membranes and face are characteristic, together with its tragus. Its powerful teeth are necessary for tackling hardbodied beetles.

coarse droppings to 1cm long

short, narrow, and concave tragus

large teeth

SIZE *Body 6–8cm; tail 4.5–5.5cm.*
YOUNG *Single young; June–August.*
DIET *Large flying insects, especially dung beetles and moths.*
ECHOLOCATION *25kHz.*
STATUS *Locally common.*
SIMILAR SPECIES *Noctule (above).*

wingspan 32–38cm

Brown Hare

Lepus europaeus (Lagomorpha)

A widespread British species, Brown Hares have long ears and powerful legs which can generate speeds of up to 75km per hour for short bursts. Unlike a Rabbit (below), the tail is held depressed when running. Their activity takes place mostly at dusk and dawn, but they can be active at any time. Field signs include flattened patches of grass, or forms, where they rest by day and rear their young.

FREQUENTS *open agricultural fields and pastures, also hedgerows and woodland.*

black tip

ears more than 8cm long

front to 5cm long

hind to 15cm long

droppings 1cm wide

tail blackish above

rich brown fur, reddening in winter

SIZE *Body 50–70cm; tail 7–10cm.*
YOUNG *About three litters of up to four; February–October.*
DIET *Grazes herbs, cereals, and grasses; browses low shrubs and strips bark.*
STATUS *Common, though declining in parts.*
SIMILAR SPECIES *Rabbit (below).*

Rabbit

Oryctolagus cuniculus (Lagomorpha)

The Rabbit is a familiar part of the British countryside. Its fur is generally grey-brown above and paler below, but a wide range of colour variations from black to white can persist in the wild after escapes from captivity. The tail is brown above and white below; when running, the tail is held erect to display the white fur. The legs are short, yet powerful, and the ears are long.

OCCUPIES *grassland and farmland, with hedges; signs include burrows and droppings in communal latrines.*

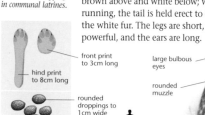

front print to 3cm long

hind print to 8cm long

rounded droppings to 1cm wide

large bulbous eyes

rounded muzzle

used for territorial marking

LATRINE

SIZE *Body 35–45cm; tail 4–8cm.*
YOUNG *Three to seven litters of up to 12 young; February–August.*
DIET *Plant material; strips bark in the winter.*
STATUS *Common.*
SIMILAR SPECIES *Brown Hare (above) and Mountain Hare (Lepus timidus).*

Red Squirrel

Sciurus vulgaris (Rodentia)

A remarkably variable species over much of its range, the Red Squirrel can be any colour from red, through all shades of brown, to black, though always with white underparts. In winter, all variations assume a more greyish appearance. This agile species spends much of its time in trees, where the long bushy tail is used for balance.

OCCUPIES *coniferous and deciduous woodland, where its nests (dreys) are built in the fork of a tree.*

long bushy tail

ear-tufts

front print to 3cm long

nibbled at top

hind print to 5cm long

droppings to 8mm wide

EATEN NUTS

white underparts

SIZE *Body 18–25cm; tail 24–20cm.*
YOUNG *One or two litters of 3–5; March–September.*
DIET *Tree seeds, buds, bark, roots, fungi, birds' eggs, and nestlings.*
STATUS *Near-threatened; locally common.*
SIMILAR SPECIES *Grey Squirrel (below).*

Grey Squirrel

Sciurus carolinensis (Rodentia)

The Grey Squirrel has displaced the Red Squirrel (above) from most of England and Wales. Less arboreal than Red Squirrels, they feed extensively on the ground, and hide caches of acorns and other fruit for future use. The grey fur is variable in colour and the ears are never strongly tufted. Field signs are similar to those of Red Squirrels.

INHABITS *all kinds of woodland, parkland, and gardens with a ready supply of food.*

whitish tail fringe

reddish tone on flanks

front print to 3cm

hind print to 5cm

droppings 8mm wide

DREY

stripped bark

TREE DAMAGE

SIZE *Body 23–30cm; tail 20–24cm.*
YOUNG *One or two litters of 3–6; May–October.*
DIET *Seeds, bark, insects, eggs, and nestlings.*
STATUS *Introduced from North America; very common and still extending its range.*
SIMILAR SPECIES *Red Squirrel (above).*

Bank Vole

Clethrionomys glareolus (Rodentia)

This blunt-nosed vole climbs trees well, making it easier to observe than most other voles. As its activity is mostly under the cover of darkness, identification of its feeding signs is important. These range from small cones stripped of scales and seeds (less frayed than those eaten by squirrels) to hazelnuts with a large, neat, round hole, and no teeth marks outside the opening.

LIVES in scrubby grassland and in deciduous and mixed shrubby woodland.

large ears and eyes

russet-brown back

pale underparts

front to 1cm

hind to 1.8cm

droppings to 4mm

inner bark

AERIAL BARK STRIPPING

SIZE Body 8–11cm; tail 3.5–7cm.
YOUNG Four or five litters of 3–5; April–October, year round if conditions are good.
DIET Buds, leaves, fruit, seeds, and fungi; some invertebrates.
STATUS Common.
SIMILAR SPECIES Field Vole (below).

Field Vole

Microtus agrestis (Rodentia)

Also known as the Short-tailed Vole, the Field Vole has a tail that is shorter than many other voles, and is distinctly dark above. Its long, shaggy fur almost covers its small ears, which are partially hairy inside, especially at the base. Differentiation of the *Microtus* voles by their characteristic teeth details is of little value in the field, but useful for remains found in owl pellets.

FAVOURS marshes, tall grassland, and open woodland; shreds leaves and grass forming clear pathways.

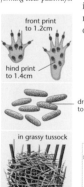

front print to 1.2cm

hind print to 1.4cm

droppings to 4mm

in grassy tussock

NEST

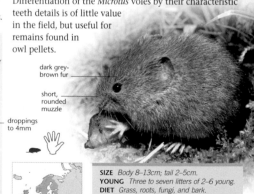

dark grey-brown fur

short, rounded muzzle

SIZE Body 8–13cm; tail 2–5cm.
YOUNG Three to seven litters of 2–6 young.
DIET Grass, roots, fungi, and bark.
STATUS Common; may be a pest.
SIMILAR SPECIES Bank Vole (above); Common Vole (M. arvalis), only on Guernsey and Orkney.

Water Vole

Arvicola terrestris (Rodentia)

A large, blunt-nosed vole with a furry tail, the Water Vole is usually found in or near aquatic habitats. The fur is variable in colour – usually brown, but a large proportion of voles can be almost black. Shredded bark, cut grass leaves, and irregularly gnawed nuts are often the best evidence of its presence, as it is largely active at twilight or before sunrise.

FOUND *in freshwater habitats – listen for the "plop" as it dives for safety; also in meadows and pastures.*

swims high in water

blunt muzzle

front to 2cm

hind to 3.5cm

green, with rounded ends

to 0.8cm

serrated edge to hole

GNAWED NUT

SIZE *Body 12–22cm; tail 6–12cm.*
YOUNG *Two to five litters of 2–6, March–October.*
DIET *Wide range of plant material.*
STATUS *Locally common, but severely declining due to pollution and habitat loss.*
SIMILAR SPECIES *Other smaller voles.*

House Mouse

Mus domesticus (Rodentia)

Worldwide the most widely distributed mammal, apart from humans, the House Mouse is typically grey-brown above and dusky grey below, and there is no sharp line between the colour of the upper- and underparts. Its hairless, thick tail has 140–175 prominent rings and is as long as the head and body length. A distinctive feature of the teeth of the House Mouse is that the upper incisors have a notch at the tip.

FOUND *mainly in buildings, where it is active by night, usually making a nest of paper and fabric.*

dark grey-brown above

small ears and eyes

usually paler below

hairless thick tail

front print to 1cm long

hind print to 1.8cm long

droppings to 6mm

SIZE *Body 7–10cm; tail 7–9.5cm.*
YOUNG *Up to 10 litters of 4–8; year-round if sufficient food is available.*
DIET *Grain, stored food; some invertebrates.*
STATUS *Common.*
SIMILAR SPECIES *Wood Mouse (p.286) and Yellow-necked Mouse (Apodemus flavicollis).*

Wood Mouse

Apodemus sylvaticus (Rodentia)

One of the commonest European mammals, the Wood Mouse is found throughout Britain. It can be confused with the House Mouse (p.285), but it has larger ears, eyes, and feet. It sometimes has a yellowish chest spot. It is very agile, with a bounding, kangaroo-like gait across open ground, and climbs nimbly up trees. Feeding signs to look out for are fir cones with scales neatly gnawed off, and hazelnuts with teeth marks around the outside of the hole.

OCCURS *in woodland, forest edges, grassland, marshes, rocky areas, and cultivated land; frequently to be found in buildings.*

large, beady eyes

large ears

yellow-brown flanks

greyish white underparts

front to 1.2cm

hind to 2cm

droppings to 6mm long

SIZE *Body 8–11cm; tail 7–11.5cm.*
YOUNG *One or two litters of 4–8; March–October.*
DIET *Seeds, cereal crops; insects and snails.*
STATUS *Common.*
SIMILAR SPECIES *Yellow-necked Mouse (A. flavicollis) always has a yellowish chest spot.*

Harvest Mouse

Micromys minutus (Rodentia)

The smallest European rodent, the Harvest Mouse is a very agile climber, using its feet with opposable outer toes to grip grass stems, and the semi-prehensile tail for additional support. The end 2cm of the tail can be curled around a stem, or held out straight for balance. Mainly nocturnal, it remains active throughout the year, although winter months are spent mostly on or below the ground.

OCCUPIES *grassland, scrub patches, river banks, edges of reedbeds, and among cereal crops.*

front to 8mm

hind to 1.5cm

NEST

blunt snout

short hairy ears

orange-brown fur above

whitish underparts

long, semi-prehensile tail

SIZE *Body 5–8cm; tail 5–7cm.*
YOUNG *Three to seven litters of up to eight; May–October.*
DIET *Grain and other seeds; flowers, and fruit; insects and young birds and rodents.*
STATUS *Near-threatened.*
SIMILAR SPECIES *Hazel Dormouse (right).*

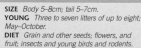

Hazel Dormouse

Muscardinus avellanarius (Rodentia)

A small, orange-brown, largely arboreal rodent, the Hazel or Common Dormouse is nocturnal and hibernates from October to April in a tightly curled position to conserve heat. It is rather sensitive to cold, and even during its active period, cold weather can induce periods of torpor. The nest is a spherical ball of woven grass, moss, and bark strips, positioned in dense undergrowth, or in tree forks or nesting boxes. As befits its climbing habit, its feet are prehensile for grasping branches, and have well-developed pads to enable it to grip well. Its long furry tail may occasionally have a white tip.

FAVOURS *deciduous, often coppiced, woodland, scrub, and thick hedges; rather elusive, so best located by looking for feeding signs, especially hazelnuts with a neat round hole.*

pale below

SLEEPING

NOTE

A classic habitat for the Hazel Dormouse is coppiced Hazel, abundant Bramble, and Climbing Honeysuckle, the latter providing bark strips to line its nest with.

long whiskers

large eyes

orange-brown fur

furry tail

front to 1cm

hind to 1.5cm

droppings to 5mm

smooth inner margin

NIBBLED HAZELNUT

SIZE Body 6–9cm; tail 5.5–8cm.
YOUNG One or two litters of 4–7; June–August.
DIET Flowers, insects, and fruit that is seasonally available in its habitat.
STATUS Near-threatened; scarce and declining due to habitat fragmentation.
SIMILAR SPECIES Harvest Mouse (left), which is a similar size and colour, but has a hairless tail.

Common Rat

Rattus norvegicus (Rodentia)

The Common Rat is also known as the Brown Rat. Its fur is generally a mid-brown colour, but there is some variability. A robust species, the Common Rat is distinguished by its thick tail, which is shorter than the head and body length, as well as being dark above and pale below, and small, hairy ears. They are good swimmers and are largely nocturnal.

OCCURS *in urban, industrial, and other developed areas, farms, refuse tips, river banks, and sewage systems.*

front print to 1.8cm

hind print to 3cm

droppings to 2cm

NIBBLED GRAIN

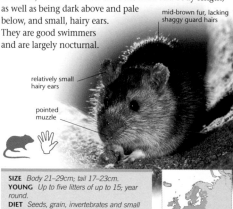

mid-brown fur, lacking shaggy guard hairs

relatively small hairy ears

pointed muzzle

SIZE *Body 21–29cm; tail 17–23cm.*
YOUNG *Up to five litters of up to 15; year round.*
DIET *Seeds, grain, invertebrates and small vertebrates; scavenges from human waste.*
STATUS *Introduced from Asia; common.*
SIMILAR SPECIES *Ship Rat (R. rattus).*

Red Fox

Vulpes vulpes (Carnivora)

Worldwide the most abundant and widespread carnivore, the Red Fox, as it name suggests, is usually a red-brown colour. Its underparts are usually white or pale, as is the tip of its long, bushy tail. The lower part of the legs and the backs of the erect, triangular ears are blackish. Mainly crepuscular and nocturnal, it is most easily noticed by its droppings, the musky odour of its urine, or its nocturnal high-pitched barks.

OCCUPIES *a vast range of habitats, from woodland and farms to mountains and city centres; often secretive.*

reddish brown fur

darker fur patch on narrow muzzle

front print to 5cm long

hind print smaller

tapered droppings 5–10cm long

SIZE *Body 55–90cm; tail 30–45cm.*
YOUNG *Single litter of 4–5; March–May.*
DIET *Omnivorous: rabbits, rodents, birds and their eggs; ground invertebrates; fruit; carrion and food scavenged from refuse tips and bins.*
STATUS *Common.*
SIMILAR SPECIES *None.*

American Mink

Mustela vison (Carnivora)

An introduction in the 1920s, the American Mink has colonized Britain and Europe as a result of escapes from fur-farms. It has now occupied most of Britain and Ireland, and is considered to be a major factor in the recent decline in Water Vole (p.285) numbers. It is typically dark brown; other farmed colour forms that have escaped revert to dark brown after a few generations.

INHABITS *a variety of waterside habitats, even rocky coasts; the droppings are similar to an Otter's but lack their "sweet" smell.*

front to 2.5cm

hind to 4m

twisted, tapering droppings to 8cm

glossy dark brown fur

long, bushy tail

partially webbed toes

white fur on lower lip

SIZE *Body 30–45cm; tail 13–20cm.*
YOUNG *Single litter of 4–6; April–May.*
DIET *Rodents, birds, amphibians, and fish.*
STATUS *Locally common and spreading.*
SIMILAR SPECIES *Otter (p.290), which is larger; Western Polecat (M. putorius), which has a paler face.*

Stoat

Mustela erminea (Carnivora)

The rich chestnut upperparts of this slender, agile predator, contrast sharply with white below, and distinguish the Stoat from all its relatives, except the Weasel (p.290). However, the Weasel never has a black-tipped tail. In winter, all Stoats develop some white fur on the flanks and neck, but in more northerly areas, they assume the "ermine" coat – all white except the black tip to the tail.

FOUND *in most terrestrial habitats with sufficient cover, in woodland, marshes and mountains.*

chestnut upperparts

hind print to 3.5cm

front print to 2cm

droppings to 2cm

long, sinuous body

WINTER COAT

SIZE *Body 18–31cm; tail 9–14cm.*
YOUNG *Single litter of 6–12; April–May.*
DIET *Preys upon rodents (often pursued in their burrows), Rabbits, and birds.*
STATUS *Common.*
SIMILAR SPECIES *Weasel (p.290), which is smaller and does not have a black-tipped tail.*

Weasel

Mustela nivalis (Carnivora)

In Britain, the Weasel is usually distinguishable from the similar Stoat (left) by its smaller size, and shorter tail with no black tip. However, the same is not true across its European range, where Weasels differ considerably in size and winter colour. An inquisitive predator, given its tiny size and high metabolic rate, it must eat several times a day; twenty-four hours without food would lead to starvation.

OCCURS *in all terrestrial habitats, from grassland to woodland, and coasts to mountain tops.*

chestnut fur

short tail

white underparts

hind print to 3cm

front print to 2cm

narrow, twisted droppings to 6cm long

SIZE *Body 13–30cm; tail 3–10cm.*
YOUNG *Single or double litters of 4–6; April–August.*
DIET *Rodents, Rabbits, and birds; needs up to 10 meals each day.*
STATUS *Common.*
SIMILAR SPECIES *Stoat (p.289).*

Otter

Lutra lutra (Carnivora)

A predominantly aquatic mammal, the Otter is generally seen in or near water. However, it will travel long distances overland at night, its main activity period. On land, it travels with an awkward, bounding gait, but in water it is very agile and playful. It swims low in the water, with just the head exposed. When underwater, it has a silvery appearance due to bubbles of air trapped in the fur.

FAVOURS *rivers, lakes, estuaries, and sheltered rocky coasts, without significant disturbance.*

sleek brown fur

whitish throat

fully webbed feet

flattened head

small ears

long, thick, tapering tail

JUVENILE

front to 7cm

hind to 9cm

blackish droppings to 10cm long

SIZE *Body 55–90cm; tail 35–50cm.*
YOUNG *Single litter of 2–5; May–August, but can be all year round.*
DIET *Fish, crustaceans, rodents, and water birds; molluscs in coastal areas; carrion.*
STATUS *Generally scarce; locally common.*
SIMILAR SPECIES *American Mink (p.289).*

Pine Marten

Martes martes (Carnivora)

The Pine Marten's sinuous shape, long legs, and long, bushy tail are useful features for its partly arboreal lifestyle – most of its hunting being done in trees. It climbs with agility despite its relative bulk. Largely nocturnal, it makes a den in a natural hole or crevice in rocks or trees. The most distinctive feature of its generally dark brown coat is the pale throat patch, which is rather variable in colour, from cream to pale orange.

LIVES *mainly in woodland (especially coniferous and mixed), but also colonizes scrub, rocky, and cliff habitats.*

pale patch

dark brown coat

long, bushy tail

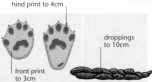

hind print to 4cm

droppings to 10cm

front print to 3cm

NOTE

Formerly found throughout the British Isles, Pine Martens were perscuted almost to extinction in the 19th century. They are now spreading again and have started to recolonize northern England and Wales, benefiting from the afforeststion of the uplands.

SIZE *Body 40–55cm; tail 18–25cm.*
YOUNG *Single litter of 3–5; April–May.*
DIET *Rodents (mainly squirrels), frogs, birds, and eggs; fruit, berries, and fungi; honey.*
STATUS *Locally common.*
SIMILAR SPECIES *None, although Red Squirrel (p.283) may look similar but is smaller if glimpsed in the treetops.*

Badger

Meles meles (Carnivora)

The Badger's complex burrow system (sett) with an often extensive series of holes 20cm or more across is distinctive. The characteristic black and white facial stripes of this nocturnal mammal are surprisingly visible even in twilight conditions, when most badgers are observed. Heavily built, the Badger has a small pointed head and short neck, widening to a powerful body, with short, strong limbs and a small tail.

OCCURS *in a range of habitats; setts are in woodland, scrub, or hedges; forages in open areas.*

front to 12cm
hind to 10cm

grey upperparts

small, white-fringed ears

black and white striped head

SETT

SIZE *Body 67–80cm; tail 12–18cm.*
YOUNG *Single litter of 2–4; January–March.*
DIET *Omnivorous; earthworms, insects, small mammals, amphibians, grain, and carrion.*
STATUS *Common.*
SIMILAR SPECIES *None; the Red Fox (p.288) has similar burrows, but lack the spoil heaps.*

Wild Cat

Felis sylvestris (Carnivora)

The size of a large domestic cat, Wild Cats can be very difficult to tell apart from feral tabbies and especially hybrids. Solitary and nocturnal, the Wild Cat is an agile climber, although it hunts mainly on the ground. This species is relatively short-legged, and so is unable to tolerate snow deeper than 20cm for long periods.

INHABITS *woodland, scrub, and rocky areas, mainly in mountains; makes dens in hollow trees, and rock crevices.*

footprints to 4cm long

droppings to 5cm long

yellow-green eyes

dark markings forming stripes, not blotches

black-tipped, bushy tail with 3–5 dark rings

SIZE *Body 48–65cm; tail 20–35cm.*
YOUNG *Single litter of 2–4; April–September.*
DIET *Rabbits, hares, rodents, birds, lizards, and frogs; exceptionally takes lambs.*
STATUS *Vulnerable, scarce and local, threatened by interbreeding with domestic cats.*
SIMILAR SPECIES *Domestic cats and hybrids.*

Grey Seal

Halichoerus grypus (Pinnipedia)

Male Grey Seals are very large, about a third larger than the females, and both sexes have variably blotchy grey upperparts and paler undersides. In profile, the forehead runs straight into the muzzle and the nostrils are widely separated. Pups are born white and remain on land for several weeks. Almost half of the world population of Grey Seals breeds around the British coastline.

FOUND *along coasts and in coastal marine waters; breeds on rocky islets and grassy coastal strips.*

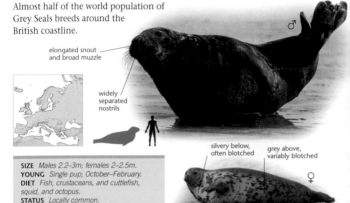

♂

elongated snout and broad muzzle

widely separated nostrils

silvery below, often blotched

grey above, variably blotched

♀

SIZE *Males 2.2–3m; females 2–2.5m.*
YOUNG *Single pup; October–February.*
DIET *Fish, crustaceans, and cuttlefish, squid, and octopus.*
STATUS *Locally common.*
SIMILAR SPECIES *Common Seal (below) is smaller and has a dog-like facial profile.*

Common Seal

Phoca vitulina (Pinnipedia)

Also known as the Harbour Seal, the Common Seal is one of the smaller members of its family, with a grey or brownish coat speckled with black. Its nostrils form a V-shaped pattern. Pups are born with a colour similar to their parents, and are capable of swimming almost immediately after birth. Common Seals can, therefore, breed on tidal flats.

OCCUPIES *shallow coastal waters and estuaries; rocks and sand banks at low tide; swims up rivers.*

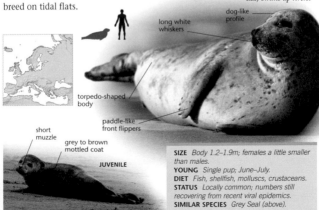

dog-like profile

long white whiskers

torpedo-shaped body

paddle-like front flippers

short muzzle

grey to brown mottled coat

JUVENILE

SIZE *Body 1.2–1.9m; females a little smaller than males.*
YOUNG *Single pup; June–July.*
DIET *Fish, shellfish, molluscs, crustaceans.*
STATUS *Locally common; numbers still recovering from recent viral epidemics.*
SIMILAR SPECIES *Grey Seal (above).*

Harbour Porpoise

Phocoena phocoena (Cetacea)

The commonest (and smallest) cetacean in European waters, the Harbour Porpoise is a relatively nondescript, steely grey above and whitish below. The dorsal fin is located centrally down the back. It has a rounded head and spade-shaped teeth. Unlike most dolphins, the snout is not extended into a beak; nor is it typically as agile as a dolphin, as Harbour Porpoises do not leap clear of the water.

OCCURS *in shallow coastal waters and estuaries right around Britain, including North Sea and Channel waters.*

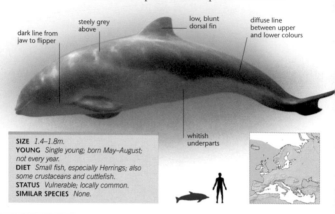

dark line from jaw to flipper

steely grey above

low, blunt dorsal fin

diffuse line between upper and lower colours

whitish underparts

SIZE *1.4–1.8m.*
YOUNG *Single young; born May–August; not every year.*
DIET *Small fish, especially Herrings; also some crustaceans and cuttlefish.*
STATUS *Vulnerable; locally common.*
SIMILAR SPECIES *None.*

Bottlenose Dolphin

Tursiops truncatus (Cetacea)

With resident populations off parts of the Scottish and Welsh coasts, this is the most frequently seen dolphin species. It has greyish upperparts, a short beak, and a long, curved dorsal fin. Despite its bulky appearance, it is very acrobatic, often leaping clear of the water, and it can be very inquisitive, approaching swimmers and boats closely.

OCCURS *worldwide in tropical and temperate seas, from shallow estuaries to deep oceanic water.*

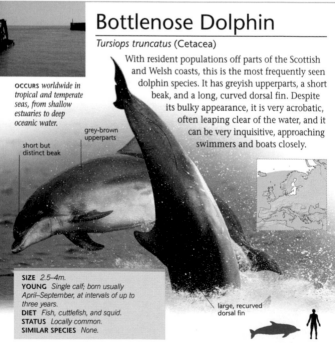

short but distinct beak

grey-brown upperparts

large, recurved dorsal fin

SIZE *2.5–4m.*
YOUNG *Single calf; born usually April–September, at intervals of up to three years.*
DIET *Fish, cuttlefish, and squid.*
STATUS *Locally common.*
SIMILAR SPECIES *None.*

Red Deer

Cervus elaphus (Artiodactyla)

The mature male Red Deer with a full set of antlers is a magnificent sight. All adult animals can be distinguished by their uniform red-brown coat (young fawns are spotted with white), and their buff-coloured rump. These large deer leave many signs of their presence, including mud wallows, and damage to saplings and the bark of larger trees.

FAVOURS *open deciduous woodland, riverine marshes, open mountains and moorland; descends into woodland in winter.*

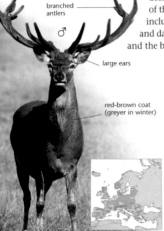

branched antlers

♂

large ears

red-brown coat (greyer in winter)

hind print to 7cm long

front print to 8cm long

acorn-shaped droppings to 1.5cm long

SIZE *Body 1.6–2.6m; tail 10–15cm.*
YOUNG *Single young; born May–June.*
DIET *Grazes, and browses heather, conifers, birch, and other trees; strips bark.*
STATUS *Locally common.*
SIMILAR SPECIES *Sika Deer (Cervus nippon), which is smaller and has a white rump.*

Fallow Deer

Dama dama (Artiodactyla)

A familiar and widespread deer, the Fallow Deer is found over much of Britain and Europe. The ground colour of a Fallow Deer's coat is usually orange-brown, boldly spotted with white in summer and greyer and almost unspotted in winter. At all seasons, the white rump with a black border and long tail with a blackish upper surface are distinctive, as are the flattened, palmate antlers of an adult male.

OCCUPIES *open woodland and parkland, and adjacent agricultural habitats.*

♂

white-spotted summer coat

antlers with single basal point

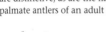

white rump patch

♀

front and hind prints to 6.5cm

pellets to 1.6cm

SIZE *Body 1.3–1.6m; tail 16–20cm.*
YOUNG *Single young; born June–July.*
DIET *Grazes in open woodland or on nearby crops; browses saplings and larger trees; acorns and fruit; strips bark in the winter.*
STATUS *Widely introduced and common.*
SIMILAR SPECIES *Sika Deer (Cervus nippon).*

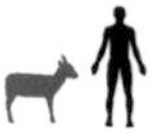

Roe Deer

Capreolus capreolus (Artiodactyla)

The most widespread European deer, and the smallest native species, the Roe Deer is a secretive, solitary, and nocturnal woodland inhabitant, although it is increasingly found in suburban habitats. Red-brown above, turning grey in winter, its most distinctive feature is the white rump patch and short white tail. As with most deer, the fawns are spotted with white. The antlers of the male are short, with at most three points each.

FAVOURS *deciduous and coniferous woodland with dense shrubs, open farmland, reedbeds, and moorland.*

NOTE

Field signs of Roe Deer include frayed tree bark; it rubs against bark to help remove the "velvet" from its developing antlers, and also to act as a territorial marker for the rut.

♀

unspotted red-brown coat

white-spotted coat

small antlers

♂

FAWN

white upper lip and chin

front and hind prints to 4.5cm

front print splayed

droppings to 1.8cm

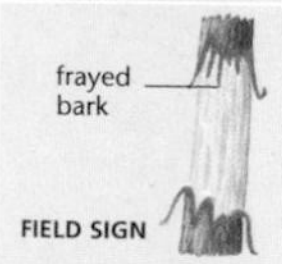

frayed bark

FIELD SIGN

SIZE *Body 1–1.4m; tail 2–3cm.*
YOUNG *Single litter of one, occasionally two; May–June.*
DIET *Browses woodland-edge shrubs and low trees; also eats crops and autumn berries.*
STATUS *Common and increasing.*
SIMILAR SPECIES *Muntjac (Muntiacus reevesi) and Chinese Water Deer (Hydropotes inermis) are both smaller and have a different rump pattern.*

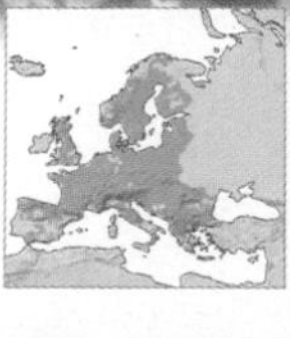

Birds

It is no wonder that birds are admired by so many people, with their bright colours, pleasing song, and great diversity of form. Watching and identifying birds in their natural habitat is an absorbing, and often challenging, pastime. Birds are found in every habitat, but with its long coastline, Britain is particularly important as a migration and wintering site for thousands of waders and ducks, and its sea-cliffs and offshore islands are the principal breeding site for many seabirds.

ROBIN

MARSH HARRIER

KINGFISHER

LONG-EARED OWL

Mute Swan

Cygnus olor (Anatidae)

The huge, elegant Mute Swan is one of the most familiar of waterfowls. It holds its neck in a graceful curve, distinctive at long range, and has a longer tail than the two tundra-breeding swans. Territorial pairs are aggressive, driving off intruders with arched wings and loud hisses.

BREEDS *and feeds on lakes, reservoirs, rivers, estuaries, sheltered coasts, and marshes, as well as nearby fields and urban parks.*

outstretched neck

large black knob; smaller on female

all-white plumage

orange-red bill, angled down

♂

long tail

long, often curved neck

grey-brown plumage

♀

grey bill

VOICE *Strangled trumpeting, snorting, and hissing notes; wings throb loudly in flight.*
NESTING *Huge pile of vegetation at water's edge; 5–8 eggs; 1 brood; March–June.*
FEEDING *Plucks plants from short grass and shallow water; upends in deeper water.*
SIMILAR SPECIES *Bewick's Swan (C. columbianus), Whooper Swan (C. cygnus).*

Pink-footed Goose

Anser brachyrhynchus (Anatidae)

This short-billed goose has a shorter neck than other geese, and a strong contrast between its very dark head and pale breast – features that are often obvious in flight. It occurs in tens of thousands at favoured sites, such as arable land near coast, feeding in dense flocks by day and making spectacular mass flights to its roosts in the evening.

ROOSTS *on estuaries, lakes, islands; feeds on marshes and coasts.*

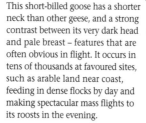

dark underwings

dark, round head

bill with pink band

white-barred, pale grey back

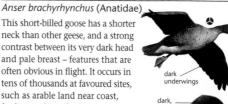

pale grey wings

pale pinkish breast

dark bars on flanks

pale to rich pink legs

VOICE *Resonant ahng-unk and frequent, higher wink-wink.*
NESTING *Down-lined nest on open tundra or rocky slope; 4–6 eggs; 1 brood; June–July.*
FEEDING *Eats grass, waste grain, sugar beet tops, carrots, and potatoes, feeding in flocks.*
SIMILAR SPECIES *Greylag Goose (right), Bean Goose (A. fabalis).*

Greylag Goose

Anser anser (Anatidae)

The heaviest of the grey geese, the Greylag Goose looks pale in soft light but its colours look more contrasted in strong sun. It has a very pale forewing, and its white stern is often conspicuous. Its honking calls are familiar, betraying the fact that it is a direct ancestor of domestic geese.

FEEDS *on coastal marshes, pastures, and farmland in winter. Breeds by lakes and coastal inlets.*

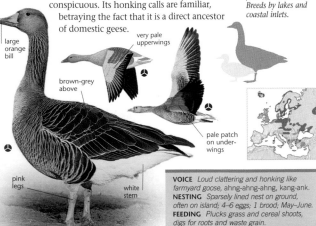

large orange bill

very pale upperwings

brown-grey above

pale patch on under-wings

pink legs

white stern

> **VOICE** *Loud clattering and honking like farmyard goose, ahng-ahng-ahng, kang-ank.*
> **NESTING** *Sparsely lined nest on ground, often on island; 4–6 eggs; 1 brood; May–June.*
> **FEEDING** *Plucks grass and cereal shoots, digs for roots and waste grain.*
> **SIMILAR SPECIES** *Pink-footed Goose (left), White-fronted Goose (A. albifrons).*

Canada Goose

Branta canadensis (Anatidae)

A large goose with a black head and neck and a distinctive white "chinstrap", the Canada Goose is a native of North America that has become common in Britain and other parts of northern Europe. Originally migratory, this species is largely resident apart from annual movements to moulting grounds on quiet estuaries. Flocks of Canada Geese usually draw attention to themselves by their loud, honking calls.

LIVES *on lakes, rivers, marshes, reservoirs, and surrounding grassland; also town parks and estuaries.*

black bill

black head and neck

brown upperparts

white rump

tail held high

white stern

black legs

> **VOICE** *Deep, loud, trumpeting ah-ronk!; loud, honking effect from flock in flight.*
> **NESTING** *Down-lined scrape on ground; loosely colonial; 5–6 eggs; 1 brood; April–June.*
> **FEEDING** *Grazes on grass and cereals in fields close to water; takes some aquatic plants.*
> **SIMILAR SPECIES** *Barnacle Goose (B. leucopsis).*

Brent Goose

Branta bernicla (Anatidae)

This small, very dark goose occurs as two main races, dark-bellied and pale-bellied; the black-bellied North American race is a rare vagrant. All have black heads and a distinctive white neck patch. Flocks often feed on the water, upending like ducks to reach vegetation growing beneath the surface.

WINTERS *on muddy estuaries and harbours, salt marshes, and nearby arable land. Breeds on tundra.*

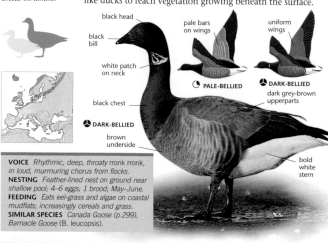

black head

black bill

white patch on neck

black chest

pale bars on wings

🌓 **PALE-BELLIED**

uniform wings

🌑 **DARK-BELLIED**

dark grey-brown upperparts

🌑 **DARK-BELLIED**

brown underside

bold white stern

VOICE *Rhythmic, deep, throaty rronk rronk, in loud, murmuring chorus from flocks.*
NESTING *Feather-lined nest on ground near shallow pool; 4–6 eggs; 1 brood; May–June.*
FEEDING *Eats eel-grass and algae on coastal mudflats; increasingly cereals and grass.*
SIMILAR SPECIES *Canada Goose (p.299), Barnacle Goose (B. leucopsis).*

Shelduck

Tadorna tadorna (Anatidae)

Looking black and white at a distance, but revealing rich chestnut patches and a bright red bill at close range in breeding plumage, the Shelduck is a handsome, erect, rather goose-like duck that lives mainly on coasts and estuaries. In eclipse plumage, it is less distinctive, but still easy to identify. It is usually seen in pairs or small, loose flocks.

FEEDS *and breeds on sandy or muddy shores, especially on sheltered estuaries; some breed near inland lakes.*

brown-black cap

pink or grey bill

tawny orange band

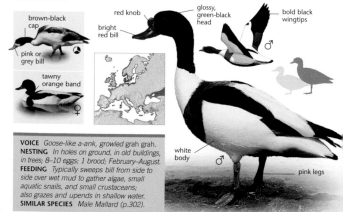

red knob

bright red bill

glossy, green-black head

bold black wingtips

♂

♀

white body

♂

pink legs

VOICE *Goose-like a-ank, growled grah grah.*
NESTING *In holes on ground, in old buildings, in trees; 8–10 eggs; 1 brood; February–August.*
FEEDING *Typically sweeps bill from side to side over wet mud to gather algae, small aquatic snails, and small crustaceans; also grazes and upends in shallow water.*
SIMILAR SPECIES *Male Mallard (p.302).*

Wigeon

Anas penelope (Anatidae)

Although it often nests far from the sea in its northern breeding grounds, the Wigeon is a characteristic duck of coastal estuaries and salt marshes in winter. The often large grazing flocks advance across the ground in a tightly packed mass. Squat and short-legged on the ground, Wigeon are transformed into swift and elegant birds in flight.

BREEDS *on edges of moorland pools and lakes in Britain. Winters on estuaries, freshwater marshes, or around reservoirs.*

dull grey wings

♀

♂❄

sharp tail

reddish flanks

rounded grey body; paler than male Teal's

♂❄

chestnut head and neck

retains white on wing

♂❄

round head

black tip

♀

black-and-white stern

pinkish breast

white belly

VOICE Male has loud, musical whistling whee-oo; female gives deep, harsh growls.
NESTING Down-lined hollow on ground among tallish vegetation, near water; 8–9 eggs; 1 brood; April–July.
FEEDING Grazes on short grasses; also feeds by dabbling and upending in shallow water.
SIMILAR SPECIES Male Teal (below).

Teal

Anas crecca (Anatidae)

The Teal is the smallest of the common European surface-feeding ducks. Outside the breeding season, it is usually seen in smallish flocks. Taking off almost vertically, the fast-flying birds wheel and turn with great agility, co-ordinating their actions precisely like a flock of small waders.

LIVES *in freshwater marshes and on boggy heathland and moorland. Winters mainly on fresh waters and estuaries.*

♀

white midwing bars

cream-edged green band

chestnut head

white centre to underwings

♂❄

grey bill

green patch

pale streak by tail

finely barred grey body

♀

streaked brown

VOICE Male has far-carrying, high-pitched, piping crik crik; female utters high quacks.
NESTING Down-lined hollow near water; 8–11 eggs; 1 brood; April–June.
FEEDING Dabbles and upends mainly for seeds, but also small snails, fly larvae, and other aquatic animals in breeding season.
SIMILAR SPECIES Male Wigeon (above).

Gadwall

Anas strepera (Anatidae)

An elegant, exquisitely marked bird at close range, the Gadwall can appear rather drab-looking at a distance. It has a smaller, squarer head than the similar Mallard (below), which gives it a different character; the male also has a darker body than a Mallard or Wigeon (p.301). In spring, pairs are often seen flying over their territories, calling loudly.

FEEDS *and breeds on lakes and rivers with reeds or wooded islands. Winters on open waters.*

protruding head

steep forehead

pale brown head ♂❋

pale area

white patch near base of wings

♂❄

white belly

black stern

mottled brown body

♂☼

narrow, straight, black bill

grey body

pale, yellowish orange legs

white patch

paler head than Mallard

♀

white patch

VOICE *Male has high, whistling* pee *and deep, croaking* ahrk; *female gives loud quack.*
NESTING *Nest is down-lined hollow on ground near water; 8–12 eggs; 1 brood; April–June.*
FEEDING *Dabbles and upends for plant matter in shallow water; also takes insects.*
SIMILAR SPECIES *Mallard (below).*

Mallard

Anas platyrhynchos (Anatidae)

Common, widespread, and adaptable, able to thrive in all kinds of environments from town parks to coastal marshes, the Mallard is the most familiar of all the ducks. The breeding male's glossy green head and white neck-ring are instantly recognizable, and both sexes sport a characteristic purple-blue wing patch or speculum throughout the year.

FEEDS *on arable land and muddy lake margins. Breeds on and near all kinds of waters.*

white underwings

blue hindwings

♂

orange legs

♀

dark belly

♂❋

white neck-ring

pale body

curly central tail feathers

blue speculum

♀

purple-blue, white-edged speculum

becomes browner

♂☼

VOICE *Male whistles quietly; female gives loud, descending quacks, quark quark quark.*
NESTING *Usually on ground in down-lined hollow; 9–13 eggs; 1 brood; January–August.*
FEEDING *Takes aquatic invertebrates and plant matter while upending or dabbling.*
SIMILAR SPECIES *Gadwall (above), Shoveler (p.304), Pintail (p.304).*

Pochard

Aythya ferina (Anatidae)

Pochard often appear in large flocks on lakes in autumn, feed for a day or two and then move on. A winter male is striking, with a rich red head, black breast, and grey body; the female is greyish with pale "spectacles", but has a similar grey-patched bill. Often sleepy by day, they sit on the water in tight, frequently single-sex flocks.

WINTERS *on open lakes and estuaries; breeds by reedy lakes, rivers, and marshes.*

pale grey wingbars

♂❄

pale grey back

peaked crown

rich red head

dark bill with pale patch

black breast

dull grey-brown

dark cap

brown with pale flanks ♀

♂☼

dull head

brownish red head ♂♨

VOICE *Wheezing rise-and-fall call from displaying male; purring growl from female.*
NESTING *Pad of leaves and down on ground near water; 8–10 eggs; 1 brood; April–July.*
FEEDING *Dives from surface, taking seeds, shoots, and roots; often feeds at night.*
SIMILAR SPECIES *Female Tufted Duck (below), Scaup (A. marila).*

Tufted Duck

Aythya fuligula (Anatidae)

The drooping crest and black-backed, pied plumage of the male Tufted Duck are distinctive in winter, but females and summer males are dark, dull, and easy to confuse with Scaup (*A. marila*). A Tufted Duck has a larger black tip on the bill, which helps to identify it at close range.

BREEDS *in long grass around lakes and rivers; winters on lakes and sheltered coastal waters.*

golden eyes

♂

♀

bold white wingbars

long, wispy tuft on nape

black body with white flanks

blue-grey bill with large black tip

♂❄

slight tuft

dull brown body ♂☼

short crest ♀

VOICE *Deep, grating growl; male gives nasal whistles during courtship.*
NESTING *Down-lined hollow concealed in dense, tall vegetation close to water; 8–11 eggs; 1 brood; May–June.*
FEEDING *Dives for molluscs and insects.*
SIMILAR SPECIES *Female Pochard (above), Scaup (A. marila).*

Pintail

Anas acuta (Anatidae)

Arguably the most elegant of all the surface-feeding ducks, the Pintail is a big, slim, long-necked bird. The striking breeding plumage of the males, acquired as with other ducks in winter, is unmistakable, but females and immatures need separating from those of other dabbling ducks. Good clues are the long neck, slim bill, and more pointed tail.

FEEDS at wintering sites on estuaries and fresh marshes; breeds by tundra and upland pools or lowland coastal marshes.

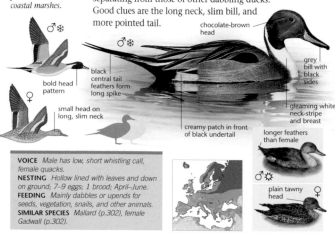

♂❋

bold head pattern

♀

small head on long, slim neck

black central tail feathers form long spike

chocolate-brown head

grey bill with black sides

gleaming white neck-stripe and breast

creamy patch in front of black undertail

longer feathers than female

♂❊

plain tawny head ♀

VOICE Male has low, short whistling call, female quacks.
NESTING Hollow lined with leaves and down on ground; 7–9 eggs; 1 brood; April–June.
FEEDING Mainly dabbles or upends for seeds, vegetation, snails, and other animals.
SIMILAR SPECIES Mallard (p.302), female Gadwall (p.302).

Shoveler

Anas clypeata (Anatidae)

Male Shovelers in breeding plumage look superficially like male Mallards (p.302), however, they are easily distinguished by their low-slung bodies, gleaming white breasts that contrast with the dark green head and chestnut flanks, and above all, by their outsized, broad, shovel-like bill. The bill and body shape of the female helps separate them from other dabbling ducks.

WINTERS and breeds by reedy pools, mainly in lowlands.

streaked, pale brown body

♀

huge bill

dark head

♂❊

pale crescent

dark rufous flanks

yellow eye

huge, long, broad bill

♂❋

pale blue forewings

♂

grey forewings

♀

VOICE Often silent birds; rival males give nasal took took calls; females may give soft quacks.
NESTING Hollow lined with down, near water; 8–12 eggs; 1 brood; March–June.
FEEDING Dabbles on surface for seeds and invertebrates.
SIMILAR SPECIES Mallard (p.302), female Garganey (A. querquedula).

Eider

Somateria mollissima (Anatidae)

A big, bulky, entirely marine duck with a characteristic wedge-shaped head, the Eider is usually easy to identify. A winter male is boldly pied black and white, with green patches on its head and a pink flush on its breast. Females have brown plumage with close dark bars that provide superb camouflage on the nest. Highly sociable, Eiders often form large rafts offshore, but they are equally familiar around coastal rocks.

BREEDS *on low-lying northern coasts and islands with rocky shores and weedy bays. Winters at sea, often in sandy bays and over mussel beds.*

black outer wings

dark hindwings

white rear flanks

♂

♀

pale line above eye

brown, closely barred body

dark belly

♀

black crown

green patch

wedge-shaped bill

black underparts

white upperparts

pinkish breast

♂❄

white patch

black stern

♂☀ — unbarred dark body, often piebald

pale band over eye ◐

NOTE

The male Eider is the only duck that combines a white back and breast with black flanks and belly – features that are readily seen at long range.

VOICE *Male gives sensuous, cooing aa-ahooh; females respond with deep growls and a mechanical kok-kok-kok.*
NESTING *Hollow on ground, liberally lined with down, either exposed or well hidden; 4–6 eggs; 1 brood; April–June.*
FEEDING *Eats mainly molluscs, especially mussels, diving from surface to gather them from rocks; also crustaceans such as crabs and shrimps, starfish, and marine worms.*
SIMILAR SPECIES *Velvet Scoter (Melanitta fusca), female Mallard (p.302).*

Goosander

Mergus merganser (Anatidae)

The Goosander is the largest of the sawbills with a thick, strongly-hooked bill. The male is white with a salmon-pink tinge, and has a drooping crest on its green-black head. The smaller female is mostly blue-grey with a dark rufous head and a white throat. It is a shy, wary bird.

FEEDS *mainly on fresh water, on lakes and rivers. In summer, breeding pairs prefer upland reservoirs and shallow streams.*

dark eyes

plum-red bill

black back

striped face

greyish body

blue-grey body

long tail

dark brown head

salmon-pink to white body

large white wing patch

elongated look in flight

VOICE *Usually silent, male croaks during courtship; female cackles and give harsh karrr.*
NESTING *Usually hole in tree near water; 8–11 eggs; 1 brood; April–July.*
FEEDING *Dives from surface, travelling long distances underwater in lakes, to take fish.*
SIMILAR SPECIES *Male Mallard (p.302), Red-breasted Merganser (M. serrator).*

Ruddy Duck

Oxyura jamaicensis

Striking and distinctive, the breeding male Ruddy Duck has a chestnut body, white cheeks, and gaudy blue bill. During his dramatic courtship display, he vibrates his bill against his breast, creating a flurry of bubbles on the water surface. The Ruddy Duck is a strictly freshwater bird, typically feeding in family parties on the reedy shores of small lakes in summer.

BREEDS ON *reedy pools, flooded gravel pits, and sand pits, moving to larger, more open lakes and reservoirs in autumn and winter.*

dull grey-brown body

blackish bill

all-dark wings

white face

black cap and nape

rounded back

dark grey bill

cheek stripe

stiff tail, laid flat or angled upward

VOICE *Mostly silent, but male grunts during display; female gives hisses and squeaks.*
NESTING *Large, floating pile of vegetation in tall reeds; 6–10 eggs; 1 brood; April–June.*
FEEDING *Dives for insect larvae and seeds from surface, reappearing like bobbing cork.*
SIMILAR SPECIES *Smew (Mergellus albellus), Common Scoter (Melanitta nigra).*

Red Grouse

Lagopus lagopus (Tetraonidae)

This is a thickset bird of heather-clad moors. It looks rather like a larger, darker partridge, but is more evenly mottled, rather than streaked and barred. In flight, it reveals darker wings and almost black sides to the short tail, and distinctive white underwings. Its echoing calls are a characteristic of upland moors.

short stout bill

red wattle over eye

FOUND *mainly on dry heather moorland on northern hills of the British Isles.*

stiff dark wing

short dark tail

♂

yellow-brown plumage

heavily mottled body

♀

plain dark wings

short blackish tail

feathered feet

VOICE Deep, staccato calls, kau-kau-kau-ka-ka-karrr-rrr-g'back, g'back, bak.
NESTING Sparsely lined scrape on ground in heather; 6–9 eggs; 1 brood; April–May.
FEEDING Plucks shoots and seeds from heather; also takes a variety of berries and seeds; chicks feed on insects.
SIMILAR SPECIES Grey Partridge (p.308).

Red-legged Partridge

Alectoris rufa (Phasianidae)

An elegant gamebird with a bright red bill, the Red-legged Partridge is surprisingly well camouflaged and often hard to spot. It favours warm, open, stony slopes, or farmland with sandy soils. Its plumage looks unmistakable, but in many parts of its range, this bird is easily confused with hybrids resulting from crosses with the introduced Chukar Partridge (*A. chukar*).

BREEDS *on open slopes with bare ground and dry, sandy arable land; also on grassy heaths and coastal dunes.*

plain pale brown above

black, grey, and brown bars on flanks

white stripe

dark red-brown tail

black-streaked "necklace"

straight, stiff wings

red legs

rufous tail

VOICE Deep, gobbling and hissing or chuckling mechanical calls, chuk-uk-ar, k'chuk-ar, k'chuk-ar.
NESTING Grass-lined scrape beneath low vegetation; 7–20 eggs; 1 brood; April–June.
FEEDING Takes leaves, shoots, berries, nuts, and seeds from ground; chicks eat insects.
SIMILAR SPECIES Grey Partridge (p.308).

Grey Partridge

Perdix perdix (Phasianidae)

LIVES *mainly on farm-land, especially grassy meadows with rich insect life; also on heaths, low moorland, and dunes.*

This neat gamebird is typical of old-fashioned farmland with hedges. It feeds secretively in long grass, in tight flocks, pausing to raise its head and look around. If disturbed, it rockets off with whirring wings, alternating with short glides on bowed wings.

dull brown bill

orange-brown face

orange tail sides

pale brown wings

streaked back

finely barred grey breast

bold red-brown bars on flanks

dull brown legs

broad, brown belly patch

♂

VOICE *Distinctive low, rhythmic, mechanical, creaky kieeer-ik or ki-yik.*
NESTING *Well-hidden, shallow scrape on ground; 10–20 eggs; 1 brood, April–June.*
FEEDING *Takes seeds, leaves, and shoots from ground; feeds insects to chicks.*
SIMILAR SPECIES *Red-legged Partridge (p.307), juvenile Pheasant (below).*

Pheasant

Phasianus colchicus (Phasianidae)

INHABITS *mainly in wood-land edge, arable land, reedbeds, heaths, and moorland edge.*

The male pheasant is a conspicuous, noisy bird, although very variable, with or without a white neck-ring but always with a bold red wattle around the eye. The female is more anonymous-looking and secretive, but the long, pointed tail is very distinctive.

bare red skin

long neck

orange-copper flanks

♂

tail longer than female's

white neck-ring

often has pale rump

♀

long pointed tail

black markings

♀

white markings

♂

VOICE *Loud, explosive corr-kok! with sudden whirr of wings; loud clucking in flight.*
NESTING *Hollow on ground, beneath cover; 8–15 eggs; 1 brood; April–July.*
FEEDING *Takes a variety of food from ground, from seeds and berries to insects and lizards.*
SIMILAR SPECIES *Female like female Grey Partridge (above), Black Grouse (Tetrao tetrix).*

Capercaillie

Tetrao urogallus (Tetraonidae)

The magnificent Capercaillie is by far the largest of the grouse. The male in particular is a massive, dark, turkey-like, aggressive bird; the female is much smaller, but still big in comparison with other grouse, with an orange breast and a broad tail. Males display competitively in spring, attracting females with their remarkable voices and wing-flapping leaps. Generally shy and secretive, the Capercaillie is sensitive to disturbance and is now seriously threatened in many parts of its range, including Scotland.

LIVES *in ancient pine forests and boggy forest clearings with bilberry, juniper, and heather; less often in mature pine plantations.*

short, stout, pale, hooked bill

red comb

♀

dark bars on orange tail

♂

big, rounded tail

brown wings

"beard" of spiky feathers

black tail, speckled with white

bold white shoulder spot

broad, round tail when fanned in display

huge, blackish body

♂

brown wings

dark bars on rufous-ginger body

cream with black and rufous bars

orange breast

♀

NOTE

Despite its size, the Capercaillie roosts in the trees, and often feeds up in the branches in winter. In summer, it is more likely to be found at ground level. It rarely allows a close approach, but sometimes sits tight until it is forced to burst up from underfoot in a cacophony of flapping wings.

VOICE Pheasant-like crowing; male in spring utters bizarre "song" of clicks and belches, ending with cork-popping and wheezy gurgling.
NESTING Hollow on ground, often at base of tree, lined with grass, pine needles, and twigs; 5–8 eggs; 1 brood; March–July.
FEEDING Eats shoots, leaves, and buds of several shrubs and trees, berries of various herbs and shrubs, especially bilberry, and pine needles taken from treetops in winter.
SIMILAR SPECIES Female Black Grouse (T. tetrix).

Little Grebe

Tachybaptus ruficollis (Podicipedidae)

INHABITS *freshwater lakes, ponds, flooded pits, and rivers. Winters on larger waters or sheltered coastal waters.*

The smallest European grebe, this dark, short-billed, rotund, and almost tailless bird swims buoyantly and dives often. Longer-necked and less portly in winter, it can look like a Black-necked Grebe *(Podiceps nigricollis)*. In summer, its whinnying trills are a good clue to its presence.

all-dark wings

trailing feet

blackish cap

rufous on face and neck

pale yellow spot on short bill

buff foreneck

buffish face

"sawn-off" rear end due to very short, buff tail

VOICE *When breeding, distinctive high-pitched, rapid trill that fades away.*
NESTING *Floating mound of weed, anchored to branch; 4–6 eggs; 1 brood; April–June.*
FEEDING *Dives to catch small fish, insects, and molluscs.*
SIMILAR SPECIES *Moorhen (p.320), Black-necked Grebe (Podiceps nigricollis).*

Great Crested Grebe

Podiceps cristatus (Podicipedidae)

COURTS *and breeds on flooded gravel pits, reservoirs, or big lakes and rivers; winters on fresh waters or sheltered coastal waters.*

Largest of European grebes, this is a striking bird in spring and summer, when pairs use their spectacular head ruff and spiky head tufts in face-to-face head-shaking courtship displays. They also dive, surfacing with weed in their bills to offer one another. Winter birds are hard to distinguish from scarcer Red-necked Grebes *(P. grisegena)*.

black head plumes

dagger-like pink bill

unique ruff

slender white neck and white breast

drooping neck

two bold white patches

VOICE *Loud growls and barks while courting and nesting; juveniles make loud whistles.*
NESTING *Semi-floating pile of wet weed; 3–4 eggs; 1 brood; February–June.*
FEEDING *Dives to catch mainly fish, also aquatic insect larvae and small amphibians.*
SIMILAR SPECIES *Red-necked Grebe (P. grisegena).*

striped head

pink bill

pale greyish

white over eye

white foreneck

Fulmar

Fulmarus glacialis (Procellariidae)

Although it has gull-like plumage, the Fulmar is a tube-nosed petrel more closely related to the albatrosses. It holds its wings straight when gliding, unlike a gull, and has a distinctive thick neck and black eye-patch. Fulmars are often seen soaring on updraughts around coastal cliffs, although they spend much of their time at sea.

FEEDS *at sea; breeds on steep coastal cliffs or on remote grassy banks near sea.*

black eye-patch

yellowish white head

tubular nostrils

short, thick neck

hooked bill

pale patch

stiff, straight wings

grey wingtips

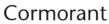

pale grey rump and tail

weak legs (cannot stand)

VOICE *Loud, harsh, throaty cackling heard only at nesting ledge; generally silent at sea.*
NESTING *On cliff or earth ledge, or rarely on building; 1 egg; 1 brood; April–June.*
FEEDING *Takes mostly fish offal from trawlers, small fish, jellyfish, squid, and other marine animals.*
SIMILAR SPECIES *Herring Gull (p.331).*

Cormorant

Phalacrocorax carbo (Phalacrocoracidae)

Bigger and bulkier than a Shag (p.312), and slightly less snaky in shape, the Cormorant has a thicker bill, a low, flat forehead, and no crest. Cormorants swim with their backs almost awash, and typically perch with their wings half-open.

LIVES *on coasts in sheltered estuaries and bays; also inland on lakes, rivers, and pools. Breeds on cliffs.*

yellow near bill

white on face

blue gloss on head and neck

white below

neck kinked in flight

bill tilted up

blackish above, with bronze gloss

brown above

long, broad tail

VOICE *Growling and cackling at nests and communal roosts, but otherwise a quiet bird.*
NESTING *Bulky nest of sticks in a tree or on a cliff ledge, often marked by white splashes beneath; 3–4 eggs; 1 brood; April–May.*
FEEDING *Catches fish, such as eels, in long underwater dive from surface.*
SIMILAR SPECIES *Shag (p.312).*

Shag

Phalacrocorax aristotelis (Phalacrocoracidae)

This large, long-bodied diving bird is black overall with an oily green gloss, the only colour being the bright yellow patch at the base of its bill. Although sometimes solitary, Shags tend to feed in flocks, favouring the fast tide races and rough water under rocks and cliffs.

SEEN *off rocky coasts and islands; not common around harbours. Breeds on coastal cliffs.*

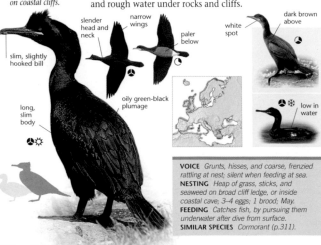

slender head and neck

narrow wings

paler below

white spot

dark brown above

slim, slightly hooked bill

long, slim body

oily green-black plumage

low in water

VOICE *Grunts, hisses, and coarse, frenzied rattling at nest; silent when feeding at sea.*
NESTING *Heap of grass, sticks, and seaweed on broad cliff ledge, or inside coastal cave; 3–4 eggs; 1 brood; May.*
FEEDING *Catches fish, by pursuing them underwater after dive from surface.*
SIMILAR SPECIES *Cormorant (p.311).*

Gannet

Morus bassanus (Sulidae)

Largest of all European seabirds, the adult Gannet is typically seen offshore as a brilliant white bird with black wingtips, flying steadily, singly or in straggling lines, or circling and diving for fish with spectacular plunges. Juvenile birds, by contrast, are very dark with white specks.

FEEDS *at sea, many moving south for the winter; breeds in dense, noisy colonies on rocky islands.*

pale blue eyes

white plumage

webbing across all four toes

yellowish head

blackish above with white spots

piebald; turns white with age

white band above tail

black wingtips

large black wingtips

VOICE *Croaks at nesting colony; cackling from groups feeding at sea; otherwise silent.*
NESTING *Pile of seaweed and debris on broad ledge high above sea, in dense, often very large colony; 1 egg; 1 brood; April–July.*
FEEDING *Catches fish underwater, in dive from air; also scavenges from fishing boats.*
SIMILAR SPECIES *Arctic Skua (p.330).*

Bittern

Botaurus stellaris (Ardeidae)

This very secretive, large, bulky bird is more often heard than seen, when males proclaim their territories by a remarkable booming "song", audible up to 5 km away. Restricted to large wet reedbeds, the Bittern is very local and scattered across its British range.

BREEDS *in large, wet reedbeds. More widespread in winter, when it may be forced by frost to feed in smaller patches of reed or open water.*

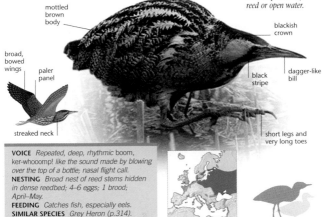

mottled brown body

blackish crown

broad, bowed wings

paler panel

black stripe

dagger-like bill

streaked neck

short legs and very long toes

VOICE *Repeated, deep, rhythmic* boom, ker-whooomp! *like the sound made by blowing over the top of a bottle; nasal flight call.*
NESTING *Broad nest of reed stems hidden in dense reedbed; 4–6 eggs; 1 brood; April–May.*
FEEDING *Catches fish, especially eels.*
SIMILAR SPECIES *Grey Heron (p.314).*

Little Egret

Egretta garzetta (Ardeidae)

This dazzling white bird is the most widespread of Europe's white herons. Found in both freshwater wetlands and along coasts, it is steadily spreading northwards in western Europe. It is much smaller than the Great White Egret. Often active and agile in search of prey, it also spends much time wading slowly or standing still.

SEEN *feeding in small loose flocks by or in water, on lakes and shores.*

all-white plumage

pointed breast plumes

rather bowed wings

no head or back plumes

black legs

yellow feet

VOICE *Usually silent except when breeding, when it utters snarling and croaking calls.*
NESTING *Stick nest in tree, often with other herons and cormorants; 3–4 eggs; 1 brood; April–July.*
FEEDING *Eats small fish, frogs, and snails.*
SIMILAR SPECIES *None in the British Isles, except other, very much rarer, egrets.*

Grey Heron

Ardea cinerea (Ardeidae)

INHABITS *fresh and salt water habitats, from estuaries and rocky shores to lakes, floods, and even garden ponds.*

Standing still as a statue or walking slowly through the shallows, the Grey Heron will suddenly straighten its neck and grab a fish in its bill with lightning speed. Long-necked, long-legged, and mainly grey and white, it can however look hunched, with its neck drawn in. It flies with deeply bowed wings.

wispy black plume

pale grey body

dagger-like yellowish bill; orange in spring

black streaks on white foreneck

broad, bowed, grey and black wings

head with grey cap; lacks crest

grey sides of head and neck

VOICE *Loud, harsh fraink; squawking, croaking, and bill-snapping at nest.*
NESTING *Large nest of stout sticks, usually in treetop colony; 4–5 eggs; 1 brood; January–May.*
FEEDING *Seizes fish, frogs, small mammals, and other prey, typically after long stalk.*
SIMILAR SPECIES *None in the British Isles.*

Osprey

Pandion haliaetus (Pandionidae)

CATCHES *fish in lakes, rivers, estuaries, and in coastal waters. Breeds in tall trees or on cliffs near water.*

A big, long-winged, eagle-like bird of prey, yet surprisingly like an immature gull at long range, the Osprey is uniquely equipped for diving into the water to catch fish. It is rarely seen far from water, but like many birds of prey it spends much of its time perched, when its white, black-banded head is usually obvious.

dark brown above; juvenile has bright buff feather edges

glides on kinked wings

dark brown above

variable breast-band

blackish band along middle of underwings

long, broad wings

white underparts

bluish grey feet

large, sharp claws

VOICE *Loud yelps and repeated, high, liquid, whistled pyew pyew pyew near nest.*
NESTING *Stick nest on tree or cliff, or ruined building; 2–3 eggs; 1 brood; April–July.*
FEEDING *Snatches fish from water using feet, sometimes hunts from perch.*
SIMILAR SPECIES *Immature Great Black-backed Gull (p.334).*

Marsh Harrier

Circus aeruginosus (Accipitridae)

This is the biggest and heaviest of the harriers, and also the darkest – it can be taken for a dark Buzzard (below) when soaring. Marsh Harriers hunt in classic harrier fashion, patrolling slowly at low level with their wings raised in a "V" when gliding, and dropping into reeds or long grass to seize their prey.

SEARCHES *for prey on marshland and coastal open country. Breeds in large reedbeds, among long grass, or tall crops.*

creamy cap and throat

broad black wingtips

♂

cream patch on wings

♀

"V" shape when gliding

very dark brown plumage

♀

grey on wings

♂

dark brown

VOICE *Shrill kee-yoo in display flight; hoarse kyek-ek-ek-ek or kyi-yi-yi-yi, or high whistles.*
NESTING *Large platform of reed stems among dense reeds over water, or among crops; 4–5 eggs; 1 brood; April–July.*
FEEDING *Dives to catch small birds and mammals, also frogs; scavenges for carrion.*
SIMILAR SPECIES *Hen Harrier (C. cyaneus).*

Buzzard

Buteo buteo (Accipitridae)

One of the most common and widespread British birds of prey, the Buzzard is often seen soaring on broad wings in wavering, rising circles as it scans the ground for prey. Its plumage varies from pale cream to blackish brown, but from below its flight feathers are always pale with a dark trailing edge.

SOARS *over, hunts, and breeds in wooded farmland, on moors, and mountains; also on coastal cliffs.*

cream head

PALE

hunched shoulders

rich brown above

pale "U" below

soars with wings slightly raised

short head

pale, barred tail

dark wrist patch

VOICE *Frequent, loud, high, ringing pee-yaah or weaker mew; calls often while flying.*
NESTING *Stick nest in tree, or beneath bush on cliff ledge; 2–4 eggs; 1 brood; March–June.*
FEEDING *Catches voles, rabbits, beetles, worms, and some birds; eats a lot of carrion.*
SIMILAR SPECIES *Honey Buzzard (Pernis apivorus), Rough-legged Buzzard (B. lagopus).*

Red Kite

Milvus milvus (Accipitridae)

An agile, long-winged, aerobatic bird of prey, the Red Kite is exceptionally graceful in the air, with a light, buoyant, elastic flight style that has few equals. Identifying the Red Kite is no problem, for its rusty plumage, bold white wing patches, and contrasting black wingtips are distinctive. The forked tail often glows almost orange in bright sun. Where common, it may gather in large numbers to exploit good food sources.

WINTERS *at lower altitude, foraging around towns. Breeds in wooded valleys, hunting over open country.*

soars on bowed wings

pale eyes

whitish head

pale band on upperwings

black flight feathers

forked tail

pale tawny to rust-red body

whitish to pale red below tail

bold white patch

NOTE

At a distance, the long, narrow wings and flight style separate a kite from a Buzzard (p.315). White underwing patches and a reddish body identify a Red Kite.

paler than adult

paler upperwings

rusty-brown, forked tail

VOICE High, long-drawn-out, wailing or squealing weieie-ee-ow, higher pitched than the call of a Buzzard.
NESTING Large nest of sticks, rags, earth, and rubbish in tree, usually well hidden; 2–4 eggs; 1 brood; March–June.
FEEDING Scavenges from the carcasses of dead animals such as rabbits or sheep; catches birds up to size of crow or gull in surprise dash; also feeds on insects, earthworms, and voles.
SIMILAR SPECIES Buzzard (p.315).

White-tailed Eagle

Haliaeetus albicilla (Accipitridae)

A huge, heavy-billed bird with very long, broad, plank-like wings and a very short tail, the White-tailed Eagle has a distinctive flight silhouette. Adults have pale heads, yellow bills, and white tails, but immatures are darker overall. It has been reintroduced to its former range in Scotland.

WINTERS *mainly on large, coastal plains; hunts on rocky coasts, estuaries, and remote marshes in summer.*

dark tail

glides on flat wings

head and neck protrude

saw-toothed trailing edge

big yellow bill

short white tail

pale and dark blotches

VOICE *Shrill yaps near nest in summer, otherwise usually a silent bird.*
NESTING *Huge pile of sticks on cliff ledge or flat tree crown; 2 eggs; 1 brood; March–July.*
FEEDING *Picks dead and sick fish, and fish offal, from water with feet; catches seabirds and hares; takes carrion on land.*
SIMILAR SPECIES *Golden Eagle (below).*

Golden Eagle

Aquila chrysaetos (Accipitridae)

A huge, supremely elegant raptor, the Golden Eagle favours remote mountains and crags. Its wide, slow, circling flight is often sufficient to identify it. It holds its long, broad wings in a shallow "V" when soaring, the primaries swept up at the tips.

pale tawny to golden crown

HUNTS *over remote peaks or upland forests and more rarely on steep coasts, far from settlements and roads.*

bulky body and wings

dark brown body plumage

soars with wings raised in shallow "V"

white wing patches

barred dark underwings

long tail, paler at base

white on tail

VOICE *Occasional shrill yelps and whistling twee-oo of alarm, but generally silent.*
NESTING *Immense pile of sticks, on broad cliff ledge or in old pine tree; 1–3 eggs, 1 brood; February–June.*
FEEDING *Hunts mainly for crows, rabbits, and marmots; eats much carrion in winter.*
SIMILAR SPECIES *White-tailed Eagle (above).*

Sparrowhawk

Accipiter nisus (Accipitridae)

HUNTS *in wide variety of habitats. Breeds in wooded farmland and forest; winters in more open country.*

The short, broad wings and long tail give this bird great manoeuvrability in pursuing prey through forests. It often dashes to low level with a distinctive flap-flap-glide action, then jinks and swerves to disappear through a tight gap.

short, small head

glaring yellow eyes gives fierce expression

orange on face

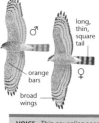

♂

long, thin, square tail

orange bars

♀

broad wings

pale line

brown bars

darker grey above

grey bars

♀

♂

long, thin, yellow legs

VOICE *Thin squealing peee-ee.*
NESTING *Platform of twigs close to tree trunk; 4–5 eggs; 1 brood; March–June.*
FEEDING *Hunts small birds, males take mainly tits and finches, larger females take thrushes and pigeons.*
SIMILAR SPECIES *Kestrel (below), Goshawk (A. gentilis).*

Kestrel

Falco tinnunculus (Falconidae)

LIVES *in wide variety of habitats. Common around woodland and over rough grassland.*

A common falcon of open spaces, the Kestrel is familiar to most people as the bird that hovers over roadsides for long periods. The smaller male has a blue-grey head and tail while the female's upperparts are all brown, spotted with black.

dark eyes

rufous back

♂

buff below spotted black

rufous inner wings

♀

paler outer wings than male

pale brown inner wings

black claws

blue-grey tail with black tip

black-barred back and inner wings

♀

VOICE *Nasal, complaining, whining keee-eee-eeee and variants, especially near nest.*
NESTING *On bare ledges on cliffs, on derelict buildings, in disused crows' nests or tree holes; 4–6 eggs; 1 brood; March–July.*
FEEDING *Catches small mammals, also eats beetles, lizards, earthworms, and small birds.*
SIMILAR SPECIES *Sparrowhawk (p.318).*

Hobby

Falco subbuteo (Falconidae)

A dynamic aerial hunter with the speed and agility to catch dragonflies, swallows, and even swifts, the scythe-winged Hobby is like a smaller version of the Peregrine (below). An adult is deep grey above, with a black cap and "moustache" that contrast with its pale cheeks and throat. It has dense, dark streaks on its underside.

NESTS *in abandoned crows' nests; hunts over open ground, and especially areas with flooded pits where it eats flying insects.*

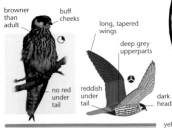

browner than adult

buff cheeks

long, tapered wings

deep grey upperparts

no red under tail

reddish under tail

dark head

yellow legs

whitish cheeks and throat

dark streaks on underside

short, narrow, plain tail

VOICE Clear, musical, whistled *kyu-kyu-kyu-kyu*, especially near nest.
NESTING Uses old nest in tree, usually of crow family; 2–3 eggs; 1 brood; June–August.
FEEDING Catches fast-flying small birds in flight, and eats many large flying insects, such as dragonflies and airborne beetles.
SIMILAR SPECIES Peregrine (below).

Peregrine

Falco peregrinus (Falconidae)

The big, powerfully built Peregrine is a bird-killing falcon, famous for the high-speed diving "stoop" that it often uses to kill its prey in mid-air. When hunting, it often patrols at great height, looking like a tiny black anchor in the sky. It spends much of its time perched, when it looks particularly bulky.

dull black head

broad white breast

HUNTS *over estuaries and marshes in winter. Breeds on hills and rocky coasts with cliffs; also in cities.*

darker wingtips

broad, pale rump

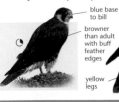

blue base to bill

browner than adult with buff feather edges

yellow legs

VOICE Loud, raucous calls at nest include throaty *haak-haak-haak-haak* and whining *kee-keee-eeeeee* and *wheeee-ip*.
NESTING On broad ledge or earthy scrape on cliff; 2–4 eggs; 1 brood; March–June.
FEEDING Kills birds of sizes ranging from thrush to pigeon or grouse, sometimes larger.
SIMILAR SPECIES Hobby (above), Kestrel (left).

blue-grey upperparts

Coot

Fulica atra (Rallidae)

Bigger and sturdier than its relative the Moorhen (below), the quarrelsome Coot also differs in having lobed toes, like grebes. It forms larger, more cohesive feeding flocks, which dive often to feed underwater, bobbing up to the surface like corks.

WINTERS *on larger, more open lakes. Breeds mainly on lakes and flooded pits, with fringing vegetation or overhanging branches.*

pale trailing edge

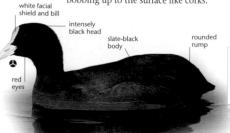

white facial shield and bill

intensely black head

slate-black body

rounded rump

red eyes

VOICE Loud kowk! high-pitched, metallic pik or teuwk; juvenile gives loud whistles.
NESTING Heap of weed on bank or overhanging branch; 6–9 eggs; 1–2 broods; April–August.
FEEDING Eats grass, aquatic plants, seeds, tadpoles, and other small aquatic animals.
SIMILAR SPECIES Moorhen (below).

yellowish bill

whitish face and throat

big grey feet with lobed toes

Moorhen

Gallinula chloropus (Rallidae)

Widespread and common on and near all kinds of waters from wet ditches to large lakes, the Moorhen is easily distinguished from the similar Coot (above) by its red and yellow bill and green legs. It has an oddly nervous manner, and usually runs or swims into cover at any hint of danger.

BREEDS *on small ponds with overgrown edges; feeds near ponds, lakes, and rivers, on open, wet, grassy ground.*

rich brown back

green legs

brown head; bill greenish yellow

brown body

white under tail

long green toes

diagonal white stripe

VOICE Loud, throaty or metallic notes, kurruk or kittik, high kik, stuttering kik-kikikikik-ik.
NESTING Shallow bowl of leaves and stems in vegetation, usually just above water; 5–11 eggs; 2–3 broods; April–August.
FEEDING Picks seeds, fruit, shoots, snails, and insects from damp ground or shallows.
SIMILAR SPECIES Coot (above).

Water Rail

Rallus aquaticus (Rallidae)

This is a skulking, secretive bird of dense reeds and water-side vegetation, often hard to see but readily identified by its long red bill. When venturing into the open, it soon slips out of sight between plant stems. It can often be detected at dawn or dusk by its squealing calls.

FEEDS *and breeds in wet reedbeds, swampy willow thickets, and overgrown riversides.*

dark streaked above

red, slightly curved bill with black tip

red eyes

barred flanks

dull legs — untidy bars below

pink legs

grey chest and face

slate-grey below

VOICE *Hard, repetitive, kipkipkipkipkip, extra-ordinary, loud, pig-like squealing, grunting.*
NESTING *Shallow, raised nest in vegetation; 6–11 eggs; 2 broods; May–August.*
FEEDING *Eats mainly insects and molluscs; also seeds, berries, voles, birds, and carrion.*
SIMILAR SPECIES *Spotted Crake (Porzana porzana).*

Oystercatcher

Haematopus ostralegus (Haematopodidae)

With its dazzling black and white plumage and stout, carrot-coloured, blade-like bill, the Oystercatcher is one of Britain's most unmistakable, and common, waders. A noisy bird, its loud, piercing calls are equally distinctive. The powerful bill is adapted for prising or hammering open cockles, mussels, and other bivalve molluscs.

ROOSTS *in often huge flocks. Breeds on sandy, muddy, and rocky shores; some inland on grass or river shingle.*

red eyes with orange eye-ring

big, bright orange-red bill

portly, black and white body

dark tip to bill

white "V"

white collar

browner back

broad white wingbar

bill with dark tip

short, sturdy, pale pink legs; duller in juvenile

VOICE *Loud, strident klip, kleep or kleep-a-kleep; shrill chorus from big flocks.*
NESTING *Shallow scrape in shingle or sand; 2–3 eggs; 1 brood; April–July.*
FEEDING *Probes for molluscs and marine worms; eats earthworms inland.*
SIMILAR SPECIES *Black-tailed Godwit (Limosa limosa).*

Grey Plover

Pluvialis squatarola (Charadriidae)

Like a silver version of the Golden Plover (below) in breeding plumage, but bigger and with a larger bill, the Grey Plover is a more coastal bird that typically feeds on mudflats, and roosts in rather static flocks on nearby fields at high tide. It is easily identified in flight by its black "wingpits".

FEEDS *on large muddy estuaries and other shores from autumn to spring; breeds on northern tundra.*

bold white wingbars

white rump

black wingpits

bold white band from forehead to side of chest

patchy plumage

spangled silver and black

black underside

LATE MOULTING

mottled grey

pale below

VOICE *High, plaintive 3-syllabled twee- oo-wee! and loud, melancholic, fluted song.*
NESTING *Scrape on ground in short vegetation; 4 eggs; 1 brood; May–July.*
FEEDING *Pulls worms, molluscs, and crustaceans from mud in winter.*
SIMILAR SPECIES *Golden Plover (below), Knot (p.325).*

Golden Plover

Pluvialis apricaria (Charadriidae)

In winter, flocks of Golden Plover feed on lowland fields, often with Lapwings (right). Their winter plumage is like that of the Grey Plover (above), but lacks black "wingpits", and they have slimmer bills. In summer, birds from the north develop more black on the face and underside than those that stay to breed in Britain.

FEEDS *on low-lying arable fields, pastures, and salt marshes in winter; breeds on high moorland and tundra.*

mottled face

weak white wingbars

white belly

dark rump

white on underwings

SOUTHERN RACE

golden yellow, white, and black spangled

brownish black back

pale yellow breast

buff-yellow spots

white-sided black belly

VOICE *Plaintive, whistled tleee, higher tlee, treeoleee; song phee-oo, pheee-oo in flight.*
NESTING *Shallow scrape, lined with lichen and heather, on ground in heather or grass; 4 eggs; 1 brood; April–July.*
FEEDING *Takes insects in summer, mainly earthworms in winter.*
SIMILAR SPECIES *Grey Plover (above).*

Lapwing

Vanellus vanellus (Charadriidae)

Distinguished by its unique wispy crest, the Lapwing is Britain's largest and most familiar plover. At a distance it looks black and white but a close view reveals glossy greenish upperparts. Very sociable, it breeds in loose colonies on undisturbed ground, males performing spectacular tumbling aerial displays while calling loudly. Outside the breeding season it forms large flocks on fields and pastures, often with Golden Plovers (left) and Black-headed Gulls (p.332). It gets its name from its flappy, instantly recognizable flight style, and has broad, rounded wings.

WINTERS *on arable fields and salt marsh. Breeds on wet moors, riverside pastures, and upland fields.*

white under-wing

broad, rounded wings

buff fringes to feathers

short crest

shorter crest than summer

green back with buffish feather edges

black cap extends into wispy crest

purple and copper gloss on dark green back

shorter crest than male

mottled throat

♂

♀

white underparts

♂

cinnamon patch under tail

dull pinkish legs

NOTE

If a Lapwing dives at you in summer with a shrill weew-ee call, it is trying to protect its eggs or young, so watch where you walk in case you step on them.

VOICE *Nasal, strained weet or ee-wit; wheezy variations on this theme; passionate song in spring, whee-er-ee, a wheep-wheep! accompanied by loud throbbing from wings.*
NESTING *Shallow hollow on open ground, lined with grass; 3–4 eggs; 1 brood; April–June.*
FEEDING *Tilts forward to pick insects and spiders from ground, or pull earthworms from soil; often taps foot on ground to attract or reveal prey.*
SIMILAR SPECIES *None, this species is unmistakable.*

Ringed Plover

Charadrius hiaticula (Charadriidae)

A small, pale plover with a striking head and breast pattern and bright orange legs, the Ringed Plover is typically found feeding on sandy beaches in summer, or in tight flocks with other waders at high tide. Migrants may move inland, especially in spring and autumn.

BREEDS *on sandy and shingly beaches. Also locally but increasingly inland, on river banks or gravel pits.*

dull head

white over eyes

dull legs

white wingbars

dull bill

weak band

black and orange bill

broad black breast-band

orange legs

VOICE *Fluty whistle, a bright, mellow too-lit, repeated too-wee-a too-wee-a in song-flight.*
NESTING *Shallow scrape lined with pebbles or grass; 4 eggs; 2–3 broods; April–August.*
FEEDING *Picks small insects and worms from ground, using run-tilt action.*
SIMILAR SPECIES *Little Ringed Plover (C. dubius).*

Avocet

Recurvirostra avosetta (Recurvirostridae)

The Avocet is a distinctive wader, handsome and graceful, with a strongly upturned bill. Conservation and habitat management have helped provide it with its special needs – shallow, brackish water and oozy mud for feeding, and drier islands for nesting. As a result, it has thrived and spread.

WINTERS *in close flocks that fly and feed on muddy estuaries. Breeds on shallow, saline coastal lagoons and by muddy pools.*

black bars on wings and back

brown tips to feathers

curved black band on each side of back

fine, black, upcurved bill

black cap

rather blunt black wingtips

tilts forward when feeding

long blue-grey legs

VOICE *Loud, fluty klute or kloop.*
NESTING *Scrape on low islet or dry mud, bare or lined with shell fragments and grass; 3–4 eggs; 1 brood; April–July.*
FEEDING *Sweeps upcurved bill sideways through water to detect and snap up tiny shrimps and worms.*
SIMILAR SPECIES *None.*

Knot

Calidris canutus (Scolopacidae)

Marbled black, buff, and chestnut with coppery underparts, the Knot is among the most colourful of waders in spring and summer. In winter, it is a dull pale grey, yet it is still spectacular for it forms vast flocks of many thousands that often take to the air, swooping through the sky in dramatic aerial manoeuvres.

pale grey rump and tail

pale stripe

ROOSTS *in dense flocks on muddy estuaries, and feeds on a wide variety of shores. Breeds on tundra.*

straight black bill

pale grey plumage

chestnut and copper

apricot-tinged below

short grey legs

VOICE *Rather quiet; dull, short nut, plus occasional bright, whistled note.*
NESTING *Shallow hollow on ground near water, on tundra; 3–4 eggs; 1 brood; May–July.*
FEEDING *Eats molluscs, crustaceans, and marine worms in winter.*
SIMILAR SPECIES *Grey Plover (p.322), Dunlin (p.326).*

Sanderling

Calidris alba (Scolopacidae)

In winter, the Sanderling is by far the whitest of small waders. It has a unique feeding style: very quick and nimble, it darts back and forth along the edge of waves as they move in and out to snatch food carried by the surf. In spring and autumn, its back and breast are marbled chestnut, but its belly stays pure white.

FEEDS *in flocks on broad, sandy beaches and estuaries. Breeds on northern tundra.*

black spangled grey

marbled chestnut

broad white wingbar

bright white underparts

black bill

black legs

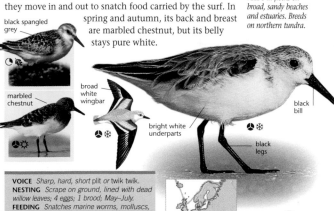

VOICE *Sharp, hard, short plit or twik twik.*
NESTING *Scrape on ground, lined with dead willow leaves; 4 eggs; 1 brood; May–July.*
FEEDING *Snatches marine worms, molluscs, and crustaceans such as sandhoppers and insects from the edge of waves.*
SIMILAR SPECIES *Dunlin (p.326), Little Stint (C. minuta).*

Dunlin

Calidris alpina (Scolopacidae)

The Dunlin often occurs in huge flocks that feed and roost together on mudflats and marshes, and perform perfectly co-ordinated aerobatic flights. Its winter plumage is quite drab, unlike breeding birds in summer that are rich chestnut and black above, with a squarish black patch on the belly.

WINTERS *on estuaries, inland marshes, and lake shores. Breeds on damp moorlands.*

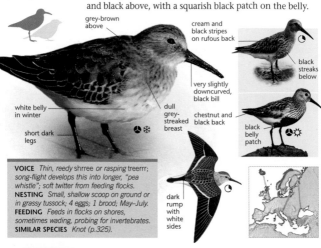

grey-brown above

cream and black stripes on rufous back

black streaks below

very slightly downcurved, black bill

white belly in winter

dull grey-streaked breast

chestnut and black back

black belly patch

short dark legs

dark rump with white sides

VOICE *Thin, reedy shrree or rasping treerrr; song-flight develops this into longer, "pea whistle"; soft twitter from feeding flocks.*
NESTING *Small, shallow scoop on ground or in grassy tussock; 4 eggs; 1 brood; May–July.*
FEEDING *Feeds in flocks on shores, sometimes wading, probing for invertebrates.*
SIMILAR SPECIES *Knot (p.325).*

Ruff

Philomachus pugnax (Scolopacidae)

In spring, male Ruffs grow a huge ruff of feathers around the neck and curly crown-tufts, very varied in colour and pattern. These help them attract the much smaller females at communal mating grounds (leks). Winter adults are variable; the small head and drooping bill are distinctive features.

BREEDS *in lowland wet meadows; migrants and wintering birds live by lakes, marshes, and coastal lagoons.*

ruff of feathers

head often white

blotched back

orange legs

short, barely curved bill

bright ochre-buff head and breast

white rump sides

bright buff feather edges

pale ochre to greenish legs

VOICE *Usually silent; occasionally utters a low, gruff wek call.*
NESTING *Well hidden grass-lined scrape; 4 eggs; 1 brood; April–July.*
FEEDING *Probes into soft mud for worms, insects and their larvae; also eats some seeds.*
SIMILAR SPECIES *Redshank (right), Wood Sandpiper (Tringa glareola).*

Snipe

Gallinago gallinago (Scolopacidae)

A heavily streaked wader with a very long bill, the Snipe can feed only in areas where soft, oozy mud allows it to probe deeply for prey. Less elusive than the Jack Snipe *(Lymnocryptes minimus)*, it rises from cover with harsh, dry calls. In spring, males dive through the air with stiff outer tail feathers fanned to produce a strange bleating hum.

LIVES *in boggy heaths and wet freshwater marshes with soft mud, moving to coasts in freezing conditions.*

dark brown back with cream stripes

white tail tip

striped head with cream central stripe

streaked breast

very long bill

white belly

barred flanks

probes deep for food

rufous-centred tail

VOICE *Short, rasping scaap; in spring musical chip-per, chip-per; also throbbing "bleat" from tail feathers during switchback display flight.*
NESTING *Grass-lined scrape in dense vegetation; 4 eggs; 1–2 broods; April–July.*
FEEDING *Probes soft mud for worms.*
SIMILAR SPECIES *Jack Snipe (Lymnocryptes minimus).*

Redshank

Tringa totanus (Scolopacidae)

Very conspicuous, thanks to its loud voice and bold white upperwing bands, the Redshank is common on many coasts but scarcer inland in areas where drainage has destroyed wet grassland. A wary bird, it flies off with noisy calls, alerting other birds to danger.

SEEN *in estuaries, salt marshes, freshwater marshes, and muddy lake shores. Breeds on salt marshes, wet pastures, and moors.*

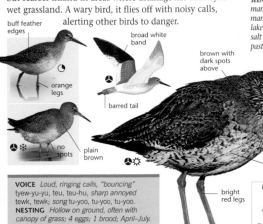

buff feather edges

broad white band

brown with dark spots above

orange legs

barred tail

straight, red-based bill

no spots

plain brown

whitish belly with black spots

bright red legs

VOICE *Loud, ringing calls, "bouncing" tyew-yu-yu, teu, teu-hu, sharp annoyed tewk, tewk; song tu-yoo, tu-yoo, tu-yoo.*
NESTING *Hollow on ground, often with canopy of grass; 4 eggs; 1 brood; April–July.*
FEEDING *Probes and picks at mud, taking insects, worms, crustaceans, and molluscs.*
SIMILAR SPECIES *Knot (p.325).*

Bar-tailed Godwit

Limosa lapponica (Scolopacidae)

Although they breed only on the Arctic tundra, Bar-tailed Godwits are far more widespread on coasts of Britain in winter than the larger Black-tailed Godwits (*L. limosa*). Flocks disperse to probe for food in the mud; these often have a habit of rolling and twisting as they fly in to roost at high tide.

WINTERS on broad estuaries and sheltered muddy and sandy beaches, rarely inland.

long, slightly upcurved bill

pale buff breast

streaked grey-brown and buff

🐦1ST ❄

quite short, dark legs

plain upperwings with dark tips

coppery red below

♂ ☀

barred tail

streaked bright buff

VOICE Rapid, yelping *kirruk kirruk* flight call.
NESTING Shallow scrape on ground, on drier ridge or mound in mainly swampy tundra; 4 eggs; 1 brood; May–July.
FEEDING Probes in mud and sand for large marine worms and molluscs.
SIMILAR SPECIES Black-tailed Godwit (*L. limosa*), Curlew (below).

Curlew

Numenius arquata (Scolopacidae)

Britain's largest wader, the Curlew has a very long, downcurved bill, distinctive calls, and lovely song. At long range on mudflats or roosting on sand spits, Curlews tend to look large and dark, but close views reveal a pale sandy-brown colour that is streaked above and on the breast.

WINTERS mainly on big, muddy estuaries; breeds on northern moorland and bogs.

gull-like wing shape

two-tone upperwings

broad white "V"

whiter belly

long, evenly curved bill

quite short, greyish legs

white rump

streaked brown above and on breast

spotted flanks

VOICE Loud *whaup, whoy, cur-li; song starts slowly, accelerating to ecstatic bubbling trill.
NESTING Shallow hollow on ground, lined with grass; 4 eggs; 1 brood; April–July.
FEEDING Probes for and picks up worms, crabs, molluscs, starfish, and insects.
SIMILAR SPECIES Bar-tailed Godwit (above).

Common Sandpiper

Actitis hypoleucos (Scolopacidae)

A small, slim, long-tailed wader, the Common Sandpiper can be recognized by the strong "hook" of white on its flank, and the way it bobs its head and swings its tail end up and down. It usually feeds in small, loose groups; when disturbed they fly off at low level with rapid, flickering wingbeats and stiff-winged glides, piping noisily.

BREEDS on rocky streams and lakesides with shingle and grass banks. Migrants live in all waterside habitats, including estuaries.

mottled, dark back; plainer in winter

mid-brown above

bold white bars

long tail

white crescent in front of wing

pale-flecked feather edges

VOICE *Loud, ringing, sharp tew-tew-tew or tyew-yu-yu; summer calls include fast, trilling teu-i teu-i teu-i, chip, tidledi tidledi tidledi.*
NESTING *Small, grass-lined hollow on ground or bank; 4 eggs; 1 brood; April–July.*
FEEDING *Skips and saunters along waterside snatching insects, worms, and molluscs.*
SIMILAR SPECIES *Green Sandpiper (below).*

greenish or ochre legs

Green Sandpiper

Tringa ochropus (Scolopacidae)

A larger and stockier bird than the Wood Sandpiper (*T. glareola*), often seen feeding in twos and threes on muddy shores, the Green Sandpiper usually looks very dark above and white below. It bobs like the Common Sandpiper (above), but not so continuously, and is quick to alarm and take to the air, flying off with loud calls and shooting around the sky.

INHABITS shores of salt marsh creeks, pools, streams, and reservoirs. Breeds in boggy forests.

pale line

dark wings

thick bars

streaked breast

diffuse buff spots

white-speckled, dark grey-brown upperparts

bright white below

greenish legs

VOICE *Loud, full-throated, liquid, almost yodelling tlu-eet, weet-weet!*
NESTING *Old nest of thrush or similar, in tree near forest bog; 4 eggs; 1 brood; May–July.*
FEEDING *Picks insects, crustaceans, and worms from water, often wading up to belly.*
SIMILAR SPECIES *Common Sandpiper (above), Wood Sandpiper (T. glareola).*

Turnstone

Arenaria interpres (Scolopacidae)

Most waders like to feed on soft mud or sand, but the stocky, short-billed Turnstone favours areas of stones, weed, or other debris that it can flick through in search of small animal food. Noisy, active, and often tame, it is colourful in summer but very dark above in winter, with a piebald look in flight.

FEEDS *on sea coasts of all kinds, especially rocky shores and gravelly tidelines. Breeds on rocky northern coasts.*

white wing patch

white wingbars

black and white pattern on head

black, white, and chestnut above

white below

bold black breast-band

short, vivid orange legs

dull brown and black above

VOICE *Fast, hard, abrupt, staccato calls, tukatukatuk, teuk, tchik.*
NESTING *Scantily lined scrape on ground close to shore; 4 eggs; 1 brood; May–July.*
FEEDING *Stirs up and turns seaweed, shells, and stones on beach to find invertebrates.*
SIMILAR SPECIES *Purple Sandpiper (Calidris maritima).*

Arctic Skua

Stercorarius parasiticus (Stercorariidae)

The slender, sharp-winged Arctic Skua is one of the most beautifully shaped seabirds in flight. It occurs in both pale and dark forms, which can be confusing, but its clean-cut profile is distinctive. It obtains a lot of its food by piracy, harassing terns and small gulls until they disgorge fish. The swift, acrobatic pursuit can be quite spectacular.

FEEDS *near coasts on migration; winters out at sea. Breeds on coastal moorland and northern tundra.*

white wing flash

dark cap

PALE FORM

brown back

white wing flash

DARK FORM

sooty brown

DARK FORM

grey-brown or yellowish breast-band

PALE FORM

whitish underside

VOICE *Gives loud, nasal wailing in summer, ahh-yeow, eee-air, ka-wow; silent at sea.*
NESTING *Shallow scrape on ground, in small colony; 2 eggs; 1 brood; May–June.*
FEEDING *Robs birds of fish; also catches fish and small birds; eats some berries and insects.*
SIMILAR SPECIES *Immature Common Gull (p.333), Pomarine Skua (S. pomarinus).*

Great Skua

Stercorarius skua (Stercorariidae)

The largest, heaviest, boldest, and most predatory of the skuas, the Great Skua is always dark brown with pale buff streaks and big white wing patches. Able to steal from a Gannet (p.312) and kill a Kittiwake (p.333), its success in recent years has caused problems for other seabirds.

BREEDS *on northern moors near sea; at other times usually lives well offshore, but sometimes near coasts.*

dark cap

pale streaks on neck

streaked dark brown above

stout, hooked, dark bill

bold white wing patch

tapered wings

dark underparts

thick blackish legs

VOICE Barking uk-uk-uk; silent at sea.
NESTING Simple hollow on ground on moorland, dives fearlessly at intruders into its nesting territory; 2 eggs; 1 brood; May–June.
FEEDING Steals fish from other seabirds; kills birds, takes eggs, or scavenges for carrion.
SIMILAR SPECIES Arctic Skua (left), Pomarine Skua (S. pomarinus).

Herring Gull

Larus argentatus (Laridae)

The big, noisy Herring Gull is mainly a bird of sea cliffs in summer, but roams over all kinds of shores and far inland in winter, when its white head and neck are streaked brownish. Paler than the Yellow-legged Gull (*L. michahellis*), it has pink legs and fierce-looking pale eyes.

FEEDS *on beaches, estuaries, reservoirs, and refuse tips. Breeds on cliffs, islands, and rooftops.*

yellow bill with red spot

blotched brown

grey-brown streaks

pale grey back

white spots

pale pink legs

VOICE Loud, squealing notes, yelps, barks, kyow, kee-yow-yow-yow, ga-ga-ga, kuk-kuk.
NESTING Grass-lined nest on ground, cliff ledge, or building; 2–3 eggs; 1 brood; May.
FEEDING Takes fish, molluscs, insects, fish offal, and scraps from ground or water.
SIMILAR SPECIES Common Gull (p.333), Lesser Black-backed Gull (p.334).

Black-headed Gull

Larus ridibundus (Laridae)

Common and familiar, this is a small, agile, very white-looking gull. It is never truly "black-headed", because in breeding plumage its hood is dark chocolate brown and does not extend to the back of its head. In other plumages, it has a pale head with a dark ear spot. Its dark underwing gives a flickering effect in flight. It has always been a frequent bird inland, but numbers have increased still further in response to abundant food provided by refuse tips and safe roosting sites on reservoirs and flooded pits.

FEEDS *on coasts, lakes, reservoirs, farmland, refuse tips, and along rivers. Common in towns and cities. Breeds from coastal marshes to upland pools, widespread but local.*

NOTE

Look out for a striking white wedge-shaped marking along the leading edge of each outer wing; no other common gull has this feature.

dark brown hood

deep red bill

white eye-ring

very pale grey back

deep red legs

brown on neck and back

black-tipped

neck and back become grey

dark hind edge

🐦1ST❄

🐦1ST❄

white leading edge

dark grey underwings with white outer edge

black trailing edge

dark spot

vivid red bill with black tip

vivid red legs

VOICE *Loud, harsh, squealing, laughing, and chattering calls, kwarrr, kee-arr, kwuk, kuk-kuk; particularly noisy at breeding colonies.*
NESTING *Pile of stems on ground in vegetation in marshland, in colony; 2–3 eggs; 1 brood; May–June.*
FEEDING *Takes worms, seeds, fish, and insects from ground and water, also catches insects in flight.*
SIMILAR SPECIES *Common Gull (right), Little Gull (L. minutus), Mediterranean Gull (L. melanocephalus).*

Common Gull

Larus canus (Laridae)

Rather like the Herring Gull (p.331) in its general pattern, but much smaller, the Common Gull has a smaller bill with no red spot, a rounder head, and a dark eye, giving it a more gentle expression. Compared to the slightly smaller Black-headed Gull (left), it has no dark hood or ear spot, and no white leading edge on its outer wing. It is not as common as either species.

BREEDS *on coasts and moors; winters on coasts, farmland, lakes, and reservoirs.*

grey-brown on head

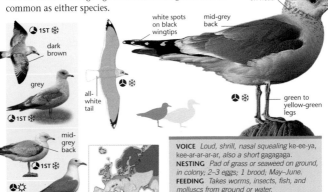

1ST

dark brown

grey

white spots on black wingtips

mid-grey back

all-white tail

mid-grey back

1ST

green to yellow-green legs

1ST

green legs

VOICE *Loud, shrill, nasal squealing ke-ee-ya, kee-ar-ar-ar-ar, also a short gagagaga.*
NESTING *Pad of grass or seaweed on ground, in colony; 2–3 eggs; 1 brood; May–June.*
FEEDING *Takes worms, insects, fish, and molluscs from ground or water.*
SIMILAR SPECIES *Herring Gull (p.331), Black-headed Gull (left).*

Kittiwake

Larus tridactyla (Laridae)

One of the most maritime of gulls, the Kittiwake comes to land only to breed in noisy colonies on sheer cliffs. Its very white head and black wingtips are distinctive in flight, and its call is unmistakable. In winter, the adult has a grey nape and a dark ear patch.

BREEDS *on coastal cliffs. Winters at sea, when scarce on coasts. Rare but regular inland on migration.*

black triangle

white head and breast

blue-grey back

pale outer wings

black collar

black zigzag

short blackish legs

grey collar

1ST

black zigzag

dull plumage

1ST

dark spot

VOICE *Ringing, nasal, rhythmic kiti-a-wake! often repeated; also high, thin, mewing note.*
NESTING *Nest of weed on ledge on cliff or seaside building; 2–3 eggs; 1 brood; May–June.*
FEEDING *Takes mostly fish in shallow dive or from surface; also fish offal from trawlers.*
SIMILAR SPECIES *Common Gull (above), Herring Gull (p.331), Little Gull (L. minutus).*

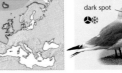

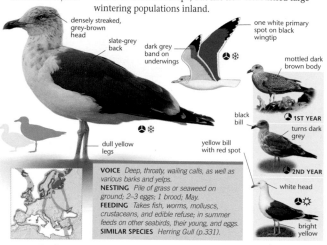

Lesser Black-backed Gull

Larus fuscus (Laridae)

A handsome bird in slate-grey and pure white with vivid yellow legs and bill, this gull is almost as big as the Herring Gull (p.331), but slimmer and darker. It used to be a summer visitor to western Europe, but has now established large wintering populations inland.

BREEDS *on cliffs, islands, moorland, and rooftops. Feeds on beaches and fields.*

densely streaked, grey-brown head

slate-grey back

dark grey band on underwings

one white primary spot on black wingtip

mottled dark brown body

1ST YEAR

turns dark grey

2ND YEAR

black bill

dull yellow legs

yellow bill with red spot

white head

bright yellow

VOICE *Deep, throaty, wailing calls, as well as various barks and yelps.*
NESTING *Pile of grass or seaweed on ground; 2–3 eggs; 1 brood; May.*
FEEDING *Takes fish, worms, molluscs, crustaceans, and edible refuse; in summer feeds on other seabirds, their young, and eggs.*
SIMILAR SPECIES *Herring Gull (p.331).*

Great Black-backed Gull

Larus marinus (Laridae)

Powerful, heavy-billed, and fiercely predatory, the Great Black-backed is the world's largest gull. The size of its bill is a good guide to its identity, when it resembles an oversized Herring Gull (p.331). Adults are blacker than the southern races of the Lesser Black-backed Gull (above), although the black plumage fades browner as it ages.

FOUND *on rocky coasts, often in flocks around coastal pools. Winters on beaches and harbours.*

whitish head

1ST

chequered back

2ND

pure white head

black back

large white patch on wingtips

dark flight feathers

pale greyish, whitish, or pink legs

VOICE *Deep barking notes, short hoarse yowk, gruff, guttural ow-ow-ow.*
NESTING *Shallow scrape on cliff ledge or pinnacle; 3 eggs; 1 brood; May–June.*
FEEDING *Takes seabirds and voles; catches fish; scavenges for edible scraps on beaches.*
SIMILAR SPECIES *Lesser Black-backed Gull (above), immature Herring Gull (p.331).*

Common Tern

Sterna hirundo (Sternidae)

A typical black-capped, pale-bodied tern, the Common Tern is well named. It is widespread on coasts from spring to late autumn and is the most likely tern to be seen inland. It closely resembles the Arctic Tern (below), and often mixes with it, but is rather stouter, with a shorter tail and a longer red bill with a black tip.

FEEDS in coastal waters and rivers. Breeds on coasts, islands, salt marshes, and locally near fresh waters.

black cap

pale grey upperparts

long neck

white forehead

dark shoulder

forked white tail

white body

red legs, longer than Arctic Tern's

dark nape

VOICE Grating, thin, kreee-yair of alarm, sharp kik kik, ringing keeer, rapid kirrikirrikirrik.
NESTING Scrape on ground, in colonies near water; 2–4 eggs; 1 brood; May–June.
FEEDING Dives into water for prey; also insects and fish from water surface in flight.
SIMILAR SPECIES Arctic Tern (below), Sandwich Tern (p.336).

Arctic Tern

Sterna paradisaea (Sternidae)

Similar to the Common Tern (above), the Arctic Tern is a more strictly maritime bird. Its wings have translucent outer primaries, and a narrow, more tapered dark trailing edge beneath. Uniquely, the Arctic Tern spends the northern winter in the Southern Ocean, thereby enjoying more summer daylight than any other bird.

LIVES on northern offshore islands, and sandy and gravelly beaches. Winters in Southern Ocean, as far as Antarctic pack ice.

rounded head with black cap

very pale outer wings

bill shorter than Common Tern's

short neck

grey back

short red bill

white forehead

black bill

dark crescents on back

long outer tail streamers

pale grey below

short red legs

VOICE Grating, sharp kee-yaah, rising pee-pee-pee, sharp kik, kreer.
NESTING Scrape in sand, hollow in rocks in colonies; 2 eggs; 1 brood; May–June.
FEEDING Plunge-dives for small fish; insects from freshwater pools and crustaceans.
SIMILAR SPECIES Common Tern (above), Roseate Tern (S. dougallii).

Sandwich Tern

Sterna sandvicensis (Sternidae)

The Sandwich Tern is a large, active, noisy bird with a spiky black crest, a long, sharp bill, and long, angular wings that it often holds away from its body, slightly drooped. It looks very white in the air, diving for fish from high up and hitting the water with a loud smack.

FOUND *on sand dunes, shingle beaches, and islands. Winters in coastal waters of Africa.*

long black bill, yellow at tip

black cap, spiky at rear

very pale silver-grey back

very pale silver-grey wings

white underside

white tail

black legs

short tail with shallow fork

dark chequers and bars on "saddle"

dark streaks

dark tail corners

white forehead

VOICE *Loud, harsh, rhythmic ker-ink, short kik or kear-ik!*
NESTING *Shallow scoop in sand or shingle; 1–2 eggs; 1 brood; May–June.*
FEEDING *Catches fish, especially sandeels, by plunge-diving from air.*
SIMILAR SPECIES *Common Tern (p.335), Black-headed Gull (p.332).*

Black Tern

Chlidonias niger (Sternidae)

The marsh terns of the genus *Chlidonias* are smaller, more delicate birds than the sea terns, and feed by dipping to the water surface instead of plunge-diving. The Black Tern is the most widespread species. In summer, it is mainly blackish and smoky grey; its plumage is less distinctive in autumn.

FEEDS *on marshes, lagoons, salt pans, estuaries, lakes, and reservoirs. Breeds on lakes and marshes.*

dark smoky grey above

pale underwings

blackish bill

white under tail

blackish legs

dark chest spot

browner body

sharp wings

VOICE *Usually a rather quiet bird, but may give short, nasal flight calls, kik, or kik-keek.*
NESTING *Nest of waterweed in shallow water or on mat of floating vegetation, in marsh or nearby drier land; 3 eggs; 1 brood; May–June.*
FEEDING *Dips to take insects, small fish, crustaceans, and amphibians from the water.*
SIMILAR SPECIES *Little Gull (Larus minutus).*

Guillemot

Uria aalge (Alcidae)

A slim, long-bodied auk with a slender bill, the Guillemot is one of the commonest breeding seabirds at cliff colonies. It often nests alongside the more thickset Razorbill (below), which has a deeper bill. It can often be seen flying low and fast off headlands, and swimming in large groups below the cliffs.

BREEDS *in colonies on narrow ledges on sea-cliffs and flat-topped stacks. Winters at sea, well offshore.*

pointed bill

dark brown to black above

white sides to rump

white face

black eye-stripe

white below

smudgy greyish streaks on flanks

VOICE Loud, whirring, growling chorus at colony, arrrr-rr-rr; juveniles whistle at sea.
NESTING On bare ledge on sheer cliff, in colony; 1 egg; 1 brood; May–June.
FEEDING Dives from surface to catch fish deep underwater, propelled by wings.
SIMILAR SPECIES Razorbill (below), Manx Shearwater (Puffinus puffinus).

Razorbill

Alca torda (Alcidae)

More heavily built than the very similar Guillemot (above), and not usually as numerous, the Razorbill has a pointed tail and a distinctive deep, flattened, blade-like black bill with a fine white line near the end. It breeds in company with Guillemots, but less conspicuously because it nests in cavities rather than open ledges.

LIVES *on rocky coasts on cliffs with crevices, or among boulder scree, feeding at sea. Winters out at sea.*

black head

broader, longer white sides than Guillemot

white throat and breast

black cap

pointed tail, often cocked

black upper-parts

white below

VOICE Prolonged, tremulous growls and grunts at colony, deep urrr.
NESTING On sheltered cliff ledge, or cavity between boulders; 1 egg; 1 brood; May–June.
FEEDING Dives, often very deeply, from surface to pursue and catch fish, using its wings to "fly" underwater.
SIMILAR SPECIES Guillemot (above).

Puffin

Fratercula arctica (Alcidae)

Few seabirds are more instantly recognizable than the Puffin in summer, with its clown-like eyes, and huge, flamboyantly coloured bill. In winter, it is less striking, as the colourful eye ornaments and horny plates at the edges of its bill fall away; its face is also darker.

SEEN *on coastal clifftops, mainly on islands, feeding in nearby waters. Winters well out to sea.*

plain black wings

deep, triangular bill, striped bluish, orange, yellow, and red

dark eyes with bluish scale above

black upperparts and neck

grey-white facial disc

black back

dusky grey face

white below

VOICE Loud, cooing growl at nest, aaarr, karr-oo-arr; usually silent outside breeding season.
NESTING Digs or occupies ready-made burrow at or near clifftop, or suitable cavity between boulders; 1 egg; 1 brood; May–June.
FEEDING Dives from water surface to catch fish; also takes small squid and crustaceans.
SIMILAR SPECIES Razorbill (p.337).

Turtle Dove

Streptopelia turtur (Columbidae)

The purring song of the Turtle Dove used to be a common feature of high summer, but it is becoming less familiar as its woodland and hedgerow habitats are eliminated by intensive agriculture. Similar to the Collared Dove (p.340), it has a darker back, neatly chequered brown-black, and a striped bluish white and black neck patch.

LIVES *in wooded farmland, broadleaved woods with sunny clearings, and tall, dense, old hedgerows.*

blue-grey midwing

dark spots on orange-brown above

white tip to tail

pink breast

no neck patch

duller body

white belly

VOICE Deep, purring, crooning rooorrr rooorrr.
NESTING Small, flimsy platform of thin twigs in hedge or low branches of tree; 2 eggs; 2–3 broods; May–July.
FEEDING Takes seeds and shoots of arable weeds on ground.
SIMILAR SPECIES Collared Dove (p.340), Kestrel (p.318).

Rock Dove

Columba livia (Columbidae)

The wild ancestor of the town or feral pigeon, the Rock Dove is a bird of rocky coasts and crags. It is paler, with an ash-grey back, a green and purple gloss on its neck, two broad black wingbars, and a white rump. Feral pigeons have very varied plumage patterns, and interbreeding between the two forms has made the genuine wild Rock Dove a rarity.

BREEDS *on coastal cliffs and mountains. Feral birds widespread from coasts to cities, and on farmland.*

tiny white patch

larger white patch

glossy purple and green on neck

FERAL PIGEON

two long, broad, black bars on wings

pale grey back

dark below

white underwing

white rump

VOICE *Deep, rolling, moaning coo, oo-ooh-oorr, oo-roo-coo.*
NESTING *Loose, untidy, sparse nest on ledge or in cavity; 2 eggs; 3 broods; all year.*
FEEDING *Forages for seeds, buds, berries, and small invertebrates on ground.*
SIMILAR SPECIES *Woodpigeon (p.340), Stock Dove (below), Peregrine Falcon (p.319).*

Stock Dove

Columba oenas (Columbidae)

A compact pigeon of farmland, parks, and uplands, the Stock Dove resembles a small Woodpigeon (p.340) but has a shorter tail, more bluish plumage, and no white markings. The two dark bars on its folded wing are a lot smaller and its head smaller and rounder than those of the similar Rock Dove (above).

FOUND *in a wide variety of places, from flooded fields and farmland with trees to rocky upland moors.*

glossy green neck patch

deep wine-pink breast

black trailing edge and wingtips

pale midwings

grey underwings

dark tail band

two short dark bars on wings

blue-grey body

VOICE *Rhythmic, booming coo, repeated with increased emphasis, ooo-woo ooo-woo.*
NESTING *Tree hole, ledge or cavity in cliff or building; 2 eggs; 2–3 broods; all year.*
FEEDING *Takes seeds, buds, shoots, roots, and berries from ground, but not in gardens.*
SIMILAR SPECIES *Rock Dove (above), Woodpigeon (p.340).*

Woodpigeon

Columba palumbus (Columbidae)

A large, common, boldly marked pigeon, often found in large flocks, the Woodpigeon is usually identifiable by its white neck patch, pink breast, white wingbar, and plump, small-headed look. Although tame in city parks, it is shy in rural areas where it is persecuted as a pest.

FEEDS *mainly on farmland; breeds in a variety of woodland and farmland with trees, also town parks and big gardens.*

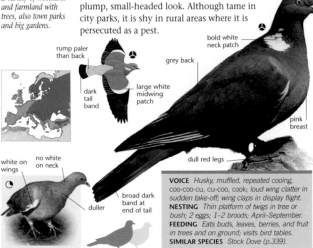

rump paler than back

dark tail band

large white midwing patch

bold white neck patch

grey back

pink breast

dull red legs

white on wings

no white on neck

duller

broad dark band at end of tail

VOICE Husky, muffled, repeated cooing, coo-coo-cu, cu-coo, cook; loud wing clatter in sudden take-off; wing claps in display flight.
NESTING Thin platform of twigs in tree or bush; 2 eggs; 1–2 broods; April–September.
FEEDING Eats buds, leaves, berries, and fruit in trees and on ground; visits bird tables.
SIMILAR SPECIES Stock Dove (p.339).

Collared Dove

Streptopelia decaocto (Columbidae)

Identifiable by its pale, grey-brown body, its thin, black half-collar, and monotonous triple coo, the Collared Dove is common on farms and in suburbs. It prefers to nest and roost in tall conifers. The male has a dramatic display flight, rising steeply and gliding down in wide arcs on flat wings, with harsh nasal calls.

SEEN *in woodland, parks, gardens, around farm buildings, and in villages and towns.*

grey area on upperwings

dark wingtips

white-tipped tail

pale, grey-brown body

black half-collar

pinkish head and breast

no collar

VOICE Loud, repeated triple cu-cooo-cuk; also a nasal gwurrrr call in flight.
NESTING Small platform of twigs, rubbish; 2 eggs; 2–3 broods (or more); all year.
FEEDING Picks grain, seeds, and shoots from ground; often takes seeds from bird tables.
SIMILAR SPECIES Turtle Dove p.338, Rock Dove (p.339), Kestrel (p.318).

sandy-buff

Cuckoo

Cuculus canorus (Columbidae)

The Cuckoo's call is well known, but few people are familiar with the bird itself: a quite large, long-tailed bird that resembles a small-headed hawk or falcon with barred under-parts. It often perches on trees or on overhead wires, its wings drooped and tail fanned.

pale band

PARASITIZES *nests of small birds in woods, reedbeds, on wooded farmland, bushy moorland, and heaths.*

yellow bill base and eyes

pale spot on nape

wedge shape

medium grey upperparts

grey bars on white underside

dark tail with white spots

dark wingtips

yellow legs and feet

barred above

VOICE *Familiar bright cuc-coo, sometimes cuc-cuc-oo; female has odd bubbling call.*
NESTING *Lays eggs in other birds' nests; 1–25 (usually 9) eggs, 1 per nest; May–June.*
FEEDING *Drops to ground to take large, hairy caterpillars; also eats small insects.*
SIMILAR SPECIES *Sparrowhawk (p.318), Kestrel (p.318), Stock Dove (p.339).*

Barn Owl

Tyto alba (Tytonidae)

Often seen by day, especially when it has young to feed, this is a strikingly pale owl with a heart-shaped face and black eyes. It often hunts in flight, flying low over the ground with quick, deep wingbeats. The buff-breasted European form is rare in the British Isles.

heart-shaped facial disc

BREEDS *and hunts in open country, from farmland to marshes and young moorland, and young plantations.*

black eyes

thin bars

pale buff upperparts

grey and black spots

white under-wings

buff below

white below

T. a. guttata

legs may dangle

VOICE *Hissing, snoring calls from nest, nasal hi-wit, shrill, rolling shrieks and high squeals.*
NESTING *Big hole in tree, stack of hay bales, or building; 4–7 eggs; 1 brood; May–June.*
FEEDING *Hunts from perch or in low flight, for voles, mice, rats, and sometimes birds.*
SIMILAR SPECIES *Short-eared Owl (p.343), Tawny Owl (p.342).*

Tawny Owl

Strix aluco (Strigidae)

HUNTS *in all kinds of woodland, wooded farmland, and also in urban parks and large gardens with trees, even in big cities.*

A big-headed, bulky woodland owl that is generally strictly nocturnal, the Tawny Owl is responsible for the hooting and loud *ke-wick* notes often heard after dark. Beautifully camouflaged, it is hard to spot while roosting in the trees unless betrayed by the mobbing of small birds.

large black eyes

obvious facial disc

large, round head

brown back with row of white spots on each side

short wings and tail

pale spots and bars

VOICE *Loud, excited, yapping ke-wick!, long, quavering hoot, hoo hoo-hooo hoo-o-o.*
NESTING *Hole in tree or building, or old stick nest of crow; 2–5 eggs; 1 brood; April–June.*
FEEDING *Drops down to take rodents, frogs, beetles, and worms; also small roosting birds.*
SIMILAR SPECIES *Long-eared Owl (right).*

Little Owl

Athene noctua (Strigidae)

PERCHES *on posts and branches on farmland, open rocky slopes, and even semi-desert areas with rocks and cliffs.*

The small, chunky, flat-headed, short-tailed Little Owl frequently perches out in the open by day, when it often attracts the noisy attention of small birds. It can look very round and solid – although it may stretch upwards when alarmed and take off in a low, fast, bounding flight, like that of a thrush or woodpecker.

broad head with spotted crown

pale yellow eyes

brown back with cream-buff spots

round wings

brown and cream bars

wavy dark streaks

quite long legs

flattish white eyebrows

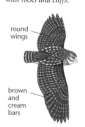

VOICE *Loud, musical, plaintive calls, rising keeeooo, sharper werro! short kip kip kip.*
NESTING *In long, narrow hole in tree, bank, or building; 2–5 eggs; 1 brood; May–July.*
FEEDING *Mostly takes small rodents, large insects, and worms from ground.*
SIMILAR SPECIES *Tawny Owl (above), Short-eared Owl (right).*

Long-eared Owl

Asio otus (Strigidae)

A large, upright owl, with long ear tufts that it raises when alert, the Long-eared Owl is typically strictly nocturnal. Migrants can sometimes be seen by day, when they can be confused with Short-eared Owls (below), but the Long-eared Owl is slightly less buoyant in flight and never glides on raised wings. Also, the pattern on its wings is less contrasted.

ROOSTS *in thorn and willow thickets, old hedgerows, and similar thick cover. Breeds mainly in conifer woods or shelter belts.*

mottled inner wings

ear tufts relaxed

slanting white eyebrows

faint bars

dark wrist patch

deep orange outer wings

dark, closely streaked underside

> **VOICE** *Song deep, moaning, short hoot, oo oo oo or uh uh.*
> **NESTING** *Old nest of crow or hawk in tree, squirrel drey, or scrape on ground beneath bushes; 3–5 eggs; 1 brood; March–June.*
> **FEEDING** *Hunts from perch or in flight, catching rodents on ground or birds in trees.*
> **SIMILAR SPECIES** *Short-eared Owl (below).*

Short-eared Owl

Asio flammeus (Strigidae)

One of few owls that regularly appears in broad daylight, the Short-eared Owl has a buoyant flight and yellow eyes that give it a fierce expression, often visible at long range. It is very like the Long-eared Owl (above) in flight, but has a pale belly and bolder bars on the tail.

large round head with tiny ear tufts, usually hidden

PREYS *over grassland, plantations, marshes, heaths, and upland moors. Erratic breeder in south of range.*

whitish underwings

complex buff marbling on upperparts

black-rimmed, cold yellow eyes

orange-buff to yellowish outer wings

blunt head

narrow dark bar

pale belly

scarcely streaked pale belly

bold bars on tail

white trailing edge

dark wrist patch

> **VOICE** *Nasal bark, kee-aw, or hoarse, whip-like ke-ow; male's song a deep, booming hoot, boo-boo-boo-boo, given in display flight.*
> **NESTING** *Unlined scrape on the ground; 4–8 eggs; 1–2 broods; April–July.*
> **FEEDING** *Rodents and other small mammals.*
> **SIMILAR SPECIES** *Long-eared (above), Tawny (left), and Barn (p.341) Owls; female harriers.*

Kingfisher

Alcedo atthis (Alcedinidae)

Usually glimpsed as a streak of electric blue as it flies over water, the Kingfisher can be surprisingly hard to see when perched in the dappled shade watching for prey. Its shape is unique: dumpy, almost tailless, with a long, heavy spike of a bill. It is often best located by its shrill whistled calls.

FOUND *along rivers and canals, on marshes, and flooded pits; also on coasts, especially in winter.*

vivid blue streak ♂

white neck patch

barred blue cap ♂

red on base of bill ♀

electric blue

rusty orange below ♂

dagger-like black bill

white throat patch

VOICE Quite loud, sharp, high kit-cheeee or cheee; high, fast trill in spring.
NESTING Deep tubular tunnel, lined with fish bones, in earth bank over water; 5–7 eggs; 2 broods; May–July.
FEEDING Catches fish, frogs, and aquatic insects, in dive from perch or mid-air hover.
SIMILAR SPECIES None.

Nightjar

Caprimulgus europaeus (Caprimulgidae)

The strange, nocturnal Nightjar is best known for its song – a protracted mechanical trill that sounds wooden and rattling at close range. Invisible by day, thanks to its superb camouflage, it can be seen hawking for flying insects at twilight, in wonderfully light, buoyant, agile flight.

HUNTS *over heaths and open ground with low undergrowth, or in forest clearings.*

tiny bill

flat head

white line on cheek

elongated body and tail ♂

long wings ♀

white on tail corners ♂

subtly barred, mottled, grey-brown body

white spots ♀

VOICE Frog-like, nasal gooik; song prolonged, mechanical churring, varying in pitch.
NESTING Unlined scrape on ground; 2 eggs; 1–2 broods; May–July.
FEEDING Catches insects, mainly moths, in flight, mostly at dusk and dawn.
SIMILAR SPECIES Song like Grasshopper Warbler's (Locustella naevia) but lower.

Green Woodpecker

Picus viridis (Picidae)

Easily detected, especially in spring, by its loud laughing calls, this big, pale woodpecker forages mainly on the ground. A wary feeder, it is often spotted as it flies up and into cover. Adults are mainly bright green with crimson crowns; young birds are mottled.

LIVES in and around broadleaved and mixed woodland, and heaths with bushes and trees. Feeds on grassy areas with ants.

black around whitish eye

vivid red cap (in both sexes)

red and black moustache; no red in female

♂

bright greenish yellow rump

blackish spots and streaks

apple-green upperside

♂

dark wingtips with pale bars

greenish yellow rump

VOICE Loud, shrill, bouncing keu-keu-keuk; song a descending kleu-kleu-kleu-keu-keu.
NESTING Bores nest hole in tree; 5–7 eggs; 1 brood; May–July.
FEEDING Eats ants, ants' eggs, and larvae, mainly on ground, using tongue to probe nests.
SIMILAR SPECIES Female Golden Oriole (Oriolus oriolus), which has a plain head.

Lesser Spotted Woodpecker

Dendrocopos minor (Picidae)

The size of a sparrow, this Woodpecker is the smallest of British woodpeckers and one of the most secretive. It forages high in the slender branches of trees, creeping over the bark and searching for insects with rapid pecks of its small, sharp bill. Its territorial drumming has a rattling quality.

LIVES in woodland, copses, orchards, and tall hedges with old or diseased trees.

red cap

black cheek patch

barred wings; no big white shoulder patches

♂

less red than male

barred back

black cap

♀

variable streaks below

closely barred back

♂

VOICE Sharp, weak tchik; nasal, peevish pee-pee-pee-pee-pee-pee; weak drum.
NESTING Bores nest hole in tree; 4–6 eggs; 1 brood; May–June.
FEEDING Takes insects from under bark and also from woody stems of ground plants.
SIMILAR SPECIES Great Spotted Woodpecker (p.346), Kestrel (call) (p.318).

Great Spotted Woodpecker

FEEDS in gardens and scrub as well as mature woodland; breeds in both deciduous and conifer woods.

Dendrocopos major (Picidae)

The rapid "drum roll" of this bird is a common sound of spring woodland. The woodpecker itself is often easy to locate, propped on its tail as it hammers at bark or timber. If disturbed, it swoops away in a deeply undulating flight.

big white shoulder patch

♂

all-red crown; less on female

no red

♀

red patch on back of head

black and white above

vivid red under tail ♂

bright buff below

VOICE *Explosive tchik! fast rattle of alarm; loud, fast, very short drumming.*
NESTING *Bores nest hole in tree trunk or branch; 4–7 eggs;1 brood; April–June.*
FEEDING *Digs insects and grubs from bark with strong bill; also eats seeds and berries.*
SIMILAR SPECIES *Lesser Spotted Woodpecker (p.345).*

Sand Martin

BREEDS in colonies in earth banks and sand quarries, often near water, excavating rows of nest holes.

Riparia riparia (Hirundinidae)

The smallest of the European swallows and martins, with the most fluttering flight, the Sand Martin is the first to appear on its northern breeding grounds in spring. At this time it usually hunts over water, where it can rely on a supply of flying insect prey. It feeds on the wing, swooping after flies with fast in-out flicks of its wings. Always gregarious, it roosts in noisy flocks.

all-brown above

angled-back wings

white underparts

tail with shallow fork

brown breast-band

perches at nest hole

VOICE *Low, dry, rasping or chattering chrrrp; song rambling, chattering, weak twitter.*
NESTING *Bores long hole into earth or soft sandstone; 4–5 eggs; 2 broods; April–July.*
FEEDING *Catches insects in flight, often over water; sometimes feeds on bare ground.*
SIMILAR SPECIES *House Martin (right), Swift (p.348).*

House Martin

Delichon urbica (Hirundinidae)

Small, stocky, with pied plumage and a bold white rump, the House Martin is a common breeding bird in many towns and villages in northern Europe. It feeds entirely in the air on small flies and similar prey, circling high up over the rooftops or low over fresh waters. It comes down to the ground only to gather mud, which it uses to build its distinctive nest.

dark wings

PERCHES in flocks on wires before migration. Breeds on house walls, feeding over wetlands and open areas.

nest on outside wall

white rump

blue-black cap

forked tail

blue-black back

white throat

white underside

VOICE Hard, quick, chirping prrit or chrrit, tchirrup; twittering song of similar notes.
NESTING Enclosed mud nest with top entrance, under house eaves or (in south of range) cliff overhang; 4–5 eggs; 2–3 broods; April–September.
FEEDING Catches insects in flight, high up.
SIMILAR SPECIES Swallow (below).

Swallow

Hirundo rustica (Hirundinidae)

The glossy, fork-tailed Swallow is a common sight around farmsteads in summer, since it prefers to nest in barns and sheds close to a steady supply of its favourite prey, large flies. It catches these on the wing, often swooping low with a graceful action, using its long tail to steer. Its tail streamers and deep red chin are usually conspicuous in flight.

PERCHES on wires, especially in autumn before migrating to Africa. Breeds in and around villages and farms.

deep rust-red chin

dark rufous forehead

dark cap

deep, glossy blue upperparts

long, slender wings

pale undertail coverts

pale below

whitish to deep peach-buff underparts

brown wings

long tail

VOICE Call liquid swit-swit-swit, nasal vit-vit-vit, tsee-tsee; song quick, chirruping warble.
NESTING Open cup of mud and straw, on beam or ledge in outbuilding; 4–6 eggs; 2–3 broods; April–August.
FEEDING Flies low to catch flying insects.
SIMILAR SPECIES House Martin (above), Swift (p.348).

Swift

Apus apus (Apodidae)

The only swift to occur over most of Europe, the common Swift is usually instantly identifiable by its scythe-like wings and loud, screaming calls. It spends most of its life in the air, only landing at the nest, and never perches like a swallow. In bad weather, it flies very low, giving good views.

BREEDS *in holes in old buildings; rarely in cliffs nowadays; hunts over open country, villages, towns, and some large cities.*

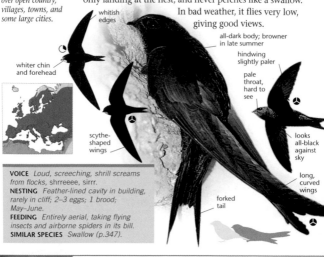

whitish edges

all-dark body; browner in late summer

hindwing slightly paler

whiter chin and forehead

pale throat, hard to see

scythe-shaped wings

looks all-black against sky

long, curved wings

forked tail

VOICE Loud, screeching, shrill screams from flocks, shrreeee, sirrr.
NESTING Feather-lined cavity in building, rarely in cliff; 2–3 eggs; 1 brood; May–June.
FEEDING Entirely aerial, taking flying insects and airborne spiders in its bill.
SIMILAR SPECIES Swallow (p.347).

Meadow Pipit

Anthus pratensis (Motacillidae)

The tinkling song of the Meadow Pipit is one of the evocative sounds of summer in the open hills. Often seen from a distance as it rises in a song flight, or flutters up jerkily with squeaky calls, the bird has a hesitant, nervous manner. A close look is needed to appreciate the subtle distinctions of its plumage.

FOUND *on grassland, heaths, dunes, and moors, from coasts to uplands; on farmland and marshes near coasts in winter.*

slim dark bill

pale stripe

streaked brown back

soft blackish streaks on brown back

dark tail with white sides

olive-buff or cream below

evenly streaked flanks and chest

very long hind claw

VOICE Call sharp, weak pseeep, quiet pip, in winter flock; song long series of notes and trills in parachuting song flight.
NESTING Nest a cup of grass on ground; 4–5 eggs, 2 broods; May–July.
FEEDING Eats insects and some seeds.
SIMILAR SPECIES Skylark (right), Tree Pipit (A. trivialis), Rock Pipit (A. petrosus).

NOTE

Song-flight very like that of Tree Pipit (A. trivialis), but it usually begins and ends it on ground, while Tree Pipit flies from perch to perch.

Skylark

Alauda arvensis (Alaudidae)

The silvery song of the Skylark is a familiar sound over the farmlands and pastures of the British Isles. A typical streaky lark on the ground, it has a distinctive appearance in flight, with its angular wings and short, white-edged tail. In winter, large flocks gather to feed on farmland.

SINGS *over open fields, especially with cereal crops, moorland, heaths, and pastures. Feeds on arable land in winter.*

narrow whitish trailing edge to wing

whitish over eye

dark stripes on back

pale-centred cheeks

closely streaked, pale to warm tan-brown above

blackish tail with wide white sides

flattened crest

grey underwings

white belly

long hind claw

VOICE Calls chirruping shrrup, trrup, *higher* seee; song fast, rich, from perch or in high, soaring flight, sounding thinner at distance.
NESTING Grassy cup on ground, in crops or grass; 3–5 eggs; 2–3 broods; April–July.
FEEDING Forages on ground in grass or on bare earth, eating seeds, shoots, and insects.
SIMILAR SPECIES Woodlark (Lullula arborea).

Yellow Wagtail

Motacilla flava (Motacillidae)

A male Yellow Wagtail in summer is elegant, colourful, and distinctive, but autumn birds, particularly juveniles, are easy to confuse with other species. Unlike other wagtails, it is never seen in Europe in winter, since it migrates to Africa to feed among the grazing herds on the tropical grasslands.

SNATCHES *prey from beneath feet of farm animals on wet fields; often near water.*

pale line

white lines

buff

bright yellow stripe

green crown; blue-headed race occasional in spring

green back

pale line

grey-green

♂

two white wingbars

♀

bright yellow below

♂

white-sided black tail

VOICE Call full, flat or rising tsli, or tsweep; song repetiton of brief chirping phrases.
NESTING Grassy cup in vegetation on ground; 5–6 eggs; 2 broods; May–July.
FEEDING Takes insects from ground; skips and leaps after flies in short flycatching sallies.
SIMILAR SPECIES Grey Wagtail (p.350), juvenile Pied Wagtail (p.350).

Grey Wagtail

Motacilla cinerea (Motacillidae)

The extensive yellow in the Grey Wagtail's plumage can lead to confusion with the Yellow Wagtail (p.349), but its back is grey instead of green, and the summer male's black bib is distinctive. In winter, it often occurs near puddles, even in cities, when the Yellow Wagtail is far away in Africa.

BREEDS *along clean, often tree-lined rivers or open upland streams; widespread near water in winter, including briefly in urban areas.*

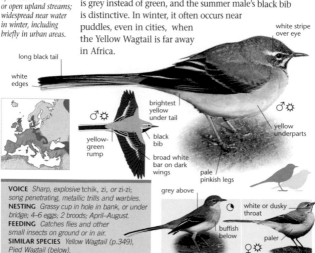

white stripe over eye

long black tail

white edges

♂ ☼ brightest yellow under tail

yellow-green rump

black bib

broad white bar on dark wings

♂ ☼

yellow underparts

pale pinkish legs

grey above

♀ ☼ white or dusky throat

buffish below

paler

VOICE *Sharp, explosive tchik, zi, or zi-zi; song penetrating, metallic trills and warbles.*
NESTING *Grassy cup in hole in bank, or under bridge; 4–6 eggs; 2 broods; April–August.*
FEEDING *Catches flies and other small insects on ground or in air.*
SIMILAR SPECIES *Yellow Wagtail (p.349), Pied Wagtail (below).*

Pied Wagtail

Motacilla alba (Motacillidae)

Common throughout Europe, this boldly patterned wagtail occurs in two forms. The darker Pied Wagtail of Britain and Ireland has a black back, dark flanks and blackish wings.

The mainland European form, the White Wagtail, is a scarce migrant in spring and autumn in the British Isles. It has a pale grey back and rump.

ROOSTS *in trees in towns; feeds on rooftops and roadsides; also in fields, often by water.*

greyer back

♀ PIED

♂♀ PIED

pale grey back and rump

WHITE WAGTAIL
M.a.alba

black cap, chin, and throat; white chin and throat in winter

white feather edges

sooty flanks

white belly

♂ ☼ PIED

buffish below

♂ ☼ white streaks on wings

VOICE *Call loud, musical chirp, chuwee, chrruwee, grading into harder tissik or chiswik.*
NESTING *Grassy cup in cavity in bank, wall, cliff, or woodpile, in outbuilding or under bridge; 5–6 eggs; 2–3 broods; April–August.*
FEEDING *Feeds actively on ground, or flying in pursuit of flies; takes insects and seeds.*
SIMILAR SPECIES *Grey Wagtail (above).*

Dipper

Cinclus cinclus (Cinclidae)

The Dipper is quite unmistakable, thanks to its unique hunting technique. It feeds underwater, often by walking into a fast-flowing stream and foraging along the bottom. Out of the water it has a distinctive springy character, often bobbing and flicking its tail, and flies low and fast along watercourses.

HUNTS *aquatic prey in clean upland streams, moving to lowland rivers and even coasts in hard winters.*

greyer body

stout dark bill

deep brown head

blackish back

plump body

blackish tail

bold white chest

chestnut band

stout black legs

big feet

VOICE *Call sharp dzit or djink; song loud, rich warbling with explosive, grating notes.*
NESTING *Nest of grass in hole or under overhang; 4–6 eggs; 2 broods; April–July.*
FEEDING *Forages for aquatic insect larvae, small fish, crustaceans, and molluscs.*
SIMILAR SPECIES *Ring Ouzel (Turdus torquatus).*

Wren

Troglodytes troglodytes (Troglodytidae)

A tiny, plump, finely-barred bird with a surprisingly loud voice, the Wren has a habit of raising its very short tail vertically. It also has a distinctive flight – fast and direct, often plunging straight into dense cover. Wren populations decline in cold winters, but usually recover quite quickly.

SINGS *from exposed perches; seen foraging at low level in woods and thickets.*

very slightly downcurved, fine bill

pale stripe over eye

dark barring

short, rounded tail

rusty-brown above with barred wings

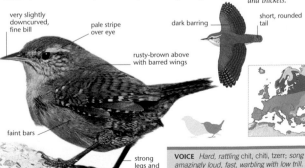

faint bars

strong legs and feet

VOICE *Hard, rattling chit, chiti, tzerr; song amazingly loud, fast, warbling with low trill.*
NESTING *Small, loose ball of leaves and grass in bank; 5–6 eggs; 2 broods; April–July.*
FEEDING *Forages for insects under hedges, in ditches, and other dark, damp places.*
SIMILAR SPECIES *Dunnock (p.352), Robin (p.353).*

Dunnock

Prunella modularis (Prunellidae)

Although it is one of many small, streaky, sparrow-like birds, the Dunnock has a fine bill, grey head and breast, and forages on the ground with a distinctive, jerky, creeping shuffle. If disturbed, it generally flies at ground level into the nearest thick bush.

FORAGES *for food in low, dense scrub and bushes, on heaths and moors, and in forests, woods, parks, and gardens.*

red-brown eyes

fine, dark bill

grey throat

row of pale spots on wings

browner head

rich brown with black streaks

orange-brown legs

black-streaked brown wings and back

VOICE Loud, high, penetrating pseep, vibrant teee; song high, fast warble.
NESTING Small grassy cup lined with moss, hair, in bush; 4–5 eggs; 2–3 broods; April–July.
FEEDING Picks small insects and seeds from ground, shuffling under and around bushes.
SIMILAR SPECIES Robin (right), Wren (p.351), House Sparrow (p.374).

Nightingale

Luscinia megarhynchos (Turdidae)

Famous for the male's rich and varied song, the Nightingale can be frustratingly difficult to see. It skulks in thick vegetation, often close to the ground. With its almost anonymous, brown plumage, it resembles a large juvenile Robin (right) or a Garden Warbler (p.360), but it has a longer rufous-brown tail, conspicuous in flight.

SINGS *in thickets in overgrown gardens, bushy gullies, heaths, and coppiced woodland.*

plain brown wings

rufous tail

warm brown back

pale ring around large, dark eyes

spotted above

grey neck side

rusty rump and tail

grey-buff below

tail often raised

bright rump

VOICE Calls include low, mechanical, grating kerrr, loud, bright tweet; song brilliant, varied.
NESTING Small cup of leaves, lined with grass and hair, built in low bush; 4–5 eggs; 1 brood; May–June.
FEEDING Eats worms, beetles, and berries.
SIMILAR SPECIES Juvenile Robin (right), Garden Warbler (p.360), Redstart (p.354).

Robin

Erithacus rubecula (Turdidae)

The round-bodied, slim-tailed Robin is a shy, skulking woodland bird over most of its range. It is adapted to animals such as wild boar and pigs, taking small invertebrates that the animals disturb from the ground. In the British Isles, it follows gardeners in a similar way, taking worms and grubs turned up by their spades. It is perhaps the easiest of all birds to become hand-tame, given a regular diet of mealworms or other grubs, which it finds irresistible. Nevertheless, nesting Robins remain secretive and shy, quick to desert their eggs if disturbed.

LIVES *in open forests and woods, on bushy heaths, and in parks and gardens with hedges and shrubs.*

NOTE

Robins have developed the habit of singing at night under artificial lights, both in suburban areas and alongside car parks and industrial sites.

warm brown above

white breast spot

big black eye

bluish grey on sides of neck and chest

orange-red breast

mottled brown body

VOICE *Sharp* tik, *quick* tik-ik-ik-ik, *high, thin* seep; *song rich, sweet, musical, varied warble.*
NESTING *Domed nest of leaves and grass in bank or bush; 4–6 eggs; 2 broods; April–August.*
FEEDING *Takes spiders, insects, worms, berries, and seeds, mostly from ground.*
SIMILAR SPECIES *Dunnock (left), Nightingale (left), Redstart (p.354).*

Redstart

Phoenicurus phoenicurus (Turdidae)

A male Redstart is an extremely handsome bird in spring and summer, best located in its breeding wood by its short, sweet song. The female, less distinctive, shares the male's habit of constantly flicking its rust-red tail up and down. They like old woods with open space beneath the canopy.

SEEN *in open woodland with sparse under-growth. Migrants seen near coasts or lakes.*

white forehead

whitish mottling

♂

♀

pale buff below

rusty rump

orange-rufous below

♂

bluish grey from crown to back

♂

pale rust-red tail with dark centre

VOICE *Clear, rising wheet, sharp tac; song brief, musical warble, ending with weak trill.*
NESTING *Grassy nest lined with feathers or hair, in hole; 5–7 eggs; 1 brood; May–June.*
FEEDING *Forages in foliage or on ground for insects, spiders, small worms; some berries.*
SIMILAR SPECIES *Nightingale (p.352), Robin (p.353), Black Redstart (P. ochruros).*

Stonechat

Saxicola torquata (Turdidae)

Small, chunky, and upright, the Stonechat is a bird of open, bushy terrain, such as gorse thickets above coastal cliffs. It likes to perch on the tops of bushes, where its scolding calls and the male's pied head-neck pattern make it conspicuous. It often darts down to snatch prey from the ground, flying back to its perch on whirring wings like a giant bumblebee.

PERCHES *prominently in open places with bushes and heather, on heaths, coasts, and moorland.*

black head and throat

paler head and throat

white neck patch

white wing patch

♂

paler head

♀

mottled chest

♀

rust-red breast

short dark tail

♂

♂

VOICE *Hard, scolding tsak or tsak-tsak, sharp wheet; song rapid, chattery warble.*
NESTING *Grassy cup, often in grass with entrance tunnel; 5–6 eggs; 2 broods; May–July.*
FEEDING *Takes insects, spiders, worms and seeds from ground; also catches insects in air.*
SIMILAR SPECIES *Wheatear (right), Redstart (p.354), Whinchat (S. rubetra).*

Wheatear

Oenanthe oenanthe

In summer, the Wheatear is a bird of open, rocky habitats, but it often turns up along coasts, on farmland, and even on golf courses while on migration. It has a distinctive habit of flying ahead of people, then perching before moving on again, flashing its white rump every time it moves.

bold black "T"

white rump

♀

♂

BREEDS IN *mainly upland areas that combine boulders, scree, or cliffs with open grassland.*

pale grey crown

white stripe above eye

black patch through eye

brownish above

small eye-patch

♀♂

plumage like autumn adult

♀♂

♂

buff below, fading to white

black legs

VOICE *Hard chak-chak, bright wheet- chak-chak; song rambling, scratchy warble.*
NESTING *Grassy cup in hole in ground, stone wall, burrow; 5–6 eggs; 1–2 broods; April–July.*
FEEDING *Hops and runs after insects and spiders on open ground; also leaps for flies.*
SIMILAR SPECIES *Stonechat (left).*

Blackbird

Turdus merula (Turdidae)

A smart, plump thrush with a distinctive habit of raising its tail on landing, the Blackbird is a familiar garden bird. The glossy black male is easy to recognize, but the brown female can be confused with other thrushes despite her darker plumage. Males sing superbly, especially from high perches towards dusk.

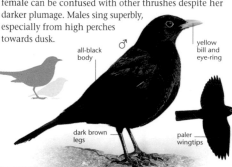

all-black body

♂

yellow bill and eye-ring

dark brown legs

paler wingtips

LIVES *in woods with leaf litter, also parks and gardens, and farmland with tall hedges.*

gingery body

dull black

dark bill

♂♀ 1ST ❄

dark brown

♀

mottled below

VOICE *Low, soft chook, frequent pink-pink-pink, fast alarm rattle, high srreee; song superb, musical, varied, full-throated warbling.*
NESTING *Grass and mud cup in shrub or low in tree; 3–5 eggs; 2–4 broods; March–August.*
FEEDING *Finds worms, insects, and spiders on ground; fruit and berries in bushes.*
SIMILAR SPECIES *Ring Ouzel (T. torquatus).*

Fieldfare

Turdus pilaris (Turdidae)

A large, handsome thrush with a striking combination of plumage colours, the Fieldfare is usually identifiable by its blue-grey head and white underwing. It is a winter visitor to most of Europe, like the smaller Redwing (below), and the two often feed together in mixed flocks, stripping berries from fruiting trees and shrubs.

FEEDS *on farmland, bushy heaths, shrubs, woods, orchards, and gardens in winter; breeds in woodland.*

white under-wings

pale grey rump

black tail

dark brown back

blue-grey head with black mask

black and yellow bill

orange-buff breast with heavy black spots

whiter flanks

dense black chevrons on white flanks

VOICE *Loud, chuckling* chak-chak-chak, *low, nasal* weeip; *song a rather unmusical mixture of squeaks, warbles, and whistles.*
NESTING *Cup of grass and twigs in bush or tree; 5–6 eggs; 1–2 broods; May–June.*
FEEDING *Mostly eats worms and insects on the ground; also fruit from trees and bushes.*
SIMILAR SPECIES *Mistle Thrush (right).*

Redwing

Turdus iliacus (Turdidae)

A small, sociable thrush with a bold head pattern and well-defined streaks below, the Redwing is named for its distinctive rusty-red underwings and flanks. It is a winter visitor to much of Europe from the taiga forests of the far north, and typically forages in flocks for berries, often with Fieldfares (above). In hard winters, it often visits large gardens for food.

FOUND *on farmland with hedges and bushy heaths. Breeds in conifer and birch woods.*

reddish underwing

dark brown back

short, square tail

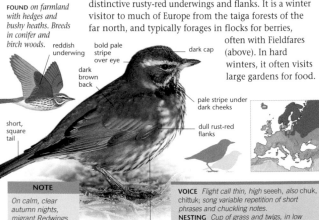

bold pale stripe over eye

dark cap

pale stripe under dark cheeks

dull rust-red flanks

silvery white below, with dark streaks

NOTE

On calm, clear autumn nights, migrant Redwings can often be heard flying overhead, calling to each other to stay in contact.

VOICE *Flight call thin, high* seeeh, *also* chuk, chittuk; *song variable repetition of short phrases and chuckling notes.*
NESTING *Cup of grass and twigs, in low bush; 4–6 eggs; 2 broods; April–July.*
FEEDING *Worms, insects, and seeds taken from ground, berries in winter.*
SIMILAR SPECIES *Song Thrush (right).*

Song Thrush

Turdus philomelos (Turdidae)

Small, pale, and neatly spotted below, the Song Thrush is a familiar bird with a wonderfully vibrant, varied, full-throated song. Well known for its habit of smashing the shells of snails to extract their soft bodies, it also hauls many earthworms from their burrows. It is declining in many areas, particularly on farmland.

BREEDS *and feeds in broadleaved woodland, farmland with trees and hedges, parks and gardens with shrubs.*

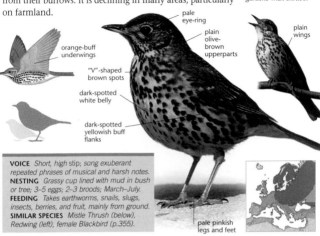

orange-buff underwings

pale eye-ring

plain olive-brown upperparts

plain wings

"V"-shaped brown spots

dark-spotted white belly

dark-spotted yellowish buff flanks

pale pinkish legs and feet

VOICE *Short, high* stip; *song exuberant repeated phrases of musical and harsh notes.*
NESTING *Grassy cup lined with mud in bush or tree; 3–5 eggs; 2–3 broods; March–July.*
FEEDING *Takes earthworms, snails, slugs, insects, berries, and fruit, mainly from ground.*
SIMILAR SPECIES *Mistle Thrush (below), Redwing (left), female Blackbird (p.355).*

Mistle Thrush

Turdus viscivorus (Turdidae)

Big, bold, and aggressive, the Mistle Thrush is the largest of the European thrushes. It has a tall, long-necked look compared to the Song Thrush (above), and often flies much higher when disturbed. Males often sing from the tops of tall trees in all weathers, and in winter single birds defend berry-laden trees against Fieldfares (left), Redwings (left), and other birds.

LIVES *on farmland with tall trees, edges of moorland near forest, woodland clearings, orchards, and parks.*

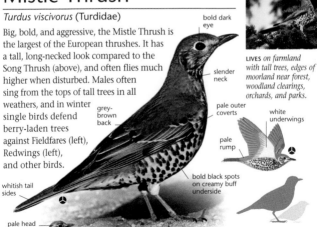

bold dark eye

slender neck

grey-brown back

pale outer coverts

white underwings

pale rump

bold black spots on creamy buff underside

whitish tail sides

pale head

pale spots

VOICE *Loud, rattling chatter, tsairrk-sairr-sairr-sairk; song repeated wild, fluty phrases.*
NESTING *Loose cup of twigs and grass high in tree; 3–5 eggs; 2 broods; March–June.*
FEEDING *Hops on ground, taking seeds and invertebrates; also eats berries and fruit.*
SIMILAR SPECIES *Song Thrush (above), Fieldfare (left), female Blackbird (p.355).*

Sedge Warbler

Acrocephalus schoenobaenus (Sylviidae)

A small, well-marked, active bird with a loud, fast, varied song, the Sedge Warbler is common in waterside and boggy habitats. It often occurs among reeds, but not always, for it prefers to forage among a variety of vegetation that may include willow and hawthorn scrub, and hedges beside wet ditches.

SINGS from the tops of reeds and bushes in reedbeds and wetlands, also in short song-flights. May also occur in thorn bushes.

silvery white stripe over eye

buff on chest and flanks

tawny back, streaked greyish

whitish below

tawny-buff rump

VOICE *Call dry rasping tchrrr, sharper tek; song fast mix of whistles, clicks, and trills.*
NESTING *Deep nest of grass, moss, and cobwebs; 5–6 eggs; 1–2 broods; April–July.*
FEEDING *Insects, spiders, and some seeds, taken from reeds, sedges, nettles, and bushes.*
SIMILAR SPECIES *Reed Warbler (below).*

Reed Warbler

Acrocephalus scirpaceus (Sylviidae)

Although it occasionally nests in willows growing over water, the Reed Warbler is basically a reedbed specialist, adept at grasping vertical stems and shuffling through the dense reeds in search of food. Very like the slightly plumper Marsh Warbler (*A. palustris*), it is best identified by its repetitive, conversational song.

LIVES in extensive, wet reedbeds, reedy ditches, and willows beside lakes and rivers. Migrants can be seen on coasts.

long wing feathers with pale fringes

plain brown above

long tail

pale eye-ring

rump brighter than back

dark legs

white throat

bright buff underside

VOICE *Call low churr or chk; song rhythmic trik trik, chrr chrr, chewe chewe trrt tiri tiri.*
NESTING *Deep grass nest woven around reed stems; 3–5 eggs; 2 broods; May–July.*
FEEDING *Insects and spiders taken from mud and thick, wet vegetation; some seeds.*
SIMILAR SPECIES *Marsh Warbler (A. palustris), Sedge Warbler (above).*

Dartford Warbler

Sylvia undata (Sylviidae)

A skulking, secretive bird of warm heaths and sunny slopes, the Dartford Warbler is often hard to see clearly as it flicks from one bush to another and slips from sight. But in warm, still weather it may perch in full view, when it is easy to recognize. A year-round resident, it can suffer declines in hard winters.

FOUND *in heaths with gorse, heather, and small bushes, and on warm, bushy slopes with thorn scrub.*

red eye and eye-ring

duller than male

paler below

brownish grey back

♀

long, slender, dark tail

dark red-brown underside

♂

VOICE *Call distinctive, low, buzzy chrrr; song quick, rattling warble, sometimes given in air.*
NESTING *Grassy cup nest, low in gorse or heather; 3–5 eggs; 2–3 broods; April–July.*
FEEDING *Searches for insects and many spiders in low vegetation.*
SIMILAR SPECIES *Whitethroat (p.360).*

Lesser Whitethroat

Sylvia curruca (Sylviidae)

Smaller and neater than the Whitethroat (p.360), with a dark eye-patch and darker legs, the Lesser Whitethroat is a secretive warbler of woodland edges and hedgerows. Although easy to locate by its song, it often moves to a new perch. In autumn, it can be easy to find feeding on shrubs and trees with berries.

LIVES *in tall, dense thickets at the edges of woods, patches of scrub, and old, thick, overgrown hedgerows.*

white eye-ring

♂

slim tail, edged white

♂

dark eye-patch

grey cap

head paler in spring

♀

plain brown wings

dull grey-brown back

white throat

whitish underside, washed pink

dark grey legs

♂

VOICE *Sharp metallic tak, thin chi; song a rattling, wooden chikachikachikachikachika.*
NESTING *Cup of twigs or grass built in shrub; 4–6 eggs; 1 brood; May–June.*
FEEDING *Picks insects from foliage; also eats many berries in late summer.*
SIMILAR SPECIES *Whitethroat (p.360), Blackcap (p.361).*

Whitethroat

Sylvia communis (Sylviidae)

Typically a bird of open spaces with low bushes and scrub, the Whitethroat often skulks in low, thick vegetation. It gives itself away by its irritable calls, and often emerges to scold intruders. It sings quite often, sometimes from a low perch or a high wire, but also during a short, bouncing song-flight.

SINGS *from perches in bushy, dry, and heathy places with low thorny scrub; also thickets, hedges, dense herbs.*

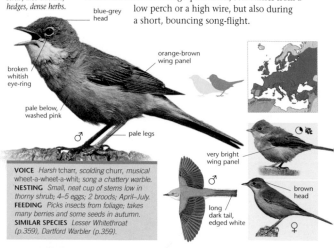

blue-grey head

orange-brown wing panel

broken whitish eye-ring

pale below, washed pink

pale legs

♂

very bright wing panel

♂

long dark tail, edged white

brown head

♀

VOICE *Harsh* tcharr, *scolding* churr, *musical* wheet-a-wheet-a-whit; *song a chattery warble.*
NESTING *Small, neat cup of stems low in thorny shrub; 4–5 eggs; 2 broods; April–July.*
FEEDING *Picks insects from foliage; takes many berries and some seeds in autumn.*
SIMILAR SPECIES *Lesser Whitethroat (p.359), Dartford Warbler (p.359).*

Garden Warbler

Sylvia borin (Sylviidae)

This short-billed, round-faced warbler has no obvious patterning and few distinctive features apart from its song, which is a beautiful outpouring of mellow warbling notes. Normally solitary, it may join other warblers to feed on berries in late summer to fuel its migration. Despite its name, it rarely visits gardens unless they are large and overgrown, or to feed when on migration.

BREEDS *and feeds in open woods, wooded parkland, tall thickets, shrubs, and trees.*

dull, pale wings

grey neck patch

thin, pale eye-ring

large, dark eyes

pale buff-brown above

pale feather edges, sharper on juvenile

pale buff underside

VOICE *Call thick, soft* tchak, churr; *song rich, throaty, musical, fast warbling.*
NESTING *Shallow, skimpy cup of grass and moss in bush; 4–5 eggs; 1 brood; May–July.*
FEEDING *Takes insects and spiders from foliage, berries and seeds in autumn.*
SIMILAR SPECIES *Blackcap (right), Reed Warbler (p.358), Spotted Flycatcher (p.363).*

Blackcap

Sylvia atricapilla (Sylviidae)

The Blackcap is a stocky warbler with a typical, hard, unmusical call. Its song, however, is beautiful, rich, and full-throated, less even than the similar song of the Garden Warbler (left). It may overwinter in northwest Europe, when it visits gardens to take seeds and scraps, often driving other birds away from feeders.

SINGS *brilliantly from perches in woods, parks, and large bushy gardens, with plenty of thick undergrowth.*

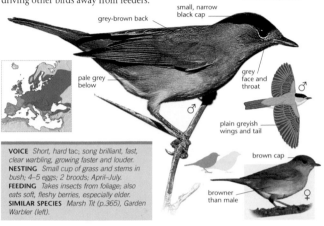

small, narrow black cap

grey-brown back

pale grey below

grey face and throat

♂

plain greyish wings and tail

brown cap

browner than male

♀

VOICE *Short, hard tac; song brilliant, fast, clear warbling, growing faster and louder.*
NESTING *Small cup of grass and stems in bush; 4–5 eggs; 2 broods; April–July.*
FEEDING *Takes insects from foliage; also eats soft, fleshy berries, especially elder.*
SIMILAR SPECIES *Marsh Tit (p.365), Garden Warbler (left).*

Wood Warbler

Phylloscopus sibilatrix (Sylviidae)

One of the biggest of the *Phylloscopus* warblers, the Wood Warbler is also the brightest, with areas of pure lemon-yellow and clear green in its plumage. It feeds quietly, high in the foliage of mature deciduous trees, and can be hard to spot. In early summer, the male is best located by his metallic, trilling song, delivered with such force that the bird's entire body vibrates with the effort.

TRILLS *ecstatically from branches in mature broadleaved woods with open ground beneath the canopy.*

long wings

clear green upperside

long, broad yellow stripe over eye

pale sulphur-yellow chin and upper breast

silky white underside

VOICE *Call loud song low, sweet* sioo sioo sioo, *or sharp ticking, accelerating into silvery trill,* ti-ti-ti-ti-ti-ti-tik-ik-ik-ikrrrrrrrrrrrrr.
NESTING *Domed grassy nest in dead leaves on ground; 6–7 eggs; 1 brood; May–June.*
FEEDING *Insects and spiders, from foliage.*
SIMILAR SPECIES *Willow Warbler (p.362), Chiffchaff (p.362).*

Chiffchaff

Phylloscopus collybita (Sylviidae)

By sight the Chiffchaff is almost impossible to distinguish from the Willow Warbler (below), although the slightly plumper Chiffchaff's habit of dipping its tail downward is a useful clue. When it sings, it betrays its identity by repeating its name over and over again – and luckily it sings a lot, particularly in spring. Some Chiffchaffs spend the winter in western Europe, unlike Willow Warblers.

REPEATS *its name from perches in woodland, parks, bushy areas, and large gardens; favours taller trees in summer.*

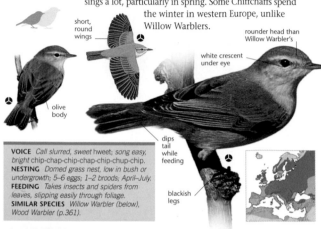

short, round wings

rounder head than Willow Warbler's

white crescent under eye

olive body

dips tail while feeding

blackish legs

VOICE *Call slurred, sweet* tweet; *song easy, bright chip-chap-chip-chap-chip-chup-chip.*
NESTING *Domed grass nest, low in bush or undergrowth; 5–6 eggs; 1–2 broods; April–July.*
FEEDING *Takes insects and spiders from leaves, slipping easily through foliage.*
SIMILAR SPECIES *Willow Warbler (below), Wood Warbler (p.361).*

Willow Warbler

Phylloscopus trochilus (Sylviidae)

The most common and widespread of the leaf warblers, this small, slim bird closely resembles the Chiffchaff (above). It is most easily recognized by the simple, yet wonderfully evocative song that heralds its arrival in the north in spring. It usually feeds alone, slipping easily through foliage as it searches for insects and other prey.

SINGS *with beautiful fluid cadence in light woodland, scrub, and thickets, especially of birch and willow.*

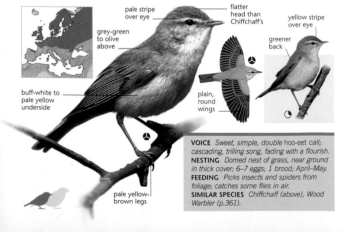

pale stripe over eye

flatter head than Chiffchaff's

grey-green to olive above

yellow stripe over eye

greener back

buff-white to pale yellow underside

plain, round wings

pale yellow-brown legs

VOICE *Sweet, simple, double* hoo-eet *call; cascading, trilling song, fading with a flourish.*
NESTING *Domed nest of grass, near ground in thick cover; 6–7 eggs; 1 brood; April–May.*
FEEDING *Picks insects and spiders from foliage; catches some flies in air.*
SIMILAR SPECIES *Chiffchaff (above), Wood Warbler (p.361).*

Goldcrest

Regulus regulus (Sylviidae)

Britain's smallest bird, the agile, busy Goldcrest frequently forages very close to people, apparently oblivious of their presence. This needle-billed, round-bodied bird often gives its high-pitched calls as it searches restlessly for food. It has a plainer face than its close relative, the Firecrest (*R. ignicapillus*).

FEEDS *in coniferous and mixed woodland, thickets, and large gardens, throughout the year.*

yellow inner stripe on black crown

buff below

broad white "V"

olive-green back

blackish wings

> **VOICE** *High, sibilant see-see-see call; high, fast song, seedli-ee seedli-ee seedli-ee.*
> **NESTING** *Cup of cobwebs and moss, slung from branch; 7–8 eggs; 2 broods; April–July.*
> **FEEDING** *Picks tiny insects, spiders, and insect eggs from foliage, often hovering briefly.*
> **SIMILAR SPECIES** *Willow Warbler (left), Chiffchaff (left), Firecrest (R. ignicapillus).*

Spotted Flycatcher

Muscicapa striata (Muscicapidae)

Sharp-eyed and constantly alert, the Spotted Flycatcher specializes in targeting flying insects from a vantage point on an open perch. Launching itself with a burst of rapid wingbeats, it seizes its quarry in mid-air and usually returns to the same perch – a technique that makes it quite distinctive despite its unremarkable grey-brown plumage.

HUNTS *flying insects from perches in open woodland, parkland, and gardens with bushes and trees.*

streaked head

long, narrow wings

spotted crown

cream spots on back

soft brown streaks on breast

silvery white below

long brown tail held downwards

> **VOICE** *Short, scratchy tzic or tzee, tzee-tsuk tsuk; song short, scratchy, weak warble.*
> **NESTING** *Cup of grass, leaves, moss in vine or cavity; 3–5 eggs; 1–2 broods; June–August.*
> **FEEDING** *Catches insects in air, sallying from perch and usually returning to same perch.*
> **SIMILAR SPECIES** *Garden Warbler (p.360), female Pied Flycatcher (p.364).*

Pied Flycatcher

Ficedula hypoleuca (Muscicapidae)

A breeding male Pied Flycatcher is boldly pied and hard to mistake as he dashes out from a forest perch to seize flying insects on the wing. After the autumn moult, males resemble the browner females, but the white wing and tail patches are distinctive in both.

PREFERS *to breed in nest boxes, in mature broadleaved woodland, with clear air beneath canopy for hunting.*

one or two white spots on forehead

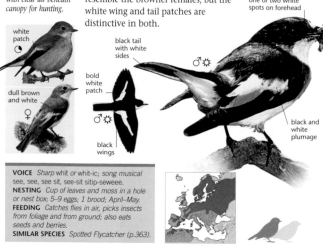

white patch ☾

dull brown and ♀

black tail with white sides

bold white patch

♂☀

black wings

♂☀

black wings

black and white plumage

VOICE *Sharp whit or whit-ic; song musical see, see, see sit, see-sit sitip-seweee.*
NESTING *Cup of leaves and moss in a hole or nest box; 5–9 eggs; 1 brood; April–May.*
FEEDING *Catches flies in air, picks insects from foliage and from ground; also eats seeds and berries.*
SIMILAR SPECIES *Spotted Flycatcher (p.363).*

Bearded Tit

Panurus biarmicus (Timaliidae)

The tawny, long-tailed Bearded Tit lives almost exclusively in large reedbeds, although in winter it may briefly occupy tall grasses or reedmace when forced to move on by overcrowding. On windy days it stays out of sight, but in calm weather it can sometimes be located by its loud "pinging" call.

INHABITS *reedbeds, where it breeds and finds most of its food. Sometimes found in nearby tall vegetation.*

bright blue-grey head

tawny, cream, and black above

pale brown head

big black "moustache"

♀

black back ☾

round wings

pale tawny underside

♂

long tail

VOICE *Metallic psching, pink, or ping.*
NESTING *Deep cup of leaves, stems, and reed flowers, low down in reeds standing in water; 5–7 eggs; 2–3 broods; April–August.*
FEEDING *Caterpillars and reed seeds, taken from among reeds.*
SIMILAR SPECIES *Long-tailed Tit (right), Reed Warbler (p.358).*

Long-tailed Tit

Aegithalos caudatus (Aegithalidae)

The tiny rounded body and slender tail of the Long-tailed Tit give it a ball-and-stick shape that is quite unique among British birds. In summer, family parties move noisily through bushes and undergrowth, but in winter they often travel through woodland in much larger groups, crossing gaps between the trees, one or two at a time.

LIVES *in deciduous or mixed woods with bushy undergrowth; also scrub. Increasingly visits garden feeders.*

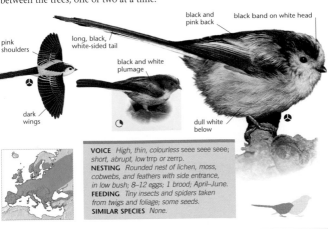

pink shoulders

dark wings

long, black, white-sided tail

black and white plumage

black and pink back

black band on white head

dull white below

VOICE High, thin, colourless seee seee seee; short, abrupt, low trrp or zerrp.
NESTING Rounded nest of lichen, moss, cobwebs, and feathers with side entrance, in low bush; 8–12 eggs; 1 brood; April–June.
FEEDING Tiny insects and spiders taken from twigs and foliage; some seeds.
SIMILAR SPECIES None.

Marsh Tit

Poecile palustris (Paridae)

Virtually identical to the Willow Tit (*P. montana*) in its appearance, the slightly slimmer, neater Marsh Tit is most easily identified by its distinctive *pit-chew* call. Despite its name, it is not found in marshes, but prefers mature broadleaved woodland where it often feeds at low level among thick undergrowth.

FORAGES *among tall deciduous trees in woodland and parks, especially beech and oak; also in gardens.*

glossy black cap and back of neck

black bib, smaller than Willow Tit's

pale grey-buff underside

neck slimmer than Willow Tit's

neat, plain grey-brown upperparts

rounded grey-brown wings

VOICE Bright pit-chew! and titi-zee-zee-zee; song rippling schip-schip-schip-schip.
NESTING Grass and moss cup in pre-existing tree hole; 6–8 eggs; 1 brood; April–June.
FEEDING Mostly insects and spiders in summer; seeds, berries, and nuts in winter.
SIMILAR SPECIES Willow Tit (P. montana), Coal Tit (p.366), Blackcap (p.361).

Crested Tit

Lophophanes cristatus (Paridae)

The jaunty crest of this species makes it unique among British tits, aiding identification if one has a clear view of its head. But it often feeds high in pine trees, where it is best located by its stuttering call. In Britain it is restricted to northern Scotland, mainly in ancient forests of Scots pine.

FEEDS *and breeds in mature pine forests, but may occur in mixed or deciduous woods in parts of mainland Europe.*

mottled black and white crest

brown tail

white face with black cheek edge

black bib

brown wings

plain wings

warm brown back

VOICE *Quick, low, stuttering trill, b'd-rrr-rup; also thin, high zit or zee typical of tits.*
NESTING *Cup of moss and hair in decaying tree stump; 5–7 eggs; 1 brood, April–June.*
FEEDING *Small insects and spiders; seeds in winter, many from stores made in spring.*
SIMILAR SPECIES *Coal Tit (below), Marsh Tit (p.365), Willow Tit (P. montana).*

Coal Tit

Periparus ater (Paridae)

Although often seen in gardens, the diminutive white-naped Coal Tit is typically a bird of conifer trees, where it makes the most of its minute weight by searching the thinnest twigs for food. Active and fearless, it often joins up with other species of tits in autumn and winter, roaming through woodlands and gardens in large, loose, mixed flocks.

FORAGES *among pines and other conifer trees, but also feeds in low shrubbery and visits garden bird feeders.*

yellower cheek

black head

white nape patch

greyish back

dark wings with two white bars

bright buff underside

black bib

white cheek

VOICE *Call high, sweet tseu, thin tsee, bright psuet; song quick wi-choo wi-choo wi-choo.*
NESTING *Cup of moss and leaves in hole in tree or wall; 7–11 eggs; 1 brood; April–June.*
FEEDING *Takes tiny insects and spiders from foliage; also seeds and nuts; visits feeders.*
SIMILAR SPECIES *Marsh Tit (p.365), Willow Tit (P. montana), Great Tit (right).*

Blue Tit

Cyanistes caeruleus (Paridae)

Colourful, tame, and noisy, the Blue Tit is mainly yellow and greenish as well as blue. It is a common visitor to bird feeders where its acrobatic skills make it a favourite garden bird. Its black-and-white face pattern is distinctive. A thin, dark central streak often shows on its yellow underside.

VISITS *gardens to feed from nut baskets and other feeders. Lives in woods of all kinds, as well as parks, gardens, and bushy places.*

bright blue cap

white bars on blue wings

♂

♂

blue tail

yellow below

greenish cap

less blue

♀

♀

VOICE *Thin, quick tsee-tsee-tsee, scolding churrrr; song trilled tsee-tsee-tsee-tsisisisisisi.*
NESTING *Small cup of moss and hair in tree hole/nest box; 7–16 eggs; 1 brood; April–May.*
FEEDING *Mainly seeds, nuts, insects, and spiders; often visits garden feeders.*
SIMILAR SPECIES *Coal Tit (left), Great Tit (below), Goldcrest (p.363).*

Great Tit

Parus major (Paridae)

The bold, even aggressive Great Tit is one of the most familiar garden and woodland birds. Its calls can be confusing, but it is easily identified by the broad black stripe on its yellow breast. Less agile than the smaller tits, it feeds on the ground more often.

BREEDS *and feeds in wide variety of mixed woodland, as well as parks and gardens. Often uses nest boxes.*

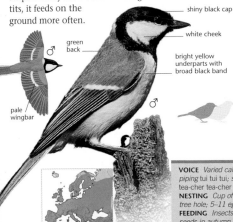

shiny black cap

green back

white cheek

bright yellow underparts with broad black band

♂

pale wingbar

♂

yellow cheeks

♀

band narrower than male

VOICE *Varied calls include ringing chink and piping tui tui tui; song repeated two-note tea-cher tea-cher or see-too see-too.*
NESTING *Cup of moss, leaves, and grass in tree hole; 5–11 eggs; 1 brood; April–May.*
FEEDING *Insects, seeds, nuts, especially tree seeds in autumn, winter; often visits feeders.*
SIMILAR SPECIES *Coal Tit (left).*

Nuthatch

Sitta europaea (Sittidae)

Identified by its blue-grey and buff plumage and oddly top-heavy look, the Nuthatch is an agile climber that (unlike other birds) often descends trees head-first, as well as climbing upwards. It wedges nuts and seeds in bark so it can crack them open, with loud blows of its long, grey, chisel-like bill.

FOUND *high in trees and on the ground in deciduous and mixed woodland, parkland, and large gardens, all year round.*

broad blue-grey wings

buff below, with rusty flanks

acrobatic pose

black stripe

dagger-like grey bill

strong feet for clinging to bark

short tail

VOICE *Loud, liquid whistles, pew pew pew, chwee chwee; fast ringing trills, loud chwit.*
NESTING *Typically plasters mud around old woodpecker hole lined with bark and leaves; 6–9 eggs; 1 brood; April–July.*
FEEDING *Variety of seeds, berries, and nuts, often wedged in bark for easy cracking.*
SIMILAR SPECIES *None.*

Treecreeper

Certhia familiaris (Certhiidae)

The slender-billed Treecreeper searches for insect prey by shuffling up the trunks and branches of trees like a mouse, clinging to the bark with its strong toes and propped up on its stiff tail. It usually spirals up one tree, then flies down and lands near the bottom of another to start its next search. This habit makes it easy to identify, even in silhouette.

PROBES *bark of trees in mixed, deciduous, or coniferous woods. Also occurs in tall hedges, parks, and gardens with mature trees.*

white stripe over eye

fine, curved bill

mottled brown back

silky white underside

pale feather shafts on notched brown tail

rounded wings

pale wingbars

VOICE *Call thin, high seee and more vibrant sreee; song high, musical series of tsee notes ending in falling trill with final flourish.*
NESTING *Untidy nest behind loose bark or ivy; 5–6 eggs; 1 brood; April–June.*
FEEDING *Takes insects and spiders from bark, probing with bill while shuffling up trees.*
SIMILAR SPECIES *None.*

Jay

Garrulus glandarius (Corvidae)

Noisy but shy, the Jay often keeps to thick cover and beats a swift retreat if disturbed, flying off with a flash of its bold white rump. It has a curious habit of allowing ants to run over its plumage, probably to employ the ants' chemical defences against parasites. In town parks, it may become a little less elusive, and can be seen feeding on the ground, using long, bouncing or leaping hops. In gardens, this bird can even be bold enough to visit bird feeders, hanging on clumsily while taking peanuts, pieces of cheese, or lumps of fatball. However, it remains wary and unapproachable even here.

BREEDS *in woodland and parks, especially with oak trees, and visits gardens.*

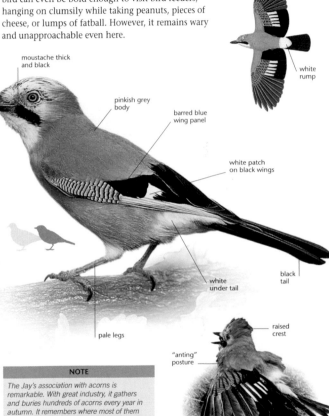

moustache thick and black

pinkish grey body

barred blue wing panel

white patch on black wings

white rump

black tail

white under tail

pale legs

raised crest

"anting" posture

NOTE

The Jay's association with acorns is remarkable. With great industry, it gathers and buries hundreds of acorns every year in autumn. It remembers where most of them are and digs them out to eat late in the winter or spring, when other food is scarce. The Jay even feeds sprouting acorns to its chicks in spring if other food is in short supply.

VOICE Nasal, mewing pee-oo, short bark; loud, harsh, cloth-tearing skairk!
NESTING Bulky stick nest, low in dense bush; 4–5 eggs; 1 brood; April–June.
FEEDING Takes a variety of foods, ranging from caterpillars to small rodents; eats mainly insects in summer, with some eggs and nestlings; stores acorns in autumn for use in winter.
SIMILAR SPECIES Mistle Thrush (p.357), Jackdaw (p.371).

Magpie

Pica pica (Corvidae)

A handsome crow with boldly pied plumage and a long, tapered tail, the Magpie is unmistakable. In sunlight it has an iridescent sheen of blue, purple, and green. It has a reputation for wiping out songbirds, but research shows that its fondness for eating eggs and chicks has little overall effect on populations.

FOUND *on farmland with hedges, woodland edges, and parks. Visits gardens to find food.*

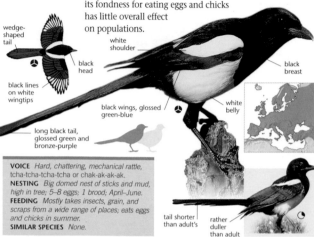

wedge-shaped tail

white shoulder

black head

black lines on white wingtips

black wings, glossed green-blue

long black tail, glossed green and bronze-purple

black breast

white belly

tail shorter than adult's

rather duller than adult

VOICE *Hard, chattering, mechanical rattle, tcha-tcha-tcha-tcha or chak-ak-ak-ak.*
NESTING *Big domed nest of sticks and mud, high in tree; 5–8 eggs; 1 brood; April–June.*
FEEDING *Mostly takes insects, grain, and scraps from a wide range of places; eats eggs and chicks in summer.*
SIMILAR SPECIES *None.*

Chough

Pyrrhocorax pyrrhocorax (Corvidae)

Sociable, noisy, exuberant, and spectacularly agile in the air, the Chough is a bird of wild rocky places with ancient grassland, where it gets most of its food by probing in the turf. Family parties and larger flocks soar and dive around cliffs, with total mastery of the turbulent air currents, their ringing calls echoing off the rocks.

LIVES *on rocky coasts, high-altitude pastures, gorges, crags, and quarries; also feeds on beaches in winter.*

square-ended wings with long "fingers"

longish red bill

glossy black body

square tail

red legs

paler, orange-red bill

VOICE *Explosive, ringing, pee-yaa or chia, also shorter chuk and kwarr calls.*
NESTING *Nest of sticks and hair in cavity in rock or ruin; 3–5 eggs; 1 brood; May–July.*
FEEDING *Eats ants on old pastures, insects dug from soil, and lichen prised from rocks.*
SIMILAR SPECIES *Rook (right), Carrion Crow (p.372).*

Jackdaw

Corvus monedula (Corvidae)

A small, short-billed crow with a black cap and a pale grey
nape, the Jackdaw is a sociable bird that often flies in flocks,
performing spectacular aerobatics with much calling. It also
feeds in mixed flocks with Rooks (below), when its compact
shape becomes obvious.

SEEN *around cliffs,
quarries, old buildings,
woods, farmland with
mature trees, or towns
and villages where
there are old houses
with chimneys.*

rounded
wings

black cap

grey nape

pale
eyes

short,
thick
bill

dark grey
underwings

grey-black
body

VOICE *Noisy kyak or tjak! with squeaky,
bright quality; some longer calls like chee-ar.*
NESTING *Pile of sticks lined with mud, moss,
and hair, in hole in tree, cliff, or building, or in
chimney; 4–6 eggs; 1 brood; April–July.*
FEEDING *Takes worms, seeds, and scraps
from ground; also caterpillars and berries.*
SIMILAR SPECIES *Rook (below).*

NOTE

*Although similar to
other black crows
such as the Rook
(below), the Jackdaw
is distinctly smaller,
with shorter legs and
a shorter bill.*

Rook

Corvus frugilegus (Corvidae)

Well known for its loud cawing calls, the
Rook is a big, black, intensely social
crow. The adult is distinguished
by the bare, parchment-
white face that gives it a very
long-billed look. It has a peaked,
rather than flat-topped crown.
Ragged thigh feathers give it
a "baggy trouser" effect.

peaked
crown

BREEDS *in treetop
colonies, typically in
farmland, parks, and
villages or small towns
with scattered tall trees
for nesting.*

glossy
black
body

black
bill
base

narrow,
rounded
tail

loose, ragged
thigh feathers

rounded
tail

VOICE *Loud, raucous, but relaxed cawing,
plus variety of strangled or metallic notes.*
NESTING *Big nest of sticks lined with grass,
moss, and leaves, in treetop colony; 3–6
eggs; 1 brood; March–June.*
FEEDING *Eats worms, beetle larvae, seeds,
grain, and roots from ground; also roadkill.*
SIMILAR SPECIES *Carrion Crow (p.372).*

Carrion Crow

Corvus corone (Corvidae)

The all-black Carrion Crow is easy to confuse with other crows, particularly a juvenile Rook (p.371), but its head has a distinctly flatter crown and its body plumage is much tighter and neater-looking, with no "baggy trouser" effect. It is usually seen alone or in pairs, but may gather to feed and roost in flocks in autumn and winter, and often feeds alongside other crows.

INHABITS *all kinds of open areas, from farm-land and upland moors to city centres; also feeds on coasts and estuaries.*

thick, arched bill

flat-topped head

squarer wingtips than Rook

neat, tight body feathering

glossy black body

square tail

VOICE *Loud, harsh, grating caw, krra krra krra, metallic konk, korr, and similar calls.*
NESTING *Big stick nest, in tree, bush, on cliff or building; 4–6 eggs; 1 brood; March–July.*
FEEDING *Feeds on ground, taking all kinds of invertebrates, eggs, grain, and various scraps; usually in pairs but sometimes flocks.*
SIMILAR SPECIES *Rook (p.371), Raven (right).*

Hooded Crow

Corvus cornix (Corvidae)

A close relative of the all-black Carrion Crow (above), and sometimes considered a subspecies of it, the Hooded Crow is a much more distinctive bird with a different range. Where the two meet, they interbreed to produce a range of hybrids, with varying amounts of grey plumage.

FOUND *in a wide range of open habitats; appears to prefer poorer land to Carrion Crow in breeding season.*

black hood

black wings

black wings and tail

pale body

black wings and tail

VOICE *Very like Carrion Crow's; often a more hard, rolling croak repeated 3–4 times.*
NESTING *Large stick nest, in tree or bush, some on cliffs, 4–6 eggs; 1 brood; March–July.*
FEEDING *Wide range of animal food, including carrion, grain, and food scraps.*
SIMILAR SPECIES *Jackdaw (p.371).*

Raven

Corvus corax (Corvidae)

The world's largest perching bird, the Raven is a heavier, more powerful bird than the Carrion Crow (left). It often increases the apparent size of its head by bristling up its throat feathers, giving it a bearded appearance. The first clue to the presence of a Raven is usually its loud, deep, croaking call, which echoes from the surrounding peaks and crags.

LIVES *in large forests, mountain regions, open moorland, and hills with crags and isolated trees.*

long, fingered wings

wedge-shaped tail

tail diamond-shaped when spread

very large, deep, arched bill

all-black plumage; metallic green and purplish gloss in strong light

long tail

VOICE *Loud, abrupt, echoing crronk crronk crronk various clicking, or quiet musical notes.*
NESTING *Huge nest of sticks, wool, grass, and heather, used for many years, on cliff or in tall tree; 4–6 eggs; 1 brood; February–May.*
FEEDING *Catches small mammals and birds; eats carrion; forages for scraps on shore.*
SIMILAR SPECIES *Carrion Crow (left).*

Starling

Sturnus vulgaris (Sturnidae)

A common, sociable, but quarrelsome bird, the Starling is instantly recognizable by its strong-legged walk and waddling run as it pokes and pries in the soil for insect grubs and seeds. Superficially black, its plumage is glossed with iridescent green and purple in summer, and spotted with buff in winter.

GATHERS *in big winter flocks in forests, city centres, bridges, and piers. Breeds in woods, gardens, and towns.*

glossy black body with green and purple sheen

sharp yellow bill

blue-grey bill base; pale pink on female

silvery face with dark mask

dull head last to get adult colours

short, squarish tail

long, strong, red-brown legs

MOULTING

dark bill

VOICE *Loud, slightly grating cheer, musical, whistled tswee-oo, song fast mixture of trills.*
NESTING *Bulky nest of grass and stems, in tree hole, cavity in wall or building, or large nest box; 4–7 eggs; 1–2 broods; April–July.*
FEEDING *Forages for invertebrates and seeds on the ground; catches flying ants in mid-air.*
SIMILAR SPECIES *Blackbird (p.355).*

House Sparrow

Passer domesticus (Passeridae)

PREFERS *cities, towns, villages, farms, and on farmland; rarely found far from human habitation.*

This common, noisy sparrow is one of the most familiar small birds due to its habit of nesting in buildings. The male has a bold black bib and distinctive grey cap, but the female can be confused with a female finch. Although House Sparrow populations have declined, they are still widespread.

grey cap

big black bib

red-brown above, with dark streaks

unmarked grey below

whitish wingbar ♂

greyish rump

♂☀

pale stripe

♀

plain plumage

VOICE *Lively chirrup, chilp, as loud chorus from flock; song a simple series of chirps.*
NESTING *Untidy nest of grass and feathers in cavity; 3–7 eggs; 1–4 broods; April–August.*
FEEDING *Takes seeds, nuts, and berries, mainly from ground, plus insects for young.*
SIMILAR SPECIES *Tree Sparrow (below), female Chaffinch (right).*

Tree Sparrow

Passer montanus (Passeridae)

INHABITS *farmland with scattered trees, in parks, woods, and woodland edges; also in towns and cities.*

Over much of its range the Tree Sparrow is a less suburban bird than the House Sparrow (above), preferring woods and farmland. The sexes are almost identical, both having the black mask, brown cap, black cheek patch, and white collar. This sparrow often feeds on the ground in company with finches and buntings.

rich brown cap

black mask and bib

white cheek with square black patch

buffish rump

black and brown streaked back

two whitish wingbars

plain grey-buff below

VOICE *Call loud chirruping and cheeping, plus a disyllabic tsu-wit, hard tek-tek in flight.*
NESTING *Domed nest of grass in holes in tree or building; 4–6 eggs; 2–3 broods; April–July.*
FEEDING *Picks seeds from ground, plus some insects and buds; visits bird feeders.*
SIMILAR SPECIES *House Sparrow (above).*

NOTE

Superficially similar to the male House Sparrow (above), this bird has a distinctive hard flight-call as well as a different head pattern.

Chaffinch

Fringilla coelebs (Fringillidae)

One of the least specialized of the finches, the Chaffinch is also one of the most successful and abundant. Unusually for finches, pairs breed in separate territories, proclaimed by males singing loudly from prominent perches. At other times they are social and often very tame.

BREEDS *in coniferous and deciduous forests, woods, hedges, parks, and gardens; some winter in fields.*

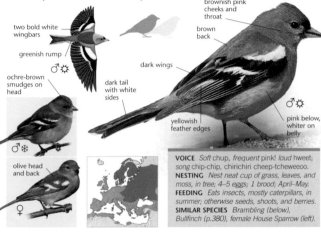

two bold white wingbars

greenish rump

♂ ☀

ochre-brown smudges on head

dark tail with white sides

♂ ❄

olive head and back

♀

brownish pink cheeks and throat

brown back

dark wings

yellowish feather edges

♂ ☀

pink below, whiter on belly

VOICE Soft chup, *frequent* pink! *loud* hweet; *song* chip-chip, chirichiri cheep-tcheweeoo.
NESTING Nest neat cup of grass, leaves, and moss, in tree; 4–5 eggs; 1 brood; April–May.
FEEDING Eats insects, mostly caterpillars, in summer; otherwise seeds, shoots, and berries.
SIMILAR SPECIES Brambling (below), Bullfinch (p.380), female House Sparrow (left).

Brambling

Fringilla montifringilla (Fringillidae)

Very like the Chaffinch (above), but with a white rump and a darker back, the Brambling is generally less common and absent from Britain in summer. In winter, Bramblings may gather in huge feeding flocks, especially in central Europe, but numbers fluctuate from year to year with the supply of beech-mast and other tree seeds.

SEEN *in farmland and parks, in winter, especially areas with beech, birch, and spruce; breeds in northern forests.*

black head and back

♂ ☀

"scaly" head

♀ ❄

duller

♂ ❄

dark spots on flanks

white rump

♂ ❄

big orange-buff upper wingbar

bright yellow-orange breast and shoulder

white belly

VOICE Call hard chek, distinctive nasal tsweek; song repeated nasal, buzzing dzeeee.
NESTING Cup of lichen, bark, and stems, in tree or bush; 5–7 eggs; 1 brood; May–June.
FEEDING Eats insects in summer, seeds at other times; takes beech-mast from ground.
SIMILAR SPECIES Chaffinch (above), female House Sparrow (left).

Goldfinch

Carduelis carduelis (Fringillidae)

Flocks of colourful Goldfinches feed on waste ground, farmyards, and field edges, picking soft, milky seeds from thistles, tall daisies, and similar plants with their pointed bills. They are agile feeders, often swinging head-down from seedheads, and have a distinctive dancing flight and tinkling calls.

FORAGES *in weedy places with tall seed-bearing flowers; also in alder and larch.*

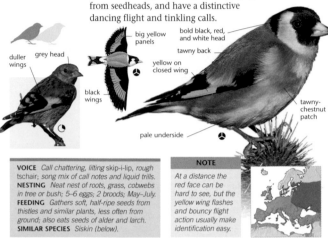

duller wings

grey head

big yellow panels

bold black, red, and white head

tawny back

yellow on closed wing

black wings

pale underside

tawny-chestnut patch

VOICE *Call chattering, lilting skip-i-lip, rough tschair; song mix of call notes and liquid trills.*
NESTING *Neat nest of roots, grass, cobwebs in tree or bush; 5–6 eggs; 2 broods; May–July.*
FEEDING *Gathers soft, half-ripe seeds from thistles and similar plants, less often from ground; also eats seeds of alder and larch.*
SIMILAR SPECIES *Siskin (below).*

NOTE

At a distance the red face can be hard to see, but the yellow wing flashes and bouncy flight action usually make identification easy.

Siskin

Carduelis spinus (Fringillidae)

A specialist at feeding on tree seeds, the neat, slender Siskin is particularly associated with conifers and spruces. It usually feeds high in the trees, displaying tit-like agility, and in spring the males often sing from treetops. In winter, Siskins forage in flocks, often with Common Redpolls *(C. flammea)*.

VISITS *gardens for peanuts, but breeds in spruce and pine forest. In winter, found in alder and larch along rivers.*

black cap and chin

dark streaks on green back

yellow patch each side of black tail

♂

lime-green to yellowish breast

bold yellow wingbars

♂

greyer head than male

like greyer female

♀

VOICE *Whistled tsy-zee; hoarse purr; song mixes calls with trills and hard twittering notes.*
NESTING *Tiny nest of twigs and stems, lined with down, high in tree; 4–5 eggs; 1–2 broods; May–July.*
FEEDING *Eats the seeds of pine, larch, alder, birch, and various other trees.*
SIMILAR SPECIES *Greenfinch (right).*

Greenfinch

Carduelis chloris (Fringillidae)

Males are easy to identify by their green plumage with
bright yellow flashes, and a "frowning" look; the duller
females and juveniles are also stocky and stout-billed, but
trickier to distinguish. In spring, males sing during circling,
stiff-winged display flights. Their songs are simple on the
face of it, but actually quite varied in rhythm, pattern, and
pitch, the best of them being surprisingly musical. If they
choose to nest in tall evergreen hedges or mature conifers,
Greenfinches add a lot to the atmosphere of a garden in
spring and summer, especially
in suburban housing areas.

FEEDS *on sunflower
seeds at garden feeders;
breeds in open woods,
hedges, large gardens.*

dark patch

yellow
patches
on tail ♂

flashes of
yellow
on outer part
of grey wings

yellow
stripe

bright olive
green

♂☼

NOTE

*Male and female
Greenfinches are
very alike, but on
average the male
has broader yellow
edges to the wing
and tail feathers.*

browner
than adult

streaked
all over

greyer
above

♂❄

duller
than male

♀

VOICE *Flight call fast, tinny chatter, tit-it-it-it, nasal dzoo-ee, hard
jup-jup-jup; song series of rich trills, mixed with buzzy dzweee, often
given from high perch but also in fluttering, bat-like song.*
NESTING *Bulky nest of grass and twigs in tree; 4–6 eggs; 1–2 broods;
April–July.*
FEEDING *Takes seeds from trees, herbs, and ground; also berries and
nuts; often visits bird feeders in gardens.*
SIMILAR SPECIES *Siskin (left).*

Linnet

Carduelis cannabina (Fringillidae)

Lively and sociable, the Linnet is usually seen in tightly co-ordinated flocks that travel and feed together throughout much of the year. In winter, when the males lose much of their bright colour, the flocks usually feed on the ground. In the breeding season, small parties can be seen foraging for insects in bushes to feed their nestlings.

FLIES *in tight flocks, which feed on heaths, upland meadows, and coastal marshes. Breeds in thickets and hedges.*

browner head

tawny-buff chest

♂※

♀

pale cheek spot

pink-red chest

♂※

light grey head

whitish streaks on dark wings

♂※

VOICE *Twittering, flight call, tidit tidititit; song rich, musical, mixed with chattering notes.*
NESTING *Nest of stems and roots, in bush near ground; 4–6 eggs; 2–3 broods; April–July.*
FEEDING *Takes seeds from ground, especially arable weeds; feeds young on insects.*
SIMILAR SPECIES *Common Redpoll (C. flammea).*

Lesser Redpoll

Carduelis cabaret (Fringillidae)

The Lesser Redpoll breeds in Britain and is smaller and darker than the Common Redpoll (*C. flammea*). It is commonest in the north but numbers and range fluctuate – in the 1970s it was commoner as a nesting bird in southern Britain, where it is now known mostly as a winter visitor.

FEEDS *on seeds in alders, larches, and birches, often seen with siskins and sometimes goldfinches.*

black chin

streaked plumage

pink chest

♂※

red cap

buff wingbar

black legs

♀

forked tail

VOICE *Metallic, abrupt chattering notes; longer trill in spring song; nasal tsoo-weee.*
NESTING *Small cup of twigs and leaves in bush; 4–6 eggs; 1–2 broods; April–June.*
FEEDING *Eats seeds of trees and shrubs, including birch seeds from ground; caterpillars in summer.*
SIMILAR SPECIES *Linnet (above).*

Crossbill

Loxia curvirostra (Fringillidae)

This large, powerful finch is specialized for eating the seeds of spruces, pines, and other conifers, using its hooked, crossed bill to prise the cone scales apart so it can extract the seeds with its tongue. It feeds acrobatically and often noisily in the treetops, but has to drink frequently to moisten its diet of dry seeds.

LIVES *in extensive woods of spruce, larch, and pine, with easy access to water.*

dark wings

♂

brightest red on rump

orange-red to strawberry-red plumage

hooked bill with crossed mandibles

brownish wings

dark tail

brown wings

♀

green body

pale, streaked

VOICE *Loud, abrupt calls, jup-jup-jup, quiet conversational notes while feeding; song mixes buzzy notes, calls, warbles, and trills.*
NESTING *Small nest of twigs and moss high in conifer; 3–4 eggs; 1 brood; January–March.*
FEEDING *Eats seeds of conifers such as spruce and pine; also berries, buds, insects.*
SIMILAR SPECIES *Hawfinch (below).*

Hawfinch

Coccothraustes coccothraustes (Fringillidae)

The immensely powerful bill of the Hawfinch is adapted for cracking the toughest seeds, such as cherry stones and olive pits. It usually feeds in the treetops, where it can be elusive and difficult to see well, although its bulky silhouette is distinctive. In winter, it feeds on tree seeds on the ground, where it is more visible, although it flies up if disturbed.

FEEDS *and breeds in deciduous woodland, orchards, olive groves, and large gardens.*

♂✽

broad, diagonal, buff and white wingbars

very deep, powerful bill

greyer wingbar

scaly back

barred beneath

♀

blue-black wings

♂✽

broad white tip to tail

VOICE *Call short, sharp, metallic tik or tzik, thin tzree, tikitik; weak scratchy song.*
NESTING *Nest of twigs, roots, and moss, in old tree; 4–5 eggs; 1 brood; April–May.*
FEEDING *Takes large tree seeds and berries from trees; picks seeds from ground in winter.*
SIMILAR SPECIES *Chaffinch (p.375), Crossbill (above), Bullfinch (p.380).*

Bullfinch

Pyrrhula pyrrhula (Fringillidae)

Heavily built, rather sluggish, and often hard to see as it feeds quietly in dense cover, the Bullfinch is unmistakable when it emerges into the open. The male is a striking sight, with his bold red, grey, and black plumage and bright white rump. Generally shy, its caution may be warranted, because it is often treated as a pest due to its taste for soft buds of fruit trees. It is seriously declining in some regions.

RAIDS *flowering fruit trees in woodland, farmland with hedges, thickets, orchards, parks, and gardens.*

no dark cap

plumage like female

dull brownish back

♀

beige-grey below

grey-white band on dark wing

red-pink below

♂

black cap, bill, and chin form distinct hood

pale grey back

white under tail

black tail

♂

VOICE Call low, clear whistles, peuuw or phiu; song infrequent, warble mixed with calls.
NESTING Cup of twigs, lined with moss and grass, in dense bush or tree; 4–5 eggs, 2 broods, April–June.
FEEDING Eats soft buds, seeds, berries, and shoots from bushes, shrubs, and fruit trees.
SIMILAR SPECIES Chaffinch (p.375).

Snow Bunting

Plectrophenax nivalis (Emberizidae)

The stark black and white of the breeding male Snow Bunting is well suited to its snowy northern breeding habitat, but in Britain it is seen only in its subdued winter plumage, when the sexes look very alike. They have a distinctive low-slung look on the ground, owing to their short legs.

FEEDS *on shingle banks and muddy coastal marshes in winter as well as on mountain slopes.*

reddish or orange-brown cheeks

stocky body

♂ ❄

long black and white wings

forked black tail with white sides

white wing panel

white underside

white below

♂ ❄

♂ ☀

brown cap

♀ ❄

VOICE Call loud, clear pyiew or tsioo, frequent trilling tiri-lil-il-il-il-ip; song short, ringing, fluty phrase, turee-turee-turee-turitui.
NESTING Nest of moss and grass in cavity among rocks; 4–6 eggs; 1–2 broods; May–July.
FEEDING Takes insects in summer, and seeds and marine invertebrates in winter.
SIMILAR SPECIES Reed Bunting (right).

Yellowhammer

Emberiza citrinella (Emberizidae)

The repetitive song of the male of this species is a typical sound of warm summer days on farmland and bushy heaths. During colder months, Yellowhammers form small groups, often with other buntings, to roam the fields in search of seeds.

GATHERS *to eat seeds in winter; breeds on pastures, heaths, and farmland with hedges.*

yellow head with dusky stripes

black streaks on rufous back

more streaks

less yellow

♀

rufous, buff, and black

yellow below with fine dark streaks

♂ ❧

black tail with white sides

rufous rump

♂ ❄

VOICE *Call sharp tsik; song thin trill, with longer notes at end, ti-ti-ti-ti-ti-ti-ti-teee-tyew.*
NESTING *Nest of grass or straw in bank or below bush; 3–5 eggs; 2–3 broods; April–July.*
FEEDING *Takes seeds from ground, and also insects in summer.*
SIMILAR SPECIES *Cirl Bunting (E. cirlus), female Reed Bunting (below).*

Reed Bunting

Emberiza schoeniclus (Emberizidae)

Easy to find and identify in summer, male Reed Buntings sing monotonously from low perches among reeds and other wetland vegetation. In winter, when the males are far less striking, they are harder to recognize – especially when feeding on farmland or even in gardens.

INHABITS *wet places with reeds, sedge, rushes; also willow thickets and heaths; gardens in winter.*

hint of pale collar

♀

cream and black streaks on back

long, notched tail

black head

white collar and moustache

rufous forewing

♂ ❄

bold white tail sides

duller head pattern

brown back with black streaks

♂ ❄

streaked, whitish underside

♂ ❄

pale red-brown legs

VOICE *Call loud high tseeu, and high, thin, pure sweee, zi zi; song short, jangly phrase, srip srip srip sea-sea-sea stitip-itip-itipip.*
NESTING *Bulky nest of grass and sedge, on ground; 4–5 eggs; 2 broods; April–June.*
FEEDING *Eats seeds, plus insects in summer.*
SIMILAR SPECIES *Female House Sparrow (p.374).*

Corn Bunting

Miliaria calandra (Emberizidae)

A big, pale bunting of wide open spaces, the Corn Bunting lives up to its name by favouring farmland with large cereal fields, as well as extensive grasslands. It shares this habitat with the Skylark (p.349), but has a quite different song: a unique, jangling rattle given by the male from a prominent exposed perch or in a display flight, with dangling legs. It feeds on insects and seeds on the ground, and the widespread use of weedkillers and insecticides on modern farmland has made it virtually extinct in many intensively farmed regions. Where it is still common, it can often be seen flying overhead in small groups towards dusk, heading for its communal roosts.

PERCHES *in hedges when disturbed while feeding on meadows, rough grassland, arable fields, and coastal scrub.*

dark stripes on crown

dark lower cheeks

row of dark spots on wing coverts

plain wings

streaked, pale brown back

stocky shape

dark streaks often merge into central smudge on chest

plain brown tail, with no white at sides

heavy, pale yellowish bill

upright posture when singing

NOTE

Although it looks like a Skylark (p.349) and lives in the same places, the Corn Bunting tends to hop rather than walk, and has no white on its tail.

pale, streaked breast

VOICE *Call short, abrupt, clicking* plip *or* quit; *song jangling, dry, fast, rattled phrase resembling rattling keys or broken glass.*
NESTING *Nest of grass and roots, lined with finer material, on ground; 3–5 eggs; 1–2 broods; April–June.*
FEEDING *Forages on ground, picking up insects and seeds in summer and only seeds in winter.*
SIMILAR SPECIES *Female Reed Bunting (p.381), female Yellowhammer (p.381), Skylark (p.349).*

Reptiles and Amphibians

Due to its cool climate and island status (a result of the last ice age), Britain has a small reptile and amphibian population compared to the rest of Europe. Nevertheless, frogs, toads, and newts are a familiar sight in many garden ponds, and snakes or lizards can often be seen scurrying through grass on country walks. Unfortunately, changes in farming practices and habitat loss in the wider countryside have led to the demise of many populations of the commoner species, and gardens are now an important refuge for them.

| COMMON TOAD | ADDER | SMOOTH NEWT | VIVIPAROUS LIZARD |

Adder

Vipera berus (Squamata)

With a robust body (especially females), the Adder is a cold-tolerant species, found well into the Arctic Circle, and is the most northerly snake in the world. Its grey body, sometimes with yellow or reddish tones, is strongly marked with a dark stripe down the back, black in males and brown in females. Although it basks in sunshine, it tends to avoid the hottest conditions, and in the south hunts mostly at dusk. Some populations frequently produce dramatic melanic specimens: such animals are all black, with bright red eyes. The Adder is quite venomous and its bite requires medical attention.

PREFERS *heathland and moorland, open woods, meadows, and marshes; largely montane in the south.*

♀
brown zig-zag stripe

NOTE

Adders hibernate between September –October and February–March (according to location). Traditional hibernation sites may be used communally, and adults can navigate to them from distances of 2km or more.

red eyes with vertical pupils

HEAD

dark zig-zag stripe

dark V-mark on back of head

dark grey to black underside

♂

SIZE *50–65cm.*
YOUNG *Up to 20 live young in August, though not breeding every year.*
DIET *Small mammals (pursued in their burrows), lizards, newts, frogs, and nestling birds.*
STATUS *Common.*
SIMILAR SPECIES *The zig-zag stripe is unmistakeable; melanic animals could be confused with melanic Grass Snakes (right).*

Grass Snake

Natrix natrix (Squamata)

The only British snake that is associated with water and wetland habitats, the Grass Snake swims well, with its head and neck out of the water (the nostrils are not set at the top of the snout), and does much of its hunting in water. Hibernation takes place between October and March, often in traditional communal sites.

FAVOURS *damp areas, feeding in rivers, ponds, and marshes; also in meadows, heathland, and open woodland.*

variable back and flank spotting

dark olive-green ground colour

yellow collar, highlighted by black crescents

rounded snout

STRIPED FORM

SIZE *70–150cm.*
YOUNG *Lays up to 100 eggs.*
DIET *Amphibians, fish, small mammals, birds, lizards, and invertebrates.*
STATUS *Common.*
SIMILAR SPECIES *Smooth Snake (Coronella austriaca), which lacks the yellow collar.*

Viviparous Lizard

Zootoca vivipara (Squamata)

Also called the Common Lizard, the Viviparous Lizard is the commonest lizard in Britain. The ground colour varies from grey-brown to reddish and olive green; there are variable stripes down the back, sometimes with black blotches or ocelli, often organized into rows down the back or flanks. It can be confused with the Sand Lizard (p.386), a rare species of heaths and dunes, which is more robust and is often green in colour.

OCCUPIES *a wide range of habitats, lowland to montane, from open, dry sand dunes to damp, shady woodland; hibernates under logs or stones.*

white throat (may be blue in a breeding male)

variable black blotches

dark stripe down back

serrated collar edge

UNDERSIDE

yellow-orange below

SIZE *Body up to 6.5cm; tail 8–10cm.*
YOUNG *Up to 10 live young, born in damp areas, June–September.*
DIET *Insects, spiders, snails, earthworms, and other invertebrates.*
STATUS *Common.*
SIMILAR SPECIES *Sand Lizard (p.386).*

Sand Lizard

Lacerta agilis (Squamata)

The Sand Lizard is powerfully built, with a short head and legs, and a stocky body. It is a ground-dweller, with poor climbing abilities. One of the most variable and beautifully marked lizards, it has a band of narrow scales running down its back; this band is often a different colour to the rest of the body, but only rarely green. The entire upperpart can be blotched with black patches or, on the flanks, with white-centred ocelli.

FOUND *in dry grassy areas, hedgebanks, heathland, and woodland margins, and into montane habitats in the south.*

flanks often green

pale stripes on either side of spine

band of narrow scales

eye spots on flanks

JUVENILE

SIZE *Body up to 9cm; tail up to 15cm.*
YOUNG *One or two clutches of up to 14 eggs.*
DIET *Insects, slugs, other invertebrates; fruit, flowers; small lizards.*
STATUS *Locally common.*
SIMILAR SPECIES *Viviparous Lizard (p.385), which is less robust.*

Slow-worm

Anguis fragilis (Squamata)

Also (incorrectly) called the Blind Worm, the Slow-worm has a blunt head and its underparts are paler than the grey-brown upperparts. The females may have a dark stripe down the back, retained from the juveniles' colour, which has a deep bronze sheen.

FOUND *mostly in rather moist grassy areas, with scrub or hedgerows for refuge; also in open woodland, up to montane levels.*

round pupils

♂

may have dark back stripe

males sometimes have blue spots

snake-like, limbless body

smooth scales

uniform bronze grey-brown upperparts

SIZE *30–50cm.*
YOUNG *6–12 (sometimes more) live young, born August–September.*
DIET *Worms, slugs, and other invertebrates.*
STATUS *Common.*
SIMILAR SPECIES *Small individuals could be mistaken for large earthworms.*

Red-eared Terrapin

Trachemys scripta (Chelonia)

Introduced from North America, adult Red-eared Terrapins have a uniform dark grey-brown shell. The shell pattern of juveniles is more distinctive, with complex pale yellowish markings, making them much valued as pets. Their webbed feet aid them in swimming. The male is usually smaller than the female with a much longer, thicker tail.

FREQUENTS *lakes, ponds, canals, and slow-moving rivers; often close to human habitation.*

uniformly dark shell

bright red patch behind eyes

pale eyes

clear yellow stripes on neck

webbed feet

SIZE *Shell up to 28cm long.*
YOUNG *Lays clutches of up to 10 eggs.*
DIET *Aquatic invertebrates and plants, fish.*
STATUS *Scarce, but increasing as a result of overgrown pets being released.*
SIMILAR SPECIES *No native species; other terrapins occasionally recorded as escapes.*

shell broadens behind

SHELL FROM ABOVE

Common Toad

Bufo bufo (Anura)

A widespread and robust species, the Common Toad is generally uniform brown in colour, and its skin covered in numerous warts. Rather constant in colour, they are more variable in size, with females growing to a size considerably larger than males. The parotid glands behind the eyes exude a secretion that repel predators. They are mainly nocturnal, except when breeding.

FOUND *in marshes, woodland, heathland, gardens, and mountain pastures, with access to pools and ponds.*

large parotid glands

very warty skin

amber eyes, with horizontal pupils

eggs in long, double strings

SPAWN

♀

powerful limbs

SIZE *Body 8–15cm.*
YOUNG *Lays 1,000–8,000 eggs.*
DIET *Insects and other invertebrates; large toads feed on small reptiles and mammals.*
STATUS *Common.*
SIMILAR SPECIES *Natterjack Toad (B. calamita) has a pale stripe down its back.*

Common Frog

Rana temporaria (Anura)

ABUNDANT *in lowland meadows, marshes, and mountain pastures, with access to shallow ponds for breeding.*

The most widespread of the European frogs, the Common Frog is relatively robust, with a wide, blunt snout and two parallel ridges running down the back. Its colour is variable but the ground colour is usually yellowish to olive-brown, and the markings dark brown to almost black. The colour often intensifies during the breeding season, when the female develops a granular skin and the male's throat often turns bluish. Active during the day and the night, the northern populations hibernate under logs and stones, or in leaf mould or burrows.

smooth, variably coloured skin

dark blotches, especially on hind legs

gold-flecked brown iris

dark eye mask

large ear-drum

fully webbed hind feet

PALER FORM

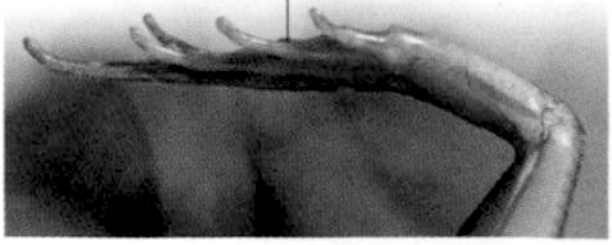

HIND FOOT

SIZE *6–8cm.*
YOUNG *Lays 1,000 to 4,000 eggs.*
DIET *Slugs, snails, insects, worms, and other invertebrates.*
STATUS *Common.*
SIMILAR SPECIES *Marsh Frog (R. ridibunda), which is larger, and often greener.*

NOTE

When frogs gather at traditional breeding pools, the males utter a low, purring croak and grab anything that moves; if it happens to be a female, she can attract a whole host of suitors, and in the ensuing melée may even be drowned.

Great Crested Newt

Triturus cristatus (Caudata)

Also known as the Warty Newt, on account of its granular skin, the Great Crested Newt has blackish skin. When breeding, its ground colour lightens, and black spots and blotches appear, along with white flecks on the head and flanks. The distinctive, jagged crest, with a gap at the base of the tail, and silvery tail flash feature only in males. Largely nocturnal, they also hibernate, usually under logs and stones.

OCCURS *in a wide range of weedy, deep, standing waters and favours sites without predatory fish.*

UNDERSIDE

spiky crest

silvery tail stripe

irregularly spotted orange belly

♂

BREEDING MALE

dark, almost black, skin

orange lower tail margin

♀

SIZE *Body up to 8cm; tail up to 7.5cm.*
YOUNG *Lays 200–400 eggs.*
DIET *Aquatic insects, worms, and other invertebrates; small and larval amphibians.*
STATUS *Common, but declining.*
SIMILAR SPECIES *Breeding male Smooth Newt (p.390), which has a smooth texture.*

Palmate Newt

Triturus helveticus (Caudata)

The smallest of the native British newts, the Palmate Newt gets its name from the black webs which develop on the hind feet of the male during the breeding season; its breeding appearance is also characterized by a prominent crest on the tail, which terminates in a distinct filament. At all times, Palmate Newts have a blackish stripe through the eye, a pale yellow belly, and unspotted throat. Most adults leave the breeding pools in late summer and hibernate under rocks and logs.

FOUND *in shallow, still, often acidic, usually well vegetated, waterbodies in woodland, heathland, farmland, and mountains; can tolerate brackish conditions.*

dark line through the eye

smooth tail crest

terminal filament

whitish throat

black webbing on hind feet

BREEDING MALE

SIZE *Body up to 4.5cm; tail up to 4.5cm.*
YOUNG *Lays 300–400 eggs.*
DIET *Invertebrates, worms, and tadpoles.*
STATUS *Common.*
SIMILAR SPECIES *Smooth Newt (p.390), which is more spotted below, especially in summer.*

pale yellow, underparts

Smooth Newt

Triturus vulgaris (Caudata)

LIVES *on land in damp woodland, marshes, and gardens; breeds in ponds, ditches, lake margins, and slow-moving rivers.*

One of the most widespread and abundant amphibians in Britain, it is not surprising that an alternative name for the Smooth Newt is the Common Newt. It is much more terrestrial than many other newts, typically living in water as an adult only for breeding, between March and July. Non-breeding animals are olive-brown, with a black-spotted throat, and two ridges on the head which join near the snout. They have darker spots and a black-spotted, orange belly. Largely nocturnal, they shelter (aswell as hibernate) under logs, stones, or leaf-litter. Breeding males, in contrast, are very showy, with a wavy crest up to 1cm high, and clear black face stripes.

bright yellow-orange beneath

NOTE

Sometimes mistaken for the Great Crested Newt (p.389) on account of its equally flamboyant crest, the most obvious point of distinction is that the crest of the breeding male Smooth Newt is continuous from the back onto the tail.

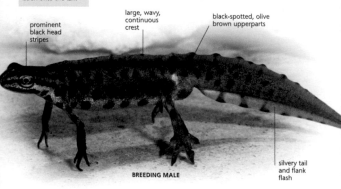

prominent black head stripes

large, wavy, continuous crest

black-spotted, olive brown upperparts

silvery tail and flank flash

BREEDING MALE

small crest on underside of tail

shiny, smooth skin

♀

SIZE *Body up to 6cm; tail up to 5cm.*
YOUNG *Lays 200–500 eggs, hatching in 2–3 weeks.*
DIET *Insects, worms, and other invertebrates; tadpoles.*
STATUS *Common.*
SIMILAR SPECIES *Great Crested Newt (p.389); Palmate Newt (p.389), which has a whitish, unspotted throat, and a smooth crest in the breeding male, and tends to be found in more acidic waters.*

Fish

Like reptiles, the number of fish species in Britain has been limited by the effects of the last ice age, though there have been successful introductions of several species from elsewhere. Recent efforts in pollution control have seen fish numbers increase significantly in many rivers, though it takes practice to recognise them when seen from above the water's surface. The species on the following pages are those that are most likely to be encountered when walking by a river, pond, estuary, or the seashore.

COMMON
CARP

BROWN
TROUT

BALLAN
WRASSE

PERCH

Common Carp

Cyprinus carpio (Cyprinidae)

The Common Carp has probably been farmed longer than any other fish. It can be recognized by its bronze-brown coloration and the two pairs of tiny barbels on its lips. The wild form has uniform-sized scales and is much slimmer than introduced fish, which have much deeper bodies and scales that vary in shape and number.

FOUND *in stagnant water of lowland lakes and rivers that have a muddy substrate and abundant vegetation.*

spine-like anterior ray of dorsal fin

red tinge on lower part of pectoral fin

long barbel at corner of mouth

uniform-sized body scales

SIZE *Rarely over 80cm long.*
DIET *Bottom-living insect larvae, blood worms, crustaceans, small snails, and water weeds.*
BREEDING *In shallow water in spring (late May).*
SIMILAR SPECIES *Crucian Carp (Carassius carassius), now found in southern Britain, is smaller and has no barbels around the mouth.*

Chub

Leuciscus cephalus (Cyprinidae)

The Chub is one of the most widespread freshwater fish. Slow to mature, it forms large schools near the water surface although larger adults tend to be more solitary. Coloured dark brown above and cream below, the Chub has a blunt-snouted head with a wide mouth. Its body is covered with large scales and the pelvic fin bases are situated anterior to the dorsal fin.

SEEN *near the surface in the mid-reaches of rivers and in large lakes.*

dark brown dorsal fin

slender body covered with large scales

blunt snout

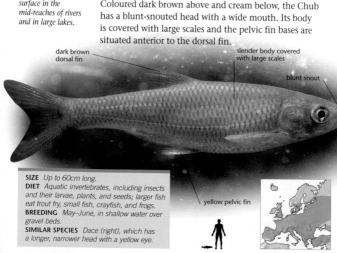

SIZE *Up to 60cm long.*
DIET *Aquatic invertebrates, including insects and their larvae, plants, and seeds; larger fish eat trout fry, small fish, crayfish, and frogs.*
BREEDING *May–June, in shallow water over gravel beds.*
SIMILAR SPECIES *Dace (right), which has a longer, narrower head with a yellow eye.*

yellow pelvic fin

Dace

Leuciscus leuciscus (Cyprinidae)

In river habitats, shoals of Dace are so common that they often outnumber the other fish. The Dace has a slender body, with a small head and distinctive mottled yellow eyes; the outer edges of dorsal and anal fins are concave. Unlike many other cyprinids that fast over winter, the Dace feeds all year round. Its fry are eaten by birds such as the Kingfisher.

THRIVES *in mid-reaches of rivers; sometimes in lakes and lowland rivers; occasionally in brackish water near river mouths.*

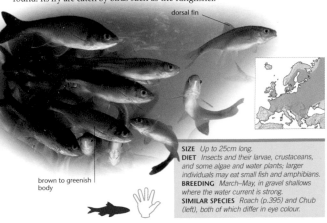

dorsal fin

brown to greenish body

SIZE *Up to 25cm long.*
DIET *Insects and their larvae, crustaceans, and some algae and water plants; larger individuals may eat small fish and amphibians.*
BREEDING *March–May, in gravel shallows where the water current is strong.*
SIMILAR SPECIES *Roach (p.395) and Chub (left), both of which differ in eye colour.*

Gudgeon

Gobio gobio (Cyprinidae)

The elongated, round-bodied Gudgeon is a bottom-dwelling shoal fish that uses its fleshy lips and sensory barbels to locate food. Its scales are moderately sized and shaded silvery white below. There are a series of dark blotches running along its sides, following the course of the lateral line (a sensory structure).

FOUND *in lakes and rivers that are well oxygenated and clean, with sandy bottoms.*

dark blotches

scales coloured green-brown above

barbel at corner of mouth

SIZE *Up to 15cm long.*
DIET *Bottom-living insect larvae, crustaceans, and molluscs.*
BREEDING *May–June, at night, in very shallow water when water temperatures reach 14°–15° C.*
SIMILAR SPECIES *Barbel (p.394), which is much larger and has a flattened body.*

cream coloured pectoral fin

Barbel

Barbus barbus (Cyprinidae)

OCCURS *in mid- and lower reaches of clean rivers where the current is moderate to fast.*

A large, bottom-dwelling fish, the Barbel can be recognized by its ventrally situated mouth, the two pairs of barbels on its lips, and a broad, flattened belly. The anterior dorsal fin ray is long and modified into a serrated edged spine and the tail fin is deeply forked. Females are always bigger than males of an equivalent age. Barbels are most active at night when they disperse to feed. During daylight hours, they gather in small schools of similar sized fish and are found in the water current near areas of turbulence, such as waterfalls. During the spawning season, males develop rows of white tubercles along their heads and backs. They pursue the females until they release their eggs, which they then swim over and fertilize.

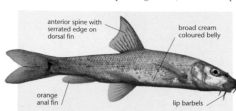

anterior spine with serrated edge on dorsal fin

broad cream coloured belly

orange anal fin

lip barbels

brown-green upper body

SIZE *Up to 50cm long (a few specimens of 90cm have been recorded).*
DIET *Bottom-living invertebrates such as water snails, Freshwater Shrimps, aquatic insect larvae, and plant debris.*
BREEDING *March–May.*
SIMILAR SPECIES *Gudgeon (p.393), which is much smaller and has only has one pair of barbels, one at each corner of the mouth. It lacks both the spiny fin ray with the serrated edge at the front of the dorsal fin and the broad flattened belly of this species.*

NOTE

During winter, when the water temperature drops below 3°C, Barbels cease feeding and activity levels drop. They move together into deeper water where they become torpid – a condition similar to mammal hibernation.

Bream

Abramis brama (Cyprinidae)

Nicknamed "skimmers" because juveniles trawl the surface waters in search of newly hatched midge larvae, the Bream can survive in water that is low in oxygen. It is a narrow, deep-bodied fish that skims over the bottom at an oblique angle when searching for food. It has a small head and in shallow water, its tail may break the surface as it moves.

OCCURS *in slow-flowing rivers, lowland lakes, and ponds with stagnant water and muddy bottoms.*

brown dorsal fin

terminal mouth

cream belly

anal fin with long base

pale pectoral fin

SIZE *Up to 80cm long.*
DIET *Insect larvae, worms, snails, bivalves, and crustaceans.*
BREEDING *May–July, where vegetation is dense; often occurs at night in shallow water.*
SIMILAR SPECIES *Silver Bream (Blicca bjoerka), which has a paler body; the eye and scales are relatively much larger.*

Roach

Rutilus rutilus (Cyprinidae)

The environment in which the Roach lives influences its shape and size – it is only in optimum conditions that it acquires any thickness or grows over 15cm in length. Its body is blue-grey dorsally, shading to silver on the sides and white below. The iris of the eye is reddish as are the pelvic and anal fins.

SEEN *in lowland rivers and lakes, preferring areas with slower currents to faster ones; tolerant of low-level pollution.*

grey-brown dorsal fin

conspicuous body scales

reddish anal fin

reddish pelvic fin

red iris

SIZE *Up to 35cm long.*
DIET *Insects and their larvae, crustaceans, and snails, as well as algae and plant matter.*
BREEDING *April–June, in dense vegetation in shallow water of at least 10° C.*
SIMILAR SPECIES *Rudd (Scardinius erythrophthalmus), which has a golden iris and a more upward-pointing mouth.*

Tench

Tinca tinca (Cyprinidae)

One of the few freshwater fish to show sexual dimorphism outside the breeding season, a male Tench is distinguishable from the female by the time it is two years of age. By then, its anal fin is longer than that of a female and the second fin ray of the anal fin also becomes greatly thickened.

FOUND *in murky water of lakes and ponds with soft bottoms, sometimes in lower reaches of rivers; tolerant of low-oxygen conditions.*

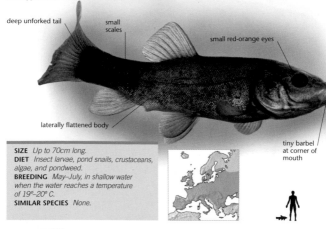

deep unforked tail

small scales

small red-orange eyes

laterally flattened body

tiny barbel at corner of mouth

SIZE *Up to 70cm long.*
DIET *Insect larvae, pond snails, crustaceans, algae, and pondweed.*
BREEDING *May–July, in shallow water when the water reaches a temperature of 19°–20° C.*
SIMILAR SPECIES *None.*

Bullhead

Cottus gobio (Cottidae)

Also referred to as the Miller's Thumb, this bottom-dwelling fish has a wide head and a tapering body that lacks scales. Its colour is variable and depends on the habitat. The dorsal fins are joined and form a continuous fin that extends along almost the entire length of the body. The Bullhead also has huge, rounded pectoral fins, and an anal fin with a long base. Unusually, the lateral line extends onto the tail fin.

FOUND *in clean, clear, shallow water with strong to moderate currents in rivers, streams, and lakes with stony substrates.*

large eyes towards top of head

rounded pectoral fin

anterior dorsal fin

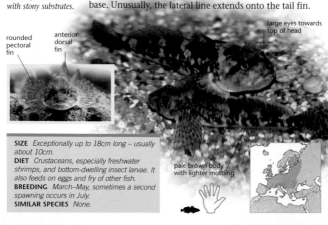

pale brown body with lighter mottling

SIZE *Exceptionally up to 18cm long – usually about 10cm.*
DIET *Crustaceans, especially freshwater shrimps, and bottom-dwelling insect larvae. It also feeds on eggs and fry of other fish.*
BREEDING *March–May, sometimes a second spawning occurs in July.*
SIMILAR SPECIES *None.*

Minnow

Phoxinus phoxinus (Cyprinidae)

This tiny fish forms an important part of the aquatic food chain because it is eaten by larger fish, such as trout and Pike (p.398), as well as being taken by birds, such as the Grey Heron (p.314). Usually seen in small schools, the Minnow has a blunt snout, short-based fins, and small, inconspicuous scales. During the breeding season, the belly of the male changes colour from white to red and both sexes may develop small tubercles on their heads. Minnows usually feed on bottom-dwelling invertebrates, but should an insect land on the surface of the water, they will swim up, take hold of its legs, and pull it under the water to eat it. Young minnows, called fry, gather in huge numbers in very shallow, warm water where they feed on algae and zooplankton.

FOUND *typically in upland areas with gravel substrates in fast-flowing, well-oxygenated rivers and streams, or high-altitude lakes with cool, clean water.*

NOTE

Minnow species have been used in laboratory experiments to determine how well fish can hear as sound travels better in water than in air.

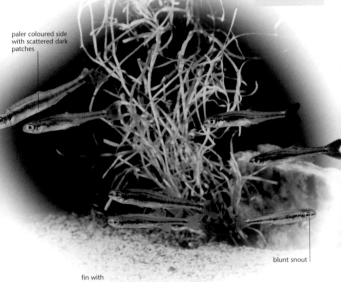

paler coloured side with scattered dark patches

blunt snout

fin with short base

dark brown back

white belly

SIZE *Rarely more than 8cm long.*
DIET *Insects and insect larvae, crustaceans, trout eggs, algae, and plants.*
BREEDING *May–mid-July, over gravel.*
SIMILAR SPECIES *Swamp Minnow (Phoxinus percnurus) is similar to the juvenile Minnow but has spots rather than scattered dark patches on the sides of the body. It is also found in a slightly different habitat, preferring well-vegetated ponds and lakes.*

Pike

Esox lucius (Esocidae)

INHABITS *varied habitats with slow currents – small ponds, large lakes, and rivers.*

The Pike is an ambush predator that lies in wait for its prey among the weeds and strikes at great speed when it is close enough. It has a distinctive torpedo-shaped body with similarly shaped, opposing dorsal and anal fins far back on the body. The jaws are lined with sharp, backward-pointing teeth. Pike tend to be brown-green in colour, flecked with yellow on their sides, so as to blend into the pond vegetation.

broad, flattened snout

powerful tail

SIZE *Up to 1.5m long.*
DIET *Fish, ducklings, and other small birds, frogs and newts, and even small mammals.*
BREEDING *March–late June, in daylight, depending on locality; spawning occurs later in the north of its range as the temperature rises more slowly in spring.*
SIMILAR SPECIES *None.*

green-brown body flecked with yellow

dorsal fin

JUVENILE

Eel

Anguilla anguilla (Anguillidae)

OCCURS *in fresh and salt water depending on the stage of its life cycle.*

A migratory fish, the Eel starts its life in the sea but moves into freshwater to grow and mature. The Eel is snake-like and has a continuous fin enveloping the hind part of the body, which is made up of fused dorsal, tail, and anal fins. Unusually for a fish, the Eel can survive short periods out of water and is capable of moving overland between different river systems.

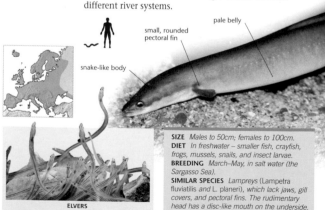

pale belly

small, rounded pectoral fin

snake-like body

SIZE *Males to 50cm; females to 100cm.*
DIET *In freshwater – smaller fish, crayfish, frogs, mussels, snails, and insect larvae.*
BREEDING *March–May, in salt water (the Sargasso Sea).*
SIMILAR SPECIES *Lampreys (Lampetra fluviatilis and L. planeri), which lack jaws, gill covers, and pectoral fins. The rudimentary head has a disc-like mouth on the underside.*

ELVERS

Atlantic Salmon

Salmo salar (Salmonidae)

Like all salmonids, the Atlantic Salmon can be recognized by the small, fleshy adipose fin on its back, located between the dorsal fin and the tail. Males are red-brown in colour dorsally while females are silver-grey; both have white bellies. During the spawning season, the males develop a well-defined hook on the lower jaw. Salmon return to the rivers in which they hatched, to breed. Because they stop feeding at this time, they lose about 40 per cent of their body weight and most die of exhaustion after spawning.

SEEN in freshwater (November–December) and in salt water; low tolerance to pollution.

white belly

fleshy adipose fin

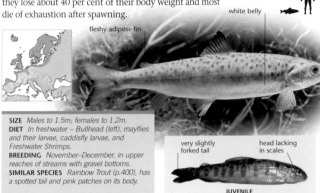

SIZE Males to 1.5m; females to 1.2m.
DIET In freshwater – Bullhead (left), mayflies and their larvae, caddisfly larvae, and Freshwater Shrimps.
BREEDING November–December, in upper reaches of streams with gravel bottoms.
SIMILAR SPECIES Rainbow Trout (p.400), has a spotted tail and pink patches on its body.

very slightly forked tail

head lacking in scales

JUVENILE

Brown Trout

Salmo trutta (Salmonidae)

There are two types of Brown Trout – one that is migratory and moves between river and sea, and one that is non-migratory and remains in freshwater, living in either lakes or rivers. The differences between them tend to be behavioural rather than genetic. The former is silver coloured with black spots while the latter is, as its name suggests, brown with both black and red spots on its back and on the sides.

INHABITS cool, clean well-oxygenated water whether fresh or salty; small streams, rivers, lakes, and the sea; intolerant of pollution.

black spots

upper jaw extends back beyond eye

ALEVINS

SIZE Up to 1m long.
DIET Small crustaceans and insect larvae, small fish.
BREEDING October–January.
SIMILAR SPECIES Rainbow Trout (p.400), which is more colourful, has a blunter head, and no red spotting; Atlantic Salmon (above), which can be confused with the sea-going Brown Trout but is larger.

Rainbow Trout

Oncorhynchus mykiss (Salmonidae)

The Rainbow Trout is now widespread in Britain and is important commercially, being farmed both for food and as a source for restocking rivers for anglers. It is easily recognized by the pink coloration along its sides and the dark spots that extend over the tail. It has a small head with a blunt snout; the body is covered in tiny scales.

FOUND *in streams, rivers, and lakes; more tolerant of pollution and high temperatures than the Brown Trout.*

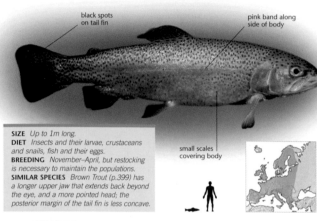

black spots on tail fin

pink band along side of body

small scales covering body

SIZE *Up to 1m long.*
DIET *Insects and their larvae, crustaceans and snails, fish and their eggs.*
BREEDING *November–April, but restocking is necessary to maintain the populations.*
SIMILAR SPECIES *Brown Trout (p.399) has a longer upper jaw that extends back beyond the eye, and a more pointed head; the posterior margin of the tail fin is less concave.*

Grayling

Thymallus thymallus (Salmonidae)

The distinctive appearance of the Grayling with its linear arrangement of body scales, elongated dorsal fin, and downward-directed mouth differentiates it not only from other salmonids, but also from all other freshwater fish. Grayling live in shoals in which all fish are of similar size, but larger individuals may be solitary.

INHABITS *fast-flowing, clear, well-oxygenated water in the upper reaches of rivers with sand or gravel.*

large dorsal fin

large scales arranged in distinct rows

pear-shaped iris in eye

SIZE *Up to 50cm long.*
DIET *Bottom-dwelling insect larvae, including stonefly nymphs, small worms, crustaceans, and molluscs. It also takes insects that land on the surface of the water. Larger individuals may consume small fish.*
BREEDING *March–May, in fast-flowing water in gravelly shallows.*
SIMILAR SPECIES *None.*

Perch

Perca fluviatilis (Percidae)

A deep-bodied fish, the Perch has a green-brown back and a white or cream belly. Its sides are more golden in colour with four to six vertical dark bands. The orange-red pelvic and anal fins add to its colourful appearance. The Perch feels rough to the touch because the body scales are covered in small tubercles. Not a particularly active fish, it lives in schools.

SEEN *in lowland lakes and ponds, and in slow-running rivers.*

anterior dorsal fin

olive-brown upper body

cream belly

orange-red pelvic fin

EGGS

SIZE *Up to 50cm long.*
DIET *Juveniles feed on invertebrates, but as adults they also feed on fish such as smaller Perch, sticklebacks, and small cyprinids.*
BREEDING *March–June (peaking in April and May), in shallow water.*
SIMILAR SPECIES *Ruffe (Gymnocephalus cernuus), which has larger scales, and yellowish pelvic and anal fins.*

Thick-lipped Grey Mullet

Chelon labrosus (Mugilidae)

A sea fish that ventures into river estuaries to feed, the Thick-lipped Grey Mullet has a streamlined body covered with large grey-blue scales that become silvery on the sides and white on the belly. The fish has two dorsal fins, the first being small, with only four fin spines. As its name suggests, the upper lip is swollen and has two or three rows of tubercles on the lower half near the mouth.

FOUND *in coastal waters and in river estuaries.*

dark grey pectoral fin

large scales that extend onto head

deeply forked tail

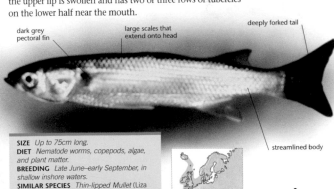

streamlined body

SIZE *Up to 75cm long.*
DIET *Nematode worms, copepods, algae, and plant matter.*
BREEDING *Late June–early September, in shallow inshore waters.*
SIMILAR SPECIES *Thin-lipped Mullet (Liza ramada) is thinner and lacks tubercles on the upper lip; Golden-Grey Mullet (Liza aurata) has a gold spot behind each eye and gill.*

Shanny

Lipophyris pholis (Blenniidae)

INHABITS *coastal habitat; in rock pools from the high-water mark down to a water depth of 300m.*

Abundant in rock pools, the Shanny has a blunt head, large eyes, and an elongated, smooth scale-less body. The dorsal fin is long and has a dark red or black spot between the first and second fin rays. There is a small depression in the dorsal fin margin between the spiny and soft, rayed sections. The pelvic fins, situated just behind the head and anterior to the pectoral fins, are reduced and spine-like. The anal fin is as long as the soft, rayed section of the dorsal fin. The Shanny remains hidden under stones and seaweed while the tide is out, but at high water leaves its pool to forage on the shore for food.

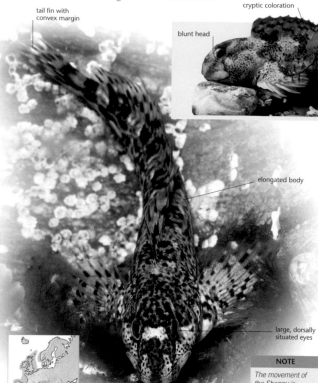

tail fin with convex margin

cryptic coloration

blunt head

elongated body

large, dorsally situated eyes

NOTE

The movement of the Shanny is dictated by the tides. If it is removed from its natural habitat, into a laboratory, this rhythmical behaviour vanishes. However, it is re-established very quickly when the fish is returned to its normal environment.

SIZE *Up to 16cm.*
DIET *Barnacles, small crabs, and other crustaceans.*
BREEDING *April–August.*
SIMILAR SPECIES *Montagu's Blenny (Coryphoblennius galerita) and the Tompot Blenny (Parablennius gattorugine), both of which have a fleshy flap between their eyes that is not present in the Shanny.*

Sea Bass

Dicentrarchus labrax (Moronidae)

A schooling fish of inshore waters, the Sea Bass can be recognized by the spines on its gill cover. On the lower edge, the spines point forwards, but the two spines on the back edge are flattened and point towards the tail. The two dorsal fins are separate, the first of them being spiny, as is the anal fin. The Sea Bass is slow to mature, but may live for 20 years.

FOUND *in inshore waters; juveniles especially enter estuaries to feed.*

spiny first dorsal fin

large head

second dorsal fin

large silver scales on sides

SIZE *Up to 1m but usually 50cm.*
DIET *Wide range of fish – fish of the herring family, sand-eels, squids, and crustaceans.*
BREEDING *March–mid-June, in deep inshore seas.*
SIMILAR SPECIES *Large-mouthed Bass (Micropterus salmoides) has a continuous but notched dorsal fin, its jaw extends beyond the eye, and the gill covers lacks spines.*

Lesser Sand-eel

Ammodytes tobianus (Ammodytidae)

A shoaling, silvery fish, the Lesser Sand-eel is often abundant in the inshore zone. It has a thin, elongated body with a long dorsal fin that fits into a groove. It lacks pelvic fins and has a small forked tail. It forms the staple diet of many seabirds, including the Puffin (p.338) and terns. Unfortunately, many stocks have been over-fished on an industrial scale, and this has greatly reduced the numbers of birds that rely on Sand-eels as food for their chicks.

OCCURS *on sandy shores, from mid-tide level to the shallow sublittoral; often buried in sand, even at low tide.*

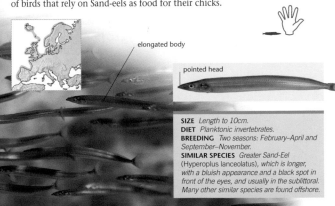

elongated body

pointed head

SIZE *Length to 10cm.*
DIET *Planktonic invertebrates.*
BREEDING *Two seasons: February–April and September–November.*
SIMILAR SPECIES *Greater Sand-Eel (Hyperoplus lanceolatus), which is longer, with a bluish appearance and a black spot in front of the eyes, and usually in the sublittoral. Many other similar species are found offshore.*

Ballan Wrasse

Labrus bergylta (Labridae)

A stout, laterally compressed wrasse, the Ballan Wrasse is very variable in colour. Most often, it is green or brown with pale spots, but reddish and purple colours often develop according to its habitat and the breeding stage. Like many related species, the fish starts its life as a female and then becomes male as it grows. Unusually among fish, the Ballan Wrasse sleeps on its side.

FAVOURS *rocky, seaweed-covered shores and rock pools, from the lower intertidal to the shallow sublittoral.*

rows of pale spots on fins

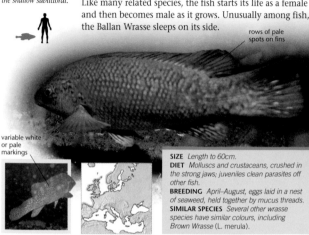

variable white or pale markings

SIZE *Length to 60cm.*
DIET *Molluscs and crustaceans, crushed in the strong jaws; juveniles clean parasites off other fish.*
BREEDING *April–August, eggs laid in a nest of seaweed, held together by mucus threads.*
SIMILAR SPECIES *Several other wrasse species have similar colours, including Brown Wrasse (L. merula).*

Sand Goby

Pomatoschistus minutus (Gobiidae)

A slender, sand-coloured fish, the Sand Goby has small scales on its body. It has two dorsal fins, rounded pectoral fins, and anteriorly positioned pelvic fins that have finger-like processes extending from the free edges. Males have a conspicuous dark patch, bordered with white, on the posterior edge of the first dorsal fin. The tail has a long base (peduncle) and a convex posterior margin.

INHABITS *marine habitats; inshore sandy areas from the mid-tide line down to 20m.*

pectoral fin

prominent, dorsally positioned eye

small body scales

SIZE *Up to a maximum of 10cm but more often about 6cm.*
DIET *Small crustaceans.*
BREEDING *March–July.*
SIMILAR SPECIES *Norway Goby (P. norvegicus) is very similar, but it lives in deeper water; Common Goby (P. microps) is stouter and has larger scales but lacks scales on the breast.*

FISH IN BURROW

Three-spined Stickleback

Gasterosteus aculeatus (Gasterosteidae)

A small scale-less fish with a torpedo-shaped body, this Stickleback is named for the three spines on its back. The first two are longer than the third, which is considerably smaller and close to the base of the second dorsal fin. Usually brown-green in colour, males develop a bright red belly during the spawning season. They become very territorial, guarding their tubular nest and displaying to passing females.

SEEN *in rivers, lakes, estuaries, and coastal waters; common in marine habitats only in Scotland.*

three spines on back

large pectoral fin

large eye

SIZE *Up to 10cm but more usually 5–8cm.*
DIET *Larval insects, small crustaceans, worms, other fish eggs, and some plant material.*
BREEDING *April–late June, in spring and early summer.*
SIMILAR SPECIES *Nine-spined Stickleback (Pungitus pungitus), which has nine spines instead of three.*

Fifteen-spined Stickleback

Spinachia spinachia (Gasterosteidae)

Also called the Sea Stickleback because it is the only wholly marine species of stickleback, the Fifteen-spined Stickleback has a very slender and elongated snout, head, and body. Males have larger pectoral fins than the females, and both are usually brown or green-brown in colour with a yellow belly. During the breeding season, females become yellower and males develop an attractive brown chequered pattern.

OCCURS *only in marine habitats, in shallow coastal waters to a depth of 10m.*

narrow tail base

elongated snout

chequered brown pattern

SIZE *Up to 22cm but usually 15cm.*
DIET *Small invertebrates – mainly crustaceans, including copepods and amphipods.*
BREEDING *April–August.*
SIMILAR SPECIES *None.*

Shore Clingfish

Lepadogaster lepadogaster (Gobiesocidae)

Also known as the Cornish Sucker, the Shore Clingfish has a flattened body with a broad triangular head and "duck-billed" snout, accentuated by thick lips. The pelvic fins are modified into a thoracic sucking disc that allows it to adhere to rocks and other substrates. Usually a reddish brown colour with darker smudges, its most obvious markings are two deep blue spots behind the eyes.

INHABITS
seaweed-covered rocky shores and rock pools, or clings to the underside of boulders at low tide.

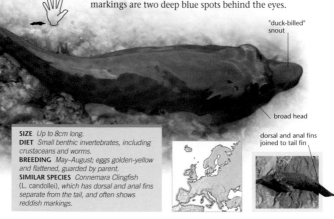

"duck-billed" snout

broad head

dorsal and anal fins joined to tail fin

SIZE *Up to 8cm long.*
DIET *Small benthic invertebrates, including crustaceans and worms.*
BREEDING *May–August; eggs golden-yellow and flattened, guarded by parent.*
SIMILAR SPECIES *Connemara Clingfish (L. candollei), which has dorsal and anal fins separate from the tail, and often shows reddish markings.*

Plaice

Pleuronectes platessa (Pleuronectidae)

The bottom-dwelling flatfish are divided into two groups according to whether their eyes are on the right or the left side of the fish. Plaice has its eyes on the upper, right side, the eyes moving into position in the juvenile stage. The upper parts are variable in colour, changing rapidly by the expansion and contraction of pigment cells; normally they are brown with orange blotches.

LIVES *on, or shallowly buried into, sandy sediments in intertidal pools and the sublittoral zone; extends a little into estuarine waters.*

anal fin extending to whole length of body

both eyes on right side

eye looking up from sand

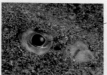
BURIED IN SAND

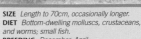

SIZE *Length to 70cm, occasionally longer.*
DIET *Bottom-dwelling molluscs, crustaceans, and worms; small fish.*
BREEDING *December–April.*
SIMILAR SPECIES *Flounder (right), which is rough along the lateral line, less distinctly spotted, and extends well into estuaries; Dab (Limanda limanda), which has a rough texture overall, a sandy colour, and is often smaller.*

Flounder

Platichthys flesus (Pleuronectidae)

Another right-eyed fish (though left-eyed specimens do occur), the Flounder is round in profile and has a row of tubercles running along the bases of the dorsal and anal fins. Feeding at night, it buries itself during the day, with its eyes showing above the substrate. It is the only flatfish that can survive in freshwater, the river Thames being one of the most important nursery areas.

FOUND *in rivers that connect to the sea, on sandy or muddy substrate; has low tolerance to pollution.*

anal fin

eyes usually on right side

dorsal fin

SIZE *Up to 51cm.*
DIET *Bottom-living invertebrates such as molluscs, worms, and crustaceans.*
BREEDING *March–May.*
SIMILAR SPECIES *Plaice (left); Dab (Limanda limanda), which lacks tubercles along the bases of the dorsal and anal fins; Lemon Sole (Microstomus kitt) has dorsal and anal fins that extend to the base of the tail fin.*

Basking Shark

Cetorhinus maximus (Cetorhinidae)

Despite its size (it is the second largest fish in the world) and fearsome gaping mouth, the Basking Shark is a harmless filter-feeder, trawling through inshore waters, collecting plankton. The first, and often only, sign of its presence is the large triangular dorsal fin, followed by the tip of its tail fin, moving from side to side as the shark slowly swims forward.

INHABITS *the open sea, moving into shallow coastal waters, especially during the summer months.*

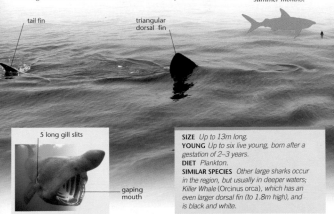

tail fin

triangular dorsal fin

5 long gill slits

gaping mouth

SIZE *Up to 13m long.*
YOUNG *Up to six live young, born after a gestation of 2–3 years.*
DIET *Plankton.*
SIMILAR SPECIES *Other large sharks occur in the region, but usually in deeper waters; Killer Whale (Orcinus orca), which has an even larger dorsal fin (to 1.8m high), and is black and white.*

Invertebrates

A majority of animal life is made up of invertebrates, which include familiar species such as butterflies, moths, spiders, and insects. Species that are less frequently encountered include centipedes, snails, and a vast diversity of marine creatures. Invertebrates occupy every habitat on earth, and are vital to the proper functioning of the ecosystem, but many of them are in danger of going extinct as they are highly susceptible to factors such as habitat loss, pollution, or changes in land management.

ORB WEB SPIDERS

BUSH CRICKETS

COMMOM STARFISH

PILL MILLIPEDES

Small Skipper

Thymelicus sylvestris (Hesperiidae)

One of the most widespread and numerous butterflies in the region, the Small Skipper's colourful and rather uniform orange-brown wings are a useful clue to its identity. However, it is easily confused with the very similar Essex Skipper (*T. lineola*), although in this species the antennal club is black underneath, whereas in the Small Skipper it is orange-brown. It usually sunbathes with its forewings slightly elevated and angled, the manner adopted by many other Skippers.

INHABITS *all kinds of grassy places, roadside verges, and grassy lowland meadows.*

antennal club orange-brown below

greenish grey tip to forewing

♂●

lacks the dark male sex-brand

♀●

up to 2.5cm long

black line or sex-brand

narrow dark margin

♂●

WINGSPAN *2.5cm.*
FLIGHT PERIOD *May–September.*
LARVAL FOODPLANT *Various meadow species of grasses (family Poaceae).*
SIMILAR SPECIES *Lulworth Skipper (T. acteon), which has a "paw-print" of yellowish spots on its upper wings; Essex Skipper (T. lineola), females in particular.*
STATUS *Common, although absent from Cumbria, Scotland, and Ireland.*

Large Skipper

Ochlodes venata (Hesperiidae)

This familiar grassland butterfly has rich colours and markings on its upperwings. Like other members of the Skipper family, the male has a conspicuous sex-brand in the form of a dark line on the forewing. Generally, it has brighter colours than the otherwise similar female. The underwings of both sexes are yellowish with a variable suffusion of greenish scaling, and faint pale spots.

FAVOURS *a wide range of grassy habitats from meadows to hedgerow margins; also hillsides up to 2,000m.*

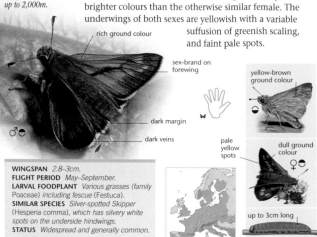

rich ground colour

sex-brand on forewing

yellow-brown ground colour

dark margin

dark veins

♂

pale yellow spots

pale yellow spots

dull ground colour ♀

up to 3cm long

WINGSPAN *2.8–3cm.*
FLIGHT PERIOD *May–September.*
LARVAL FOODPLANT *Various grasses (family Poaceae) including fescue (Festuca).*
SIMILAR SPECIES *Silver-spotted Skipper (Hesperia comma), which has silvery white spots on the underside hindwings.*
STATUS *Widespread and generally common.*

Dingy Skipper

Erynnis tages (Hesperiidae)

Although the Dingy Skipper may appear rather nondescript, its uniformly dark brown upperwings and pale brown underwings, when taken together, are unique and have diagnostic features: there are few butterflies with which it could be confused. However, observers should be aware that the buzzing flight and undeniably sombre appearance of this small butterfly do give it a distinctly moth-like appearance.

SEEN *in grassland with plenty of flowers, and also often on chalky soil.*

indistinct, pale and dark bands

pale brown ground colour

faint pale spots

small, faint marginal spots

up to 2cm long

WINGSPAN *2.5cm.*
FLIGHT PERIOD *May–August.*
LARVAL FOODPLANT *Trefoil (Lotus), Crown Vetch (Coronilla varia), and related plants in the pea family.*
SIMILAR SPECIES *None.*
STATUS *Widespread and locally common, although declining due to habitat loss.*

Grizzled Skipper

Pyrgus malvae (Hesperiidae)

Although it is a small butterfly, the Grizzled Skipper makes up for what it lacks in terms of size with the beautiful patterning on its wings. The upper surfaces are a rich brown colour, adorned with an intricate pattern of squarish pale spots. Fortunately, the butterfly frequently sunbathes with its wings open and spread out, giving observers plenty of opportunity to study them. The underwing ground colour is yellowish brown with a pattern of whitish spots similar to that seen on the upper surfaces of the wings.

INHABITS *grassy heaths, woodland margins, and clearings; often found along tracks where foodplants flourish.*

large, central white spot

yellow-brown ground colour

up to 2cm long

NOTE

The combination of its small size and the presence of squarish spots of rather uniform size and intensity across the upperwings are useful identification clues. Look also for the arc of pale spots on the upperside hindwing and the large central pale spot on the underside.

squarish pale spots

rich brown ground colour

crescent of pale spots

WINGSPAN *2cm.*
FLIGHT PERIOD *April–June, with a rare second brood in July–August in the south.*
LARVAL FOODPLANT *Wild Strawberry (see p.84), and Creeping Cinquefoil (Potentilla reptans).*
SIMILAR SPECIES *None.*
STATUS *Locally common, but under threat in many places from land development. However, new colonies have recently been discovered.*

Swallowtail

Papilio machaon (Papilionidae)

FOUND *once across wetlands in Britain, it is now confined to the damp fenland of the Norfolk Broads.*

This large and spectacular species is almost unmistakable. Although Swallowtails seem rather restless, they often remain relatively still when feeding, allowing observers excellent views of their beautiful markings. The overall colour of both surfaces of the wings is yellow, and they are patterned with a network of black veins and bands. The upperwings also reveal a marginal band of blue scaling and a colourful eyespot. Lastly, there is the trademark tail streamer on the hindwing. This characteristic feature is found in many members of this butterfly family and lends it the name "Swallowtail".

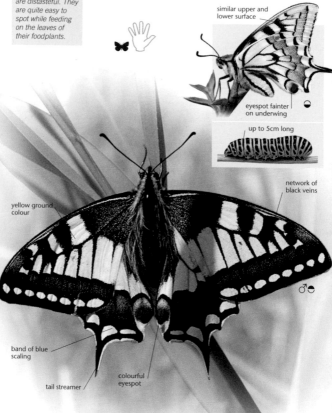

similar upper and lower surface

eyespot fainter on underwing

up to 5cm long

network of black veins

yellow ground colour

band of blue scaling

colourful eyespot

tail streamer

WINGSPAN *8–9cm.*
FLIGHT PERIOD *May–June, in favourable years a second brood may appear in August.*
LARVAL FOODPLANT *Fennel (Foeniculum vulgare), Milk Parsley (Peucedanum palustre), and other carrot family members.*
SIMILAR SPECIES *None.*
STATUS *Restricted to the Norfolk Broads, although some immigrants from Europe arrive in the far south each year.*

Orange-tip

Anthocharis cardamines (Pieridae)

The Orange-tip is one of the most distinctive spring butterflies in the region and can often be seen flitting along flowery verges and woodland rides. The male is particularly striking, with bright orange tips on its white upper forewings, which can also be seen on its underwings. The tips of the female's forewings are black rather than orange, making it quite subdued in appearance. The underside of the hindwing in both sexes is white with subtle greenish marbling.

FLIES *along flowery roadside verges, woodland rides, and meadows; sometimes appears in gardens.*

NOTE

A female Orange-tip could be mistaken for a Bath White (Pontia daplidice), so note the Orange-tip's paler appearance with fewer dark spots, and delicate flight.

green marbling

♂⬤

faint grey tip

white ground colour

dark spot

♀⬤

up to 2.5cm long

bright orange wing tip

dark spot on forewing

white ground colour

♂⬤

WINGSPAN *4cm.*
FLIGHT PERIOD *April–June.*
LARVAL FOODPLANT *Garlic Mustard (see p.64), Cuckooflower (see p.67), and other cabbage family members.*
SIMILAR SPECIES *Bath White (Pontia daplidice), which is a rare migrant.*
STATUS *Widespread and common.*

Small White

Pieris rapae (Pieridae)

This is a typical small white butterfly, with white upperwings that have a blackish tip marked with two black spots, one of which is less distinct in males. The yellow and greyish white underwings are similarly marked. The larva is a pest of cultivated plants belonging to the cabbage family.

INHABITS *areas with cabbage family plants; particularly common in gardens and on farmland.*

dark tip to forewing

white ground colour

dark spot on forewing

♂●

hindwing yellow and grey

white ground colour

♀●

up to 2.5cm long

WINGSPAN *5cm.*
FLIGHT PERIOD *April–October.*
LARVAL FOODPLANT *Members of the cabbage family, especially the genus Brassica; Nasturtium (Tropaeolum majus).*
SIMILAR SPECIES *Large White (right), which is larger; Green-veined White (below).*
STATUS *Widespread and extremely common.*

Green-veined White

Pieris napi (Pieridae)

Once this butterfly's underwings have been seen clearly, there is usually no doubt about its identity. The well-defined network of greenish grey veins that criss-cross the yellow hindwings distinguishes it from related species. The females are marginally larger than males.

FOUND *in a wide range of flowery habitats, from roadside verges and gardens, to woodland rides and damp meadows.*

black forewing tip

green-grey veins

white ground colour

♂●

yellow ground colour

twin spots

dark veins

white ground colour ♀●

up to 2.5cm long

WINGSPAN *5cm.*
FLIGHT PERIOD *March–October in two or three broods.*
LARVAL FOODPLANT *Garlic Mustard (see p.64) and other wild cabbage family members.*
SIMILAR SPECIES *Female Orange-tip (p.413).*
STATUS *Widespread and common.*

Large White

Pieris brassicae (Pieridae)

Although the adult Large White is a charming sight in the
garden, the species is notorious for its larvae, hordes of which
can be found demolishing the leaves of cabbages and other
related plants. In both sexes, the upperwings
are creamy white and show a dark tip
to the forewing; in females, two dark
spots can also be seen on the forewing.

OCCURS *in a range of
flowery places, from
meadows and roadside
verges to farmland
and town gardens.*

white forewing

dark spot
on forewing

yellow-grey
ground colour

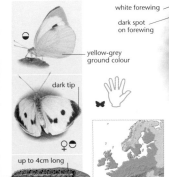

dark tip

♀

up to 4cm long

WINGSPAN *6cm.*
FLIGHT PERIOD *April–October.*
LARVAL FOODPLANT *Cabbage (Brassica
oleracea) and other cultivated cabbage family
members; Nasturtium (Tropaeolum majus).*
SIMILAR SPECIES *Small White (left); female
Brimstone (below).*
STATUS *Widespread and common.*

Brimstone

Gonepteryx rhamni (Pieridae)

For many naturalists, the sight of a Brimstone in early spring
is a sign that winter has finally ended. On sunny mornings as
early as February, this species emerges from hibernation in
search of nectar sources. The male Brimstone's bright yellow
colour is sufficient to identify even flying individuals. The
typical wing shape found in both sexes, can only be seen
in resting butterflies and is the best way
to identify a female.

SEEN *in areas of scrub,
woodland rides, and
gardens, the common
factor being the
presence of the
larval foodplant.*

lemon yellow ground
colour

♂

hook-tipped
forewing

red spots

angular
hindwing

greenish white
ground colour

♀

up to 3cm long

WINGSPAN *6cm.*
FLIGHT PERIOD *July–October, and
February–May after hibernation.*
LARVAL FOODPLANT *Buckthorn (Rhamnus)
and Alder Buckthorn (Frangula alnus).*
SIMILAR SPECIES *None, it is the only
resident yellow coloured butterfly in Britain.*
STATUS *Widespread and generally common.*

Clouded Yellow

Colias crocea (Pieridae)

This colourful butterfly is active and fast-flying, qualities that enable it to undertake long migrations north each year from its stronghold in southern Europe. The extent of the species' travels varies from year to year but in most seasons the range extends northwards as far as southern Britain. Unfortunately, its life cycle is not completed here because of the cold, wet weather in autumn. In flight, the dominant orange-yellow wing colour catches the eye. The upperwings have a broad, dark brown margin. However, resting individuals rarely, if ever, open their wings fully.

FAVOURS all sorts of flowery, grassy places. Given the species' migratory nature, it can appear in a variety of habitats within its range.

NOTE

Some female Clouded Yellows occur in a pale form that looks confusingly similar to a Pale Clouded Yellow (C. hyale). Pay attention to the upperwing colour and wing shape.

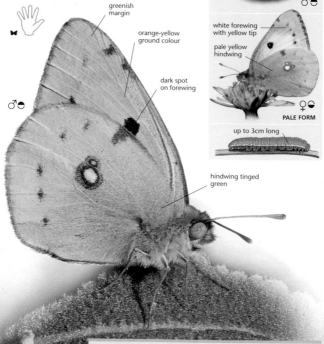

orange-yellow ground colour

broad, dark brown margin

♂●

greenish margin

orange-yellow ground colour

dark spot on forewing

♂●

white forewing with yellow tip

pale yellow hindwing

♀●
PALE FORM

up to 3cm long

hindwing tinged green

WINGSPAN 5cm.
FLIGHT PERIOD May–October.
LARVAL FOODPLANT Clover (Trifolium), Lucerne (see p.92), and other pea family members.
SIMILAR SPECIES Pale Clouded Yellow (C. hyale), which has a different wing shape and does not have dark brown upperwing margins.
STATUS An immigrant species, it is found in all parts of Britain in favourable years.

Holly Blue

Celastrina argiolus (Lycaenidae)

For many people, the Holly Blue is a familiar species as it is often found in gardens where holly and ivy are common. Both sexes have blue upperwings, although they are paler in females than males. The dark wing margins are more extensive in females.

INHABITS *diverse habitats such as woodland, inland cliffs, and gardens – the common factor being larval foodplants.*

narrow dark margin

violet-blue ground colour

faintly chequered pale fringe

♂●

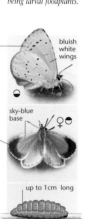

small dark spots

bluish white wings

♀●

sky-blue base

♀●

variable dark margin

up to 1cm long

WINGSPAN *3cm.*
FLIGHT PERIOD *April–May and August–September, in two distinct broods.*
LARVAL FOODPLANT *Holly (Ilex) for first and ivy (Hedera) for second brood larvae.*
SIMILAR SPECIES *Small Blue (Cupido minimus).*
STATUS *Generally common and widespread.*

Common Blue

Polyommatus icarus (Lycaenidae)

One of the Britain's commonest butterflies, the male Common Blue has blue upperwings tinged with a hint of violet, while those of the female are brown with orange spots and violet-blue at the wing base. Underwings of both sexes are grey-brown with orange and black white-ringed spots.

FAVOURS *a wide variety of grassy places, wherever the larval foodplant grows abundantly.*

bright violet-blue ground colour

white fringe

♂●

narrow dark margin

black and orange spots

dark spot on forewing cell

●

rich brown ground colour

♀●

orange submarginal spots

up to 1.5cm long

WINGSPAN *3.2cm.*
FLIGHT PERIOD *April–October, in successive broods.*
LARVAL FOODPLANT *Bird's-foot Trefoil (see p.95) and other pea family members.*
SIMILAR SPECIES *Adonis Blue (P. bellargus), which has chequered wing borders.*
STATUS *Widespread and common.*

Chalk-hill Blue

Polyommatus coridon (Lycaenidae)

A sun-loving butterfly that is characteristic of chalky grassland, the Chalk-hill Blue is a particularly attractive species. The male has bright sky-blue upperwings, which are often revealed when it is feeding or basking in the sunshine. The female is more subdued in appearance and has mainly dark brown upperwings; the hindwings are adorned with a submarginal row of orange, white, and black eyespots. In common with many other Blue butterflies, the larvae of the Chalk-hill Blue are attended by ants.

ASSOCIATED with flower-rich chalk and limestone grassland – habitats to which the larval foodplant is restricted.

pale-ringed dark spots

grey-brown ground colour

brown ground colour

♀●

up to 1.5cm long

orange spots

NOTE

The species is notoriously variable, particularly in the extent of the dark margin on the male upperwing. However, the sky-blue upperwing ground colour, and the favoured habitat are good clues to identity, of males at least.

chequered fringe

bright sky-blue ground colour

broad, dark brown margin

♂●

WINGSPAN 4cm.
FLIGHT PERIOD July–August.
LARVAL FOODPLANT Horseshoe Vetch (see p.96).
SIMILAR SPECIES None, no other "blue" in Britain has such silvery-blue wings, as the male Chalk-hill Blue. The female Adonis Blue (*P. bellargus*) is similar to the female Chalk-hill Blue but is bluer.
STATUS Locally very common in the south. Declining due to habitat destruction.

Green Hairstreak

Callophrys rubi (Lycaenidae)

In spite of its bright underside ground colour, this active butterfly can be very difficult to spot. At rest it looks exactly like a green leaf. In flight, its colours blend with the surroundings so well that it is almost impossible to follow its movements. It seldom exposes its brown upperwings when resting, showing only its underwings.

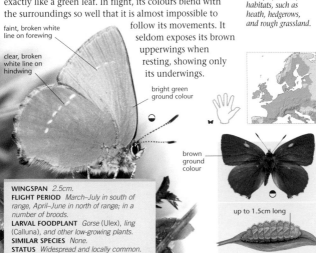

INHABITS *a wide variety of scrubby habitats, such as heath, hedgerows, and rough grassland.*

faint, broken white line on forewing

clear, broken white line on hindwing

bright green ground colour

brown ground colour

up to 1.5cm long

WINGSPAN *2.5cm.*
FLIGHT PERIOD *March–July in south of range, April–June in north of range; in a number of broods.*
LARVAL FOODPLANT *Gorse (Ulex), ling (Calluna), and other low-growing plants.*
SIMILAR SPECIES *None.*
STATUS *Widespread and locally common.*

Purple Hairstreak

Favonius quercus (Lycaenidae)

The Purple Hairstreak is often seen flitting high among the treetops. Fortunately for observers, it often descends closer to ground level on dull days (particularly after rain). Unlike some of its Hairstreak relatives, it occasionally basks with its wings open, revealing the purple markings on its sooty brown upperwings. Its under surface is buffish grey.

INHABITS *mature oak woodland but colonies are sometimes found on isolated oak trees.*

♂

grey ground colour

black-edged white streak

purple or violet iridescence

small orange spots

♂

♀

sooty-brown ground colour

small tail streamer

less extensive purple sheen

up to 2.5cm long

WINGSPAN *4–5cm.*
FLIGHT PERIOD *July–August.*
LARVAL FOODPLANT *Mainly Blackthorn (see p.39) and related species, but also birch (Betula).*
SIMILAR SPECIES *None.*
STATUS *Widespread but distinctly local, forming discrete colonies.*

Small Copper

Lycaena phlaeas (Lycaenidae)

FLIES *over all kinds of flowery, grassy places, from roadside verges to meadows and cliffs.*

Despite its small size, the Small Copper catches the eye due to its bright markings. Although some of the upperwing surface is brown, this relatively sombre background serves to highlight the vivid orange markings. The underwings have more subdued colours than the upperwings although the pattern of markings is broadly similar. A subtle variation in wing markings exists across the species' range; in particular, the extent of the orange submarginal band on the hindwing shows considerable variation.

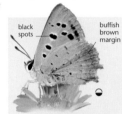

black spots

buffish brown margin

NOTE
Male Small Coppers are strongly territorial and it can be interesting to watch them defend their "home patch" against intruding rivals. They even attack male butterflies belonging to other species on occasion.

up to 1.5cm long

orange-red forewing

brown margin

brown spots

brown hindwing

pointed rear margin

submarginal orange band

WINGSPAN *3–3.8cm.*
FLIGHT PERIOD *April–October, in successive broods.*
LARVAL FOODPLANT *Sorrel and dock (both Rumex).*
SIMILAR SPECIES *None.*
STATUS *Widespread and one of the commonest butterflies in the British Isles.*

Brown Argus

Aricia agestis (Lycaenidae)

At first glance, the Brown Argus could be mistaken for a female Common Blue (p.417). However, the species is quite distinctive, the rich brown upperwings being adorned with bright orange crescent-shaped spots around the white-fringed margins. On the grey-brown underwings, there are orange spots arranged in a pattern similar to that seen on the upperwings.

FAVOURS *free-draining, dry grassland areas, seeming equally at home on chalky or slightly acidic soil.*

submarginal row of orange spots

rich brown ground colour

dark central spot

dark spots

white fringe

white streak

up to 1.5cm long

WINGSPAN *2.5cm.*
FLIGHT PERIOD *May–August, in successive broods in the south.*
LARVAL FOODPLANT *Rock-rose (Helianthemum) and stork's bill (Erodium).*
SIMILAR SPECIES *Northern Brown Argus (A. artaxerxes); female Common Blue (p.417).*
STATUS *Widespread and locally common.*

White-letter Hairstreak

Satyrium w-album (Lycaenidae)

As Hairstreak butterflies go, this is a rather distinctive species. Its best diagnostic feature is the white streak on the underside of the hindwing, shaped like the letter 'W'. The underwing ground colour is a rich brown and the hindwing is also marked with a fused row of submarginal, crescent-shaped orange spots. In addition to the tail streamer, a second, smaller projection can be seen on the margin.

W-shaped white streak

FOUND *invariably in the vicinity of elm trees and so occurs in mature hedgerows and along woodland margins and rides.*

dark brown ground colour

crescent-shaped orange marking

tail streamer

faint orange spot

up to 1.5cm long

WINGSPAN *3.5cm.*
FLIGHT PERIOD *July.*
LARVAL FOODPLANT *Elm (Ulmus).*
SIMILAR SPECIES *Black Hairstreak (S. pruni), which has black spots along the orange band on the hindwing underside.*
STATUS *Widespread but local; affected by the impact of Dutch Elm disease on elms.*

Small Pearl-bordered Fritillary

Boloria selene (Nymphalidae)

It would be difficult to separate this species from some of its close relatives by simply looking at its upperwings. What distinguishes them are the markings on the underside of the hindwing. In addition to the seven white pearl-like spots along the margin, which are strongly defined by black lines along their inner edge, the Small Pearl-bordered Fritillary has several silvery white spots at the centre and towards the base of the wing.

FOUND *in a variety of habitats where larval foodplants grow, from woodland, grassland, moors, and hillsides.*

orange ground colour

numerous black spots

several white spots

7 white spots on hindwing margin

up to 2cm long

WINGSPAN *4cm.*
FLIGHT PERIOD *June–July.*
LARVAL FOODPLANT *Violet (Viola).*
SIMILAR SPECIES *Pearl-bordered Fritillary (B. euphrosyne), which has a single silvery spot at the centre of its hindwing undersides.*
STATUS *Widespread and locally common, although habitat loss is affecting its numbers.*

Dark Green Fritillary

Argynnis aglaja (Nymphalidae)

This butterfly of open habitats is unaffected by strong winds and has a fast and direct flight. Fortunately, it frequently feeds on the flowers of thistle and knapweed, allowing for close-up views. Like most other Fritillaries, it has orange upperwings with dark spots. The undersides of the hindwings, however, are a distinctive green colour, marked with white spots.

INHABITS *grassy habitats from coastal dunes, to downland and open moors.*

greenish ground colour

striking white spots

up to 4cm long

orange ground colour

♂♀

crescent of 5 black spots on hindwing

numerous black spots

WINGSPAN *6–6.5cm.*
FLIGHT PERIOD *June–August.*
LARVAL FOODPLANT *Violet (Viola).*
SIMILAR SPECIES *High Brown Fritillary (A. adippe), which has buff rather than green underside hindwings that are marked with a crescent of chestnut spots.*
STATUS *Widespread and locally common.*

Silver-washed Fritillary

Argynnis paphia (Nymphalidae)

Across much of its range an experienced observer can identify a Silver-washed Fritillary, with a reasonable degree of confidence, by its size and flight pattern alone. It is a relatively large butterfly with a fast, gliding flight. A close view of a resting individual reveals the forewings to be rather angular while the hindwings are relatively large and rounded. In most specimens, the upperwings have a rich orange ground colour. By contrast, the buffish yellow and greenish underwings are marked with metallic, silvery bands – a feature that gives this butterfly its common name.

ASSOCIATED with wooded areas, favouring clearings, rides, and margins with brambles, which are a source of nectar for adult butterflies.

NOTE

The female Silver-washed Fritillary occurs in two colour forms. Typically, it resembles a duller, more heavily spotted version of the male, but in the form A. p. valesina the upperwings are greenish buff.

silvery bands

♀

orange-buff ground colour

♀

prominent black spots

up to 4cm long

angular forewings

♂

rich orange ground colour

rounded hindwings

WINGSPAN *6cm.*
FLIGHT PERIOD *June–August.*
LARVAL FOODPLANT *Violet (Viola).*
SIMILAR SPECIES *None.*
STATUS *Occurs locally in southern Britain and Ireland. Its numbers have been well-maintained over the last 30 years, and in Ireland its distribution has grown significantly.*

Small Tortoiseshell

Nymphalis urticae (Nymphalidae)

INHABITS *a variety of flowery wayside places, from fields, verges, and gardens in lowlands, to meadows on lower mountain slopes.*

The Small Tortoiseshell is one of Europe's most familiar and attractive butterflies. The colourful upperwings are mainly orange, but are boldly marked with black, yellow, and dark brown; discrete blue markings around the wing margins complete the mosaic effect. By contrast, the underwings are rather sombre and afford the butterfly a degree of camouflage when resting with its wings shut. Small Tortoiseshells appear in two or three successive broods each year; adults from the last generation of autumn hibernate over the winter months, often using attics and outhouses; they emerge again in early spring.

yellow and black markings on forewing

buffish yellow markings

orange ground colour

blue spots in margin

smoky brown ground colour

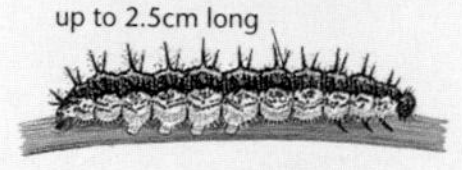

up to 2.5cm long

NOTE

If you want to attract Small Tortoiseshells to your garden, not only should you grow nectar-rich plants such as Buddleia (Buddleia) and Iceplant (Sedum spectabile) for the adults, but you must also include patches of nettle (Urtica) for the larvae.

WINGSPAN *4.2–4.5cm*
FLIGHT PERIOD *March–October, in a number of successive broods.*
LARVAL FOODPLANT *Nettle (see p.46).*
SIMILAR SPECIES *None in the British Isles.*
STATUS *Widespread and common.*

Comma

Nymphalis c-album (Nymphalidae)

This is one of the most distinctive European butterflies. The colours and shape of its wings, with ragged margins, allow recognition even in silhouette. The sombre underwings, marked with a white comma-like shape, contrast with the orange upperwings.

FOUND *in a wide range of flower-rich and way-side habitats, from verges and woodland to meadows and gardens.*

marbled brown ground colour

♂●

small white "comma" mark

up to 3.5cm long

jagged wing margin

dark markings

♂●

bright orange ground colour

WINGSPAN *4.5cm.*
FLIGHT PERIOD *March–September, in two broods; second brood adults hibernate.*
LARVAL FOODPLANT *Nettle (see p.46), hop (Humulus), and elm (Ulmus).*
SIMILAR SPECIES *None.*
STATUS *Widespread and common in Britain.*

Painted Lady

Vanessa cardui (Nymphalidae)

With its distinctively patterned salmon-pink upperwings, the Painted Lady is one of the easiest British butterflies to recognize, even on the wing. Although duller in appearance, the underwing pattern is similar to that of the upperwings. As they migrate through Britain they breed and may reach northern Scotland by late summer.

FOUND *in grassy places where flowers are in bloom, often visiting gardens on occasions.*

♂●

forewing has dark tip with white spots

salmon-pink and black pattern

submarginal eyespots

hindwing marbled grey, buffish brown, and white

●

up to 3cm long

WINGSPAN *6cm.*
FLIGHT PERIOD *April–October in the British Isles; March–November in southern Europe.*
LARVAL FOODPLANT *Thistle (Carduus/Cirsium) and Nettle (see p.46).*
SIMILAR SPECIES *None.*
STATUS *Migratory species; numbers vary from year to year; common by late summer.*

Red Admiral

Vanessa atalanta (Nymphalidae)

OCCURS *in almost any flowery habitat, from grassy meadows, verges, and hedgerows to parks and gardens.*

The fact that it is a frequent visitor to gardens, along with its bright colours and distinctive markings, makes the Red Admiral one of the Britain's most familiar butterflies. Its jet-black upperwings are marked with bands of red and white spots. The antennae have dark and light markings and a white tip.

white spots on wing tip

red hindwing margin

blue spot on hindwing base

pink patch on forewing

smoky brown hindwing

up to 3.5cm long

WINGSPAN *6cm.*	
FLIGHT PERIOD *May–October, and again in March and April after hibernation.*	
LARVAL FOODPLANT *Nettle (Urtica).*	
SIMILAR SPECIES *None.*	
STATUS *Common; it arrives from Europe early in the spring to breed, spreading throughout Britain.*	

White Admiral

Limenitis camilla (Nymphalidae)

FOUND *in mature woodland with sunny clearings and rides, and an abundance of larval foodplants.*

A widespread and familiar woodland butterfly, the White Admiral is fast-flying and alert to danger. However, it can be observed at close range if you approach it without making any sudden movements. The blackish brown upperwings are marked with distinctive white bands; the pattern of white is similar, but more extensive, on the underwings, which have a rich orange-brown ground colour.

blackish brown ground colour

orange-brown ground colour

scalloped white edging

up to 3cm long

WINGSPAN *5cm.*	
FLIGHT PERIOD *June–August.*	
LARVAL FOODPLANT *Honeysuckle (Lonicera), typically plants growing in shady settings.*	
SIMILAR SPECIES *Second-generation Map Butterflies (Araschnia levana), which have strikingly different underwings.*	
STATUS *Widespread and locally common.*	

Peacock

Nymphalis io (Nymphalidae)

Striking eyespots and gaudy colours make the Peacock an unmistakable butterfly. Like several of its colourful relatives, it is a frequent visitor to gardens, where it feeds on nectar; it is particularly fond of the flowers of buddleia and iceplant. When resting with its wings closed, the cryptic coloration of the undersides and the jagged wing margins make the species look like dead leaves or bark, affording it excellent camouflage. If startled, a resting Peacock will flash open its wings, the sudden revelation of the eyespots scaring off potential predators.

FREQUENTS *grassy and wayside habitats, from hedgerows and verges to meadows, gardens, and parks.*

marbled brown ground colour

jagged edge

up to 4cm long

NOTE

Peacock larvae live communally, constructing conspicuous silken tents on their foodplants, which are members of the nettle family. Look for these wispy structures among the clumps of nettles during summer months.

yellow, maroon, and bluish purple eyespot

reddish maroon ground colour

blue and black eyespot on hindwing

WINGSPAN *6cm.*
FLIGHT PERIOD *July–September, and after hibernation, March–May.*
LARVAL FOODPLANT *Nettle (Urtica).*
SIMILAR SPECIES *None.*
STATUS *Widespread and common. One of the commonest butterflies found in the garden.*

Small Heath

Coenonympha pamphilus (Satyridae)

Although small and not especially colourful, the Small Heath is easy to spot in the field. It can sometimes be found sitting on grass stems, allowing close inspection of the marbled grey undersurface of its hindwings and orange-brown underside of the forewings. The forewing is marked with a small, but striking black eyespot on both surfaces.

INHABITS *a range of grassy habitats, from meadows and verges, to heaths; from lower levels up to altitudes of 2,000m.*

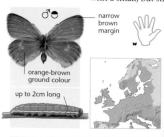

narrow brown margin

orange-brown ground colour

up to 2cm long

orange-brown forewing

black eyespot

jagged, creamy white band

marbled grey and brown hindwing

WINGSPAN *3cm.*
FLIGHT PERIOD *May–September, in successive broods.*
LARVAL FOODPLANT *Various grasses (family Poaceae), notably fescue (Festuca).*
SIMILAR SPECIES *Large Heath (C. tullia) is larger and has more eyespots on the forewing.*
STATUS *Widespread and common.*

Wall Brown

Pararge megera (Satyridae)

The boldly patterned upperwings of the Wall Brown make it a comparatively easy species to identify. It sunbathes frequently allowing excellent close-up views. The underside of the hindwings has a cryptic pattern that resembles tree bark or mottled stone, which helps the butterfly to camouflage.

FAVOURS *dry, grassy heaths, hillsides, and cliffs, typically with rocks and bare areas for sunbathing; from sea level to 2,000m.*

oblique dark band on forewing

orange-buff forewing

network of dark veins

large eyespot

orange ground colour

grey-brown marbled hindwing

orange ground colour

row of eyespots on hindwings

up to 2.5cm long

WINGSPAN *4.5cm.*
FLIGHT PERIOD *May–September, in successive broods.*
LARVAL FOODPLANT *Grasses (Poaceae).*
SIMILAR SPECIES *Speckled Wood (p.430), which has darker and more pointed upperwings.*
STATUS *Widespread but declining.*

Gatekeeper

Maniola tithonius (Satyridae)

The emergence of this familiar wayside butterfly is perceived by many naturalists to be a sign that summer is at its height. The Gatekeeper is on the wing just as bramble flowers are at their best, and groups can be seen feeding on their nectar. Its upperwings are a rich orange colour with a brown margin and an eyespot bearing twin highlights on the forewing. The underwing coloration is rather similar, although the hindwing has a more marbled appearance. Male Gatekeepers are smaller than females, with more brightly coloured wings, and have a dark sex-brand on each forewing.

FREQUENTS *meadows, grassy hedgerows, and woodland margins, typically from sea level to around 750m.*

dark patch on forewing

highlights on twin eyespot

♂●

broad brown margin with pale fringe

buffish yellow ground colour

buff-brown margin

●

up to 2cm long

NOTE

Throughout most of its range, this is the most common small- to medium-sized orange member of the Brown family, and is the species most likely to be seen feeding in groups on the flowers of bramble and other meadow and hedgerow plants.

WINGSPAN *4cm.*
FLIGHT PERIOD *July–August.*
LARVAL FOODPLANT *Various grasses (family Poaceae), such as bents (Agrostis), meadow grasses (Poa), and fescues (Festuca).*
SIMILAR SPECIES *None.*
STATUS *Widespread and common.*

Speckled Wood

Pararge aegeria (Satyridae)

This butterfly is characterized by a dark upperwing surface, marked by large, marginal, yellowish blocks and spots. Some of these have small pale centres. The upperwing surface near the body is covered with a mass of hair-like scales. The underwings are browner with eyespots around the edges.

ASSOCIATED *with woodland and typically found on the margins of sunny clearings and rides.*

eyespot on forewing

marbled hindwing with pale spots

SOUTHERN FORM

up to 2.5cm long

single eyespot on forewing

dark brown ground colour

yellow-buff spots

orange and brown ground colour

several eyespots on hindwing

WINGSPAN *4.5cm.*
FLIGHT PERIOD *March–October, in successive broods.*
LARVAL FOODPLANT *Various woodland species of grasses (family Poaceae).*
SIMILAR SPECIES *None.*
STATUS *Widespread and locally common.*

Meadow Brown

Maniola jurtina (Satyridae)

This is probably the most numerous and widespread grassland butterfly species in the region. The underwings are most commonly seen: the forewing coloured orange and buff with a striking eyespot, and the brown hindwing with a paler band containing small black spots.

FOUND *in a variety of grassy places, from meadows and roadside verges to woodland rides and hillsides up to 1,500m or more.*

orange forewings

eyespot on faint orange-buff patch

buff band with black spots

eyespot on orange band

brown ground colour

up to 2.5cm long

WINGSPAN *5cm.*
FLIGHT PERIOD *June–October.*
LARVAL FOODPLANT *Various grasses (family Poaceae), such as fescues (Festuca), bents (Agrostis), and meadow grass (Poa).*
SIMILAR SPECIES *None.*
STATUS *Widespread and locally very common.*

Ringlet

Aphantopus hyperantus (Satyridae)

This is a widespread and familiar butterfly. The upper surfaces of the wings are sooty brown; they are darkest in males, and sometimes appear almost black. Small black eyespots may or may not be visible on the upper surfaces of the wings, but the brown undersurfaces are adorned with yellow-ringed black eyespots that have white highlights.

INHABITS *grassy places from meadows, hedgerows, and verges to woodland clearings; common at low levels.*

brown ground colour

white highlights

yellow-ringed black eyespots

up to 3cm long

♂●

two faint eyespots on each wing

dark, sooty brown ground colour

WINGSPAN *4.5–5cm.*
FLIGHT PERIOD *June–July.*
LARVAL FOODPLANT *Various grasses (family Poaceae).*
SIMILAR SPECIES *None.*
STATUS *Widespread and common.*

Scotch Argus

Erebia aethiops (Satyridae)

This upland butterfly is easy to observe since it is slow-flying and often basks on vegetation. Its upperwing ground colour is rich dark brown and both wings are patterned with reddish orange bands containing eyespots with white highlights. The underside of the forewing resembles the upperside, but the hindwing is sooty brown with a lilac-grey submarginal band.

OCCURS *in grassy places in open woodland and on moors, usually between 500m and 1,500m.*

forewing underside resembles upper surface

broad lilac-grey band

♂●

eyespots with highlights

up to 2.5cm long

sooty brown ground colour

WINGSPAN *4–4.5cm.*
FLIGHT PERIOD *July–September.*
LARVAL FOODPLANT *Various grasses (family Poaceae), such as Blue Moor-grass (Sesleria caerulea) and Purple Moor-grass (Molinia caerulea).*
SIMILAR SPECIES *None.*
STATUS *Locally common.*

Marbled White

Melanargia galathea (Satyridae)

An attractive and well-marked butterfly, the Marbled White exhibits some variation in its appearance. However, typically the upperwings are pale creamy white, with an extensive pattern of linked black veins and patches. Compared to other *Melanargia* species, the proportion of black to white is evenly balanced and distributed across the wings. The pattern on the underwings is similar but many of the black markings are replaced by grey, making the wings look much paler overall. While males and females are usually alike, females often have a yellowish suffusion on the underside of the hindwing.

FAVOURS *flower-rich, grassy places such as meadows and verges; most common below 1,500m.*

pale, creamy white ground colour

grey band with eyespots

grey patches

up to 2cm long

white scalloped margin

extensive black patches and veins

WINGSPAN *5cm.*
FLIGHT PERIOD *June–August.*
LARVAL FOODPLANT *Various grasses (family Poaceae), such as Red Fescue (see p.222).*
SIMILAR SPECIES *None.*
STATUS *Widespread and locally common, typically forming discrete colonies.*

NOTE

The Marbled White is an easily recognized British species that lives mainly in the south and east of Britain, reaching as far north as Lincolnshire and east Yorkshire. Isolated colonies exist in Durham. It is thought to be colonizing new areas and extending its range.

White-shouldered House-moth

Endrosis sarcitrella (Oecophoridae)

The upperwings of this House-moth are grey-brown and heavily mottled, while its head and thorax are white. This is a common and distinctive species, often found in birds' nests, houses, and outbuildings where grain or other produce is stored. Adult moths may be seen indoors at any time of the year, and frequently come to light sources.

LIVES *in houses, barns, and outhouses; sometimes also found in old birds' nests.*

dark mottling

up to 1cm long

white head and thorax

grey-brown wings

WINGSPAN *1.3–2cm.*
TIME OF FLIGHT *Night.*
FLIGHT PERIOD *Throughout the year.*
LARVAL FOOD *Almost any vegetable matter, stored grain, wood, and birds' droppings and feathers.*
SIMILAR SPECIES *None.*
STATUS *Widespread and common.*

Green Oak Tortrix

Tortrix viridana (Tortricidae)

This moth is a member of the large family of Micro-moths known as Leaf-rollers, from the larva's habit of rolling a leaf of the foodplant into a tube in which it lives. Entirely green forewings and greyish hindwings make this Tortrix one of the more easily recognized species. It can be abundant in oak woods, and the caterpillars sometimes defoliate entire trees.

FEEDS *on the leaves of oak trees, and is common in any deciduous wood where the foodplant grows.*

reddish-brown limbs and body

wing colour blends with oak leaves

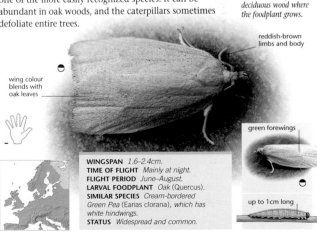

green forewings

up to 1cm long

WINGSPAN *1.6–2.4cm.*
TIME OF FLIGHT *Mainly at night.*
FLIGHT PERIOD *June–August.*
LARVAL FOODPLANT *Oak (Quercus).*
SIMILAR SPECIES *Cream-bordered Green Pea (Earias clorana), which has white hindwings.*
STATUS *Widespread and common.*

Mint Moth

Pyrausta aurata (Pyralidae)

This attractive little moth is sometimes called the Mint Moth, reflecting its main foodplant. It is most frequently seen flying in bright sunshine, but also flies at night, when it is attracted to light. It is often confused with the very similar *P. purpuralis*, but that species is usually a brighter purple, and has three distinct yellow marks forming a band across each forewing.

FOUND *wherever mint and other herbs grow: chalky downland, wetlands, wasteland, and woodland edges.*

dark purplish brown colour

single yellow spot on forewing

yellowish bar on hindwing

up to 1.5cm long

WINGSPAN *1.5–2cm.*
FLIGHT PERIOD *May–August, in two broods.*
LARVAL FOOD *Mint (Mentha), marjoram (Origanum), and other herbs.*
SIMILAR SPECIES *P. purpuralis, which is a brighter purple and has more yellow markings on the forewings.*
STATUS *Widespread and locally common.*

Twenty-plume Moth

Alucita hexadactyla (Alucitidae)

This moth gets its name from the six linked feather-like "plumes" that make up each of its wings. At rest it often adopts a triangular posture, with the plumes held tightly together, and can look like an ordinary moth until its wings are spread, revealing the individual plumes. The adult hibernates, but may fly on mild nights in the winter.

FOUND *in gardens, woodland, and commons – wherever its larval foodplant, honeysuckle, grows.*

plumes spread out

up to 0.5cm long

dark double band on forewing

feathery plumes

WINGSPAN *1.4–1.6cm.*
TIME OF FLIGHT *Night.*
FLIGHT PERIOD *Adults occur at any time of the year.*
LARVAL FOODPLANT *Honeysuckle (Lonicera).*
SIMILAR SPECIES *None.*
STATUS *Common.*

Small Magpie

Eurrhypara hortulata (Pyralidae)

One of the most attractive and familiar of the Micro-moths, the Small Magpie is easily recognized by its black and white wings, and yellow and black body. The caterpillar feeds on Nettles, and the adult moth is easily disturbed from vegetation during the day. The moth's natural time of flight is from early evening onwards, and it is attracted to light.

FREQUENTS *any habitat where Nettles grow, favouring damper areas of woodland, commons, and gardens.*

black margins

up to 2cm long

yellow and black body

white wings with black spots

WINGSPAN *3.3–3.5cm.*
FLIGHT PERIOD *May–August.*
LARVAL FOODPLANT *Common Nettle (see p.46), woundwort (Stachys), and mint (Mentha) species.*
SIMILAR SPECIES *Magpie Moth (p.442), which is much larger.*
STATUS *Widespread and common.*

Mother of Pearl

Pleuroptya ruralis (Pyralidae)

The Mother of Pearl is one of the larger Micro-moths, larger, in fact, than some of the Macro-moths. Its wings have an attractive pinkish pearly sheen, which resembles the inside of an oyster shell. Although it flies mainly at night, when it is attracted to light, it can be disturbed from Nettles during the day.

FAVOURS *areas where Nettles grow, such as gardens, wasteland, and damper woodland.*

pearly sheen

pale buff forewings

pointed wingtips

brownish markings

up to 2cm long

WINGSPAN *3.3–3.7cm.*
TIME OF FLIGHT *Night; but can be disturbed easily during the day.*
FLIGHT PERIOD *June–August.*
LARVAL FOODPLANT *Common Nettle (see p.46).*
SIMILAR SPECIES *None.*
STATUS *Widespread and common.*

White Plume-moth

Pterophorus pentadactyla (Pterophoridae)

This is the only completely white Plume moth. Although its wings are made up of feather-like plumes similar to those of the Twenty-plume Moth (p.434), the two are not closely related. Its forewings are divided into two plumes, and the hindwings into three. At rest it holds its wings outstretched. The moth flies mainly at dawn and dusk, and is often found sitting at lighted windows at night.

FOUND in grassy places, gardens, commons, hedgerows, and wherever the foodplant grows.

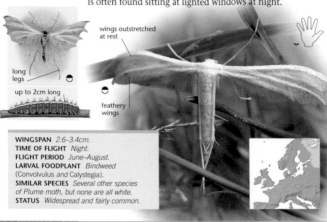

wings outstretched at rest

long legs

up to 2cm long

feathery wings

WINGSPAN 2.6–3.4cm.
TIME OF FLIGHT Night.
FLIGHT PERIOD June–August.
LARVAL FOODPLANT Bindweed (Convolvulus and Calystegia).
SIMILAR SPECIES Several other species of Plume moth, but none are all white.
STATUS Widespread and fairly common.

Pebble Hook-tip

Drepana falcataria (Drepanidae)

One of several species of moths known as Hook-tips, from the distinctive shape of their wingtips, the Pebble Hook-tip has an intricate mottled pattern on its wings, making it look like a dead leaf or a piece of bark as it rests during the day. It has a distinctive resting posture, with the forewings partly concealing the hindwings, giving the moth an almost oval outline.

FEEDS on birch; found wherever it grows, in woodland, heathland, commons, and gardens.

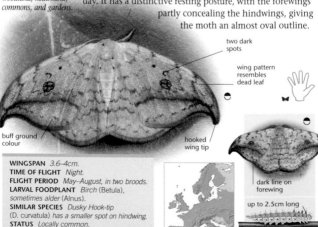

two dark spots

wing pattern resembles dead leaf

buff ground colour

hooked wing tip

dark line on forewing

up to 2.5cm long

WINGSPAN 3.6–4cm.
TIME OF FLIGHT Night.
FLIGHT PERIOD May–August, in two broods.
LARVAL FOODPLANT Birch (Betula), sometimes alder (Alnus).
SIMILAR SPECIES Dusky Hook-tip (D. curvatula) has a smaller spot on hindwing.
STATUS Locally common.

Six-spot Burnet

Zygaena filipendulae (Zygaenidae)

This attractive day-flying species can be told apart from the similar Five-spot Burnet (*Z. trifolii*) by the presence of three pairs of red spots on an iridescent greenish black or bluish green background. The hindwings, revealed in flight, are the same bright crimson-red as the forewing spots. All species of burnet moth contain cyanide, and have bright colours warning predators they are toxic. However, despite this fact, they are occasionally eaten by birds. A rare colour variant of this moth has the red areas of the wings replaced by yellow instead. The papery cocoon may be found on the foodplant after the moth has emerged.

INHABITS *downland, meadows, woodland rides, and other flower-rich places; also cliff tops and sand hills.*

NOTE

The extra red spot which separates this species from the Five-spot Burnet is at the tip of the forewing, making up three distinct pairs of spots.

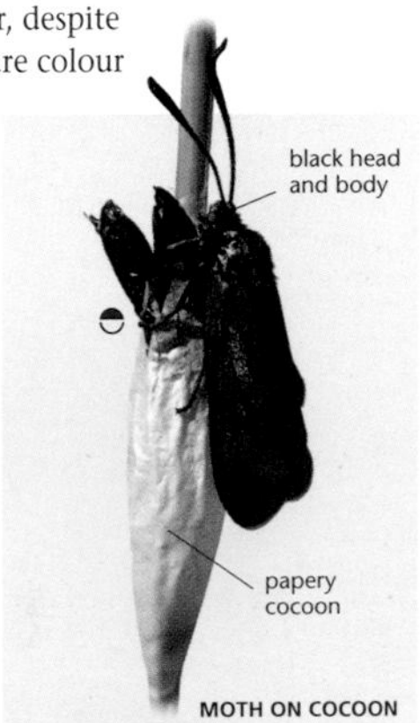

black head and body

papery cocoon

MOTH ON COCOON

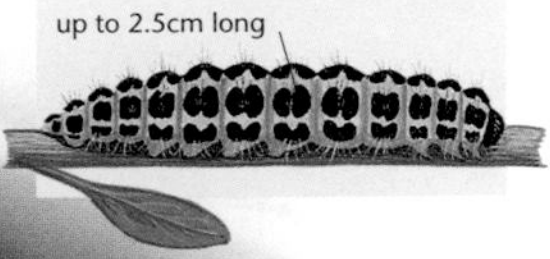

thick, clubbed antennae

up to 2.5cm long

3 pairs of red spots on forewing

iridescent blue-green ground colour

WINGSPAN *2.5–4cm.*
FLIGHT PERIOD *June–August.*
LARVAL FOODPLANT *Bird's-foot Trefoil (see p.95).*
SIMILAR SPECIES *Five-spot Burnet (Z. trifolii), which has fewer red spots on its forewing; Cinnabar (p.447).*
STATUS *Widespread and fairly common.*

Green Pug

Pasiphila rectangulata (Geometridae)

When freshly emerged, the Green Pug usually lives up to its name, with a distinctly green coloration on its wings. However, this colour quickly fades. Some specimens may also be darker, occasionally almost black. The Green Pug is strongly attracted to light, and is often found at windows or in moth traps after dark.

INHABITS *orchards and other places where fruit trees grow, such as gardens, woodland, and commons.*

wavy lines on forewing

greenish ground colour

DARKER FORM

dark line at centre of forewing

up to 1.5cm long

WINGSPAN *1.7–2.1cm.*
TIME OF FLIGHT *Night.*
FLIGHT PERIOD *June–July.*
LARVAL FOODPLANT *Flowers of fruit trees.*
SIMILAR SPECIES *V-Pug (Chloroclystis v-ata), which has a black "V" on forewings; Sloe Pug (P. chloerata), which is less green.*
STATUS *Widespread and common.*

Latticed Heath

Chiasmia clathrata (Geometridae)

On first sight, the Latticed Heath could be mistaken for a Skipper butterfly, particularly the Grizzled Skipper (p.411). However, a close view will show that the moth is usually browner, while the Grizzled Skipper is more black and white. A rather variable moth – some specimens are darker or lighter than the typical form.

FAVOURS *a wide variety of habitats, including meadows, heathland, commons, and open woodland.*

wings often held closed

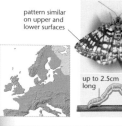

pattern similar on upper and lower surfaces

up to 2.5cm long

buff or whitish background

WINGSPAN *2.6–3.2cm.*
FLIGHT PERIOD *May–September, two broods.*
LARVAL FOODPLANT *Various clovers and trefoils (Trifolium/Lotus); also Lucerne (see p.92).*
SIMILAR SPECIES *Grizzled Skipper (p.411), Dingy Skipper (p.410).*
STATUS *Widespread and locally common.*

Garden Carpet

Xanthorhoe fluctuata (Geometridae)

The Garden Carpet may be distinguished from other small geometrid moths by the dark patch across the forewings, which extends only halfway across the wing. A common moth, even in suburban areas, it may be found during the day resting on walls, trees, or fences. It flies at dusk, and is attracted to light.

APPEARS *in various habitats with flowers, including gardens, commons, waste ground, and hedgerows.*

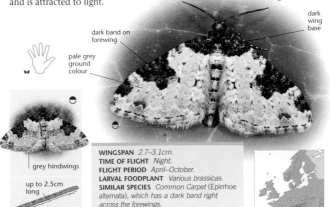

dark wing base

dark band on forewing

pale grey ground colour

grey hindwings

up to 2.5cm long

WINGSPAN *2.7–3.1cm.*
TIME OF FLIGHT *Night.*
FLIGHT PERIOD *April–October.*
LARVAL FOODPLANT *Various brassicas.*
SIMILAR SPECIES *Common Carpet (Epirrhoe alternata), which has a dark band right across the forewings.*
STATUS *Widespread and common.*

Winter Moth

Operophtera brumata (Geometridae)

The Winter Moth, as its common name suggests, flies only during the winter months. As is the case with several other geometrids, only the male moth flies; the female is almost wingless, and rather spider-like in appearance. Both sexes may be found after dark sitting on tree trunks, and the male is often seen at lighted windows on mild nights.

FOUND *wherever there are deciduous trees and shrubs. This species can be a serious pest in orchards.*

plain underside

♂

pale grey-brown ground colour

♂

faintly darker bands

up to 2cm long

WINGSPAN *2.8–3.3cm.*
TIME OF FLIGHT *Night.*
FLIGHT PERIOD *November–February.*
LARVAL FOODPLANT *Oak (Quercus), birch (Betula), sallow (Salix), and apple (Malus).*
SIMILAR SPECIES *Northern Winter Moth (O. fagata), which is larger and paler.*
STATUS *Widespread and common.*

Speckled Yellow

Pseudopanthera macularia (Geometridae)

An attractive, day-flying species, the Speckled Yellow typically lives up to its common name, although the ground colour is variable, and some individuals may be cream or almost white. It prefers warmer climates, and is commoner in the south of its European range, but may be found in mountainous areas.

OCCURS *in open woodland and scrubland, both in lowland and mountainous regions.*

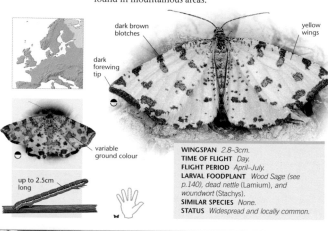

dark brown blotches

dark forewing tip

yellow wings

variable ground colour

up to 2.5cm long

WINGSPAN *2.8–3cm.*
TIME OF FLIGHT *Day.*
FLIGHT PERIOD *April–July.*
LARVAL FOODPLANT *Wood Sage (see p.140), dead nettle (Lamium), and woundwort (Stachys).*
SIMILAR SPECIES *None.*
STATUS *Widespread and locally common.*

Brimstone Moth

Opisthograptis luteolata (Geometridae)

This bright yellow geometrid moth sometimes flies by day, when it may be mistaken for a butterfly. More usually, it flies from dusk onwards, and is a common visitor to moth traps and lighted windows. This moth usually has several reddish brown marks along the leading edge of the wing, but occasional plain yellow specimens may also be found.

FOUND *in hedgerows, gardens, covered bushy places, as well as open woodland.*

unmarked hindwing

up to 3cm long

bright yellow wings

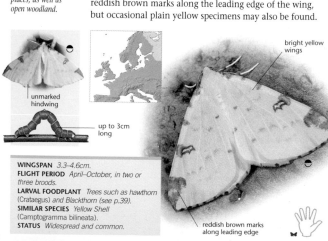

WINGSPAN *3.3–4.6cm.*
FLIGHT PERIOD *April–October, in two or three broods.*
LARVAL FOODPLANT *Trees such as hawthorn (Crataegus) and Blackthorn (see p.39).*
SIMILAR SPECIES *Yellow Shell (Camptogramma bilineata).*
STATUS *Widespread and common.*

reddish brown marks along leading edge

Blood-vein

Timandra comai (Geometridae)

The Blood-vein is a rather delicate moth with pointed tips to both the forewings and hindwings. At rest, the reddish lines on each wing join up to form a continuous stripe. The sexes are similar, but the male can be distinguished by its feathered antennae.

FREQUENTS *a wide range of habitats, including wasteland, commons, gardens, field margins, and meadows.*

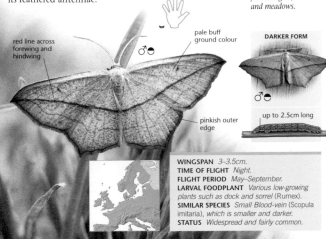

red line across forewing and hindwing

pale buff ground colour

♂●

DARKER FORM

♂●

pinkish outer edge

up to 2.5cm long

WINGSPAN *3–3.5cm.*
TIME OF FLIGHT *Night.*
FLIGHT PERIOD *May–September.*
LARVAL FOODPLANT *Various low-growing plants such as dock and sorrel (Rumex).*
SIMILAR SPECIES *Small Blood-vein (Scopula imitaria), which is smaller and darker.*
STATUS *Widespread and fairly common.*

Purple Thorn

Selenia tetralunaria (Geometridae)

The group of geometrid moths known as Thorns rest with their wings raised. The Purple Thorn can be told from similar species by its habit of holding its wings half open over its back. The moth has two, sometimes three broods each year, the later generations usually being smaller and darker than the spring brood.

OCCURS *in deciduous woodland; also in parks, gardens, and commons.*

pale "half moon" mark

●

up to 4.5cm long

●

chestnut-tipped forewing

dark brown band

horizontal bands of buff and brown

WINGSPAN *4.5–5.2cm.*
TIME OF FLIGHT *Night.*
FLIGHT PERIOD *April–August.*
LARVAL FOODPLANT *Oak (Quercus), birch (Betula), and alder (Alnus).*
SIMILAR SPECIES *Early Thorn (Selenia dentaria), which is paler.*
STATUS *Widespread and fairly common.*

Magpie Moth

Abraxas grossulariata (Geometridae)

FOUND *in gardens and allotments where currant and Gooseberry are grown; also in hedgerows and open deciduous woodland.*

This strikingly marked species is highly variable, with some forms showing very few black spots, and others being almost entirely black. However, these aberrations are usually the result of captive breeding, and are very rarely seen in the wild. The bold patterning suggests that the moth is distasteful, and serves as a warning to predators. Interestingly, the caterpillar has a similar pattern of black spots on a whitish body, and a reddish stripe along the sides. It may be a pest on currant and Gooseberry bushes.

yellow and black thorax and abdomen

yellow S-shaped line

DARKER FORM

large black patches

LIGHTER FORM

fewer black spots

white ground colour

black spots

up to 3.5cm long

NOTE

The caterpillar of the Magpie Moth is just as variable in its coloration as the adult moth. While most caterpillars are whitish with black spots, some are darker, or even completely black as in the case of the adult.

WINGSPAN *4.2–4.8cm.*
TIME OF FLIGHT *Night (occasionally day).*
FLIGHT PERIOD *July–August.*
LARVAL FOODPLANT *Currant (Ribes), Gooseberry (Ribes uva-crispa), Blackthorn (see p.39), and Hazel (see p.29).*
SIMILAR SPECIES *Small Magpie (p.435), which is much smaller and belongs to the Micro-moth group.*
STATUS *Widespread and common.*

Light Emerald

Campaea margaritata (Geometridae)

The Light Emerald's green coloration quickly fades almost to white. However, the pattern of two greenish brown lines bordered by white is usually visible, making this moth easy to identify, while a newly-emerged moth has small red-brown wing-tips. The females are larger than the males.

FOUND *in gardens, parks, woodland, hedgerows, and commons.*

faded colours

OLDER SPECIMEN

greenish white ground colour

up to 4cm long

WINGSPAN *4–5.5cm.*	
TIME OF FLIGHT *Night.*	
FLIGHT PERIOD *July–September.*	
LARVAL FOODPLANT *Oak (Quercus), birch (Betula), and hawthorn (Crataegus).*	
SIMILAR SPECIES *Large Emerald (Geometra papilionaria).*	
STATUS *Widespread and common.*	

Swallow-tailed Moth

Ourapteryx sambucaria (Geometridae)

This large, pale yellow moth has a very distinctive shape, and should not be confused with any other British species. The hindwings have projecting "tails" reminiscent of the Swallowtail Butterfly (p.412), and the forewings are also sharply pointed. This moth is strongly attracted to light, and is frequently found resting on lighted windows after dark.

OCCURS *in woodland, gardens, parks, hedgerows, and commons.*

brown lines across forewings

pointed tails on hindwings

pointed forewings

up to 5.5cm long

WINGSPAN *5–6.2cm.*	
TIME OF FLIGHT *Night.*	
FLIGHT PERIOD *June–July.*	
LARVAL FOODPLANT *Various trees and plants, including hawthorn (Crataegus), ivy (Hedera), and privet (Ligustrum).*	
SIMILAR SPECIES *None.*	
STATUS *Fairly common.*	

Peppered Moth

Biston betularia (Geometridae)

The Peppered Moth has three distinct forms – light, intermediate, and dark – and is often cited as an example of natural selection. In industrial areas, where tree trunks are blackened with soot, the lighter moths are highly visible to birds, and therefore eaten more often. The darker forms, however, are camouflaged, resulting in less predation; thus more dark moths survive to pass on their genes to their offspring. On the other hand, recent studies have shown how the darker form has become less common in areas formerly blighted by pollution, but where the situation has improved once clean air laws have taken effect. Both sexes fly at night and are strongly attracted to light.

FREQUENTS *woodland, gardens, parks, hedgerows, and commons, where there are trees for the caterpillar to feed on.*

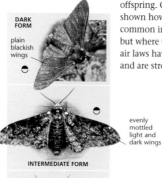

DARK FORM

plain blackish wings

evenly mottled light and dark wings

INTERMEDIATE FORM

LIGHTER FORM

lightly mottled wings

up to 6cm long

whitish background

NOTE
The three forms are genetically distinct from one another. The intermediate form cannot be reproduced by crossing the light form with the dark form. All three forms may occur in the same area, but one will usually predominate over the other two. The intermediate form is generally the least common.

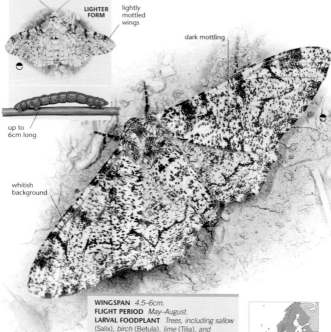

dark mottling

WINGSPAN *4.5–6cm.*
FLIGHT PERIOD *May–August.*
LARVAL FOODPLANT *Trees, including sallow (Salix), birch (Betula), lime (Tilia), and hawthorn (Crataegus).*
SIMILAR SPECIES *Brindled Beauty (Lycia hirtaria), which is more buff and brown.*
STATUS *Widespread and common.*

Yellow-tail

Euproctis similis (Lymantriidae)

The Yellow-tail contains irritating chemicals at all stages of its life cycle, which can cause a severe allergic reaction in some people if they are touched. The adult moth has an unusual defensive posture: if disturbed, it lies on its side, with its yellow-tipped abdomen projecting beyond the trailing edge of the wings. The males have small dark marks on the forewings, while the females' wings are pure white.

INHABITS *hedgerows, scrub, and other areas with bushy vegetation, where there is plenty of larval foodplant available.*

small dark marks

♂♀
furry body
display of yellow-tipped abdomen
up to 4.5cm long

white ground colour
♂♀
small dark marks

WINGSPAN *3.5–4.5cm.*
FLIGHT PERIOD *July–August.*
LARVAL FOODPLANT *Hawthorn (Crataegus), Blackthorn (see p.39), sallow (Salix), and other trees and shrubs.*
SIMILAR SPECIES *Brown-tail (Euproctis chrysorrhoea); White Satin (Leucoma salicis).*
STATUS *Widespread and generally common.*

Common Footman

Eilema lurideola (Arctiidae)

This moth rests with its long thin forewings folded flat over its back. However, if seen in flight, it appears much larger, owing to its broad yellowish hindwings. Flying from dusk onwards, it may be found feeding at thistle flowers (*Cirsium* and *Carduus*) or Traveller's Joy *(Clematis vitalba)*. Like most members of the "Footman" family, the larvae feed on lichens.

FOUND *in hedgerows, gardens, and open woodland, wherever there are lichen-covered trees for the larvae to feed on.*

long, thin forewings

pale yellow leading edge

yellow-grey ground colour

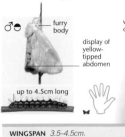

broad yellowish hindwings
up to 2.5cm long

WINGSPAN *3.1–3.8cm.*
FLIGHT PERIOD *July–August.*
LARVAL FOODPLANT *Lichens growing on trees, walls, fences, or rocks.*
SIMILAR SPECIES *Scarce Footman (Eilema complana), which rests with its wings rolled around its body.*
STATUS *Widespread and common.*

Ruby Tiger

Phragmatobia fuliginosa (Arctiidae)

One of the smaller members of its family, the Ruby Tiger has plain reddish brown forewings with two small blackish dots. The hindwings vary from orange-red with dark markings to plain black. This moth flies mainly at night, when it often comes to light, but may sometimes be found flying on sunny days.

OCCURS *in waste ground, gardens, commons, heathland, and moorland.*

red-brown ground colour

furry head and thorax

red and black hindwings

blackish spots

plain forewings

up to 3.5cm long

WINGSPAN *2.8–3.8cm.*
FLIGHT PERIOD *April–September, in two broods.*
LARVAL FOODPLANT *Various plants, including dock (Rumex) and dandelion (Taraxacum).*
SIMILAR SPECIES *None.*
STATUS *Widespread and common.*

White Ermine

Spilosoma lubricipeda (Arctiidae)

This attractive species is very variable – typical specimens have small black spots evenly scattered over the white forewings, but some may have larger or smaller spots. Occasionally, individuals may be seen with much more black, the spots being joined up to form bars. The ground colour also varies, some moths being more buff-coloured.

FREQUENTS *a wide variety of habitats, as the caterpillar is not at all fussy about what foodplants it feeds on.*

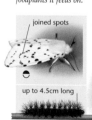

joined spots

up to 4.5cm long

furry head and thorax

white forewings

many black spots

WINGSPAN *3.8–4.8cm.*
TIME OF FLIGHT *Night.*
FLIGHT PERIOD *May–July.*
LARVAL FOODPLANT *Various plants.*
SIMILAR SPECIES *Water Ermine (Spilosoma urticae), which has two black spots on each forewing.*
STATUS *Widespread and common.*

The Cinnabar

Tyria jacobaeae (Arctiidae)

This distinctive and familiar species is sometimes seen flying by day, when the bright crimson hindwings draw attention to it. At rest, the crimson hindwings are concealed beneath the forewings, which are glossy dark grey, with red lines and spots. Unlike most members of its family, the caterpillars are gregarious, and can be found in large numbers on ragwort (*Senecio*) plants.

SEEN *wherever ragwort and groundsel grow; on waste ground, commons, and meadows.*

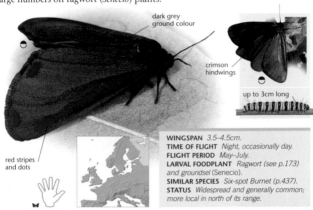

dark grey ground colour

crimson hindwings

up to 3cm long

red stripes and dots

WINGSPAN *3.5–4.5cm.*
TIME OF FLIGHT *Night, occasionally day.*
FLIGHT PERIOD *May–July.*
LARVAL FOODPLANT *Ragwort (see p.173) and groundsel (Senecio).*
SIMILAR SPECIES *Six-spot Burnet (p.437).*
STATUS *Widespread and generally common; more local in north of its range.*

Garden Tiger

Arctia caja (Arctiidae)

The large and strikingly-marked Garden Tiger has declined dramatically in many parts of its range in recent years. The complex pattern of dark brown and cream on the forewings varies from moth to moth. The contrasting hindwings are a bright orange ground colour with prominent black spots. Also orange, the abdomen is marked with black bars.

INHABITS *gardens, parks, commons, waste ground, and any habitat where low plants grow.*

cream ground colour

reddish brown head

exposed orange hindwings

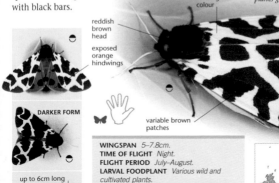

DARKER FORM

variable brown patches

up to 6cm long

WINGSPAN *5–7.8cm.*
TIME OF FLIGHT *Night.*
FLIGHT PERIOD *July–August.*
LARVAL FOODPLANT *Various wild and cultivated plants.*
SIMILAR SPECIES *None.*
STATUS *Widespread, but not as common as it once was.*

The Vapourer

Orgyia antiqua (Lymantriidae)

FREQUENTS *a wide variety of habitats, including gardens, woodland, commons, and urban areas.*

The red-brown male Vapourers are often seen flying rapidly in sunshine, but the females are wingless and rarely move far from the cocoon after hatching. Males also fly at night, and are attracted to light. The larvae have red and yellow tufts, and black and brown hairs, which can cause irritation if handled.

plain hindwings

WINGLESS FEMALE

fat, furry body ♀

white spots on forewing

up to 4cm long

red-brown ground colour

WINGSPAN	*3.5–4cm.*

TIME OF FLIGHT *Day and night.*
FLIGHT PERIOD *July–October, in two broods.*
LARVAL FOODPLANT *Many deciduous trees and shrubs.*
SIMILAR SPECIES *Scarce Vapourer (O. recens) has a white mark at forewing tip.*
STATUS *Widespread and common.*

Puss Moth

Cerura vinula (Notodontidae)

INHABITS *hedgerows, open woodland, parks, and gardens; also found at watersides, where the larval foodplants, grow.*

This large and attractive moth is tinged with a delicate green when freshly emerged. However, this colour quickly fades to a lighter shade. The white forewings of the adult moth are patterned with black lines. The caterpillar is one of the most extraordinary of the moth world. It has a large head, and two red-tipped "tails", which are actually modified hindlegs.

buff veins

black spots on thorax

intricate pattern of black lines

FRESHLY EMERGED
greenish tinge to wings

greyish white ground colour

furry head and thorax

zig-zag markings

red-tipped hindlegs up to 6.5cm long

WINGSPAN *6–8cm.*
TIME OF FLIGHT *Night.*
FLIGHT PERIOD *May–July.*
LARVAL FOODPLANT *Poplar (Populus) and sallow (Salix).*
SIMILAR SPECIES *None.*
STATUS *Widespread and fairly common throughout.*

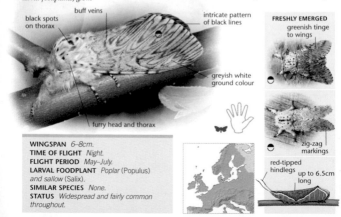

Buff-tip

Phalera bucephala (Notodontidae)

A superbly camouflaged species, the Buff-tip almost perfectly resembles a broken-off birch twig. At rest, the moth's wings are rolled around its body in a tubular shape, with the pale hindwings concealed. Most of the forewing is an intricately mottled silvery grey, with delicate black and brown lines running across it; the wingtips are a contrasting pale buff, as are the fluffy head and thorax. Like all the members of this family, the adult moths have no proboscis, and so do not feed. The Buff-tip tends to fly late at night, when it is attracted to light.

OCCUPIES *hedgerows, gardens, and open woodland, wherever there are trees for the caterpillars to feed on.*

NOTE

The yellow and black Buff-tip caterpillars are gregarious at first, later becoming solitary before pupation. They often cause severe damage to trees by stripping the leaves off branches.

scalloped forewing margins

furry buff head and thorax

up to 7.5cm long

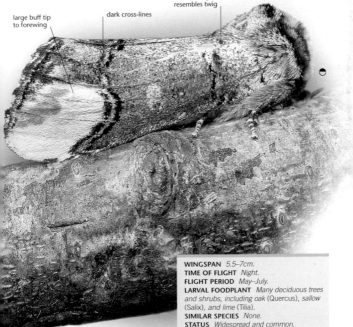

large buff tip to forewing

dark cross-lines

tubular shape resembles twig

WINGSPAN *5.5–7cm.*
TIME OF FLIGHT *Night.*
FLIGHT PERIOD *May–July.*
LARVAL FOODPLANT *Many deciduous trees and shrubs, including oak (Quercus), sallow (Salix), and lime (Tilia).*
SIMILAR SPECIES *None.*
STATUS *Widespread and common.*

Common Rustic

Mesapamea secalis (Noctuidae)

The Common Rustic, the Lesser Common Rustic (*M. didyma*), and the very rare Remm's Rustic (*M. remmi*) are very closely related species. All three are so similar that they can only be identified on the structure of the genitalia, which requires dissection by experts. As a general rule, however, the Lesser Common Rustic is smaller and darker than the other two.

OCCURS *in a wide range of grassy habitats, such as meadows, commons, gardens, and heathland.*

DARKER FORM

MOTTLED LIGHT AND DARK BROWN FORM

PLAIN BROWN FORM

whitish spot on forewing

up to 3cm long

mottled ground colour

dark brown ground colour

lacks white spot on forewing

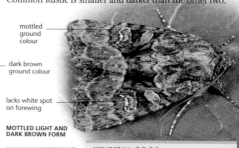

WINGSPAN 2.8–3.6cm.	
TIME OF FLIGHT *Night.*	
FLIGHT PERIOD *July–August.*	
LARVAL FOODPLANT *Various grasses (family Poaceae).*	
SIMILAR SPECIES *Lesser Common Rustic (M. didyma) and Remm's Rustic (M. remmi).*	
STATUS *Widespread and often abundant.*	

Mother Shipton

Callistege mi (Noctuidae)

This day-flying species is often found in the same habitats as Dingy (p.410) and Grizzled Skipper (p.411) butterflies, and may be mistaken for them in flight. At rest, however, its wing patterns are quite different. The moth gets its common name, Mother Shipton, from a legendary witch whose profile, with its long, hooked nose and pointed chin, is said to be reflected in the markings.

INHABITS *grassy places such as downland, meadows and heaths; also open woodland and marshes.*

"chin of witch's profile"

complex light and dark pattern

white-spotted hindwings

up to 4cm long

WINGSPAN 3–3.5cm.	
TIME OF FLIGHT *Day.*	
FLIGHT PERIOD *May–June.*	
LARVAL FOODPLANT *Clover (Trifolium).*	
SIMILAR SPECIES *Grizzled Skipper (p.411) and Dingy Skipper (p.410) butterflies are often mistaken for moths.*	
STATUS *Locally common.*	

Hebrew Character

Orthosia gothica (Noctuidae)

A very common moth, the Hebrew Character occurs in almost all habitats, including mountainous regions and within the Arctic Circle. Although it emerges to feed on sallow blossom after dark, it is also attracted to light. The black C-shaped mark is absent in some specimens, and the colour of the wings ranges from grey to red-brown.

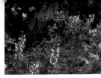

FREQUENTS *almost every possible habitat; particularly common in gardens.*

C-shaped mark on both wings

grey-brown ground colour

brown margin

PALER FORM

up to 4.5cm long

WINGSPAN *3–4cm.*
TIME OF FLIGHT *Night.*
FLIGHT PERIOD *March–May.*
LARVAL FOODPLANT *Trees and shrubs.*
SIMILAR SPECIES *Setaceous Hebrew Character (Xestia c-nigrum), which is larger, darker, and flies later in the year.*
STATUS *Widespread and common.*

Common Wainscot

Mythimna pallens (Noctuidae)

This is a rather plain species, with few distinguishing marks. The colour of the forewings varies from pale yellow to a darker orange-buff, on which the pale veins stand out more clearly. The hindwings are always white. It may be found resting on grass stems after dark, or feeding at flowers, and is strongly attracted to light.

OCCUPIES *grassy habitats, such as meadows, commons, heaths, marshes, and gardens.*

pale veins

DARKER FORM

pale yellow ground colour

orange-buff wings

up to 4.5cm long

WINGSPAN *3–4cm.*
TIME OF FLIGHT *Night.*
FLIGHT PERIOD *June–October.*
LARVAL FOODPLANT *Various grasses (family Poaceae).*
SIMILAR SPECIES *Smoky Wainscot (M. impura), which has grey hindwings.*
STATUS *Widespread and common.*

Common Quaker

Orthosia cerasi (Noctuidae)

One of the commonest of the spring-flying species, this moth can be abundant in deciduous woodland. Like many species that emerge early in the year, it feeds at sallow blossom after dark, and is drawn to light. The colour of the forewings varies from light brown to dark reddish brown.

PREFERS *deciduous woodland, but also found in gardens, parks, and hedgerows.*

PALER FORM

DARKER FORM

up to 4cm long

2 pale rings on brown forewings

pale line at rear

diffused dark line

WINGSPAN *3.5–4cm.*
TIME OF FLIGHT *Night.*
FLIGHT PERIOD *March–April.*
LARVAL FOODPLANT *Trees, including oak (Quercus) and sallow (Salix).*
SIMILAR SPECIES *Powdered Quaker (O. gracilis); Small Quaker (O. cruda).*
STATUS *Widespread and common.*

Heart and Dart

Agrotis exclamationis (Noctuidae)

One of the commonest British moths, the Heart and Dart is found in a wide range of habitats. The ground colour of the forewings ranges from light brown to dark brown, but the markings, a blackish "heart" and "dart" on each wing are fairly constant. The hindwings are pure white in colour. It feeds at flowers after dark, and is a very frequent visitor to moth traps.

FOUND *in almost every possible habitat as the larvae feed on a wide variety of plants; a particularly common garden species.*

dart-like mark

heart-shaped mark

black band

grey-brown ground colour

DARKER FORM

up to 4cm long

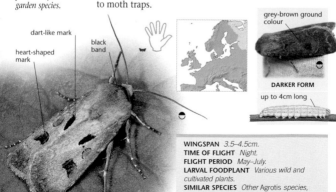

WINGSPAN *3.5–4.5cm.*
TIME OF FLIGHT *Night.*
FLIGHT PERIOD *May–July.*
LARVAL FOODPLANT *Various wild and cultivated plants.*
SIMILAR SPECIES *Other Agrotis species, which lack the "heart and dart" markings.*
STATUS *Widespread and often abundant.*

Grey Dagger

Acronicta psi (Noctuidae)

The Grey Dagger forms a species pair with the Dark Dagger (*A. tridens*). The two are so similar as adults that they can reliably be told apart only by examining the genitalia. The hindwings may offer a clue to the moth's identity; those of the Dark Dagger are usually, but not always, pure white rather than off-white. The forewings of both species have a complex pattern of black markings on a grey background.

APPEARS *mainly in deciduous woodland; also hedgerows, parks, and gardens, and wherever there are trees for larvae to feed on.*

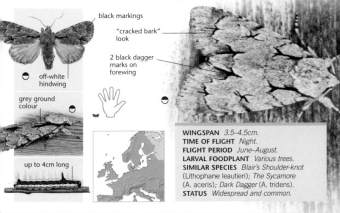

off-white hindwing

grey ground colour

black markings

"cracked bark" look

2 black dagger marks on forewing

up to 4cm long

WINGSPAN *3.5–4.5cm.*
TIME OF FLIGHT *Night.*
FLIGHT PERIOD *June–August.*
LARVAL FOODPLANT *Various trees.*
SIMILAR SPECIES *Blair's Shoulder-knot (Lithophane leautieri); The Sycamore (A. aceris); Dark Dagger (A. tridens).*
STATUS *Widespread and common.*

Angle Shades

Phlogophora meticulosa (Noctuidae)

The Angle Shades folds its wings in a unique way when at rest, giving it the appearance of a dried, dead leaf. The colour of the wings varies from olive-green to reddish brown, but the pattern is fairly constant. Some individuals migrate north each year, swelling the numbers of resident moths in northern Europe.

FOUND *in gardens, woodland, commons, and urban areas; not tied to any particular habitat as it feeds on a variety of plants.*

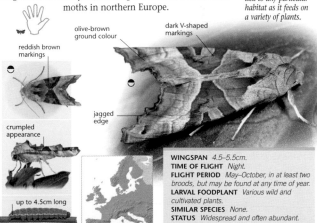

reddish brown markings

olive-brown ground colour

dark V-shaped markings

jagged edge

crumpled appearance

up to 4.5cm long

WINGSPAN *4.5–5.5cm.*
TIME OF FLIGHT *Night.*
FLIGHT PERIOD *May–October, in at least two broods, but may be found at any time of year.*
LARVAL FOODPLANT *Various wild and cultivated plants.*
SIMILAR SPECIES *None.*
STATUS *Widespread and often abundant.*

Dark Arches

Apamea monoglypha (Noctuidae)

This large brownish moth is very common throughout Britain and Europe, and is found in a wide variety of habitats. The forewings vary in colour from medium brown to almost black, the lighter forms having darker and lighter blotches and lines. Dark Arches is attracted to flowers such as Red Valerian (see p.160), and is also attracted to light.

INHABITS *a variety of grassy areas such as meadows, moorland, downland, and commons.*

mottled wings

dark line at wing margin

blackish ground colour

DARKER FORM

up to 4.5cm long

WINGSPAN *4.6–5.4cm.*
TIME OF FLIGHT *Night.*
FLIGHT PERIOD *June–October, in two broods.*
LARVAL FOODPLANT *Various grasses (family* Poaceae*).*
SIMILAR SPECIES *Large Nutmeg (A. anceps), which is smaller.*
STATUS *Widespread and often abundant.*

Silver Y

Autographa gamma (Noctuidae)

One of the great migrants of the insect world, the Silver Y sometimes arrives from warmer areas in vast numbers in spring and early summer to breed in northern Europe, including Britain. The species cannot survive the winter here, and caterpillars, pupae, and adults are all killed by the first frosts. The adult moth is active by day and night, and can be found feeding at flowers, especially at dusk.

FOUND *in almost every possible habitat in temperate climates, as the larvae feed on a variety of plants.*

double crest on thorax

mottled grey and brown ground colour

silver Y marking on forewing

scalloped wing margin

dark outer edge

up to 4cm long

WINGSPAN *3.5–5cm.*
TIME OF FLIGHT *Night and day.*
FLIGHT PERIOD *May–October.*
LARVAL FOODPLANT *Feeds on a wide variety of herbaceous plants.*
SIMILAR SPECIES *Beautiful Golden Y (A. pulchrina), which is browner.*
STATUS *Widespread and often abundant.*

Large Yellow Underwing

Noctua pronuba (Noctuidae)

This is one of the commonest and most widespread moths in Europe, occurring in almost all habitats. In some years, numbers at light traps may run into hundreds, or even thousands. The forewing colour is variable, ranging from light brown with dark markings to a uniform dark brown, with males tending to have darker wings than females.

FOUND *in almost every possible habitat as the larvae feed on a wide variety of plants; a particularly common garden species.*

Although most large moths have to warm up their wings by rapidly vibrating them before taking flight, the Large Yellow Underwing is able to take flight instantly without doing so. This sudden flight exposes the yellow and black hindwings, which scare off potential predators.

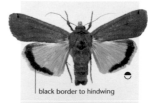

black border to hindwing

NOTE

The Large Yellow Underwing is the largest of several similar species with yellow and black hindwings. The Lesser Broad-bordered Yellow Underwing (N. janthe) has orange hindwings with broader black borders.

paler ground colour

♀ ●

up to 5.5cm long

black mark near forewing tip

yellow and black hindwing

●

dark patches on forewing

WINGSPAN *5–6cm.*
TIME OF FLIGHT *Night.*
FLIGHT PERIOD *June–September.*
LARVAL FOODPLANT *Various plants, including grasses.*
SIMILAR SPECIES *Lesser Yellow Underwing (N. comes), which is smaller; Lesser Broad-bordered Yellow Underwing (N. janthe), which has orange hindwings; several other Yellow Underwing species.*
STATUS *Widespread and often abundant.*

Old Lady

Mormo maura (Noctuidae)

The upper wings of this large moth are banded in mottled greys and browns and have a serrated fringe. The Old Lady flies at night, when it feeds on tree sap and honeydew, and it can be recognized by its slow, lazy flight with deep flaps of its broad wings. By day, it hides in dark places, such as sheds, or in hollow trees, especially near water.

INHABITS *a wide variety of habitats, including open woodland, gardens, parks, commons, and open countryside.*

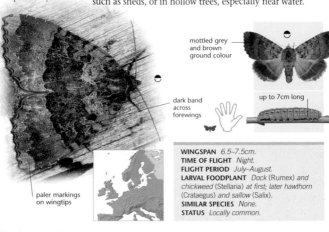

mottled grey and brown ground colour

dark band across forewings

up to 7cm long

paler markings on wingtips

WINGSPAN 6.5–7.5cm.
TIME OF FLIGHT *Night.*
FLIGHT PERIOD *July–August.*
LARVAL FOODPLANT *Dock* (Rumex) *and chickweed* (Stellaria) *at first; later hawthorn* (Crataegus) *and sallow* (Salix).
SIMILAR SPECIES *None.*
STATUS *Locally common.*

Ghost Moth

Hepialus humuli (Hepialidae)

Also known as the Ghost Swift, this is a member of one of the most primitive groups of moths, characterized by long wings and very short antennae. The males, which are pure white, may be seen in large groups hovering in a ghostly fashion over vegetation at dusk. The yellowish females are generally larger and have a pinkish brown pattern on the forewings.

FREQUENTS *grassy places such as field margins, meadows, and gardens. Also found in arable fields.*

wing veins on forewing and hindwing

silvery white wings

♂ ⬤

yellowish thorax

pinkish brown ♀ ⬤ patterns

yellowish ground colour

up to 3.5cm long

WINGSPAN 4.5–5cm.
TIME OF FLIGHT *Night.*
FLIGHT PERIOD *June–August.*
LARVAL FOODPLANT *Grasses (family Poaceae) and several other plants, including crops.*
SIMILAR SPECIES *None.*
STATUS *Widespread and generally common.*

Emperor Moth

Saturnia pavonia (Saturniidae)

The males of this spectacular moth may be seen flying in sunshine. The larger females fly at dusk, and are sometimes attracted to light. The males have feathery antennae and both sexes have large and conspicuous eyespots on all four wings. In the resting position, the hindwings of the Emperor Moth are concealed; the spots on the forewings, combined with the dark brown thorax, give the impression of the eyes and snout of a small mammal, which may deter birds from attacking it.

INHABITS *a variety of habitats such as heathland, moorland, and open woodland where the larval foodplants grow.*

feathery antennae

large furry body

large eyespots on all 4 wings

♂⚲

DARKER FORM

♂⚲

brown ground colour

red on forewing tip

♀⚲

lighter colouring than male

up to 6.5cm long

NOTE

When ready to mate, the female releases a pheromone scent, which is detectable by the male, with its sensitive feathery antennae, from up to 2km away. Several males may be attracted to the same female – this behaviour is known as "assembling".

WINGSPAN 5.5–8.8cm.
TIME OF FLIGHT *Day (male); night (female).*
FLIGHT PERIOD *May–August.*
LARVAL FOODPLANT *Mainly heather (Erica and Calluna), Bramble (see p.79), hawthorn (Crataegus), sallow (Salix), but also several other plants.*
SIMILAR SPECIES *None.*
STATUS *Widespread and locally common.*

The Drinker

Euthrix potatoria (Lasiocampidae)

The caterpillar of this large and attractive moth supposedly drinks more frequently than other species, and may be seen drinking from drops of water on leaves or other surfaces. The adult female is larger and paler than the male, and has more pointed wingtips. Both sexes fly at night, and are drawn to light, although the male is more frequently attracted than the female.

SEEN *in woodland, commons, moorland, fens, and other grassy habitats.*

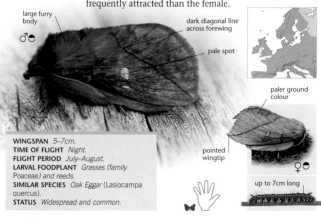

♂ large furry body

dark diagonal line across forewing

pale spot

paler ground colour

♀ pointed wingtip

up to 7cm long

WINGSPAN *5–7cm.*
TIME OF FLIGHT *Night.*
FLIGHT PERIOD *July–August.*
LARVAL FOODPLANT *Grasses (family Poaceae) and reeds.*
SIMILAR SPECIES *Oak Eggar (Lasiocampa quercus).*
STATUS *Widespread and common.*

Hummingbird Hawk-moth

Macroglossum stellatarum (Sphingidae)

This small, day-flying hawk-moth resembles a hummingbird as it hovers in front of flowers, feeding on nectar. It is particularly fond of fuchsia, jasmine, Red Valerian (see p.160), and campion. A resident of southern Europe, it breeds all year round. Some migrate north in summer, and regularly turn up in Britain.

BREEDS *wherever bedstraws are present. Migrants found near flowers, in parks, gardens, meadows, and wasteland.*

brownish forewings

dark wavy bands

long proboscis

white marks on black abdomen

orange hindwing

up to 6.5cm long

WINGSPAN *5–5.8cm.*
TIME OF FLIGHT *Day.*
FLIGHT PERIOD *Adults may occur in any month of the year.*
LARVAL FOODPLANT *Bedstraw (Galium).*
SIMILAR SPECIES *None.*
STATUS *Irregular migrant to British Isles in summer, in varying numbers.*

Elephant Hawk-moth

Deilephila elpenor (Sphingidae)

This species gets its common name from the caterpillar, which vaguely resembles an elephant's trunk. The adult moth has buff forewings, banded with pink, while the underside is mostly pink; the hindwings have white fringes. This attractive moth flies at dusk and through the night, often feeding at flowers such as honeysuckle or Red Valerian (see p.160).

FOUND *in woodland clearings, river valleys, meadows, commons, and gardens; also found in wasteland.*

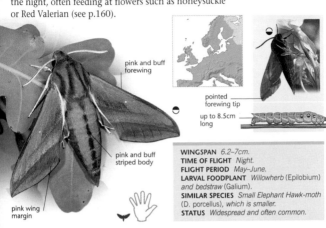

pink and buff forewing

pointed forewing tip

up to 8.5cm long

pink and buff striped body

pink wing margin

WINGSPAN *6.2–7cm.*
TIME OF FLIGHT *Night.*
FLIGHT PERIOD *May–June.*
LARVAL FOODPLANT *Willowherb (Epilobium) and bedstraw (Galium).*
SIMILAR SPECIES *Small Elephant Hawk-moth (D. porcellus), which is smaller.*
STATUS *Widespread and often common.*

Poplar Hawk-moth

Laothoe populi (Sphingidae)

Although quite closely related to the Eyed Hawk-moth (p.460), with which it can hybridize in captivity, the Poplar Hawk-moth has a very different resting position – it holds its hindwings at right angles to its body, projecting in front of the forewings. If disturbed, it flicks its hindwings forward, revealing a patch of orange-red.

FAVOURS *open woodland, waterside habitats, and wherever sallows and poplars grow. Also gardens, parks, and commons.*

large thorax and abdomen

hindwings project in front of forewings

short hindwings

red patch

grey-brown ground colour

up to 7cm long

WINGSPAN *7.2–9cm.*
TIME OF FLIGHT *Night.*
FLIGHT PERIOD *May–June.*
LARVAL FOODPLANT *Poplar (Populus), Aspen (see p.41), and sallow/willow (Salix).*
SIMILAR SPECIES *None.*
STATUS *Widespread and generally common.*

Eyed Hawk-moth

Smerinthus ocellata (Sphingidae)

When it is at rest, the mottled brown Eyed Hawk-moth resembles the bark of a tree. If disturbed, however, it will suddenly open its wings to reveal a startling pair of blue and black eyespots on the pinkish hindwings. These, combined with the centre of the thorax, which resembles the snout of a small mammal, have the effect of scaring off predators.

INHABITS *open woodland, orchards, gardens, and waterside habitats where sallows grow.*

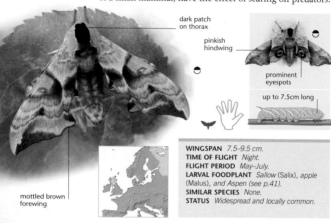

dark patch on thorax

pinkish hindwing

prominent eyespots

up to 7.5cm long

mottled brown forewing

WINGSPAN	*7.5–9.5 cm.*
TIME OF FLIGHT	*Night.*
FLIGHT PERIOD	*May–July.*
LARVAL FOODPLANT	*Sallow (Salix), apple (Malus), and Aspen (see p.41).*
SIMILAR SPECIES	*None.*
STATUS	*Widespread and locally common.*

Privet Hawk-moth

Sphinx ligustri (Sphingidae)

This is the largest hawk-moth resident in Britain, on average just a little smaller than the migrant Convolvulus Hawk-moth *(Agrius convolvuli)* and Death's-head Hawk-moth *(Acherontia atropos)*. It has a large blackish thorax and long, pointed forewings. The hindwings have pale pink bands, and the abdomen is striped pink and black. It flies at night, visiting flowers to feed, and is attracted to light.

FAVOURS *open countryside, gardens, woodland rides, hedgerows, and commons.*

black thorax

dark band across forewing

pink and black banded hindwing

up to 8.5cm long

WINGSPAN	*10–12cm.*
TIME OF FLIGHT	*Night.*
FLIGHT PERIOD	*June–July.*
LARVAL FOODPLANT	*Privet (Ligustrum), lilac (Syringa), and ash (Fraxinus).*
SIMILAR SPECIES	*Convolvulus Hawk-moth (Agrius convolvuli) lacks the black thorax.*
STATUS	*Widespread and locally common.*

The Water Springtail

Poduridae

This common, squat species is greyish blue to dark bluish black in colour. The water springtail spends its life on the surface of water in ditches, ponds, canals, boggy areas, and even rain-filled rock pools. It can be so abundant that the water surface appears dark. The spring under the body is long and flattened to ensure that it can jump effectively.

LIVE *on the surface of freshwater. It will even colonize large puddles in summer.*

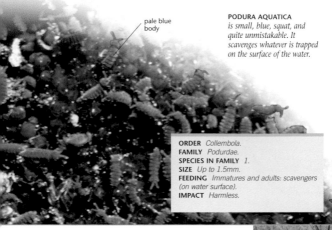

pale blue body

PODURA AQUATICA *is small, blue, squat, and quite unmistakable. It scavenges whatever is trapped on the surface of the water.*

ORDER *Collembola.*
FAMILY *Poduridae.*
SPECIES IN FAMILY *1.*
SIZE *Up to 1.5mm.*
FEEDING *Immatures and adults: scavengers (on water surface).*
IMPACT *Harmless.*

Globular Springtails

Sminthuridae

Also known as garden springtails, these species are pale to dark brown or green in colour with very rounded, almost spherical bodies. The segmentation of the abdomen is very indistinct, and the antennae are long and elbowed. Males often look different from females, and their antennae are often modfied for holding the antennae of the female during courtship.

COMMON *in a variety of habitats, including fields, pasture, leaf litter in woodland, and freshwater.*

globular abdomen

SMINTHURUS AQUATICUS *is widespread, but does not gather in such large numbers as the Water Springtail (above).*

NOTE

Sminthurus viridis, *known as the Lucerne Flea, is a widespread pest of alfalfa, clover, and some vegetables. It nibbles holes in the stems and leaves.*

shortish, bent antennae

ORDER *Collembola.*
FAMILY *Sminthuridae.*
SPECIES IN FAMILY *900.*
SIZE *1–3mm.*
FEEDING *Immatures and adults: herbivores.*
IMPACT *Several species can be pests of crop seedlings.*

Silverfish and Firebrats

Lepismatidae

OCCUPY *a range of habitats such as debris and vegetation, caves, bird nests, and warm places indoors.*

These elongated and slightly flattened, wingless insects are brown or tan in colour and usually covered in greyish or silvery scales and hairs. The end of the abdomen has three slender "tails" of a similar length. The compound eyes are small and widely separated. Lepismatids run rapidly, but unlike jumping bristletails, do not jump.

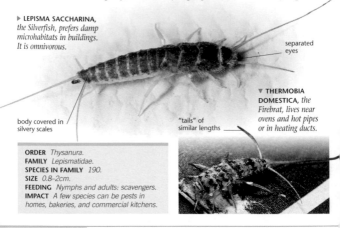

▶ LEPISMA SACCHARINA, *the Silverfish, prefers damp microhabitats in buildings. It is omnivorous.*

separated eyes

body covered in silvery scales

"tails" of similar lengths

▼ THERMOBIA DOMESTICA, *the Firebrat, lives near ovens and hot pipes or in heating ducts.*

ORDER *Thysanura.*
FAMILY *Lepismatidae.*
SPECIES IN FAMILY *190.*
SIZE *0.8–2cm.*
FEEDING *Nymphs and adults: scavengers.*
IMPACT *A few species can be pests in homes, bakeries, and commercial kitchens.*

Small Mayflies

Baetidae

THRIVE *in a wide range of aquatic habitats, such as ditches, pools, lakes, and streams.*

Small mayflies are pale or dark brown or black with yellowish, grey, or white markings. The front wings are elongated and oval with a reduced number of veins. In some species the hind wings may be small or absent. The males have large eyes, divided into upper and lower portions. The abdomen has two very long, slender tails.

NYMPHS

The small, slender nymphs are active swimmers and climb about on submerged plants.

extremely long tails

single pair of front wings

▲ CHLOEON DIPTERUM, *the Pond Olive, breeds in many freshwater habitats, including stagnant pools, water troughs, and rain butts. The adults lack hind wings.*

▼ BAETIS RHODANI *breeds in many types of water. The adults have very small hind wings and can be found all year.*

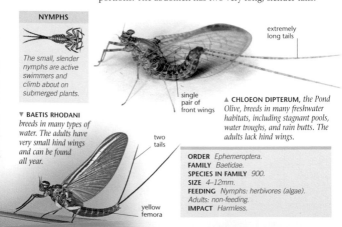

two tails

yellow femora

ORDER *Ephemeroptera.*
FAMILY *Baetidae.*
SPECIES IN FAMILY *900.*
SIZE *4–12mm.*
FEEDING *Nymphs: herbivores (algae). Adults: non-feeding.*
IMPACT *Harmless.*

Burrowing Mayflies

Ephemeridae

The wings of these large mayflies are typically clear or brownish in colour, although they have dark spots in some species. The bodies are often pale yellowish or whitish cream with characteristic dark spots or other markings, especially towards the end of the abdomen, which has two or three very long tails.

FOUND *in or near to streams, rivers, lakes, and ponds.*

EPHEMERA DANICA
is a large and distinctive species with three long tails. The adult's darkish wings may span up to 4cm.

dark, mottled wings

three long tails

abdominal gills

NYMPH

NYMPHS

Strong front legs enable the nymphs to dig into silt, which is then pushed back by the rear legs.

ORDER *Ephemeroptera.*
FAMILY *Ephemeridae.*
SPECIES IN FAMILY *150.*
SIZE *1–3.4cm.*
FEEDING *Nymphs: scavengers, predators. Adults: non-feeding.*
IMPACT *Harmless.*

Crawling Mayflies

Ephemerellidae

The commonest species in this family are pale reddish in colour and often have small, dark abdominal markings. The hindwings are relatively large and can be up to one-third as long as the forewings. The end of the abdomen carries two or (usually) three long, slender tails. Females release their eggs in one clump that separates out on the water surface.

OCCUR *in a wide variety of running water as well as ponds and margins of lakes.*

NYMPHS

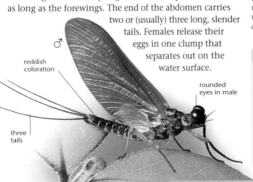

♂

reddish coloration

rounded eyes in male

three tails

Nymphs crawl on submerged plants. Their legs are usually long and the abdomen has flap-like lateral gills.

EPHEMERELLA IGNITA, *known by anglers as the Blue-winged Olive, is a reddish species with three tails. It is common near fast-flowing streams and rivers. Males have partly rounded eyes.*

ORDER *Ephemeroptera.*
FAMILY *Ephemerellidae.*
SPECIES IN FAMILY *200.*
SIZE *6–10mm.*
FEEDING *Nymphs: scavengers, predators. Adults: non-feeding.*
IMPACT *Harmless.*

Caenid Mayflies

Caenidae

The front wings of these small, delicate mayflies are very broad with highly distinctive dark longitudinal veins at the front margin and a very rounded hind margin. The hindwings are absent. The eyes in both sexes are small. The thorax is usually a little darker than the abdomen, which can be pale or greyish but always has three very long, slender tails.

OCCUPY *a variety of waterbodies such as large lake margins, ponds, and slow-flowing rivers.*

short, broad head

CAENIS HORARIA *breeds in muddy lakes, large ponds, and slow-moving rivers. Known as the "angler's curse", it appears in huge numbers.*

pale abdomen with three tails

NYMPHS

The nymphs are slightly flattened with square-shaped gill plates on the second abdominal segment.

ORDER *Ephemeroptera.*
FAMILY *Caenidae.*
SPECIES IN FAMILY *100.*
SIZE *5–12mm.*
FEEDING *Nymphs: scavengers. Adults: non-feeding.*
IMPACT *Harmless.*

Broad-winged Damselflies

Calopterygidae

Also called demoiselles, these fairly large, metallic-bodied damselflies have wings that narrow gradually towards their bases. The body is metallic green or blue. The male wings have a large dark patch or are entirely dark with a blue or purple sheen; females' wings are tinted green or brown.

INHABIT *both fast- and slow-flowing streams and rivers, as well as canals; adults also occur in woods far from water.*

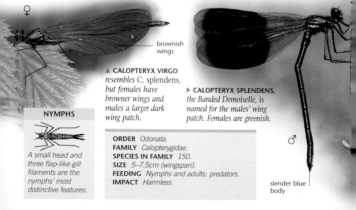

♀

brownish wings

▲ **CALOPTERYX VIRGO** *resembles C. splendens, but females have browner wings and males a larger dark wing patch.*

▶ **CALOPTERYX SPLENDENS,** *the Banded Demoiselle, is named for the males' wing patch. Females are greenish.*

NYMPHS

A small head and three flap-like gill filaments are the nymphs' most distinctive features.

ORDER *Odonata.*
FAMILY *Calopterygidae.*
SPECIES IN FAMILY *150.*
SIZE *5–7.5cm (wingspan).*
FEEDING *Nymphs and adults: predators.*
IMPACT *Harmless.*

♂

slender blue body

Narrow-winged Damselflies

Coenagrionidae

Many of these slender damselflies are beautifully coloured in shades of light blue with dark markings. Others may have blue-green or red-brown coloration, also with dark markings. The adults are generally weak fliers and rest horizontally with their clear wings folded together over the body. Towards the tip at the front margin of both pairs of wings there is a short, diamond-shaped mark called the pterostigma. In most species, the males are more brightly coloured than the females, which tend to be greenish.

OCCURS *mainly along streams and rivers, but also around ponds, stagnant pools, and swampy areas.*

NYMPHS

The slender-bodied nymphs are variable in colour with three gill filaments arising from the end of the abdomen, the middle filament being the longest.

▶ **PYRRHOSOMA NYMPHULA**, *the Large Red Damselfly, is often one of the first species to be seen flying in spring.*

dark markings

black legs

red eyes

greenish thorax

blue segment

♂

▲ **ERYTHROMMA NAJAS**, *the Red-eyed Damselfly, is an excellent flier. Females have browner eyes and lack the males' blue abdominal tip.*

♂

◀ **ISCHNURA ELEGANS** *is known as the Blue-tailed Damselfly as the male has a blue abdominal segment.*

▼ **COENAGRION PUELLA**, *the Azure Damselfly, has blue and black males and brilliant green and black females.*

diamond-shaped pterostigma

one blue segment

black and green thorax

♀

single black stripe on side of thorax

two blue segments

typical form

♀

♂

▲ **ENALLAGMA CYATHIGERUM**, *the Common Blue Damselfly, resembles Coenagrion males, but has a black club-shaped marking on the second abdominal segment. Females (left) vary from blue to brown.*

ORDER Odonata.
FAMILY Coenagrionidae.
SPECIES IN FAMILY 1,000.
SIZE Most species 2–5cm (wingspan).
FEEDING Nymphs and adults: predators.
IMPACT Harmless.

Hawkers

Aeshnidae

Also called darners, this family includes some of the largest and most powerful dragonflies. These robust insects are usually dark green, blue, or brown, with stripes on the thorax and spots or bands on the abdomen. The large eyes touch on top of the head. The wings, which are usually clear, sometimes have an amber or yellowish brown tint. Both pairs of wings have an elongated pterostigma. The end of the abdomen has a pair of claspers and, in males, a smaller appendage in between.

FOUND *usually near still waters with plenty of aquatic vegetation, but may occur along hedgerows and paths and in urban areas.*

eyes touch each other

hairy thorax

▼ **AESHNA MIXTA**, *the Migrant Hawker, is widespread in central and southern Europe. Females are yellow and brown.*

clear wings

♂

alternate small white and larger blue marks

blue eyes

paired blue spots on abdomen ♂

▶ **AESHNA CYANEA** *has blue eyes and a blue abdominal tip in males; females are yellow and green with brownish eyes.*

♂

blue tip to otherwise green-marked abdomen

▲ **BRACHYTRON PRATENSE**, *the Hairy Dragonfly, has a thick layer of hairs on the thorax. Females have yellow (not blue) spots.*

yellow stripes on thorax

apple-green thoracic markings

▲ **AESHNA GRANDIS**, *the Brown Hawker, has brownish wings and distinctive thoracic stripes.*

mainly clear wings

♂

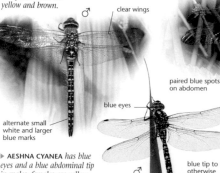

NYMPHS

The cryptically coloured nymphs have strongly built, cylindrical bodies and large eyes. They live among weeds, crawling on the bottom in search of their prey.

black stripe down back

claspers

ORDER *Odonata.*
FAMILY *Aeshnidae.*
SPECIES IN FAMILY *420.*
SIZE *6–14cm (wingspan).*
FEEDING *Nymphs and adults: predators.*
IMPACT *Harmless.*

▲ **ANAX IMPERATOR**, *the Emperor Dragonfly, is very large, with blue males and green females. It breeds in large ponds and even in weedy ditches.*

Common Skimmers

Libellulidae

These dragonflies, which represent a large proportion of the order *Odonata*, are also called darters or chasers due to their fast, unpredictable flight interspersed with short periods of hovering. They are colourful and males often differ from females, their bodies sometimes having a pale blue, powdery appearance. The wingspan is typically longer than the body length and the wings sometimes have dark bands or other markings, especially at their bases. In many species the abdomen is broad and flattened. The large eyes always touch on top of the head.

OCCUR *over still or slow-moving water in a variety of habitats, from mountains and moors to forests.*

NYMPHS

Fiercely predatory and aquatic, the nymphs are short, stocky, and slightly flattened, often with spines projecting from the abdomen. Their facial masks are hollow and large.

NOTE

Adult males are very territorial and command their patch from a perch on an exposed plant stem or twig. They dart away to chase off rival males.

clear wings

♂

black tip

blue abdomen

◀ **ORTHETRUM CANCELLATUM** *is also known as the Black-tailed Skimmer; the female is yellowish with two black stripes along the length of the abdomen.*

wings take on a golden tinge with age

♂

blood red colouring

brown wing bases

clear wings

♂

▲ **SYMPETRUM SANGUINEUM,** *the Ruddy Darter, can be found around shallow ponds, ditches, and lakes. The male is bright red while the female is yellowish. Both have a yellow mark at the base of their wings.*

▶ **LIBELLULA DEPRESSA,** *the Broad-bodied Chaser, breeds in ponds. The abdomen in females is broader than in males and is brown with yellow lateral patches.*

small dark spot

two dark marks on each wing

brown hindwing base

▶ **LIBELLULA QUADRIMACULATA** *is known as the Four-spotted Chaser on account of the small dark spot in the middle of the front margin of each wing. The sexes are quite similar.*

yellow at sides

ORDER *Odonata.*
FAMILY *Libellulidae.*
SPECIES IN FAMILY *1,250.*
SIZE *4–8cm (wingspan).*
FEEDING *Nymphs and adults: predators.*
IMPACT *Harmless.*

Common Stoneflies

Perlidae

FOUND *in a variety of flowing water bodies, such as rivers and streams with stony beds.*

Yellowish brown to dark brown in colour, these often quite stout and flat-bodied stoneflies have minute remains of the nymphal gill tufts on the underside of the thorax near the bases of the legs. The front wings have a distinctive "double ladder" made up of numerous cross veins in the basal half. Males can be much smaller than the females. The abdomen has a pair of longish tails, called cerci, which are made up of many segments. The nymphs can be patterned but always have branched gills on the thoracic segments.

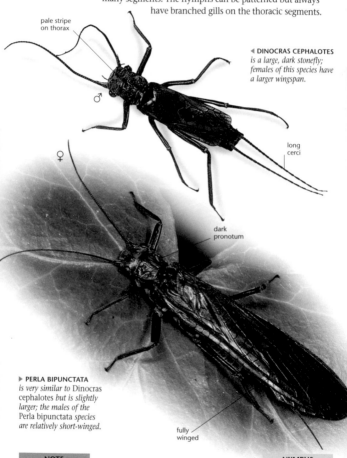

pale stripe on thorax

♂

◄ **DINOCRAS CEPHALOTES** *is a large, dark stonefly; females of this species have a larger wingspan.*

♀

long cerci

dark pronotum

► **PERLA BIPUNCTATA** *is very similar to* Dinocras cephalotes *but is slightly larger; the males of the* Perla bipunctata *species are relatively short-winged.*

fully winged

NOTE

In common with the Perlodidae, the nymphs of these stoneflies are predatory and help to control the larvae of potential pest fly species.

ORDER *Plecoptera.*
FAMILY *Perlidae.*
SPECIES IN FAMILY *400.*
SIZE *2–5cm.*
FEEDING *Nymphs: predators. Adults: non-feeding*
IMPACT *Harmless.*

NYMPHS

The nymphs may take up to five years to become adult, and moult as many as thirty times.

True Crickets

Gryllidae

The insects of this family are slightly flattened in body shape, with distinctive rounded heads and long, thin antennae, which are as long as or longer than the body. Crickets are rather drably coloured black or shades of brown. In winged species the front wings are held flat over the body at rest; males rub them together to produce songs. The end of the abdomen bears a pair of noticeable, often bristly, unsegmented cerci. In females the conspicuous ovipositor is cylindrical or needle-like. In Britain, the Field Cricket and the Wood Cricket are very rare and confined to the far south.

FOUND in all manner of herbage in woods, hedgerows, grassland, and scrub.

NOTE

Males sing mostly at night, by using their front wings, a series of small teeth on one wing rubbing over a scraper on the other.

short wings

◀ **NEMOBIUS SYLVESTRIS,** known as Wood Cricket, has short front wings and no hind wings.

pale wing base

ovipositor

▶ **GRYLLUS CAMPESTRIS,** the Field Cricket, is a stocky insect with a big head and large hind legs. It makes burrows in grassland.

♀

dark, shiny head

folded hind wings

spines

dull brown coloration

▲ **ACHETA DOMESTICA** is a nocturnally active species. It is dull brown in colour and both sexes are fully winged.

ORDER Orthoptera.
FAMILY Gryllidae.
SPECIES IN FAMILY 1,800.
SIZE 0.5–2.5cm.
FEEDING Nymphs and adults: herbivores, scavengers, predators.
IMPACT Some species can be crop pests.

Bush Crickets

Tettigoniidae

OCCUR *in a variety of habitats, both lush and sparsely vegetated, from ground level up to the treetops.*

Highly distinctive due to their long, thread-like antennae and saddle-shaped pronotum, these brownish or greenish insects are sometimes known as long-horned grasshoppers. The wings are short in some species, but in fully-winged species the folded wings extend well beyond the end of the abdomen. Females have a conspicuous, laterally flattened ovipositor, which may be short and curved like a sickle or long like a sabre, depending on where the female lays her eggs. The hind legs are enlarged for jumping. Males make a species-specific song by rubbing the front wings together. Songs can take the form of soft drumming or ticking.

NOTE

Bush cricket songs have been likened, among other things, to high-speed drills, watch winding, knife grinding, buzzing, and sliding a comb over a ruler's edge.

small, brownish red spots all over body ♀

large, sword-like ovipositor

▲ **LEPTOPHYES PUCTATISSIMA,** *the Speckled Bush Cricket, is common and widespread in well-vegetated areas such as woodland margins, hedgerows, and gardens. The wings are always very short.*

♂

◀ **TETTIGONIA VIRIDISSIMA,** *the Great Green Bush Cricket, is a large but very well-camouflaged species. It is fairly common in the southern half of Britain. The female lays eggs in the soil or leaf litter.*

brown stripe

long wings

▼ **METRIOPTERA BRACHYPTERA** *is known as the Bog Bush Cricket, but also inhabits drier places such as heathland. Its song is a train of chirps that sound like "zrit".*

♀

short wings

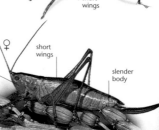

♀

short wings

slender body

sloping face

ORDER *Orthoptera.*
FAMILY *Tettigoniidae.*
SPECIES IN FAMILY *5,000.*
SIZE *1.6–6cm.*
FEEDING *Nymphs and adults: herbivores, scavengers, predators.*
IMPACT *A few species can be plant pests.*

▲ **CONOCEPHALUS DORSALIS,** *the Short-winged Conehead, is a slender species that favours moist habitats such as damp grassland, river edges, and the margins of salt marshes.*

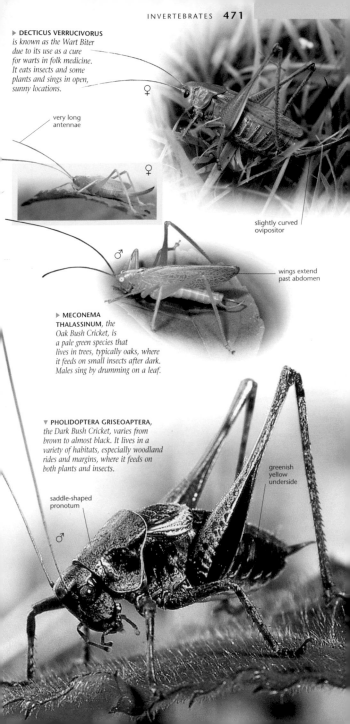

▶ **DECTICUS VERRUCIVORUS**
*is known as the Wart Biter
due to its use as a cure
for warts in folk medicine.
It eats insects and some
plants and sings in open,
sunny locations.*

♀

very long
antennae

♀

slightly curved
ovipositor

wings extend
past abdomen

♂

▶ **MECONEMA
THALASSINUM**, *the
Oak Bush Cricket, is
a pale green species that
lives in trees, typically oaks, where
it feeds on small insects after dark.
Males sing by drumming on a leaf.*

▽ **PHOLIDOPTERA GRISEOAPTERA**,
*the Dark Bush Cricket, varies from
brown to almost black. It lives in a
variety of habitats, especially woodland
rides and margins, where it feeds on
both plants and insects.*

greenish
yellow
underside

saddle-shaped
pronotum

♂

Grasshoppers and Locusts

Acrididae

These insects are active during the day and prefer hot, sunny conditions. Most species are brownish or greenish with markings and patterns of all kinds. Two distinctive characteristics are the short antennae and the large saddle-shaped pronotum. The hind legs are greatly enlarged for jumping. The jump is an escape response, but if trapped, grasshoppers can use their hind legs to kick out at enemies. The large hindwings are folded beneath the narrower and tougher front wings, but some species are short-winged. Many species have brightly coloured hindwings, which they can flash to startle enemies. Females are mostly larger than males, which sing by rubbing a row of small pegs on the inside of their hind femora against a hard, thickened vein on the edge of the front wings.

▼ **STENOBOTHRUS LINEATUS**, *the Stripe-winged Grasshopper, has a white stripe on the front wing. It likes dry habitats and has a buzzing song that changes pitch like a siren.*

white mark on wing

yellow stripe along front of wing

red tip to abdomen in male

◄ **STETHOPHYMA GROSSUM**, *the Large Marsh Grasshopper, occurs in damp places. Males make a clicking noise by kicking their hind legs past their wings.*

purple-red legs

ORDER *Orthoptera.*
FAMILY *Acrididae.*
SPECIES IN FAMILY *9,000.*
SIZE *1–6cm.*
FEEDING *Nymphs and adults: herbivores (leaves and foliage).*
IMPACT *Some species are crop pests.*

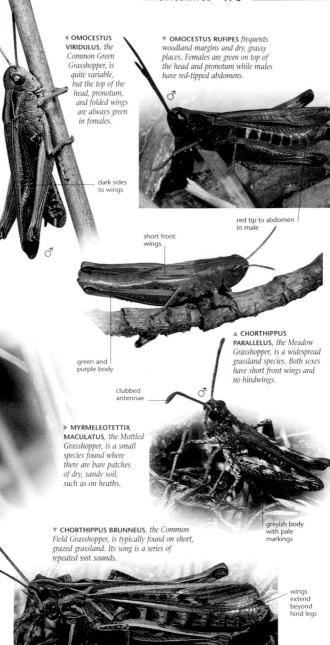

◄ **OMOCESTUS VIRIDULUS**, *the Common Green Grasshopper, is quite variable, but the top of the head, pronotum, and folded wings are always green in females.*

dark sides to wings

♂

▼ **OMOCESTUS RUFIPES** *frequents woodland margins and dry, grassy places. Females are green on top of the head and pronotum while males have red-tipped abdomens.*

♂

red tip to abdomen in male

short front wings

green and purple body

▲ **CHORTHIPPUS PARALLELUS**, *the Meadow Grasshopper, is a widespread grassland species. Both sexes have short front wings and no hindwings.*

clubbed antennae

♂

▶ **MYRMELEOTETTIX MACULATUS**, *the Mottled Grasshopper, is a small species found where there are bare patches of dry, sandy soil, such as on heaths.*

greyish body with pale markings

▼ **CHORTHIPPUS BRUNNEUS**, *the Common Field Grasshopper, is typically found on short, grazed grassland. Its song is a series of repeated ssst sounds.*

wings extend beyond hind legs

Common Earwigs

Forficulidae

These nocturnal insects are reddish brown to dark brown with paler legs and thread-like antennae. The front wings are small and toughened, covering the folded, fan-shaped hindwings. The second tarsal segment of each leg is expanded sideways. The body is flattened and the abdomen has a pair of forceps at the tip. Those of males are very curved and – as with all earwigs – used for courtship and defence; those of females are much straighter.

CRAWL *through soil, leaf litter, crevices in rocks, or under bark, sometimes in large aggregations.*

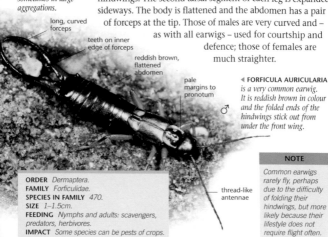

long, curved forceps

teeth on inner edge of forceps

reddish brown, flattened abdomen

pale margins to pronotum

♂

◄ **FORFICULA AURICULARIA** *is a very common earwig. It is reddish brown in colour and the folded ends of the hindwings stick out from under the front wing.*

thread-like antennae

ORDER *Dermaptera.*
FAMILY *Forficulidae.*
SPECIES IN FAMILY *470.*
SIZE *1–1.5cm.*
FEEDING *Nymphs and adults: scavengers, predators, herbivores.*
IMPACT *Some species can be pests of crops.*

NOTE

Common earwigs rarely fly, perhaps due to the difficulty of folding their hindwings, but more likely because their lifestyle does not require flight often.

Human Lice

Pediculidae

These lice are small and pale with narrow heads and pear-shaped, flattened bodies. The mouthparts are modified for piercing and sucking. The legs are short, strong, and inwardly curved. Each has a large claw for grasping and climbing through hair. Human head and body lice appear to differ only in the area of the body they occupy.

LIVE *on humans on hair and among items of clothing.*

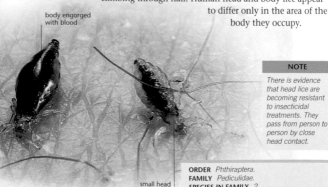

body engorged with blood

small head

NOTE

There is evidence that head lice are becoming resistant to insecticidal treatments. They pass from person to person by close head contact.

PEDICULUS HUMANUS, *the Human Head Louse, lives entirely in hair and attaches its eggs, called nits, to hair shafts with a strong glue. It is prevalent among young school children.*

ORDER *Phthiraptera.*
FAMILY *Pediculidae.*
SPECIES IN FAMILY *2.*
SIZE *1.5–3.5mm.*
FEEDING *Nymphs and adults: parasites.*
IMPACT *Body lice transmit diseases to humans.*

Booklice

Liposcelidae

These small, light to yellowish brown insects have squat, slightly flattened bodies and are quite difficult to see. The hind legs are larger than the first two pairs and the hind femora are very enlarged, allowing the insects to make small jumps. The tarsi have three segments The head, which is large in comparison to the rest of the body and appears to bulge at the front, carries a pair of small compound eyes, chewing mouthparts, and shortish, thread-like antennae. Most species are wingless; when present, the wings have rounded ends.

INFEST houses and collections of stored plants and insects; also found in scrub and woods under bark and among leaf litter.

strong mandibles

flattened, yellowish olive body

slender antennae

stout hind legs

▲ **LIPOSCELIS TERRICOLIS** *is a widespread domestic pest that eats a wide range of damp or starchy foodstuffs and gnaws damp papers and books.*

▲ **LIPOSCELIS SP.** *are prepared and mounted on glass slides for microscopic examination due to their small size and similarity.*

NOTE

Some species are pests of stored food that has become damp, including pasta, cereals, and flour. Outbreaks occur due to high humidity levels.

pale antennae

▼ **LIPOSCELIS LIPARUS** *is a common pest species in libraries and archives where conditions are dark and damp.*

small, dark eyes

swollen front to head

narrow prothorax

ORDER *Psocoptera.*
FAMILY *Liposcelidae.*
SPECIES IN FAMILY *150.*
SIZE *0.5–1.5mm.*
FEEDING *Nymphs and adults: scavengers, fungi-feeders.*
IMPACT *May be pests of stored produce.*

Pubic Lice

Pthiridae

Also called the Crab Louse, this pale to translucent louse has a squat, flat body and a head that is much narrower than the thorax. The middle and hind legs are especially stout with strong curved claws for gripping pubic hair shafts. The family includes the Human Pubic Louse, *Pthirus pubis*, and the Gorilla Pubic Louse, *P. gorillae*.

OCCUR on the bodies of humans (also on gorillas in Africa).

conspicuous eye

strong middle and hind claws

pubic hair shaft

PTHIRUS PUBIS lives on human pubic hairs and is passed on through intimate contact. These slow-moving lice cannot jump, and feed on blood.

NOTE

This species is found all over the world wherever there are humans. It is unpleasant, but is not known to transmit any diseases.

NYMPH

flattened body

ORDER Phthiraptera.
FAMILY Pthiridae.
SPECIES IN FAMILY 2.
SIZE 1.5–3mm.
FEEDING Nymphs and adults: parasites (blood).
IMPACT Parasites of humans and gorillas.

Acanthosomatids

Acanthosomatidae

Typically greenish or reddish brown with dark markings, acanthosomatids have broad bodies that taper slightly to the rear, behind the broad pronotum. The relatively small head has antennae with five segments, and can appear sunk into the front margin of the pronotum. The scutellum is large and triangular. The tarsi have two segments.

INHABIT the foliage of trees and shrubs in a variety of habitats.

▼ ACANTHOSOMA HAEMORRHOIDALE is mainly found on hawthorn, where it feeds on buds and berries. It also feeds on other deciduous tree species, such as hazel.

broad pronotum

pronotum pointed at sides

large, triangular scutellum

▲ ELASMUCHA GRISEA, the Parent Bug, shows maternal behaviour, the females guarding their eggs and newly hatched nymphs from predators.

ORDER Hemiptera.
FAMILY Acanthosomatidae.
SPECIES IN FAMILY 250.
SIZE 0.8–1.3cm.
FEEDING Nymphs and adults: herbivores.
IMPACT Harmless.

Stink Bugs

Pentatomidae

Also known as shield bugs due to their distinctive shape, stink bugs can produce powerful defensive odours (which may be strong enough to induce headaches) from glands on the thorax. Many species are brown and green, but others are very conspicuously marked black and red. The head can appear partly sunk into the pronotum, which is broad and may have sharply angled corners. The antennae typically have five segments, while the tarsi have three. The scutellum reaches midway down the abdomen.

OCCUR *on herbaceous vegetation, shrubs, and trees in a wide range of habitats.*

sharply pointed sides of pronotum

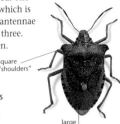

square "shoulders"

◀ **PICROMERUS BIDENS** *is a stealthy predator, sneaking up to suck the juices of a wide range of insect prey, such as caterpillars and beetle grubs.*

metallic sheen

large triangular scutellum

▲ **PENTATOMA RUFIPES**, *the Forest Bug, is associated with deciduous trees where it feeds on sap and small insects.*

bronzy area on wings

▼ **AELIA ACUMINATA** *is called the Bishop's Mitre after its distinctive shape. The bug feeds on grasses and sometimes on cereal crops such as wheat and barley.*

pale lengthwise stripes

pitted surface

bronze band across pronotum

downcurved head

▲ **PALOMENA PRASINA**, *the Green Shield Bug, is extremely common and wide-spread. It lives on a wide variety of host plants, including trees and crops.*

▲ **PIEZODORUS LITURATUS** *is called the Gorse Shield Bug but feeds on several other plants, such as broom. Adults hibernate and emerge the following spring as sexually mature, green bugs.*

▼ **DOLYCORIS BACCARUM**, *the Sloe Bug, feeds on hawthorn, sloe, raspberry, and other related plants, especially on the fruit and flowers. Close up, it looks quite hairy.*

white bands on sides of abdomen

green scutellum

NOTE

The eggs are laid in small, regular or hexagonal clusters. In many species the females guard the eggs and nymphs, standing over them when danger strikes.

ORDER *Hemiptera.*
FAMILY *Pentatomidae.*
SPECIES IN FAMILY *5,500.*
SIZE *0.5–2.5cm.*
FEEDING *Nymphs and adults: herbivores, predators.*
IMPACT *Some species are crop pests.*

Seed Bugs

Lygaeidae

FOUND *close to the
ground in leaf litter,
under stones, or
among low-growing
vegetation.*

Also known as ground bugs, these bugs are dull-coloured,
being mainly pale yellow, brown, or black, although a few
species are bright red and black. The body is quite tough
and flattened and is either elongate or oval. The head is
typically triangular but can be very broad in some species.
The antennae arise from well down the sides of the head,
below the prominent eyes. Many of the ground-living
species may be short-winged or wingless. The femora of
the front legs may be swollen, with stout spines. As their
name suggests, seed bugs are mostly seed-feeders, using
the strong, toothed or spined front legs to grasp their food.

NOTE

*Sound production
by stridulation plays
an important part in
the mating of some
species. Males may
use lengthy matings
to ensure paternity
of the offspring.*

▼ **ISCHNODEMA SABULETI**,
*the European Chinch Bug,
occurs in long- and short-
winged form. It feeds on
grasses and reeds.*

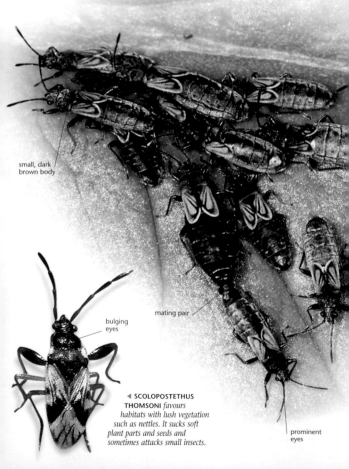

small, dark
brown body

mating pair

bulging
eyes

◄ **SCOLOPOSTETHUS
THOMSONI** *favours
habitats with lush vegetation
such as nettles. It sucks soft
plant parts and seeds and
sometimes attacks small insects.*

prominent
eyes

▼ **HETEROGASTER URTICAE**,
known as the Nettle Ground Bug,
lives entirely on stinging nettles.
It overwinters as an adult.

orange-red
spot on wing

pale yellow
markings

▲ **APHANUS ROLANDRI**
has a reddish or yellowish spot
at the top of the wing membranes.
It forages for fallen seeds on the
ground after dark.

▼ **KLEIDOCERYS RESEDAE** lives on birch,
alder, and some other trees. Both sexes make
characteristic calls before mating commences.

unusually clear,
transparent wings

spines on
front legs

▶ **GASTRODES ABIETUM**,
the Spruce Cone Bug,
hides in spruce and fir
cones during the day.
At night it feeds on
young needles.

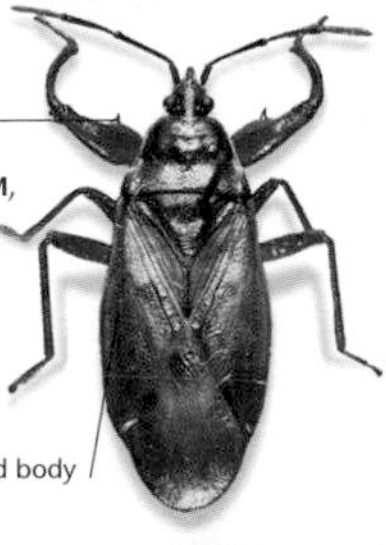

flattened body

**SHORT-WINGED
FORMS**

two dark spots

▶ **GRAPTOPELTUS LYNCEUS**
inhabits coastal cliffs and
dune systems and other dry,
sandy places.

ORDER Hemiptera.
FAMILY Lygaeidae.
SPECIES IN FAMILY 3,500.
SIZE 4–12mm.
FEEDING Nymphs and adults: herbivores.
IMPACT A few species attack cereals and
some other crops.

Squash Bugs

Coreidae

DISTRIBUTED *wherever their host plants grow, especially in grassland, heathland, and light woodland.*

Squash bugs are so named because some species feed on squash plants. Most are roughly oval in shape and dull brown. In some species, the abdomen is flattened, projects sideways, and may be lobed and angular. The head is very much narrower and shorter than the pronotum. The antennae have four segments. The hind part of the front wings has a distinctive pattern of parallel veins. All squash bugs are herbivorous as adults and nymphs, eating shoots, buds, fruits, and unripe seeds of their food plants.

NOTE

When threatened, some large species of squash bug produce unpleasant or fruity-smelling secretions from special glands in the thorax.

▼ SYROMASTUS RHOMBEUS *inhabits dry, sandy places. The lack of wings and presence of dorsal gland openings show that this specimen is a nymph.*

▶ CORIOMERIS DENTICULATUS *is a relatively slender squash bug with many short spines. It feeds on leguminous plants on well-drained soils.*

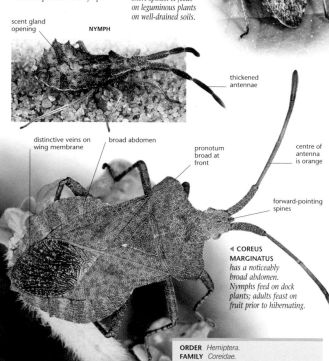

white tubercles

scent gland opening

NYMPH

thickened antennae

distinctive veins on wing membrane

broad abdomen

pronotum broad at front

centre of antenna is orange

forward-pointing spines

◀ COREUS MARGINATUS *has a noticeably broad abdomen. Nymphs feed on dock plants; adults feast on fruit prior to hibernating.*

ORDER *Hemiptera.*
FAMILY *Coreidae.*
SPECIES IN FAMILY *2,000.*
SIZE *1–1.8cm.*
FEEDING *Nymphs and adults: herbivores.*
IMPACT *Mainly harmless, although a few species are pests of crops and vegetables.*

Assassin Bugs

Reduviidae

Most of these bugs are yellowish brown, grey, or blackish, but some are reddish orange. The body shape varies from robust and oval to very elongated and slender with thread-like legs. The head has a transverse groove between the eyes and the antennae; the latter are often bent after the long, first segment, have four main segments, and many subsegments. The rostrum has three segments and is distinctively short and curved. The front legs are often enlarged.

OCCUR *on vegetation of all kinds and sometimes in houses where their prey is present.*

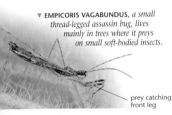

▼ **EMPICORIS VAGABUNDUS,** *a small thread-legged assassin bug, lives mainly in trees where it preys on small soft-bodied insects.*

prey catching front leg

brownish body

ORDER *Hemiptera.*
FAMILY *Reduviidae.*
SPECIES IN FAMILY *6,000.*
SIZE *0.6–1.6cm.*
FEEDING *Nymphs and adults: predators.*
IMPACT *If handled roughly, larger species may bite, piercing human skin.*

NYMPH

▲ **REDUVIUS PERSONATUS,** *the Masked Hunter, is named for the nymphs, which cover themselves with dust and debris as camouflage.*

Water Measurers

Hydrometridae

Also called marsh-treaders, these delicate, reddish to dark brown bugs are very slender, with thread-like legs. The eyes are fairly large and bulge out from the sides of the elongated head. The antennae and rostrum have four segments. Most species are wingless, but short-winged or fully-winged forms occur in some species. Water measurers are slow-moving and take small prey.

FOUND *in quiet pools, marshes, and swamps, including stagnant and brackish water. Stay at the water's edge or on floating plants.*

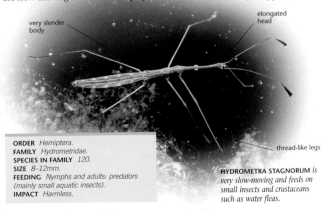

very slender body

elongated head

thread-like legs

ORDER *Hemiptera.*
FAMILY *Hydrometridae.*
SPECIES IN FAMILY *120.*
SIZE *8–12mm.*
FEEDING *Nymphs and adults: predators (mainly small aquatic insects).*
IMPACT *Harmless.*

HYDROMETRA STAGNORUM *is very slow-moving and feeds on small insects and crustaceans such as water fleas.*

Plant Bugs

Miridae

This family is the largest group of true bugs in the world. Plant bugs have a delicate structure and are variously coloured green, brown, red, and black, with a great diversity of markings. The rostrum and the antennae have four segments and the hind part of the front wings, or membrane, has one or two distinctive closed cells. Most species are fully winged, although short-winged and wingless forms occur. Diverse in their biology, plant bugs are mostly herbivores, eating seeds, fruits, leaves, and plant juices. Others are scavengers or are predators of aphids, mealy bugs, mites, and soft-bodied prey.

LIVE *in almost every habitat from ground level to the treetops.*

mainly green

◀ **LYGOCORIS PABULINUS,** *the Common Green Plant Bug, is a serious pest of a wide range of plants, including fruits such as raspberries, pears, and apples.*

brown membrane

orange-yellow patch on scutellum

▲ **CAMPLYONEURA VIRGULA** *is a tree-living predator that hunts bark lice, aphids, and other soft-bodied prey. Despite its fragile appearance, it can bite if handled.*

shiny red upperside

swollen and hairy segments

▶ **HETEROTOMA MERIOPTERA** *is recognizable by its antennae, the first two segments of which are swollen. It lives among nettles and other rank vegetation.*

▲ **PANTILIUS TUNICATUS** *feeds on hazel, birch, and alder trees. Adults are yellowish green when they first appear, becoming reddish and darker as they get older.*

pink veins

pale green legs

▼ **NOTOSTIRA ELONGATA** *is a common grass bug, found on rough, grassy verges. Females are green with a swollen abdomen; males are darker and more slender.*

swollen abdomen

♀

slender body

◀ **STENODEMA LAEVIGATUM** *has a slender, elongated body and can be found on a variety of grasses, where the nymphs and adults feed on the flower- heads and unripe seeds.*

ORDER *Hemiptera.*
FAMILY *Miridae.*
SPECIES IN FAMILY *7,000.*
SIZE *2–12mm.*
FEEDING *Nymphs and adults: herbivores, predators, scavengers.*
IMPACT *Several species attack crops.*

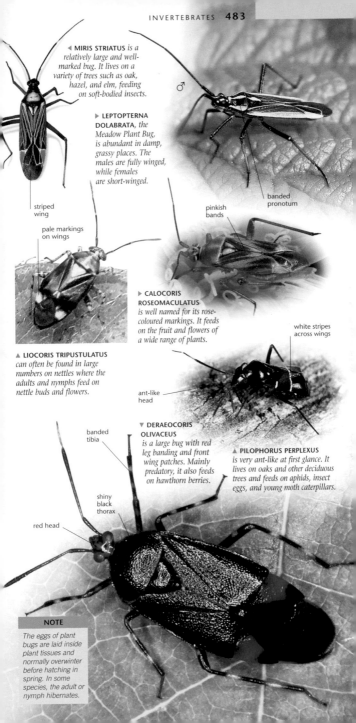

◄ **MIRIS STRIATUS** is a relatively large and well-marked bug. It lives on a variety of trees such as oak, hazel, and elm, feeding on soft-bodied insects.

♂

▶ **LEPTOPTERNA DOLABRATA,** the Meadow Plant Bug, is abundant in damp, grassy places. The males are fully winged, while females are short-winged.

banded pronotum

striped wing

pale markings on wings

pinkish bands

▶ **CALOCORIS ROSEOMACULATUS** is well named for its rose-coloured markings. It feeds on the fruit and flowers of a wide range of plants.

white stripes across wings

▲ **LIOCORIS TRIPUSTULATUS** can often be found in large numbers on nettles where the adults and nymphs feed on nettle buds and flowers.

ant-like head

▼ **DERAEOCORIS OLIVACEUS** is a large bug with red leg banding and front wing patches. Mainly predatory, it also feeds on hawthorn berries.

banded tibia

shiny black thorax

red head

▲ **PILOPHORUS PERPLEXUS** is very ant-like at first glance. It lives on oaks and other deciduous trees and feeds on aphids, insect eggs, and young moth caterpillars.

NOTE

The eggs of plant bugs are laid inside plant tissues and normally overwinter before hatching in spring. In some species, the adult or nymph hibernates.

Water Crickets

Veliidae

These bugs are also called small water striders and resemble pond skaters (below), but are generally much smaller, more robust, and have shorter, stouter legs. Most are brownish with orange undersides and orange or silver markings. The antennae and rostrum have four segments. Some species are fully winged; others can be short-winged or wingless.

LIVE *among vegetation or on the surface of still or slow-moving water in ponds, lakes, and damp forests.*

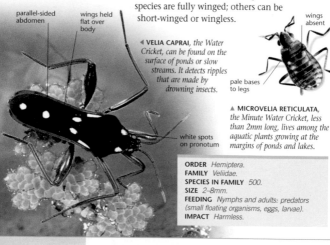

parallel-sided abdomen

wings held flat over body

◀ **VELIA CAPRAI**, *the Water Cricket, can be found on the surface of ponds or slow streams. It detects ripples that are made by drowning insects.*

wings absent

pale bases to legs

white spots on pronotum

▲ **MICROVELIA RETICULATA**, *the Minute Water Cricket, less than 2mm long, lives among the aquatic plants growing at the margins of ponds and lakes.*

> **ORDER** *Hemiptera.*
> **FAMILY** *Veliidae.*
> **SPECIES IN FAMILY** *500.*
> **SIZE** *2–8mm.*
> **FEEDING** *Nymphs and adults: predators (small floating organisms, eggs, larvae).*
> **IMPACT** *Harmless.*

Pond Skaters

Gerridae

Also known as water striders, these fast-moving and often wingless bugs are adapted to living on the surface of water. They are dark brown or blackish, with a covering of velvety hairs. The antennae and rostrum have four segments. The front legs are short for grasping prey, while the middle and hind legs are more elongated. Ripple-sensitive hairs on the legs locate struggling prey.

WALK *on the surface film of any available freshwater, including ditches and ponds, even water troughs.*

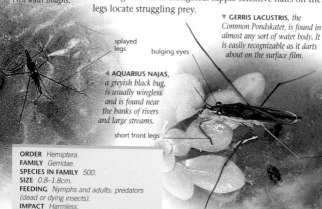

splayed legs

bulging eyes

▼ **GERRIS LACUSTRIS**, *the Common Pondskater, is found in almost any sort of water body. It is easily recognizable as it darts about on the surface film.*

◀ **AQUARIUS NAJAS**, *a greyish black bug, is usually wingless and is found near the banks of rivers and large streams.*

short front legs

> **ORDER** *Hemiptera.*
> **FAMILY** *Gerridae.*
> **SPECIES IN FAMILY** *500.*
> **SIZE** *0.8–1.8cm.*
> **FEEDING** *Nymphs and adults: predators (dead or dying insects).*
> **IMPACT** *Harmless.*

Water Scorpions

Nepidae

These brownish bugs are also known as water stick insects due to their shape. They may be oval, flattened with short legs, or cylindrical and elongated with relatively long legs. The head has rounded eyes and a short, curved rostrum. The front legs are modified for catching prey. There is a distinctive breathing siphon at the rear that may be as long as the body.

OCCURS *in either still or slow-moving water, with some species in muddy shallows and others in deeper water.*

breathing siphon

enlarged femur

wings folded over broad body

▲ **NEPA CINEREA,** or the Water Scorpion, has a long breathing siphon at its rear end. It also has powerful front legs.

▼ **RANATRA LINEARIS,** *the yellowish brown Water Stick Insect, is a predator and attacks even small vertebrates.*

narrow body

front legs gripping prey

> **ORDER** *Hemiptera.*
> **FAMILY** *Nepidae.*
> **SPECIES IN FAMILY** *250.*
> **SIZE** *1.8–3cm.*
> **FEEDING** *Nymphs and adults: predators.*
> **IMPACT** *Generally harmless, but sometimes bite if handled.*

Saucer Bugs

Naucoridae

Also known as creeping water bugs, these flat, streamlined insects have a smooth, rounded or oval body. Most species are dark greyish green or brown. The front legs are adapted for capturing prey, with curved, sickle-like tibiae that fold back like a jack-knife on to the enlarged femora. The hind legs have rows of specialized swimming hairs.

MOVE *slowly on the bottom of static or moving water bodies, or climb about on submerged vegetation.*

head appears sunk into prothorax

NOTE

Saucer bugs lack a breathing siphon: supplies of oxygen are obtained at the water surface and retained in the space under the wings.

broad, flat body

> **ORDER** *Hemiptera.*
> **FAMILY** *Naucoridae.*
> **SPECIES IN FAMILY** *400.*
> **SIZE** *1–1.5cm.*
> **FEEDING** *Nymphs and adults: predators (mainly larvae, crustaceans, snails).*
> **IMPACT** *Occasionally bite if handled.*

hairs on legs

ILYOCORIS CIMICOIDES or the Saucer Bug, is a flattened greyish green insect that has wings, but cannot fly. Instead, it uses the space beneath the wings to store air.

Water Boatmen

Corixidae

Superficially similar to backswimmers (right), these streamlined bugs are generally dark reddish- or yellowish brown, often with fine transverse markings. The upper body surface is flattened without a central keel and the under body is pale. Corixids do not swim upside-down. The short head has large dark eyes, short antennae, and a short, stout rostrum. The front legs have scoop-shaped ends for feeding; the middle legs are used for holding plants; and the clawless back legs are fringed with hairs.

FOUND *in still and slow-moving water in ponds, lakes, and occasionally streams.*

NOTE

While underwater, corixids carry bubbles of air under their wings where the concave, dorsal surface of the abdomen acts as a reservoir.

▼ **CORIXA PUNCTATA** *is common and has a wide distribution. Typically, the back is patterned and dark, while the underside is pale. This species flies and is attracted to lights at night.*

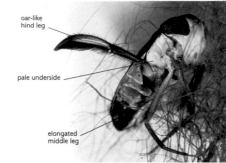

oar-like hind leg

pale underside

elongated middle leg

swimming hairs on hind leg

▲ **CORIXA SP.** *feed on algae, diatoms, and plant debris at the bottom of well-vegetated ponds, using their hair-fringed front legs to filter through the debris.*

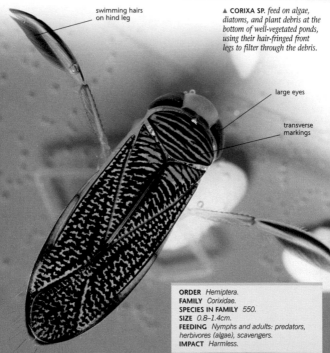

large eyes

transverse markings

ORDER *Hemiptera.*
FAMILY *Corixidae.*
SPECIES IN FAMILY *550.*
SIZE *0.8–1.4cm.*
FEEDING *Nymphs and adults: predators, herbivores (algae), scavengers.*
IMPACT *Harmless.*

Backswimmers

Notonectidae

These compact, wedge-shaped bugs swim upside-down in water, and when resting at the surface they hang from the end of their abdomen. The surface of their back is typically pale-coloured and convex, with a ridge or keel running down the middle. Their underside is dark brown to black. The stout rostrum and the very short antennae have four segments. Used for propulsion, the oar-like hind legs are fringed with hairs.

FAVOUR *still, open stretches of water such as lake margins, pools, and stream edges.*

hair fringes

pale upper surface

▲ **NOTONECTA GLAUCA,** *the Common Backswimmer, is widespread and can be found in ponds, lakes, and even canals or ditches.*

▼ **NOTONECTA MACULATA** *is found in the northern hemisphere and feeds on prey trapped by the surface film in temporary habitats.*

oar-like hind leg

mottled reddish wings

pale pronotum

dark, shiny eyes

ORDER Hemiptera.
FAMILY Notonectidae.
SPECIES IN FAMILY 350.
SIZE 0.8–1.6cm.
FEEDING Nymphs and adults: predators (varied prey up to size of small fish).
IMPACT May bite if handled.

Froghoppers

Cercopidae

These squat, round-eyed bugs are good jumpers and very similar to spittle bugs (p.490). Most species are brown, grey, or drab, but some are black with vivid red or orange markings. The head has rounded eyes and is narrower than the thorax, which can look hexagonal or angular. Like spittle bugs, the nymphs produce frothy excrement to reduce evaporation and provide protection from predators.

INHABIT *well-vegetated areas such as woods, meadows, and scrub, occurring on a variety of shrubs, trees, and herbaceous plants.*

bold red markings

rounded eyes

NOTE

This species is quite common in the south of Britain. The nymphs live underground, feeding on the root sap of host plants.

ORDER Hemiptera.
FAMILY Cercopidae.
SPECIES IN FAMILY 2,400.
SIZE 0.5–2cm. Most under 1.4cm.
FEEDING Nymphs and adults: herbivores (plant juices); nymphs feed on root sap.
IMPACT Some species are crop pests.

▲ **CERCOPIS VULNERATA** *is a very conspicuous species, with bright warning coloration to deter potential predators.*

Leafhoppers

Cicadellidae

ABUNDANT *virtually everywhere, especially in lush, well-vegetated habitats.*

Leafhoppers are generally slender with broad or triangular heads and large eyes. Many species are green or brown in colour and may have brightly striped markings. The body has parallel sides or tapers towards the rear end. One of the most distinctive features of these bugs is their excellent jumping ability. The hind legs are enlarged and the hind tibiae are slightly flattened and distinctive in having three or four regular rows of very conspicuous spines arranged along their length. All leafhoppers are herbivores: most species suck the juices of plants' phloem vessels (the main transport vessels in plants), while others suck the contents of individual plant cells.

▼ **EUPELIX CUSPIDATA** *occurs in dry, grassy areas and is recognized by its large, shovel-shaped head.*

spiny hind leg

front of head pointed

▼ **GRAPHOCEPHALA FENNAHI**, *the Candy-Striped Leafhopper, is native to the USA but is now widespread in central and southern Britain on rhododendrons.*

black stripe through eye

▼ **LEDRA AURITA** *is a large, flat-bodied species with distinctive horns on the sides of the pronotum. It is well camouflaged against the lichen-covered bark of the oak trees on which it lives.*

net-like pattern of veins

camouflaged coloration

horns on pronotum

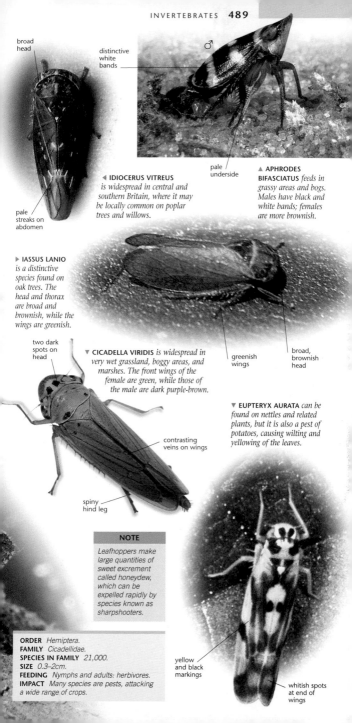

broad
head

distinctive
white
bands

♂

pale
underside

pale
streaks on
abdomen

◀ **IDIOCERUS VITREUS**
is widespread in central and
southern Britain, where it may
be locally common on poplar
trees and willows.

▲ **APHRODES
BIFASCIATUS** feeds in
grassy areas and bogs.
Males have black and
white bands; females
are more brownish.

▶ **IASSUS LANIO**
is a distinctive
species found on
oak trees. The
head and thorax
are broad and
brownish, while the
wings are greenish.

greenish
wings

broad,
brownish
head

two dark
spots on
head

▼ **CICADELLA VIRIDIS** is widespread in
very wet grassland, boggy areas, and
marshes. The front wings of the
female are green, while those of
the male are dark purple-brown.

contrasting
veins on wings

spiny
hind leg

▼ **EUPTERYX AURATA** can be
found on nettles and related
plants, but it is also a pest of
potatoes, causing wilting and
yellowing of the leaves.

NOTE

Leafhoppers make
large quantities of
sweet excrement
called honeydew,
which can be
expelled rapidly by
species known as
sharpshooters.

yellow
and black
markings

whitish spots
at end of
wings

ORDER Hemiptera.
FAMILY Cicadellidae.
SPECIES IN FAMILY 21,000.
SIZE 0.3–2cm.
FEEDING Nymphs and adults: herbivores.
IMPACT Many species are pests, attacking
a wide range of crops.

Spittle Bugs

Aphrophoridae

COMMON *in nearly all habitats on a wide range of woody and herbaceous plants.*

Spittle bugs vary from pale to dark brown with lighter mottling and markings. Some species have many colour forms. The head is almost as wide as the pronotum, the front of which is arched or curved forwards. The hind tibiae have one or two strong spines and a circle of smaller spines at their ends. These bugs are good jumpers.

variable colour and pattern

broad, thick-set head

NOTE

Nymphs produce cuckoo spit: a frothy protective covering. This is made by blowing watery excrement through a modified anus.

CUCKOO SPIT

PHILAENUS SPUMARIUS, *the Meadow Spittle Bug or Common Froghopper, lives on many plants. The nymphs' foamy mass is a familiar sight in sheltered habitats.*

ORDER *Hemiptera.*
FAMILY *Aphrophoridae.*
SPECIES IN FAMILY *850.*
SIZE *6–10mm.*
FEEDING *Nymphs and adults: herbivores (leaves, shoots, stems, and plant sap).*
IMPACT *Some species are minor crop pests.*

Planthoppers

Delphacidae

ABUNDANT *at or near ground level in grassy areas, meadows, and woodland margins, especially near water.*

These small bugs are mostly brown or greenish. Their bodies are elongated and almost parallel-sided. The antennae are short and often arise from a small indentation on the lower edge of the eyes. A distinctive feature of these insects is a flat, moveable spur at the end of the hind tibiae. Most species have short-winged and fully-winged forms.

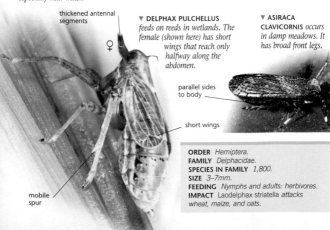

thickened antennal segments

▼ **DELPHAX PULCHELLUS** *feeds on reeds in wetlands. The female (shown here) has short wings that reach only halfway along the abdomen.*

▲ **ASIRACA CLAVICORNIS** *occurs in damp meadows. It has broad front legs.*

♀

parallel sides to body

short wings

mobile spur

ORDER *Hemiptera.*
FAMILY *Delphacidae.*
SPECIES IN FAMILY *1,800.*
SIZE *3–7mm.*
FEEDING *Nymphs and adults: herbivores.*
IMPACT *Laodelphax striatella attacks wheat, maize, and oats.*

Whiteflies

Aleyrodidae

Whiteflies are very small, white, moth-like insects with two pairs of relatively broad wings that are usually white with a distinctive dusting of white, powdery wax. The hind and front wings are of the same size and, when resting, are held horizontally over the body. The head has a pair of antennae with seven segments. Females lay their eggs on tiny stalks on the undersides of leaves.

THRIVE on both wild and cultivated plants in a range of habitats, including greenhouses.

▼ **ALEYRODES PROLETELLA** attacks brassica species such as cabbages. It can be found at almost any time of year.

empty skin

freshly emerged adult

dark spots on wings

white wings covered in powdery wax

white legs and antennae

▼ **TRIALEURODES VAPORARIORUM,** the Glasshouse Whitefly, is a pest of glasshouse crops such as tomatoes.

ORDER Hemiptera.
FAMILY Aleyrodidae.
SPECIES IN FAMILY 1,200.
SIZE 1–3mm.
FEEDING Nymphs and adults: herbivores.
IMPACT May be pests of glasshouse crops and plants in the cabbage family.

Soft, Wax, and Tortoise Scales

Coccidae

These scale insects are very variable in form, but females are usually oval and flattened with a hard, smooth, or waxy body. Wax-covered species appear white, while others may be brownish. Females are almost always sedentary on their host plant. They reproduce mainly by parthenogenesis, without the need for males. Males, which are rarely seen, may be winged or wingless and are short-lived.

FOUND on host plants, both in the wild and in fields, orchards, and greenhouses; also feed on houseplants.

mature scale

▶ **PULVINARIA REGALIS** is known as the Horse Chestnut Scale; females reproduce without males and lay as many as 3,000 eggs.

reddish brown body

mature scale insect

eggs in waxy mass

◀ **PARTHENOLECANIUM CORNI,** the Brown Scale, is a pest of some fruit trees and around 300 ornamental plant species.

ORDER Hemiptera.
FAMILY Coccidae.
SPECIES IN FAMILY 1,250.
SIZE 2–6mm.
FEEDING Nymphs and adults: herbivores.
IMPACT Many species are pests of crops, gardenplants, and houseplants.

Plant Lice, Greenfly, or Aphids

Aphididae

These small, slow-moving, soft-bodied insects make up one of the most destructive insect families. They reproduce with phenomenal speed and cause immense damage to plants, weakening them, feeding on their sap, and infecting them with plant viral diseases. Aphid life cycles can be complex, involving sexual and asexual generations on different host plants. Most species are green, but some may be pink, black, or brown. The antennae have between four and six segments. The pear-shaped abdomen ends in a short, pointed tail – the cauda – and usually has a pair of projecting tubes, or cornicles, from which a defensive secretion can be produced. In some species the entire body may be coated with a white waxy secretion. When present, the wings are held tent-like over the body and are either clear or have darkish markings; the hind wings are smaller than the front wings.

▼ **THECABIUS AFFINIS** *is a woolly aphid which causes distortion and folding of the leaves of poplar and also the leaves of some buttercups.*

NOTE

Aphid excrement (honeydew) is rich in sugar, attracting ants which feed on it. In return the ants protect the aphids from enemies such as parasitic wasps.

long hind legs

short dark cornicle

▼ **TUBEROLACHNUS SALIGNUS** *is a large and widespread aphid occurring on willow. The back of the fourth abdominal segment has a single projection called a tubercle.*

mass of eggs

▲ **LACHNUS ROBORIS** *lays eggs in clusters on oak branches. The aphids live in colonies and are attended by ants, which feed on their honeydew.*

▼ **PERIPHYLLUS ACERICOLA** *lives on the leaves of sycamore trees. The nymphs have a resting period in the height of summer.*

winged adult

aggregation of aphids

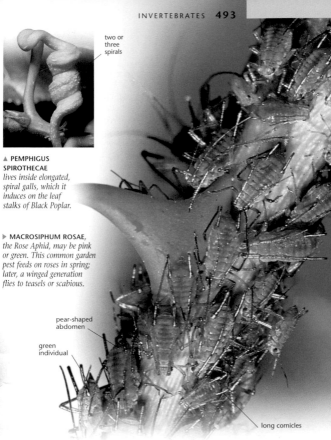

two or
three spirals

▲ **PEMPHIGUS
SPIROTHECAE**
*lives inside elongated,
spiral galls, which it
induces on the leaf
stalks of Black Poplar.*

▶ **MACROSIPHUM ROSAE**,
*the Rose Aphid, may be pink
or green. This common garden
pest feeds on roses in spring;
later, a winged generation
flies to teasels or scabious.*

pear-shaped
abdomen

green
individual

long cornicles

▼ **TUBERCULOIDES
ANNULATUS** *is a small
yellow, greenish, or pinkish
aphid that lives underneath
oak leaves.*

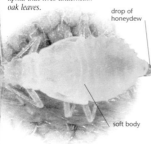

drop of
honeydew

soft body

▼ **APHIS FABAE**, *the Black
Bean Aphid or Blackfly,
attacks beans and other
plants during the summer.*

black body
with short
cornicles

ORDER *Hemiptera.*
FAMILY *Aphididae.*
SPECIES IN FAMILY *2,250.*
SIZE *2–5mm.*
FEEDING *Nymphs and adults: herbivores.*
IMPACT *Many species are pests of crops
and garden plants.*

Mealy Bugs

Pseudococcidae

OCCUR *wherever their host plant grows, in the wild or in glasshouses.*

Unlike related families of scale insects, mealy bugs have functional legs at all stages of their life history (in others, there is a sedentary stage). The sexes are very different. Females are elongated, wingless, covered with a wax coating, and possess sucking mouthparts. Males have a pair of wings, so look like typical insects, but lack developed mouthparts.

NOTE

Mealy bugs are sap-suckers and infest all parts of their host plant. Some species lay eggs in a mass of downy wax; others give birth to live nymphs.

long tail filaments

soft, waxy body

PSEUDOCOCCUS ADONIUM,
the Long-tailed Mealy Bug, is a pest of apple, pear, and citrus trees and also attacks crops and garden and house plants.

ORDER *Hemiptera.*
FAMILY *Pseudococcidae.*
SPECIES IN FAMILY *2,000.*
SIZE *1.5–4mm.*
FEEDING *Nymphs and adults: herbivores.*
IMPACT *Some species are pests of crops, gardenplants, and houseplants.*

Common Thrips

Thripidae

FAVOUR *the leaves and flowers of a vast range of plants, often including crops.*

The wings of these pale yellow, brown, or blackish thrips are narrower than in banded thrips and their ends are more pointed. The body appears flattened and the antennae usually have seven or eight segments. The front wings may have one or two longitudinal veins. In females the ovipositor curves downwards, not upwards.

wings not overlapped at rest

◀ **LIMOTHRIPS CEREALIUM,**
or the Grain Thrips, is a cosmopolitan species that attacks grasses and cereals.

▼ **TAENIOTHRIPS SIMPLEX**
can be a serious pest on Gladiolus and related flowers, leaving pale speckled marks on the flowers.

pale wings

flattened body

ORDER *Thysanoptera.*
FAMILY *Thripidae.*
SPECIES IN FAMILY *1,500.*
SIZE *0.7–2mm.*
FEEDING *Nymphs and adults: herbivores.*
IMPACT *Some species cause serious damage to field crops by feeding.*

Alderflies

Sialidae

Alderflies are day-flying insects with stout, dark brown to blackish grey bodies and a brownish or greyish tint to the wings, which are held together, tent-like, over the body. The head is blunt with large eyes and long, thread-like antennae. The pronotum is squarish. The front and hind wings are similarly sized with prominent dark veins that are not forked close to the wing margins.

SPEND long periods resting on alders and similar vegetation beside slow-moving streams, canals, and mud-bottomed pools.

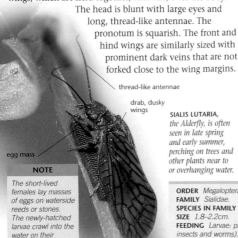

thread-like antennae

drab, dusky wings

SIALIS LUTARIA, the Alderfly, is often seen in late spring and early summer, perching on trees and other plants near to or overhanging water.

egg mass

LARVAE

The aquatic larvae have powerful jaws and seven pairs of feathery abdominal gills on each side.

NOTE

The short-lived females lay masses of eggs on waterside reeds or stones. The newly-hatched larvae crawl into the water on their well-developed legs.

ORDER Megaloptera.
FAMILY Sialidae.
SPECIES IN FAMILY 75.
SIZE 1.8–2.2cm.
FEEDING Larvae: predators (small aquatic insects and worms). Adults: non-feeding.
IMPACT Harmless.

Snakeflies

Raphidiidae

These shiny, dark brown insects have an elongated prothorax on which the head can be raised. The head is broadest across the eyes and tapers behind. The clear wings have a pterostigma and a prominent network of veins, which fork close to the wing margins. Females are a little larger than males, with a long ovipositor.

OCCUPY lush, low-growing vegetation in wooded areas.

♀ elongated prothorax

◀ **RAPHIDIA XANTHOSTIGMA** lives in woodland, where the larvae hunt small insects under bark. The sexes are identical, except for the female's ovipositor.

▼ **RAPHIDIA NOTATA** inhabits deciduous woodland, especially with oak trees. The larvae are often found in rotting stumps.

clear wings with dark veins

head narrows to rear

LARVAE

The slender larvae lack abdominal gills and have short, curved mandibles like those of adults.

ORDER Raphidioptera.
FAMILY Raphidiidae.
SPECIES IN FAMILY 85.
SIZE 1.4–2cm.
FEEDING Larvae and adults: predators (mainly aphids and soft-bodied insects).
IMPACT Harmless.

Common Lacewings

Chrysopidae

INHABITS all types of vegetation, including along woodland edges and hedgerows.

These delicate insects generally have a green body and wings and are sometimes known as green lacewings. The wings are often iridescent with delicate tints of pink, green, and blue, have many forked veins, lack markings, and are held roof-like over the body. The eyes are golden, brassy, or reddish and appear to shine. The antennae are long and slender.

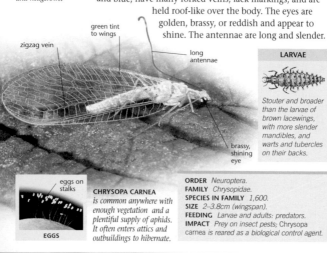

zigzag vein

green tint to wings

long antennae

brassy, shining eye

LARVAE

Stouter and broader than the larvae of brown lacewings, with more slender mandibles, and warts and tubercles on their backs.

eggs on stalks

EGGS

CHRYSOPA CARNEA *is common anywhere with enough vegetation and a plentiful supply of aphids. It often enters attics and outbuildings to hibernate.*

ORDER *Neuroptera.*
FAMILY *Chrysopidae.*
SPECIES IN FAMILY *1,600.*
SIZE *2–3.8cm (wingspan).*
FEEDING *Larvae and adults: predators.*
IMPACT *Prey on insect pests; Chrysopa carnea is reared as a biological control agent.*

Screech Beetles

Hygrobiidae

OCCUR in ponds and other waterbodies with muddy bottoms.

Screech beetles are reddish brown with dark markings, smooth, and broadly oval. The upperside of the body is convex, the underside even more so. The head is fairly broad, with bulging eyes. The legs have special swimming hairs on the tibiae, femora, and tarsi; when swimming, the legs are used alternately. When disturbed, adults make a distinctive squeaking noise by rubbing the end of the abdomen against a ridged structure on the wing cases.

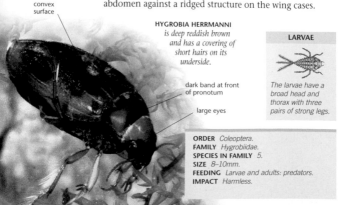

convex surface

HYGROBIA HERRMANNI *is deep reddish brown and has a covering of short hairs on its underside.*

dark band at front of pronotum

large eyes

LARVAE

The larvae have a broad head and thorax with three pairs of strong legs.

ORDER *Coleoptera.*
FAMILY *Hygrobiidae.*
SPECIES IN FAMILY *5.*
SIZE *8–10mm.*
FEEDING *Larvae and adults: predators.*
IMPACT *Harmless.*

Whirligig Beetles

Gyrinidae

These oval, streamlined beetles are typically black, with a bronze or steel-blue sheen in some species. The head has short antennae and the eyes are divided into upper and lower portions for vision above and below water. The long front legs are adapted for grasping prey, while the middle and hind legs are short, flat, and paddle-like.

FOUND on the surface of ponds, pools, slow-moving streams, and sluggish rivers.

LARVAE

The yellowish or greenish larvae are elongated with sharp mouthparts and narrow heads.

hairy upper surface

grasping front leg

▲ ORECTOCHILUS VILLOSUS, the Hairy Whirligig, has short, pale hairs on its dorsal surface. It is narrower and more elongated than other whirligig beetles.

▶ GYRINUS SP. are dark, shiny beetles that swim rapidly in circles on the water.

smooth, dark elytra

ORDER Coleoptera.
FAMILY Gyrinidae.
SPECIES IN FAMILY 750.
SIZE 4–8mm.
FEEDING Larvae and adults: predators, scavengers.
IMPACT Harmless.

Water Scavenger Beetles

Hydrophilidae

Most of these beetles live in water, carrying air under their wing cases and on their body surface. Oval in shape, they are black, brown, or yellowish. The upperside of the body is convex and smooth; the underside is flat with a covering of short, velvety hairs that looks silvery underwater. The maxillary palps (a pair of sensory mouthparts) are typically longer than the short, club-ended antennae.

FAVOUR freshwater habitats; also occur in dung, soil, and decaying vegetation.

LARVAE

Surface-breathing or equipped with gills, the predatory larvae may have warty or hairy backs.

faint striations

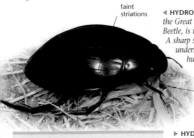

◀ HYDROPHILUS PICEUS, the Great Silver Diving Beetle, is up to 5cm long. A sharp spine on its underside can pierce human skin.

long palp

smooth, rounded outline

▶ HYDROCHARA CARABOIDES is quite a good swimmer and, like Hydrophilus piceus (above), it lays its eggs in floating cocoons. It is found in weedy, still water.

ORDER Coleoptera.
FAMILY Hydrophilidae.
SPECIES IN FAMILY 2,000.
SIZE 0.4–4.8cm.
FEEDING Larvae: predators. Adults: mainly scavengers, also predators.
IMPACT Harmless.

Ground Beetles

Carabidae

These beetles are active hunters with long, slender legs and powerful jaws; most species are nocturnal. They may be dull or shiny. The majority are brown or black, often with a metallic sheen, although a few species are green, red, and black or have yellow or green markings. The body is long, parallel-sided, and slightly flattened, usually with striations running along the elytra. The head has thread-like antennae, conspicuous eyes, and toothed jaws. The head, thorax, and abdomen tend to be clearly differentiated.

FOUND *on the ground in a wide variety of habitats, including under wood, stones, leaf litter, and debris.*

LARVAE

Most larvae live in soil or debris and are black or dark brown with long bodies that taper at both ends. They use enzymes to digest prey, then suck in the resulting liquid.

4 pale spots

▲ **DROMIUS QUADRIMACULATUS** *is easily recognized by its dark elytra with four yellowish brown spots. It hides under tree bark.*

reddish legs

▲ **HARPALUS RUFIPES** *occurs in cultivated land, waste ground, and gardens. It forages after dark for seeds, sometimes attacking strawberries.*

▼ **BRACHINUS CREPITANS** *hides under stones in dry locations. Like all bombardier beetles, it can fire hot chemicals from its rear end in defence.*

bluish or greenish elytra

flattened body

▲ **NEBRIA BREVICOLLIS** *is found in many habitats, most commonly under stones and logs in woodland and hedgerows.*

reddish brown head, thorax, and legs

▼ **CARABUS VIOLACEUS**, *better known as the Violet Ground Beetle, is a large, widespread species that feeds on a range of invertebrates, including slugs. It is commonest in woodland.*

metallic violet sheen

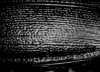

faint yellowish spot
at rear of elytra

narrow head

▲ **BEMBIDION LUNATUM**
is common and widespread near
water, especially on riverbanks.
There are many similar species.

yellow legs

▲ **CYCHRUS CARABOIDES**
crawls under moss and bark on
old tree stumps in woodland. It
emerges after dark to hunt snails.

pale spot

◀ **CICINDELLA CAMPESTRIS**, the
Green Tiger Beetle, is an active
flier and very fast runner. It likes
hot, sunny, open areas.

large jaws

pale, circular
spots

bronze sheen
to elytra

large
eyes

▲ **ELAPHRUS RIPARIUS** is
unmistakable due to its rows
of pale spots. It forages on bare
ground near ponds and streams.

broad
body

▲ **NOTIOPHILUS BIGUTTATUS**
is a squat species with very large
eyes. It is a specialist predator
of springtails, which it catches
in its strong jaws.

bronze
sheen

long, thin
antennae

prominent
striations

▲ **CALOSOMA INQUISITOR**
inhabits deciduous woodland.
Like other Calosoma species, it
hunts caterpillars among foliage.

◀ **PTEROSTICHUS NIGER**
is one of numerous similar
nocturnal species that forage on
the ground for prey or carrion.

shiny black
body

ORDER Coleoptera.
FAMILY Carabidae.
SPECIES IN FAMILY 29,000.
SIZE 0.2–2.8cm.
FEEDING Immatures and adults: predators,
scavengers; some species partly herbivores.
IMPACT Many species help to control pests.

NOTE

The larvae
of Tiger beetles live
in vertical burrows
in sandy or gravel
soil. They seize
any passing
insects and drag
them down to
eat them.

Predatory Diving Beetles

Dytiscidae

INHABIT *streams, ditches, canals, lakes, and ponds, usually in shallower water.*

These voracious predators have smooth, streamlined, shiny bodies. Many species are reddish to dark brown or black, but some have extensive yellowish or reddish bands, spots, and other markings. The head appears to be partly sunk into the pronotum and the antennae are thread-like. The hind legs, which are flattened and paddle-like with fringes of long hairs, are used for swimming; they are often longer than the other legs. The front legs are used for holding prey and the middle legs for clinging to vegetation. The males of some species have swollen structures on the front tarsi, used to hold the females' smooth backs during mating.

LARVAE

Due to their highly predatory nature, the larvae are often called water tigers. They are elongated with hairy legs and large, curved jaws and obtain air at the water surface.

▶ **GRAPHODERUS ZONATUS** *is recognized by the black bands at the front and rear of the pronotum, as well as the extensive mottling on the elytra.*

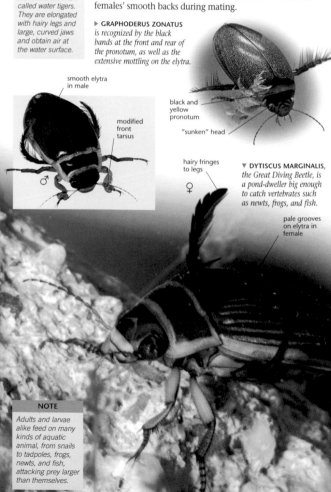

smooth elytra in male

modified front tarsus

black and yellow pronotum

"sunken" head

hairy fringes to legs
♀

▼ **DYTISCUS MARGINALIS,** *the Great Diving Beetle, is a pond-dweller big enough to catch vertebrates such as newts, frogs, and fish.*

pale grooves on elytra in female

NOTE

Adults and larvae alike feed on many kinds of aquatic animal, from snails to tadpoles, frogs, newts, and fish, attacking prey larger than themselves.

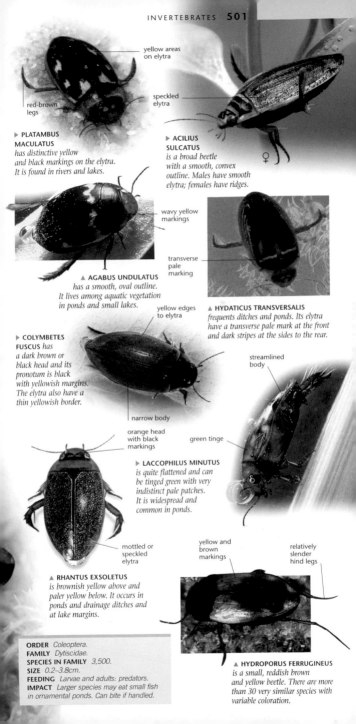

yellow areas on elytra

red-brown legs

speckled elytra

▶ **PLATAMBUS MACULATUS**
has distinctive yellow and black markings on the elytra. It is found in rivers and lakes.

▶ **ACILIUS SULCATUS**
is a broad beetle with a smooth, convex outline. Males have smooth elytra; females have ridges.

♀

wavy yellow markings

▲ **AGABUS UNDULATUS**
has a smooth, oval outline. It lives among aquatic vegetation in ponds and small lakes.

transverse pale marking

▲ **HYDATICUS TRANSVERSALIS**
frequents ditches and ponds. Its elytra have a transverse pale mark at the front and dark stripes at the sides to the rear.

yellow edges to elytra

▶ **COLYMBETES FUSCUS** has
a dark brown or black head and its pronotum is black with yellowish margins. The elytra also have a thin yellowish border.

narrow body

streamlined body

orange head with black markings

green tinge

▶ **LACCOPHILUS MINUTUS**
is quite flattened and can be tinged green with very indistinct pale patches. It is widespread and common in ponds.

mottled or speckled elytra

▲ **RHANTUS EXSOLETUS**
is brownish yellow above and paler yellow below. It occurs in ponds and drainage ditches and at lake margins.

yellow and brown markings

relatively slender hind legs

▲ **HYDROPORUS FERRUGINEUS**
is a small, reddish brown and yellow beetle. There are more than 30 very similar species with variable coloration.

ORDER Coleoptera.
FAMILY Dytiscidae.
SPECIES IN FAMILY 3,500.
SIZE 0.2–3.8cm.
FEEDING Larvae and adults: predators.
IMPACT Larger species may eat small fish in ornamental ponds. Can bite if handled.

OCCUR *on the ground close to carcasses; also under dung and in rotting fungi in damp, shady woodland.*

Carrion Beetles

Silphidae

Many of these slightly flattened, soft-bodied beetles are black or brown, often with yellow, red, or orange markings. The body surface may be dull or shiny and some have a roughened texture or ridges. The head, which is much narrower than the thorax, has round, slightly bulging eyes, strong, curved mandibles, and short, club-ended antennae. The legs of most species are strong and spiny.

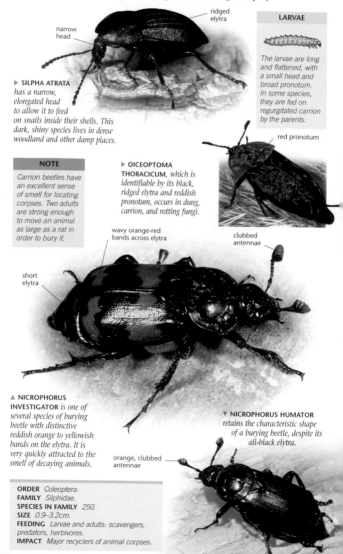

ridged elytra

narrow head

▶ **SILPHA ATRATA** has a narrow, elongated head to allow it to feed on snails inside their shells. This dark, shiny species lives in dense woodland and other damp places.

LARVAE

The larvae are long and flattened, with a small head and broad pronotum. In some species, they are fed on regurgitated carrion by the parents.

red pronotum

NOTE

Carrion beetles have an excellent sense of smell for locating corpses. Two adults are strong enough to move an animal as large as a rat in order to bury it.

▶ **OICEOPTOMA THORACICUM**, which is identifiable by its black, ridged elytra and reddish pronotum, occurs in dung, carrion, and rotting fungi.

wavy orange-red bands across elytra

clubbed antennae

short elytra

▲ **NICROPHORUS INVESTIGATOR** is one of several species of burying beetle with distinctive reddish orange to yellowish bands on the elytra. It is very quickly attracted to the smell of decaying animals.

orange, clubbed antennae

▼ **NICROPHORUS HUMATOR** *retains the characteristic shape of a burying beetle, despite its all-black elytra.*

ORDER *Coleoptera.*
FAMILY *Silphidae.*
SPECIES IN FAMILY *250.*
SIZE *0.9–3.2cm.*
FEEDING *Larvae and adults: scavengers, predators, herbivores.*
IMPACT *Major recyclers of animal corpses.*

Rove Beetles

Staphylinidae

Most rove beetles are small and smooth with elongated, parallel-sided bodies and black or brown coloration. Some species have bright colours, a sculptured surface, or dense body hairs. The head is squarish with long, sharp jaws that cross over each other; the antennae are short and thread-like. All species have distinctively short elytra that expose five or six of the abdominal segments. The full-sized hind wings are folded under the elytra when not in use. The flexible abdomen may be raised in a defensive posture.

FOUND in dung and carrion, and also in soil, fungi, leaf litter, decaying plant matter, and ant nests.

raised abdomen

matt black all over

◀ **STAPHYLINUS OLENS,** the Devil's Coach Horse, displays alarm by raising its abdomen and opening its jaws.

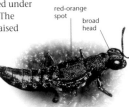

red-orange spot

broad head

▲ **STENUS BIMACULATUS** lives in marshy places. It secretes a surface tension-reducing chemical from its rear end to move over water.

▶ **TACHYPORUS HYPNORUM** is one of many similar small species with tapering bodies and red elytra.

tapering abdomen

short red elytra

▼ **EMUS HIRTUS,** the Hairy Rove Beetle, is restricted to southern Britain where it eats insects found in animal dung.

large jaws

hind wings folded beneath short elytra

orange-red prothorax

bluish green sheen to elytra

▼ **PHILONTHUS FIMETARIUS** eats fly maggots and beetle larvae. There are numerous very similar species.

flexible abdomen

black end to femur

LARVAE

The larvae are dark and elongated, with short antennae and cerci. Some larvae produce odours to trick ants into taking them into their nests and feeding them.

▶ **PAEDERUS LITTORALIS** is a flightless, orange and black species found in riverine habitats.

NOTE

Most rove beetles can fly well. Smaller species tend to be diurnal, whereas large species are generally nocturnal. A few species are associated with ants.

ORDER Coleoptera.
FAMILY Staphylinidae.
SPECIES IN FAMILY 27,000.
SIZE 0.8–2.6cm.
FEEDING Larvae: predators, scavengers. Adults: predators, scavengers, herbivores.
IMPACT Harmless.

Stag Beetles

Lucanidae

OCCUR *in deciduous woodland, especially with mature trees and decaying timber.*

These beetles are typically large, shiny, robust insects with black or reddish brown coloration, although some species are smaller or have a bluish sheen. The males of most species have greatly enlarged, toothed mandibles; females are often smaller and have proportionately smaller mandibles. The antennae are elbowed or bent in the middle with a terminal club of three or four expanded, flattened segments. The elytra are smooth and shiny with faint striations. Stag beetles are attracted to lights at night, when they may wander far from woodland.

horn on head

♂

▲ SINODENDRON CYLINDRICUM
has a very rounded shape. The male has a horn on its head and the front of its pronotum is toothed.

♂

large prothorax

▲ DORCUS PARALLELIPIDEDUS,
the Lesser Stag Beetle, has a relatively large head and prothorax. The male's jaws are curved but not enlarged.

▼ LUCANUS CERVUS,
the Stag Beetle, is unmistakable. It has declined in recent years due to the loss of rotten wood as a breeding site for its larvae.

massive mandibles

♂

large head

elbowed antennae

♀

smooth brown elytra

LARVAE

The C-shaped larvae have strong legs on the thorax. They feed on decaying logs and tree stumps and may take several years to develop.

NOTE

During courtship, male stag beetles fight pitched battles with rivals. Their jaws have teeth that lock onto a rival's pronotum to try to flip it upside down.

ORDER Coleoptera.
FAMILY Lucanidae.
SPECIES IN FAMILY 1,300.
SIZE 1.4–6.4cm.
FEEDING Larvae: wood-feeders (decaying timber). Adults: liquid-feeders.
IMPACT May try to bite if handled.

Dor Beetles

Geotrupidae

These stout insects are broadly oval and rounded. They are brown or black, shiny, and often have a metallic greenish, blue, or purplish sheen. In many species, males have tooth-like projections and horns on the head and thorax. The jaws are large and clearly visible; the club-ended antennae have 11 segments but are not elbowed. The elytra have obvious lengthwise grooves, while the tibiae of the broad front legs are armed with strong teeth for digging.

FOUND beneath dung of all kinds and in carrion, decaying wood, and fungi.

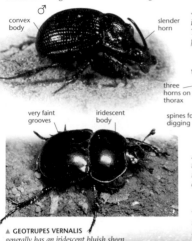

♂

convex body

slender horn

◄ **ODONTAEUS ARMIGER** is a small, dark, convex-bodied beetle. The male has upturned lobes while the female is reddish brown without lobes.

three horns on thorax

spines for digging

♂

▲ **TYPHAEUS TYPHOEUS**, the Minotaur Beetle, digs deep into sandy soil beneath piles of sheep and rabbit droppings.

very faint grooves

iridescent body

▼ **GEOTRUPES STERCORARIUS** is often infested with parasitic mites. It is black, often with a shiny metallic blue or purplish sheen underneath.

clubbed antennae

▲ **GEOTRUPES VERNALIS** generally has an iridescent bluish sheen and has less noticeable striations on the elytra than Geotrupes stercorarius.

LARVAE

The pale C-shaped larvae is found under animal dung in burrows. Larval development can take many months. They make noises by rubbing their legs on their body.

NOTE

Adult dor beetles dig tunnels many centimetres deep below dung and carry pieces of it down to provide a food source for their larvae.

ORDER Coleoptera.
FAMILY Geotrupidae.
SPECIES IN FAMILY 600.
SIZE 1–2.5cm.
FEEDING Larvae and adults: scavengers, dung-feeders.
IMPACT Harmless, beneficial.

Scarab Beetles and Chafers

Scarabaeidae

OCCUR *in a huge range of places, including decaying wood, fungi, carrion, dung, flowers, vegetation, bark, and the nests of mammals and social insects.*

Scarabs and chafers comprise a very large group of beetles and there is enormous variation in shape and size between species. The body colour varies from dull brown and black through red, yellow, and orange to metallic blues and greens. Despite this variety, a single character can identify these beetles: the antennae, which have between eight and ten segments and end in a distinctive club. The club is made up of three to seven flat, moveable, plate-like flaps, which can be separated or folded together. In many species the males have horns, used to fight for mates.

LARVAE

The larvae are white grubs with strong mandibles and a C-shaped body. Many live in the soil and feed on roots; others are found in dung, rotten wood, and decaying matter.

▶ **AMPHIMALLON SOLSTITIALIS** *is called the Summer Chafer as it can be seen flying in swarms around the tops of trees on June evenings.*

yellowish brown elytra

white hairs on thorax

◀ **PHYLLOPERTHA HORTICOLA,** *the Garden Chafer, can damage the leaves and buds of apple and pear trees by chewing them; its larvae eat the roots of grasses, including cereals.*

reddish brown elytra

long hairs on head and thorax

bee-like markings on abdomen

▶ **TRICHIUS FASCIATUS,** *the Bee Beetle, can be yellow or orange, but always has black markings and a very hairy body. Its larvae develop in rotting wood.*

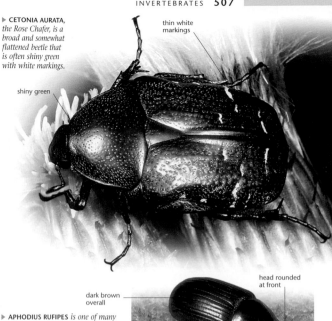

▶ **CETONIA AURATA,** the Rose Chafer, is a broad and somewhat flattened beetle that is often shiny green with white markings.

thin white markings

shiny green

head rounded at front

dark brown overall

▶ **APHODIUS RUFIPES** is one of many similar-looking beetles attracted to fresh cow, sheep, and horse dung. These species do not burrow or bury, but simply lay their eggs in the dung.

black convex shape

♂

curved horn

◀ **COPRIS LUNARIS,** the Horned Dung Beetle, has a distinctive horn on the head and a large, flat-fronted pronotum. Both sexes dig brood chambers in sandy soil.

♂

5 to 7 segments in antennal club

▶ **MELOLONTHA MELOLONTHA,** the Common Cockchafer, is also known as the May Bug since the adult emerges around this time. It flies around tree tops and is attracted to lights.

white hairs on elytra

NOTE

Dung beetles are extremely important recyclers in many regions. They clear away and bury vast amounts of dung, returning valuable nutrients to the soil.

ORDER Coleoptera.
FAMILY Scarabaeidae.
SPECIES IN FAMILY 20,000.
SIZE 0.2–15cm.
FEEDING Larvae: scavengers, fungi-feeders. Adults: liquid-feeders (nectar).
IMPACT A few species are serious pests.

Click Beetles or Skip Jacks

Elateridae

LIVE *on foliage, under bark, and in leaf litter, rotting wood, and soil.*

The most remarkable feature of these elongated, narrow-bodied beetles is their ability, when lying on their backs, to click loudly as they throw themselves into the air. Most are brownish or black, although a few are greenish. The antennae are quite long and slender, but may have a comb-like appearance. The rear angles of the pronotum are sharp and often extend backwards to form an acute point that meets the rounded shoulders of the elytra.

patterns of hair on pronotum and elytra

faint circular mark

▲ **PROSTERNON TESSELLATUM** *is black with a bronze sheen and has irregular patterns of pale hair on the pronotum.*

broad reddish brown band on elytra

▲ **AMPEDUS BALTEATUS** *is distinctive as the front two-thirds of the elytra are reddish brown while the rear one-third is blackish brown. The larvae develop in rotten wood.*

black head and pronotum

◄ **SERICUS BRUNNEUS** *is reddish brown with a central dark stripe running down the pronotum. The larvae live in the soil in cooler regions.*

dark central stripe

▼ **ATHOUS HAEMORRHOIDALIS** *is one of the commonest European click beetle species and is found in a wide range of habitats. The larvae are herbivorous.*

broad head

yellow-brown hairs on elytra

LARVAE

Often known as wireworms for their slender, elongated, cylindrical shape, and tough bodies, click beetle larvae are commonly found in rotten wood, under bark, or soil.

NOTE

The beetles can "flick" themselves upwards at an amazing 300 times the acceleration of gravity. The loud click and movement frightens predators.

ORDER *Coleoptera.*
FAMILY *Elateridae.*
SPECIES IN FAMILY *8,500.*
SIZE *0.2–3cm.*
FEEDING *Larvae: scavengers, herbivores, predators. Adults: herbivores.*
IMPACT *May be pests of crops and pasture.*

Fireflies and Glow-worms

Lampyridae

Once seen, the sight of fireflies emitting pulses of eerie greenish light as they fly through the night air is never forgotten. These slightly flattened, parallel-sided beetles are generally drab brown, but may have paler markings of red or yellow. The head, which is small with slender antennae, is concealed by the large, hood-like pronotum. Males are fully winged and the wing cases are soft and rather hairy. The females of some species look like the flattened larvae and lack wings. Only two species are found in Britain – the Glow-worm, seen mostly in southern Britain, and a smaller and very rare species called *Phosphaenus hemipterus*, which is confined to localities in one or two southern counties.

FAVOUR *woods, hedgerows, meadows, and damp grassland; also chalk grassland.*

NOTE

These insects produce light by a chemical reaction in luminous organs. The flashing is used to attract a mate and is specific to each species.

LARVAE

The broad, flattened larvae are predatory and attack snails, using their narrow head and elongate, flattened body, to push inside as they feed.

LAMPYRIS NOCTILUCA, *the Glow-worm, is mainly found in southern Britain on chalk grassland. The female, which can resemble a woodlouse, glows to attract males.*

light-emitting organs

wings absent

♀

flattened body

LARVA

dull brown elytra

pale at pronotum margins

ORDER *Coleoptera.*
FAMILY *Lampyridae.*
SPECIES IN FAMILY *2,000.*
SIZE *0.8–1.8cm.*
FEEDING *Larvae: predators. Adults: non-feeding, predators.*
IMPACT *Harmless.*

Soldier Beetles

Cantharidae

OCCUR *on flowers and other vegetation in grassland, woodland edges, and hedgerows.*

These beetles may have been named after the black and red coloration and contrasting markings of the commonest species, reminiscent of 18th- and 19th-century military uniforms. Soldier beetles are elongate, nearly parallel-sided, and have soft bodies. The head has curved, sharp jaws and relatively long, slender antennae. The pronotum is relatively short and squarish; the wing cases of some species are short and do not reach the abdomen's tip.

LARVAE

The larvae appear similar to those of ground beetles (p.498), with flattened bodies and a fine, velvety covering of short hair.

dark elytra

black spot on pronotum

red base to antennae

◀ **CANTHARIS FUSCA** *is largely black but for the reddish pronotum with a black patch at the front.*

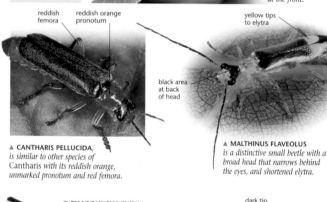

reddish femora

reddish orange pronotum

yellow tips to elytra

black area at back of head

▲ **CANTHARIS PELLUCIDA**, *is similar to other species of Cantharis with its reddish orange, unmarked pronotum and red femora.*

▲ **MALTHINUS FLAVEOLUS** *is a distinctive small beetle with a broad head that narrows behind the eyes, and shortened elytra.*

▼ **RHAGONYCHA FULVA**, *a common species in Britain, is usually seen on the flowers of umbellifers, where they mate.*

dark tip to elytra

shiny, reddish orange pronotum

ORDER *Coleoptera.*
FAMILY *Cantharidae.*
SPECIES IN FAMILY *4,000.*
SIZE *0.3–2cm.*
FEEDING *Larvae: predators. Adults: liquid-feeders (nectar), herbivores, predators.*
IMPACT *Harmless.*

Skin, Larder, and Museum Beetles

Dermestidae

Beetles in this family are small and typically broadly oval and rounded in side view. Most species are dull brown or black in colour, but others may appear variegated. They are often thickly covered with white, yellow, brown, or red scales or hair that form spots or delicate patterns. The head is mostly concealed by the pronotum, into which it fits neatly. The short, club-ended antennae can be concealed in grooves on the underside of the thorax and are often hard to see.

SCAVENGE *in all kinds of places, such as bird nests, rodent burrows, fur, stored food, and museum collections.*

LARVAE

The larvae are very hairy and the long hair tufts of many species produce nettle-like rashes in sensitive people. Anthrenus larvae are commonly called woolly bears.

◄ **ANTHRENUS VERBASCI** *is also known as the Varied Carpet Beetle. It is a small rounded beetle with distinctive patterns of white, yellow, and black scales.*

variegated pattern of scales

rounded, convex body

sombre scale patterns

◄ **ANTHRENUS FUSCUS** *lives mainly in sheds, outbuildings, and stone walls where the females lay eggs on dead insects.*

rounded body outline

pale front half of elytra

dark rear half of abdomen

▶ **DERMESTES LARDARIUS**, the Bacon or Larder Beetle, is a dry carrion feeder but will also eat dried meat, fish, skins, and a large range of other stored produce.

white patches on rear of pronotum

NOTE

The larvae feed on a range of organic materials, including spices and carpets. They may destroy entire museum collections of biological material.

▶ **ATTAGENUS PELLIO**, known as the Two-spotted Carpet Beetle or Fur Beetle, can be a serious domestic pest; it is also found outdoors.

white spots on elytra

ORDER *Coleoptera.*
FAMILY *Dermestidae.*
SPECIES IN FAMILY 800.
SIZE *2–10mm.*
FEEDING *Larvae: scavengers. Adults: liquid-feeders (nectar), herbivores (pollen).*
IMPACT *Pests of stored items and textiles.*

Furniture and Drugstore Beetles

Anobiidae

NATIVE *to woodland, but thrive in all kinds of artificial wooden structures, both outside and in buildings.*

These small, hairy, light brown to black beetles are better known to many people as woodworm, although this name strictly refers to the grub-like larvae of the wood-boring species. The adults are typically elongated and cylindrical in shape, and, from the side, the head appears partly hooded by the pronotum. The antennae have eight to eleven segments, with the last three lengthened or expanded. The legs are short and can be pulled into special grooves on the underside of the body.

▼ ANOBIUM PUNCTATUM *is very common in trees and structural timbers alike. Its larvae are called woodworm.*

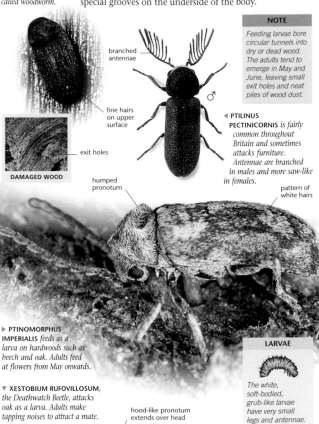

branched antennae

fine hairs on upper surface

exit holes

DAMAGED WOOD

humped pronotum

♂

◀ PTILINUS PECTINICORNIS *is fairly common throughout Britain and sometimes attacks furniture. Antennae are branched in males and more saw-like in females.*

pattern of white hairs

▶ PTINOMORPHUS IMPERIALIS *feeds as a larva on hardwoods such as beech and oak. Adults feed at flowers from May onwards.*

LARVAE

▼ XESTOBIUM RUFOVILLOSUM, *the Deathwatch Beetle, attacks oak as a larva. Adults make tapping noises to attract a mate.*

hood-like pronotum extends over head

The white, soft-bodied, grub-like larvae have very small legs and antennae.

ORDER *Coleoptera.*
FAMILY *Anobiidae.*
SPECIES IN FAMILY *1,500.*
SIZE *2–8mm.*
FEEDING *Larvae: scavengers, wood-feeders. Adults: scavengers, non-feeding.*
IMPACT *May damage furniture and timbers.*

Powder-post Beetles

Lyctidae

These beetles are small and slender in shape and brown in colour. The head has rounded, prominent eyes and antennae with eleven segments, of which the last two form a small club. The family's common name refers to the fine, powdery material that is all that is left after the larvae have burrowed into the sapwood of certain hardwoods.

SEEN *in dead and dying trees in woodland, and seasoned wood indoors.*

NOTE

Larvae bore in the sapwood of hardwoods such as oak or elm with high starch content and leave their tunnels packed with very fine powdery dust.

LARVAE

The larvae are white, quite hairless, and slightly curved. They bear three pairs of short legs.

LYCTUS BRUNNEUS *is very widespread. Females have long ovipositors to lay their eggs in cracks and fissures.*

elongated body

antennal club made of two segments

ORDER *Coleoptera.*
FAMILY *Lyctidae.*
SPECIES IN FAMILY *100.*
SIZE *3–7mm.*
FEEDING *Larvae and adults: wood-feeders.*
IMPACT *A few species are serious pests of wood.*

Soft-winged Flower Beetles

Melyridae

These beetles are narrow and elongated with a soft and flattened body. Many are brightly coloured in green and red and can be quite hairy. The head is typically short and broad with conspicuous eyes and slender antennae that have less than 11 segments. When disturbed, red sac-like swellings appear at the sides of the thorax and abdomen.

THRIVE *in woodland, meadows, grassland, and hedgerows.*

LARVAE

The larvae are long and slender, and may be slightly flattened or broader in the middle.

red margins and rear to elytra

▼ **MALACHIUS AENEUS** *has iridescent coloration and can often be seen feeding on flowers, especially buttercups.*

▼ **MALACHIUS BIPUSTULATUS** *is a common beetle of flower-rich grassland and meadows, where it hunts for small, soft-bodied prey.*

reddish orange tips to elytra

metallic green coloration

ORDER *Coleoptera.*
FAMILY *Melyridae.*
SPECIES IN FAMILY *1,500.*
SIZE *2–8mm.*
FEEDING *Larvae: predators. Adults: predators, herbivores (pollen).*
IMPACT *Harmless.*

Ladybirds or Ladybugs

Coccinellidae

OCCUR *in coniferous and deciduous woodland, heather, gardens, and parks; wherever there is prey.*

LARVAE

Often warty or spiny with dark bodies and red or white spots, larvae moult four times before pupating. Pupae are dark coloured or look like bird droppings.

These brightly marked, oval or round, sometimes almost hemispherical beetles are immediately recognizable. Ladybirds are shiny, and have a ground colour of black, red, yellow, or orange. The elytra have contrasting spots or regular markings. The bright colouring and marking of adults warns predators of their poisonous or distasteful nature. Confusingly, many species have several colour forms. The head is nearly completely concealed from view by the pronotum, and has antennae with three to six segments, and a short, terminal club. The legs are short, and can be drawn tightly into grooves on the underside of the body. Most adults and larvae are highly predacious on soft-bodied insects. There are, however, some herbivorous species (*Epilachna*) that can be a pest on plants, such as beans and squashes. The adults of many species hibernate in sheltered microhabitats and are often found in attics, and in cooler areas inside houses.

▶ **PSYLLOBORA 22-PUNCTATA** *is small with a very round outline. It lives on low vegetation, shrubs, and trees, where it feeds on mildews and moulds.*

small black spots

yellow background

warty bumps

PUPA

▲ **ANATIS OCELLATA,** *the Eyed Ladybird, is quite a large predatory species, which is associated with coniferous trees.*

pale-ringed dark spots

▼ **COCCINELLA SEPTEMPUNCTATA** *is more commonly known as the Seven-spot Ladybird. It is a common species in a wide variety of habitats throughout Britain.*

red elytra with seven black spots

white patches on pronotum

antennae

ORDER *Coleoptera.*
FAMILY *Coccinellidae.*
SPECIES IN FAMILY *5,000.*
SIZE *1–10mm.*
FEEDING *Larvae: predators, herbivores. Adults: predators, herbivores.*
IMPACT *Beneficial as predators of pests.*

NOTE

Adult ladybirds show what is known as reflex bleeding. If attacked, they can cause toxic body fluids to ooze out from the leg joints.

▶ **APHIDECTA OBLITERATA**, *the Larch Ladybird, has four, dark longitudinal marks on the pronotum. The species is associated with larch and some other coniferous trees.*

black and white markings on head

brown elytra

▼ **CALVIA 14-GUTTATA**, *the Cream-spot Ladybird, is quite small, and has no black markings. Common on trees such as alder, hazel, and whitethorn, it has also been found on flowers of Scots Pine.*

yellowish orange background

rectangular dark patches

whitish yellow spots

orangish brown background

▲ **PROPYLEA 14-PUNCTATA** is *very variable in colour. Some are all yellow or all black where all the spots seem to have joined up. This species eats aphids on shrubs and trees.*

one dark spot on each elytron

elytra predominantly red

▶ **ADALIA BIPUNCTATA**, *the Two-spot Ladybird, is a variable species, ranging from mainly black to mainly red with a large number of varieties in between.*

white patches on sides of pronotum

ADALIA BIPUNCTATA VARIANT

light orange patches on sides

dark markings predominate

ADALIA BIPUNCTATA VARIANT

LARVA

19 black spots on elytra

◀ **HARMONIA AXYRIDIS**, *the Harlequin Ladybird, is a recent arrival that threatens native ladybirds. It is large and variable, usually orange with 15–21 black spots, and has very distinctive larva.*

Pollen or Sap Beetles

Nitidulidae

These small beetles are often oval, squarish, or rectangular in outline. The majority are smooth, shiny and either dark or black, and are often marked with reddish or yellowish irregular spots. In some species, the elytra are a little shorter than the abdomen, exposing the last two segments. The short antennae have swollen or clubbed ends. The legs are short.

FOUND *on flowers, fungi, carrion, oozing sap on trees, and decaying fruit.*

clubbed antennae

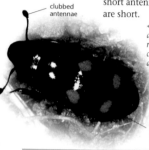

◀ **GLISCHROCHILUS HORTENSIS,** *an oval black beetle with four reddish orange spots on the elytra, can be found feeding at tree sap and the juices of ripe fruit.*

▼ **MELIGETHES AENEUS** *is often seen in large numbers in flowers where there is a good pollen supply.*

small, compact body

four orange spots on elytra

LARVAE

The larvae, which are long, pale, and slightly curved, may be pests of mustard and oilseed rape.

ORDER *Coleoptera.*
FAMILY *Nitidulidae.*
SPECIES IN FAMILY *2,800.*
SIZE *1–14mm.*
FEEDING *Larvae and adults: liquid-feeders, herbivores (pollen), predators, scavengers.*
IMPACT *Pests of crops and stored foods.*

False Oil Beetles

Oedemeridae

These beetles are soft-bodied, elongated, and parallel-sided, like soldier beetles (p.510). Many are brownish, but some are a shiny, iridescent green. The head is small and almost as wide as the pronotum, which is itself widest towards the front. The antennae are long and slender. The margins of the eyes have a small notch.

COMMON *in meadows and flower-rich grassland; the adults feed at flowers.*

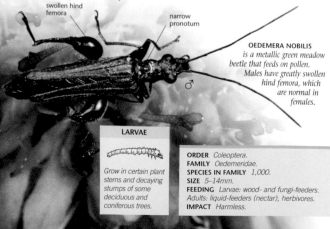

swollen hind femora

narrow pronotum

OEDEMERA NOBILIS *is a metallic green meadow beetle that feeds on pollen. Males have greatly swollen hind femora, which are normal in females.*

♂

LARVAE

Grow in certain plant stems and decaying stumps of some deciduous and coniferous trees.

ORDER *Coleoptera.*
FAMILY *Oedemeridae.*
SPECIES IN FAMILY *1,000.*
SIZE *5–14mm.*
FEEDING *Larvae: wood- and fungi-feeders. Adults: liquid-feeders (nectar), herbivores.*
IMPACT *Harmless.*

Darkling Beetles

Tenebrionidae

Darkling beetles are mostly black or very dark brown, but some species have reddish markings. The body shape ranges from small and parallel-sided to large and broadly oval, and may be smooth and shiny or dull and roughened. The antennae usually have 11 segments and can be relatively long and slender, or short with clubbed ends. The eyes do not have a circular or oval outline. In many species, the hind wings are very small.

INHABIT *virtually all terrestrial habitats, including those with very dry conditions.*

LARVAE

The larvae, known as mealworms, are elongated and cylindrical, usually with very tough bodies and short legs. Some species are reared as bird and reptile food.

◀ **CTENOPIUS SULPHUREUS** *is a brightly coloured species that is often found feeding at umbelliferous flowers in sunny places.*

dense hairs on body

sulphur-yellow elytra

dark legs

▶ **BLAPS MUCRONATA,** *the Cellar or Churchyard Beetle, lives mainly in damp, dark places close to the ground.*

▲ **LAGRIA HIRTA** *favours dry localities, where its larvae feed among leaf litter. It is sometimes placed in a separate family: Lagriidae.*

elytra fused together

distinctive striations on elytra

stout femora

short antennae

ORDER *Coleoptera.*
FAMILY *Tenebrionidae.*
SPECIES IN FAMILY *15,000.*
SIZE *0.2–2.5cm.*
FEEDING *Larvae and adults: scavengers.*
IMPACT *Some species are pests of stored grain, flour, meal, and dried fruit.*

▲ **TENEBRIO MOLITOR,** *the Yellow Mealworm Beetle, is found all over the world. It can be a pest of stored grain, meal, and flour.*

NOTE

Some of these species consume and breed on very dry food (bran and meal); they get all the water they need from digesting what they eat.

Longhorn Beetles

Cerambycidae

Named for their most distinctive feature, these beetles have antennae that are always at least two-thirds as long as the body, and sometimes up to four times as long. Coloration varies from shades of brown to very brightly marked black and yellow or orange, while some species are even bluish or violet. Often large, the beetles have long bodies with parallel sides. The eyes are notched or occasionally completely divided and the antennae are usually raised on conspicuous tubercles (swellings). Adults of many species are non-feeding, but others may feed on pollen, nectar, leaves, or roots.

LARVAE

Longhorn larvae are long and cylindrical, with tiny legs or none at all. They use their powerful jaws to eat wood, creating tunnels with a circular cross-section.

▶ **ACANTHOCINUS AEDILIS,** *the Timberman Beetle, has extremely long antennae in males. The larvae feed under the bark of dead pine trees.*

greyish or greyish brown

bluish coloration

tibia mainly yellowish-orange

body tapers towards rear

▶ **STRANGALIA MACULATA** *is often seen feeding on pollen at flowers. Its larvae feed in decaying tree trunks and stumps. It is a common and widespread species throughout Britain.*

variable yellow markings

NOTE

Longhorn beetles have been known to emerge from furniture made from attacked timber, having been hidden inside the wood as developing larvae.

yellowish brown elytra

black prothorax

▶ **LEPTURA RUBRA** *is bicoloured black and brown in males, whereas females are reddish brown. Its larvae feed on conifers such as pine.*

yellowish lower part of legs

antennae darker near tip

ORDER *Coleoptera.*
FAMILY *Cerambycidae.*
SPECIES IN FAMILY *25,000.*
SIZE *0.3–4.5cm.*
FEEDING *Larvae: wood-feeders. Adults: non-feeding, liquid-feeders (nectar), herbivores.*
IMPACT *Many species are pests of trees.*

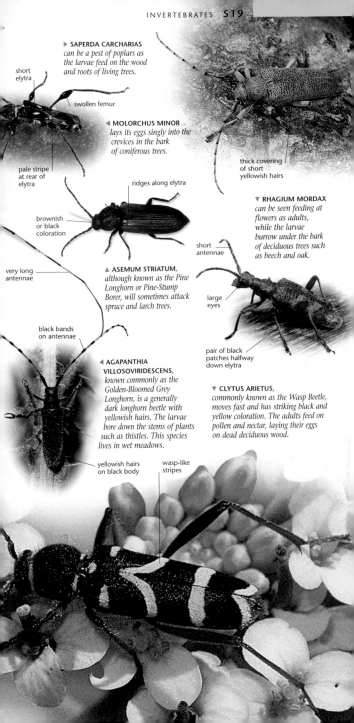

▶ **SAPERDA CARCHARIAS** can be a pest of poplars as the larvae feed on the wood and roots of living trees.

short elytra

swollen femur

◀ **MOLORCHUS MINOR** lays its eggs singly into the crevices in the bark of coniferous trees.

pale stripe at rear of elytra

thick covering of short yellowish hairs

ridges along elytra

▼ **RHAGIUM MORDAX** can be seen feeding at flowers as adults, while the larvae burrow under the bark of deciduous trees such as beech and oak.

brownish or black coloration

short antennae

very long antennae

▲ **ASEMUM STRIATUM**, although known as the Pine Longhorn or Pine-Stump Borer, will sometimes attack spruce and larch trees.

large eyes

black bands on antennae

pair of black patches halfway down elytra

◀ **AGAPANTHIA VILLOSOVIRIDESCENS**, known commonly as the Golden-Bloomed Grey Longhorn, is a generally dark longhorn beetle with yellowish hairs. The larvae bore down the stems of plants such as thistles. This species lives in wet meadows.

▼ **CLYTUS ARIETUS**, commonly known as the Wasp Beetle, moves fast and has striking black and yellow coloration. The adults feed on pollen and nectar, laying their eggs on dead deciduous wood.

yellowish hairs on black body

wasp-like stripes

Leaf Beetles

Chrysomelidae

OCCUR *on almost every type of plant in most terrestrial habitats.*

Typical leaf beetles are hairless, broadly oval when seen from above, and rounded when seen from the side. Many are brightly coloured and patterned or have a metallic sheen (such conspicuous coloration often serves to warn predators that the beetles are unpalatable). Although related to longhorn beetles (p.518), leaf beetles never have long antennae; these are usually less than half the body length. Some species look rather like ladybirds (p.514), but can be distinguished by the fact that the latter have three clearly visible tarsal segments on each leg, while leaf beetles have four.

LIFE CYCLE

Long and grub-like, leaf beetle larvae bore through plant tissues and also feed on the surface of plants. Species in the subfamily Donaciinae have aquatic larvae.

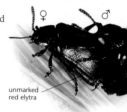

unmarked red elytra

▲ **CHRYSOMELA POPULI**, *the Poplar Leaf Beetle, feeds on the leaves of poplar and, occasionally, willow, as larvae, sometimes reducing entire leaves to skeletons.*

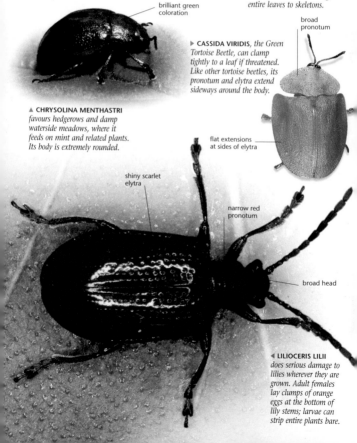

brilliant green coloration

▶ **CASSIDA VIRIDIS**, *the Green Tortoise Beetle, can clamp tightly to a leaf if threatened. Like other tortoise beetles, its pronotum and elytra extend sideways around the body.*

broad pronotum

flat extensions at sides of elytra

▲ **CHRYSOLINA MENTHASTRI** *favours hedgerows and damp waterside meadows, where it feeds on mint and related plants. Its body is extremely rounded.*

shiny scarlet elytra

narrow red pronotum

broad head

◀ **LILIOCERIS LILII** *does serious damage to lilies wherever they are grown. Adult females lay clumps of orange eggs at the bottom of lily stems; larvae can strip entire plants bare.*

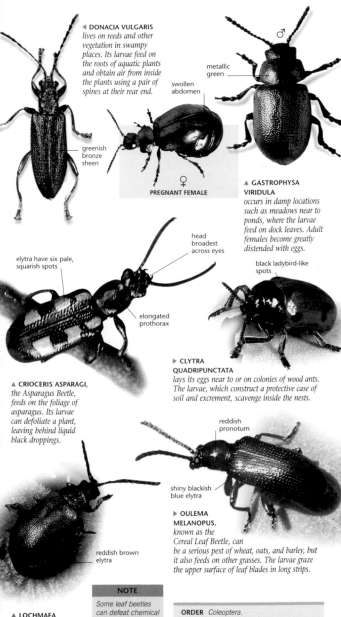

◀ **DONACIA VULGARIS** *lives on reeds and other vegetation in swampy places. Its larvae feed on the roots of aquatic plants and obtain air from inside the plants using a pair of spines at their rear end.*

greenish bronze sheen

swollen abdomen

♀
PREGNANT FEMALE

♂

metallic green

▲ **GASTROPHYSA VIRIDULA** *occurs in damp locations such as meadows near to ponds, where the larvae feed on dock leaves. Adult females become greatly distended with eggs.*

black ladybird-like spots

elytra have six pale, squarish spots

head broadest across eyes

elongated prothorax

▲ **CRIOCERIS ASPARAGI**, *the Asparagus Beetle, feeds on the foliage of asparagus. Its larvae can defoliate a plant, leaving behind liquid black droppings.*

▶ **CLYTRA QUADRIPUNCTATA** *lays its eggs near to or on colonies of wood ants. The larvae, which construct a protective case of soil and excrement, scavenge inside the nests.*

reddish pronotum

shiny blackish blue elytra

▶ **OULEMA MELANOPUS**, *known as the Cereal Leaf Beetle, can be a serious pest of wheat, oats, and barley, but it also feeds on other grasses. The larvae graze the upper surface of leaf blades in long strips.*

reddish brown elytra

▲ **LOCHMAEA CAPREA** *can be found on the foliage of birch and willow trees. The adults and larvae chew holes in the leaves, but leave the veins intact.*

NOTE

Some leaf beetles can defeat chemical plant defences. Before feeding, these species cut trenches in leaves to isolate them from the rest of the plant.

ORDER *Coleoptera.*
FAMILY *Chrysomelidae.*
SPECIES IN FAMILY *30,000.*
SIZE *0.2–2cm.*
FEEDING *Larvae: herbivores (leaves, stems, roots). Adults: herbivores (flowers, leaves).*
IMPACT *Many species are serious pests.*

Oil or Blister Beetles

Meloidae

The name "blister beetle" comes from the fact that the members of this family can produce oily defensive fluids capable of blistering skin. These beetles have a soft, leathery texture and are often bluish black, bright green, or red and black. The head is large, broadly triangular, and bent downwards, while the pronotum is often squarish and narrower than the back of the head. The elytra of ground-living species can be very short and gape to expose a large part of the swollen abdomen. In many species, the adults are herbivorous and, when present in large numbers, may completely defoliate plants.

SEEN *on the foliage and flowers of various plants, on the ground in dry grassy areas and on certain trees.*

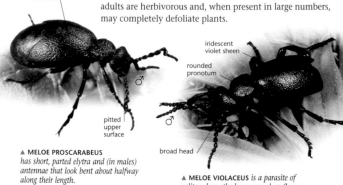

short elytra expose abdomen

iridescent violet sheen

rounded pronotum

pitted upper surface

broad head

▲ **MELOE PROSCARABEUS** *has short, parted elytra and (in males) antennae that look bent about halfway along their length.*

▲ **MELOE VIOLACEUS** *is a parasite of solitary bees: the larvae crawl up flower stems to latch onto passing bees.*

▶ **LYTTA VESICATORIA**, *called the Spanish Fly, has a very localized distribution in southern Britain. It produces a mousy defensive odour when attacked. The larvae develop in the nests of solitary bees.*

iridescent golden-green elytra

broad head on narrow "neck"

LARVAE

The newly hatched, predacious larvae seek out the eggs of grasshoppers or bees to eat, becoming increasingly grub-like with each successive moult.

NOTE

In some species, the larvae attach themselves to a bee when it is visiting flowers. They travel to the bee's nest, then eat the eggs and food provisions.

ORDER *Coleoptera.*
FAMILY *Meloidae.*
SPECIES IN FAMILY *2,000.*
SIZE *0.5–3.5cm.*
FEEDING *Larvae: predators, parasites. Adults: herbivores, liquid-feeders (nectar).*
IMPACT *Many produce oily defensive fluids.*

Cardinal Beetles

Pyrochroidae

Also called fire-coloured beetles, these insects are usually flattened and soft-bodied. The head narrows at the rear, giving the appearance of a broad neck, and the antennae are slender or comb-like (those of males may be feathery). The elytra broaden noticeably towards the rear of the body.

OCCUPY *deciduous woodland, where adults are found crawling on fallen trees and stumps.*

dark spot on pronotum

branched antennae

black legs

body tapers towards rear

red head

▲ **SCHIZOTUS PECTINICORNIS,** *the Black-headed or Scarce Cardinal Beetle, can be found in upland areas across Britain, but is uncommon.*

LARVAE

The slightly flattened larvae live under bark and feed on fungal threads or smaller insects.

ORDER *Coleoptera.*
FAMILY *Pyrochroidae.*
SPECIES IN FAMILY *150.*
SIZE *0.6–1.8cm.*
FEEDING *Larvae: predators, scavengers, fungi-feeders. Adults: herbivores, predators.*
IMPACT *Harmless.*

▲ **PYROCHROA SERRATICORNIS** *can be told from the very similar but slightly larger species Pyrochroa coccinea by the latter's black head.*

Leaf-rolling Weevils

Attelabidae

These beetles are closely related to weevils (p.524). They vary from oval to moderately elongated and are often bright reddish and black. The head is sometimes "pinched" at the rear to form a neck; its rostrum can be short and broad or long and narrow. The antennae are not elbowed, but the last three segments form a club.

OCCUR *on host species in scrubland, hedgerow, and woodland, especially on some coppiced species.*

LARVAE

Larvae feed on wilting tissue inside leaf rolls made by the female and fully grown ones drop out.

▶ **DEPORAUS BETULAE,** *the female of the Birch Leaf Roller, lays eggs on birch leaves, rolled into a tube.*

clubbed antennae

shiny red elytra

distinct "neck"

shiny black elytra

◀ **APODERUS CORYLI** *is a fairly common species. The head is tapered behind the eyes.*

ORDER *Coleoptera.*
FAMILY *Attelabidae.*
SPECIES IN FAMILY *1,800.*
SIZE *3–7mm.*
FEEDING *Larvae and adults: herbivores.*
IMPACT *A few species can be serious pests of fruit trees and soft fruit.*

red femora

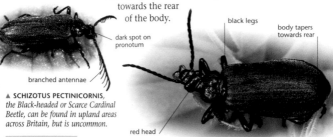

Weevils

Curculionidae

Weevils form the largest family in the animal world. Also known as snout beetles, they possess a snout, or rostrum, which is a prolongation of the head. It carries the jaws at its end and it may be short and broad or slender and as long as the body. The antennae, which arise from the rostrum, are normally "elbowed" and have clubbed ends. Most weevil species are covered by small scales and are cryptically coloured, although some are bright green or pinkish. This family also includes the bark beetles, which live on coniferous and deciduous trees. They are compact, either brown or black, and lack a conspicuous rostrum. Their head is usually almost hidden from view by a hood-like shield covering the thorax.

WIDELY *distributed in all land habitats and associated with almost every species of plant.*

NOTE

Bark beetles carry fungal spores on the head and thorax, and thus infect trees when they lay eggs. As the fungal growth spreads, it may kill the host tree.

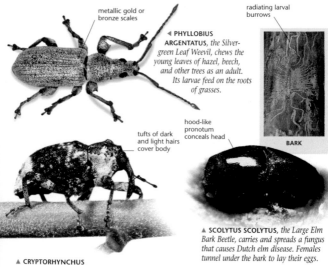

metallic gold or bronze scales

◀ **PHYLLOBIUS ARGENTATUS**, *the Silver-green Leaf Weevil, chews the young leaves of hazel, beech, and other trees as an adult. Its larvae feed on the roots of grasses.*

radiating larval burrows

BARK

hood-like pronotum conceals head

tufts of dark and light hairs cover body

▲ **SCOLYTUS SCOLYTUS**, *the Large Elm Bark Beetle, carries and spreads a fungus that causes Dutch elm disease. Females tunnel under the bark to lay their eggs.*

▲ **CRYPTORHYNCHUS LAPATHI**, *commonly known as the Poplar and Willow Borer, has effective camouflage. The larvae burrow under the bark of alders and sometimes birch.*

very long, curved snout

♀

LIFE CYCLE

The pale, legless, grub-like larvae feed on roots or inside plant tissues; a few eat foliage. Bark beetle larvae hatch in brood galleries cut under bark by the adult female.

▲ **CURCULIO NUCUM** *feeds on pollen and nectar. The snout is very long and curved in females, which use it to make holes in hazelnuts before they lay their eggs.*

ORDER *Coleoptera.*
FAMILY *Curculionidae.*
SPECIES IN FAMILY *50,000.*
SIZE *0.3–2.4cm.*
FEEDING *Larvae: fungi- and wood-feeders, herbivores. Adults: fungi-feeders, herbivores.*
IMPACT *Many species are pests of plants.*

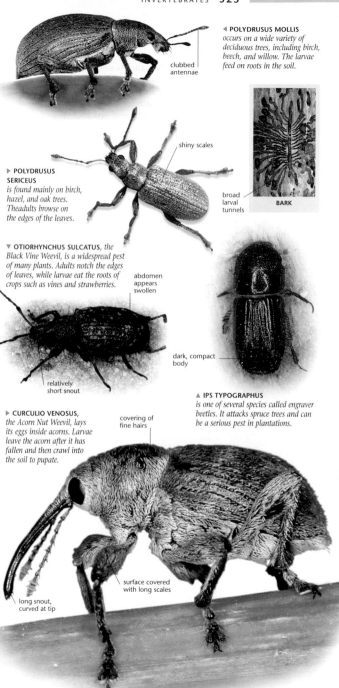

◀ **POLYDRUSUS MOLLIS**
occurs on a wide variety of deciduous trees, including birch, beech, and willow. The larvae feed on roots in the soil.

clubbed antennae

shiny scales

broad larval tunnels

BARK

▶ **POLYDRUSUS SERICEUS**
is found mainly on birch, hazel, and oak trees. Theadults browse on the edges of the leaves.

▼ **OTIORHYNCHUS SULCATUS,** *the Black Vine Weevil, is a widespread pest of many plants. Adults notch the edges of leaves, while larvae eat the roots of crops such as vines and strawberries.*

abdomen appears swollen

relatively short snout

dark, compact body

▲ **IPS TYPOGRAPHUS**
is one of several species called engraver beetles. It attacks spruce trees and can be a serious pest in plantations.

▶ **CURCULIO VENOSUS,**
the Acorn Nut Weevil, lays its eggs inside acorns. Larvae leave the acorn after it has fallen and then crawl into the soil to pupate.

covering of fine hairs

surface covered with long scales

long snout, curved at tip

Common Fleas

Pulicidae

PARASITES *on a range of mammals, such as dogs, cats, hedgehogs, rabbits, and humans.*

Fleas are immediately recognizable by their small size, dark brown or black coloration, winglessness, laterally flattened bodies, and – above all – remarkable jumping ability. The head is fused to a small thorax and carries short antennae concealed in grooves at the side. The simple lateral eyes are quite well developed and the mouthparts are modified for piercing skin and sucking blood. On many fleas, there is a comb of stout bristles at the back of the pronotum and at the sides of the head. Fleas are prolific breeders; owners of untreated pets risk having flea eggs and larvae in their home.

NOTE

In general, fleas avoid light and are attracted to a variety of hosts. Hungry fleas may jump hundreds of times an hour for several days to find a host.

▶ **SPILOPSYLLUS CUNICULI**, *the Rabbit Flea, is a major vector of the rabbit disease myxomatosis.*

"comb" on pronotum

piercing mouthparts

◀ **PULEX IRRITANS** *is called the Human Flea but is more often found attacking pigs and goats. People are more likely to be bitten by cat and dog fleas.*

"comb" on pronotum

long, spiny hind legs

flat, shiny abdomen

LARVAE

Flea larvae are tiny and elongated. They feed on detritus in the host's nest, the faeces of adult fleas, and dried blood. When fully grown, they each spin a silken cocoon.

▼ **CTENOCEPHALIDES FELIS**, *the Cat Flea, is capable of a high jump of 34cm at up to 130 times the acceleration of gravity.*

▲ **CTENOCEPHALIDES CANIS**, *the Dog Flea, also lives on wolves. It is the intermediate host for the tapeworm Dipylidium caninum, which also infects cats.*

ORDER *Siphonaptera.*
FAMILY *Pulicidae.*
SPECIES IN FAMILY *200.*
SIZE *1–8mm.*
FEEDING *Larvae: scavengers (dried blood and faeces). Adults: blood-feeders.*
IMPACT *Bites may cause allergic reactions.*

Common Scorpionflies

Panorpidae

The head of these brownish yellow and black insects is elongated downwards to form a beak that carries biting mouthparts. The wings often have dark markings. Males have an upturned abdomen with bulbous genitalia; the abdomen of females tapers towards the rear.

FOUND *in low-growing vegetation, usually in shady places such as groves and woodland.*

LARVAE

The larvae look like caterpillars, with eight pairs of short abdominal feet and (often) spines.

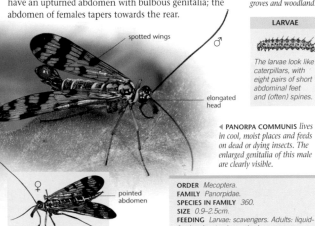

spotted wings

♂

elongated head

◀ **PANORPA COMMUNIS** *lives in cool, moist places and feeds on dead or dying insects. The enlarged genitalia of this male are clearly visible.*

♀

pointed abdomen

ORDER *Mecoptera.*
FAMILY *Panorpidae.*
SPECIES IN FAMILY *360.*
SIZE *0.9–2.5cm.*
FEEDING *Larvae: scavengers. Adults: liquid-feeders (nectar, honeydew), scavengers.*
IMPACT *Harmless.*

Non-biting Midges

Chironomidae

These pale green, brown, or grey flies are delicate and look a bit like mosquitoes (p.529), but lack scales on the wings and their mouthparts are very short or absent. Males have very feathery antennae and a slender body, while females have hairy antennae and a stoutish body.

SWARMS *at dusk near to ponds, lakes, and streams. Larvae occur in all aquatic habitats.*

LARVAE

The long, slender larvae occasionally have gills at the rear of the body. Their coloration varies.

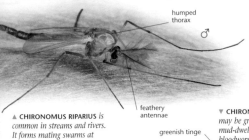

humped thorax

♂

feathery antennae

▲ **CHIRONOMUS RIPARIUS** *is common in streams and rivers. It forms mating swarms at certain times of year.*

greenish tinge

▼ **CHIRONOMUS PLUMOSUS** *may be greenish in colour. Its mud-dwelling larvae, known as bloodworms, contain haemoglobin.*

ORDER *Diptera.*
FAMILY *Chironomidae.*
SPECIES IN FAMILY *5,000.*
SIZE *1–9mm.*
FEEDING *Larvae: scavengers, predators. Adults: liquid-feeders.*
IMPACT *May be a nuisance, but do not bite.*

Crane Flies

Tipulidae

LIVE *near water and lush vegetation; larvae occur in diverse places such as rotting wood, soil, and water.*

Also known as "daddy-long-legs", crane flies are easy to identify due to their slender, fragile bodies, elongated wings, and long, thread-like legs. A highly characteristic feature of these flies is that their legs are shed very easily if they are trapped or handled. The body is brown, black, or grey, often with yellow, orange, or pale brown markings, and there is a distinctive V-shaped groove on top of the thorax.

dark marks on wings

yellow bands on abdomen

♀

▲ **NEPHROTOMA CROCATA** *is a black crane fly with three bright yellow bands on the abdomen.*

feathery antennae

♀

▲ **TIPULA MAXIMA** *is a very large species with clear dark marks all over the wings. The thorax is greyish and abdomen reddish brown.*

▶ **CTENOPHORA ORNATA** *males have a swollen abdominal tip, while the females are slender with a reddish abdomen.*

♂

dark spot on wings

LARVAE

The brown or grey larvae are long and cylindrical and are called leatherjackets due to their texture. They may be partly aquatic, aquatic, or terrestrial in habit.

NOTE

Large species of crane fly rest with their wings fully outstretched, while smaller species tend to fold their wings back along the body.

wings held open at rest

brown front edge to wing

pointed tip to abdomen

◀ **TIPULA OLERACEA** *is a very abundant species. Its wings have a brown marking along the front margin.*

♀

ORDER *Diptera.*
FAMILY *Tipulidae.*
SPECIES IN FAMILY *15,000.*
SIZE *1–6cm (wingspan).*
FEEDING *Larvae: scavengers. Adults: liquid-feeders (plant sap, nectar).*
IMPACT *Pests of grasses and some crops.*

Mosquitoes

Culicidae

It might not be easy to spot these very slender, delicate flies, but they produce a high-pitched whine in flight that is a sure sign of their presence. The head is small and rounded with very long and slender, forward-facing sucking mouthparts. The body and legs are covered with tiny scales and appear pale brown to reddish brown, although some species have bright markings. The wings are long and narrow with scales along the veins and margins. The antennae are feathery in males and slightly hairy in females. Females suck blood from vertebrate hosts; males feed on nectar or honeydew.

REMAIN *near to the larval breeding grounds in a range of aquatic habitats, from puddles to ponds and lakes.*

LARVAE

The larvae, known as "wrigglers" after the way in which they thrash about in water, are mainly scavengers, but a few are predators. Most obtain air at the surface.

biting mouthparts

◀ **CULEX PIPIENS** *is a very common greyish brown mosquito with pale bands on the abdomen. It rarely bites humans.*

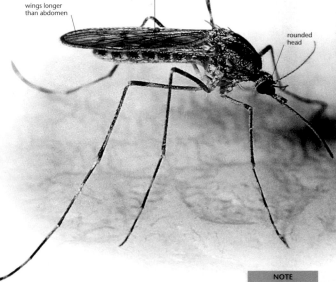

banded abdomen

wings longer than abdomen

rounded head

▲ **CULISETA ANNULATA**, *a large species, has spotted wings and banded legs. It can breed in quite polluted water and often enters houses.*

ORDER Diptera.
FAMILY Culicidae.
SPECIES IN FAMILY 3,100.
SIZE 3–9mm.
FEEDING Larvae: scavengers. Adults: blood-feeders (females), liquid-feeders (males).
IMPACT Bites are painful; transmit diseases.

NOTE

The eggs are laid in almost any standing water. Although they tend to remain near water, the adults may be common in shady woodland and forest at dusk.

Biting Midges

Ceratopogonidae

These small flies are similar to but somewhat smaller than non-biting midges (p.527), with shorter front legs. They often have dark patterns on their wings. The rounded head is not concealed from above by the thorax and the antennae of males are feathery. The mouthparts, especially those of the females, are short and piercing for sucking up fluids.

PLENTIFUL *near the margins of ponds, lakes, and rivers, and in boggy areas.*

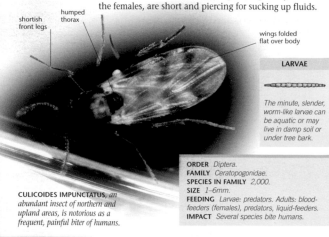

shortish front legs

humped thorax

wings folded flat over body

LARVAE

The minute, slender, worm-like larvae can be aquatic or may live in damp soil or under tree bark.

CULICOIDES IMPUNCTATUS, *an abundant insect of northern and upland areas, is notorious as a frequent, painful biter of humans.*

ORDER *Diptera.*
FAMILY *Ceratopogonidae.*
SPECIES IN FAMILY *2,000.*
SIZE *1–6mm.*
FEEDING *Larvae: predators. Adults: blood-feeders (females), predators, liquid-feeders.*
IMPACT *Several species bite humans.*

Black Flies

Simuliidae

Black flies have stout bodies, short legs, and a distinctively humped thorax. The head is relatively large and rounded with short, thick mouthparts, which, in the females of most species, are used for cutting skin and sucking blood. The antennae are short with no more than nine segments. The wings are broad at the base and narrow towards the end with distinct veins at the leading edge.

THRIVE *around rivers and other fast-flowing bodies of water.*

SIMULIUM SP. *appear at certain times of the year in swarms and attack humans and domesticated animals. Their bites are very painful, itchy, and can cause serious allergic reactions.*

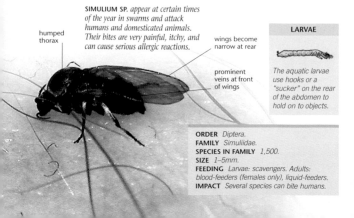

humped thorax

wings become narrow at rear

prominent veins at front of wings

LARVAE

The aquatic larvae use hooks or a "sucker" on the rear of the abdomen to hold on to objects.

ORDER *Diptera.*
FAMILY *Simuliidae.*
SPECIES IN FAMILY *1,500.*
SIZE *1–5mm.*
FEEDING *Larvae: scavengers. Adults: blood-feeders (females only), liquid-feeders.*
IMPACT *Several species can bite humans.*

Owl Midges

Psychodidae

Also called moth flies due to the long hairs or scales covering their bodies, wings, and legs, these small flies are greyish or brownish. The eyes are large and the antennae are made up of 10 to 14 bead-like segments. The wings are usually broad with pointed tips and have few, if any, cross-veins. Like night-flying moths, owl midges are largely nocturnal and are often attracted to lights after dark.

FOUND *in damp and shady places such as woods and bogs; often rest in cracks, crevices, or burrows by day.*

LARVAE

Owl midge larvae are elongated and cylindrical. They live in decaying matter, often in sewers.

PERICOMA FULIGINOSA is found wherever its semi-aquatic larvae breed in mud; also often found in outbuildings and at windows after dark.

moth-like overall shape

patterns of long hairs

ORDER *Diptera.*
FAMILY *Psychodidae.*
SPECIES IN FAMILY *1,500.*
SIZE *1.5–5mm.*
FEEDING *Larvae: scavengers. Adults: liquid-feeders.*
IMPACT *Harmless.*

March Flies

Bibionidae

These flies are stout-bodied, black or dark brown insects, often with very hairy bodies and shortish legs. The heads of males and females are differently shaped: the former are larger and have large compound eyes that meet on top of the head; females have narrower heads, and eyes which do not meet. March flies are common in spring, when males can swarm in large numbers.

PLENTIFUL *on flowers in pastures, meadows, gardens, and other similar habitats.*

hairy black thorax

clear wings

BIBIO MARCI *is distinctively hairy and slow-flying; males are often found in numbers flying over short grasses in spring.*

shortish legs

LARVAE

The larvae are large, elongated, slightly flattened, and large-headed, with strong mouthparts.

ORDER *Diptera.*
FAMILY *Bibionidae.*
SPECIES IN FAMILY *800.*
SIZE *5–11mm.*
FEEDING *Larvae: scavengers, herbivores. Adults: non-feeding.*
IMPACT *Some damage seedlings of cereals.*

♀

Horse Flies

Tabanidae

Also called deer flies, clegs, or gad flies, these insects are stout-bodied, hairless, and fast-flying. They are black, grey, or brown and often have bright yellow or orange bands or other markings. The head is large, hemispherical, and flattened; the short antennae are the most typical feature. The large eyes, which occupy most of the head, are green or purple with iridescent bands and spots. The females' mouthparts are adapted to cut skin and lap blood.

SEEN *near mammals, often far from larval breeding grounds in marshy areas or near water.*

NOTE

Female horse flies approach victims with great stealth and feed in hard-to-reach places. Their bites are painful and may cause allergic reactions.

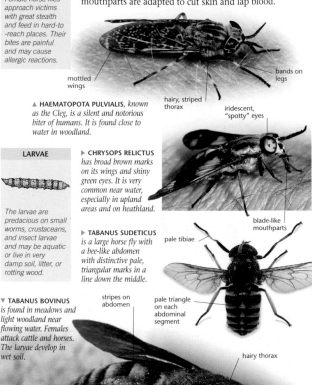

mottled wings

bands on legs

hairy, striped thorax

▲ **HAEMATOPOTA PULVIALIS**, *known as the Cleg, is a silent and notorious biter of humans. It is found close to water in woodland.*

iridescent, "spotty" eyes

blade-like mouthparts

LARVAE

The larvae are predacious on small worms, crustaceans, and insect larvae and may be aquatic or live in very damp soil, litter, or rotting wood.

▶ **CHRYSOPS RELICTUS** *has broad brown marks on its wings and shiny green eyes. It is very common near water, especially in upland areas and on heathland.*

▶ **TABANUS SUDETICUS** *is a large horse fly with a bee-like abdomen with distinctive pale, triangular marks in a line down the middle.*

pale tibiae

pale triangle on each abdominal segment

▼ **TABANUS BOVINUS** *is found in meadows and light woodland near flowing water. Females attack cattle and horses. The larvae develop in wet soil.*

stripes on abdomen

hairy thorax

ORDER *Diptera.*
FAMILY *Tabanidae.*
SPECIES IN FAMILY *4,100.*
SIZE *0.6–2.8cm.*
FEEDING *Larvae: predators. Adults: blood-feeders (females), liquid-feeders (males).*
IMPACT *Severe nuisance with painful bite.*

Soldier Flies

Stratiomyidae

These robust, rather flattened flies sometimes have yellow, green, or pale abdominal markings. Some large species resemble wasps, while others are smaller, and coloured brown, green, or metallic bluish black. The eyes cover a large area of the broad, hemispherical or very rounded head, especially in males. The short antennae are distinctive, with the third segment bent outwards from the basal segments. The wings are folded flat over the body at rest. Although they are not particularly strong fliers, some can hover.

FOUND *mainly in damp areas on the flowers of willow, hawthorn, irises, and umbellifers.*

green thorax

LARVAE

The larvae of the soldier flies are elongate and flattened; their tough and leathery bodies are impregnated with calcareous deposits.

▶ **CHLOROMYIA FORMOSA** *has a rather blunt-ended, broad abdomen. It is bronze coloured in males and bluish in females.*

smoky-tinged wings

yellow scutellum

yellow stripes on head

◀ **OXYCERA RARA** *is a stout-bodied species with strong yellow on black markings. It favours sunny clearings in wet areas, such as fenland.*

pale tibia

broad abdomen

elbowed antennae

◀ **STRATIOMYS CHAMELEON** *has a broad black abdomen with yellow patches on the sides. The scutellum has two long spines.*

black central stripe

ORDER *Diptera.*
FAMILY *Stratiomyidae.*
SPECIES IN FAMILY *1,800.*
SIZE *2–17mm.*
FEEDING *Larvae: scavengers, predators, herbivores. Adults: liquid-feeders (nectar).*
IMPACT *Harmless.*

▲ **ODONTOMYIA VIRIDULA** *has a black, hairy thorax and a broad, flattened abdomen. It is found in wet meadows.*

lime green sides to abdomen

Robber or Assassin Flies

Asilidae

Robber flies are aerial or ambush hunters with excellent eyesight. Most are brownish or black with reddish orange or yellow markings and the body varies from slender and relatively hairless to stout and hairy. The head has a groove between the separated, bulging eyes and the face has a tuft of long hairs, called the beard. The forward-pointing proboscis is stiff and sharp for stabbing and sucking. The legs are strong and bristly for catching insect prey in flight.

FOUND in a variety of habitats, but prefer sunny sites in open or lightly wooded areas.

LARVAE

The ground-living larvae are cryptically coloured, elongated, and tapered at both ends. They are scavengers or prey on the eggs, larvae, and pupae of other insects.

◀ PHILONICUS ALBICEPS inhabits sandy areas, including coastal sand dunes. It is pale yellowish grey, with a "dusty" appearance.

long, cylindrical abdomen

yellowish bristles on abdomen sides

widely separated eyes

dusky wings

▲ LEPTOGASTER CYLINDRICA flies holding its front and middle legs forward, ready to catch prey. It hunts aphids, small flies, and bugs.

four yellow abdomen segments

bee-like abdomen

facial tuft

▲ ASILUS CRABRONIFORMIS is a very large, wasp-like fly that makes short, darting flights to seize large prey such as crane flies (as here).

NOTE

Most species perch on an exposed twig or stone to spot passing prey, then give chase. They quickly stab victims and inject a protein-dissolving saliva.

▼ DIOCTRIA BAUMHAUERI has a less-developed facial hair tuft than other genera of robber flies. It occurs in cool, deciduous woodland.

very hairy legs

◀ LAPHRIA SP. can seem very bee-like due to their large size and hairy bodies. Their larvae burrow inside wood and eat wood-boring beetle larvae.

dark, slender wasp-like body

ORDER Diptera.
FAMILY Asilidae.
SPECIES IN FAMILY 5,000.
SIZE 0.3–2.8cm.
FEEDING Larvae: predators, scavengers. Adults: predators.
IMPACT Harmless.

Bee Flies

Bombyliidae

As the name implies, bee flies can look very similar to bees. Some are stout-bodied and very hairy. Their body colour is usually brown, red, and yellow. The wings may be clear or have dark bands or patterned markings, particularly at the leading edge. The head is often rounded, and the proboscis can be very long for sucking nectar from deep flowers.

SEEN feeding or flying in open, sunny locations or resting on bare sandy ground.

hairy, bee-like body

dark area on front of clear wing

▶ **VILLA MODESTA** *looks quite bee-like. It has a rounded head, short proboscis, and a furry body.*

head pale at sides

clear wings

▲ **BOMBYLIUS MAJOR** *looks like a bee and hovers like a hover fly. It has a long proboscis that projects in front of the head.*

ORDER *Diptera.*
FAMILY *Bombyliidae.*
SPECIES IN FAMILY *5,000.*
SIZE *2–18mm.*
FEEDING *Larvae: parasitic, predators. Adults: liquid-feeders (nectar).*
IMPACT *Harmless.*

LARVAE

Some larvae eat eggs of grasshoppers in the soil. Most are parasitic on other insect larvae.

Dance Flies

Empididae

These flies' common name refers to the mating swarms in which the males fly up and down as if dancing. Most are small with a stout thorax and a slender, tapering abdomen. The coloration varies from dark brown and black to yellow or light brown. The rounded head has large eyes, antennae with three segments, and a long, downward-pointing proboscis. Dance flies are all predators, but may drink nectar as well.

FOUND on vegetation in moist locations, often resting on tree trunks or branches and sometimes on water.

LARVAE

The spindle-shaped larvae can retract their head and live in leaf litter, humus, wood, and water.

almost spherical head

◀ **HYBOS FEMORATUS** *flies slowly, hunting small flies such as midges. Its thorax is noticeably humped.*

enlarged hind femora

ORDER *Diptera.*
FAMILY *Empididae.*
SPECIES IN FAMILY *3,500.*
SIZE *2–11mm (body length).*
FEEDING *Larvae: predators. Adults: mainly predators; also nectar-feeders.*
IMPACT *Harmless.*

▶ **EMPIS TESSELLATA** *preys on other small flies, but can also be seen feeding on nectar at flowers such as hawthorn.*

brownish wings

striped thorax

Hover Flies or Flower Flies

Syrphidae

Hover flies are the most easily recognizable of all the flies due to their often wasp-like or bee-like appearance and their ability to hover. These superb aerial acrobats can move in all directions, including backwards, and can hold a fixed position in the air even in gusty conditions. The adults are typically slender-bodied with black and yellow or white stripes; some are stout and hairy. The eyes are large and in males meet on top of the head. The wings have a characteristic false vein running down the middle (a simple thickening of the wing membrane) and a false margin at the edge (the joining together of the outer wing veins). Despite the wasp-like markings, and the bee-like appearance of many species, hover flies are harmless nectar feeders.

INHABIT *a range of habitats, particularly localities with plenty of umbelliferous (flat-topped) flowers.*

NOTE

Most hover flies are important as plant pollinators and pest controllers. Often it is possible to find four or five different species feeding on a single flowerhead.

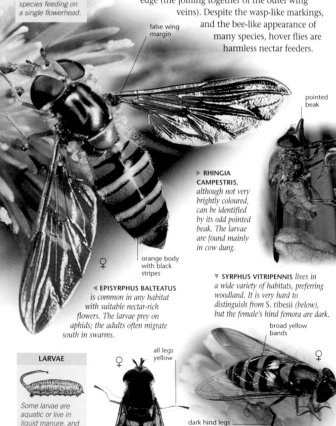

false wing margin

pointed beak

▶ **RHINGIA CAMPESTRIS,** *although not very brightly coloured, can be identified by its odd pointed beak. The larvae are found mainly in cow dung.*

♀

orange body with black stripes

◀ **EPISYRPHUS BALTEATUS** *is common in any habitat with suitable nectar-rich flowers. The larvae prey on aphids; the adults often migrate south in swarms.*

▼ **SYRPHUS VITRIPENNIS** *lives in a wide variety of habitats, preferring woodland. It is very hard to distinguish from S. ribesii (below), but the female's hind femora are dark.*

broad yellow bands

♀

LARVAE

Some larvae are aquatic or live in liquid manure, and possess a breathing tube (above). Many others are slug-like and fierce predators of aphids and other soft-bodied pests.

all legs yellow

♀

dark hind legs

false margin

◀ **SYRPHUS RIBESII** *commonly occurs in gardens, where its larvae are major aphid predators. The adults feed on nectar, so planting suitable flowers will improve pest control.*

◀ **VOLUCELLA BOMBYLANS** *may have a reddish or a whitish tail and mimics the red- and buff-tailed bumble bees, but can be distinguished by its large eyes and single pair of wings.*

DARK FORM

large, stout, hairy body

separated eyes

black posterior of abdomen

♀

very broad abdomen

▶ **VOLUCELLA ZONARIA**, *a very big hover fly, resembles a large wasp or hornet. Its larvae develop in wasps' nests, while the adults feed on nectar in sheltered habitats.*

▲ **VOLUCELLA PELLUCENS** *is often to be seen feeding at bramble blossom. Its larvae live inside the nests of wasps and bees, where they are scavengers.*

▶ **XYLOTA SEGNIS** *is recognized by the broad orange band on its slender abdomen. The adults feed on honeydew and sap, while the larvae live in rotten wood.*

orange band

furry, bee-like thorax

♀

▼ **HELOPHILUS PENDULUS**, *also called the Sun Fly as it likes to bask, favours damp habitats. The larvae inhabit rotting matter such as liquid manure.*

three black stripes on thorax

♀

orange-brown body

yellow face

▲ **ERISTALIS TENAX** *is known as the Drone Fly for its resemblance to male honey bees. Its larvae, called Rat-Tailed Maggots, live in shallow, nutient-rich or stagnant water.*

white patches

♂

shiny black thorax

brownish veins on wings

▼ **MYATHROPA FLOREA** *looks like a paler version of the Drone Fly (above left). Like Rat-Tailed Maggots, the larvae have a breathing siphon at their rear end, but live in water-filled tree holes.*

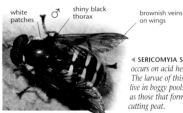

◀ **SERICOMYIA SILENTIS** *occurs on acid heathland. The larvae of this species live in boggy pools, such as those that form after cutting peat.*

ORDER *Diptera.*
FAMILY *Syrphidae.*
SPECIES IN FAMILY *6,000.*
SIZE *0.4–2.8cm (body length).*
FEEDING *Larvae: predators and scavengers. Adults: liquid-feeders, herbivores.*
IMPACT *Beneficial as predators of aphids.*

orange hairs

♀

Anthomyiid Flies

Anthomyiidae

These rather ordinary-looking flies are very similar in general appearance to house flies (p.540), although some may be larger or smaller. The body colour may be dull yellowish brown, grey, brown, or black, and the slender, bristly legs are yellowish brown or black. The wings may be clear or have a light smoky tinge. The adults of many species feed on pollen and nectar at umbelliferous and other flowers, while some species are predators of small insects. The larvae can be terrestrial or semiaquatic and show a wide range of feeding types.

INHABIT *a very wide range of habitats from cultivated land and grassland to woodland and gardens; widespread and ubiquitous.*

LARVAE

The herbivorous white larvae are found as stem borers, gall formers, and leaf miners in the roots, stems, flower heads, and leaves of a huge range of host plants.

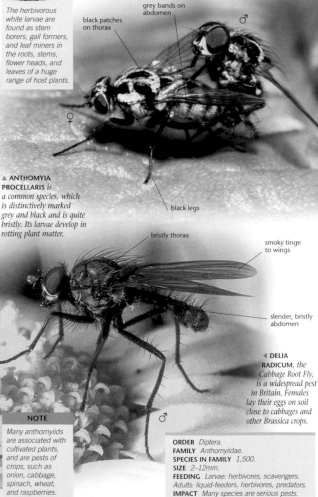

grey bands on abdomen

black patches on thorax

♂

♀

▲ **ANTHOMYIA PROCELLARIS** *is a common species, which is distinctively marked grey and black and is quite bristly. Its larvae develop in rotting plant matter.*

black legs

bristly thorax

smoky tinge to wings

slender, bristly abdomen

◄ **DELIA RADICUM**, *the Cabbage Root Fly, is a widespread pest in Britain. Females lay their eggs on soil close to cabbages and other Brassica crops.*

♂

NOTE

Many anthomyiids are associated with cultivated plants, and are pests of crops, such as onion, cabbage, spinach, wheat, and raspberries.

ORDER *Diptera.*
FAMILY *Anthomyiidae.*
SPECIES IN FAMILY *1,500.*
SIZE *2–12mm.*
FEEDING *Larvae: herbivores, scavengers. Adults: liquid-feeders, herbivores, predators.*
IMPACT *Many species are serious pests.*

Dung Flies

Scathophagidae

Dung flies are black, yellow, grey, or brown and sometimes show two of these colours in striking contrast. These flies may look superficially like house flies (p.540), but the commonest species are very hairy or bristly, some looking almost furry. The wings are usually clear but may have darkish tinges or spots. The abdomen is slender, but, in males, is enlarged at the rear end.

FOUND *in a variety of habitats, often on dung or in boggy areas.*

hairy body

LARVAE

The pale-coloured larvae are cylindrical and taper sharply to a point at the head end.

strong bristles on legs

♀

flies gathered to breed

SCATHOPHAGA STERCORARIA, *the Yellow Dung Fly, is abundant on sheep and cow dung, where its larvae develop. It also breeds in the faeces of poultry, horses, and humans.*

ON DUNG

ORDER *Diptera.*
FAMILY *Scathophagidae.*
SPECIES IN FAMILY *250.*
SIZE *3–11mm.*
FEEDING *Larvae: herbivores, dung-feeders, predators. Adults: predators.*
IMPACT *Generally harmless.*

Lesser House Flies

Fanniidae

Like smaller and more slender house flies (p.540), these flies are generally dark, although the legs or abdomen may be wholly or partly yellowish. The eyes of the males can be large and may even touch each other, while those of the females are smaller and separated. Males swarm in the shade of branches or overhangs and will fly indoors, where they dart about and land on the underside of ceiling lights.

COMMON *near decaying matter, in sheltered, well-vegetated locations, and under trees at woodland margins, parkland, or gardens.*

dull-coloured body

clear wings

LARVAE

The larvae taper to the front. Each segment has long, branched, fleshy extensions.

pale patch at base of abdomen

NOTE

The larvae of some lesser house fly species are more commonly called latrine flies from the fact that they breed in liquid excrement.

ORDER *Diptera.*
FAMILY *Fanniidae.*
SPECIES IN FAMILY *280.*
SIZE *5–6mm.*
FEEDING *Larvae: scavengers, dung-feeders. Adults: liquid-feeders, herbivores (pollen).*
IMPACT *Some can be a nuisance indoors.*

FANNIA CANICULARIS, *the Lesser House Fly, is slightly smaller than the House Fly. It is a widespread and very common species.*

House Flies and their relatives

Muscidae

The House Fly is a typical member of this family. These flies can be slender or stoutish, dull black, grey, or yellowish in colour, with clear wings. All parts of the body usually have strong, dark bristles. The legs are slender and quite long. The mouthparts act like a sponge and draw in liquid foods, except in blood-feeding species, which have piercing mouthparts. Identification of species relies on bristle patterns and structure of the genitalia. Muscids are found on flowers, excrement, and decaying organic matter. Blood-feeding species are associated with their hosts.

LIVE *wherever there is excrement, carcasses, and rotting matter; ubiquitous in all habitats.*

LARVAE

The larvae are typically maggot-shaped, tapering towards the front and blunt at the rear. They develop quickly in rotting material, and pupate in just over a week.

yellowish orange at base of wings

▼ **STOMOXYS CALCITRANS**, *the Stable Fly, looks like a House Fly with a striped thorax, and lightly chequered abdomen.*

sharp proboscis

▲ **MESEMBRINA MERIDIANA** *is an unmistakable large, shiny, dark fly, identified by the yellowish orange patches at the wing bases.*

grey patches on abdomen

abdomen with orange patches

▼ **POLIETES LARDARIUS** *is grey with a bluish tinge, a longitudinally striped thorax, and a dark-marked abdomen.*

clear wings

▲ **MUSCA DOMESTICA**, *the House Fly, is dark grey with lighter, longitudinal stripes down its thorax.*

silvery stripes on thorax

reddish eyes

NOTE

Many of these flies transmit harmful micro-organisms via their mouthparts and feet, which cause diseases such as dysentery and typhoid.

ORDER *Diptera.*
FAMILY *Muscidae.*
SPECIES IN FAMILY *3,000.*
SIZE *2–12mm.*
FEEDING *Larvae: scavengers, herbivores. Adults: predators, scavengers, herbivores.*
IMPACT *Some bite, others transfer disease.*

Blow Flies

Calliphoridae

Typical species, often called "bluebottles" or "greenbottles", are stout-bodied, medium to large, metallic green or blue flies that are attracted to carrion, as well as fresh and cooked meat and fish. Some species are shiny black or drab coloured. Most are usually the same size or bigger than a house fly. The tips of the antennae are distinctively feathered, and the proboscis is short. In some species, the sexes are different colours.

OCCUR *on all habitats, with the larvae on soil, dung, and carcasses.*

▶ LUCILIA CAESAR *is a cosmopolitan, shiny, metallic green species that breeds on rotting carcasses and dung.*

metallic green coloration

LARVAE

The larvae are typical white maggots that taper at the front end and are blunt ended at the rear. The head is narrow with dark, hook-like mouthparts.

shiny blue abdomen

◀ CALLIPHORA VOMITORIA *is a common "bluebottle". The dark thorax has faint longitudinal stripes and the abdomen has a metallic blue sheen.*

yellowish hairs

▶ POLLENIA RUDIS, *also known as the Cluster Fly, has distinctive, golden-yellow hair on its thorax.*

dark red eyes

bristly rear of abdomen

◀ CALLIPHORA VICINA *is very similar to C.* vomitoria, *but can be separated from it by the "cheeks" of the head below the eyes, which are red, not black, in colour.*

NOTE

Many species in this family are of medical and veterinary importance. Besides flesh-eating larvae, some calliphorids carry diseases such as dysentery.

ORDER *Diptera.*
FAMILY *Calliphoridae.*
SPECIES IN FAMILY *1,200.*
SIZE *4–16mm.*
FEEDING *Larvae: scavengers, parasites. Adults: scavengers, liquid-feeders, herbivores.*
IMPACT *Can infest livestock and humans.*

hair

wings

CALLIPHORA VICINA

Giant Casemakers or Large Caddisflies

LIVE *near slow-moving rivers and streams and around ponds, lakes, and marshes.*

Phryganeidae

These insects are light brown or grey, often mottled, and their wings can be quite brightly marked with black and yellow-orange or have dark margins and stripes. The antennae are quite short: in some cases about as long as the front wings. The front, middle, and hind tibiae bear two, four, and four spurs respectively.

LARVAE

The larvae move around in beautifully regular cases made of plant fibres and lined with silk.

▼ **PHRYGANEA GRANDIS,** *a common species, lays its eggs in jelly-like masses on aquatic plants.*

smoky brown wings

shortish antennae

▼ **PHRYGANEA VARIA** *is attractively mottled and well camouflaged at rest. It flies at dusk.*

mottled upperside

ORDER *Trichoptera.*
FAMILY *Phryganeidae.*
SPECIES IN FAMILY *500.*
SIZE *1–2.8cm.*
FEEDING *Larvae: predators, scavengers. Adults: non-feeding.*
IMPACT *Harmless.*

Long-horned Caddisflies

ABUNDANT *around lakes, large ponds, and medium to large rivers.*

Leptoceridae

As their common name implies, these caddisflies have slender antennae that are typically two to three times longer than the front wings. The basal segment of the antenna is bulbous and about as long as the head. The front wings are long, narrow, and very hairy, often with dark cross bands. The front tibiae may have one or two spurs or none; the middle and hind tibiae always have two spurs.

LARVAE

The larval cases are mostly made of sand grains, small stones, and plant material.

extremely long antennae

ORDER *Trichoptera.*
FAMILY *Leptoceridae.*
SPECIES IN FAMILY *850.*
SIZE *0.6–1.6cm.*
FEEDING *Larvae: scavengers, herbivores, predators. Adults: non-feeding.*
IMPACT *Harmless.*

OECETIS OCHRACEA *is widely distributed and has very long antennae typical of its family.*

Horntails or Woodwasps

Siricidae

The common names for these large, stout-bodied sawflies refer to a spine-like structure at the end of their abdomen, which is short and triangular in males and long and spear-like in females. In addition, females have an even longer ovipositor, with which they drill into wood to lay a single egg. Despite their large size and (sometimes) wasp-like appearance, these insects do not sting. The head is quite large, broadest behind the eyes, and usually has long and slender antennae. The wings are generally clear, but may be dark or tinged yellowish.

OCCUR *in coniferous or deciduous forests, where females attack diseased, weakened, or fallen trees.*

▼ **UROCERUS GIGAS**, *the Horntail, has strikingly wasp-like females with long ovipositors; males are smaller and less wasp-like.*

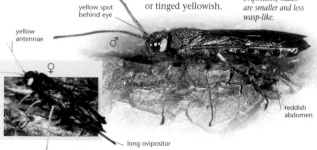

reddish orange antennae

yellow spot behind eye

yellow antennae

♂

♀

long ovipositor

reddish abdomen

greenish tinge to thorax

blue-violet abdomen

♀

reddish base to antennae

reddish brown end to abdomen

▲ **SIREX JUVENCUS** *lays its eggs in spruce and pine. The abdomen is bluish in females and reddish brown in males.*

LARVAE

Woodwasp larvae have a stout spine at their rear end, with which they push themselves through tunnels in heartwood. Their development takes up to two years.

NOTE

Despite their large size and alarmingly long ovipositors, which are often mistaken for stings, these insects are entirely harmless to humans.

ORDER Hymenoptera.
FAMILY Siricidae.
SPECIES IN FAMILY 100.
SIZE 2–4cm.
FEEDING Larvae: wood-feeders, fungi-feeders. Adults: liquid-feeders.
IMPACT Many species are pests of trees.

Common Sawflies

Tenthredinidae

Common sawflies vary a great deal and may be quite narrow-bodied and wasp-like or broader and more robust. The body colour is typically brown, black, or green but many are brightly marked with yellow or red. The slender antennae can be made up of anything between 7 and 13 segments, but usually have 9 segments. The tibiae of the front legs have two apical (near the tip) spurs, and in many species the sexes have different coloration.

LIVE in nearly all land habitats, especially gardens, pastures, and woodland, as far north as the Arctic.

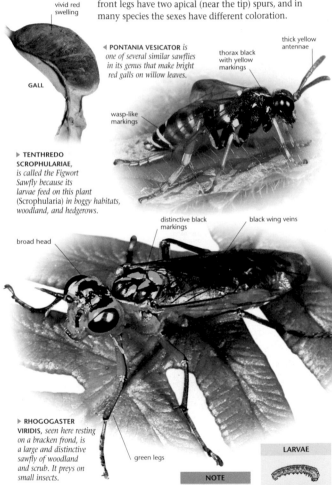

vivid red swelling

GALL

◀ **PONTANIA VESICATOR** *is one of several similar sawflies in its genus that make bright red galls on willow leaves.*

thick yellow antennae

thorax black with yellow markings

wasp-like markings

▶ **TENTHREDO SCROPHULARIAE,** *is called the Figwort Sawfly because its larvae feed on this plant (Scrophularia) in boggy habitats, woodland, and hedgerows.*

distinctive black markings

black wing veins

broad head

▶ **RHOGOGASTER VIRIDIS,** *seen here resting on a bracken frond, is a large and distinctive sawfly of woodland and scrub. It preys on small insects.*

green legs

LARVAE

The caterpillar-like larvae may have warning coloration or be cryptically coloured. Some are smooth, while others have spines, hairs, and bumps.

NOTE

Females use their ovipositor to cut egg-laying slits in the leaves, twigs, and shoots of host plants. Most larvae browse on foliage; some produce galls.

ORDER Hymenoptera.
FAMILY Tenthredinidae.
SPECIES IN FAMILY 4,000.
SIZE 4–15mm (body length).
FEEDING *Larvae:* herbivores (leaves). *Adults:* predators, liquid-feeders.
IMPACT Many species are pests of crops.

Ichneumon Wasps

Ichneumonidae

Ichneumons are generally slender-bodied with antennae at least half as long as the body and composed of a minimum of 16 segments. Many species are uniformly coloured pale yellowish- or reddish brown to black, while others are brightly patterned with yellow and black. The slender, sometimes laterally flattened abdomen is joined to the thorax by a slender stalk of variable length. Most species are fully winged with a prominent pterostigma on the leading edge of the front wings.

COMMON *almost everywhere, above all in damp habitats. Strongly attracted to umbelliferous (flat-topped) flowers and lights.*

♀ ──── ovipositor sheath

ovipositor in use

red legs

▲ **NETELIA SP.** *parasitize the caterpillars of moths. If handled, females will try to "sting" fingers with their ovipositors.*

▶ **LISSONOTA SP.** *parasitize wood-feeding moth larvae, which females drill down to reach.*

yellowish brown all over

▶ **PROTICHNEUMON PISORIUS** *can be seen at flowers; females lay their eggs inside hawk moth caterpillars.*

pale bands on antennae

▶ **DIPLAZON LAETATORIUS** *is very widespread. Females lay their eggs inside the eggs of hover flies.*

very long ovipositor

banded hind femura

▶ **RHYSSA PERSUASSORIA,** *the Sabre Wasp, drills into the trunks of pine trees to locate the larvae of wood wasps deep within the wood.*

black and white body

♀

reddish legs

LARVAE

Pale and maggot-like, the larvae may have a tail that gets shorter with age. Most are internal parasites that eventually kill the host organism.

ORDER *Hymenoptera.*
FAMILY *Ichneumonidae.*
SPECIES IN FAMILY *20,000.*
SIZE *0.3–4.2cm (body length).*
FEEDING *Larvae: parasites. Adults: liquid-feeders.*
IMPACT *Many species control other pests.*

NOTE

Females use their long ovipositors to lay eggs on or inside the larvae or pupae of insects such as beetles, flies, moths, butterflies, sawflies, and other wasps.

Gall Wasps

Cynipidae

THRIVE *in a range of habitats, wherever suitable host trees or plants grow.*

Gall wasps are tiny and have shiny black or blackish brown bodies. The thorax has a characteristic humped appearance in side view. Most species are fully winged, with much reduced vein patterns; some are short-winged or wingless. Males are typically smaller than females, which have an oval abdomen flattened from side to side. The galls that these wasps induce on their host plants are unique to each species and much easier to identify than the wasps themselves as they vary greatly in size, colour, texture, and location. Gall wasps have complex life cycles, often involving sexual and asexual (no males involved) generations that occur at different times of year.

hairy surface

GALLS

▲ **LIPOSTHENES GLECHOMAE** *makes small, globular, hairy galls on ground ivy (Glechoma species). Inside each gall is a single developing larva.*

▶ **DIPLOLEPIS EGLANTERIAE** *causes rounded, green or red galls on the underside of wild and cultivated roses. A single larva feeds inside each gall.*

GALLS

pea-like shape

irregular, elongated form

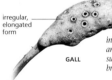

GALL

◀ **DIASTROPHUS RUBI** *induces swollen galls on the shoots and young stems of Rubus species such as raspberry, dewberry, and bramble. Each contains many larvae.*

▶ **BIORHIZA PALLIDA** *has a unisexual generation (shown right) that develops in galls on oak tree roots. This emerges to lay eggs on oak buds, producing Oak Apple Galls (below). These in turn give rise to a bisexual generation.*

smooth, shiny abdomen

♀

large thorax

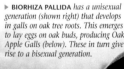

reddish and spongy

GALL

GALL

hard and
knobbly gall

▲ **ANDRICUS QUERCUSCALICIS**
*induces knobbly galls to grow
from the base of acorns of the
English Oak. Each houses a
larva of the asexual generation.*

spherical,
woody galls

green first,
then brown
when mature

GALLS

▲ **ANDRICUS KOLLARI** *causes
Marble Galls on oak trees.
These were once collected as
their high tannin content was
important in ink-making.*

hard, scaly
orange galls

GALLS

▲ **NEUROTERUS
QUERCUSBACCARUM** *is one of several
species to produce Spangle Galls on the
underside of oak leaves. Some leaves
may be completely covered with galls.*

GALL

▲ **DIPLOLEPIS ROSAE**
*causes the Rose Bedeguar
Gall, or Robin's Pincushion,
on wild roses and sometimes
on cultivated varieties. The
gall contains many larvae.*

extensive
"mossy"
growth

green at first,
then turn red

GALLS

▼ **CYNIPS
QUERCUSFOLII**
*has two generations.
The second, bisexual
generation lays eggs
on the lower surface
of oak leaves, creating
Cherry Galls (left).*

♀

humped
thorax

shiny abdomen

ORDER Hymenoptera.
FAMILY Cynipidae.
SPECIES IN FAMILY 1,250.
SIZE 1–8mm.
FEEDING Larvae: herbivores, parasites.
Adults: liquid-feeders.
IMPACT High infestations weaken host plants.

NOTE

Some gall wasps do
not form galls,
instead share those
of other species;
some are parasitic
on the larvae of
dipteran flies or
parasitic wasps.

LARVAE

The pale, smooth,
grub-like larvae
hatch from eggs laid
inside plant tissues,
inducing the plant
to produce galls
that both protect
and nourish the
developing larvae.

Common Wasps, Paper Wasps, and Potter Wasps

Vespidae

FOUND *practically wherever there is suitable prey, including woodland, parkland, and gardens.*

The commonest species in this family are yellow-jackets, which live in colonies inside rounded paper nests and catch insects, often caterpillars, to feed their larvae. Most species are black or brown with yellow or white markings. Vespid's eyes are notched on the internal margins and may look crescent-shaped. At rest, the wings are folded in longitudinal pleats along the sides of the body. Paper wasps, which are occasionally found in Britain, make nests of combs that are never enclosed by an outer carton. The solitary potter wasps make small mud nests on stems and in natural cavities. Nests of common wasps are not reused and only the queen wasps survive the winter to start a new colony in the spring.

LARVAE

The wrinkled body is broadest about a third of the way from the head. The larvae are fed by workers which live in colonies inside individual nest cells.

NOTE

Nest shape, colour, and location help to identify social wasps, which may look very similar. Wasps remove many garden pests to feed their larvae.

▶ **VESPULA GERMANICA**, *the German Wasp, has three small black spots on its face. This species makes greyish coloured nests underground, in hollow trees, or inside sheds and attics.*

antennae — eyes — longitudinally pleated wings — yellow tibia

▶ **VESPULA VULGARIS**, *the Common Wasp, has a small anchor-shaped mark on its face. This worker (right) is scraping wood fibres from a tree to make paper for its nest.*

antennae — yellow stripes on thorax

large nest on roof timbers

NEST

ORDER *Hymenoptera.*
FAMILY *Vespidae.*
SPECIES IN FAMILY *4,000.*
SIZE *8–26mm.*
FEEDING *Larvae: carnivorous. Adults: predators, liquid-feeders (nectar).*
IMPACT *Very beneficial but can sting.*

▼ **DOLICHOVESPULA MEDIA,** *the Median Wasp, has a small black spot or bar on the face, and a slim "7"-shaped line at the sides of the thorax. It builds nests in bushes and shrubs.*

antennae

variable markings on abdomen

chestnut brown thorax

yellow head

◀ **VESPA CRABRO,** *the Hornet, is a very large species. The front of the abdomen is largely chestnut brown; the posterior part is dull yellow with dark markings.*

▼ **EUMENES COARCTATUS** *is the Potter Wasp. Common on heathland, females gather mud with their mandibles to construct the elegant vase-shaped nests.*

very slender first abdominal segment

stout thorax

vase-shaped mud nest

NEST

Solitary Hunting, Digger, and Sand Wasps

Sphecidae

ACTIVE in sandy, open localities, especially in bright sunshine, and often visit flowers.

These wasps paralyse insects as food for their larvae. Some species are stocky; in others the abdomen is elongated and thread-like where it joins the thorax. The body is typically black with yellow or reddish markings. The head is fairly broad and the pronotum is narrow, collar-like, and does not extend back towards the wing bases. Both sexes are fully winged. Females often have a comb-like, digging structure on their front legs.

LARVAE

The carnivorous larvae are pale creamy white and have dark mouthparts. The body is tapered slightly at both ends and is usually slightly curved.

▶ **CERCERIS ARENARIA** *is shown here stinging a weevil, with which to stock her nest. The female pushes soil out of her burrow backwards, using her abdomen.*

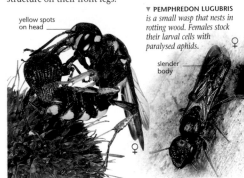

yellow spots on head

▼ **PEMPHREDON LUGUBRIS** *is a small wasp that nests in rotting wood. Females stock their larval cells with paralysed aphids.*

slender body

♀

♀

▼ **AMMOPHILA SABULOSA** *is a species of sand wasp that hunts for large caterpillars to stock its nests with. Females deposit one paralysed victim in each nest, sealing it with sand before feeding on it.*

slender abdomen, narrow at front

♀

large jaws for carrying prey

◀ **PHILANTHUS TRIANGULUM,** *the Bee Killer or Bee Wolf, fills its nests with paralysed honey bees, with up to six bees in each larval cell.*

broad head

yellow legs

ORDER *Hymenoptera.*
FAMILY *Sphecidae.*
SPECIES IN FAMILY *8,000.*
SIZE *0.6–2.4cm.*
FEEDING *Larvae: carnivorous (paralysed prey provided by adults). Adults: liquid-feeders.*
IMPACT *Help to control certain pests.*

Leaf-cutter and Mason Bees

Megachilidae

Most of these bees are solitary. Leaf-cutter bees cut circular pieces of leaves to line their nests' brood cells, while mason bees make mud cells under stones and in burrows. The former are typically stout-bodied and many species are dark brown to black, often with yellow or pale markings. Mason bees are short, broad, and metallic blue or green. The mouthparts are long and pointed and the wings may be clear or smoky.

OCCURS *especially where dead wood and pithy plant stems provide nest sites.*

LARVAE

The larvae of these bees are rather fat, especially near the rear of the body. Most feed on pollen or honey provided by the female, but a few are parasites in other bees' nests.

▶ **ANTHIDIUM MANICATUM,** *known as the Common Carder Bee, nests in old beetle or moth larvae burrows.*

♀

yellow edging to black abdomen

bright yellow hairs

densely hairy abdomen

clypeal horns

pollen carried in a brush of hairs below abdomen

◀ **HOPLITIS SPINULOSA** *nests inside empty snail shells and uses sheep or rabbit dung to make the walls between adjacent cells.*

▲ **OSMIA RUFA,** *the Red Mason Bee, nests in natural cavities and holes in walls. It can be encouraged to nest using bundles of dry bamboo.*

NOTE

A group of species known as carder bees use their jaws to strip the hairs from woolly-leaved plants, which they then tease out to make cell linings.

stout body

◀ **MEGACHILE CENTUNCULARIS** *is a common leaf-cutter bee. Leaves with semicircular holes along the edges are evidence that a nest is nearby.*

pieces cut by female leaf-cutter

DAMAGED LEAF

ORDER *Hymenoptera.*
FAMILY *Megachilidae.*
SPECIES IN FAMILY *3,000.*
SIZE *0.7–2.1cm.*
FEEDING *Larvae: pollen- and honey-feeders. Adults: pollen- and nectar-feeders.*
IMPACT *Essential plant pollinators.*

Ants

Formicidae

FOUND *in virtually every habitat across the region.*

Ants are familiar and ubiquitous social insects, and may be pale yellow, reddish to brown, or black. The individuals commonly seen are the wingless workers, but the reproductive males and females that appear from time to time are fully winged. The second, or second and third segments of the abdomen are constricted to form a waist, called the pedicel, which may have bumps or spine-like processes. The head carries strong jaws, and the antennae are elbowed immediately after the long first segment.

reddish thorax of worker

NOTE

Ants are essential elements of all terrestrial habitats, and they are often the most abundant and significant carnivorous group of insects present.

▼ **FORMICA RUFA**, *the Wood Ant, is an active predator, but also likes honeydew. The ants shown below are tending a colony of aphids.*

worker tending aphid

black workers

LARVAE

The white larvae are grub-like, slightly curved, and may have fine body hairs. They are fed by worker ants and moved to a new site if the nest is disturbed.

ORDER *Hymenoptera.*
FAMILY *Formicidae.*
SPECIES IN FAMILY *8,800.*
SIZE *1–12mm.*
FEEDING *Larvae and adults: predators, herbivores, liquid-feeders.*
IMPACT *May sting, bite, or spray formic acid.*

▲ **LASIUS NIGER**, *the common Black Garden Ant, occurs in soil under stones and pavements. In late summer, large mating swarms of winged ants are produced.*

▶ **MYRMICA RUBRA**
*is a common reddish
brown species (males
are darker) that is
found in many
habitats, including
gardens. The
pedicel is made up
of two segments.*

ant larva

pedicel

reddish
brown
workers

yellowish brown
thorax

dark head

black abdomen

▶ **LASIUS BRUNNEUS** *nests
in old trees. The abdomen
is darker than the petiole or
the thorax, unlike* L. niger,
which is uniformly brown.

nest mound

ANT NEST

▼ **LASIUS FLAVUS,** *the
Yellow Meadow Ant, is
similar in all but colour to*
L. niger. *It nests in meadows
and rough grassland.*

pupa inside
cocoon

yellowish
brown
workers

Bumble Bees and Honey Bees

Apidae

SEEN *in almost any flower-rich habitat. Bumble bees are particularly common in northern regions and in mountains.*

These familiar social bees live in complex and often very large colonies with a queen, males, and sterile worker females. Bumble bees are very hairy, stout-bodied, and brownish or orange to black with yellow markings. Their body hairs are typically yellow, orange, or black. Honey bees are smaller, more slender, and golden brown with pale hairs. The females of most species have a specialized pollen-carrying structure called the corbiculum on the outer surface of the hind tibiae.

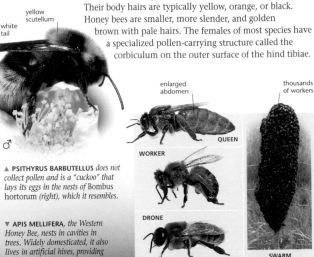

yellow scutellum

white tail

♂

enlarged abdomen

thousands of workers

QUEEN

WORKER

DRONE

SWARM

▲ **PSITHYRUS BARBUTELLUS** *does not collect pollen and is a "cuckoo" that lays its eggs in the nests of* Bombus hortorum *(right), which it resembles.*

▼ **APIS MELLIFERA,** *the Western Honey Bee, nests in cavities in trees. Widely domesticated, it also lives in artificial hives, providing honey, wax, and other products.*

NOTE

Western Honey bees have been spread all over the world by commerce. The value of the crops that they pollinate exceeds that of their honey and wax.

yellow collar

yellow front of abdomen

red tail

▲ **BOMBUS LAPIDARIUS,** *the Red-tailed Bumble Bee, is common in open habitats and nests in the ground under stones. The male has a yellow collar.*

♀

▶ **BOMBUS HORTORUM,** *the Large Garden Bumble Bee, has a yellow collar, yellow at the rear of the thorax and the first abdominal segment, and a white tail.*

yellow collar

▲ **BOMBUS PRATORUM** *inhabits light woodland and gardens. Workers have a yellow collar, a yellowish second abdominal segment, and a red "tail".*

yellowish abdominal segment

orange collar

▲ **BOMBUS TERRESTRIS,** *the Buff-tailed Bumble Bee, is an abundant species. It makes nests underground and can find its way back after foraging trips to 13km.*

orange-yellow second abdominal segment

LARVAE

The pale, grub-like larvae are fed pollen and honey in brood cells made of wax. At first, the larvae produce female workers to build up the colony; males appear later.

▼ **BOMBUS LUCORUM** *is a very common species which rests underground and sometimes in grass tussocks.*

pollen on leg

yellow collar

ORDER *Hymenoptera.*
FAMILY *Apidae.*
SPECIES IN FAMILY *1,000.*
SIZE *0.3–2.7cm (body length).*
FEEDING *Larvae: herbivores (pollen), honey-feeders. Adults: herbivores, honey-feeders.*

Cuckoo, Digger, and Carpenter Bees

Anthophoridae

THRIVE *in a variety of flower-rich habitats, especially in sunny, open localities.*

Cuckoo bees are black and yellow or brown and white, lack pollen baskets on their hind legs, are relatively hairless, and can look extremely wasp-like. Digger bees are typically bumble bee-like and hairy. Carpenter bees can be divided into two main groups: very large, hairy, blackish or bluish species; and small, relatively bare, dark bluish green species. Female digger and carpenter bees have densely hairy pollen baskets on their hind legs.

long antennae in male

golden, hairy body

pinched "wasp-like" waist

◀ **EUCERA LONGICORNIS** *nests on the ground, often in groups. Males are attracted to the Bee Orchid and attempt to mate with it, thus serving as the flower's pollinators.*

short, straight antennae

black and yellow markings

▲ **NOMADA FLAVA**, *a very wasp-like cuckoo bee, does not make a nest of its own but is a parasite of various mining bees, in whose nests it lays its eggs.*

▼ **ANTHOPHORA PLUMIPES** *has distinct sexes: males are yellowish brown, while females are blackish. Nests are excavated in soil or the soft mortar of old walls.*

▼ **XYLOCOPA VIOLACEA**, *the Violet Carpenter Bee, is a very large, noisy-flying species that has been breeding sporadically in Britain in recent years. It nests in old wood.*

resembles small bumble bee

purplish blue wings

huge, robust body

entirely black

LARVAE

These bees' larvae may be fat-bodied or slender and pale or yellow. Cuckoo bee larvae develop in the nests of other bees, killing the resident larvae and eating their food.

NOTE

Also known as the long-tongued bees, this family is notable for its members' long tongues, which in some cases may exceed the length of the body itself.

ORDER *Hymenoptera.*
FAMILY *Anthophoridae.*
SPECIES IN FAMILY *4,200.*
SIZE *0.5–2.2cm.*
FEEDING *Larvae: pollen- and honey-feeders. Adults: pollen- and nectar-feeders.*
IMPACT *Essential plant pollinators.*

Phalangiids

Phalangiidae

These harvestmen usually have soft bodies and may have many spiny projections. Typical species are brownish or greyish with a dark area on the upper surface known as the saddle. On the front edge of the carapace there is often a cluster of three closely grouped spines, called the trident. Leg segments may have longitudinal ridges, which are sometimes spined. Males and females can look different, especially in the shape of the chelicerae, which are enlarged in males.

LIVE *under stones and among leaf litter in wooded and grassy areas; some also found in buildings.*

trident of short spines at front of head

second leg is up to 1.8cm long

reddish-brown body

▲ OLIGOLOPHUS TRIDENS *has a brown body with a black central mark, which is broad at the front and more parallel-sided towards the rear.*

▶ **PHALANGIUM OPILIO** *is one of the few day-active species in gardens. Males (shown here) have horn-like extensions on the chelicerae.*

horned chelicerae in male

pale sides

second leg up to 4cm long

▲ MITOPUS MORIO *is variable in general body colour, but always has a very broad, saddle-shaped dark band running down its back. It lives among low-growing vegetation and bushes.*

ORDER *Opiliones.*
FAMILY *Phalangiidae.*
SPECIES IN FAMILY *200.*
SIZE *1–12mm.*
FEEDING *Immatures and adults: predators, scavengers.*
IMPACT *Harmless.*

Gall Mites

Eriophyidae

It is extremely difficult indeed to see these tiny mites, but very easy to recognize the galls that they make on the leaves of their host plants and inside which they develop. Each species of mite produces a uniquely shaped gall, often on a specific host plant. Gall mites range from white to yellowish, pinkish, or transparent and are widest just behind the head, giving them a distinctive, carrot-like shape. The thorax and abdomen are completely fused and, unlike any other mites, which have four pairs of legs, gall mites have only two pairs of legs. Many species are parthenogenetic.

FOUND in woodland, parkland, gardens, hedgerows, and wherever their host species grow.

GALLS

◀ **ERIOPHYES MACROCHELUS** galls found on the surface of Field Maple leaves, are green and hairy. They grow up to 5mm across, and occur in groups of up to 4.

silver-white hair

▶ **ACERIA FRAXINIVORUS** inhabits the flower buds of ash trees. Growing up to 2cm, the galls are green but darken as they mature.

GALLS

▶ **PHYTOPUS AVELLANAE** occurs on the buds of Hazel. This causes the buds to swell and open, making them more conspicuous than normal buds.

swollen Hazel bud

irregular shape

GALLS

two pairs of legs

pale tapered body

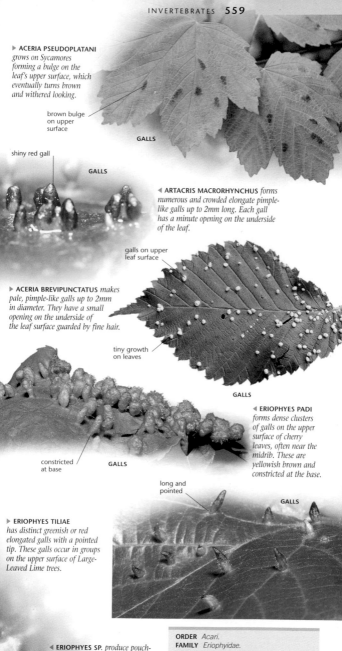

▶ **ACERIA PSEUDOPLATANI**
grows on Sycamores
forming a bulge on the
leaf's upper surface, which
eventually turns brown
and withered looking.

brown bulge
on upper
surface

GALLS

shiny red gall

GALLS

◀ **ARTACRIS MACRORHYNCHUS** forms
numerous and crowded elongate pimple-
like galls up to 2mm long. Each gall
has a minute opening on the underside
of the leaf.

galls on upper
leaf surface

▶ **ACERIA BREVIPUNCTATUS** makes
pale, pimple-like galls up to 2mm
in diameter. They have a small
opening on the underside of
the leaf surface guarded by fine hair.

tiny growth
on leaves

GALLS

◀ **ERIOPHYES PADI**
forms dense clusters
of galls on the upper
surface of cherry
leaves, often near the
midrib. These are
yellowish brown and
constricted at the base.

constricted
at base

GALLS

long and
pointed

GALLS

▶ **ERIOPHYES TILIAE**
has distinct greenish or red
elongated galls with a pointed
tip. These galls occur in groups
on the upper surface of Large-
Leaved Lime trees.

◀ **ERIOPHYES SP.** produce pouch-
like galls with a small opening
guarded by dense hairs. The
mites live and feed inside
the gall, sucking the
contents of plant cells.

ORDER Acari.
FAMILY Eriophyidae.
SPECIES IN FAMILY 2,000.
SIZE 0.1–0.3mm.
FEEDING Immatures and adults: herbivores.
IMPACT Make galls on a range of plants that
is detrimental to the health of the host plants.

Hard Ticks

Ixodidae

These flattened, yellowish red to dark brown or almost black ticks have a very tough (sometimes patterned) plate on the back of the body. In males, this plate covers the whole body, but in females and immatures it covers only the front half. Some species are distinctively marked. The abdomen is soft and flexible to allow large blood meals to be taken from the animal hosts on which these ticks are found. Hard ticks transmit disease and may carry viral diseases that affect humans, such as encephalitis.

OCCUPY grassland, scrub, or woodland, in association with their bird or mammal hosts.

flattened abdomen

tough dorsal shield

sucking mouthparts

IXODES RICINUS, *the Sheep Tick, actually sucks blood from a wide range of hosts. It is greyish to reddish brown with a dark dorsal plate and head.*

ORDER *Acari.*
FAMILY *Ixodidae.*
SPECIES IN FAMILY 650.
SIZE 2–10mm.
FEEDING *Immatures and adults: blood-feeders (mammals and birds).*
IMPACT *Serious pests of domestic animals.*

NOTE

Females gorge on blood after mating, then drop off to lay their eggs. There are two immature stages: a six-legged larva and an eight-legged nymph.

Spider Mites

Tetranychidae

These tiny, soft-bodied mites are orange, red, greenish, or yellow in colour and have a spider-like appearance. Large numbers infest and feed on plants, which may then develop pale blotches and wither or die. Spider mites produce silk from glands in the front part of the body and often cover affected plant parts with a fine webbing. The plants attacked include a number of commercially important crops such as wheat, citrus and other fruit trees, cotton, and coffee; yields may suffer dramatically.

OCCUR in a variety of habitats on shrubs, trees, and herbaceous plants.

▼ **TETRANYCHUS URTICAE** *feeds on a wide range of host plants. It hibernates deep in leaf litter in winter.*

greenish in colour

pale, fine body hairs

NOTE

The eggs of spider mites are reddish, rounded, and quite large. They are laid on the bark of host plants. Immatures – and adults – live under the leaves.

ORDER *Acari.*
FAMILY *Tetranychidae.*
SPECIES IN FAMILY 650.
SIZE 0.2–0.8mm.
FEEDING *Immatures and adults: herbivores.*
IMPACT *Several species are important pests of grasses, clovers, and crops.*

Lace-webbed Spiders

Amaurobiidae

Named for their distinctive webs, these small spiders make irregular or tangled webs with a tube-shaped retreat in dark or concealed places. The silk produced by these spiders has a bluish appearance when fresh. The spiders have a

WEBS *of these spiders can be found in holes in walls and bark, underneath stones, and in leaf litter.*

dark reddish brown cephalothorax with eight eyes in two rows at the front. The abdomen is dark or greyish brown with lighter, sometimes chevron-shaped, markings.

funnel-like retreat

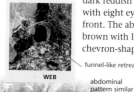

WEB

abdominal pattern similar in both sexes

AMAUROBIUS FENESTRALIS *spins its webs under the bark of old trees or stumps but is most commonly found in the crevices of stone walls.*

dark head

NOTE
A vibrating tuning fork held to the web of a lace-webbed spider will lure it out of its retreat. The webs are produced at night under the cover of darkness.

ORDER *Araneae.*
FAMILY *Amaurobiidae.*
SPECIES IN FAMILY *350.*
SIZE *4–14mm (body length).*
FEEDING *Immatures and adults: predators.*
IMPACT *Beneficial and harmless.*

Nursery-web Spiders

Pisauridae

These large, long-legged hunting spiders are very similar in habit and appearance to wolf spiders (p.564), but differ in the size of their eyes. Viewed from the front, the two eyes forming the second row of eyes are quite small. The carapace is oval, with longitudinal markings. They do not make webs, but run and hunt on the ground, on the surface of still water, and on aquatic plants.

WIDESPREAD *on grassland, heathland, woodland rides and margins, and also in marshy areas.*

▼ **DOLOMEDES FIMBRIATUS**, *the Fishing Spider, lives in wet habitats and hunts for prey on the surface of water.*

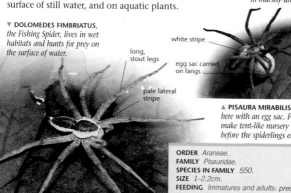

white stripe

long, stout legs

egg sac carried on fangs

pale lateral stripe

▲ **PISAURA MIRABILIS** *is seen here with an egg sac. Females make tent-like nursery webs just before the spiderlings emerge.*

ORDER *Araneae.*
FAMILY *Pisauridae.*
SPECIES IN FAMILY *550.*
SIZE *1–2.2cm.*
FEEDING *Immatures and adults: predators.*
IMPACT *Beneficial and harmless. Dolomedes fimbriatus is protected by law in the UK.*

Orb Web Spiders

Araneidae

The most distinctive feature of these spiders is their vertical and circular webs, which have a central hub with radiating lines and spirals of sticky and non-sticky silk. The structure of the web is often species specific. The spider usually sits at the hub of the web, awaiting the arrival of prey. These species often have very large, egg-shaped abdomens, which can be brightly coloured and patterned with all manner of bands, spots, and irregular markings. There are eight eyes, the middle four often forming a square, with two pairs further out towards the side of the head. The legs of most orb web spiders have numerous bristles and spines.

OCCUR *in a wide variety of habitats, from heathland to woodland and gardens to meadows.*

NOTE

Orb web designs differ between species. The spider usually sits at the hub of the web, although some hide close by, to wait for prey.

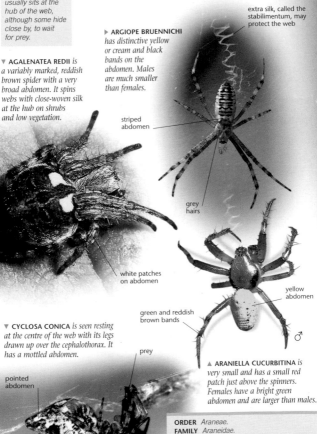

▶ **ARGIOPE BRUENNICHI** *has distinctive yellow or cream and black bands on the abdomen. Males are much smaller than females.*

extra silk, called the stabilimentum, may protect the web

▼ **AGALENATEA REDII** *is a variably marked, reddish brown spider with a very broad abdomen. It spins webs with close-woven silk at the hub on shrubs and low vegetation.*

striped abdomen

grey hairs

white patches on abdomen

green and reddish brown bands

yellow abdomen

▼ **CYCLOSA CONICA** *is seen resting at the centre of the web with its legs drawn up over the cephalothorax. It has a mottled abdomen.*

prey

pointed abdomen

▲ **ARANIELLA CUCURBITINA** *is very small and has a small red patch just above the spinners. Females have a bright green abdomen and are larger than males.*

ORDER *Araneae.*
FAMILY *Araneidae.*
SPECIES IN FAMILY *4,000.*
SIZE *3–16mm.*
FEEDING *Immatures and adults: predatory.*
IMPACT *Beneficial and harmless, although some larger species may bite in defence.*

▲ **ARANEUS MARMOREUS** *has two colour forms; the rarer one has a variably marked, brownish abdomen. The other (above) has a much paler abdomen with a dark patch towards the rear.*

bristly legs

▼ **ARANEUS QUADRATUS** *has four spots in a squarish pattern on its abdomen. This species spins webs low down on heathland shrubs.*

cross-shaped markings

▲ **ARANEUS DIADEMATUS,** *the Garden Cross Spider, is extremely common. It is very variable in colour, but always seems to have a cross-shaped mark on its abdomen.*

▶ **LARINIOIDES CORNUTUS** *makes its webs between grass stems and other plants, often near freshwater or in coastal areas. The female has a less distinct abdominal pattern.*

four pale spots on the abdomen

♂

dark, flattened body

patterning on the abdomen

▲ **NUCTENEA UMBRATICA,** *common and widespread in Britain, hides under the bark of dead trees and other crevices during the day, and spins a web to trap nocturnal flying insects.*

Wolf Spiders

Lycosidae

OCCUR *everywhere from grassland to marshes and mudflats, on low vegetation.*

NOTE

Although wolf spiders look similar to nursery-web spiders, their middle forward-facing eyes are much larger than the other eyes.

Drably coloured, the bodies of wolf spiders are densely covered with light and dark hairs that form patterns. These spiders have very good eyesight for hunting prey. The head has eight eyes: four small eyes in a row at the front, and above this a much larger pair of forward-facing eyes; another pair, further back, point sideways. Females often carry their egg sacs around with them, attached to their spinnerets. When the young spiderlings hatch, the mother may carry them on her back for a week or so. Most species live on the ground among leaf litter or on low-growing vegetation. Wolf spiders are fast runners.

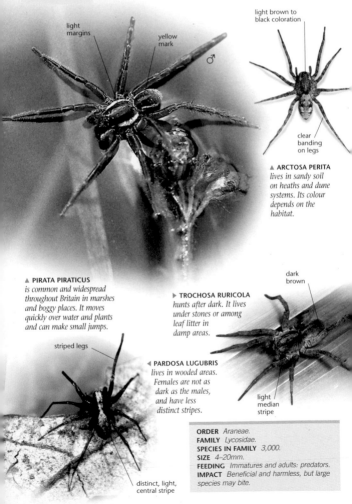

light margins

yellow mark

♂

light brown to black coloration

clear banding on legs

▲ **ARCTOSA PERITA** *lives in sandy soil on heaths and dune systems. Its colour depends on the habitat.*

▲ **PIRATA PIRATICUS** *is common and widespread throughout Britain in marshes and boggy places. It moves quickly over water and plants and can make small jumps.*

▶ **TROCHOSA RURICOLA** *hunts after dark. It lives under stones or among leaf litter in damp areas.*

dark brown

striped legs

◀ **PARDOSA LUGUBRIS** *lives in wooded areas. Females are not as dark as the males, and have less distinct stripes.*

light median stripe

distinct, light, central stripe

ORDER *Araneae.*
FAMILY *Lycosidae.*
SPECIES IN FAMILY *3,000.*
SIZE *4–20mm.*
FEEDING *Immatures and adults: predators.*
IMPACT *Beneficial and harmless, but large species may bite.*

The Water Spider

Argyronetidae

This unique spider lives permanently underwater, and makes a dome-shaped, silk diving bell attached to submerged plants. Prey items are dragged back to the bell for eating. The water spider has a reddish brown cephalothorax and a dark brown abdomen with a distinctive dense pile of short hair. The third and fourth pairs of legs are much hairier than the first two pairs.

FOUND in very slow-flowing and still water with plenty of aquatic vegetation.

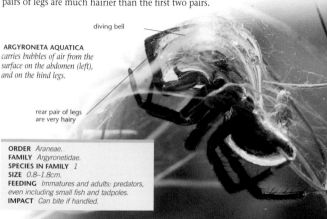

diving bell

ARGYRONETA AQUATICA
carries bubbles of air from the
surface on the abdomen (left),
and on the hind legs.

rear pair of legs
are very hairy

ORDER *Araneae*.
FAMILY *Argyronetidae*.
SPECIES IN FAMILY *1*
SIZE *0.8–1.8cm*.
FEEDING *Immatures and adults: predators,
even including small fish and tadpoles.*
IMPACT *Can bite if handled.*

Cobweb Spiders

Agelenidae

These spiders are also called funnel-weavers due to their web – a flat, tangled silk sheet with a funnel-shaped tube at one side. They are often long-legged and the front of the cephalothorax is narrowed, with eight smallish eyes grouped together. The abdomen is quite slender, oval, and may be patterned.

LIVE in grassland, meadows, gardens, and similar habitats, often entering houses.

chevron
markings

long
legs

oval
abdomen

funnel-shaped
tube

▶ **AGELENA LABYRINTHICA**
spins a sheet web among
grasses, low-growing
vegetation, or bushes,
resting in the funnel-
shaped retreat.

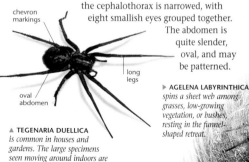

▲ **TEGENARIA DUELLICA**
is common in houses and
gardens. The large specimens
seen moving around indoors are
usually males looking for mates.

ORDER *Araneae*.
FAMILY *Agelenidae*.
SPECIES IN FAMILY *700*.
SIZE *4–16mm (body length)*.
FEEDING *Immatures and adults: predators*.
IMPACT *Entirely harmless, but responsible
for frightening arachnophobic householders.*

Six-eyed Spiders

Segestriidae

LIVE *in tubular nests in holes in walls, and sometimes in bark.*

Despite their common name of six-eyed spiders, segestriids are not the only family of spiders with six eyes. The eyes are arranged in three groups of two – a close-set pair in the middle, facing forward, and one pair on each side. A good recognition feature for these spiders is that the first three pairs of legs are held forwards. They also lay threads like trip wires radiating from the nest entrance.

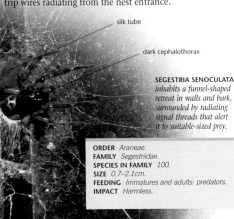

silk tube

dark cephalothorax

SEGESTRIA SENOCULATA
inhabits a funnel-shaped retreat in walls and bark, surrounded by radiating signal threads that alert it to suitable-sized prey.

ORDER *Araneae.*
FAMILY *Segestriidae.*
SPECIES IN FAMILY *100.*
SIZE *0.7–2.1cm.*
FEEDING *Immatures and adults: predators.*
IMPACT *Harmless.*

Daddy-Long-Legs Spiders

Pholcidae

FOUND *in caves and buildings, especially near ceilings and in dark corners.*

Also known as cellar spiders, these small spiders make irregular, tangled webs of criss-cross threads. They quickly wrap prey in silk before biting it. The carapace is rounded in outline and the legs are much longer than the body, giving a spindly appearance similar to crane flies (p.528). The head has a pair of small eyes flanked by two groups of three closely-set eyes.

NOTE

The males look very similar to females but have a slender abdomen and are slightly smaller. The mating of these spiders can last for hours.

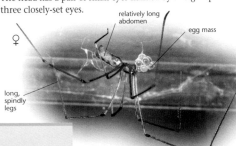

relatively long abdomen

egg mass

♀

long, spindly legs

ORDER *Araneae.*
FAMILY *Pholcidae.*
SPECIES IN FAMILY *350.*
SIZE *3–14mm (body length).*
FEEDING *Immatures and adults: predators.*
IMPACT *Beneficial and harmless, although sometimes regarded a nuisance in houses.*

PHOLCUS PHALANGIOIDES
is very common in buildings. When disturbed, it vibrates its body and web rapidly to blur its outline, confusing potential predators.

Crab Spiders

Thomisidae

These spiders are named for their typically squat shape and characteristic sideways, scuttling movement. The carapace is nearly circular and the abdomen is short and often blunt-ended. The first two pairs of legs, which are used to seize prey, are larger and more spiny than the other two pairs and are turned to face forwards. The head has eight small, dark and beady, equally-sized eyes arranged in two rows.

OCCUR *on a variety of plants, especially the flowerheads, and on the bark of trees.*

▲ **TIBELLUS OBLONGUS** *conceals itself among grass and other low-growing foliage by holding its legs stretched out.*

camouflage posture

pale lower half of legs

▶ **XYSTICUS CRISTATUS** *has cryptic coloration to blend in with dried leaves on bushes and the ground, where it lies in wait for prey.*

reddish abdomen contrasts with greenish cephalothorax

◀ **DIAEA DORSATA** *drops on a thread when threatened, holding its first two pairs of legs straight out sideways.*

NOTE

Crab spiders rely on superb camouflage to ambush their prey. Some species can change their body colour in the space of a day to blend in better.

large abdomen

WHITE FORM

dark stripes on cephalothorax

♀

large front legs

▼ **PHILODROMUS AUREOLUS** *lives on or near the ground. The male has dark markings, while the female is larger and light brown.*

chelicera

YELLOW FORM

palps

♀ ▲ **MISUMENA VATIA** *has a white or yellow female, which changes colour to match its background. The male is far smaller, with dark markings.*

long legs

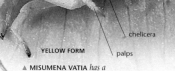

♂

slightly iridescent

ORDER *Araneae.*
FAMILY *Thomisidae.*
SPECIES IN FAMILY *2,500.*
SIZE *3–12mm (body length).*
FEEDING *Immatures and adults: predators.*
IMPACT *Beneficial and harmless.*

Himantariids

Himantariidae

These pale yellowish to brown, slender centipedes have a slightly flattened, ribbon-like appearance. The trunk segments are broadest in the middle of the body and become narrow towards either end, especially towards the head. The head is broader than long and always much narrower than the first trunk segment. The antennae are quite short and compressed.

INHABIT *soil, leaf litter, and debris in woods and grassland.*

short antennae

slim, flexible body

HAPLOPHILUS SUBTERRANEUS *is a pale yellowish species with as many as 80 pairs of short legs. It feeds in soil and leaf mould.*

short legs

ORDER *Geophilida.*
FAMILY *Himantariidae.*
SPECIES IN FAMILY *100.*
SIZE *2.5–8cm.*
FEEDING *Immatures and adults: predators.*
IMPACT *Harmless.*

Lithobiids

Lithobiidae

Most lithobiids are reddish brown and the body is tough and quite flattened. The plates that cover the upper surface of the body segments are alternately large and small. There are 15 pairs of legs, with the last two pairs being longer than the others. The antennae are slender and tapering.

LIVE *in cracks and crevices, mainly in woodland but also in grassland, upland, and coastal areas.*

LITHOBIUS VARIEGATUS *is common among the leaf litter of deciduous woods. It climbs trees in search of food.*

poison claw

light and dark bands on legs (sometimes hard to see)

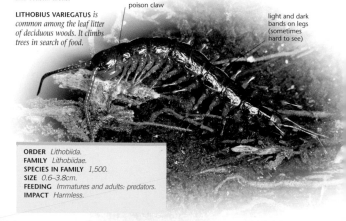

ORDER *Lithobiida.*
FAMILY *Lithobiidae.*
SPECIES IN FAMILY *1,500.*
SIZE *0.6–3.8cm.*
FEEDING *Immatures and adults: predators.*
IMPACT *Harmless.*

Cylinder Millipedes

Julidae

Cylinder millipedes vary from shortish, pale-coloured species to longer dark or black species with reddish stripes. The antennae are fairly long and slender. Most species are tough-bodied and relatively broad. As the common name implies, they have a circular cross-section. These are slow-moving species, which are good at pushing through soil and leaf litter. Like most millipedes, the species in this family have a pair of defence glands located on each of the body segments that are able to produce a range of chemicals to deter enemies.

LIVE *in a wide variety of habitats including grassland, heaths, and woodland, in soil and leaf litter and under stones and rotting wood.*

NOTE

This family is the largest in Britain, comprising 18 of the 52 species present. The millipedes are important in decomposition and nutrient recycling.

two yellow-brown stripes down body

▲ **OMMATOIULUS SABULOSUS**, *the Striped Millipede, is found all over Britain and is commonly found in areas with light or sandy soils. It has dorsal stripes that may become broken up into spots or patches.*

relatively long antennae

dark legs

shiny body

pale legs

▲ **TACHYPODOIULUS NIGER**, *the White-legged Snake Millipede, is a common species in Britain except for the very far north. It is a shiny back-bodied species with contrasting white legs.*

ORDER *Julida.*
FAMILY *Julidae.*
SPECIES IN FAMILY *450.*
SIZE *0.8–5cm.*
FEEDING *Immatures and adults: scavengers, herbivores.*
IMPACT *Harmless.*

Pill Millipedes

Glomeridae

OCCUR *in many habitats, but especially in woodland, rough pasture, and farmland.*

Pill millipedes are small. Their trunk has 13 segments, and the shape of the body plates allows them to roll into a tight ball with the head tucked in. These species should not be confused with pill woodlice (right), which can also roll up for protection. Millipedes have many more legs, and two pairs of legs for each body segment. The young have only three pairs of legs when they hatch. They reach the full complement of 15 pairs at adulthood.

tough, shiny body

saddle-shaped segment behind head

GLOMERIS MARGINATA *is very widespread and common. It has a shinier body than the pill woodlouse.*

rolled-up position

ORDER *Glomerida.*
FAMILY *Glomeridae.*
SPECIES IN FAMILY *200.*
SIZE *0.2–2cm.*
FEEDING *Immatures and adults: scavengers, herbivores.*
IMPACT *Harmless.*

Porcellionid Woodlice

Porcellionidae

WIDESPREAD *where there is a humid microhabitat provided by rotting plant matter.*

The body surface of these woodlice can be smooth and slightly glossy or warty, but is usually grey or greyish brown with other markings. The last section of the antennae, called the flagellum, is composed of two segments. The body of some species is narrow, and these species can run quickly. Woodlice excrete ammonia gas and this gives large colonies a characteristic smell.

pitted surface

flagellum with two segments

PORCELLIO SCABER *is also known as the Common Rough Woodlouse. It is usually grey, but can sometimes be yellowish or orangish, and speckled.*

seven pairs of walking legs

greyish body segments

ORDER *Isopoda.*
FAMILY *Porcellionidae.*
SPECIES IN FAMILY *500.*
SIZE *0.9–2cm.*
FEEDING *Immatures and adults: scavengers, dung.*
IMPACT *Harmless.*

Pill Woodlice

Armadillidiidae

Light brown to black with yellow patches, these woodlice
have a convex cross-section and a rounded hind margin.
They are also known as pill bugs. When threatened, many
can roll up into a ball to protect themselves. Some species,
such as *Armadillidium vulgare* and *A. pictum*, make a
more perfect ball than other species.

OCCUR *in many
habitats from shoreline
to mountains; in leaf
litter and debris in
woodland and gardens.*

rolled up for
defence

convex body

flagellum
with two
segments

ORDER *Isopoda.*
FAMILY *Armadillidiidae.*
SPECIES IN FAMILY *250.*
SIZE *0.5–2cm.*
FEEDING *Immatures and adults: scavengers,
herbivores, dung.*
IMPACT *Harmless.*

**ARMADILLIDIUM
VULGARE,** *the
Pill Woodlouse, occurs
with other species but
can tolerate drier
conditions than them.*

NOTE

*Pill woodlice have
several narrow tail
segments, whereas
pill millipedes have
a single, broad tail
segment. They also
roll into a looser ball
than pill millipedes.*

Swimming Crabs

Portunidae

This family includes the swimming crabs and the common
shore crabs. The carapace has clear symmetrical patterns and
is typically trapezoidal in outline, being broad at the front
and narrow at the rear. The edge of the carapace has three
blunt teeth between the eyes and five sharp teeth on either
side of the eyes. The colour of the carapace is greenish grey
to brownish or reddish in adults. Portunids are generally
nocturnal and eat bivalve molluscs such as clams,
oysters, and mussels.

THRIVES *in a very
wide range of
marine and
estuarine habitats.*

greenish grey
carapace

CARCINUS MAENAS, *the Common
Shore Crab or Green Crab, can be
found all around the British coastline
in the intertidal zone and in the sea
to 400m deep.*

ORDER *Decapoda.*
FAMILY *Portunidae.*
SPECIES IN FAMILY *120.*
SIZE *Carapace to 9cm wide.*
FEEDING *Predators and scavengers.*
IMPACT *Some species are invasive and can
damage shellfisheries. Others are eaten.*

Rock Crabs

Cancridae

These crabs are generally heavily built with an oval-shaped body. The carapace of the best-known species, the Edible Crab, has distinctive crimped edges like that on a piecrust. The claws of males are typically larger than those of females. The abdomens of females are wider than that of males. Rock crabs are nocturnal to avoid predators such as seals and wolf fish, and hide in deep cracks or lie buried in the substrate during the day. They feed on molluscs, small fish, other crustaceans, and echinoderms.

FOUND *on British coasts from the intertidal zone to 100m deep.*

abdomen folded under carapace

oval-shaped body

large claw with black tip

CANCER PAGARUS, *the Edible Crab or Cromer Crab, is orange-brown in colour and is distinguished by its large size and black-tipped claws.*

ORDER *Decapoda.*
FAMILY *Cancridae.*
SPECIES IN FAMILY *15.*
SIZE *Carapace to 25cm wide.*
FEEDING *Predators and scavengers.*
IMPACT *Some species are commercially important.*

Prawns

Palaemonidae

Also known as shrimps, these crustaceans have an elongated body with a cylindrical carapace and an abdomen composed of six segments. The carapace is extended forwards in the form of a rostrum, which may be straight or curved, and bears a number of sharp tooth-like projections along the upper and lower edges.

INHABIT *rock pools and sea grass beds down to depths of 50m.*

eye stalks

PALAEMON ELEGANS, *the Rock Pool Prawn, grows to 6cm in length and inhabits intertidal pools on rocky shores all around Britain.*

brown, yellow, and blue spots

ORDER *Decapoda.*
FAMILY *Palaemonidae.*
SPECIES IN FAMILY *425.*
SIZE *Up to 15cm long.*
FEEDING *Predators and scavengers.*
IMPACT *Some species are caught commercially.*

Barnacles

Balanidae

Barnacles are sedentary crustaceans that live permanently cemented to the substrate and are surrounded by a calcareous shell, which they add to as they grow. These barnacles have a shell composed of 4–6 heavily ridged plates, which together have an irregular outline. They feed by waving a pair of specially modified feathery limbs called "cirri" in the water. The flow of water that is generated carries tiny suspended planktonic food particles towards the mouth.

ATTACHES *permanently to rocks in the intertidal zone; can colonize low-salinity estuarine waters.*

conical profile

more columnar growth when crowded

SEMIBALANUS BALANOIDES, *the Northern Acorn Barnacle, is the most widespread species in the north, and has a membranous shell-base, unlike other species that have calcified bases.*

ORDER *Thoracica.*
FAMILY *Balanidae.*
SPECIES IN FAMILY *45.*
SIZE *Up to 15cm in diameter and height; British species are much smaller.*
FEEDING *Omnivorous suspension feeders.*
IMPACT *Can foul ships' hulls and pilings.*

Periwinkles

Littorinidae

Periwinkles have strong conical or globular shells, typically with a pointed apex. Some species can be a brightly coloured yellow, orange, or red with contrasting bands, but most are greyish brown. The whorls are often finely grooved and the lip of the aperture is thin.

OCCUPIES *rocky shores with a good covering of seaweeds; also in brackish estuaries.*

globular shell

short, pointed spire

usually greyish brown in colour

LITTORINA LITTOREA, *the Common or Edible Periwinkle, is very common and widespread on rocky shores all around the British coastline. Its colour varies from blackish to greyish brown.*

ORDER *Mesogastropoda.*
FAMILY *Littorinidae.*
SPECIES IN FAMILY *75.*
SIZE *Shell to 4cm tall.*
FEEDING *Algal grazers.*
IMPACT *Some species are collected as human food.*

Limpets

Patellidae

STICKS *"like a limpet" on intertidal rocks, especially on exposed rocky shores; not common where there is lots of seaweed.*

With unmistakable conical, uncoiled shells and no operculum, or bony plate, limpets cling tightly to rocks to avoid the effects of desiccation when they are exposed at low tide. The shells of some species are tall while others are more flattened and many have radiating ribs or ridges and distinctive growth rings. Larger specimens may become encrusted with barnacles. The keyhole limpet has a small hole at the apex and its shells are lined with mother-of-pearl.

muscular foot

conical shell

PATELLA VULGATA, *the Common Limpet, has a home scar, a shallow depression in the rock made by abrasion, to which it returns after grazing.*

ORDER *Archaeogastropoda.*
FAMILY *Patellidae.*
SPECIES IN FAMILY *8.*
SIZE *Typically less than 6cm in diameter.*
FEEDING *Herbivorous (algal grazer).*
IMPACT *Can foul ships' hulls and other structures; sometimes eaten.*

Pond Snails

Lymnaeidae

FOUND *very commonly in well-vegetated ponds and lakes, often near the surface.*

The pond snails generally have a large last whorl and a number of smaller whorls forming a tall slender spire. The aperture is quite large and not closed by an operculum. Most species are shiny but drably coloured in shades of brown, yellow, and cream. The surface of the shell has fine lines and striations running parallel to the lip.

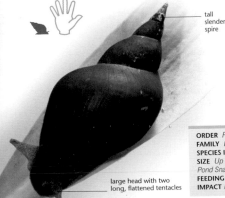

tall slender spire

LYMNAEA STAGNALIS, *the Great Pond Snail, is the largest pond snail in Britain. It grazes plants and carrion, but has been known to attack other snails, insect larvae, and even small fish and newts.*

large head with two long, flattened tentacles

ORDER *Pulmonata.*
FAMILY *Lymnaeidae.*
SPECIES IN FAMILY *100.*
SIZE *Up to 8cm long; the shell of the Great Pond Snail can reach up to 6cm long.*
FEEDING *Omnivorous.*
IMPACT *Harmless.*

Land Snails

Helicidae

Land snails are air-breathing gastropods. The large muscular foot produces mucus to aid locomotion. Their shells can be flattened, conical, or globular, depending on the species. The shells can be thick, mottled, or otherwise patterned although some are thin and translucent or even hairy. The head has four tentacles, the larger upper pair carrying the eyes. The mouth is situated under the tentacles and houses the radula, a file-like structure for grasping food.

FAVOURS *a wide range of habitats from sand dunes and mountains to meadows and woodland.*

hard thin shell

brownish shell marked with yellow

brownish tentacle

HELIX ASPERSA, *the Garden Snail, is widely distributed in Britain, except in the far north where it is confined to the coastal regions.*

ORDER *Pulmonata.*
FAMILY *Helicidae.*
SPECIES IN FAMILY *230.*
SIZE *Up to 5cm in height.*
FEEDING *Herbivores and scavengers.*
IMPACT *Important food source for other species; some species are horticultural pests.*

Limacid Slugs

Limacidae

These slugs have a small, chalky shell, which is typically enclosed completely by the mantle and a keel, or raised ridge, that runs down the middle of the body from behind the mantle to the tail. The pneumostome, the opening to the lung cavity, is situated on the right of the body and well towards the rear of the mantle.

OCCUPIES *gardens, grassland, hedgerows, and agricultural land.*

pneumostome

DEROCERAS RETICULATUM, *the Netted Slug, is probably the commonest slug found all over Britain. It grows up to 5cm in length. The skin of the mantle has a pattern that resembles a fingerprint.*

ORDER *Pulmonata.*
FAMILY *Limacidae.*
SPECIES IN FAMILY *15.*
SIZE *Up to 30cm long.*
FEEDING *Herbivores and scavengers.*
IMPACT *Some are significant agricultural and horticultural pests.*

Arionid Slugs

Arionidae

FOUND in all kinds of terrestrial habitats – gardens, parks, meadows, and lawns throughout Britain.

These slugs have a very small internal shell, enclosed by the mantle. The opening to the respiratory cavity, the pneumostome, is situated in front of the midline of the mantle. The head has two pairs of tentacles, the upper pair carrying the eyes. When disturbed, arionids can contract themselves into a tight hemispherical ball. Like all slugs, they are only active at night or in wet weather.

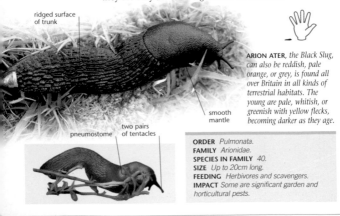

ridged surface of trunk

smooth mantle

pneumostome

two pairs of tentacles

ARION ATER, the Black Slug, can also be reddish, pale orange, or grey, is found all over Britain in all kinds of terrestrial habitats. The young are pale, whitish, or greenish with yellow flecks, becoming darker as they age.

ORDER Pulmonata.
FAMILY Arionidae.
SPECIES IN FAMILY 40.
SIZE Up to 20cm long.
FEEDING Herbivores and scavengers.
IMPACT Some are significant garden and horticultural pests.

Marine Mussels

Mytilidae

ATTACHED to rocks and other hard substrates on rocky coasts, often forming dense beds.

Mussels are bivalve molluscs that typically attach themselves to the substrate by tough golden-coloured byssus threads, which are secreted by a gland in the foot. Some mussel species are found in burrows. The shell is roughly triangular to pear-shaped, and smooth-edged with clear concentric growth lines. A layer known as the periostracum, which may be thin or tough and horny, and with whiskers or spines, covers the outside of the shell. Mussels feed by extracting bacteria, plankton, and dissolved organic matter from the seawater.

deep blue to purple in colour

shell sculptured with concentric lines

MYTILIS EDULIS, the Common or Edible Mussel, is an important food source for many marine species and birds such as Eider (p.305) and Oystercatcher (p.321).

ORDER Mytiloida.
FAMILY Mytilidae.
SPECIES IN FAMILY 90.
SIZE Up to 24cm long.
FEEDING Suspension feeder.
IMPACT Some commercial species; can foul submerged structures and pipes.

Cockles

Cardiidae

Cockles have heart-shaped shells and the two valves are similar in shape and size. The shells are strong and typically have a number of radiating ridges and furrows. In some species, the ridges bear blunt projections or strong sharp spines. Two adductor muscles hold the halves of the shell together, the wavy or serrated margins fitting tightly against each other. Cockles have a large foot.

BURROWS *in the upper 5cm of sand, muddy, and fine gravel shores, all around the British coastline.*

shell rounded and humped

opened cockle

opened cockle

CERASTODERMA EDULIS, *the Common Cockle, can tolerate the low salinity of estuaries where they can be harvested in huge numbers.*

shell with radiating ribs

ORDER *Veneroida.*
FAMILY *Cardiidae.*
SPECIES IN FAMILY *180.*
SIZE *Up to 12cm long.*
FEEDING *Suspension feeders.*
IMPACT *Some important commercial species; important food source for wading birds.*

Razor Clams

Solenidae

These marine bivalve molluscs are instantly recognizable by their very long, narrow and equally sized shells, which look like a cut-throat razor. The shells may be straight or slightly curved. The muscular foot is long and powerful and protrudes from one end, enabling these molluscs to burrow very quickly into the bottom sediment. The glossy perisotracum peels away from the surface quite readily.

LIVES *in permanent burrows in firm sand at lower shore levels; may be very abundant in sheltered locations.*

ENSIS ENSIS, *the Common Razor Shell, is common in shallow waters all around the coast of Britain wherever the bottom is made of fine sand or mud.*

pale shell with brown patches

muscular foot

concentric growth rings

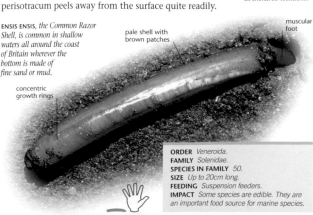

ORDER *Veneroida.*
FAMILY *Solenidae.*
SPECIES IN FAMILY *50.*
SIZE *Up to 20cm long.*
FEEDING *Suspension feeders.*
IMPACT *Some species are edible. They are an important food source for marine species.*

Sea Anemones

Actiniidae

INHABITS all rocky shore habitats, from exposed to sheltered; favours rock pools.

Anemones are solitary organisms that attach themselves to a solid substrate by an adhesive foot or disc. The stalk (column) of the anemone is capable of contraction and terminates in an oral disc in the centre of which is the mouth. Elongate tentacles, armed with stinging cells called nematocysts, surround the oral disc. When touched by prey or a predator, the nematocysts explode, releasing a tiny dart loaded with paralysing toxins.

5–6 rows of tentacles

ring of warts at top of stalk

ACTINIA EQUINA, *the Beadlet Anemone, is common on rocky shores all around the British coast and can be found fastened to rocks from the middle of the shore to depths of 10m.*

retracts tentacles out of water

ORDER *Actiniaria.*
FAMILY *Actiniidae.*
SPECIES IN FAMILY *300.*
SIZE *Up to 35cm diameter and 10cm high.*
FEEDING *Carnivorous.*
IMPACT *Some species used in genetic and biomedical research.*

Starfish

Asteriidae

FOUND on rocky shores all around the British coast, especially in mussel beds where it can be a pest.

Starfish are echinoderms typically with five arms radiating from a central disc. They have a skeleton made up of calcified elements called ossicles. The upper surface is covered with tubercles, spines, and tiny tweezer-like structures called pedicellaira, which nip off anything that settles on the arms. The lower surfaces of the arms are covered with numerous tube-feet with which they move around and hold their prey.

row of pale spines along middle of each arm

ASTERIAS RUBENS, *the Common Starfish, typically has five arms and its colour varies from reddish orange to brown or even purplish.*

ORDER *Forcipulatida.*
FAMILY *Asteriidae.*
SPECIES IN FAMILY *60.*
SIZE *Up to 90cm diameter.*
FEEDING *Predators and scavengers.*
IMPACT *Important source of food for other marine species. Used in biomedical research.*

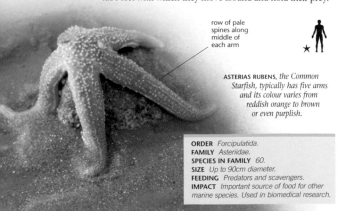

Freshwater Leeches

Erpobdellidae

These leeches, which do not feed on blood, are also known as swallowing leeches as they consume prey items such as worms, insect larvae, and crustaceans whole. Freshwater leeches have a cylindrical or slightly flattened body and are brownish or yellowish in colour. The head has a small sucker and lacks the powerful jaws present in other leech families.

INHABITS rivers, ponds, lakes, and fens throughout Britain and does well in water polluted with organic matter.

slender body

rounded head

ERPOBDELLA OCTOCULATA is up to 4cm long with a slightly flattened body that has variable patterns of dark marks. The head of this species has 8 tiny eyes in two rows. It eats the larvae of non-biting midges (Chironomidae) and small worms.

ORDER Arhynchobdellida.
FAMILY Erpobdellidae.
SPECIES IN FAMILY 50.
SIZE Up to 6cm long.
FEEDING Predators and scavengers.
IMPACT Used in freshwater toxicology research.

Earthworms

Lumbricidae

Earthworms have segmented bodies with eight short, stiff bristles on each segment to assist with locomotion. Sexually mature individuals have a swollen band around the body called the clitellum. This structure is used in the mating process and its secretions form a cocoon around the eggs that are produced. Earthworms make permanent vertical burrows in the soil and come to the surface to mate and feed.

COMMON and abundant in soil in most British terrestrial habitats.

swollen clitellum

flattened tail end

ORDER Haplotaxida.
FAMILY Lumbricidae.
SPECIES IN FAMILY 350.
SIZE Up to 30cm long.
FEEDING Herbivore and decomposer.
IMPACT Play a key role in soil formation and fertility. Important food source for vertebrates.

LUMBRICUS TERRESTRIS, the Common Earthworm or Lob Worm, flattens the tail end of its body to anchor itself in its burrow. Abundantly found, in lawns these worms can reach densities of 40 worms per square metre.

Glossary

Many of the terms defined here are illustrated in the general introduction to each plant or animal group. Words in *italics* are defined elsewhere in the glossary.

ABDOMEN In mammals, the portion of the body between the thorax and pelvis; the segmented, third section of an insect's body in which digestive, excretory, and reproductive organs are located; rear main section of an arthropod's body, except in myriapods, where there is only a head and a trunk.

ACHENE A dry, one-seeded, non-splitting fruit, often with a *pappus*.

ADIPOSE FIN A fleshy *dorsal fin* that lack spines or fin rays and is found only in members of the salmon family.

ADNATE Used to describe *gills* of fungi that are joined to the stem by their entire depth.

ADNEXED Used to describe *gills* that are narrower where they are attached to the stems.

AESTIVATE To undergo a period of dormancy during summer.

ALTERNATE Leaves borne singly, in two vertical rows or spirally.

ANAL FIN A medial fin on the belly of a fish that provides stability and steering.

ANTHER The male part of the flower that bears the pollen.

APICAL SPUR A blunt, spine-like structure at the end of a leg segment, usually a *tibia*.

ARIL A fleshy, often brightly coloured, coat on a seed.

AURICLED With small, ear-like lobes.

AWN Stiff bristle-like projection often found on flowers.

AXIL The angle between two structures, such as the leaf and stem or the midrib and a small vein of a leaf.

BIPINNATE Twice *pinnate*, i.e. with the divisions themselves pinnately divided.

BOSS A rounded projection on a petal.

BRACT A small, leaf-like structure found at the base of a flower stalk or in the *cone* of a conifer.

BRACTEOLE A small leaf-like organ at the base of secondary branches of the flower stalk.

BULBIL A small, bulb-like organ that breaks off to form a new plant.

CALCAR In bats, a hollow *spur* extending from the hind limbs and helping to support the membrane between these.

CALYX The collective name for the *sepals* of a flower.

CAPSULE Dry fruit that splits open to disperse ripe seed.

CARAPACE The shell-like *dorsal* surface that covers part of the body of some crustaceans, tortoises, and the *cephalothorax* of arachnids.

CASTE Any group of individuals in a colony of social insects that are structurally or behaviourally different from individuals in other groups, as seen in Isoptera and some Hymenoptera.

CATKIN An unbranched and often pendulous flower cluster of a single sex.

CEPHALOTHORAX The front section of an arachnid made of the head and *thorax* fused together.

CERCI (sing. **CERCUS**) A pair of sensory appendages at the rear end of an insect's *abdomen*.

CHELICERAE The first, usually pincer-like, pair of appendages on the *cephalothorax* of an arachnid.

CLADODE A modified stem that looks like a leaf.

CLEISTOGAMOUS Used to describe self-pollinating flowers, whose petals and sepals never open.

CLITELLUM The thickened portion about one third the way along the body of a sexually mature earthworm, which secretes the egg sac.

COLUMNAR Taller than broad, with parallel sides.

COMPOUND EYES The eyes of arthropods, which are made up of many light-gathering units called ommatidia.

CONE The fruiting structure of conifers. In horsetails, the spore-bearing reproductive structure produced at some stem tips.

CORBICULUM The pollen basket of honey bees, being a concave, shiny area on the hind *tibiae*, fringed with stiff hairs.

CORNICLE One of a pair of spout-like structures on the back of an aphid's *abdomen* which carry defensive secretions.

CORTINA Fine, cobweb-like threads usually joining the cap margin of a fungus to the stem.

COVERT A small feather in a well-defined tract, on the wing or at the base of the tail, covering the base of the larger flight feathers.

COXA (pl. **COXAE**) The first segment of an insect's leg, joining the rest of the leg to the *thorax*.

CREPUSCULAR Active at twilight or before sunrise.

CUCKOO A species in which the *larvae* develop eating food stored by another species for its own larvae.

CULTIVAR A selection made by humans and maintained in cultivation.

CUTICLE A general term referring to the outermost layer or skin of fungal *fruitbodies*.

CYME A flower cluster with lateral branches, each ending in a flower.

DABBLE To feed in shallow water, with rapid movements of the bill, sieving water through comb-like teeth to extract food.

DECURRENT Used to describe *gills* that join the fungal stem and extend downwards along it.

DIMORPHIC Occurring in two distinct forms: sexually dimorphic means that the male and female of a species look different; otherwise indicates two colour forms.

DISC FLORET In the Daisy family, a flower in the central part of the flowerhead, whose petals are fused into a tube.

DIURNAL Active during the day.

DORSAL FIN A medial fin or fins on the back of a fish that provide stability and steering.

DOUBLE FLOWER Describes a flower with more petals than in the normal wild state, and with few, if any, *stamens*.

DRUMMING Sound made by woodpeckers with rapid beats of the bill against a hard object, or by a snipe, diving through the air with vibrating tail feathers.

DRUPE A fleshy fruit whose seeds are surrounded by a tough coat.

EAR TUFT A bunch of feathers on the head of an owl, capable of being raised as a visual signal and perhaps to assist camouflage.

ECLIPSE The plumage of male ducks that is adopted during the summer, when they moult and become flightless for a short time.

ELYTRA (sing. **ELYTRON**) The rigid front wings of beetles, modified as covers for the *hindwings* and not used in flight.

EPICALYX A ring of *sepal*-like organs just below the true sepals (*calyx*) of a flower.

EYESPOT A distinctive eye-like marking, typically on the wings of some insects, especially butterflies; its function can be to alarm and deter a potential predator.

FALL PETAL In the Iris family, one of three outer petals that droop down.

FAMILY A unit of classification, grouping together related units called *genera*. For example, the *species* Amanita muscaria belongs to the *genus* Amanita, this is placed in the family Amanitaceae.

FEMUR (pl. **FEMORA**) The part of an insect's leg corresponding to the mammalian thigh.

FILTER-FEEDER Fish or some invertebrates that feed on minute particles that are filtered from the water, for example, by passing over gill rakers.

FLIGHT FEATHER Any one of the long feathers on a bird's wing (*primaries* and *secondaries*).

FLORET One of a group of small or individual flowers usually clustered together to form a flowerhead.

FOREWING The front part of a wing, including the outer *primaries*, primary *coverts*, and *secondary* coverts.

FREE GILLS Used to describe *gills* that do not attach to a fungal stem.

FROND The leaf of a seaweed or fern.

FRUITBODY A general term for any *spore*-producing fungal structure; more correctly called a sporophore.

FRY A stage of the fish life-cycle referring to newly hatched fish.

GALL An abnormal plant growth caused by a bacterium, virus, fungus, mite, or insect.

GEMMAE An asexual reproductive structure in liverworts and mosses that detaches from the adult plant to form a new plant.

GENUS (pl. **GENERA**) A category in classification: a group of closely related species, whose relationship is recognized by the same first name in the scientific terminology, e.g. *Larus* in *Larus fuscus*.

GILLS The thin, flattened, *spore*-bearing structures of cap and stem fungi. Also, the respiratory organ in fish, molluscs, insects, crustaceans, and amphibians.

GLUME Small scale in the inflorescence of a grass or sedge.

HALTERES The modified hind wings of Diptera insects which serve as balancing organs.

HEMIMETABOLOUS Developing by incomplete or gradual metamorphosis, such as in Orthoptera and Hemiptera insects. Immature stages are called *nymphs*.

HERBACEOUS Non-woody plants, dying back at the end of the growing season and overwintering by means of underground rootstocks.

HIBERNATION A period of dormancy undergone by animals, typically during the winter months.

HINDWING In birds, the rear part of the wing, including the secondary feathers, especially when it has a distinctive colour or pattern; in insects, one of a pair of back wings.

HOLDFAST A root-like structure that anchors seaweed to rocks but does not absorb nutrients like a true root.

HOLOMETABOLOUS Developing by complete metamorphosis such as in Coleoptera and Diptera insects. Immature stages are called *larvae*.

HYMENIUM A layer of fertile, *spore*-producing cells spread over *gills*, *tubes*, *spines* etc.

INDUSIUM (pl. **INDUSIA**) Tissue covering a *sorus* on a fern *frond*.

INNER WING In a bird, the inner part of the wing, comprising the *secondaries* and rows of *coverts* (typically marginal, lesser, median, and greater coverts).

KEEL PETAL The lower, fused petals of a peaflower, folded and curved like the keel of a boat.

LANCET A lance-shaped muscular projection on the face of a horseshoe-bat.

LARVA (pl. larvae) The immature stage of an insect that undergoes complete metamorphosis.

LATERAL LINE Sensory system of a fish that runs along the side of the body and detects pressure waves in the water.

LEK A gathering of birds at which males display communally, with mock fighting, while females choose which one to mate with.

LENTICEL A small pore found on shoots and fruit through which air can pass.

LIP A protruding petal, as in members of the Orchid and Mint families.

LOCALIZED More than 90 per cent of the population occurs at ten sites or less.

LOCALLY COMMON Abundant in particular parts of its range; even though it may be scarce or rare in other parts.

MACRO-MOTH A term commonly used to distinguish certain families of usually larger moths from the other families, called *micro-moths*, which are generally less easily identified.

MANTLE A fleshy layer of tissue that surrounds the body of molluscs. In many species, the outer cell layer of the mantle secretes the shell.

MAXILLARY PALPS A pair of segmented sensory mouthpart structures in insects, used to taste food.

MERICARP A one-seeded portion of a fruit formed by splitting from the rest.

MESOTHORAX The middle section of an insect's *thorax*, carrying the middle pair of legs and, usually, the front pair of wings.

METATARSAL TUBERCLE A prominent hard swelling under the hind foot of many species of frog and toad.

METATHORAX The rear section of an insect's *thorax*, carrying the hind pair of legs and, usually, the hind pair of wings.

MICRO-MOTH A term commonly used to distinguish certain families of usually smaller, and less easily identified moths from the *macro-moths*.

MINE A variously shaped hollow space between the upper and lower surface of a leaf caused by a feeding insect *larva*.

MOULT The shedding and renewing of feathers in a systematic way; most birds have a partial moult and a complete moult each year.

MYCELIUM (adj. **MYCELIAL**) The vegetative body of a fungus (usually below the surface) formed by a mass of fine, thread-like cells called hyphae.

MYCORRHIZAL The symbiotic relationship between a fungus and a plant, in which the fungus penetrates the plant and exchanges nutrients with it, often to their mutual benefit.

NATURALIZED A non-native plant or animal, introduced by human activity into a region, now forming self-sustaining populations in the wild.

NEMATOCYST A specialized stinging cell of cnidarians, which can be discharged to trap prey.

NOSE-LEAF A thin, broad, membranous fold of skin on the nose of many species of horseshoe-bats. It varies greatly in size and form.

NOTCHED Used to describe *gills* of fungi that turn abruptly up, then down, as they join the stem or to describe a petal with V- or U-shaped indentations.

NYMPH The immature stage of an insect showing incomplete metamorphosis, such as Hemiptera and Orthoptera (Exopterygota) insects.

OCELLI Simple light-receptive organs on the head of many insects.

OCHREA A papery, tubular sheath around the stem of some plants, notably docks.

OPERCULUM A horny or calcareous plate attached to the foot of certain gastropods, which exactly fits and seals the shell aperture. It protects the snail from desiccation and to a certain extent, from predators.

OPPOSITE Borne in pairs on opposite sides of the stem.

ORBITAL RING A thin, bare, fleshy ring around the eye, sometimes with a distinctive colour.

ORDER A category in classification: families grouped to indicate their close relationship or common ancestry; usually a more uncertain or speculative grouping than a *family*.

OSSICLE A single calcified component that makes up the skeleton just under the epidermis of echinoderms.

OUTER WING In birds, the outer half of a wing, comprising the primaries, their coverts, and the alula, or bastard wing (the "thumb").

OVIPOSITOR An organ, often tube-like, for laying eggs.

PALMATELY COMPOUND Fan-shaped and divided into leaflets.

PALPS A pair of segmented sensory appendages associated with an insect's mouthparts.

PANICLE A branched flower cluster, with stalked flowers.

PAPPUS A tuft of hairs on *achenes* or other fruits, which aids wind dispersal.

PARAPODIA (sing. **PARAPODIUM**) The flap-like locomotory appendages on the body segments of polychaete annelid worms, which usually have bristles.

PAROTID GLAND One of a pair of wart-like glands located behind the eyes in many amphibians, particularly conspicuous in toads. It may produce a noxious secretion.

PARTIAL VEIL A layer of tissue stretching from the cap margin of fungi to the stem; it may form a cobweb-like veil or a membranous ring.

PARTHENOGENESIS Reproduction without the need for fertilization.

PEA-LIKE Describes a flower structure typical of members of the Pea family, with the *sepals* fused into a short tube, and usually with an erect upper petal, two wing petals, and two lower petals forming a keel.

PECTORAL FINS Paired fins on the side of the body of a fish that aid manoeuvrability and braking.

PEDICELLARIA Tiny, two- or three-jawed organs on the surface of an echinoderm that keep it clear of encrusting organisms and parasites.

PEDIPALPS In arachnids, the second pair of appendages on the *cephalothorax*. They are tactile organs also variously used for handling and killing prey, and in male spiders, are organs of copulation.

PEDUNCLE In fish, the fleshy base of the tail fin; in plants, the stalk of an inflorescence.

PELVIC FINS *Ventrally* positioned paired fins that aid manoeuvrability and braking.

PERIOSTRACUM A thin layer of protein that covers the outside of the shell of many molluscs such as gastropods and bivalves. It can be tough and horny, thin, or even hairy.

PERSISTENT Remaining attached to the plant.

PHEROMONES Chemical "messengers" released by an animal in order to attract a member of the opposite sex of the same species.

PINNATE Describes a compound leaf with the leaflets (pinna) arranged as in a feather. Pinnately lobed leaves have lobes, rather than leaflets, arranged in this manner.

PINNULE Subdivision of pinna on a *pinnate* leaf or *frond*.

PLANKTON Microscopic organisms that drift in the sea. There are two types, phytoplankton (plants), which are photosynthetic and zooplankton (animals).

PNEUMOSTOME The respiratory opening of an air-breathing land snail or slug, which connects to a simple lung.

POLYMORPHIC Having more than two forms.

POLYPORE Common name for fungi with woody or tough *fruitbodies* and with a *pored*, tubular *spore*-producing layer.

PORES The openings of the tubular *spore*-producing layer on fungi such as boletes and *polypores*.

PRIMARY Any one of the long feathers or quills of a bird, forming the tip and trailing edge of the *outer wing*, growing from the "hand".

PROBOSCIS The coiled but extensible "tongue" of a butterfly or moth.

PROLEG The unsegmented leg of an insect *larva* (different from the segmented thoracic legs).

PROTHORAX The first segment of an insect's *thorax*, carrying the front pair of legs.

PTEROSTIGMA A coloured panel near the front edge of insect wings.

PTERYGOTA Winged insects. The larger subclass of the class Insecta.

PUPA The stage in the life cycle of a butterfly or moth that follows on from the *larva* and from which the adult insect emerges.

RACE *See* SUBSPECIES.

RACEME An unbranched flower cluster where each flower is clearly stalked.

RADULA The toothed, file-like feeding structure found in the mouths of most molluscs (not present in bivalves), which is used to graze or rasp food.

RANK A linear arrangement of leaves – 2-ranked leaves are arranged in opposite pairs along a stem; 4-ranked leaves are arranged in opposite pairs, each pair at right angles to the pair next to it.

RAY/RAY FLORET The outer, distinctively flattened flower of a daisy-type flowerhead.

RHIZOME A (usually underground) thickened stem which serves as a food storage organ.

RHIZOMORPHS Thick, cord-like strands of *mycelium*, looking rather like roots.

RING-ZONE A zone at the top of the stem of a fungus where a *partial veil* was once attached.

ROSTRUM The tubular, slender sucking mouthparts of insects such as the Hemiptera. The prolonged part of the head of weevils and scorpionflies. In crustaceans, a projecting anterior part of the carapace that extends forwards in front of the eyes.

RUT An annually recurring condition or period of sexual excitement and reproductive activity in male deer.

SAPROPHYTE a plant which feeds on rotting vegetation in the soil.

SCALE(S) Tiny, flattened plates that cloak the wing surfaces of most butterflies and moths. In fungi, pieces of surface tissue (often on cap or stem) which break away or peel back.

SCAPE A leafless stem bearing flowers.

SCAPULAR Any one of a group of feathers on the shoulder of a bird, forming an oval patch each side of the back, at the base of the wing.

SCENT GLAND A gland inside the body of insects that produces a secretion, often for defensive purposes.

SECONDARY Any one of the long *flight feathers* forming the trailing edge of the *inner wing*, growing from the ulna or "arm".

SELECTION see *CULTIVAR*

SELLA A saddle-shaped anatomical structure on the face of a horseshoe-bat.

SEPAL The usually green parts of a flower outside of the petals, collectively called the *calyx*.

SEX BRAND A patch or line of scent-emitting scales that is found on the forewing of a male butterfly.

SILIQUA A fruit of the Cabbage family, long and linear or pod-like.

SIPHON(S) Tube-like structures through which oxygenated water and suspended food particles flows in (inhalant siphon) and water and wastes flow out (exhalant siphon) of the body of certain molluscs.

SORUS (pl. **SORI**) A distinct group of minute, *spore*-producing structures on the *frond* of a fern.

SPADIX A fleshy *spike* with many unstalked flowers.

SPATHE The large, hooded *bract* that encloses a *spadix*.

SPAWNING The process of laying and fertilizing eggs in fish and amphibians.

SPECIES A unit of classification that embraces a group of genetically similar individuals, members of which are capable of reproducing with one another and of producing viable offspring.

SPECULUM A colourful patch on a duck's *hindwing*, formed by the secondary feathers. In plants, a shiny, shield-like patch on the petals of some orchids.

SPIKE An unbranched flower cluster, with unstalked flowers.

SPICULE A slender hard structure, which is often needle-like.

SPINES Tooth, peg, or spine-like structures over which the *spore*-producing layer of fungi is spread.

SPIRACLE The breathing holes of insects, leading to the tracheal system.

SPORE The basic unit of reproduction in many non-flowering plants such as fungi, ferns, and mosses.

SPORANGIUM (pl. **SPORANGIA**) Minute spore-producing organ on the underside of the *fronds* of ferns.

SPUR A hollow, cylindrical or pouched structure projecting from a flower, usually containing nectar. In animals, it refers to a pointed, projecting structure on the limbs.

STAMEN Male part of a flower, composed of an *anther*, normally borne on a stalk (filament).

STAMINODE An infertile, modified *stamen*.

STANDARD PETAL The upright, upper petal of a peaflower, often larger than the others.

STIGMA The female part of the flower that receives the pollen.

STIGMA-RAY A *stigma* that forms a star with radiating branches.

STING The modified *ovipositor* of some Hymenoptera insects, used for injecting venom.

STIPULE A leaf-like organ at the base of a leaf stalk.

STYLE The part of the female reproductive organ that joins the ovary to the *stigma*.

SUBMARGINAL Used in the context of a band of colour, or perhaps a row of spots, that are found on the area of a wing just inside the margin.

SUBSPECIES (abbrev. **SUBSP.**) A category of classification, below species, defining a group within a species, isolated geographically but able to interbreed with others of the same species.

SUPERCILIARY STRIPE In birds, a stripe of colour running above the eye, like an eyebrow.

TARSUS (pl. **TARSI**) The foot of an arthropod. It is attached to the end of the *tibia* and is made up of several tarsal segments.

TEPAL Petals and sepals that cannot be distinguished.

TERMINAL Located at the end of a shoot, stem, or other organ.

TERTIAL Any one of a small group of feathers, sometimes long and obvious, at the base of a bird's wing adjacent to the inner *secondaries*.

THORAX (adj. **THORACIC**) In insects, the middle section of an adult's body and the one to which the legs and wings are attached.

TIBIA (pl. **TIBIAE**) The lower leg segment of insects; the shin of mammals.

TRAGUS In most bats, a small cartilaginous flap in front of the external opening of the ear.

TUBERCLE A raised, wart-like structure on the surface of an arthropod.

TUBES In fungi, fleshy or woody, cylindrical or tubular structures, usually gathered together in a layer and in which the *spore*-producing layer is spread.

UMBO (adj. **UMBONATE**) A bump or hump, usually at the centre of a fungus cap.

UNIVERSAL VEIL A layer of tissue completely surrounding the fungus; the veil may be thin and cobweb-like, thick, or even glutinous and sticky.

VARIETAS (abbrev. **VAR.**) A naturally occurring variant of a species.

VEIL A layer of tissue which protects a fungus especially during some early stages of its growth. See also *partial veil* and *universal veil*.

VENT The area of feathers between the legs and the undertail *coverts*, surrounding the cloaca.

VENTRAL The under or lower surface.

VOLVA Remains of a *universal veil* left at the base of the stem of a fungus as a sack-like bag or scaly swelling as the fungus expands during growth.

WARREN A series of interconnected underground tunnels in which rabbits live.

WING PETAL The lateral petals of many flowers, particularly orchids and peaflowers.

WINGBAR A line of colour produced by a tract of feathers or feather tips, crossing the closed wing of a bird and running along the spread wing.

Index

Acknowledgments

The RSPB works for a healthy environment rich in birds and wildlife. It depends on the support and generosity of others to make a difference. It works with bird and habitat conservation organizations in a global partnership called BirdLife International. For more information on the RSPB, its work, and how to join, visit www.rspb.org.uk, telephone RSPB UK headquarters on 01767 680551, or write to The Lodge, Potton Road, Sandy, Bedfordshire SG19 2DL.

a million voices for nature

Dorling Kindersley would like to thank the following for their kind permission to reproduce the photographs:

Key: b-bottom, c-centre, l-left, r-right, t-top.

A D Schilling: 24tl, 49tr; Alan Outen: 274tl, 288tl, 394lc, 396bl, 401br, 482-483, 492-493, 494tl, 502, 511, 518-519, 520-521, 524-525, 528, 542bl, 545, 548-549, 575br, 576bl; Andrew Mackay: 434bl, 449cr, 451tr; Ardea London Ltd: Chris Knights 376tl; Ardea: Pat Morris 403tr; Barry Hughes: 68tl, 72bl, 94bl, 81br, 100bl, 231rc, 232bl, 233br, 234bl, 235br, 236cl, 237tr, 238tl, 239tr, 231tr, 241br, 242bl, 243tr, 243br, 244bl, 245tr, 245br, 248bl, 249tr, 251tr, 251br, 252tl, 252bl, 253tr, 253br, 254tl, 255tr, 256tl, 256bl, 257br, 259tr, 264bl, 265br, 266tl, 267tr, 267br, 268bl, 269br, 270bl, 324tl; Beat Fecker: 478-479, 511, 512, 513tr, 543; Beat Wermelinger: 478-479, 543, 557, 560bl; Bernd Liebermann: 139br; Bob Glover: 322tl, 322bl, 339tr, 339br, 378tl; Bruce Coleman Ltd: Kim Taylor 526; © Florian Möllers: 289tr; © Sascha Hooker/SeaPics;com: 294bl; Carlos Sanchez Alonso: 351br, 352tl, 362tl; Chris Gibson: 24lb, 25tr, 26tl, 32bl, 34bl, 38bl, 39tr, 40tl, 78tl, 82tl, 82bl, 83br, 99tr, 101tr, 112bl, 115tr, 124bl, 131br, 132bl, 158tl, 194tl, 438bl, 443br, 445br, 446tl, 446bl, 451br, 452tl, 456bl, 458tl, 458bl, 472-473, 488-489, 492-493, 539tl, 548-549, 554-555, 558-559, 562-563; Chris Gomersall

Photography: 300bl, 301tr, 302bl, 303tr, 303br, 305cr, 317br, 319br, 338tl, 340tl, 343tr, 343br, 345tr, 350tr, 352tl, 354tl, 356bl, 357tr, 357br, 359tr, 366tl, 366bl, 370tl, 370bl, 371tr, 371br, 372tl, 372bl, 373tr, 373br, 374tl, 374bl, 376bl, 377cr; Chris Knights: 299br, 342bl; Colin Varndell: 368bl, 375tr; David Bradford: 565tr; David Cottridge: 344tl, 345br, 246tl, 359tl, 360tl, 360bl; David Element: 476bl, 478-479, 480, 488-489, 512, 513br, 514-515, 552-553; David Fenwick (www.aphotoflora.com): 399tr, 574tl, 574bl, 576tl, 578tl; David Hosking: 44bl, 313tr; David Kitching: 465, 467; David Lang: 93br, 97tr, 197tr, 197br; David Tipling: 314tr, 334tl, 334bl; Dennis Avon: 497tr; Diego Reggianti: 490tl, 505, 506-507, 522, 530tl, 534, 552-553; Dorn: 107tr; Doug Perrine/SeaPics.com: 294bl; Dr. E. Elkan: 526;; E.A Janes: 325tr; Erling Svensen: 395br, 396tl, 399br, 402cl, 404bl; F Merlet: 363tr; FLPA: 364bl, 365tr; Frank Koehler: 500-501, 509, 517bl; Geoffrey Kibby: 246tl, 266bl;George McCarthy: 329tr, 346bl, 347tr, 349br, 350tl, 368tl; George McGavin: 492-493; Gerald Downey: 315br; Goran Ekstrom: 248tl;György Csóka: 464bl, 482-483, 490bl, 492-493, 504, 514-515, 520-521, 524-525, 544, 546-547, 551, 558-559; Hanne & Jens Eriksen: 301br; Heather Angel: 393br, 397tr, 398bl, 400tl, 400bl, 401tr, 407tr, 579tr; Henriette Kress: 121tr, 190bl; Holt Studios International: 491tr, 491br, 494bl, 558-559, 569; Howard Rice: 21tr; Huttenmoser: 348bl; Ian Fisher: 312tl; IliaraPimpinelli:384lc; J Benn: 237br; J;A;L; Cook: 461br; Jarmo Holopainen: 530bl; Jeff Foott: 461tr; Jeff Higgott: 452bl; Jens Petersen: 255tr; Jens Schou: 56tl, 121br, 122tl, 122bl, 130tr, 165tr, 165br, 198tl, 435tl, 435br, 436tl, 436bl, 439tr, 439br, 440bl, 441tr, 453tr, 482-483, 534, 541, 557; Jon Olav Bjørndal: 392bl; Jordi Vila: 262tl; Josef Hlasek: 284tl, 284bl, 287cr, 290bl, 293br, 466-466, 488-489, 496tl, 498-499, 505, 508, 510, 518-519, 520-521, 523tr, 524-525, 548-549; Joseph Strauch: 21br; Karl Soop: 234tl, 235tr, 240tl, 254tl; Keith Edkins: 478-479, 482-483, 482-483, 488-489, 514-515, 520-521, 548-549; Keith Rushforth: 41br; Laurie Campbell Photography: 347br; Mario Maier: 417tr, 417br, 423cr, 425tr, 427cr, 431br, 432lc; Mark Hamblin: 298tl, 300tl, 304bl, 318tl, 341tl, 341br, 342tl, 344bl, 354bl, 355tr, 363br, 364tl, 367tl, 367br, 369cr, 375br,

379br, 380tl; **Martin B Withers:** 42tl, 338bl, 340bl; **Melvyn Grey:** 279cr; **Michal Hoskovec:** 481tr, 500-501, 518-519, 557; **Mike Lane:** 298bl, 299tr, 302tl, 326tl, 349tr, 350bl, 353cr 355br, 356tl, 358bl, 361tr, 361br, 362bl, 365br; **Mike Read:** 282bl, 285tr, 285br, 295tr, 295br, 296lc, 324bl, 405tr; **N.H.P.A.:** A. Bannister 481br; **N.W. Legon:** 232tl, 233tr, 238bl, 242tl, 247cr, 263br; **Natural History Museum, London:** 475, 486; **Neil Fletcher:** 22lc, 23cr, 25br, 26bl, 27tr, 27br, 28lc, 29tr, 29br, 30tl, 33tr, 33br, 34tl, 35cr, 36tl, 36bl, 37cr, 38tl, 38br, 40bl, 41tr, 42bl, 43cr, 44tl, 46tl, 47tr, 47br, 48tl, 48bl, 49br, 50tl, 50bl, 51tr, 51br, 52lc, 53tr, 53br, 54tl, 55tr, 56bl, 57tr, 57br, 58lc, 59tr, 59br, 60tl, 60bl, 61tr, 61br, 62tl, 63tr, 63br, 64tl, 64bl, 65tr, 65br, 66tl, 66bl, 67tr, 67br, 68bl, 69tr, 69br, 70tl, 70bl, 71tr, 71br, 72tl, 73tr, 73br, 74tl, 75cr, 76tl, 76bl, 77tr, 78bl, 79tr, 79br, 80lc, 81tr, 83tr, 84tl, 84bl, 85tr, 85br, 86tl, 86bl, 87tr, 87br, 88lc, 89tr, 91tr, 91br, 92tl, 93cr, 94tl, 95br, 96tr, 97br, 98cl, 99br, 101bl, 102tl, 102bl, 103tr, 103br, 104tl, 104bl, 105tr, 105br, 106lc, 107tr, 108tl, 108bl, 109tr, 109br, 110tl, 110bl, 111tr, 111br, 113tr, 13br, 114tl, 114bl, 115br, 116tl, 116bl, 117tr, 117br, 118tl, 118bl, 119br, 120lc, 123cr, 124tl, 125tr, 125br, 126tl, 126bl, 127tr, 127br, 128tl, 128bl, 129tr, 130tl, 130bl, 131tr, 132tl, 133tr, 133br, 134tl, 134bl, 135tr, 135br, 136tl, 136bl, 137tr, 137br, 138tl, 138bl, 139tr, 140tl, 140bl, 141tr, 141br, 142tl, 142bl, 143br, 144cr, 145tr, 145br, 146tl, 146bl, 147tr, 147br, 148tl, 149tr, 149br, 150cl, 151tr, 151br, 152tl, 153tr, 153br, 154tl, 154bl, 155tr, 155br, 156tl, 156tl, 157tr, 157br, 158bl, 159tr, 159br, 160tl, 160bl, 161cr, 162tl, 162bl, 163tr, 163br, 164tl, 166tl, 166bl, 166tr, 167br, 168tl, 168bl, 169tr, 169br, 170tl, 170bl, 171tr, 171br, 172tl, 172bl, 173tr, 173br, 174tl, 174bl, 175tr, 175br, 176tl, 177cr, 178bl, 179tr, 179br, 180tl, 180bl, 181tr, 181br, 182tl, 182bl, 183tr, 183br, 184tl, 184bl, 185tr, 185br, 186tl, 186bl, 187cr, 188tl, 191tr, 191br, 192tl, 192bl, 193tr, 193br, 194bl, 195tr, 195br, 196tl, 196bl, 198bl, 199tr, 199br, 200lc, 201br, 202tl, 202bl, 203br, 204tl, 204bl, 205tr, 219br, 239br, 240bl, 244tl, 249br, 250lc, 258lc, 259tr, 264tl, 265tr, 268tl, 271tr, 271br, 276tl, 276bl, 278bl, 280tl, 282tl, 293tr, 386bl, 387bl, 388lc, 412cl, 418lc, 428tr, 431tr, 433br, 453br, 462bl, 463tr, 463br, 463tl, 465, 466, 467, 469, 470-471, 474tl, 475, 477, 485br, 488-489, 495tr, 497br, 502, 504, 518-519, 520-521, 528, 539br, 545, 548-549, 550, 561tr, 562-563, 565br, 568tl; **Neil Harris:**

269tr; **Nick Legon:** 248tl; **Nigel Catlin:** 475, 475; **Nigel Hicks:** 288bl; **Paolo Mazzei:** 428br, 429cr, 437cr, 442lc, 444lc, 445tr, 447tr, 447br, 448tl, 448bl, 454tl, 454bl, 455cr, 456tl, 457cr, 459tr, 459br, 460tl, 460bl, 467, 468tl, 469, 477, 478-479, 480, 482-483, 484bl, 486, 487tr, 498-499, 500-501, 503, 504, 505, 506-507, 509, 514-515, 518-519, 520-521,522, 524-525, 527tr, 527bl, 529, 532, 533, 536-537, 540, 541, 545, 548-549, 554-555, 556, 560tr, 561br, 562-563, 564, 568bl; 570tl; **Paolo Mazzei:** 385tr, 385br, 389tr; **Paul Doherty:** 336tl; **Peter Cairns:** 283tr, 283br, 291cr, 292tl, 292bl; **Peter Harvey:** 482-483, 534, 562-563, 564, 567; **Planet Earth:** Steven Hopkin 531tr; **Premaphotos Wildlife:** Ken Preston Mafham: 538; **Rene Pop:** 337tr, 337br; **Roar Solheim:** 289br, 290tl; **Robin Chittenden:** 304tl, 306tl; **Rod Preston Mafham:** 566tl; **Roger Key:** 468tl, 469, 470, 477, 478-479, 480, 482-483, 488-489, 488-489, 495br, 496bl, 498-499, 500-501, 502, 503, 504, 506-507, 509, 510, 512, 516tl, 517, 518-519, 523br, 524-525, 528, 529, 531br, 532, 533, 534, 535tr, 535br, 536-537, 538, 542tl, 543, 544, 545, 546-547, 548-549, 550, 551, 552-553, 556, 562-563, 564, 566bl, 567, 569, 570bl, 571tr; **Roger Tidman:** 306bl, 310tl, 310bl, 312bl, 314tl, 315tr, 316lc, 317tr, 318bl, 321br, 321cr, 325tr, 328bl, 328bl, 329br, 330tl, 332cl, 335tr, 379tr, 382lc; **Roger Wilmshurst:** 308bl, 311tr, 319tr, 319br, 32tl, 330bl, 333tr; **Rollin Verlinde:** 277tr, 277br, 278tl, 280tl, 281tr, 286tl, 286bl; **RSPB Images:** 307tl, 308tl, 335br, 336bl; **Rudolf Svensen:** 392tl; **Science Photo Library:** Eye of Science 474bl, 476tl; **Silvestris:** 358tl; **Simon Brown:** 398tl; **Simon Curson:** 438tl, 450tl, 450bl; **Stanley Porter:** 326bl; **Steve Young:** 311br, 320tl, 320bl, 327tr, 327br, 331tr, 331br, 333br, 380bl; **Ted Benton:** 74bl, 90tl, 90bl, 96bl, 409cr, 410tl, 410bl, 411cr, 413cr, 414tl, 414bl, 415tr, 415br, 416cl, 419tr, 416br, 421tr, 421br, 422tl, 422bl, 424lc, 425tr, 426tl, 426bl, 430tl, 430bl, 431tr, 440tl, 470, 465, 466, 467, 469, 472-473, 487br, 536-537, 550, 551, 554-555, 556; **Tim Loseby:** 313br, 381br; **Tony Hamblin:** 309cr; **Van Der Voort:** 386tl; **Wendelin Dorn:** 62bl, 77br, 152bl; **Windrush Photos:** Alan Petty 321tr; **Yves Adams:** 281br, 387tr;

All other images © Dorling Kindersley. For further information see: www.dkimages.com